Social Problems in India

Social Problems in India

FOURTH EDITION

Fully Revised, Expanded and Updated

Ram Ahuja

RAWAT PUBLICATIONS

Jaipur • New Delhi • Bangalore • Guwahati • Kolkata

ISBN 978-81-316-1172-2 (HB)
ISBN 978-81-316-1173-9 (PB)

First Edition, 1992
Second Edition, 1997
Third Edition, 2014
Fourth Edition, 2021

Reprinted, 2025

Published by
Prem Rawat for **Rawat Publications**
Satyam Apts, Sector 3, Jawahar Nagar, Jaipur 302 004 (India)
Phone: 0141 265 1748 / 265 7006
E-mail: info@rawatbooks.com
Website: www.rawatbooks.com

New Delhi Office
4858/24, Ansari Road, Daryaganj, New Delhi 110 002
Phone: 011 23263290

Also at *Bangalore, Guwahati* and *Kolkata*

Typeset by Rawat Computers, Jaipur
Printed at Nice Printing Press, New Delhi

Contents

Preface to the First Edition

All change is not progress. India has changed in the last 40 years and it continues to change even today. But what is the direction of change? What is the logic of change? Who is being benefitted by this change? Violence, despite determined declaration, continues abated, communalism is on the upsurge. Unemployment despite the reassuring promises continue to increase. Atrocities against women, *Harijans* and weaker sections are not on the decline. Youth are becoming more and more frustrated and taking to agitations. Politics has been criminalised. Secessionism has been curbed but terrorism is becoming more and more strident, raucous. Corruption has not been curbed. It exists with different labels. Peasants, industrial workers and government employees are in distress. Social values are fast deteriorating. More and more people are becoming the victims of mental illness. Crime, delinquency, drug abuse and alcoholism are on increase. The country is facing innumerable social problems.

It is time to analyse and understand the nature and magnitude of these social problems. It is time that social scientists try to use a theoretical perspective in their evaluation of these problems. It is time that the planners and power elites think of suitable remedial measures to streamline the existing sub-systems, structures, institutions and laws to contain them.

A humble attempt has been made to examine the current social problems in India with a sociological perspective. Most of the chapters are based on the data collected though my own empirical studies. Besides, the analysis is also based on the thinking and research of several scholars and academic professionals. Obviously, it is not possible to acknowledge every individual social thinker. The quality of their work was the inspiration behind this book. Above all, I am indebted to all those unknown scholars and known friends whose knowledge and useful ideas provided me a theoretical insight to analyse varied social problems in Indian context.

10 August 1991

Ram Ahuja
Ex-Professor of Sociology
University of Rajasthan, Jaipur

Preface to the Fourth Edition

This is the fourth edition of the book. Since its first publication, it is widely regarded as the leading book in the field as it combines theoretical rigour with an authoritative overview of relevant and up-to-date research. Over the years, the book has become a well-established text in the field of sociology. The revised edition of this popular book explains why it is so important to understand social problems in India. After its first publication in 1992, this best selling text, written by an influential academic practitioner, has established itself as the standard and authenticated source for not only students pursuing undergraduate and postgraduate courses in sociology, but also for thousands of aspirants preparing for competitive examinations, particularly civil services examinations, conducted by public service commissions. Revising a textbook such as this is a humbling experience. There is no end of ideas on any problem in society. Besides, new measures are taken by the government over the years for containing the problems. On content, there is more disagreement about what is needed. Some students and teachers feel that there should be an expanded coverage of statistics, while others hold that giving figures and statistics should be eliminated altogether. There is no right or wrong position in disagreements such as these. There are only differences in what is liked or disliked in different academic settings. Therefore, such changes in the book have been made which enhance the academic importance of the contents.

What distinguishes this edition from the previous one is that it has updated data on every problem, and new arguments and comments, wherever necessary, have been added. All chapters are discussed in greater depth than before. We hope that reader will find the additions useful and valuable, appreciating the importance of clear and logical thinking and a more rigorous issue-based analysis. However, it is virtually a new book and will be of immense value to all including those who have read its previous versions.

In the absence of our late father, who had authored this book, the task of revision/updation has been very meticulously handled by Shri Prem Ahuja. We are thankful to him. In most of the cases, as far as possible, the latest data/information has been made available. But still we feel that there might be some shortcomings for which we are solely responsible. We shall be thankful if these are brought to our notice so that the next edition of this valuable book could be further improved.

Mukesh Ahuja
Sanjay Ahuja

1

Social Problems

Concept and Approaches

Social problem is an aspect of the society that people are concerned about and would like to change. Social problems arise due to the occurrence of significant differences between values in society with the reality or the reality of the matter in the field, that can be measured or experienced. A social problem is any condition or behaviour that has negative consequences for large number of people and that needs to be addressed. The existence of social problems in a society is defined by the community itself, usually by an institution that has special authority, such as community leaders, community meetings, social organization, or government. A social issue is a problem that influences a considerable number of individuals within a society. It is often the consequence of factors extending beyond an individual's control. Anything that affects a considerable amount of people in a community/society can be heeded as a 'social problem'.

Today, 'social problems' is considered a sub-discipline of Sociology. Sociology is a very vast field, encompassing such sub-disciplines as the sociology of family, sociology of crime and delinquency, sociology of education, sociology of environment, etc.

Drug abuse, alcoholism, ageing, population explosion, corruption, AIDS, inequality, child abuse, terrorism, pollution, poverty, environmental degradation, unemployment and crime against women are not individual problems but affect the society at large. An individual problem is one which affects one individual or one group. Its resolution lies within the immediate milieu of the individual/group. Against this, a societal issue is one which affects the society as a whole, or the larger part of society. The sociologist's job is to understand the complexity of these problems and their relatedness to social structure, to study the operation of varied patterns of interrelationships in the society and how people are affected by them, and observe how social systems need to be reorganized and restructured in dealing with them.

The Concept of Social Problem

A social problem is a condition or set of events that some people in society view as being undesirable. A social problem has been defined as 'a situation confronting a group or a section of society which inflicts injurious consequences that can be handled only collectively' (Reinhardt, 1952: 14). Thus, one or a few individuals are not responsible for the appearance of a socially problematic situation, and the control of this situation is also beyond the ability of one or a few persons. This responsibility is placed upon society at large. Walsh and Furfey (1961: 1) have defined a social problem as a 'deviation from the social ideal remediable by group effort'. Two elements are important in this definition: (a) a situation which is less than ideal, that is, which is undesirable or abnormal; and (b) one which is remediable by collective effort. Though, it is not easy to determine which situation is ideal and which is not, and there is no definite standard which could be used to judge it, yet it is clear that a social ideal is not something arbitrary and the term 'social problem' is applied only to that 'issue' which social ethics (which describes human conduct as right and wrong in group relations), and society (which is concerned with the promotion of the common good or the welfare of its members and the preservation of public order) consider as unfavourable. The 'issue' should also be such as is beyond an individual to handle it by himself. If an individual wants a job and has to compete with others for getting it, then it is merely an individual's problem. Likewise, if an individual has become addicted to drugs and has to seek admission to a psychiatric institute or a community centre for deaddiction, that is his/her personal problem. On the other hand, if 35 million persons are unemployed in villages and cities in a country, and no single individual can do anything effective about it, what is needed to solve the problem is an organized group or social effort. Thus, a problem may be an individual problem under one set of circumstances and a social problem under another.

But social problems change with the passage of time. What was not considered a social problem a few decades ago may become a crucial social problem today or two decades later. For example, the population explosion in our country was not viewed as a social problem up to the late 40s of the 20th century but from the early 1950s, it has come to be perceived as a very crucial socio-economic problem. Social change creates new conditions in which an issue is identified as a social problem. Similarly, youth unrest in India was not a problem upto the 1940s but in the 1950s and the 1960s it became a problem and in the 1970s and the 1980s it became a very serious one and continues to be so even today.

Let us examine a few more viewpoints on the concept of 'social problem'. Fuller and Myers (1941: 320) have defined a social problem as 'a condition which is defined by a considerable number of persons as a deviation from some social norms which they cherish'. Merton and Nisbet (1971: 184) hold that a social problem is 'a way of behaviour that is regarded by a substantial part of a social order as being in violation of one or more generally accepted or approved norms'. This definition may apply to some problems like alcoholism, corruption and communalism, but not to problems like population explosion. Some problems are created not by the abnormal and deviant behaviour of the individuals but by the normal and accepted behaviour. Raab and Selznick (1959: 32) maintain that a social problem is 'a problem in human relationships which seriously threatens society or impedes the important aspirations of many people'. According to Carr (1955: 306), 'a social problem exists whenever we become conscious of a difficulty, a gap between our preferences and reality'. Blumer (1971: 19) writes that 'social problems involve actions or patterns of behaviour that are viewed by a substantial number of persons in the society as being deleterious to the society or in violation of societal norms, and about which ameliorative action is seen as both possible and desirable'. Landis (1959) is of the opinion that 'social problems are men's unfulfilled aspirations for welfare'. Case (1976: 310) has said that 'a social problem refers to any situation which attracts the attention of a considerable number of competent observers within a society and appeals to them as calling for readjustment or remedy by social (that is, collective) action of some kind or other'.

Horton and Leslie (1970: 4) write that a social problem is 'a condition affecting a significant number of people in ways considered undesirable, about which it is felt that something can be done through collective social action'. Though this definition emphasizes that a social problem is a condition 'affecting a significant number of people' it does not give the exact number of people who must be affected. It only points out that 'enough people' should be affected so that notice is taken of it and people begin to talk and write about it. One way of 'measuring public concern' about a condition is to assess the number of articles devoted to it in popular magazines. Thus, the problem of 'environmental pollution' in India was not taken up earnestly till the beginning of the 1980s, manifested by the fact that not many articles appeared on this issue in newspapers and magazines. The appearance of numerous articles in the last twenty years or so indicates that the condition has attracted widespread consideration, and has become a social problem.

Another element in the definition which needs attention is 'in ways considered undesirable'. The custom of *sati* in India was not a social problem as long as most people thought it was desirable. When Raja Ram Mohan Roy took initiative and a considerable number of people came to support him and started criticizing the practice as harmful and awful, only then did the custom turn into a social problem. In recent times, it was only after the incident of Roop Kanwar, a 21-year-old Rajput girl, who committed *sati* on the funeral pyre of her husband in Deorala in Sikar district in Rajasthan in September 1987 that this practice came to be condemned, and an Act was passed in February 1988 in the state of Rajasthan prescribing serious penalty for persons forcing a woman to commit *sati*.

A social problem, thus, involves a value judgement, a feeling that a condition is detrimental and requires change. Political corruption came to be viewed as a social problem only after the 1970s, though it was prevalent in our country earlier too. Issues like wife battering and child abuse are yet to be accepted as serious social problems.

Conditions that cannot be changed or evaded are also not accepted as social problems. Thus, famine was not considered a social problem until recently because of the widespread belief that the scantiness of rains was the result of the wrath of the rain-god. Today, famine in states like Rajasthan is viewed as a social problem and is seen to be the result of the failure on the part of government to complete the Rajasthan Canal because of the scarcity of economic resources and such similar reasons. The scarcity of drinking water became a social problem only when it was realized that it was not a misfortune to be endured but 'something could be done' to remove this scarcity. Thus, it is the belief and hope in the possibility of prevention and treatment that causes people to consider situation as a social problem.

The last portion in the definition of Horton and Leslie is 'collective action'. A social problem cannot be solved by an individual or a few individuals. All social problems are social in treatment, that is, it is believed that they can be tackled only by public concern, discussion, opinion formation and pressure.

According to Weinberg (1960: 4), social problems are 'behaviour patterns or conditions which arise from social processes and are considered so objectionable or undesirable by many members of a society that they recognize that corrective policies, programmes and services are necessary to cope with them'. Weinberg gives six characteristics of social problems as under:

1. Social problems arise by being collectively defined as objectionable by many members of the community. Thus, adverse conditions not defined by the community as reprehensible are not considered as social problems. For example, if taking alcohol is not regarded as objectionable by society, it is not considered as a social problem. But as society recognizes and discusses the problems inherent in alcohol consumption, studies its consequences and devises a plan of corrective action to control it, it comes to be defined as a social problem even though the original situation may not have changed.
2. Social problems change when the concerned behavioural patterns are interpreted differently. For example, till a few decades ago, mental illness was viewed as insanity and it was considered so disgraceful that the families kept the member's mental illness a secret. Now, the behaviour of a mentally-ill person is seen only as one type of 'deviant behaviour' which requires psychiatric and social treatment. Thus, the problem of mental illness today is met more realistically and effectively.
3. Mass media (newspapers, internet, television, radio, movies) play an important role in creating awareness about the scope and urgency of social problems.

4. Social problems have to be viewed in the context of society's values and institutions; for example, the problem of racial conflict in the United States is different from the problem of untouchability in India.
5. Social problems need to be analysed in terms of the influences upon them by group processes and social relationships.
6. Since social problems vary historically, contemporary social problems are society's concern, that is, the problem of refugee settlement in India in 1947–48 was different from the problem of settling refugees from Assam in 1968, or the Tamils from Sri Lanka in 1988–89, or the Indians from Kuwait and Iraq in September 1990. Similarly, the problem of immigrants in the United Kingdom in 1988 was different than it was in 1967 or 1947.

Definition of Social Problem

Some important definitions of social problems are given below:

1. *Lindbergh:* It is any deviant behaviour in a disapproved direction of such a degree that it exceeds the tolerance limit of the community.
2. *L.K. Frank:* Any difficulty of misbehaviour of a fairly large number of persons which we wish to remove or correct.
3. *Horton and Leslie:* It is often defined as a condition which many people consider undesirable and wish to correct.
4. *Fuller and Myers:* A social problem starts with the awakening of people in a given locality, with the realization of certain cherished values that are threatened by the conditions which have become acute.

We can say that an undesirable and unwanted disturbing situation, which has no ready-made solution, is called a social problem.

In social problems two things must be present: (a) an objective condition, the presence and magnitude of which can be observed, verified and measured by impartial social observers; and (b) a subjective definition by some members of the society that the objective condition is a 'problem' and must be acted upon. A social issue is a problem that influences a considerable number of individuals within a society. It is often the consequence of factors extending beyond an individual's control and is the source of conflicting opinion on the grounds of what is perceived as a morally just personal life or societal order.

Characteristics of Social Problems

Salient features and characteristics of social problem are that it changes the situation in such a way that a problem is created to the extent that existing social order has to be changed. It also means that it is difficult to solve the problem but to feel that such a solution is inevitable or undesirable is not correct. But one of the significant characteristics is that it becomes a problem only when the people begin to feel and take it in that sense. As long as people are not aware of the problem, even though it exists, there is no social disharmony, but maladjustment comes to the front only when the masses become conscious of it.

On the basis of the above definitions, we can identify the following characteristics of social problems:

1. All social problems are situations which have injurious consequences for society.
2. All social problems are deviations from the 'ideal' situation.
3. All social problems have some common basis of origin.
4. All social problems are social in origin.
5. All social problems are caused by pathological social conditions.
6. All social problems are interconnected.
7. All social problems are social in their results, that is, they affect all sections of the society.
8. The responsibility for social problems is social, that is, they require a collective approach for their solution.
9. All social problems occur in all societies.

Classification of Social Problems

So far, no universally accepted classification has been formed about a social problem. Sociologists have tried to give different classifications. Harold A. Phelps has classified such problems as biological (physical defects), bio-psychological (feeble mindedness, juvenile delinquency) and economic (poverty and unemployment). Another classification is based on heritage, e.g. physical heritage, biological heritage, and social heritage. But so far, no classification has been universally accepted. The primary reason for this is that in society no problem is absolute. Every problem is relative and is also linked with one or more aspects of our life.

Elements of a Social Problem

The important elements of a social problem are:

1. A condition or situation identified as objectionable by a significant number of people.
2. It is considered undesirable because of its harmful consequences.
3. All social problems want correction through collective action.
4. All unusual behaviours or deviations from accepted norms are termed as social problems such as crime, juvenile delinquency, drug addiction, domestic violence, ethnic or communal tension.
5. Social problems are not static but change with time and space. Changes in law and mores, change the concept of the social problem.

Reactions to Social Problems

Different people react differently to social problems. The differences may be explained in terms of the following four factors:

1. *An attitude of unconcern*: Many people remain indifferent to a problem thinking that it does not affect them. Sometimes their own individual problems like family tensions and job pressures keep them so engaged that they do not find time to be interested in what affects others. It is only when their own interests are involved that they become agitated and start taking interest in the problem.
2. *Fatalism*: Some people are so fatalistic that they attribute everything to destiny. Issues like poverty and unemployment are explained in terms of misfortunes and past *karma*. They, therefore, suffer the misfortune quietly and wait for some miracle to happen.
3. *Vested interest*: Some people take no interest in the existing problems because they stand to gain as long as the problem exists. Motivated by self-interest, they describe the problem as insoluble and talk about its eradication as a waste of time.
4. *Absence of expert knowledge*: Some people, though deeply concerned about the problem, do not take much interest in it believing that its solution is impossible unless people change their attitudes and values. As the changes must be initiated by a change in outlook, they remain unconcerned about finding alternative possibilities of treatment. Dowry is one such problem in our society.

Some people have incorrect, unreliable and superficial knowledge or fallacies about social problems. We can point out eight such feelings.

One, it is wrong to believe that there is agreement among all people on the nature of the social problems. For example, some people think that drug abuse is a social problem in India while others are convinced on the basis of the empirical studies conducted in different parts of the country pointing out to the low magnitude of drug abuse, that it cannot be perceived as a social problem. Similarly, for some people in India, untouchability is no longer a social problem after the measures adopted since independence to emancipate the *Harijans*, whereas for others, it is still a social problem. They even refer to the harassment and beating up of the *Harijans* who were prevented from entering the Nathdwara Temple in Rajasthan in September 1988 which provoked the then President of India R. Venkataraman to declare that he was willing to lead a procession of *Harijans* to enter the Nathdwara temple. Thus, on some problems there may be complete agreement and on others there may be little agreement as to their existence.

Two, it is fallacious to believe that social problems are caused by nature and are, therefore, inevitable. In fact, no social problem is beyond human control if certain social arrangements are changed.

Three, it is a misnomer to believe that social problems are caused by selfish, brutal, exploitative and indifferent people or by the wilful wickedness of a few. In fact, many problems are caused by the good people because they either mind their own business or they remain indifferent and callous to certain issues. For example, the growth of slums, which promotes family disorganization and increases certain kinds of crime, is the result of the callousness of rich persons and politicians. However, these people do not have any 'evil motive' in their indifference or thinking and behaviour. It may, therefore, be said that a social problem is the product of certain social practices and not of wilful wickedness of certain individuals.

Four, it is wrong to believe that social problems are created by talking about them. The problems are caused not because people irresponsibly talk about them and thus incite others or stir up trouble or evoke hatred and so on. In fact, people are often mobilized to solve problems and initiate action against the factors that perpetuate the problem.

Five, it is incorrect to assume that all people like to see the social problems solved, for example, the conservative Brahmins may not be interested in taking up the issue of untouchability for discussion; or many scheduled castes, scheduled tribes and other backward castes/classes people may prefer to remain 'backward' for fear of losing out on the reservation benefits; or many capitalists may not be in favour of full employment for fear of not getting adequate workers at low wages; or many landlords may not be interested in constructing more houses and reducing the problem of housing shortage for fear of getting low rents; or owners of one-room tenements in slum areas may not be interested in slum clearance because of their vested interests. Thus, a sizeable number of people can be found to be disinterested in solving social problems because of vested interests.

Six, it is not correct to believe that social problems if left on their own will solve themselves. The feeling that time will solve all problems is unsound and unrealistic in this age. It is only a rationalization for inactivity. It may, in fact, aggravate the problems, especially problems like poverty, pollution and population.

Seven, the feeling that unravelling facts will solve the problem is not correct. Though it is true that no problem can be intelligently understood without collecting complete facts about it, it is also true that without scientifically interpreting the gathered data, measures cannot be taken to solve a problem. For example, the mere collection of the facts on the magnitude of the problem of drug abuse among youth, the nature of drugs used by them, the methods of using drugs, the sources of getting drugs and the withdrawal syndromes will not help much in suggesting measures to control the drug misuse unless we analyse and interpret facts like the reasons for taking drugs, the role of peer group and the role of family in controlling drug abuse. Thus, data in itself is nothing; it is the objective interpretation of the data which is meaningful.

Eight, it is untrue to think that problems can be solved without institutional changes. In a way, it is impossible to solve problems without planning, without structural changes, without adjustments and adaptations, or without altering the existing institutions and practices. For example, we cannot eradicate corruption unless people change their values and beliefs, the laws are enacted, the courts set examples by giving retributive and deterrent punishment to corrupt people in high positions, including corrupt politicians, and so on. Many a time, a solution to one of the problems creates many new problems to be solved. Since change in institutions and values comes slowly, solving a problem is not easy and quick and takes considerable time. Sometimes we succeed in changing some conditions and thus in partly reducing the magnitude or the frequency of the problem. We may not be able to eliminate crime completely but we can surely reduce the rate of crime in society by checking the frustrations of people and providing them with alternatives to compensate failure in one field with success in another. It may not be possible to eliminate family disorganization but it is surely possible to find means to reduce tensions in family. Thus, it may not be possible to locate solutions to all problems, but there are prospects of achieving some success in reducing the personal suffering due to social problems.

Sources of Social Problems

1. Social problems occur because modern society is complex and complicated in its internal organization, so an inconsistent social structure cannot help but generate strains and social tensions.
2. Although modern society is highly productive, it still has a dark side to it. There are costs and casualties to any social system.
3. Many developmental systems have brought different types of problems for the people.
4. Social change frequently alters the social structure and therefore disrupts established relations among social groups.

The major social problems India is facing today are:

1. *Corruption* is a major menace in India. Recently conducted survey highlights that as many as 75–80 per cent of people have paid bribes in the last 10 years to get their work done.
2. *Child marriage.* It is also one of the cause of rising population. One report claims that about 47 per cent of Indian girls get married before the legal age of 18 years.
3. *Unplanned urbanization.* More than 17 per cent of urban dwellers live in slums. Slums are homes to crimes, illegal activities and epidemics.
4. *Caste-based discrimination* is still prevalent in India. It sometimes creates violence and makes working of democracy difficult. The different castes can easily be mobilized in elections.
5. *Women related issues* such as female infanticide, gender discrimination, dowry-related deaths, the crime against women are still on the rise. The patriarchal attitude is prevalent in each section of society.
6. *Communalism* was the major factor in pre-independent India which led to the creation of Pakistan. Some instances of religion led to violence are still prevalent in India.
7. *Poverty* is a major obstacle in the development and inclusion of people. As many as 22 per cent of people are still under the incidence of poverty.

Causes of Social Problems

Social problems arise out of pathological social conditions. They occur in all societies – simple (that is, small, isolated and homogeneous with a strong sense of group solidarity, and which changes slowly) as well as complex (which are characterized by impersonal secondary relations, anonymity, loneliness, high mobility and extreme specialization, and where change is faster). What it means is that, wherever and whenever a relationship is affected between a group of individuals, it leads to maladjustments and conflicts.

Three factors are important in understanding of the causal factors in social problems:

1. The causal conditions are numerous. Broadly, the potential causes of social problems found in social environment are: (a) contradictions in social systems, (b) malfunctioning of economic systems, (c) lack of change in religious systems, and (d) defective functioning of political systems.
2. Social problems provide a strong basis of common causal factors.
3. Social problems are interrelated and interdependent in the sense that they are cumulatively promotive and provocative, that is, they foster and encourage one another.

Reinhardt (1952: 7–12) has referred to three factors in the development of social problems:

1. Differentiation and Multiplication of Interests and Functions

The principle that the greater the number of parts in a machine or an organism, the greater will be the probability of maladjustment among the parts, holds good for human societies too, where there is increased opportunity for the collision of interests of various individuals, groups, institutions and systems. Untouchability, communal riots and political crimes are the social problems which are the result of the clash of interests of different castes and classes.

2. Accelerating Frequency of Social Change or Growth of Civilization

This has been made possible due to the multiplication of scientific and mechanical innovations. For example, the invention of machines has destroyed many old forms of employment resulting in the migration of millions of people, and has given rise to class conflicts. It is, thus, the structural and functional maladjustments arising from revolutionary inventions, which create many social problems.

3. Man's Developed Insight to Make a Scientific Analysis

Ever since man has developed his social insight of looking into the working of nature, issues which were formerly regarded as simple are now perceived as the result of various kinds of natural conditions which influence men and society.

Theoretical Approaches to Social Problems

Social problems have been analysed scientifically. Below we examine some of the theoretical approaches which present universal explanations for all types of social problems:

Social Disorganization Approach

Social disorganization is a condition of a society, community or group in which there is a breakdown of social control, a social order, formal and informal norms, that define permissible behaviour. It is characterized by lack of cooperation, common values, unity, discipline and predictability. Warren (1949: 83–87) has described it as a condition involving (a) lack of consensus (disagreement about group purposes), (b) lack of integration of institutions (often working at cross purposes), and (c) inadequate means of social control (preventing individuals from playing their individual roles due to confusion). Elliott and Merrill (1950: 20) have defined it as a process by which relationships between members of a group are broken or dissolved.

Social disorganization occurs when there is a change in the equilibrium of forces, a breakdown of the social structure so that the former patterns no longer apply, and the accepted forms of social control no longer function effectively. This disruptive condition of society, which is evidenced by normlessness, role conflict, social conflicts, and demoralization, increases social problems. For example, increasing industrialization, spread of education, and women taking up paid work have affected the relations between husband and wife, and between parents and children. Many of the old norms which governed the intra-family and inter-family relations seem to have broken down. Many people feel frustrated and unhappy. This is the condition of social disorganization, in which changes in the basic conditions of life, causing breakdown of traditional norms, have resulted in widespread discontentment and disillusionment. In other words, change has disrupted the organization of the formal system of behaviour. Talking of social disorganization in slum life, Whyte (1955: 268) has referred to deviant or non-approved group organization in slums.

However, according to one school of thought, the state of social disorganization does not always create social problems. For example, during Hitler's regime, Germany was not a disorganized society nor during Stalin's regime was the Soviet Union in a state of disorganization; yet many conditions in these countries were shocking 'deviations from the social ideal, demanding social action', that is, there were social problems. Reacting to this view, some scholars say that even if the social disorganization theory may not explain all social problems, it does explain some of the social problems, for example, mental illness may not be a symptom of a disorganized society but corruption in the society does lead to the malfunctioning of institutions, lack of perfect consensus and the evasion of social control by some citizens.

In employing the social disorganization approach to social problems (Horton and Leslie, 1970: 33), one looks upon factors like: What were the traditional norms and practices? What were the major changes that made them ineffective? What are the old rules which have broken down partially or completely? What is the nature and direction of social change? Who are the disgruntled groups and what solutions do they propose? How do various proposed solutions fit in with the trend of social change? What may become the accepted rules in the future?

Cultural Lag Approach

Culture lag is a situation in which some parts of a culture change at a faster rate than other related parts resulting in the disruption of integration and equilibrium of the culture; for example, the material culture changes more rapidly than the non-material culture in industrial societies through rapid advances in science and technology (Ogburn, 1966). The theory of culture lag, in particular, holds that in modern societies there has been a tendency for change in the political, educational, family and religious institutions to fall behind technological changes. It is thus easy to see how culture lag can create social problems. Even after rapid industrialization in the last quarter of the 19th century and in the first quarter of the 20th century, some people were so influenced by the rigid restrictions of the caste system that they refused to work with members of other castes in the industries and preferred to remain unemployed and poor. The first quarter of the 20th century, thus, remained a period of culture lag. It took more than a generation to adapt ourselves to technological development in agriculture and industry. Our social institutions, thus, retained the traditional flavour whereas technology advanced in the world.

Though the culture lag theory explains some of the social problems (like AIDS, population explosion, etc.), it does not explain all social problems. It, therefore, cannot be accepted as a universal explanation of all social problems.

Value Conflict Approach

A value is a generalized principle of behaviour to which the members of a group feel a strong, emotionally-toned positive commitment and which provides a standard for judging specific acts and goals. Each member of the group is expected to remain committed to the values accepted by the group. Values, thus, provide the generalized standards of behaviour. Examples of values are equality, justice, communal harmony, patriotism, mobility, collectivism, compromise, sacrifice, adjustment and so forth. Because of the strong emotional feeling attached to values and because they serve as standards for judging concrete goals or actions, they are often regarded as absolute (Theodorson and Theodorson, 1969: 456).

Different groups have different systems of values. Incompatibility between the values of two or more groups to the extent that the role performance of individuals is interfered with is called 'value conflict'. This state of conflict may last only for a short while or it may be a persistent problem. For example, conflict in values of workers and employers leads to industrial unrest, strikes and lockouts; or conflict in values between land owners and landless labourers leads to agrarian unrest or agricultural labourers' movements; or the liberal businessmen may believe in encouraging hard work, thrift, honesty and ambition and may reward these virtues financially, but on the other hand, the conservatives may differ profoundly with this view and may believe in the profit motive and individual initiative. Liberals and conservatives thus differ not only on matters of policies but more profoundly on those of values.

The value conflict theorists like Waller, Fuller, Cuber and Harper hold that clashes in value system are of basic importance in the origin and development of social problems. Waller (1936: 924) has referred to the conflict between 'organizational' and 'humanitarian' values. The former favour private property and individualism, while the latter are votaries of remedying the misfortunes of others.

But this theoretical approach is too vague. The propounders have not explained their views in concrete details. It is true that our current values overemphasize money and material possessions and this attitude encourages corruption, smuggling, drug trafficking, black marketing and taking of bribes, but problems like white-collar crime cannot be reduced to a conflict of values. The problem of divorce may be the result of value conflict but all family problems cannot be explained merely in terms of disagreements between husband and wife or parents and children. Agreement on common values helps in maintaining harmonious interpersonal relations within the family or outside it, but it is not the only thing needed for family stability or group success. Thus, the value conflict theory may be useful in some areas like economics, and in the analysis of social problems, but it certainly cannot be accepted as a universal explanation.

On applying the value conflict approach, questions generally asked (Horton and Leslie, 1970: 40) are: What are the values that are in conflict? How deep is the value conflict? What groups in the society hold to each of the competing values? How powerful are they? Which values are more consistent with other larger values such as democracy and freedom? What value sacrifices would each solution require? Are some problems insoluble at present because of certain irreconcilable value conflicts?

Personal Deviation Approach

Deviation is non-conformity to social norms. It is different from abnormal behaviour because the latter connotes psychological illness rather than social maladjustment or conflict. Thus, people who deviate from social norms are not necessarily mentally ill.

In the social disorganization approach to social problems, one looks to the rules that have broken down and the changes that have taken place because of the breaking of the rules. In personal deviation approach, one looks to the motivation and behaviour of the deviants who are instrumental in causing the problems. Two factors that need explanation in the personal deviation approach are: (a) How does personal deviancy develop? (b) What types of personal deviation are frequently involved in social problems? Personal deviancy develops because of either (i) an individual's inability to follow generally accepted norms, or (ii) an individual's failure to accept generally accepted norms. The first is caused because of a person's emotional, social or biological deficiency, that is, some persons are so constituted biologically, emotionally, or socially that they are incapable of adhering consistently to generally accepted standards. The socially deficient do not truly violate norms, rather they manifest an inability to learn and follow the norms. The cause of emotional deficiency is bio-psychological. These deviants that constitute social problems and also contribute to problems often require medical, psychiatric and environmental or social therapies. On the other hand, an individual's failure to accept social norms has something to do with deficiency in socialization. These individuals, though have learnt the norms and values like honesty, truthfulness, integrity, justice and cooperation, they cannot put them into practice. They remain disposed to telling lies, cheating, exploiting, defaming others when it suits their purposes. Their deviance does not produce any guilt feeling or shame in them. They may change sides abruptly and completely on a social issue, if it serves their purpose. They care little whether social problems exist and whether they are solved or not as long as the situation can be used for their vested interest.

Horton and Leslie (1970: 35–36) have referred to three types of personal deviations: (a) Deviation that results from conformity to norms of diverse reference groups. Because of cultural variability, most people are exposed to different sets of norms that may be in conflict with one another. For example, a person may belong to one religion or caste but his professional role may literally force him to deviate from the norms of his religion/caste. Similarly, a clerk as well as an officer may accept bribe because it serves economic interests. (b) Deviation that results from the existence of deviant sub-cultures, for example, the criminal norms in slum areas of large cities. (c) Outright deviation from generally accepted norms. Deliberately hiding one's income while filing income tax returns provides a good example of this type of deviation.

In applying the personal deviation approach to social problems, the questions asked (Horton and Leslie, 1970: 37) are: What deviant persons/groups are involved? Are deviants themselves the problem or they help create the problem? What deviant sub-cultures are involved? What alternatives are there for dealing with the deviants?

Anomie Approach

This approach was propounded by Merton. Anomie is a condition characterized by the relative absence or weakening or confusion of norms and values in a society or a group. The concept of anomie was originally developed by Durkheim to explain division of labour and suicide but it was

Merton who used this concept 41 years after the publication of Durkheim's book *Suicide* to explain deviant behaviour in terms of functioning of social and cultural structures in the society (Merton, 1938: 672–73). Anomie involves a breakdown in the cultural structure, occurring particularly when there is disjunction between cultural norms and goals and the socially structured capacities of members of the group to act in accordance with them.

Anomie is the counterpart of the idea of social solidarity. Just as social solidarity is a state of collective ideological integration, anomie is a state of confusion, insecurity and normlessness. According to Merton, the disjunction between goals and means and the consequent strain leads to the weakening of men's commitment to the culturally prescribed goals or institutionalized means, that is, to a state of anomie. Merton maintains that people adapt themselves to this disjunction either by rejecting the cultural goals or the institutionalized means or both. He gives four varieties of deviant behaviour. Merton, thus, locates the sources of strain not in the characteristics of individuals but in the culture and/or social structure. He says, 'the social problem arises not from people failing to live upto the requirements of their social statuses but from the faulty organization of these statuses into a reasonably coherent social system' (Merton and Nisbet, 1971: 823). However, Merton's theory is incomplete and inadequate. All social problems cannot be perceived as the result of the responses to strains or mode of adaptation and adjustment.

Types of Social Problems

Social problems encountered in a society are usually diverse in nature. The factors responsible can be categorized as follows: (a) *economic*, usually in the form of poverty, unemployment, etc. (b) *cultural*, usually in the form of divorce, juvenile delinquency, etc. (c) *biological*, usually in the form of infectious diseases, food poisoning, etc. and (d) *psychological*, usually in the form of neurological disease, a cult, etc.

Case (1964: 34) has described four types of social problems on the basis of their origin: (a) which are rooted in some aspect of the physical environment; (b) which are inherent in the nature or distribution of the population involved; (c) which results from poor social organization; and (d) which evolve from a conflict of cultural values within the society.

According to Fuller and Myers (1941: 367), there are three types of problems: (a) *physical problems*: though these are problems for the society but their causes are not based on value conflicts, for example, floods and famines; (b) *ameliorative problems*: there is consensus about the effects of these problems but there are differences pertaining to their solutions, for example, crime, poverty, and AIDS; and (c) *moral problems*: there is no consensus pertaining to the nature or causes of these problems, for example, gambling, alcoholism, drug abuse and divorce.

Social problems encountered in the community are usually very diverse. However, the diversity of social problems can be categorized into four main factors, namely as follows:

1. Economic factors, usually in the form of poverty, unemployment, and so on.
2. Cultural factors, usually in the form of divorce, juvenile delinquency, and so on.
3. Biological factors, usually in the form of infectious diseases, food poisoning, and so on.
4. Psychological factors, usually in the form of the neurological disease, a cult, and so on.

Sociologists distinguish between two types of social problems. First, problems of social organization which are created by the way the community or the society is organized. Community or society produces situations that some members of the society refuse to accept as right or necessary or even inevitable. These are, for instance, communalism, regionalism, poverty, population, environmental imbalance. Second, problems of deviance having to do with the adjustment of people to conventional ways of living. These include delinquency, drug addiction, alcoholism and other behaviours, most of which are forbidden by law.

Social problems may lead to the following undesirable effects:

1. *Emotional stress*: Social problems of any kind causes immense stress, sadness and worry.
2. *Economic hardship*: In the context of a wider society, social problems can damage the running of economy.
3. *Awkward relationships*: In context of a friendship, they make chatting in groups difficult rather than fun.
4. *Material hardships*: Poverty and discrimination lessen people's quality of life.
5. *Loneliness*: People who have social anxiety can feel very lonely.

Methods of Studying Social Problems

While scientific methods are basically similar for all sciences, scientific techniques differ, for techniques are the particular ways in which scientific methods are applied to a particular problem. Each science, therefore, develops a series of techniques which fits the body of material it studies. What are the techniques of sociological research in studying social problems? Three methods have mainly been used in studying social problems, namely, (a) case study method, (b) social survey method, and (c) multiple factor method. Each method has certain advantages as well as limitations.

Case Study Method

The case study is a complete, detailed account of an event, situation, or development. This method is qualitative instead of quantitative. It analyses the social process involved in the development of a social problem as well as in the causal analysis. It focuses on the sequence of events, motivations of persons, social influences affecting persons and events, social relations, sub-cultures and so forth (Bettelheim, 1955: 318). For collecting information, it depends on both primary and secondary sources like documents, letters and newspapers (Gordon, 1942). Depending on the nature of the social problem, the case study can be used to study a sub-culture of deviants such as that of organized criminals, black marketeers, smugglers, drug addicts, etc.

Perhaps, the greatest value of the case study is in the suggestion of hypotheses, which can then be tested by other methods. For instance, much of our reliable knowledge about adult crime, female crime, juvenile delinquency and crime against women has developed through the testing of hypotheses which were suggested by early case studies of criminals, delinquents, victims of violence, etc. These hypotheses are not often tested by the case study method but by other methods. A generalization cannot be based on a single case, for a case can be found to 'prove' almost anything (Horton, 1984: 34). Generalizations are based on a large mass of carefully processed data and the collection of many case studies is expensive. Also, it is difficult to 'add up' a number of case studies or compute averages or other statistical computations. Therefore, case studies are seldom used when seeking to test a hypothesis.

In analysing the causes of a social problem, the case study method is a qualitative procedure which seeks to formulate generalizations about the development of subject's behaviour. One example of this is the analysis of causes of drug addiction. By exhaustive probing of case after case and the comparing of crucial cases, Lindesmith (1948: 13–15) compared addicts with non-addicts who received drugs for a long time without becoming addicted. This enabled him to isolate the causal processes of addiction that were absent in cases of non-addiction.

This method requires a capacity for cultivating the cooperation and trust of subjects as well as a skill for intensive guided interviewing (Weinberg, 1960: 69).

Social Survey Method

Sometimes the facts we need are not recorded anywhere and we collect them by interviewing people. Interview and questionnaire studies, or the social survey method, thus, is a valuable technique for studying social problems in contemporary society. It collects data from samples of respondents representing a cross-section of a given population through a schedule or a questionnaire. This instrument is frequently used in the field of sociology to answer concrete as well as abstract questions.

The survey method does not necessarily start with a hypothesis. It can end in developing a hypothesis or it may not at all be concerned with a hypothesis. When it seeks answers to questions, it does not test a hypothesis. For example, what is the magnitude of abuse of girl children in a particular type of industry is a practical question, which the information gathered in the survey will answer. But, the survey can test the hypothesis too. For example, this author tested the hypothesis that 'familial maladjustment is the most important cause of criminality among females' (Ahuja,

1966); and also the hypothesis that crime/violence against women is caused by 'social structural conditions that create anxieties and stresses which affect the adjustment, attachment and commitment of man'. 'Maladjustment, unattachment and non-commitment lead to frustrations and relative deprivations which in turn determine man's attitude toward women. Depending on his personality traits and the resistance potential of the victim, the man uses violence against women' (Ahuja, 1987).

Questionnaires, surveys and interviews are the systematic ways of collecting data under scientific controls. But these methods have their pitfalls too which are avoided by sociologists in all possible ways. Assuming that these techniques have a margin of error, they are still very useful, for they are more reliable than guesswork.

Multiple Factor Method

This method determines the relationship between several factors and a social problem. Factors such as the nature of associations, socio-economic status, sub-culture, marital status, residential background, intra-family relations, frustrations and inherited traits can be correlated positively or negatively with the social problem under investigation; for example, the relationship between crime and poverty or between drug addiction and peer group associations and high economic status or between wife battering and inferiority complex and alcoholism or between suicide and feeling of social isolation, marital status, and religion.

The multi-factor approach is used both in single disciplinary studies as well as in interdisciplinary studies of social problems, for instance, collaborative studies on drug addiction by medical scientists, psychologists, sociologists and criminologists in India (Mohan, 1980).

Evaluation Research

The scientific research to analyse the effectiveness of the measures taken to contain a social problem, or to reduce the problems of the sufferers, or to assess the social action programmes such as rehabilitation of drug addicts, job training of the handicapped, and the like, is called 'evaluation research'. Evaluation research uses different techniques of data collection with the objective of gathering knowledge in deciding what programmes should continue and how to improve them. In theory, though the purpose of evaluation research is to assess the 'success' of the programme started for the people but in practice, the purpose is to find out whether the funding of the programme should be continued or not.

In evaluation research, many variables are controlled. Often, the findings of various evaluation studies are so conflicting that no firm conclusions can be drawn. For example, a number of studies have been conducted in India on students' agitations in educational institutions, atrocities against the weaker sections of society, strikes in industries, bonded labourers, etc.

and it has been found that the reported results vary so widely that no clear conclusion is possible. Even when numerous studies do agree, they are disbelieved and ignored. Studies critical of the functioning agency are quietly buried and those whose conclusions conflict with the popular beliefs are disregarded. Despite these difficulties and pitfalls, evaluation research on social problems is the most rapidly growing area of sociological research.

Stages in the Development of a Social Problem

Fuller and Myers (1941: 320–28) have referred to three stages through which a problem passes in the process of being defined and solved:

1. *Awareness*: In this stage, people become convinced that the problem exists, the condition is undesirable, and that something can be done about it. In the beginning, only a few people raise questions but gradually more people become aware of the existence of the problem.
2. *Policy Determination*: As awareness spreads to larger segments of the society, possible solutions come to be discussed, for example, discussion of population explosion in India and various means of family planning in the 1950s, 1960s, 1970s, 1980s and 1990s. Thus, the emphasis in the second stage shifts from what should be done to how it should be done.
3. *Reform*: As basic solutions and policies are decided upon, the stage of action is reached, for example, not only a plan for clearing the slums is put into practice but people living there are also accommodated elsewhere. No wonder, this stage is called the stage of implementation rather than the stage of decision.

Blumer (1971: 290–309) has referred to five stages in the course of a social problem: (a) emergence of a problem, (b) legitimation of a problem, (c) mobilization of action, (d) formulation of an official plan, and (e) implementation of the official plan. He says that movement from one stage to another is not automatic but it depends on many contingencies.

Spector and Kitsuse (1977: 141–50) have talked of four stages in the development of a social problem. These are:

1. *Agitation*: The people feel aggrieved about the existing situation in the society. They agitate against this grievance (a) to convince others that the problem exists, and (b) to initiate action to improve conditions and to attack the alleged cause of the grievance. The agitation is started not necessarily by the victims but even by moral crusaders on behalf of the victims, for example, the prohibition movement is started not by alcoholics but by social workers and social reformers. Thus, the agitation is to convert private troubles into public issues by declaring them to be harmful, offensive and undesirable. However, it is not necessary that their efforts should succeed. The efforts fail either because the claims made are too vague, or because the group that makes

these efforts is insignificant or powerless, or because the group creates conflicting interests.

2. *Legitimation and Capitation*: When the group in power or the power holders acknowledge the existence of the problem, the problem acquires legitimacy. Whereas in the first stage, the claimants of the problems are viewed as peculiar individuals, in this stage they are viewed as legitimate spokesmen of the aggrieved people. They are, therefore, co-opted for discussing alternative solutions, for example, giving representation to workers in factories, in management bodies or to students in the academic councils.
3. *Bureaucratization and Reaction*: When the focus in the first stage is on the complaint group, in the second stage it is on the decision-makers, and in the third stage, it is the bureaucrats and their efficiency which attracts attention. The extent to which the bureaucrats look for solutions of the problem and the extent to which they are able to fob off vested interests will determine whether the agitation will take the form of a movement or not.
4. *Re-emergence of the Movement*: The defective policies of the decision-makers and the bureaucrats and their disinterestedness vis-à-vis the problem rekindle the feelings of the aggrieved people and their crusaders who start a movement to force the power holders to adopt ameliorative measures for solving the problem.

Thus, according to Spector and Kitsuse (1977: 20), 'social problems are pre-eminently a political process through which the problem comes to be publicly accepted as such and through which particular institutional responses to the problem are shaped and then reshaped'.

Solving Social Problems

Since the ancient times, man has been applying his mind to find out a solution to the social problems. In the primitive days, he employed the method of trial and error and frequently resorted to magic and supernatural powers. This was in accordance with his concept of causes of social problems. The modern man does not deal with the social problems through magic or supernatural forces but instead undertakes a scientific analysis of the social problem. The modern approach at present is more realistic and effective. There are two current methods to deal with social problems – remedial and preventive. The remedial method treats the symptoms or consequences of a problem instead of the underlying causes. The preventive method makes painstaking research to find out all the facts underlying each problem before taking a preventive action. The remedial method is now the more common method.

Some reformers advocate an immense variety of cure-all remedies for the solution to most or all of our social problems. Karl Marx regarded the capitalist system as the cause of our problems and held communism as the only way out of most of our problems. Sorokin felt that salvation lies in a return to more spiritual values, to a stage of idealism. Solution to social problems is beset with many hurdles. First, the problem should be accepted by the members of a society as a problem. The existing social structure is supported by powerful sentiments and vested interests. Sometimes these vested interests argue that the remedies proposed would cause greater evils than the problem they are designed to solve. Second, some societies do not want to expose their ways of thinking, feeling and living to scientific inquiry. Third, finances may be a hurdle. Finally, there is the problem of implementation. Some thinkers advocate a *laissez-faire* philosophy to social problems. According to Hebert Spencer, man is automatically moving toward a better adjustment to life conditions and meddling in this evolutionary process is inadvisable. Sumner and Keller, too, held that man's adjustment to conditions of life is automatic. According to them, large-scale effective planning may have disastrous results if it is opposed to the mores and folkways. Thus, we find the thinkers advocating different solutions to social problems according to their concept of causation. But a single solution can not be offered for all the problems. Each social problem is to be scientifically and separately studied and solutions are to be found out accordingly. Social problems must be dealt with as they come up. Some of the major solutions are as follow:

1. Mass awareness
2. Education
3. Humanity
4. Positive attitude
5. Tolerance

A perusal of social problems that affect mankind today indicates that it is not the nature of these problems, but the level of their operation that causes them.

Solving of a social problem depends upon finding out the causes of troublesome social conditions which create the problem. As already stated, though every social problem is caused by multiple factors, but it is always possible to find out the chief factor, the cooperative factors and the minor aggravants in the origin and development of the problem. Every problem is likely to be unique and is likely to have individualistic traits which may differentiate it from other problems. Many a time, the nature of the social problem is such that the control becomes extremely difficult, if not impossible. This happens when a social problem is occasioned by natural factors like droughts or floods or when the conflict of social interests blocks the application of curative programmes, or a revolution is needed to change the existing political or economic systems. But after understanding and judging social problems, the society has to be effective and has to take some action whether it is by attempting to alter the established social institutions or by trying to alleviate them by adopting measures without trying to change the existing institutions. Further, action can be organized or personalized. The former is action through group effort like giving a share to industrial workers in the management of the industry, whereas the latter is action through individual life and influencing others by living a life in accordance with good principles. Gandhiji used the second method for solving the problem of untouchability – by living with untouchables and treating them with sympathy and kindness. When others imitated his example and followed him, the effect became greater and greater, and the government was ultimately forced to enact a law in 1955 prohibiting the practice of untouchability.

Organized action, thus, can be taken by the state or a political party or by the panchayat or an official group. An important point in organized action is the distribution of functions between state agencies and those not connected with the state. Sometimes the problem is solved by the combination of organized and personalized actions.

Social problems can be solved only when individuals in a society possess the following four feelings: (a) feeling that a situation can be corrected, (b) determination to correct the situation, (c) confidence in the people and a belief that there is no limit to progress because of their intelligence and efforts, and (d) the use of technological and rational knowledge and skill for correcting the situation.

The following three points have to be remembered while trying to reach an effective solution to a social problem:

1. *Multiple-factor Approach*: Each social problem is caused by a number of factors, for example, the problem of crime cannot be contained unless it is collectively perceived in terms of poverty, unemployment, social associations, functioning of social structures, strains and frustrations, and so on.
2. *Interrelatedness*: No social problem can be perceived atomistically. Each problem has some relation to the other problems.
3. *Relativity*: Each social problem is related to time and space. What is considered a problem in one society, may not be considered so in the other.

Social Problems and Social Changes in India

Societies often face problems because of social and cultural changes. Social change is a change in the patterned roles, or a change in the network of social relations, or a change in the structures and organization of a society. Social change is never complete or total; it is always partial. It can be minor or fundamental. Further, the change can be spontaneous or planned. Planned change is to achieve some set collective ideals. After independence, India also had set some collective goals to achieve.

Some of the important changes that we find in our society in the last six decades are: change from tradition to modernity in certain values and institutions, from ascribed status to achieved status, from predominance of primary groups to predominance of secondary groups, from informal means of control to formal means of control, from collectivity to individualism, from sacred values to secular values, from folklore to science and rationalism, from homogeneity to heterogeneity, and increasing processes of industrialization and urbanization, increasing awareness of rights among various sections of society due to the spread of education, weakening of the caste system, weakening of traditional sources of security, an increase in the aspirations of minority groups, occupational mobility, enactment of several social laws, and de-linking religion from politics.

Thus, though we have achieved many of the set collective goals, many contradictions have also set into our system. For example, aspirations of the people have become high but the legitimate means for achieving these aspirations are neither available nor accessible. We preach nationalism but practise casteism, linguism and parochialism. Many laws have been enacted but either these laws are full of loopholes or they are not properly implemented. We talk of egalitarianism but we enforce discrimination. We aspire for an ideational culture but what is emerging is the sensate culture. All these contradictions have increased discontentment and frustrations among people which in turn have resulted in many social problems. Youth unrest, tribal unrest, peasant unrest, labour unrest, student unrest, minority unrest, violence against women, and so forth, have all led to agitations, riots, insurgency and terrorism in the country.

Sociology, Sociologists and Social Problems

Before we analyse the relationship between sociology and social problems, we need to answer a question: Why do we study social problems in sociology? It is not because most people consider them 'bad' and these need to be eliminated. In fact, sociology as a social science, like natural sciences, attempts to approach its subject matter objectively. If we approach the study of social problems assuming that they are bad, we are not being objective and will not achieve a sociological understanding.

The three issues which need analysis with regard to the relationship between sociology and social problems are: (a) how does sociology perceive social problems; (b) what sociological principles does sociology offer about the social problems; and (c) to what extent is the knowledge of the sociologists about social problems impartial, confirmed and concrete?

As far as the sociologists' perspective is concerned, they view social problems as problems which arise out of the functioning of systems and structures in a society, or which are the result of group influences. They are also concerned with social relationships which emerge and are sustained because of the social problems. Thus, in analysing alcoholism, whereas a doctor will be concerned with its effects on the body, a psychiatrist will be concerned with its effects on attitudes and behaviour, and a sociologist will be concerned with its effects on social relations and roles, that is, the relations with family members, with colleagues in the office, and with neighbours and friends as well as its effect on work efficiency, status, and so on.

The study of social problems in sociology aspires towards a body of valid and logically related principles, and in some cases towards a systematic theory too (Rose, 1957: 189–99). Sociological knowledge of social problems is not complete. We have considerable knowledge about some social problems like crime and drug abuse, but inadequate knowledge about others like suicide, bonded labour, black marketing, mental illness, etc. According to Weinberg (1960: 64), this unevenness in knowledge about social problems is because our approach to social problems is generally 'problem-centred' rather than 'theory-centred'. Most sociologists study social problems because of the practical interest of the community rather than for building a theory, or filling up the theoretical gaps. As regards bias in the sociologists' knowledge, though it is true that their orientation and their values can influence their study of social problems, yet they try to interpret facts without any distortion (Kolb, 1954: 66–67). For example, a sociologist from a lower or a middle class is likely to have a bias towards his/her own class, yet he/she does not analyse corruption in upper class on the basis of his/her personal predilections. He/she remains impartial without being affected by any pressures. However, one possibility that exists is that persons involved in many social problems (that is, subjects) can directly influence the knowledge which emerges. For example, a sociological study of wife battering is possible in a society like India on a 'snowball' method because the complaints of assault are never lodged with the police. The study generally points out the involvement of women from lower income groups. Hence, we do not have much knowledge about battered women in upper-middle or upper income groups. The fact that data on all types of battered women is not available is bound to affect the sociological conclusions or hypotheses. Similarly, the study of role adjustment of working women restricted to the lower class rarely points to separation, desertion or divorce between husband and wife but the study of working women in middle and upper classes would probably show a higher likelihood of these steps.

One more fact in the study of social problems by the sociologists is that some sociologists think that the only role of a sociologist is that of an analyst, that is, he/she is to understand social problems but not take interest in their solution. Others think that a sociologist has not only to study social problems but has to devise ways and means to correct them. Knowledge cannot be detached completely from concerted corrective action. It has to be used in alleviating social problems. But, the fact to be remembered is that a sociologist by himself/herself cannot solve a social problem. Much depends on the officials, politicians, agencies and general public.

What is the task of a sociologist? The time has come when sociologists decide to undertake 'management of change in society' like management of business or management of administration. The central concerns of sociology are order and change. The concern for change includes the directionality of change, and sociologists have to move from delving deep into the hoary past through Indology and ancient history and from postulating concepts and theories suitable to study Indian social reality to futuristic plans and to identifying and dealing with crises in the society.

Here, a question may be raised: should sociologists be concerned with applied programmes directed at finding solutions to our social problems and in the basic research activities designed to support them? Our answer would be in the affirmative. The depth of a society's problems may require deeper structural and cultural changes. While sociologists have always been involved in analysing and understanding established practices, now they have to be called upon to suggest new structures and new practices. In doing so, the question arises as to what are the appropriate ways for the sociologists to suggest changes? The first question is, how directly should the sociologists involve themselves in effecting a change in public policy? Should sociologists remain dispassionate scientists, only providing data for others to use, or should they become actively involved as impassioned advocates of change? There is a school which stresses direct action in public policies on the part of the sociologists. We have to support this school. Sociology is a science which has to be pursued for its fruits, for the sake of what it can do. In its initial stages, the gifts of sociology may not have been great, but after the labour that has been put in developing this science during the last five to six decades, the fruits may be plucked not for their beauty but for their utility. Earlier, we might have been bogged down in explaining various concepts or in historically tracing the growth and functioning of various social institutions and communities but today our discipline has to take up the questions of the present and the future imbalances seriously. In this, questions of relevance and priorities in researches are significant. Why have top Indian sociologists remained indifferent to studying problems and critical issues like insurgency in North-East India, terrorism in Punjab, linguistic mobilization in Assam, cultural polarization in Mizoram, anti-reservation agitations in Gujarat, Madhya Pradesh, Andhra Pradesh, Delhi, Uttar Pradesh and Bihar, communal riots in Uttar Pradesh, Gujarat and Maharashtra, and police torture and criminalization of politics in Bihar? Is it because they are afraid of displeasing the establishment by their unbiased and critical evaluations and losing their positions in councils and committees and commissions, or is it because they think that these issues do not fall within the scope of their pure science? We are not trying to be critical but only pointing to the need for sociologists to take interest in the management of change in society. If sociology and sociologists alienate themselves from the immediate issues and problems of our society, both our discipline and our scholars will render themselves irrelevant to the nation as well as to humanism. It is time that the sociologists develop better predictive capabilities and present the options to the public in a comprehensible manner. This alone will help the society in tackling social problems effectively.

To conclude, it may be said that the sociologists' role in studying social problems is to create an awareness about these problems, analyse the causes of the problems, develop theories about the problems, discuss effects of social problems on individuals, groups and society, and examine the consequences of alternate plans suggested for solving problems.

References

Ahuja, Ram, *Female Offenders in India*, Meenakshi Prakashan, Meerut, 1969.

Becker, Howard S., *Social Problems: A Modern Approach*, John Wiley & Sons, New York, 1966.

Blumer, H. and Hruser, O., *Movies, Delinquency and Crime*, The Macmillan Co., New York, 1933.

Bredemeier, H.C. and Toby, J., *Social Problems in America*, John Wiley & Sons Inc., New York, 1960.

Carr, Lowell J., *Analytical Sociology*, Harper, New York, 1955.

Cuber, John F. and Harper, Robert A., *Problems of American Sociology: Values or Conflict*, Holt, New York, 1948.

Elliott, Mabel A. and Merrill, Francis E., *Social Disorganisation*, Harper and Brothers, New York, 1950.

Fuller, Richard C. and Myers, Richard R., 'The Natural History of a Social Problem', *American Sociological Review*, Vol. 6, 1941.

Gillin, J.L., Dittmen, C.G., Colbert, R.J. and Kastler, N.M., *Social Problems*, The Times of India Press, Bombay, 1965.

Hermon, Abbon P., *An Approach to Social Problems*, Ginn, Boston, 1949.

Horton, Paul B. and Leslie, Gerald R., *The Sociology and Social Problems* (4th edn), Appleton Century Crofts, New York, 1970.

Landis, Paul H., *Social Problems*, J.B. Lippincott Co., Chicago, 1959.

Laskin, Richard (ed.), *Social Problems*, McGraw Hill Co., New York, 1964.

Lindesmith, Alfred R., *Opiate Addiction*, Principia Press, Bloomington Indiana, 1948.

Merton, R.K., 'Social Structure and Anomie', *American Sociological Review*, Vol. 3, No. 5, 1938.

Merton, R.K., *Social Theory and Social Structure*, Free Press, Glencoe, New York, 1957.

Merton, Robert K. and Nisbet, Robert A. (eds), *Contemporary Social Problems*, Harcourt Brace, New York, 1971.

Mohan, D., *Drug Abuse in India*, AIIMS, Delhi, 1980.

Neumeyer, M.H., *Social Problems and the Changing Society*, Princeton, New Jersey, 1953.

Phelps, Harold A. and Henderson, David, *Contemporary Social Problems*, Prentice Hall, Englewood Cliffs, New Jersey, 1952.

Raab, Earl and Selznick, G.J., *Major Social Problems*, Row Peterson and Co., Illinois, 1959.

Reinhardt, James M., Meadows, Paul and Gillette, John M., *Social Problems and Social Policy*, American Book Co., New York, 1952.

Rose, Arnold, 'Theory for the Study of Social Problems', *Social Problems*, Vol. 4, No. 2, 1957.

Spector, Malcolm and Kitsuse, John, *Constructing Social Problems*, Cumnings, Menlo Park, CA, 1977.

Stark, Rodney, *Social Problems*, Random House, New York, 1975.

Walsh, Maty E. and Furfey, Paul H., *Social Problems and Social Action* (3rd edn), Prentice Hall, Englewood Cliffs, New Jersey, 1961.

Weinberg, Kirson S., *Social Problems in Our Times*, Prentice Hall Inc., Englewood Cliffs, New Jersey, 1960.

2

Poverty

Facts on Poverty in India

Tribals, Dalits and labour class including farm workers in villages and casual workers in cities are still very poor and make the poorest class in India. Sixty per cent of the poor still reside in the states of Bihar, Jharkhand, Odisha, Madhya Pradesh, Chhattisgarh, Uttar Pradesh and Uttarakhand. The reason for these states to be in the category of the poorest states is that 85 per cent of tribal people live there. According to the Global Hunger Index (GHI) report 2012, by the International Food Research Institute, India ranks 97th in global hunger index. Though there is no shortage of food production in India, our nation still has the highest percentage of underweight children under five. India is working hard to become a superpower, but what about these poor people in India, as our nation still lags behind in improving GHI.

India, at present, has a greater share of the poor around the world. Thirty years ago, India was home to one-fifth of the world's poor but now it is home to one-third of poor people. This means we now have a larger share of poor in India than thirty years ago, 6.5 crore Indians live in extreme poverty, about 4.9 per cent of the population. About 41.6 Indians escape poverty every second. India is on track to eradicate extreme poverty by 2030.

Meaning of Poverty

Poverty refers to a situation when people are deprived of sufficient food, shelter and other basic necessities of life. When a big portion of the population is deprived of the minimum living standard and survives only on the survival level, then it is said that poverty is widely spread in the population.

It is only in the second half of the 20th century that poverty and the poor have gained our concern and obligation. After a long neglect of the poor during the British rule, the measures adopted after independence signify the recognition of poverty and the social responsibility for alleviating it. How did this happen? What have we done? How far have we succeeded? Before attempting to answer these questions, let us first discuss the concept of poverty.

The Concept

The definition of poverty matters because how it is defined determines how much poverty there is believed to be. The definition can also influence the explanations of poverty and the possible solutions that are put forward. As Ruth Lister puts it, 'How we define poverty is critical to political, policy and academic debates about the concept. It is bound up with explanations and has implications of solutions' (cited in Holborn and Haralambos, 2008: 214).

Poverty is a situation that gives rise to a feeling of a discrepancy between what one has and what one should have. What one should have is an internal construct; hence, each person's feeling and experience of poverty is individual and unique. But, the feeling of 'powerlessness' and 'resourcelessness' is possessed by all poor people. Henry Bernstein (1992) has identified the following dimensions of poverty:

1. Lack of livelihood strategies
2. Inaccessibility to resources (money, land, credit)
3. Feeling of insecurity and frustrations
4. Inability to maintain and develop social relations with others as a consequence of lack of resources

Three precepts are often used to define poverty: (a) the amount of money required by a person to subsist, (b) the life below a 'minimum subsistence level' and 'living standard' prevalent at a given time in a given place, and (c) the comparative state of well-being of a few and the deprivation and destitution of a majority section in society. The last approach explains poverty in terms of relativity and inequality. Whereas the first two precepts refer to the economic concept of absolute poverty, the third one views it as a social concept, that is, in terms of the share of the total national income received by those at the bottom. We will explain each of the three views separately.

The First View

In terms of minimum income required for subsistence, poverty has been defined as an inability to gratify the physiological needs, that is, need for survival, safety and security. These physiological needs are different from the social needs (ego satisfaction and self-esteem), the need for autonomy, the need for independence and the need for self-actualization. The minimum requirements for fulfilling the physiological needs are food and nutrition, shelter, and preventive and protective health care. This requires 'minimum' income (varying from society to society) to buy necessities and availing of facilities.

Here 'poverty' is perceived in terms of 'poverty line' which is determined by the prevailing standards of what is needed for health, efficiency, nurturing of children, social participation, and the maintenance of self-respect (Becker, 1966: 436). In practice, however, the poverty line is drawn on the basis of a barest minimum desirable nutritional standard of calorie intake. In India, the poverty line was drawn in 1978 on the basis of a per capita (adult) daily intake of 2,400 calories for the rural and 2,100 calories for the urban areas.

The Second View

This view maintains that poverty has three main aspects of want of material goods or materialistic possessions: (a) those necessary to avoid physical suffering and needed to fulfil the requirements of hunger and shelter, that is, those needed to survive; (b) those essential to meet human needs of health, that is, to get nutrition and to avoid diseases; and (c) those needed to maintain a minimum subsistence level. In simple terms, this refers to a minimum amount of food intake, adequate housing, clothing, education and health care.

Gross and Miller (1946: 83) attempted to explain poverty in terms of three factors: income (covert and manifest), assets, and availability of services (educational, medical, recreational). The assets or the materialistic possessions, therefore, cannot be the basis of specifying poverty. Likewise, poverty cannot be related to the 'income' factor. If there is an increase in the 'price level', people may not be able to provide the necessities of life for their family members. Obviously then, poverty has to be related to time and place.

The Third View

This view defines poverty as a condition of falling below the minimum standards of subsistence appropriate to each society, or 'the absence of enough money to secure life's necessities', or 'a condition of acute physical want – starvation, malnutrition, disease, and want of clothing, shelter and medical care'. The latter is measured by comparing the condition of those at the bottom of the society with the other segments of the population. It is, thus, a matter of subjective definition rather than of objective conditions. Poverty is determined by the standards that exist within a society. Miller and Roby (1970: 34–37) have said that in this approach, poverty is sharply regarded as 'inequality'. From a sociological point of view, this definition is more important in terms of the impact which inequality of income has on the life situation and life chances of the poor. Absolute poverty can be reduced/eliminated by putting money into the hands of the poor but 'inequality' cannot be solved by moving people above a certain relative line. As long as there are people at the bottom of the income scale, they are poor in some way. Such a condition will continue to exist as long as we have social stratification.

Harrington (1958: 83) defined poverty with reference to 'deprivation'. According to him, poverty is the deprivation of those minimal levels of food, health, housing, education, and recreation which are compatible with the contemporary technology, beliefs and values of a particular society. Rein (1968: 116) identifies three elements in poverty: subsistence, inequality and externality. Subsistence emphasizes the provisions of sufficient resources to maintain health and working capacity in the sense of survival, and capacity to maintain physical efficiency. Inequality compares the lot of individuals at the bottom layer of stratified income levels with that of the more privileged people in the same society. Their deprivation is relative. Externality focusses on the social consequences of poverty for the rest of society, apart from the impact on the poor themselves.

Sociologically speaking, the poor are caught up in vicious circles. Being poor means living in poor neighbourhood, which means being unable to send children to school, which means not only the poor themselves but their children too will have low-paying jobs or no jobs at all, which means being doomed to remain poor for ever. Also, being poor means eating poor food, which means having poor health, which in turn means being handicapped or too weak to handle the heavy manual work, which also means accepting low paid work, which leads to remaining poor for ever. Thus, each circle begins and ends with being poor. No wonder, sociologists like Thomas Gladwin (1967: 76–77) give more importance to 'inequality' or the social concept of poverty.

The Problem of Poverty

India is recognized as a poor country even after around 70 years of independence. Especially in the rural sector of India, the condition is worse. Though during the planning periods, the national income of India and the per-capita income has increased, social welfare has increased, literacy level has risen and people have been able to fulfil more and more of their requirements but poverty (and especially rural poverty) is still present in its alarming form.

Absolute Poverty: It is the extreme kind of poverty involving the chronic lack of basic food, clean water, health and housing. Absolute poverty results in extreme hunger, starvation and malnutrition. People in absolute poverty tend to struggle to live. This type of poverty is usually long term in nature and often handed to them by generations before them.

Relative Poverty: This kind of poverty is usually in relation to other members and families in society. For example, a family can be considered poor because the rest of the community have access to superior services and amenities. Relative poverty may cause people to indulge in social vices such as drugs and petty crimes as a means to meet their immediate needs.

Situational Poverty: People or families can be poor because of some adversities like a serious illness. Sometimes, people can help themselves out of this situation quickly, if they are given a bit of assistance, as the cause of their situations was just one unfortunate event.

Generational or Chronic Poverty: This is when poverty is handed over to individuals and families from generations before them.

Measurements of Poverty

First, researchers have disputed whether poverty should be measured in 'absolute' or 'relative' terms. Sane writers have argued that there is a common minimum standard that can be applied to all societies below which individuals can be said to be in poverty.

Measures of absolute poverty are usually based upon the idea of subsistence. In other words, people are in poverty if they do not have the resources to maintain human life.

Supporters of the concept of relative poverty, however, tend to dismiss this view. They argue that a definition must relate to the standards of a particular society at a particular time. According to this view, the point at which the dividing line separates the poor from other members of society is drawn, will vary according to how affluent that society is.

Now, the question arises: What are the measurements of poverty? The important measurements are: malnutrition, low consumption expenditure, low income, chronic illness or poor health, illiteracy, unemployment and/or underemployment, and unsanitary housing conditions. Broadly, the poverty of a given society is expressed in terms of poor resources, low national income, low per capita income, high disparity in income distribution, weak defence, and the like.

Till 2004–05, the poverty line was constructed using the recommendation of the Lakdawala Committee (1993) which essentially recommended that consumption expenditure should be calculated based on calorie consumption. The state-specific poverty lines should be constructed and these should be updated using the consumer price index of industrial workers (CPI-IW) in urban areas and consumer price index of agricultural labour (CPI-AL) in rural areas. In the year 2005, the Tendulkar Committee recommended four major changes: (a) a shift away from calorie consumption based poverty estimation; (b) a uniform Poverty Line Basket (PLB) across rural and urban India; (c) a change in the price adjustment procedure to correct spatial and temporal issues with price adjustment; and (d) incorporation of private expenditure on health and education while estimating poverty.

Poverty in India

India represents a dichotomy in development. According to UNIDO's 'Yearbook of Statistics 2010' India has emerged as one of the world's top ten countries in industrial production. It ranks ninth in world industrial production and tenth in Gross National Production (GNP), yet it has a large population that is extremely poor. The United Nations Human Development Index (2013), based on three indicators – life expectancy, access to education and income levels – ranks India 136th among 186 countries.

According to Ansari and Akhtar (2012), at the beginning of the new millennium, 26 crore people in India did not have income to access a consumption basket which defines the poverty line. Of these, 75 per cent were in the rural areas. India is home to 22 per cent of the world's poor. Such a high incidence of poverty is a matter of concern in view of the fact that poverty eradication has been one of the major objectives of the development planning process.

In India, the last decade of the 20th century has seen a visible shift in the focus of development planning from, mere expansion of production of goods and services and the consequent growth of per capita income, to planning for enhancement of human well-being. The notion of human well-being itself is broadly conceived to include not only consumption of goods and services in general, but more specifically to ensure that the basic material requirements of all sections of the population, especially those below the poverty line, are met and that they have access to basic services such as health and education. This approach has resulted in the reduction in poverty along with overall improvement in the quality of life.

According to the data released by the Planning Commission, though poverty has shown biggest drop, one in five Indians is still below poverty line as the share of BPL population in the total population is 21.9 per cent, or 27 crore (the government has set the bar low, defining as BPL anyone earning ₹ 27.20 or less in rural areas and up to ₹ 33.30 a day in urban areas).

In spite of reduction in the number of poor across the country, income disparity between rich and poor is growing rapidly.

Causes of Poverty

Main causes of poverty in India are as follows:

1. *Climatic factors*: Climatic conditions constitute an important cause of poverty. Unfavourable climate and weather hinders the work and production. Frequent floods, famines, earthquakes and cyclones cause heavy damage to agriculture. Moreover, absence of timely rainfall, excessive or deficient rain, severely affect country's agricultural production. This increases poverty.
2. *Demographic factors*: The rapid growth of population aggravates the poverty of the people. The growth of population exceeds the rate of growth in national income. Population growth not only creates difficulties in the removal of poverty but also lowers the per capita income which tends to increase poverty.
3. *Economic causes*:
   (a) *Low agricultural productivity:* Poverty and real income are very much interrelated. Increase in real income leads to a reduction of the magnitude of poverty.
   (b) *Unequal distribution of land and other assets:* Land and other forms of assets constitute sources of income for the rural people but,

unfortunately there has been an unequal distribution of land and other assets in our economy. The size-wise distribution of operational holdings indicates a very high degree of concentration in the hands of a few farmers leading to the poverty of many in the rural sector.

(c) *Decline of village industries:* At present upto industrialization new factories and industries are being set up in rural areas. Village industries fail to compete with them in terms of quality and price. As a result, they are closed down. The workers are thrown out of employment and lead a life of poverty.

(d) *Lack of employment opportunities:* Unemployment is the reflection of poverty. Because of lack of employment opportunities, people remain either unemployed or under-employed. Most of these unemployed and under-employed workers are the small and marginal farmers and the landless agricultural labourers.

4. *Social causes*:

(a) *Education*: Education is an agent of social change and social equality. However, the present education system is more idealistic than realistic. Poverty is also said to be closely related to the levels of schooling, and these two have a circular relationship. The work by Hnatkovska and Lahiri (2012) shows that education has indeed been pivotal in bridging the wage gap between scheduled castes and scheduled tribes on one hand and non-scheduled castes on the other. This suggests an important role of education in eradicating poverty.

(b) *Caste system*: The caste system in India has always been responsible for rural poverty. The subordination of the low caste people by the high caste people caused poverty of the former. Due to the caste system, people have to carry on their traditional work, even if it is unprofitable. That is why the rich people of old times did not accept small or low-grade jobs.

(c) *Joint family system*: The joint family system provides social security to its members but some people take undue advantage of it. They live upon the income of others and become idlers. Their normal routine of life consists of eating, sleeping and begetting children. In this way, poverty gets aggravated through the joint family system.

(d) *Social customs and traditions*: The ruralites spend a large percentage of their annual earnings on social ceremonies like marriage, death feast, etc. For the sake of their own customs and traditions, the illiterate people spend thousands of rupees, and take loans for their traditions and stay strangulated in poverty. There are several social evils like dowry, child marriage, *purdah* system, etc. which have several bad effects and help in raising poverty.

5. *Growing indebtedness*: In the rural sector, most of the ruralites depend on borrowings from the moneylenders and landlords to meet even their

consumption expenses. Moneylenders, however, exploit the poor by charging exorbitant rates of interest and by acquiring the mortgaged land in the event of non-payment of loans. Indebted poor farmers cannot make themselves free from the clutches of moneylenders. Their poverty is further made more noticeable because of indebtedness. Such indebted families continue to remain under the poverty line for generations because of this debt-trap.

6. *Lower growth rate*: The growth rate of the Indian economy is very low. Sixty years of the planning period, the average growth rate has been 3.5 per cent which has deepened the roots of poverty.
7. *Unemployment in India*: The increasing rate of unemployment has spread more problems. Due to increasing unemployment, poverty has taken a more serious form. It is expected that the population in India will reach upto 1.5 billion by 2026 and then, India will be the largest nation in the world. This means shortage of jobs. For this much population, near about 20 million new jobs would be required. The number of poor will keep on increasing if such a big number of jobs won't be created.
8. *Political causes*: The long bondage of the country has slowed the pace of the economy. The foreign invaders took no interest in the development of basic industries. The *zamindari* system started in the country which exploited the farmers completely. Their agricultural policies gave birth to landless farmers and their exploitation. Poverty also increased their exploitation.
9. *Traditional production techniques*: In the fields of agriculture and manufacturing, the production techniques are traditional which have lowered the production level due to which poverty has increased.
10. *Inflation*: In India, inflation has taken an alarming shape. Due to this, people are unable to fulfil the basic requirements of their families. Today 30 per cent of the population of our country is covered under the poor class.
11. *Dependency on agriculture*: Most of the population in India depends on agriculture for their living. Each family has a small piece of land and lives with difficulty and due to the dependency only on agriculture, they remain poor.
12. *Alcoholism*: Poverty has also increased due to alcoholism. Each day, millions of people are destroying their money and health due to the habits of alcoholism. Thus, alcoholism is one of the reasons for the increase in this problem in India.
13. *Belief in fate*: Most of the population in India give importance to conservative attitude and analyse each aspect on the basis of fate. People become inactive on the thought that it is their fate that is making things happen and live lifelong in the lap of poverty.
14. *Adverse environment and climate*: On the peaks of Himalayas, there is always snowfall, Rajasthan is also under the same climate in another form. Due to the desert, farming is not possible there and poverty has

increased. Thus, the adversity of the environment and the climate has a deep impact on the growth of the nation.

15. *Lack of natural resources*: The places where the land is infertile, there is absence of resources for production. Coal or iron, minerals, etc. are also not available there, people of that place are poor. Due to geographical reasons, there are several places in India where 100 per cent of the population is poor. Like, the land of the hilly areas is not at all fit for agriculture. Moreover, due to the lack of resources for agriculture also people are poor.
16. *Harm by insects*: The termites attack the south Indian crops even today and destroy the crops. Moreover, many kinds of insects and rats destroy the wheat, maize, paddy, etc. The grains stored by the traders are also destroyed by these insects and rats. On an estimate, about 15 to 20 per cent of the crops are destroyed by them. Thus, this is also one of the reasons for Indian poverty.
17. *Lack of industries*: The opportunity of industrial development came after independence but due to the policies of the British rule, the industries could not develop properly. The cottage industries also could not get protection. This gave rise to the unbalanced growth of industries.

Thus, it can be concluded that the most important causes of poverty in India are poor agriculture, growing population, a gap between rich and poor, corruption and black money and high population growth rate. This further leads to high level of illiteracy, poor health care facilities and lack of access to financial resources. Also, high population growth affects the per capita income and makes per capita income even lower. It is expected that the population in India will reach upto 1.5 billion by 2026 and then India will be the largest nation in the world. But India's economy is not growing at the same pace. This means a shortage of jobs. Poor people move from villages to towns and from one town to another in search of employment/work. Since they are mostly illiterate and unskilled, there are very few employment opportunities open for them. Due to unemployment, many poor people are forced to live an unfulfilled life.

There are two extreme perspectives on the basis of which we can analyse the causes of poverty – the old and the modern. One view of poverty is that it is providential and it is the result of an individual's past *karmas* (deeds) or sins. The other view ascribes poverty to be the result of failure of an individual's working abilities or due to his/her lack of motivation. Describing the richness of a rich person in terms of his/her destiny and the poverty of a poor person in terms of his/her lack of abilities serves the economic interest of the rich people as they escape paying high taxes to be used for uplifting the poor. One modern view links poverty with factors which are beyond an individual's control, the other describes the functioning of social systems in the society as the cause of poverty.

David Elesh (1973: 359) has given three causes of poverty: individual, culture or sub-culture of poverty, and social structure.

Individual

The ideology of individualism which finds the cause of poverty within the individual is that success and failure of an individual are his personal matters. If one ends up in poverty, it is his own fault, because he is lazy, dull, inefficient or lacks initiative. This ideology maintains that poverty is good for society because the fittest will survive. Another aspect of this ideology is the Protestant Ethics described by Max Weber, which emphasizes on individual's success through his hard work, virtue, and honesty. If he fails, he has no one but himself to blame, for he has vices, is idle and has bad habits. The typical 'victimblamer' is a middle-class person who is enjoying reasonably good material success and has a good job and steady income. He says: 'I had to struggle to make it; why can't the poor? There must be something wrong with them'. Spencer, Carnegie and Lane believe in this ideology.

Culture or Sub-culture of Poverty

The second cause of poverty is the culture of poverty, or the way of life of the poor. Such a culture blocks all attempts of the society to change the values, norms, beliefs and lifestyle of the poor. The 'culture of poverty' concept suggests that despite economic changes, the poor have remained so because of their culture or sub-culture. The culture of the poor fosters behaviour and values associated with poverty; it has kept the poor out of the mainstream of industrial society. Oscar Lewis popularized the notion of culture of poverty in 1959. He maintained that it was a special culture that passes on poverty from generation to generation. This conservative concept, often shared by the politicians and the public, has given our society a reason for doing little or nothing about the poor and poverty as a social problem. Advocates of this ideology identify lower-class culture and assume that the lifestyle of the poor is the cause of continued poverty. Ryan and Chilman believe in this school of thought.

Social Structure

While 'individual' and 'culture of poverty' are accepted as causes of poverty by the conservatives, the liberals, the radicals, and the sociologists link poverty to social structure or to 'miserable and unjust social conditions'. Our social institutions, our economy, low educational attainment, lack of employable skills, long-term unemployment or underemployment cause and perpetuate poverty. Change in social and economic structures is not brought about, or hindered by the vested interests. Sociologist Herbert Gans has pointed out three functional gains – economic, political and social – that the middle-class derive from having a poverty-group in the society. These range from getting society's 'dirty work' done to preserve one's high status or keeping oneself in power. Thus, the fault of poverty lies with those individuals/groups who do not want to change the social structure, values and norms for their vested interests.

Concluding the discussion on the causes of poverty, it may be said that poverty in India needs to be perceived in relationship to three factors: (a) diverse historical and cultural roots of Indian attitudes, ideas, beliefs and values, that is, people's strong linkages with the past; (b) fundamental relationship between the biological and psychological characteristics of man; and (c) changes in Indian society pertaining to public policy, particularly during and after liberation from the British rule. As such, if poverty existed in India, it was because of the economic policies of the British government, lack of incentives to the people, lack of education and technological knowledge, lethargy, callousness and exploitation of the rural people, and religious and social barriers to control the family size. If after independence efforts are being made to contain poverty, it is through family planning, new industrial and agricultural policies, spread of education, and giving subsidy and training to the needy people.

However, the combination of following measures may prove to be more helpful in reducing poverty: (a) reducing the fiscal deficits by the central and the state governments; (b) lifting import restrictions and boosting up exports; (c) controlling the borrowings; (d) selling units in public sector which are constantly undergoing losses; (e) collecting more taxes; (f) improving cost effectiveness by monitoring welfare expenditure; (g) making additional funds available in the field of trade and commerce and controlling the bank rate as well as the capital erosion by making the realization of bad debts easier; (h) loans to the weaker sections of society may be provided at preferred rates while the extent of subsidy may be kept within reasonable limits; (i) though many licensing restrictions have been removed, there is still a need to review the remaining licensed items so that competition, intensified and dynamism may be imparted to Indian industry; (j) lowering customs tariffs for making the Indian economy internationally competitive; (k) removing constraints on capital-intensive infrastructure industries, such as power, irrigation and telecommunications so that these may develop competitive market structures; (l) our labour legislation till now is so designed as to provide workers with maximum security in terms of employment and wages. It is now time that labour laws are linked with labourers' performance and security is provided both to the workers and the employers; (m) growth in agricultural economy must be accelerated since two-third population is till dependent on agriculture. This requires action on several fronts, including resolving the problems of land tenure, raising the levels of investment, increasing availability of credit, ensuring appropriate pricing policies, developing new technologies to increase productivity, decontrol of prices of certain fertilizers, and setting up public investment in agriculture and rural development; (n) integrating various schemes of rural development; and (o) reducing subsidies, government expenditure and government employees.

If we unhaltingly go on with our reforms, we can overcome the severe constraints on our economy, reduce poverty, and assure a prosperous future for our people.

Poverty in Rural India

It is said that rural India is the heart of India. In spite of all the efforts, the condition of villagers is far from satisfactory, that is extremely poor. The report on Socio-Economic and Caste Census (2011) reveals the following facts:

1. *SC/ST of the rural households:* Around 18.46 per cent belongs to scheduled castes, and around 10.97 per cent belongs to scheduled tribes.
2. *A major source of income*: Manual casual labour jobs and cultivation are the major sources of income for rural people. Nearly 51 per cent of all households are economically engaged in manual casual labour and nearly 30 per cent of them are engaged in cultivation.
3. *Land ownership*: Around 56 per cent of village households do not own a land.

The number of poor people in India, according to the country's Eleventh National Development Plan, amounts to more than 300 million. The country has been successful in reducing the proportion of poor people, but almost one-fifth of the country's population of more than 11 billion continues to live below the poverty line, and a large proportion of poor people live in rural areas. Poverty remains a chronic condition for almost 30 per cent of India's rural population. The incidence of rural poverty has declined somewhat over the past three decades as a result of rural to urban migration.

Poverty is the deepest among the members of SCs/STs in the country's rural areas. On the map of poverty in India, the poorest areas are in parts of Rajasthan, Madhya Pradesh, Uttar Pradesh, Bihar, Jharkhand, Odisha, Chhattisgarh and West Bengal. Large number of India's poorest people live in the country's semi-arid tropical region. In these areas shortages of water and recurrent droughts impede the transformation of agriculture that the Green Revolution has achieved elsewhere. There is also a high incidence of poverty in flood-prone areas such as those extending from eastern Uttar Pradesh to the Assam plains, and especially in northern Bihar.

Poverty affects tribal people in forest areas also, where loss of entitlement to resources has made them even poorer. In coastal fishing communities people's living conditions are deteriorating because of environmental degradation, stock depletion and vulnerability to natural disasters.

Causes of Rural Poverty

The following causes of poverty in rural areas may be identified:

1. Inadequate and ineffective implementation of anti-poverty programmes.

2. Low percentage of population engaged in non-agricultural pursuits.
3. Non-availability of irrigational facilities and erratic rainfall in several states.
4. Low agricultural productivity resulting from dependence on traditional methods of cultivation and inadequate knowledge of modern skills.
5. Non-availability of electricity for agricultural as well as industrial use in most of the villages.
6. Poor quality of livestock.
7. Imperfect and exploited credit market.
8. Lack of link roads, communication facilities and markets (i.e. infra-structure).
9. Low level of education. The general literacy level in the rural areas in the country is low while for females it is very low.
10. Absence of dynamic community leadership.
11. Failure to seek women's cooperation in developmental activities and associating them with planned programmes.
12. Inter-caste conflicts and rivalries.
13. Spending a large percentage of annual earnings on social ceremonies like marriage, death feast, etc. and people being unwilling to break the expensive customs.

Poverty in Urban India

Half of the urban growth is due to natural factors and the rest due to migration from the country-side.

1. Poor people migrate from rural areas to cities and towns in search of employment/financial activity.
2. The income of more than 8 crore urban people is estimated to fall below the poverty line (BPL). In addition to this, there are around 4.5 crore urban people whose income level is on the borderline of the poverty level.

   The percentage of persons below poverty line in 2011–12 was estimated as 25.7 per cent in rural areas, 13.7 per cent in urban areas and 21.9 per cent in the country as a whole.
3. The income of the urban poor is highly unstable. A large number of them are either casual workers or self-employed. Banks and financial institutions are reluctant to provide them with loan because of their unstable income.
4. Five states that constitute around 40 per cent of all urban poor of India are Uttar Pradesh, Bihar, Rajasthan, Odisha and Madhya Pradesh.
5. Around 35 per cent of the total population of the four metro cities (Delhi, Kolkata, Chennai and Mumbai) consists of slum population.
6. The initiatives taken to deal with the problem of urban poverty have not yielded the desired results.

Effects of Poverty

1. *Illiteracy*: Poor people constitute a greater share of the illiterate population. Education becomes extremely difficult when people are deprived of basic necessities of life.
2. *Child labour*: In India, a large number of young boys and girls are engaged in child labour.
3. *Nutrition and diet*: Poverty is the leading cause of insufficient diet and inadequate nutrition. The resources of poor people are very limited, and its effect can be seen in their diet.
4. *Poor living condition and housing problems*: They do not get proper living conditions. They have to fight the hardship of poverty to secure food, clothes and shelter. A large number of poor families live in houses with one room only.
5. *Unemployment*: Poor people move from villages to towns and from one town to another in search of employment/work. Since they are mostly illiterate and unskilled, there are very few employment opportunities open for them. Due to unemployment, many poor people are forced to live an unfulfilled life.
6. *Hygiene and sanitation*: These people have little knowledge about hygiene and proper sanitation system. They are not aware of the harmful consequences of not maintaining proper hygiene. The government is taking initiatives to make available clean and safe water and proper sanitation system to them.
7. *Feminization of poverty*: Women are the worst victims of poverty. Poverty affects a greater number of women than men. The total of poor women outnumbers the total population of poor men. The causes include low income, gender-inequality, etc. They are deprived of proper diet, medicines and health treatment.
8. *Social tensions*: Poverty is often characterized by income disparity and unequal distribution of national wealth between the rich and the poor. The concentration of wealth in the hands of a few rich people leads to social disturbances and revolts. Fair or even distribution of wealth leads an overall improvement in the general standard of living of people.

Action Plan for Alleviating Rural Poverty

For reducing poverty in the rural areas, following plan of action may be suggested:

1. Strengthening credit disbursing agencies.
2. Providing cheap power supply for agricultural and industrial use.
3. Activating cooperative societies for selling products of household industries.
4. Making allocations in poverty alleviation programmes flexible and sanctioning special allocations to districts/blocks/villages showing good results.

5. Integrating varied poverty alleviation programmes in one or two schemes and making the availability of benefits easier.
6. Developing human resources by focussing on education, health and skill programmes.
7. Introducing double distributive system for the destitutes and the extremely poor.
8. Creating social awareness to arrest increasing debt growth among the poor.
9. Improving animal husbandry and developing dairy and poultry farming.
10. Activating panchayats to focus on adult education programme, road construction and maintaining tree plantations.
11. Activating NGOs in role-play like digging of tanks, tree plantations, training of youth, imparting skills to women, creating social awareness among the people, and so forth.

Problems of the Poor and the Pains of Poverty

After 70 years of planning, India is still one of the poorest countries in the world. Other countries, much smaller than India, have surged forward. Of the world's poor, every third person is an Indian, and the number is on the increase.

Some of the variables on which the poor differ from others are degree of participation in the labour force, kind of employment, characteristics of family, degree of knowledge of the larger society, political awareness, awareness of social and economic rights, and value orientations in politics, religion and social customs. Ross and Blum (1967: 3941), however, maintain that the poor are different but in matters of degree rather than of kind.

The important problems the poor in our society face are: (a) social discrimination and social condemnation, (b) housing, and (c) sub-culture of poverty.

Social Discrimination

The employers, the rich, the officials and even the government looks down upon the poor. They are considered lethargic, inefficient and a burden on the society. They are harassed, humiliated and discriminated at every level. Being unrepresented and powerless, they are always the targets of attack and hostility by the powerful. They have to face the challenges of illiteracy and social prejudice. They receive little or no attention in offices they visit. Whenever a theft or a crime is reported to the police, the police first rushes to the areas inhabited by the poor, as if it is only the poor who commit crimes. They are rarely considered reliable, dependent and trust-worthy. The hostile attitude of the society at every stage thus, lowers their self-image, creates in them a feeling of inferiority and curbs their efforts of gaining means to help themselves.

Housing

Houselessness, overcrowding, slums and rental laws are serious problems in urban areas. The family's dwelling unit and the neighbourhood within which it is located are important elements in the problems associated with poverty. The houses of the poor are not only overcrowded but lack privacy. Poverty forces to live in the substandard houses and leaves little for the pre-requisites of decent living. The deficient housing contributes to the weakening of family solidarity also.

Sub-culture of Poverty

When poverty is transmitted over generations, it becomes a culture, according to Oscar Lewis. Kriesgberg (1963: 335–36) has said that although the membership of the poor changes to an important degree over the generations, the successive generations resemble each other in behaviour and values as a product of the common experiences of being poor and of being subjected to similar social pressures. The children of the poor inherit a sub-culture of violence in which physically aggressive responses are either expected or required by all members. The use of violence in such a sub-culture is not viewed as illicit conduct and the users do not have to deal with feelings of guilt about their aggression. Violence becomes a part of their lifestyle, the medium for solving difficult problems and is used primarily between persons and groups who themselves rely upon the same supportive values and norms. On one hand, this sub-culture is seen as the effect of poverty, that is, it refers to the similarities in behaviour and thinking patterns of the people, and on the other hand, it is seen as the cause of poverty.

After 70 years of independence, the growth rate of income per capita has only tripled. In many countries, it has increased five or six times. The disparities between the poor and the rich are increasing, instead of narrowing down. An average Indian cannot look beyond survival, and even bare survival is now in doubt.

Strategies for Alleviating Poverty in India

Three distinct strategies for reducing poverty in India may be identified as below:

1. Initially, in the 1950s, the policy makers stressed maximization of economic growth by stepping up investment assuming that the benefits arising out of it would 'trickle down' and diffuse among all sectors of the society. But, in the 1970s, it was realized that the benefits of agricultural growth did not percolate to the rural poor.
2. This gave birth to the second approach led by the structural school which pleaded for the establishment of egalitarian society and suggested distribution of assets through land reforms, community development programmes, cooperative farming, and nationalization of big industries. But, this also did not work.
3. Then came the idea in the 1980s that suggested attack on poverty through rural development programmes, such as IRDP, TRYSEM, NREP and RLEGP, which later on merged in JRY programme. In recent

years, a landmark scheme to alleviate rural poverty in the country, called Mahatma Gandhi National Rural Employment Guarantee Scheme (MNREGS), has been launched.

Before analysing these anti-poverty programmes, we shall first evaluate the role of five-year plans, nationalization and 20–point programme in poverty alleviation.

The Five-Year Plans

The Planning Commission set up in 1950 has been formulating five-year plans for country's development taking an overall view of the needs and resources of the country. Between the Third Plan, started in 1961 and the Fourth Plan, started in 1969, three annual plans were also launched.

The *First Five-Year Plan* (1951–56) was designed to rectify the imbalances created by the Second World War and the partition of the country in 1947 and the maladies persisting in the economy as a legacy of the British rule. Though the plan aimed at achieving an all-round balanced development, it accorded top priority to agriculture and irrigation investing 44.6 per cent of the total plan budget on this sector. This was to reduce the country's dependence on agricultural imports and save foreign exchange. The industrial sector was not assigned much importance in this plan and less than 5 per cent of the plan outlay was spent on industries. However, the plan did give some importance to the development of power, rural development (community projects) and development of social welfare programmes. Of the total budget of the plan (₹ 2,378 crore), only two-third (65.6%) was actually spent. At the end of the plan, the country's national income increased by 18 per cent and per capita income by 11 per cent.

The *Second Five-Year Plan* (1956–61) aimed at achieving rapid industrialization of the economy and bringing about greater equality in income and wealth for the establishment of a socialistic pattern of society in India. It stressed that the benefits of development should accrue more to the relatively underprivileged sections of society and that there should be a progressive reduction in the concentration of income. It focussed on the growth of basic and heavy industries, expansion in employment opportunities and increase of 25 per cent in the national income. The total amount spent during this plan (₹ 4,672 crore) was double the amount spent in the First Plan. However, the performance of the plan did not justify the hopes that had been placed on it. Achievements in almost all the sectors of the economy were lower than the plan targets. Consequently, as against a near 13 per cent fall in price index during the First Plan, the Second Plan witnessed a 12.5 per cent rise in price level.

The *Third Five-Year Plan* (1961–66) aimed at securing a marked advance towards self-sustaining growth. It listed a set of five objectives, namely, increase in annual national income by 5 per cent, self-sufficiency in agriculture, growth of basic industries (like steel, power, chemicals), maximum use of manpower resources, and decentralization of economic power. Agriculture was once again given top priority and about 35 per cent of the outlay was allocated to this sector. As compared to this, 23 per cent was accounted to industries and 25 per cent to transport and communications. The plan aimed at increasing the national income by about 30 per cent and the per capita income by about 17 per cent. The total amount spent (₹ 12,767 crore) during the plan period was 9 per cent more than the allocated amount (₹ 11,600 crore).

The performance of the Third Plan was also as disheartening as that of the Second Plan. Over the five year period, the national income grew by 2.6 per cent as against the target of 5 per cent. In the agricultural sector also, the production suffered a setback. The industrial production turned out to be 7.9 per cent as compared to the target of 11 per cent. The price index in 1965–66 was 32 per cent higher than in 1960–61. The Indo-Pakistan war, the Sino-Indian conflict, and the successive failures of the monsoon were the factors beyond human control.

The shape of the economy was in fact so bad at the end of the Third Plan that the Fourth Plan, which was to be launched in March 1966 had to be abandoned and was replaced by three annual plans. The three-year period between 1966 and 1969, sometimes described as a period of 'plan holiday', was devoted to rectifying the ills that had crippled the planning process during the operation of the Third Plan. The main objective of the three annual plans was to continue the unfinished tasks of the Third Plan.

The *Fourth Five-Year Plan* (1969–74) aimed at increasing national income by 5.5 per cent, creating economic stability, reducing inequalities in income distribution, and achieving social justice with equality. Simultaneous growth of both agricultural and industrial sectors was fully recognized under the Fourth Plan. Though the total amount spent during this plan was ₹ 22,862 crore, this plan could not ensure economic growth. Neither could it achieve self-sufficiency in foodgrains, nor could the generation of employment opportunities make any significant dent in the widespread unemployment problem. The inflationary situation was also aggravated. With 1960–61 as the base, the wholesale price index jumped from 165.4 in 1968–69 to 281.7 by the end of 1973–74, an increase of 70 per cent in a five-year period.

The *Fifth Five-Year Plan* (1974–79) was formulated when the economy was facing severe inflationary pressures. It mainly aimed at removal of poverty and attainment of self-reliance. The aim was to bring larger sections of the poor masses above the poverty line by assuring a minimum income of ₹ 40 per person per month calculated at 1972–73 prices. The plan also aimed at an increase in employment opportunities, self-sufficiency, policy of minimum wages, removal of regional imbalances, and encouragement of exports. The plan targeted an annual growth rate of 5.5 per cent in the national income.

The plan ended during the *Janata* regime in 1978 instead of 1979 and the Sixth Plan was started as the 'rolling plan'. But, when the Congress once again came to power in 1978, the period of the Fifth Plan was described as being from 1974 to 1979. The Fifth Plan was uniquely unlucky. It was indeed a collection of annual development programmes. It could not achieve its targets in any field, except in the increase of foodgrains.

The *Sixth Five-Year Plan* (1980–85) was formulated after taking into account the achievements and shortcomings of the past three decades of planning. Removal of poverty was the foremost objective of the plan, even though it was recognized that this objective could not be achieved in a short period of five years. Stress was laid on economic growth, elimination of unemployment, bringing down of inequality in distribution of income, self-sufficiency in technology, raising the lifestyles of the weaker sections of society, improving the public distribution system and control of the increasing population. The total amount spent during this plan was ₹ 1,58,710 crore.

The *Seventh Five-Year Plan* (1985–90) had three priorities that were, increasing food, work and productivity. With its emphasis on generating substantial productive employment, the plan aimed at a significant reduction in the incidence of poverty and an improvement in the quality of life of the poor. The poverty ratio was expected to decline from 37 per cent to 26 per cent by 1990. The plan had a total allocation of ₹ 1,80,000 crore (₹ 3,48,148 crore at 1989–90 prices). However, this plan also failed totally in achieving its targets. There was a severe setback on the agricultural front, in the manufacturing sector, in creating employment, and in the balance of payments position of the country.

The *Eighth Five-Year Plan* (1992–97) which was to be started in 1990 was actually enforced from April 1992. The 1990–91 and 1991–92 years were considered to be yearly plans. The Eighth Plan's total budget was of ₹ 7,98,000 crore at 1990–91 prices. This means that the country spent about ₹ 159.6 thousand crore a year or about ₹ 3,069 crore a week. Of this amount, 45 per cent was spent by the government, and 55 per cent by private industries and businesses.

The plan was supposed to be oriented towards employment generation. More investment was supposed to be made in small industries which were expected to be job-intensive. The plan aimed at achieving an overall GDP growth rate of 5.5 per cent to 6.5 per cent, agricultural growth rate of 5 per cent, industrial growth rate of 7.5 per cent, service sector growth rate of 8 per cent to 10 per cent and export growth rate of 10 per cent. The plan size was nearly the double of the previous plan, but then all plans had been twice the size of the previous plans. The growth rate was also more or less what the previous plans aimed at. The fact that they rarely reached the target except in the First and the Sixth Plans is a different matter. The Eighth Plan was thus no different from the earlier plans, and neither were its results.

The plan failed to achieve most of its targets. For example, in power against the set target of 31,000 MW, only about 15,000 MW (or 48% of the target) were available by the end of the Plan. Resource mobilization by the states was nowhere in sight. On the contrary, many states had diverted plan funds to meet day-to-day expenditure. The implementation of various projects in the plan was so indifferent and careless that an additional amount of ₹ 21,000 crore had to be paid by the exchequer on account of delays and the consequent rise in the cost of plan projects (*Hindustan Times*, 20 January 1997).

The *Ninth Five-Year Plan* (1997–2002) was described as ambitious and growth-oriented. The plan's thrust areas were: agriculture, employment, poverty and infrastructure. In agriculture, the top priority was to be given to irrigation. The target for annual growth rate of GDP was 7 per cent of which 4.5 per cent was to come from agriculture and 9.3 per cent from industries. In the Eighth Plan, the target was 5.5 per cent and the actual achievement was 6.2 per cent. The Ninth Plan aimed to encourage small-scale labour-intensive industrial development with appropriate incentives. The target for public savings was 26.2 per cent of the GDP as against 23.7 per cent during the Eighth Plan. The improvement was to come about through improvement in tax structure. The planned reforms were expected to phase out obsolete technologies and usher in higher material and energy efficiency. The efficiency and productivity of five infrastructure sectors – irrigation, power, mining, railways and communication – was also expected to improve. The plan was described as 'delivery-oriented'.

The *Tenth Five-Year Plan* (2002–07) was approved by the National Development Council (NDC) on 21 December 2002. It further developed the NDC mandated objectives of doubling the per capita income in ten years and achieving a growth rate of 8 per cent of GDP per annum. Since economic growth was not the only objective, the plan aimed at harnessing the benefits of growth to improve the quality of life of the people by setting the following key targets: reduction in the poverty ratio from 26 per cent to 21 per cent by 2007; decadal population growth to reduce from 21.3 per cent in 1991–2001 to 16.2 per cent in 2001–11; growth in gainful employment, at least, to keep pace with addition to the labour force; all children to be in school by 2003 and to complete five years of schooling by 2007; reducing gender gaps in literacy and wage rates by 50 per cent; literacy rate to increase from 65 per cent in 1999–2000 to 75 per cent in 2007; providing potable drinking water to all villages; infant mortality rate to be reduced from 72 in 1999–2000 to 45 in 2007; maternal mortality ratio to be reduced from four in 1999–2000 to two in 2007; increase in forest/tree cover from 19 per cent in 1999–2000 to 25 per cent in 2007; and cleaning of major polluted river stretches.

The Eleventh Five-Year Plan: The Planning Commission of India first started talking of 'inclusive growth' as an objective while formulating the Eleventh Plan which was in operation from 2007 to 2012. But we find that while this plan succeeded in achieving a remarkable rate of growth, it also witnessed impoverishment and exclusion of large sections of the populations from benefits of development. This was because of the singular focus of the planners on growth and not on distribution with the assumption that accelerated growth would trickle down to benefit all. Unfortunately, this did not happen. On the contrary, the disparities seem to have increased.

The Twelfth Five-Year Plan (2012–17): The Twelfth Plan aimed at a growth rate of 8 per cent. This is the revised rate when compared to the initial approach paper. The Twelfth Plan period presented both challenges and opportunities. The Twelfth Plan has therefore, proposed a two-pronged strategy focussing initially on the need to bring the macroeconomic imbalances under control and to reverse the slowdown, while also pushing for structural reforms in many areas that were critical for maintaining medium-term growth. The Twelfth Plan proposed an ambitious set of government programmes, to achieve the objective of rapid and inclusive growth. These programmes added up to a total plan size for the centre of 43,33,739 crores, which comes to about 6.35 per cent of GDP. This compared with 20,25,130 crores in the Eleventh Plan, which was 5.96 per cent of GDP. The total plan size of the states is 37,16,385 crore or 5.45 per cent of GDP, as compared to 17,25,848 crore in the Eleventh Plan, which was 5 per cent of GDP.

Despite an average 7.9 per cent growth in GDP (Gross Domestic Product) during the Eleventh Plan period – sometimes also peaking to 9 per cent – the performance of India in terms of the Human Development Index (indicative of inclusive growth and the extent of population benefiting from development) saw a downward slide from 128th and 127th positions in 2000 and 2005 respectively to 134th position in 2009 and 2011. While a handful are reaping benefits and have entered the billionaires club, millions are being forced into deprivation and disempowerment. For the first time in history, four Indians found a place amongst the 10 richest people of 2009, but three out of every ten poor people in the world in the same year were also Indians – an unusual phenomenon of continuing poverty and marginalization in the midst of galloping plenty.

If we make an appraisal of all the twelve plans completed so far, we find that we have completed seven decades of planning. All our plans have been oriented towards self-reliance in agricultural production, employment generation, rapid industrialization and industrial growth, power generation, growth in GDP, etc.

Nationalization

Nationalization has some negative effects too. Judged from the standpoint of efficiency, the quantum of profits, the standard of service to the general public or even deposit mobilization, the banks have not been the pace-setters which the government claims them to be. Lack of efficiency, initiative and commitment have been the casualties of nationalization. Only in two areas – branch expansion and grant of credit to the weaker sections – have the banks done better than expected. The loans advanced by the banks are not given to the really needy people but are sanctioned to people having some political or social backing.

20-Point Programme

This programme was propounded in July 1975 for reducing poverty and economic exploitation, and for the upliftment of the weaker sections of the society. The five important goals of this programme were: (a) controlling inflation, (b) giving incentive to production, (c) welfare of the rural population, (d) lending help to the urban middle classes, and (e) controlling economic and social crimes. The programmes included in the 20–point programme were: increase in irrigational facilities, increase in production programmes for rural employment, distribution of surplus land, minimum wages to landless labourers, rehabilitation of bonded labour, development of scheduled castes (SCs) and scheduled tribes (STs), growth of housing facilities, increasing power production, family planning, tree plantations, extension of primary health facilities, programmes for the welfare of women and children, increase in primary education, strengthening of the distribution system, simplification of industrial policies, control of black money, betterment of drinking water facilities, and developing internal resources.

The programme was discontinued with the change of government. However, in January 1982, the programme was implemented again with a revised format. Among other things, the revised programme included an increased tempo of rural development and a direct attack on rural poverty, besides specific schemes for the upliftment of the SCs and STs.

The fact that the rural people and the urban poor are more discontented and feel more frustrated today points to the failure of the 20-point programme in fulfilling its commitments.

Poverty Alleviation Programmes

Several poverty alleviation programmes have been launched by the government for the rural poor, comprising the small and marginal farmers, landless labourers and rural artisans, as well as urban poor. These poverty alleviation programmes are classified into (a) self-employment programmes; (b) wage employment programmes; (c) food security programmes; (d) social security programmes; and (e) urban poverty alleviation programmes. Here, we will be discussing mainly those programmes/schemes that are targeted for the benefit of rural poor.

Integrated Rural Development Programme

Integrated Rural Development Programme (IRDP) can be viewed in different ways with special emphasis on its objectives, content, process, structure, outcome and effect. The programme had been thought about because according to the Sixth Five-Year Plan, the project or sectoral approach was not adequate for overall development of the area and distribution of benefits to the local population, particularly the weaker sections of the society.

It was, therefore, necessary 'to plan for integration of various programmes and to establish appropriate linkages for optimal utilization of local endowments, consistent with the plan objectives, local needs and environment balance'. At the planning stage itself the integration was thought of as clubbing together of various programmes for total development.

The need for total development had not occurred all of a sudden, it had a long history behind it. Community development was introduced with so much enthusiasm and everyone expected that it would bring changes. However, the Balwantrai Mehta Committee (1957) found it to be a failure and suggested a three-tier system of administration to enhance the participation of people.

Though the Panchayati Raj system was introduced in many states, it was not uniform in many ways and made the system more politically inclined and catered more to the elite, the high class and high caste people. Such an administration could not create a healthy atmosphere for the effective implementation of the developmental activities. On the contrary, many a time it had been a hindrance. Of course, in states like Maharashtra and Rajasthan, the Panchayati Raj system is functioning well in implementing developmental activities.

Assistance had to be provided to the poorest among the poor, in other words, *'antyodaya'* approach had to be followed in selecting the beneficiaries.

Indira Awaas Yojana (IAJ)

The scheme was primarily launched to provide grant for the construction of houses to the members of SCs and STs, freed bonded labourers and to non-SC/ST rural poor who live below poverty line. Though it was launched by the central government during 1985–86, under the Rural Landless Employment Guarantee Programme (RLEGP), it became a sub-scheme under Jawahar Rozgar Yojana (JRY), and since 1 January 1996, it has become an independent scheme.

The target group covered under this scheme has now been extended to ex-servicemen, widows, next-of-kin of defence personnel and paramilitary forces killed in action, irrespective of the income criteria, subject to the condition that they (a) live rural areas, (b) so far have not been covered under any other project, and (c) are in need of shelter or house upgradation. There is a 60 per cent reservation for the SC and ST categories and non-SCs and STs constitute the remaining 40 per cent.

The identification of beneficiaries is done by the Gram Sabha after getting the allotment list for each panchayat from DRDA/Zila Parishad. There is no approval required from the panchayat union for the selection done by the Gram Panchayat, provided the order of priority for selection shall be, according to the guidelines given in the IAY scheme.

The allotment of houses is done in the name of the womenfolk of the family. Alternatively, it can be allotted in the name of both husband and wife. The family labour contribute their entire labour to the construction of the houses and no contractor is allowed in the construction of IAY houses. In other words, the beneficiaries or the occupants construct the house with the minimum engagement of skilled labour.

Low cost and durable technology and materials is used for the construction, which should be eco-friendly in nature. The state government provides all necessary information in this regard to the beneficiaries. Provision for drinking water, fuel-efficient *chullahs* and sanitation is ensured. The state governments also ensure environmental improvements through social forestry. Involvement of NGOs in supervision, guidance and monitoring of construction is encouraged and especially in the aspects of sanitary latrines and smokeless *chullahs*.

The monitoring and evaluation is done by the respective state governments/union territories through DRDA or other agencies. Reputed research institutions are engaged to conduct evaluation studies and the reports shall be submitted to the Government of India. Remedial action taken based on the evaluation is also be reported to the central government.

Pradhan Mantri Gramodaya Yojana – Gramin Awaas

Taking into consideration the magnitude and the urgency, the Government of India decided to introduce a comprehensive programme to promote housing among the rural poor living below poverty line. Though Indira Awaas Yojana (IAY) is in operation, the Gramin Awaas Yojana is an additional programme to provide rural shelter. The target group, identification of beneficiaries, allotment of houses, priorities, location, involvement of beneficiaries, monitoring and evaluation are similar to that of IAY.

The scheme was introduced in the year 2000–01 and ₹ 104.79 crore was allotted to focus on primary health, primary education, rural housing, drinking water and nutrition. The important feature is that the coverage is only in rural areas.

Sampoorna Gramin Rozgar Yojana

Explosion of population, failure of monsoon, natural calamities and other similar factors lead into the problems of unemployment and underemployment in India and especially in villages. It is observed that the volume of those unemployed or underemployed has increased from time to time and hence the Government of India proposes various schemes for providing employment opportunities with food security as it was envisaged that larger and efficient use of available human resources is one of the effective ways of alleviating poverty, reducing inequality and improving nutritional level.

With this background the Government of India merged the already existing schemes such as Employment Assurance Scheme (EAS) and the

Jawahar Gram Samridhi Yojana (JGSY) as a new scheme and named it Sampoorna Gramin Rozgar Yojana (SGRY) with effect from 25 September 2001.

The SGRY has been primarily launched to promote additional wage and employment in villages and thereby provide food security and improve the nutritional level. In addition to that, creation of community, social and economic assets and infrastructural development in villages, are the secondary objectives.

As the programme is self-targeting in nature, it covers all the rural poor who require employment, either unskilled or manual. Though it is a central scheme, 25 per cent of the share shall be borne by the concerned state governments; for the union territories the entire grant is supported by the central government. However, the food grains supplied for this scheme shall entirely be given by the central government free of cost. The target groups covered under the scheme are agricultural labourers, marginal farmers, women, SCs, STs, parents of child labour withdrawn from hazardous occupations, parents of disabled children, etc.

This scheme is implemented through PRIs and special safeguards are provided for women and weaker sections. The allocation to women is 30 per cent and to SC and ST categories it is 22.5 per cent. Since food grains form part of the wages, the beneficiary should be supplied with 5 kg of food grain a day.

The cash payment shall be in accordance with the Minimum Wages Act and there should be equal remuneration for both men and women and they shall be paid on a fixed day for every week. The committees for monitoring and evaluation shall be constituted at the district, state and panchayat union level to supervise the scheme. Periodical evaluation studies should be conducted and reports should be sent to the central government in the proper format.

As a special component, the areas affected by calamity, especially for the damages caused to agriculture, shall be aptly responded by this scheme in the form of generating additional wage employment in the affected area after due notification and acceptance by the Ministry of Agriculture. There are provisions for reservation of certain percentage of food grains for this cause.

Antyodaya Anna Yojana

It is a centrally sponsored scheme aimed at Hunger Free India by providing food grains to the poor. The scheme was launched in 2000. It envisages the identification of one crore families comprising around 5 crore poorest of the poor people who would be supplied with 25 kg of food grains per month at the rate of ₹ 2 per kg for wheat and ₹ 3 per kg for rice.

With the involvement of PRIs, local bodies and NGOs, the government intended to implement the scheme more transparently by ensuring more quality in the public distribution system.

National Rural Employment Guarantee Scheme

The National Rural Employment Guarantee Scheme was introduced in 2004 to cover all the rural BPL households by providing employment to the eligible labourers.

The scheme envisaged guarantee to the eight categories of work such as water conservation, water harvesting, drought proofing, irrigation canals, renovation of traditional bodies, land development, floor control and rural roads and connectivity. Total outlay estimated for this scheme is ₹ 39,372 crore. The scheme guaranteed one hundred days' wage employment to the adult labourers belonging to unskilled and manual category.

The scheme also guaranteed unemployment allowance to the eligible worker who is not offered work within the prescribed time limit of 15 days. The allowance shall not be less than one-fourth of the wage rate for the first 30 days and half of the wage rate for the subsequent days of the financial year.

Swarnajayanti Gram Swarozgar Yojana

To commemorate the celebration of fifty years of our independence, the Government of India launched this scheme on 1 April 1999, incorporating the already existing six central schemes into it as under:

1. Integrated Rural Development Programme (IRDP)
2. Training of Rural Youth for Self-Employment (TRYSEM)
3. Development of Women and Children in Rural Areas (DWCRA)
4. Supply of Improved Toolkits to Rural Artisans (SITRA)
5. Ganga Kalyan Yojana (GKY)
6. Million Wells Scheme (MWS)

Hence, these six schemes ceased to exist from April 1999.

All the aspects of self-employment components under these six schemes have been integrated into this scheme, such as organization of the poor into self-help groups, training, credit, technology, infrastructure and marketing. Though the scheme is a central programme, 75 per cent of the funds are met by the centre and the remaining 25 per cent by the concerned state governments. The various agencies involved in the implementation process are banks, rural banks, cooperative banks, PRIs, district rural development agencies, NGOs and technical institutions.

To help the *'swarozgaris'* (SHGs) to increase the income level to ₹ 2,000 per month within three years and to support at least 30 per cent of the BPL families in each panchayat union to come out of the clutches of poverty within five years, are the specific objectives of this scheme. To uplift the weak and vulnerable sections, there are also provisions of reservation: for scheduled castes (SCs) and scheduled tribes (STs), as high as 50 per cent, for women, 40 per cent and for disabled, 3 per cent and so on. Subsidy under SGSY is given at the rate of 30 per cent of the project cost or to the maximum of ₹ 7,500. For SCs and STs, the subsidy is payable at the rate of 50 per cent or to the maximum of ₹ 10,000. For group of *swarozgaris*, the subsidy is 50 per cent of the project cost subject to per capital subsidy of ₹ 10,000 or ₹ 1.25 lakh, whichever is less.

Minimum skill requirement for each activity is ascertained by the agencies meant for this purpose. Once an individual or a group of individuals is identified for assistance their training needs are to be assessed too. Those *swarozgaris* having the minimum required skills are further put into the basic orientation programmes such as record maintenance, marketing, product costing, product pricing and familiarization with financial institution. The resource persons should include bankers, BDOs, line departments, marketing personnel, NGOs and trainers meant for this purpose. The persons who require the minimum or additional skills will be given training by government institutions, ITIs, polytechnics, universities, NGOs, etc. The *Swarozgaris* are paid stipend if the training is for more than a week and they become eligible only when they complete this training.

Self-Help Groups (SHGs)

1. The scheme provides opportunities to organize SHGs from among the families living below poverty line. Under this scheme, group activities are given preference and progressively more funding is allotted for group activities.
2. The membership may range from 10 to 20 for a group. The group with disabled persons may be organized even if the minimum number is five. The group should not have more than one person from the same family and also an individual should not be a member of more than one group. The group can be a registered group under the Societies Act or an informal group. The individual or all the members of the group can benefit from the scheme.
3. DRDA/Zila Parishad in each district should initiate the process of social mobilization for poverty eradication programmes by organizing them into various groups, especially SHGs.

After independence, poverty eradication has been one of the major objectives of development of planning process in India. Reduction of poverty is the prime issue for the attainment of international goals – developing rural areas. Particularly the dimensions relating to education, health and other basic services have been systematically and progressively internalized in the planning process in India. The central and the state governments are trying to make sufficient allocations for the provisions of health, education and other facilities for the well-being of the rural poor. Anti-poverty strategies and programmes have certainly provided opportunities of employment and income to the rural people.

Self-Employed Women's Association (SEWA)

This is a trade union of women workers in the informal sector. Its main goal is to organize women workers for full employment and self-reliance through the strategy of struggle and development. This is both an organization and a movement. A SEWA bank is operating to reach the maximum number of poor women workers engaged in the unorganized sector and provides them with suitable financial services for their socio-economic empowerment and self-development through their own management and ownership. In the year 1993, SEWA Bank began its banking activities through the formation of SHGs. Through SHGs, the Bank aimed at providing banking services at the doorstep of the poor women in order to pull them out of the vicious circle of poverty and free them from unscrupulous moneylenders. In brief, since its operation through SHGs, many vulnerable women in rural Gujarat are now in the mainstream of the society.

MNREGS/MNREGA

Objectives

MGNREGA which is the largest work guarantee programme in the world, was enacted in 2005 with the primary objective of guaranteeing 100 days of wage employment per year to rural households. Second, it aims at addressing the causes of chronic poverty through the 'works' (projects) that are undertaken and thus, ensuring sustainable development. Finally, there is an emphasis on strengthening the process of decentralization by giving a significant role to Panchayati Raj Institutions (PRIS) in planning and implementing these works.

Key Features:

1. *Legal right to work*: Unlike the previous employment guarantee schemes, this act provides a legal right to employment for adult members of rural households. At least one-third beneficiaries have to be women. Wages must be paid according to the wages specified for agricultural labourers in the state under the Minimum Wages Act, 1948 unless the central government notifies a wage rate.
2. *Programme bound guarantee of work and unemployment allowance*: Employment must be provided within 15 days of being demanded failing which an 'unemployment allowance' must be given.
3. *Decentralized planning*: Gram Sabhas must recommend the works that are to be undertaken and at least 50 per cent of the works must be executed by them. PRIS are primarily responsible for planning, implementation and monitoring of the works that are undertaken.
4. *Worksite facilities*: All work sites should have facilities such as crèches, drinking water, and first aid.

5. *Transparency and accountability*: There are provisions for proactive disclosure through wall writings, citizen information boards, management information systems and social audits. Social audits are conducted by Gram Sabhas to enable the community to monitor the implementation of the scheme.
6. *Funding*: Funding is shared between the centre and the states. There are three major items of expenditure – wages (for unskilled, semi-skilled and skilled labour), material and administrative costs. The central government bears 100 per cent of the cost of unskilled labour, 75 per cent of the cost of semi-skilled and skilled labour, 75 per cent of the cost of materials and 6 per cent of the administrative costs.

MGNREGA was implemented in phases, starting from February 2006, and at present, it covers all districts of the country with the exception of those that have a 100 per cent urban population. The act provides a list of works that can be undertaken to generate employment related to water conservation, drought proofing, land development, and flood control and protection works.

Mahatma Gandhi National Rural Employment Guarantee Act (MGNREGA) was passed on 5 September 2005 and came into force in February 2006. The programme is seen as a significant opportunity by the government as well as civil society organizations to transform rural economy in selected districts/states as it guarantees 100 days employment per family and provides adequate resources for the improvement of infrastructure including productive assets of the village. The initial three quarters since operationalization of the programme have been invested not only in building systems and procedures, but also in developing operational details. Further, many states have moved towards effectively implementing the programme and generating employment for the poor families. The process of implementation has therefore generated ground-level data at the household, village, and panchayat levels about the initial bottlenecks and operational hurdles.

The *goals of the scheme* are as under:

1. Strong social safety arrangement for the vulnerable groups by providing a fallback employment source, when other employment alternatives are scarce or inadequate. Growth machinery for sustainable development of an agricultural economy.
2. Providing employment in areas that result in chronic poverty, e.g., drought, deforestation, and soil erosion.
3. Empowerment of rural poor through the processes of a rights-based law.
4. New ways of doing business, as a model of governance reform anchored on the principles of transparency and grassroots democracy.

Adult members of every rural household who are willing to do casual manual work at the statutory minimum wage may apply to the Gram

Panchayat for registration. Registration is valid for a period not less than five years and is renewable. Employment is to be provided to every registered person within 15 days of receipt of an application. Applications are to be for at least 14 days of continuous work. Gram Panchayat is to accept valid applications and issue a dated receipt to the applicant. Applicants provided with work to be notified in writing. Employment is to be provided within a radius of 5 km If work is provided beyond 5 km, it is to be provided within the block, and the labourers paid 10 per cent of the daily minimum wages extra.

Thus, MGNREGA covers the entire country with the exception of districts that have a 100 per cent urban population. The scheme under this Act is implemented as a centrally sponsored scheme on a cost-sharing basis between the centre and the states as determined by the Act.

Wages are to be paid every week not later than a fortnight. In case of any delay in the payment of wages, labourers are entitled to compensation as per the Payment of Wages Act. No gender bias is permitted. Provisions are made for compensation and treatment in case of injury, for on-site safe drinking water, care of small children, periods of rest, and a first-aid box. At least 60 per cent of the expenditure under any project is to be on wages. At least 50 per cent of the projects, in terms of value, to be implemented through the Gram Panchayats which must prepare a development plan. The programme officer will be responsible for the implementation of the employment guarantee programme in the block.

MGNREGS has thus marked a paradigm shift from all precedent wage employment programmes. The significant aspects of this paradigm shift are: it provides a statutory guarantee of wage employment and rights-based framework for wage employment. Employment is dependent upon the worker exercising the choice to apply for registration, obtain a job card, and seek employment for the time and duration that the worker wants. Unlike the earlier wage employment programmes that were allocation based, MGNREGS is demand driven. Resource transfer under MGNREGS is based on the demand for employment and this provides another critical incentive to states to leverage the Act to meet the employment needs of the poor. It has inbuilt transparency safeguard documents: Job cards recording entitlements (in the custody of workers), written application for employment, muster rolls, measurement books and asset registers processes, acceptance of employment application, issue of dated receipts, time-bound work allocation and wage payment, Citizen Information Boards at worksites, Vigilance Monitoring Committees, regular block, district and state-level inspections, and social audits. The public delivery system has been made accountable, as it envisages an annual report on the outcomes of MGNREGS to be presented by the Central Government to the parliament and to the State Legislature by the State Government. Specifically, personnel responsible for implementing the Act have been made legally responsible for delivering the guarantee under the Act.

As the centre gears up to implement MGNREGA across all the districts in the country, instances of corruption and irregularities in implementing the scheme are tumbling out, e.g. fudged job cards, incomplete muster rolls, missing names or signatures and more. A government-sponsored study on the MGNREGA has found large-scale corruption and irregularities in the implementation of the programme in several states with authorities in some areas misappropriating central funds.

The Ministry of Rural Development's official data also shows that the average days of work provided was less than 40 days in 2017–18, against mandated 100 days of work in a year to each willing household.

The *successful implementation* of the scheme depends on the following:

1. The capacity (including technical) and willingness of panchayats and local government to plan works and run the programme effectively.
2. Dissemination about the programme and its guidelines to local people who can make use of it to register and demand for work.
3. Mobilization to run social audits without fear of repression.
4. MGNREGA contains many safeguards in terms of transparency and accountability. These are likely to be resisted by vested interests at every level and should be continuously fought through local mobilization.

Food Security Scheme (2013)

The National Food Security Act, 2013 provides for food and nutritional security in human life cycle approach, by ensuring access to adequate quantity of quality food at affordable prices to people to live a life with dignity and for matters connected therewith or incidental thereto. It includes the Midday Meal Scheme, Integrated Child Development Services Scheme and the Public Distribution System. Further, the NFSA 2013 recognizes maternity entitlements. The Midday Meal Scheme and the Integrated Child Development Services Scheme are universal in nature whereas the PDS will reach about two-thirds of the population (75% in rural areas and 50% in urban areas). The state government shall be responsible for the implementation and monitoring of the scheme under the Act. The scheme extends to the whole of India and shall be deemed to have come into force from 5 July 2013.

Priority households are entitled to 5 kg of foodgrains per person per month, and *antyodaya* households to 35 kg per household per month. The combined coverage of priority and antyodaya households (called 'eligible households') shall extend up to 75 per cent of the rural population and up to 50 per cent of the urban population. The PDS issue prices would be ₹ 3/2/1 per kg for rice/wheat/millets respectively, which may be revised after three years. Similarly, children between the age 6 months and 14 years are also entitled to free meal under the scheme. The concerned Act does not specify criteria for the identification of households eligible for scheme. It is left to state governments, and is to be completed within a year.

The Act also provides for the creation of State Food Commissions aimed to monitor the implementation of the scheme, give advice to the state governments and their agencies, and inquire into violations of entitlements. State Commissions also have to hear appeals against orders of the District Grievance Redressal Officer (DGRO). The Food Commissions have powers to impose penalties. If an order of the DGRO is not complied with, the concerned authority or officer can be fined up to ₹ 5,000. State governments must also put in place an internal grievance redressal mechanism which may include call centres, help lines, etc. Mandatory transparency provisions include: (a) placing all PDS related records in the public domain; (b) conducting periodic social audits of the PDS and other welfare schemes; (c) using information and communication technology to ensure transparent recording of transactions at all levels; and (d) setting up vigilance committees at all levels to supervise all schemes under the Act.

Effective Measures for Poverty Alleviation

Poverty alleviation has to go hand in hand with a vigorous drive for reforms. A former member of the Planning Commission suggested the following measures for economic reforms in India:

1. *Distribution of income*: Not only income has to be increased by stimulating policies of economic growth by the government (i.e. growth of output and employment) but distribution of income also has to be given importance in the country. The reforms must have a positive impact on the poor.
2. *Encouraging private investment*: Investment of capital in private industries has lagged behind in our country. There is a belief that profitability will increase over a period of time. Adopting liberalization can assure such beliefs.
3. *Raising resources and planning expenditure*: Until the private investment increases, there has to be a substantial public investment in infrastructure. This requires raising resources and planning expenditure. The latter has to focus on cutting expenditure or reducing non-essential expenditure and raising revenue. The revenue can be raised not by increasing taxes but by increasing tax collection. At present, a very small fraction of people pay income tax. We have to double the number of those who should be taxed compared to what we have today.
4. *Containing inflation*: Inflation may be contained by increasing production.
5. *Creating independent banking institutions*: In a market-based system, we must have institutions which are independent. We must, therefore, work for more autonomy of the Reserve Bank. But, the interest rates and the foreign exchange rate should not be entirety deregulated. The fundamental rates should be stable.
6. *Reframing of disinvestment policy*: The policy pertaining to disinvestment in public sector needs to be framed in such a way that if the unit is

incurring losses, the government must get out. We have to have an exist policy. Then there are units which have to be improved. The government can sell their shares and use the money for improvement. But there are units which are making huge profits. Selling the shares of such units is quite like selling the assets. It is a bad policy.

The economists thus, believe that only economic reforms can really help in reducing poverty in our country. However, the Leftists feel that a mixed economic system in the country obstructs alleviation of poverty. The absence of a minimum wage policy has increased discontentment among the labourers who today take more interest in strikes than in increasing production. The capitalists think that lack of free licensing policy has hampered industrial growth. The socialists maintain that measures like control over prices of manufactured commodities, fixing the profit margin of industrialists, action against black money, and control over urban property will alleviate poverty in the country. Intellectuals believe that change in the tax structure, control over conspicuous consumption, reduction in administrative expenses, change in the distribution system and added incentives to medium class entrepreneurs will contain poverty.

Broadly speaking, the measures for alleviating poverty can be classified into four groups: (a) those affecting the demand for work; (b) those affecting training in skilled labour; (c) those affecting the transfer of income; and (d) those affecting change in the existing social system. All these necessitate the following measures for eradicating poverty or at least reducing it significantly.

Creating Employment

The experience so far has shown that certain kinds of economic activities do not create jobs. All large industries, all industries using a lot of capital, and all industries which require import of machinery, components and raw materials belong to this group. These industries only produce goods which increase the well-being of the upper and upper-middle classes. They generate little employment for the poor. As such, small and cottage industries and agriculture, which now remain neglected as employment-generating sources, need to be identified and the credit and tax incentives need to be channelized more intensely to these areas.

Creating employment by such means as the MNREGS is not enough. Now, initiatives in the eco-political policy are also needed. If the estimated 20 million people who are unemployed and therefore also unproductive become productive in the process of being employed, they would become an enormous productive asset for the community.

Some new schemes for generating work and increasing income of the poor people in villages could be: (a) dissemination of knowledge in eco-technologies to cultivators; (b) training in horticulture, tree plantation, and use of unused lands; (c) creating artisan units in villages; (d) establishing micro-enterprises for women; (e) establishing community facility centres; and (f) mobilizing role of NGOs in villages.

Decentralizing Planning and its Execution

For the success of such anti-poverty/rural development programmes, it is necessary that they should be planned by the village panchayats. Unless the planning and its execution is decentralized, unless the families living in poverty are objectively identified by individual village panchayats at the local level, the programmes will not benefit the persons for whom they are made. In the urban areas also, the municipal councils should plan the self-employment programmes based on local resources and the skills of the slum dwellers. Decentralized plans alone can help in reducing and ridding ourselves of poverty.

Other Measures

Besides the above-mentioned measures, the following measures can also contribute to poverty alleviation: (a) Forming a time-bound and result-oriented action plan for rapid industrialization. The upsurge in industrial investments will provide employment to millions of people. (b) Participation in the emerging global markets. (c) Change in budgetary outlays to reduce irrelevant government expenditure. (d) Generating power substantially, improving transmission losses and controlling distribution. (e) Encouraging term-lending institutions. (f) Providing seed money to voluntary organizations through people-sponsored programmes. (g) Developing the mass rapid transit system in big cities with the help of the Asian Development Bank. (h) Establishing subsidized training centres for training youth in computers, electronic trade, and small-scale industries. (i) Helping women to be self-reliant through a carefully planned programme. (j) Constituting dedicated teams of committed bureaucrats and technocrats in every state for formulating, implementing and moderating job-oriented programmes. (k) Arranging full participation and involvement of people in development programmes. (l) Strengthening the PRIs so that they can become institutions of democratic management of rural development, both at the district and block levels. The government officials at the district and village levels can provide technical, managerial and marketing support on one hand and on the other hand stimulate social awareness and mobilize the poor households. (m) The help of non-government organizations may be taken in the administrative arrangements for the implementation of rural and urban development programmes. It calls for keeping the formal staff to the minimum and increasing the non-formal staff as part of full-time consultants drawn from academic or voluntary organizations. Non-government organizations here include professional/technical institutes, polytechnics, agricultural universities, university faculties, management institutes, research organizations, welfare/voluntary organizations and professional resources of business organizations and banking sectors.

Besides the above measures, some measures like, land redistribution, elimination of industrial monopolies, plugging of national drainage, efficient and democratic management of public sector enterprises, also help in reducing poverty in our country. So as long as we have a double mind about what path of developmental style to adopt, we will fail economically in our goals. It is not lack of resources or technical skills which are hindrances in our development, it is lack of the political policies. Planning is to be based on the fact that poverty is not a cause but a result. Elimination of poverty is not merely a question of economic upliftment but is a social and a political issue related to the level of the awareness of people.

Solutions

Poverty is a complex issue that affects millions of people, but some of the problems that cause it to exist can be fixed.

1. As over two-third of the population lives in rural areas, public investment should focus on developing agriculture and basic infrastructures. It is time to improve agricultural productivity and employ the jobless or underemployed migrating to the cities. There is a need to provide technological support to traditional craftsmen and agriculture-based small scale industries.
2. If we want to change the scenario, then change is required in the economic policies, in our attitude towards poor and we have to accept the fact that without supporting rural economy we can not alleviate poverty.
3. India needs to adopt the right development model. It has to realize that by blindly following GDP growth, it is only promoting inequality that sustains by keeping the poor in poverty.
4. India needs an economy that supports millions of small and medium enterprises that are suitable to employ low skilled poor people. It needs to promote women empowerment through education and health care; it will greatly help in dealing with poverty led by the population growth.
5. It is time when the government should start implementing its policies, ensure rule of law and simplify tax regime to encourage entrepreneurship.

Stress Points

1. Farmers must get all facilities for irrigation.
2. They should be trained and educated.
3. Agriculture must be made profitable.
4. The ever-rising population should be checked.
5. Family planning schemes should be introduced.
6. More and more industries should be set up to meet the needs of our country.
7. Activating panchayats to focus on eradication of superstitions.

8. Developing human resources by focussing on education, health and skill programmes.
9. Improving animal husbandry and developing dairy and poultry farming.

Conclusion

According to the world bank, between 2004 and 2011, poverty declined in India from 38.9 per cent of the population to 21.2 per cent (2011 purchasing power parity at $1.9 per person per day). Defining extreme poverty as living on less than $1.9 a day. A recent study says that by 2022, less than 3 per cent of Indians will be poor and extreme poverty could be eliminated altogether by 2030. The assumption that India would be able to eliminate extreme poverty by 2030 seems realistic given the country's record in the past 10 years in reducing poverty and its ability to meet the millennium development goals. But GDP must continue to grow at 7–8 per cent for the remaining period. Poverty is a national problem and it must be solved on a war footing. The government is taking a number of steps to mitigate poverty. Eradication of poverty would ensure a sustainable and inclusive growth of economy and society. Most of the schemes are clouded with implementation challenges. These programmes need to be centralized under one organization so that leakages can be prevented at multiple levels. Programmes are plagued by leakages on subsidies that limit its impact on the poor. We all should do everything possible and within our limits to help alleviate poverty in our country. Poverty must be eradicated in India as every person has the right to live a healthy life. One of the main causes of poverty is the growth in population and other economic problems unless these causes are not solved, the statistics of poverty in India is expected to increase and may not be alleviated in targeted dates as what the government may set.

References

Ansari, Iqbal Zafar and Akhtar, Sahail, 'Incidence of Poverty in India: Issues and Challenges', *Zenith,* Vol. 2, Issue 3, March, pp. 443–45.

Bagachee, S., 'Poverty Alleviation Programmes in Seventh Plan: An Appraisal', *Economic and Political Weekly,* Bombay, 24 January, 1987.

Becker, Howard, *Social Problems: A Modern Approach,* John Wiley & Sons Inc., New York, 1966.

Bernstein, Henry, *Rural Livelihoods: Crises and Responses,* Oxford University Press, Oxford, 1992.

Bhagwati, Jagdish, and Panagariya, Arvind, *India's Reforms: How They Produced Inclusive Growth.* Oxford University Press, New York, 2012.

Centre for Policy Research, *Population, Poverty and Hope,* Uppal Publishing House, New Delhi, 1983.

Chand, Attar, *Poverty and Underdevelopment: New Challenges,* Gian Publishing House, Delhi, 1987.

Dantwala, M.L., 'Garibi Hatao: Strategy Options', *Economic and Political Weekly,* 16 March, 1985.

Elesh, David, 'Poverty Theories and Income Maintenance: Validity and Policy Relevance', *Social Science Quarterly*, Vol. 26, 1973.

Ghate, P., *Direct Attacks on Rural Poverty*, Concept, New Delhi, 1984.

Gladwin, Thomas, *Poverty*, Little Brown, Boston, 1967.

Holborn, Martin and Haralambos, Mike, *Sociology: Themes and Perspectives* (7th edn), HarperCollins, London, 2008.

Kriesberg, Louis, 'The Relationship between Socio-Economic Rank and Behaviour', *Social Problems*, Vol. 10, 1963.

Miller, S.M. and Roby, Pamela, *The Future of Inequality*, Basic Books, New York, 1970.

Ornati, Oscar, 'Poverty in America', *Social Problems*, Vol. 14, 1964.

Rein, Martin, 'Problems in the Definition and Measurement of Poverty', in L.A. Ferman, J.L. Kornbluh and Alan Haber (eds), *Poverty in America*, University of Michigan Press, Michigan, 1968.

Ross, Peter H. and Blum, Zahava D., *Class, Status and Poverty*, Basic Books, New York, 1967.

Sagar, Deep, 'Rural Development Policies of India: A Historical Analysis', *The Indian Journal of Public Administration*, Delhi, Vol. 36, No. 2, 1990.

3

Unemployment

A man has to perform many roles in his life, the most crucial of which is, that of an earning member. It is crucial not because a man spends approximately one-third of his lifetime performing this role but because it determines both his livelihood and status. It also enables an individual to support his family and fulfil his social obligations towards the society. It makes possible for him to achieve power, too. If a person, with a capacity and potential to work, refuses to work or fails to obtain work, he not only loses status in society but also comes to suffer from several emotional and social problems. His plight affects him, his family, and the society too. No wonder, unemployment has been described as the most significant sociological problem in society. Opportunity for employment then becomes imperative in all such cultures which claim to be democracies. Equal employment opportunity is a prerequisite for equal accessibility to achieve status. Attempts to deal with unemployment have hitherto been two-pronged: one, to alleviate the status of the unemployed, and two, to abolish unemployment itself. After independence, though the governments – both central and state – have taken the problem into their hands, they have remained ineffective in tackling this and in providing assistance to persons unable to support themselves. Unemployment is still viewed as an economic rather than a social phenomenon.

What is 'Unemployment'?

One of the major problems of India is unemployment. Unemployment means the fate of being without any opportunity of earning one's livelihood. Unemployment occurs when a person who is actively searching for employment is unable to find work. Unemployment is often used as a measure of the health of the economy. The most frequent measure of unemployment is the unemployment rate, which is the number of unemployed people divided by the number of people in the labour force.

If a man with a PhD degree works as a petty clerk in an office, he will not be considered an unemployed person. At most, he would be viewed as an 'underemployed' person. An unemployed person is 'the one who having potentialities and willingness to earn, is unable to find a remunerative work'. Sociologically, it has been defined as 'forced or involuntary separation from remunerative work of a member of the normal working force (that is, of 15–59 age group) during normal working time at normal wages and under normal conditions'. D'Mello (1969: 24) has defined it as 'a condition in which an individual is not in a state of remunerative occupation despite his desire to do so'. Naba (1968) has explained unemployment as a 'condition of involuntary idleness'. The Planning Commission of India has described a person as 'marginally unemployed' when he remains without work for six months in a year. Against this, the ILO considers that person as 'employed' who remains with work for 15 hours (two days) in a week (of five days). This definition may be accepted in a developed country which provides social security to the unemployed but it cannot be accepted in a developing country like India which has no Unemployment Insurance Scheme.

In India, there is a tendency to conflate employment and work. But employment is only that part of work that is remunerated, and in India, a vast amount of work is actually unpaid and often not even socially recognized. Once we recognize that, a lot of what appears to be inexplicable about Indian employment trends becomes easier to understand. Employment figures in India are derived by applying two important parameters, Labour Force Participation Rate (LFPR) and the Unemployment Rate (UR), on estimates of working-age population.

Unemployment has three elements: (a) an individual should be capable of working, (b) an individual should be willing to work, and (c) an individual must make an effort to find work. On this basis, a person who is physically and/or mentally disabled, or who is chronically ill and unable to work, or a *sadhu* who because of his status as an incharge of a *math*, considers it beneath his dignity to work, or a beggar who does not want to work, cannot be included in the definition of unemployed persons. A society is believed to be in a 'condition of full employment' if the period of enforced idleness remains minimum. A society with full employment has four characteristics: (a) an individual takes very little time to find remunerative work according to his capabilities and qualifications, (b) he is sure of finding remunerative work, (c) the number of vacant jobs in the society exceeds the number of job seekers, and (d) work is available on 'adequate remuneration'.

Differences in Theories of Unemployment

Many variations of the unemployment rate exists with different definitions concerning who is an 'unemployed person' and who is in the 'labour force'. For example, US Bureau of Labour Statistics commonly cites the 'U-3' unemployment rate as the official unemployment rate, but this definition of unemployment does not include unemployed workers who are discouraged by a tough labour market and are no longer looking for work.

Usually, unemployment is measured by the term unemployment rate. The unemployment rate is usually given by the following formula as shown below:

Unemployment rate = ((number of unemployed persons/labour force)*100)

Additionally, thoughts of various schools of economic differ on the cause of unemployment. Natural unemployment is frequently defined as the lowest rate of unemployment an economy will reach. It is 'natural' because its causes are the things other than the problems caused due to a bad economy. No matter how robust the economy is, there will always be people who are unemployed while in such situations. Two of the most common economic changes creating structural unemployment are technological advances and rapid relocation of available jobs. Another factor that makes up natural unemployment is surplus unemployment. This occurs when wage controls are put in place by unions or minimum wage laws. This causes employers to cut their workforce to stay within budgetary constraints. Unemployment is a serious problem in India. It is becoming severe day by day. India has a population of about 1.20 billion. Many of the Indians are jobless.

According to the National Sample Survey Office (NSSO) report, the unemployment rate was at an all-time high of 6.1 per cent in 2017–18. The report also says that male youth had an unemployment rate of 17.4 per cent and 18.7 per cent in rural and urban areas, respectively while women youth had rates of 13.6 per cent and 27.2 per cent respectively in 2017–18. The employees in the country are estimated to grow by 8 million per annum for the next decade and a half, which is a little part of the job requirements in the economy, with a lot of workforce still finding employment.

Magnitude

Indian labour market is characterized by part-time workers, seasonality of work, underemployment and social factors which restrict many women from joining the labour force. Though it is often repeated that there has been an alarming rise in unemployment in our country since independence, the exact number of unemployed persons is not yet known. In India, the National Sample Survey Office (NSSO) conducts surveys on employment/unemployment scenario in the country. The figures given are based only on estimates. The estimates take into consideration only the number of persons registered in the employment exchanges and these employment exchanges cover mainly the urban areas. Registration with the employment exchanges being voluntary, not all the unemployed register their names in the exchanges. Further, some of the registered persons are already employed but register again to seek better employment. However, most of the social scientists are of the opinion that quite a large proportion of the working population is not regularly employed in our country and that these unemployed and underemployed people and their families are dependent upon their family members or kin even for their bare necessities.

With fears that India is experiencing jobless growth and uncertainty abounding that the country may not be able to cash in on its 'demographic bonus', – the world's largest working-age population of 869 million by 2020 – because of limited progress on health, education and job skills. Seven warning signs are:

1. In the case of women living in urban areas, the unemployment rate was 12.4 per cent, while in rural areas, it was 6.4 per cent. The overall unemployment among women was 7.7 per cent across the country.
2. As many as 60 per cent of those with jobs do not find employment for the entire year, indicating widespread 'under-employment' and temporary jobs.
3. The formation of companies has slowed down to 2009 levels.
4. Companies are growing at 2 per cent, the lowest in five years.
5. With large corporations and public-sector banks financially stressed, the average size of companies in India is reducing, at a time when well-organized large companies are central to creating a job.
6. The statistics show the unemployment rate in India from 2007 to 2017 was estimated to be 3.6 per cent.
7. Unemployment rate in India increased to 6.10 per cent in 2018 form 3.52 per cent in 2017. There are around 3 crore unemployed seeking jobs now.

Types of Unemployment

The most accepted classification of unemployment recognizes two broad types: voluntary and involuntary unemployment.

Voluntary unemployment arises when an individual is not under any employment out of his own desire not to work. This could be from their total apprehension towards the concept itself, or it may be that an individual is unable to find work paying their desired wages and they do not want to settle.

Involuntary unemployment encompasses all those factors that prevent a physically fit individual willing to work, from getting an appointment. According to John Maynard Keynes, 'involuntary unemployment arises due to the insufficiency of effective demand which can be solved by stepping up aggregate demand through government intervention'. Involuntary unemployment is further categorized into the following subheads:

1. *Structural*: Such unemployment stems from any structural change in the economy that leads to the decline of specific industries. Long-term changes in the market conditions, reorganization of the same, and sudden changes in the technological sector create, a skill gap in the existing workers, where workers fail to find jobs and employers with available jobs fail to find workers. This problem is created by some inherent long-term change in the economy.

2. *Regional*: Globalization and the relocation of jobs also lead to unemployment as workers are often unable to move to the new location where the employers currently hold positions. Agricultural labourers, farmers, workers of sugar mills, rice sellers, cotton ginning units and ice factories are included in seasonal unemployment. Agro-based industries and tourism industries are examples of this form of unemployment.
3. *Frictional*: This type of unemployment happens when the labour is either transitioning between jobs or is trying to find a job more suited to their skill set. Friction is generally referred to as the time, energy and cost that a person invests while searching for a new job. This type of unemployment is caused by situations like new graduates just starting their search for a job, people leaving a job to move to another city, or people quitting their jobs to look for a better one.
4. *Casual*: Some occupations can only offer temporary employment to individuals and their engagement is subject to termination as soon as the demand subsides. Daily labourers who work on a day-to-day basis are an example of such types of unemployment.
5. *Disguised*: This is a scenario when more people are employed in a job than that is actually required. This is the hallmark of developing economies where availability of labour is abundant. It is a common feature in agriculture when more than the required human-resource has been engaged in the cultivation of the same plot. It is a sort of underemployment.

   Unemployment may be further classified either as rural and urban, or as seasonal, cyclical, and technological. Urban unemployment has been sub-classified as educational and industrial.
6. *Seasonal unemployment* is inherent in the agricultural sector and certain manufacturing units like sugar and ice factories. The nature of work in a sugar factory or an ice factory is such that the workers have to remain out of work for about six months in a year.
7. *Agricultural unemployment* is caused on account of a number of factors. First, the landholdings are so small that even the family members of the working age groups are not absorbed by the land. Second, the nature of work is seasonal. Broadly speaking, a cultivator in India remains unemployed for about four to six months in a year.
8. *Cyclical unemployment* is caused because of the ups and downs in trade and business. When the entrepreneurs earn high profits, they invest them in business which increases employment, but when they get less profits or suffer from losses or their products remain unsold and pile up, they reduce the number of workers in their industries which causes unemployment. A boom is generated when investments exceed savings, and similarly a depression results when savings exceed investment. This is probably an over simplification of the concept of cyclical unemployment but still it is essentially true. Several external factors like wars, strikes and political disturbances, natural calamities that affect business cycle are also contributors to cyclical unemployment.

9. *Industrial unemployment* is caused because of a large-scale migration of people from rural to urban areas, losses incurred by industries, slow growth of industries, competition with foreign industries, unplanned industrialization, defective industrial policies, labour strikes or employers' lockouts, rationalization, and so on.
10. *Technological unemployment*: This type of unemployment refers to the situation when people have been put out of work by the introduction of a superior technology in their area of operation or through the inclusion of technology that the current labour force is ill-adapted to. It is caused due to the introduction of automation or other technological changes in industry or other work places. It is also caused due to the reduction in man power necessary to produce a finished product. In long run, it is true that technological improvements may increase employment in related service industries (Elliott and Merrill, 1950: 607–8). Nevertheless, continued improvements in mechanical devices mean that employment opportunities have to increase proportionately or there will be an added residue of unemployment.
11. *Educated unemployment* arises when a large number of educated people are unemployed or unable to secure a job. This form of unemployment also happens when people with advanced degrees are unable to procure an engagement that is suited to their level of training. Educational unemployment is caused because the system of education is largely unrelated to life. In fact, one of the University Grants Commission's (UGC) annual reports stated clearly that the present system of education is generating much waste and stagnation. The (education) system is irrelevant because of the stress it lays on higher education which can be given only to a small minority, most of whom would in any case be unemployed or unemployable once they graduate. The education is of little relevance to the needs of the nation.

The situation is poorer for youth with certain level of technical training. Though such technical training/qualifications are quite sought after in the country and are supposed to provide market ready applied skills to the candidates. As a result, contrary to expectations, more than one-fourth of youth with technical training are without any gainful employment.

We can also classify youth according to their skill level – a combination of their general, vocational and technical education. We may consider youth with at least secondary level of general education and some vocational/technical training as *moderately skilled* and those with graduate level of education and some vocational/technical training as *highly skilled*. We observe that unemployment among moderately skilled youth is 27 per cent while that among highly skilled youth is about 20 per cent. On an aggregate about one-fourth of skilled youth are without jobs. Incidence of skilled unemployment is higher among females compared to males and in rural areas relative to urban areas. As against this, unemployment among unskilled youth – those with less than 10 years of schooling or without any vocational/technical training is just about 6 per cent. It is thus evident that unemployment among educated youth is a serious problem in India. This has a regional setting too with states like Kerala, Odisha, Jharkhand, Assam, Bengal and Jammu & Kashmir are consistently having higher levels of educated youth unemployment compared to national average. On the other hand, unemployment among educated youth is relatively less than national average in the states of Gujarat, Madhya Pradesh, Maharashtra, Chhattisgarh and Karnataka.

Unemployment among the educated youth, poses another set of problems. It makes the youth so angry and frustrated that they become militants, rebels and a threat to the unity of the country. The widespread and gruesome agitation that followed the announcement of the acceptance of the Mandal Commission recommendations in August–September 1990 provides good testimony to the deep emotions that the question of employment stirs among the youth.

Underemployment

Open unemployment is not a true indicator of the gravity of the unemployment problem in an economy such as India, characterized as it is by large-scale underemployment and poor employment quality in the unorganized sector, which accounts for over 90 per cent of the total employment. The organized sector contributes only about 9 per cent to the total employment. Underemployment in various segments of the labour force is quite high. Even when an economy is running at full strength, these types of unemployment will still occur. There is no economic or market 'fix' for them. This is why most economists state that when an economy reaches the natural unemployment rate, the economy is at full employment. Most economists agree that the natural rate of unemployment is around 4 per cent. Unemployment in India is projected to increase from 17.7 million in 2016 to 17.8 million in 2017 and 18 million next year.

Causes of Unemployment

No one reason can be held responsible for the widespread unemployment in India but the following are the main causes of the problem:

1. *Uncertainty in agriculture*: Even after the development of science, agriculture in India is dependent on the mercy of nature. Each year millions of labourers have to lose their jobs because of droughts and floods and other natural calamities due to which uncertainty in agriculture and unemployment arises.
2. *Improper attitude*: One of the main reasons in this country is the want of a job by the educated people. They do not want to start their own production unit. Unemployment has also increased due to this improper attitude.

3. *Employment to women*: During the decade of 1950 to 1960, very few women were working, but now-a-days their number and percentage have increased. This has also increased unemployment among men.
4. *The wide gap between wages and productivity*: Inflation is continuing in the country due to which prices keep increasing. Many find it difficult to work below their qualification level. Affected by this, the labourers demand more wages and incentives due to which the cost and price of commodities increase, but demand decreases. This is followed by reduced production and thus, increases unemployment, low wages or salary below the market rate.
5. *Irrational mechanization*: The government has intentionally encouraged labour substitution activities, keeping in view development of heavy industries, due to which difficulties in the progress of employment opportunities have arised. It is definite that labour substitution through irrational mechanization would naturally increase unemployment.
6. *Lack of an extensive employment policy*: India has always lacked an extensive and short-term employment policy. It is true that unless a solid employment-oriented development policy is not evolved and implemented by a stable government, the solution of the problem of unemployment is difficult. Apart from this, the hurdles in production activities, social environment, social evils, religious superstitions, political instability and industrial unrest are increasing the problem of unemployment.
7. *The poor condition of cottage industries*: In villages, unemployment is due to lack of cottage industries. The cottage industries are in a winding state. They give whole-time occupation to only a fraction of the people who depend on them.
8. *Theoretical education*: Chronic unemployment is in some quarters attributed to the system of education prevailing in our country. Our education is too theoretical. It turns too many arts graduates and very few skilled workers.
9. *Lack of full employment in industries*: In the industrial segment, there are not many mills and factories and the number of people employed in them is not large. Even the mills and factories that we have, do not work to their maximum capacity either due to lack of requisite machinery or because of lack of adequate supply of materials.
10. *Defective planning*: Planning work has been going on in the country since independence, but this planning has been defective. Scholars opine that unemployment has also increased due to this reason.
11. *Lack of alternative opportunities for agricultural workers*: In rural India, the picture is equally discouraging. Agriculture is the principal occupation of the majority of the rural population. However, agriculture keeps the cultivators engaged for a limited part of the year. For many months every year, the agriculturist remains idle and lives miserably.

12. *Advanced technology*: Earlier for a task, hundreds or thousand people were required but now due to the advanced technology even one person can do many people's work. With the advanced technology, companies are hiring fewer persons to operate the machines. A command on the computer gets the work done and this has cut off the employment for many.
13. *Corruption*: In the government sector and even in private sector to some extent, people get the job by giving bribe, even though the candidate is not that qualified. If he gives bribe he gets the job, so the qualified candidate remains unemployed.
14. *The rapid increase in population*: The present increase in population in India has created an imbalance in the demand and supply in the labour market. The increase in techniques, capital formation, natural resources, etc. is not at the same rate as the rate of increase in population, due to which people are not getting employment and unemployment is increasing. The population of our country is ever-rising which is why the problem of employment is getting more and more acute every year. There are employment opportunities in India, but the rising population problem creates unemployment. If the population grows at the same rate, the next generation will face more problems.
15. *Educated unemployment in India*: In India, there has been an alarming phase of mass-unemployment among the educated youth. Post-graduates and graduates are walking pillar to post in search of employment. When the economy slows down, there is a surge in the number of educated unemployed people. This chronic unemployment is in some quarters attributed to the system of education prevailing in our country. To make up for this deficiency government has opened several technological institutes in different parts of India. However, this attempt, good as it is, will not solve the problem of unemployment. Already there are more technically trained people than there is employment for them.
16. *Old businesses*: Many age-old businesses that are not able to cope-up with the changing demand and economic scenario are either closed down or heavy retrenchment takes place in them. When there is a slump in business, many people find themselves without jobs.
17. *Inadequate industrial progress*: Increase in industrial progress and national wealth has not kept pace with the increase in population.
18. *Automation of works*: This has complicated the unemployment problem in India. The highly sophisticated machinery is run by skilled and trained people. On one hand, the skilled people get employed in these large industries. But, the large masses of unskilled Indians find it hard get a job that suits their skills.
19. *Education system*: Our education system is also no less responsible for the seriousness of this problem. Education is too theoretical. Education of today is cut off from the realities and practical problems of life. It is unfortunate that degrees do not provide them with a suitable job. There

are a large number of educated people who are unemployed. The problem of employment among educated youth is a serious one.

20. *Other factors*: The other factors that are responsible for unemployment in India are:
    (a) Excessive burden of population on cultivation;
    (b) Low productivity in the agriculture sector;
    (c) Defective economic planning; and
    (d) Large-scale production and mechanization.

Economists have explained unemployment in terms of lack of capital, lack of investment and high production. Some believe that unemployment has its roots in the decline in the business cycle following a period of industrial prosperity. A few hold that dislocations in the industries and an inability to forecast the market have put a sizeable proportion of men out of work. Yet others are of the opinion that sudden economic deflation and impersonal forces of economic competition cause loss of work. Improvements in machine technology, over-production, falsely stimulated speculation, social emphasis upon monetary success and the inevitable depressions – all these cause crippling disruption in the demand of labour.

The classical school of thought places the essential cause of unemployment on the 'Wage Fund Theory', according to which the wages of the workers are fixed in advance but because of lack of capital, the manufacturers engage only a small number of workers which results in unemployment. They say that the remedy for unemployment lies in lowering the wage rate. But how much down the wages could be brought? Could the labour be denied the minimum living standard to which it got accustomed, and which in fact was its due? If that were done, how much suffering and misery would it cause? This led the Cambridge professor John Maynard Keynes to enunciate a theory in 1936 (in his book *General Theory of Employment, Money and Interest*) which stated that national output, effective demand, and employment were interrelated and that total volume of employment in an economy at any point of time, depended upon the level of effective demand which meant total volume of the country's output of goods and services. If national output is rising constantly, employment would be doing so *ipso facto*. However, at times there could be some distortions in this framework. If savings exceeded investments, effective demand for goods and services would decline and with that would decline the demand for labour, this would result in some amount of unemployment. However, this could be remedied, so goes the Keyne's theory, by the state intervening and stimulating investments through proper fiscal measures and raising consumption level by injecting into the market new purchasing power, by producing deficit budgets.

Keynesian Theory of Employment

According to this theory, since the demand for goods and services is not so much that the total actual resources may be utilized, unemployment arises.

In Keynes view, the level of employment of any country depends on its effective demand. Effective demand depends on the total supply of production and the total demand.

According to Keynes, the three main reasons for spreading of unemployment are:

1. Lack of effective demand
2. Deficiency of outlay on consumption
3. Deficiency of investment

After this, as after Second World War full employment came to be accepted as the goal of the monetary policies to be pursued by governments, budget deficits came to be looked upon as not only legitimate but also the most desirable instrument for 'social engineering'. However, this was nothing but the distortion of Keynesian theory, which made inflation a perennial feature of the economic scene both in developed and developing economies.

The new classical school believes unemployment to be the result of overproduction. Overproduction reduces the prices of the commodities which necessitates reducing the workers, which in turn increases unemployment.

Some economists have referred to the imbalance between demand and supply as the cause of unemployment. When effective demand declines for the products of industry, prices drop, factories close down, wages stop, and men are shifted from the employed to the unemployed status through no fault of their own. Less demand was the result of slow rate of development in early years, or postponing investments due to poor trade and commerce, and/or shift (of investment) from the industrial to the non-industrial sector.

Lionel Edie (1926: 422) is of the opinion that unemployment is caused by the disruption of economic structure. Elliott and Merrill (1950: 606) have said that unemployment is primarily a result of the decline in the business cycle following a period of industrial prosperity. Advances in technical skills and highly specialized division of labour also make it impossible for able-bodied and capable men to secure jobs. Bartlett (1949: 6–9) has said that the virtually monopolistic industries, like iron and steel industry, have been major factors in producing depressions. These industries, he charges, do not lower their prices sufficiently during the period of declining price levels in other industries to make it possible to keep up their production.

Social Factors

Several scholars have now maintained that unemployment cannot be ascribed only to economic factors. Social and personal factors equally contribute to unemployment. In sociological terms, unemployment can be described as the product of a combination of social factors like degrading social status, geographical immobility, rapid growth of population, and defective educational system; and personal factors like lack of experience, vocational unfitness, and illness and disability.

Degrading social or work status causes unemployment, in the sense that some people consider it below their dignity to take up certain jobs and prefer to remain unemployed. Sometimes young persons refuse to accept certain jobs because they consider their family's position too high to accept the job they have been offered. It is good to have high aspirations and a growing desire for a high standard of living but it is unwise to refuse to accept substitute interests and preferences.

The upsurge in the birth rate or the rapid growth of population is a factor which immensely affects the availability of work. For a number of reasons, the pattern of responsibility to be borne by the joint family system has been changing. Maintaining unemployed dependents by nuclear families is not economically feasible for most families. This detachment not only weakens the family ties but also creates many problems for the society. The increasing unemployment due to the unchecked growth of population, thus, not only increases the responsibilities of the society but also leads to degradation as well as loss of social esteem for the unemployed individual.

Unemployment is triggered off by *geographical immobility* too. There is surplus labour in one place and inadequate labour in another place, when people refuse to move from one region to other. The immobility may also be due to the lack of information regarding the availability of jobs in other cities or because of language issues or family responsibilities.

Unemployment is also a result of the *defective educational system*. The educational system introduced by the British can no longer be described as 'purposeful' today. The education system is inadequate because it does not give due priority to primary education and what it imparts at the higher levels, at a great cost to the exchequer, does not instill attitudes needed for nation building. The benefit of education is confined to a minority comprising middle and high income groups and has not been able to help young persons find employment.

As regards the personal factors, lack of experience of a person (seeking a job) because of his young age, old age affecting one's capacity to work, lack of vocational training, physical disabilities and illness – all go against the unemployed and the unemployable.

Consequences of Unemployment

Unemployment affects an individual, family and society, or it may be said that unemployment causes personal disorganization, family disorganization and social disorganization.

From the point of view of *personal disorganization*, the unemployed person faces disillusionment and falls prey easily to cynicism. Having no outlet to release their depression, young persons tune their creative energies into wrong channels which explains the rise of the number of youthful bandits, highway robberies and bank hold-ups. These anti-social activities offer a chance to the undisciplined and recalcitrant youth to extract a living. Most of the criminals are undoubtedly recruited from boys with a history of earlier delinquencies, but there has been an increase in the number of daring criminals with the decrease in work opportunities. On the other hand, the plight of an earning person who loses his job is equally sad. Ex-wage-earners are more liable to physical illness, tension, suicide and crime, because lack of working opportunities makes it impossible for them to support their dependents. Their own dependency on others is very often morally sapping because of the humiliation that follows. Some people in this state are even known to turn to unlawful activities like smuggling and drug trafficking rather than squarely facing up the actual situation. During economic depressions, the reduction in wages and the increase in part-time jobs is further frustrating. Wages are often unbelievably low because of the competition for jobs, and the increase in unemployment further reduces the chance of finding a job and depreciates the wages. The underemployed and underpaid are subjected to nearly as many difficult adjustments as those who are completely out of work.

Family disorganization because of unemployment is easy to measure. Unemployment affects the unity of interests of family members, the unity of objectives, as well as the unity of personal ambitions. The disharmonious functioning of the members creates discord within family, which means that not only do the tensions between the unemployed husband and wife increase but conflicts between parents and children also arise. Sometimes the wife of an unemployed person wants to take up a job but the idea of a wife taking up a job irritates the husband with traditional and conservative values so much that there is tremendous conflict within the family. Many husbands object to any substantial assumption of authority by their wives in the fields which they (the husbands) consider traditionally their own. On the other hand, the conflict between husband and wife may arise when the unemployed husband wants his wife to take up a job and the wife is reluctant to do so because of the presence of young children at home.

Social disorganization caused by unemployment is hard to measure. Social disorganization is a breakdown of the social structure, or change because of which old forms of social control no longer function effectively, or a process by which social relationships between members of a group are broken or dissolved. The activities of the unemployed are so restricted and their attitudes so bitter that in this phase of disillusionment and discouragement, they lose their desire to work and their skills may deteriorate with a resultant loss to the whole community (Colcord, 1941).

Measures Taken to Contain Unemployment in India

The first measure adopted to contain unemployment was the introduction of Prime Minister's cash programme in 1972–73 (during the Fourth Five-Year Plan). The introduction of various wage employment programmes in the 1970s and the 1980s like *Kam Ke Badle Anaj* programme in 1977–78, IRDP in 1978–79, NREP in 1980–81, RLEGP in 1983 and JRY in April 1989 were very significant to tackle the growing rural unemployment. The Narasimha Rao government's Prime Minister Rozgar Yojna was started in 1993–94.

Our policy planners brought employment generation into focus in the Eighth Five-Year Plan with other parameters set so as to achieve a 3 per cent growth per year in employment.

In 1999, to commemorate the fifty years of the country's independence, the Government of India launched the Swarnajayanti Gram Swarozgar Yojana, incorporating the already existing six schemes, viz., IRDP TRYSEM, DWCRA, SITRA, GKY and MWS. Then, in 2001, the Sampoorna Grameen Rozgar Yojana was introduced by merging EAS and JGSY with the objective of providing additional wage employment and food security, alongside creation of durables assets in rural areas.

Agriculture is the most labour-absorbing sector of the economy. In recent years, there has been a decline in the dependence of population on agriculture partly because of disguised unemployment. Some of the surplus labour in agriculture has moved to either the secondary or the tertiary sector. In the secondary sector, small-scale manufacturing is the most labour-absorbing. In the case of the tertiary sector, various new services are now appearing like biotechnology, information technology and so on.

National Career Service Scheme

The Government of India has initiated the national career service scheme whereby a web portal named National Career Service Portal (www.ncs.gov.in) has been launched by the Ministry of Labour and Employment. Through this portal, job-seekers and employers can avail the facility of a common platform for seeking and updating job information. Not only private vacancies, contractual jobs available in the government sector are also available on the portal.

An important scheme, launched by the Government of India to contain unemployment, especially in rural areas, in the history of independent India, is the Mahatma Gandhi National Rural Employment Guarantee Scheme (MNREGS), which aims at enhancing the livelihood security of people living in rural areas by guaranteeing 100 days of wage employment in a financial year. It was implemented all over the country in 2006 and is more comprehensive in nature.

Apart from the Employment Exchange, the Government of India publishes a weekly newspaper titled *Employment News*. It comes out every Saturday evening and gives detailed information about vacancies for government jobs across India. Along with the list of vacancies, it also has the notifications for various government exams and recruitment procedures for government jobs.

Evaluating the measures adopted to contain unemployment in the country, it can be stated that unemployment has been a major election plank of the parties which have been in power but a satisfactory solution still eludes the policy planners. The important reason is that in most cases employment generation schemes are not backed up with adequate resources.

After independence, it came to be believed by the policy planners that unemployment can be reduced only through state intervention. This view lasted till 1991 when the government took a u-turn in its economic policy and planning strategy. The new measures for generating employment aimed at (a) liberalization, (b) doing away with controls and regulations, (c) mobilizing resources in the private sector, and (d) encouraging competitiveness in the monopolistic spheres. The economic reforms were not confined to the industrial sector alone. The sustained growth in the agricultural sector was also not neglected. The Eighth Plan had paid special attention to employment in the rural areas.

Rural Unemployment

For a number of years now, the government has announced a number of employment guarantee programmes, perceiving them as poverty alleviation strategies. There was the Food for Work Programme, renamed as the National Rural Employment Programme (NREP). Then came the Rural Landless Employment Guarantee Programme (RLEGP) both of which were subsequently merged into the Jawahar Rozgar Yojana (JRY). To this, the government added the Employment Guarantee Scheme in March 1990, but the scheme never took off despite periodic announcements about adopting the Maharashtra model, said to be functioning well.

Why have these schemes failed? Let us take up the RLEGP launched in 1983 and fully funded by the central government. The basic objective of this programme was to improve and expand employment opportunities in the rural areas for the landless labour, guaranteeing employment to at least one member of a rural landless household upto 100 days in a year. In 1989, the programme was merged with the JRY.

What is our agricultural policy and what are our goals? Is our goal to accelerate the growth rate of agricultural output, or achieve national food self-sufficiency, or keep enriching the large farmers with periodic hikes in procurement and support prices, or make work available to all cultivators in the villages? So far, our emphasis has been to give highest priority to production of foodgrains. There has been significant rise in cultivated area under commercial crops like oilseeds, cotton, sugarcane, etc. This points out to the basic question that we should find alternative sources of work for the rural people which will solve the twin problems of rural poverty and unemployment. Unless reforms and programmes of structural adjustments and infrastructural development in rural areas are not launched, the targeted economic and social objectives may not be achieved. Can freeing agriculture from the shackles of government controls and subsidies be a solution? Will such a step enable agricultural sector to offer much greater volume of employment as compared to the present? Or will this step affect the small and marginal farmers, the food prices, and the food-deficit states? The question is indeed debatable.

For educated unemployed, the Government of India has also launched a self-employment scheme, called Prime Minister's Rozgar Yojana (PMRY), to provide loans through banks for self-employment. The central government provides capital subsidy for this purpose and routes it through the Reserve Bank of India. From 1994–95 the existing Self-Employment Scheme for the Educated Unemployed Youth (SEEUY) was subsumed in PMRY. But, like the other rural employment schemes, the PMRY has not done much. The number of educated persons getting loans is decreasing continuously, and so is the subsidy released by the central government. Besides the law and order machinery, the political system would also come under greater strain in the years to come because of the rising unemployment.

The question is: In the present situation of our country, is the guarantee of right to work feasible? With cold hard statistics, can a concrete blueprint of an employment generation programme be worked out? The feeling is that the slogan of 'right to work' is nothing but a digressive, escapist, tangential, flippant, and a comic proposal. Mere making of a promise or a provision in the Constitution is not likely to provide work for anyone, except perhaps for the politicians who are experts in making impossible promises. They find nothing wrong in adding one more promise of 'right to work' without giving substantial thought to comprehensive economic policies, innovative employment generation schemes, efficient organization of the economic system, and other pragmatic and result-oriented techniques. The 'right to work' is neither viable nor enforceable without massive inputs. It is a distant fantasy and an empty shibboleth. Where are the resources and billions and trillions of rupees to give jobs to about 4 crore unemployed persons, considering the large amount of money that is needed per year to create even one job? Will this slogan not lead to wholesale frustration and disillusionment all around? Is 'right to work' not linked with obtaining a mandate from a court of law to get a job and the right of employer to terminate the employee's services, collective bargaining, and so forth? Is it not contradictory to the right of reservation ? Do we, therefore, not find a pathological fallacy in the thinking of the politicians who give such populist slogans and promises?

Will Unemployment Insurance be a Right Policy?

The ideal state today is considered to be one which is a welfare state, i.e. one which accepts the responsibility of freeing its citizens from want and fear. Arrangement of universal education, provision of health care, security against unemployment, protection against physical disabilities, and providing secure wages, ample leisure time and a generous pension are regarded as essential functions of the state. No doubt, all this is a noble endeavour. People in many countries see it as their due and as a work of civility of their society. But can the economic and fiscal cost of the welfare programme be ignored in this ideal? If unemployment insurance scheme is introduced in India, can this be funded in a sustainable way? With the increasing unemployment and increased cost of living, how can our government fulfil the rising expectations of the people? Further, it has also come to be realized in many developing countries having social security schemes that social security system is a contributory cause of the present day high rate of unemployment.

Remedies

The real remedy lies in, an addition to the national wealth, increased production of industrial goods. If there are more industries, there will be more avenues for employment, particularly for men and women with professional and technological training. Already the river valley projects and power-plant projects are finding employment for a large number of people. It is only in a rapid industrialization of the country that we have a key to the solution of our economic problem. If more and more industries are established and more commodities are produced, there will be vacancies not merely for technically trained university people but also for labourers skilled and unskilled.

What are the open job avenues have been suggested to the new entrants in the employment market? The following measures have been suggested for the galloping jobless conundrum in the country: (a) encouraging self-employment, (b) drastic reorganization of vocational courses, and (c) identification of skills needed in the present-day context required by industrial units, and designing courses and curricula relevant to such identified skills in demand in the employment market.

The innumerable opportunities for self-employment can be found not only in urban areas but in rural areas too. In rural areas, these include: farming on modern scientific lines, small-scale industries, agro-industries, forest-based industries, dairy farming, poultry farming, village arts and crafts (like handmade paper, pottery, leather goods, hand-printing and dyeing of textiles, carpets, rugs, etc.), small business and trade, nurseries, and hire and repair of farming equipment.

Some people suggest that economic growth is the best solution for tackling unemployment. This may be true for some time but not for ever. This is because of three reasons: First, economic growth has its limits. Second, advances in technology tend to displace labour in traditional occupations and industries. Third, these economies, over the years, develop structural rigidities which prevent adaptation to changing situation. The economic relations developed in decades of high growth rates cannot be sustained during the economic stagnation periods. However, a developing country like India does need the policy and programme of economic growth. Along with this, the policy of free trade will also create many employment opportunities and reduce unemployment. Depending upon the developed countries for helping the developing countries like India in their development programmes will be like living in a fool's paradise in this age because such countries are bound to impose their ideas and ideologies on the country seeking their economic help. India has to depend on its own resources. Of course, some aid in the form of loans at concessional rates of interest for development projects, some capital investments, and starting of some joint ventures in selected sectors may be helpful in development of our economy, and in mitigating the problem of spreading unemployment.

It may thus be pointed out that the remedial measures for reducing unemployment must lay greater emphasis on: (a) creation of opportunities for self employment; (b) augmentation of productivity and income levels of the working poor; (c) shift in emphasis from creation of relief type of employment to building up of durable productive assets in the rural areas; (d) instead of attempting to revert somewhat to protectionist policy, liberalization of policy may be given a serious trial and the pace of privatization may be accelerated; (e) encouraging entrepreneurship among the youth of the country; and (f) increasing production in agriculture and industrial sectors.

Suggestions

1. *Control on population growth*: It is disturbing as well as distressing to find that the standard of living of an individual is still below the desired level and unemployment is on the increase. The growth of population should be checked in order to solve unemployment problem. It is only when a real welfare state comes into existence that the curse of unemployment will disappear from our country.
2. *Development of non-agricultural subsidiary industries*: In India agriculture witnesses seasonal unemployment. Thus, in villages, some agriculture-related industries must be developed so that the farmer is able to earn something during his free time. For this, the subsidiary activities of animal husbandry, poultry farming, gardening, milk business, etc. can be developed.
3. *Development of small and cottage industries*: Small and cottage industries should be encouraged so that people get employment at low capital investment. For this, such small-scale industries must be developed which are labour intensive. This will give part-time occupation to agriculturists and relieve the poor people who depend on these small decaying industries such as weaving, making carpets and mats or utensils of bell-metal. The government alone can help them with a loan and find a market for their goods. If these industries are revived, the rural people will live in happiness and peace.
4. *Full capacity utilization*: Many industries are working at less than their full capacity. Such industries must be encouraged to utilize their full capacity, so that employment opportunities may be increased in such industries. Investment in heavy and basic industries and consumer goods industries should be increased to provide more employment with more production.
5. *Exploitation of natural resources*: The government should search for such natural resources by which new industries may be established. It is a

known fact that natural resources are in abundance in India, that is why it was named as the 'golden bird'.

6. *Increase in investment*: To increase the employment opportunities, household savings must be encouraged, so that more capital formation may be done leading to increase in investments. This would assist in the establishment of new industries and employment opportunities would increase.
7. *Demand and supply of labour*: The demand and supply of labour should be coordinated in various production areas. For this, the future demand and supply of labour should be estimated and arrangements for their training, etc. be made accordingly, so that the labourers in excess of the demand may find employment, elsewhere.
8. *Establishment of powerhouses in villages*: About 80 per cent of the population of the country lives in villages. To remove unemployment among the 80 per cent population the 'Bhagwati Committee' gave suggestions for the establishment of powerhouses in villages so that small industries may develop and no working be stopped in villages at night due to darkness.
9. The villages should become self-sufficient in their economy so that the villagers would not run to the cities in search of jobs. This would ensure that the large-cities are not overcrowded with a huge population. It would help maintain the balance between the job/vacancy and the job seekers.
10. *Promote industrialization:* So that more job opportunities can be created for the workers. The focus should be on heavy industries that employ thousands of man-power of varied skills. There is a growing demand for skilled people in various industries.
11. Other suggestions for the solution of the problem of unemployment and underemployment:
    (a) Predetermination of a national policy for employment.
    (b) Formation of all India manpower services.
    (c) Change in the education policy.
    (d) Rapid industrial development.
    (e) Survey the human resources of the country.
    (f) Strengthen the job counselling services.
    (g) Maintain at least one office at each community development division.
    (h) Provide facilities to construct rural houses.
    (i) Expansion of small irrigation facilities.
    (j) Agricultural service centres to be established so that the technical people get employment in villages also.
    (k) There is a need for industrial, vocational and technical education.
    (l) Large-scale industries should be encouraged so as to create increased avenues for employment.
    (m) Planning should be on right lines so that public money may be properly utilized.

Conclusion

One of the most disturbing problems in India has been the mounting rate of unemployment, both in the rural and urban sectors. In case of the rural sector, there has been both unemployment and underemployment. In the urban sector, there has been both educated and industrial unemployment. Unless the unemployment problem is solved, the future cannot be bright. There will be no peace and prosperity in the country if jobless people do not get a proper channel. More attention should be given, otherwise this problem can make jobless youth go in the wrong direction.

Every able-bodied man and woman must get employment. If not, the problem of unemployment will create difficulties in the development of the country.

References

Bartlett, Roland W., *Security for the People,* Wilcox and Follett Co., Chicago, 1949.

Chand, Attar, *Poverty and Underdevelopment,* Gian Publishing House, Delhi, 1987.

D'Mello, Rudolf Gyan, 'The Educated Unemployed: The Dispossessed', *Seminar,* Vol. 120, August, 1969.

Douglas, Paul H. and Director, Aaron, *The Problem of Unemployment,* The Macmillan Company, New York, 1931.

Edie, Lionel D., *Economics: Principle and Problems,* Thomas Y. Crowell Co., New York, 1926.

Elliott, Mabel A. and Merrill, Francis E., *Social Disorganization* (3rd edn.), Harper and Brothers, New York, 1950.

Keynes, John Maynard, 'An Economic Analysis of Unemployment' in *Unemployment as a World Problem,* The University of Chicago Press, Chicago, 1932.

Khanna, R.S., 'Liberalization and Unemployment in India', *The Indian Journal of Public Administration,* Vol. XLII, July–September, 1996.

Majumder, Rajarshi and Mukherjee, Deepa, 'Unemployment among Educated Youth: Implications for India's Demographic Dividend', University of Burdwan, Working Paper, May, 2013.

Myrdal, Gunnar, *Population,* Harvard University Press, Cambridge, Massachusetts, 1940.

Naba, Gopal Das, *Employment, Unemployment and Full Employment in India,* 1968.

4

Population Growth

Being a densely populated nation, India suffers from human overpopulation. The total population of India in the year 2018 is estimated to be 1,35,11,22,408 (1.35 billion). Within the next 10 years, India will become the most populous country in the world leaving behind China (most populous country in 2018). India will replace China as the world's most populous country does not mean that its demographic transition is not happening. The demographic transition is the process in which a country's death rates and birth rates decline with economic development. As death rates start declining earlier than birth rates, there is an initial phase of rapid increase in population. While India's population growth has slowed remarkably over the last few years, it's still growing faster than China and is expected to surpass China in terms of population by 2028, when both will have about 1.55 billion people. Although the crown of the world's most populous country has been on China's head for decades, according to PRB (a private non-profit, collect and analyses demographic data from across the world) India in next 10 years will surpass China to become the world's most populous country.

With the population growth rate of 1.2 per cent, India is predicted to have more than 1.53 billion people by the end of 2030. India's population will touch almost 1.7 billion by 2050 but its child population (those below 15 years of age) is projected to come down by 20 per cent over the next 32 years. More than 50 per cent of India's current population is below the age of 25 and over 65 per cent is below the age of 35. According to Registration System 2018 Report, nationally 46.3 per cent of the family population was below 25 years of age compared to 47.4 per cent of males. About 72.2 per cent of the population lives in some 6,38,000 villages and the rest 27.8 per cent in about 5,480 towns and urban agglomerations. The birth rate (childbirths per 1,000 people per year) is 22.22 births/1,000 population while death rate (deaths per 1,000 individuals per year) is 6.4 deaths/1,000 population. The fertility rate is 2.72 children born and the woman and the infant mortality rate is 30.15 deaths/1,000 live births. India has the largest illiterate population in the world. The literacy rate of India as per 2011 population census is 74.04 per cent, with male literacy rate at 82.14 per cent and female at 65.46 per cent. Every year, India adds more people than any other nation in the world.

A rapid growth rate in the population of the country was observed after independence as a result of a decline in death rates due to various health interventions. The average annual addition of population from 2001–2011 was almost 2.3 times the average annual addition of population during 1951 to 1961. However, according to the World Bank projections, the average annual addition of population is expected to reach 19.3 million by 2021 and will decline to 13.6 million by 2031.

Table 1

Population Growth and Projections by Sex

(in millions)

Year	*Males*	*Females*	*Total*	*Decennial Growth*	*Sex Ratio (Females per 1,000 males)*
1951	185.53	175.56	361.09	...	946
1961	226.30	212.94	439.24	78.15	941
1971	284.05	264.11	548.16	108.92	930
1981	353.37	329.95	683.32	135.16	934
1991	439.36	407.06	846.42	163.10	927
2001	532.16	496.45	1028.61	182.19	933
2011	623.27	587.58	1210.85	182.24	943
2021*	727.04	676.84	1403.88	193.03	931
2031*	795.53	744.38	1539.91	136.03	936

* Projections.

The reasons for India's rapidly growing population are poverty, illiteracy, high fertility rate, rapid decline in death rates or mortality rates and immigration. Alarmed by its swelling population, India started taking measures to stem the growth rate quite early. In fact India, by launching the national family planning programme in 1952 became the first country in the world to have a population policy. Though the family planning programme yielded some noticeable results but failed to achieve the ultimate goal and the population of India since independence increased almost three times.

In the midst of political uncertainty and communal fury over the past few decades, the problem of population growth has been relegated to the background. Neither social scientists nor the political parties or the governments seem to consider it necessary to focus attention upon what is surely the most crucial problem faced by the nation. There is no dearth of studies and views of the scholars to highlight the fact that India is falling behind in the race for economic and human resources development mainly because it has not shown much progress in containing its population growth.

Increase in Population

The disaster of galloping population in India can be recognized from the following facts:

1. India with a population of about 1,210 million (in 2011) is almost equal to the combined population of USA, Indonesia, Brazil, Pakistan, Bangladesh and Japan – the population of these six countries totals 1,214 million. At present, a little more than one out of every six persons in the world is from India.
2. India accounts for a meagre of 2.4 per cent of the world's surface area of 135.79 million square kms, whereas it supports and sustains a whooping 17.5 per cent of world's population.
3. As China is constantly showing lower growth in its population over the last few years, it is now estimated that by 2030, India will most likely overtake China to become the most populous country on the earth.
4. The four big states of Rajasthan, Uttar Pradesh, Madhya Pradesh and Bihar account for approximately 40 per cent of country's total population and still have an alarming high crude birth rate.
5. At the present rate of growth, life for most Indians would be unbearable – medical facilities would be difficult to provide, expenses on education, housing, etc. would be exorbitant, technical and professional education would become the exclusive prerogative of the elite, and the scarcity of food would once again plunge more than half of the nation below the poverty line.

Thus, there is an immediate need to focus serious attention on containing population growth in India. As India, with the second largest population in the world, fights valiantly to overcome a historical legacy of social and economic backwardness, a steep population growth not only negates the little achievements but also puts tremendous pressure on our already overloaded system.

In Malthus's opinion, the growth of population could become unsustainable. Mortality would then rise dramatically as it would be impossible to meet the food requirements. However, this has proved wrong for Malthus, with production of cereals and general wealth growing faster than its population.

Components of Population Change

One birth every 1 second	Births per day 69,069
One death every 3 seconds	Deaths per day 27,123
One net migrant every 1 minute	Net migrations per day 1,342
Net gain of one person every 2 seconds	Net change per day 40,604

The Myth of India's Population Explosion

No there is no population explosion. Not only is the population growth rate falling, but the pace of the decline has also actually picked up in the last few decades. In fact, India's total fertility rate, a measure of the number of children born to a woman during her lifetime, was down from 5.9 in 1951 to 2.3 in 2011. A figure for ensuring a broadly stable population. India is expected to reach replacement level fertility of 2020 and far from the one-child policy.

Causes of Population Growth

We may identify the following important causes for population explosion:

Widening Gap Between Birth and Death Rates

The average annual birth rate in India, which was 42 per thousand population in 1951–61, came down to 24.8 per thousand in 2011. The death rate also came down from over 27 per thousand population in 1951–61 to just 8 in 2011 (Census of India, 2011). Although, since birth rate has shown a moderate decline but the death rate has gone down rather sharply, and the widening gap has increased our population rapidly. The total fertility rate (average number of children born per woman) came down from about six in the fifties to three in 2011. Yet, for the past ten years, the median household size in India has stayed out at less than four children in cities and between four and five children in villages.

Increased Life Expectancy

While the average annual birth rate in India, which was 42 per thousand in 1951–61, decreased to 24.8 per thousand in 2011, the country has seen its decadal death rate decline to 8.5 in 2001–2011 from 42.6 in 1901–1911. Since the death rate has also gone down sharply, the population has tended to grow very fast in India.

Lack of Family Planning

If we add the number of miscarriages (6.20 lakh in 2010–11) in the country with an estimated number of births (2.05 crore in 2010–11) in one year, even in this age of family planning, one woman, on an average, is pregnant at any time in the age group of 15–45 years. All this happens because a large number of people in our country are illiterate with no awareness of the various advantages of family planning and the ill-effects of overpopulation on society. The failure of family planning is directly related to large-scale illiteracy which also contributes to marriage at an early age, low status of women, high child-mortality rate, etc. Uneducated families cannot grasp the issues and problems caused by the increasing population rate. They are least aware of the various ways to control population, usage of contraceptives and birth control measures.

Early Marriage

Child marriage is one of the major social problems of our country. Even today, a large number of boys and girls are married at an age when they are not prepared for family responsibilities either socially, emotionally, physically or mentally. Marriage at an unripe age also leads to a higher mortality rate of infants. Early marriages not only lead to high-population and thwart the progress of our young population, they entail an enormous amount of trouble to young mothers. These young girls, in most cases, are not healthy enough to bear the burden of a child.

High Illiteracy

Family planning has a direct link with female education, and female education is directly associated with age at marriage, general status of women, their fertility and infant mortality rate and so forth. According to the provisional report of the 2011 Census, the overall literacy percentage in India is 74.04 as compared to 64.83 ten years ago. The male literacy percentage is 82.14 while the female literacy percentage is 65.46. Education makes a person liberal, broad-minded, open to new ideas, and rational. If both men and women are educated, they will easily understand the logic of planning their family, but if either of them or both of them are illiterate, they would be more orthodox, illogical and religious-minded. This is evident from the fact that Kerala which has the overall literacy rate of 92.92 per cent and female literacy rate of 91.98 per cent (in 2009) has the lowest birth rate (14.70 per thousand) while Rajasthan's appallingly low female literacy rate of 52.66 per cent (in 2009) gives rise to the third highest birth rate in the country (27.20%), the highest having been registered in Uttar Pradesh (28.70%), followed by Madhya Pradesh (27.70%). These statistical figures hold good for most of the other states too.

Religious Reasons

Another factor that encourages the growth-rate is religion. Some communities consider any mandate or statutory method of prohibition to be sacrilegious. India being a secular state, it cannot exercise any check or restraint on religious grounds. The people who are conservative and orthodox are opposed to the use of family planning measures. Women in such families are not allowed to take part in family planning because they are not supposed to go against the wishes of God. There are also women who argue that children are born with God's will and women are destined to give birth to children.

Religious Attitude Towards Family Planning

The religiously orthodox and conservative people are against the use of family planning measures. In India, Muslims have a higher birth rate as well as fertility rate than the Hindus (Muslim women having fertility rate of 4 as compared to 3 among Hindu women). According to surveys conducted among the Muslims from time to time, it is found that despite awareness about modern family planning methods, most of the respondents – both male and female – were either against using them on religious grounds or they lacked clear and adequate knowledge about them.

The Problem of Mindset

Generally, illiterate and uneducated children inherit their father's behaviour and choose to give birth to as many children as is necessary to increase the income of their family. As a son is supposed to be the bread earner of the family, the poor desire to be ultimately blessed by a male child.

Other Causes

Some of the other causes responsible for the increase in population are: joint family system and lack of responsibility of young couples in these families to bring up their children, lack of recreational facilities, and lack of information or wrong information about family planning, etc.

Many poor parents produce children not because they are ignorant but because they need them. This is evident from the fact that there are some 13 million child workers in our country. If families stop those children from working, their family income will not be supplemented.

Compulsions of Poverty

Poverty is another reason for the increase in population in our country. Many poor parents have more children not because they do not know about contraceptives, but because they require children to assist them in earning their livelihood. It is clear from the fact that there is an unending number of child labourers in our country. If poor families stop the children from working, their family income tends to fall way short of meeting their basic needs. Having more children by poor people illustrates the paradox of the population–poverty interrelationship. Poverty is both the cause and effect of the population growth.

Problems of Overpopulation

Health Issues

Overpopulation i.e. high population density is the cause to many health issues in the country. Due to an increase in proximity between people at places of residence, the chance of spreading infections is quite higher.

Dirty and unhygienic surroundings and overpopulated localities catch up diseases faster. This is because too much activity and human waste accumulate at a faster rate. This applies even to the public transport system and places like parks, hotels, halls, etc. So decrease in population will contribute to a cleaner and hygienic environment.

Unemployment

Employment is an option for one to work and earn. But the number of positions are always fixed and limited in any sort of business. So higher the population, the difficult it would be to accommodate everyone into jobs. When there are no sufficient jobs and means of livelihood, the chances of criminal activities and theft tends to grow causing disturbance to the society. The issue is even more critical due to the advancements in artificial intelligence and automation. Automation leads to job losses occurring in production sectors. E-commerce has failed to pick up so far due to job cuts.

Poverty

The abnormal population growth is commonly believed to be one of the principal causes of India's poverty and very low standard of living for people. Overpopulation leads to the vicious circle of illiteracy, unemployment and poverty. Lack of education deprives the people of the opportunities to earn their livelihood and fulfil the bare necessities of their lives. However, it is also a fact that we cannot exercise any effective check on population unless there is an appreciable rise in the standard of living for the common people.

Lawlessness

Law and order situation is controlled by law monitoring personnel and also proper technical vigil. When the population is so huge, it becomes quite tough to manage law and order situation as the people to security personnel ratio has a wide gap. Also other factors due to overpopulation like unemployment, poverty, etc. encourage citizens to neglect and violate the law.

Unequal Education

Due to the huge population, it would be tough for any nation to provide better education resources to all the people who wish to study. Since education is expensive, many like to pursue it at minimal cost. But due to a huge population there is a huge competition for the seats and some have to miss the desired opportunities. So, many a times talented and intelligent candidates are unable to pursue their education in high populous countries and try to move to other countries for better options.

Manipulation of Democracy

People of one religion or ethnic background enhance their population drastically in comparison to another sect in the same country. In doing so, they tend to vote en masse to certain political parties which encourage them. Thus, population growth is a tool to exploit democracy by unethical means. Also, the political parties go to any extent to appease such communities to get votes and retain power. This sometimes goes against the national interest.

Effects of Overpopulation on the Environment

Overpopulation problems are not limited to society alone. It can also destroy the environment due to overuse of natural resources. More the population, the more is the requirement of natural resources like water, minerals, petroleum, etc. Due to larger demand, there is greater exploitation of groundwater, mines and minerals. Less population will help avoid this overuse of natural resources. The increasing pressure of population on natural resources will retard the economic progress and minimize the scope for social services in the form of education, wealth, housing, etc. which are essentially needed for a progressive state.

Pollution

Pollution is harmful contamination of natural resources which can be detrimental to human health. There are different types of pollution like air, water, land, etc. Due to more population, there is a high human activity like more travel, more vehicles, more release of sewage water, etc. These issues lead to enhancement in pollution. Most Indian cities are badly polluted and have little fresh air. This leads to countless airborne diseases and skin infections.

Deforestation

The presence of at least 30 per cent of forests in a country is a good sign of a natural environment. But in many countries other than in Europe, you do not find this ratio because of excess deforestation. To meet the demands of the large population, governments go for deforestation to provide housing, land for agriculture, airports, roads, etc. In doing so, most of the natural habitat for wild animals is destroyed and they get extinct.

Widening the Rich–Poor Gap

Overpopulation leads to an unequal distribution of wealth and income. Consequently, the gap between the rich and the poor is widened further.

Migration of the Population

Migration is a natural human trait. When the burden of the population in any area becomes imbalanced compared to the available financial resources, people tend to move away from their original location. It is comparable to the phenomenon of the beehive – when it is completely filled, flies leave it and go elsewhere. Similarly, human beings stop at one place for a time and then feel the urge to move on again. For this reason, human beings generally do not live anywhere permanently except for a few exceptions.

The impact of human transformation is especially felt in terms of culture, but economic effects are also important. People who make the change are often young people, while the old and the children follow them.

The following are some of the other similar problems generated by overpopulation:

Shortage of drinking water, sewage treatment, inadequate rainfall, rapid depletion of natural resources, extinction of many plant and animal species due to deforestation and loss of eco-systems, increased level of life-threatening air and water pollution, high infant and child mortality rate and hunger due to extreme poverty, nutrition problems, housing problems, starvation and famine, infectious diseases and epidemics, increasing population pressure on the cities and development of slums, the heavy burden on most resources, decrease in agricultural areas, continuous destruction of forests, threat to the environment including wildlife, political instability, war, social evils and corruption, etc.

Overpopulation weakens the economy in many respects, therefore, a planned growth of our economy requires some effective check on population. The efforts to remove the curse of population problem have only been partially effective. Consequently, the rate of population increase has gone down, but the balance between the optimum population growth and a healthy nation is far to be achieved. Both men and women should realize the dangers of over-population.

Effects of Population Growth

The growth of population has a direct effect on the living standards of the people. This is why, despite our spectacular progress in the agricultural and industrial spheres since independence, our per capita income has not risen appreciably.

How has the population growth affected India? It is estimated that about 2 million people are homeless, 97 million people have no access to safe drinking water, 272 million people are illiterate, 43 per cent children below five years are underweight, and country as a whole has 136th position in the World Human Development Index. The appalling overcrowding of our cities (which like cancerous growths are mushrooming unchecked with slums proliferating) have brought about a virtual breakdown of transportation, electricity and other services. It has also led to the rise of crime and an increase in violence in the urban and the semi-urban areas. All this has been directly fuelled by the addition of about 16 million people every year. If the population continues to increase at this rate, in a few years from now, we will have an army of unemployed, hungry and desperate people who will threaten the very foundations of the social, economic and political systems and institutions of the country. All sectoral demands have a numerical dimension. Whether it is education, employment, health, housing, water supply or any other sector, the perennial question is for how many? Even for the present population of 121 crore (in 2011), it is futile to think of jobs or shelter or health care programmes for all, especially when another 2 crore people would be added every year and, hence, need to be accommodated.

It has been calculated that for every addition of about 10 crore people in our country, we will require 1.50 lakh primary and middle schools, 10 thousand higher secondary schools, 50 lakh primary and middle school teachers, 1.5 lakh higher secondary school teachers, 5,000 hospitals and dispensaries, 2,000 primary health centres, two lakh hospital beds, 50 thousand doctors, 25 thousand nurses, 20 million tonnes cereals, 25,000 metres of cloth and 2,500 million houses.

The impact of the population boom on the quality of life is now being examined in terms of Household Misery Index (HMI), i.e. in terms of people's deprivations and basic needs. The HMI has five parameters: *pucca* housing, safe drinking water, electricity, sanitation (toilets), and fuel for cooking. Some scholars have examined it in terms of effect on human resources (literacy, health, etc.).

Our country has to either come to terms with the highly competitive world economy or go bust. India will be looking for a policy framework which can be bold enough to take up the issue of containing population explosion seriously. Unless India can do so, its future is doomed.

Need for Controlling the Growth of Population

Overpopulation is indeed a serious socio-economic problem of India. This problem has adversely affected the progress of the economy and the standard of living of the people. The problem is an urgent one and needs an immediate solution. There is an absolute need to contain the rapid growth of population. If this growth is not checked, it is going to adversely affect the various aspects of our economy. The rapid growth brings down per capita and national income which brings down the standard of living of the people. It becomes difficult to face the challenges of poverty, unemployment and underemployment. Basic needs of the people cannot be met with, political unrest and immorality cannot be effectively dealt with. Overpopulation is related to the size of the population and the utilization of the country's resources. The problem should be tackled from both the sides. First, production should be increased to meet the needs of the people. Second, the size of the population should be controlled and reduced.

(a) Measures to Increase Production

Growing population of the country can be supported through increased production. Agricultural and industrial productions are to be increased for this purpose.

1. *Increase in agricultural production*: It is necessary to resort to modern scientific cultivation in order to increase agricultural output. Use of irrigation, high yielding seeds, rotation of crops, utilization of chemicals, fertilisers, manures and such other means are to be adopted for this purpose. Production should keep pace with increasing population, if possible, should outstrip it.
2. *Increase in industrial production*: The process of industrialization is to be accelerated. Modern sophisticated technology must be used for industrial production. The industrial strategy should be such that it should be able to increase production and at the same time provide job facilities to a sizeable number of people. Industries are to be established in different places by making use of the locally available raw materials and human resources.
3. *Development of trade and commerce*: The development of trade and commerce will contribute to additional income and help the country to support the growing population.

(b) Measures to Control and Reduce Population

The problem of overpopulation can be effectively dealt with only if the rapid growth rate of population is contained. Various measures are to be undertaken in this regard.

Population Policy

A 'policy' is a 'plan of action, statement of aims and ideals, specially one made by a government, a political party, a business company, etc.' It guides the present and the future decisions. 'Population policy', in its narrower sense, according to the UN (1973: 632), is 'an effort to affect the size, structure and distribution or characteristics of population'. In its broader range, it includes 'efforts to regulate economic and social conditions which are likely to have demographic consequences'. Nortman (1975: 20) describes the narrower meaning as 'explicit policy' which directly affects the population characteristics, and the broader meaning as 'implicit policy' which affects the characteristics indirectly, sometimes without any explicit intention.

Any public policy, including population policy, is a step towards the future and an attempt to achieve desired goals. As such, it is to be laid down in terms of goals, past and present trends towards the achievement of these goals, social conditions accounting for the direction and intensity of these trends, projections for probable future, and alternatives likely to be achieved in reaching the desired goal(s). This means that the policy (population) has to be associated with participants, values or goals, institutions and resources.

Theories of Population

Thomas Robert Malthus proposed the first systematic theory of population in his book, *Essay on the Principle of Population* (1978). Malthus proposed that human populations grow exponentially (1, 2, 4, 8, 16, 32, ...) while food production grows at an arithmetic rate (1, 2, 3, 4, 5, 6 ...). This scenario of arithmetic food growth with simultaneous geometric human population growth predicted a future when humans would have no resources to survive and to avoid such a situation, Malthus urged control on population growth.

Optimum Theory of Population

According to this theory, there is a direct relationship between the size of the population and available resources in the country. The countries can be divided into three categories:

1. *Overpopulated*: If due to increase in the population per capita income begins to fall, the country is said to be overpopulated
2. *Underpopulated*: If the number of people are less than the resources of the country and they are unable to make full use of these resources, the country is said to be underpopulated.
3. *The optimum size of population*: When the size of the population is according to the size of natural resources, per capita output will be

maximum and the country is said to have an ideal size of the population or optimum population.

Two types of population policies have been suggested: (a) the ante-natal policy which aims at discouraging the growth of the population, and (b) the distributional policy which deals with the distributional imbalances of the population. The National Academy of Sciences has discerned population policy as one (a) which influences the demographic processes according to a pre-set objective (for example, encouraging people to move from urban to suburban areas), and (b) which will cope with the demands created by the demographic processes (for example, providing basic facilities to people in suburban areas).

The population policy of a developing country like India has to aim at (a) decreasing birth rate, (b) limiting the number of children in family to two, (c) decreasing the mortality, (d) creating awareness among the masses regarding the consequences of galloping population, (e) procuring necessary contraceptives, (f) enacting laws like legalizing abortion, and (g) giving incentives as well as disincentives. On the other hand, it also has to aim at (a) checking the concentration of people in congested areas, (b) providing necessary public services for effective settlement in new areas, and (c) relocation of offices to less populated areas.

Once the need for the population policy is realized, it has to be framed by appointing various committees and commissions for studying and advising and consulting experts. It has then to be implemented through various programmes and also evaluated from time to time.

India's population policy is the direct result of (a) the total size of the population, (b) a high growth rate, and (c) the problem of uneven distribution in rural and urban areas. Since our policy needs to aim at 'enhancing the quality of life', and 'increasing individual happiness', it has to act as a means to attain a broader objective of achieving individual fulfilment and social progress. Initially, the policy framed in 1952 was ad-hoc in nature, flexible, and based on a trial and error approach. Gradually, it was replaced by more scientific planning.

The sub-committee on population appointed in 1940 under the chairmanship of Radha Kamal Mukherjee by the National Planning Committee (appointed by Indian National Congress in 1938) laid emphasis on self-control, spreading knowledge of cheap and safe methods of birth control and establishing birth control clinics. It also recommended raising the legal statutory age of marriage, discouragement of polygamy, and an eugenic programme of sterilizing persons suffering from transmissible diseases. The Bhore Committee of 1946 appointed by the government criticized self-control approach and advocated 'deliberate limitation of families'.

After independence, a Population Policy Committee was created in 1952 and a Family Planning Research and Programmes Committee in 1953. A Central Family Planning Board was created in 1956 which emphasized on sterilizations. During the 1960s, a more vigorous family planning programme was advocated for stabilizing the growth of population over a reasonable period. While earlier, it was assumed by the government that the family planning programme had created enough motivation among the people and the government was only to provide facilities for contraception, but later it was realized that people needed motivation and masses had to be educated.

The primary objective of the Fourth Five-Year Plan (1969–74) was to reduce the annual birth rate to 32 by 1974 and family planning was given high priority. The Medical Termination of Pregnancy (MTP) Act was passed in 1971. The Fifth Five-Year Plan integrated family planning programme with maternal and child health programmes.

In April 1976, the Minister of Health and Family Planning, presented before the parliament the National Population Policy framed after prolonged and intensive consultations with governmental and non-official organizations, academic institutions, as well as eminent demographers and economists. This policy covered a wide spectrum of programmes including raising the statutory age of marriage, introducing fiscal incentives to states which perform well in the field of family planning, paying special attention to improving female literacy, public education through all available media (radio, television, press, films), introducing direct monetary incentives for adoption of vasectomy and tubectomy operations, and a new thrust towards research in reproductive biology and contraception. Since then, the policy of almost all governments in the states and at the centre has been so lopsided that the growth rate of population which was expected to have fallen below the 1 per cent mark, is still around 1.64 per cent (2011).

In a nutshell, according to the National Commission on Population, following are the milestones in the evolution of the population policy in India:

1. *1946*: Bhore Committee Report.
2. *1952*: Launching of Family Planning Programme.
3. *1976*: Statement of National Population Policy.
4. *1977*: Policy Statement on Family Welfare Programme.
   Both statements were laid in parliament, but never discussed or adopted.
5. *1983*: The National Health Policy of 1983 emphasized the need for 'securing the small family norm, through voluntary efforts and moving towards the goal of population stabilization'. While adopting the Health Policy, the parliament emphasized on the need for a separate National Population Policy.
6. *1991*: The National Development Council (NDC) appointed a Committee on Population with Karunakaran as the Chairman. The Karunakaran Report (Report of the National Development Council – NDC Committee on Population) endorsed by NDC in 1993 proposed the formulation of a National Population Policy to take a 'a long-term

holistic view of development, population growth and environmental protection' and to 'suggest policies and guidelines (for) formulation of programmes' and 'a monitoring mechanism with short, medium and long term perspectives and goals'. It was argued that the earlier policy statements of 1976 and 1977 were placed on the table. However, parliament never really discussed or adopted them. Specifically, it was recommended that 'a National Policy of Population should be formulated by the government and adopted by the parliament'.

7. *1993*: An Expert Group headed by M.S. Swaminathan was asked to prepare a draft of a National Population Policy that would be discussed by the cabinet and then by the parliament.
8. *1994*: Report on National Population Policy by the Expert Group headed by Dr Swaminathan was circulated among the Members of Parliament, and comments were requested from central and state agencies. It was anticipated that a National Population Policy approved by the NDC and the parliament would help produce a broad political consensus.

The policy draft submitted by the Swaminathan Committee (1994) suggested a holistic approach to health and some structural changes to implement the policy. The important measures suggested by this committee were: (a) Stabilizing population by achieving a total fertility rate of 2.1 by 2010 AD. (b) Implementing a speedy and effective minimum needs programme. (c) Replacing the present vertically structured family welfare programme with decentralized, democratic planning through panchayats, *nagar palikas* and state legislatures. (d) Involving all agencies in population control measures. (e) Abandoning the idea of fixing targets for the use of specific contraceptive methods by the central and state governments, except the goal of achieving the national average of fertility rate. (f) Discontinuing incentives in cash or kind to contraceptive users and motivators. Instead, a Population and Social Development Fund may be set up out of the funds available from government and international donor agencies. This fund will be utilized for filling the gaps in the effective implementation of the village, town, district and state level socio-demographic charters. (g) Appointing a State Population and Social Development Commission to plan, implement and monitor the population policy of the country. The sub-committees of PSDC will also be set up at the state, district and panchayat levels comprising elected representatives of people from different political parties, professionals, representatives of NGOs and women and youth organizations. (h) Family planning has become a responsibility for women alone. As such there is a need for checking the trend of putting the entire responsibility for family limitation on women.

Some socio-economic and medical goals set by the committee in the field of population welfare for forming a necessary part of the national population policy were: (a) reducing the incidence of marriage of girls below the age of 18 years to zero; (b) increasing the percentage of deliveries conducted by trained personnel to 100 per cent; (c) reducing the infant and maternal mortality rates; (d) universal immunization of children against tuberculosis, polio, diphtheria, whooping cough, tetanus and measles; (e) provision for primary health care for all; (f) providing information to individuals on birth limitation methods so that they have the fullest choice in planning their families; (g) making available and accessible the quality contraceptive services on a universal basis; and (h) universalization of primary education.

But, the experts have criticized the recommendations of this committee and have suggested that they should be rejected outrightly. Their main arguments are: (a) The report lacks in-depth analysis, justification and urgency. The approach suggested is purely managerial and the strategies pointed out are at best a reiteration of the failed aphorism that 'development is the best contraception'. (b) Minimum needs have no relationship with population control. How could all the goals which could not be achieved in the past four decades in spite of eight Five-Year Plans and eleven general elections with all the political promises be achieved by 2010 AD and more so when our population has already crossed the 975 crore (in 1996) mark with about 32 crore still below the poverty line? (c) A political population commission will be ineffective. (d) The committee has not recommended any disincentive for those who violated family planning norms. The Karunakaran Committee had proposed the introduction of disincentives – even if unpopular – to make the family planning programmes more effective. One such programme was introduced by the Government of Rajasthan according to which no individual can contest any election if he has more than three children. However, this programme exists only on paper. It is yet to be put in practice. (e) The report does not spell out why we failed in controlling our rapid population growth, though the population programmes have been going on in India uninterrupted since 1951. Is this failure because of the drawbacks in the administrative set up or because of wrong policies or faulty or tardy implementation? This is the fundamental issue which is ignored by the report. Without this analysis, the structural changes as proposed in the report may be quite irrelevant. (f) The biggest hurdle in the success of population control in India is political apathy, but the committee did not give any importance to this aspect. The political leaders have to be bold in enacting such legislative measures which may focus on the urgency of the issue. Denying promotions, debarring from holding any elected office, not giving reservation benefits, refusing bank loans, etc. to those who do not observe small family norm of two children could be some disincentives through legislation.

9. *1997*: On the 50th anniversary of India's independence, the then Prime Minister promised to announce a National Population Policy. During November 1997, the Union Cabinet approved the draft National

Population Policy with the direction that this be placed before parliament. However, this document could not be placed in either house of parliament as the respective houses stood adjourned followed by dissolution of the Lok Sabha.

10. *1999*: Another round of consultations was held during 1998, and another draft National Population Policy was finalized and placed before the cabinet in March 1999. The cabinet appointed a Group of Ministers (headed by Deputy Chairman, Planning Commission) to examine the draft policy. The Group of Ministers met several times and deliberated over the nuances of the population policy. In order to finalize a view about inclusion/exclusion of incentives and disincentives, the Group of Ministers invited a cross-section of experts from among academia, public health professionals, demographers, social scientists, and women representatives. The Group of Ministers finalized a draft population policy, and placed the same before the cabinet. This was discussed in cabinet on 19 November 1999. Several suggestions were made during the deliberations. On that basis, a fresh draft was submitted to the cabinet.
11. *2000*: The National Population Policy provided a policy framework for advancing goals and prorating strategies during the next decades to meet the reproductive and child health needs of the people of India. This policy stated that the objective of economic and social development is to improve the quality of lives people lead to enhance their well-being and to provide them with opportunities and choices to become productive assets in society. The immediate objective of this new policy was to address the unmet needs of contraception, health infrastructure, health personnel and to provide integrated service delivery for basic reproductive and child health care. The long-term target is to achieve a stable population by 2045. In pursuance of these objectives, a number of socio-demographic goals have been formulated. These are:
    (i) Making school education compulsory and to reduce drop outs.
    (ii) Reduce Infant Mortality Rate (IMR) to 30 per 1,000 live births.
    (iii) Reduce Maternal Mortality Rate (MMR) to below 100 per 1,00,000 live births.
    (iv) Promote delayed marriage of girls.
    (v) Achieve 80 per cent institutional deliveries.
    (vi) Prevent and control communicable diseases.
    (vii) Promote vigorously the small family norm to achieve replacement levels to Total Fertility Rate (TFR).

    The policy also suggests some promotional and motivational measures to promote adoption of the small family norm, viz:
    (i) Reward PRIs for promoting small family norm.
    (ii) Incentives to adopt two-child norm.

(iii) Couples below poverty line, with not more than two living children, having sterilization will be eligible for health insurance plan.
(iv) Strengthening abortion facility scheme.

Two-child Policy

Multiple Indian states have adopted a limited two-child policy. The policies are implemented by prohibiting persons with more than two children from serving in government. The most recent policy to be implemented was by Assam in 2017. Some states have repealed the policies; Chhattisgarh introduced a policy in 2001 and repealed it in 2005. A criticism of these policies is that it decreases the number of women in government positions, and encourages sex-selective abortions. As of 2014, there were 11 Indian states that implemented the two-child policy, in hopes to reduce the number of children per family. The policy was geared mainly towards politicians, future and aspiring, to limit their number of children to two or less, and set an example for the community. Government servants may also face consequences on exceeding the two-child limit.

Solutions to Control Population Growth

Family Planning

Family planning is; now-a-days, considered an indispensable method of controlling population. The motto of family planning is – 'child by choice and not by chance' or 'child by desire not by accident'. The size of the family must be limited voluntarily. Family planning facilities should be provided to rural and poor people which at present are easily available in urban and semi-urban areas. It is a good sign that the middle class are gradually becoming population conscious and are taking an active interest in the methods devised and recommended for population control.

Controlled Birth Rate

Overpopulation can only be solved by spreading awareness of and implementing measures like birth control and access to birth control devices. Birth rate must be kept within reasonable limits to make a definite advancement towards a higher standard of living, which is the primary need of India. The task will certainly be much easier if people get a chance of reaching a higher standard of living. It will then by itself serve as a kind of incentive to birth control.

Provision of Social Security

In the absence of comprehensive social security especially, in old age, sickness, unemployment and accident, people have tended to depend on large families for security. The poor, in particular, consider children as their wealth. It is necessary to introduce various social insurance and social security schemes to help the poor to develop confidence to face the future. People with a higher standard of living normally opt for a small family. Hence, it is necessary to increase the standard of living of the masses.

Reduction in Infant Mortality

By resorting to suitable medical steps the rate of infant mortality is to be reduced. If it is reduced, then parents will definitely feel that their children will survive and live longer.

Improving the Status of Women

Experience in the West has shown that high status of women is closely associated with a low birth rate. The desire to rise in the social scale develops a strong feeling for a smaller family. The educated, employed urban women exhibit a desire for a small family. Efforts must be made to encourage the rural women to go in the direction of a small family.

Propaganda in Favour of a Small Family

The benefits of family planning schemes initiated by the government are being emphasized in many ways. Nevertheless, it requires persistent propaganda work before a public opinion can be fully mobilized for a planned growth of population. Enough publicity is to be given regarding the benefits of a small family to the general masses. Mass media of communication like the press, radio, television and movies are of great help in this regard.

Creation of Awareness

In order to ensure that a society does not have to deal with the negative effects of overpopulation, conducting awareness through campaigns can be of great help. Teaching people about the importance of having fewer children is likely to help change attitudes towards reproduction.

1. *Reducing incentives*: Governments should reduce or eliminate incentives or programmes that encourage childbearing.
2. *Guarantee education*: Making it possible for all girls and boys to learn upto the highest level which can help control early pregnancies. People who are committed to secondary education are unlikely to become pregnant as they will focus more on their academic work.
3. *Population stability policies*: Encouraging leaders to focus more on policies that can help stabilize population growth can also help in management.
4. The benefits of family planning schemes initiated by the government are being emphasized in many ways. Nevertheless, it requires persistent propaganda work before a public opinion can be fully mobilized for a planned growth of population.
5. We must make an all-out drive to educate the masses about the methods of family planning. It is a good sign that a section of our people

especially those belonging to the middle class are gradually becoming population conscious and are taking an active interest in the methods devised for population control.

6. Birth rate must be kept within reasonable limits to make a definite advancement towards a higher standard of living, which is the primary need of India. The task will certainly be much easier if people get a chance of reaching a higher standard of living. It will then by itself serve as a kind of incentive to birth control.

Advantages of Population Growth

Economic Growth

The advantages of population growth include increased economic development, availability of labour and possibility of innovation. However, population growth may result in high unemployment rates, environmental degradation, food shortage and high dependency rates. The growth of population equates to increased purchases of items such as clothing, educational material, food and other household goods. In addition, an increased number of family members encourages the movement of families into larger houses. This results in an increased trade, which in essence supports several sectors of the economy like manufacturing, agriculture, construction and home improvement industries. Moreover, an increased population translates to an increase in tax revenue. This enables the government to have easy access to resources for its normal operations, security and infrastructural development.

Availability of Labour

Population growth causes an increase in the labour force. This ensures efficient utilization of resources and optimal productivity in sectors such as agriculture and manufacturing. Availability of labour is an essential tool for economic development.

Innovation

Population growth encourages innovations in fields such as medicine, agriculture and production. In addition, population growth has led to a greater consciousness for more industrial and agricultural productivity to meet the demand of a large number of people. For example, the assembly line was devised as an adaptation for the need for more industrial production.

Disadvantages of Population Growth

Environmental Degradation

Rising populations may lead to deforestation so as to create more land for human settlement and agriculture. Deforestation greatly affects the weather cycle and may lead to climate change. An increased population translates to more environmental pollution through the release of greenhouse gases from industrial machinery and improper waste disposal. This results in environmental degradation and may cause loss of biodiversity and health complications.

Unemployment

In some situations, the rapid increase in population may surpass the number of employment opportunities created in the economy. This results in widespread unemployment. Unemployment has several negative effects on the society such as increased crime rates, political instability, reduced standards of living and a decline in economic development.

Food Shortage

Unchecked population growth without an equivalent agricultural development may lead to food shortage. Factors such as reduced agricultural land and environmental degradation contribute to reduced agricultural yields, hence shortage of food.

Ageing Dependency

Increased population growth coupled with high life expectancy rates result in an increase in the number of aged population. This leads to high dependency rates, hence limiting economic development.

Property Shortage

Population growth encourages rural to urban migration in search of better employment and business opportunities. This leads to overcrowding in urban areas, resulting in shortage of housing and other social amenities. The shortage of housing in some underdeveloped countries led to the growth of informal settlements and slums.

National Population Register (NPR)

The NPR is a register of 'usual resident' of the country including non-residents. A usual resident is defined as a person who has resided in an area for the past six months and more or who intends to reside in that area for next six months. It is prepared under provisions of the Citizenship Act 1955 and the Citizenship Rules, 2003. The aim of NPR is to better target the benefits and services under the government schemes or programmes, improve planning and prevent identity fraud. The 2010 exercise was the first attempt to build a national database of all residents of India including foreigners, followed by updation in 2015. The registry of usual resident was never published, ruling out any claims and objections. Though the data was shared with various central and state government agencies for formulation of targeted entitlement schemes.

The 2020 NPR will be update of the 2010 NPR. However, 2020 version adds (i) Name and place of birth of parents and spouse, (ii) Last place of residence, (iii) Aadhar ID, (iv) Driving License, (v) Voter ID and (vi) Mobile number. The door to door survey for the population register coincides with the house-listing phase of Census 2021. The census also helps to understand the socio-economic conditions of the country and the impact of different government schemes. It is mandatory under the law for people to respond to the population register questionnaire. Registering in the NPR is mandatory for every usual resident of India. Lying in the declaration has been listed as crime. NPR 2020 is not applicable in Assam, as the Supreme Court has already mandated NRC there. In the annual report of the home ministry for 2018–19, it is clearly mentioned that NPR is the first step towards the creation of National Register of Citizens (NRC). NPR is a database for policy while NRC is the process where people are asked to prove citizenship. The updating process of NPR is to be carried out under the aegis of the Registrar General and ex-Office Census Commissioner, India. Union cabinet has allocated around ₹ 500 crores for updating of NPR.

NPR and Census are not the same. The decennial census helps to collect a variety of statistical information on different characteristics of the people of India. This includes information on demography, income, literacy, education, etc. However NPR database only includes demographic and biometric particulars.

Family Planning in India

India was the first country to evolve a government-backed family planning programme in the 1950s. Developing countries like Indonesia, Thailand and South Korea that followed suit have successfully stabilized their population growth but India, even after 70 years, is trailing behind. A separate Department of Family Planning was created in 1966 under the Union Ministry of Health. During the notorious emergency regime between 1975 and 1977, the government at the Centre implemented a forced sterilization programme against popular wishes and even used such harsh and coercive methods that today one is reluctant to talk of family planning to the populace. The programme is still criticized and is blamed for creating a public aversion to family planning, which hampered government programmes for decades.

In 1977, the government formulated a new population policy ruling out compulsion. The acceptance of the programme was made purely voluntary. The Family Planning Department was rechristened as the Family Welfare Department, and tasks beyond its competence embracing all aspects of family welfare, including improvement of women's educational level, were included in it. In its family planning awareness drive, the Government of India adopted the UNFP guideline of delaying the first child and spacing the subsequent birth(s).

The methods adopted in family planning are: sterilization, loop, pill, withdrawal, rhythm, sheath and diaphragm. The condom and the pill seem most popular among the high socio-economic groups, the withdrawal method and the condoms among the middle socio-economic groups and sterilization is preferred by people belonging to the low social strata. Operations for family planning are not very popular among the socially well-placed, as this group is exposed to other methods of birth control. A good number of women use more than one method, depending on the circumstances, availability and the mood of the moment.

Family Welfare Programme

It is a centrally sponsored programme. For this, the states receive 100 per cent assistance from Central Government. The current policy is to promote family planning on the basis of voluntary and informed acceptance with full community participation. The emphasis is on a two-child family. Also, the emphasis is on spacing methods along with terminal methods. The services are taken to every doorstep in order to motivate families to accept the small family norm. A social policy with a new integrated approach to population stabilization has now been adopted. Following are the components of this new approach:

Target-free Programme

A significant shift in the family planning programme is the introduction of target-free programme from April 1996. Targets were a major obsession in our family planning programme in which village *patwaris*, school teachers and government functionaries had to achieve the minimum targets of sterilization and other measures. Postings, promotions and transfers of functionaries depended on the fulfilment of targets. A target-free approach is indeed a welcome change. Though, only time will show the extent to which the estimated 2.5 lakh personnel involved in family planning activities will succeed through the new package of reproductive and child health (RCH) without emphasizing on achieving the set targets.

Bottom-up Approach or Decentralized Participatory Planning

Hitherto, planning was done at the top level and percolated down to the grassroots for implementation. Now, the programme is to be chalked out at the village level in consultation with health workers of sub-centre and PHC, i.e, male and female workers (ANMs), panchayat members and active individuals. Planning for the district will be the aggregation of PHC plans plus the requirements of district hospitals. These District Plans will together make the State Plan and the State Plans will be aggregated to prepare the National Plan.

State-specific Reproductive and Child Health (RCH) Strategy

Since states display a wide variation in health parameters, such as infant mortalities, maternal mortalities, birth rates, etc. area-specific RCH approach has been worked out separately for three groups of states plus the special category states where considerable infrastructure input flows from state health system projects.

Integrated RCH Package

It provides a minimum model framework for reproductive health services at different levels in the district, namely, sub-centre, PHC and district hospitals. These services are related to prevention and management of unwanted pregnancy, maternal care, services for the new-born and infants, and management of STDs.

Comprehensive Integrated Training

Emphasis will be laid on the training of personnel to improve efficiency of interventions, interpersonal communication, and management. The responsibility of training would be that of a district. The central and the state governments will support the district in training of trainers, providing training material and periodic evaluation.

Increased Involvement of NGOs

More NGOs will be involved in clinic-based interventions, in strengthening community participation in implementing project activities, and in the training of trainers for technical skills. Private rural medical practitioners, including those of indigenous systems of medicines will also be involved in the plans.

Independent Evaluation of Programme

The programme will be monitored and evaluated for qualitative performance. Eighteen Population Resource Centres (PRCs) have been established which are at present engaged in working out formats for annual surveys. Eight regional teams have also been constituted by the government for cross-checking of activities.

Impact of Family Planning/Welfare Programmes

India launched a nation-wide family planning programme in 1952, which was later expanded to cover maternal and child health, family welfare and nutrition. The efforts of the government in implementing the programme have significant impact. Various family welfare activities have gone a long way in enlightening the people about contraception and its merits.

The efforts of the government in implementing the Family Planning Programme in the country have significant impact as shown from the following:

1. Knowledge of contraception is nearly universal: 98 per cent of women and 99 per cent of men of age group. 15–49 know one or more methods of contraception.

2. Among the permanent modern family planning methods, female sterilization is the most popular. Over 97 per cent of women and 95 per cent men know about female sterilization. Male sterilization, by contrast, is known only by 79 per cent of women and 87 per cent of men.
3. Ninety-three per cent of men know about condoms, compared with 74 per cent of women.
4. More than 80 per cent women and men know about contraceptive pills.
5. Knowledge of contraception is widespread even among adolescents: 94 per cent of young women and 96 per cent of young men have heard of a modern method of contraception.

Evidence from India's last census in 2011, confirmed by data from the national family health survey 2017 (NFHS-4), shows that fertility in India is fast approaching replacement levels. This means that couples will have children who will essentially replace their number, to stabilise population growth. The NFHS-4 shows that in the past decade, the average number of children per family has come down from 2.7 to 2.2. With replacement fertility being 2.1 children per woman, this is a good news for the land and the people.

Attitudes Towards Family Planning

The attitude of a woman towards family planning is influenced by her education, age, income background, husband's occupation, and her (working) status among other factors. In terms of age, it has been found that the percentage of women approving family planning decreases as the age group increases. But, the acceptance is about two-third even among the older age groups. This clearly shows that the great majority of Indian women approve of family planning, irrespective of age.

The situation has now changed a lot. An analysis of 2011 Census data reveals that the slogan '*Hum do, hamare do*' seems to finally come true, as the median household size in urban India is now less than four for the first time in history. According to data, 56 per cent of households in urban India have now four or less members. This is a marked change from the last census conducted in 2001 when the median household size in urban India was between four and five. However, in rural India, the median household size is between four and five, but closer to four than it has ever been. As many as 47.1 per cent of rural households now have four or less members, compared to 40 per cent in 2001.

To predict the need of family planning methods, family planning managers often rely on unmet needs derived by measuring the contraceptive demand. However, woman's intention and her background knowledge of family planning methods have not received as much attention as a measure of family planning methods demand.

Education brings about a change in the attitude towards family planning. If a woman remains unexposed to family planning methods, she continues to be conservative and holds on to superstitious beliefs and fears.

Informal education also affects the practice of family planning methods. Many young women are in favour of family planning but do not know how to go about it. The illiteracy of the husband also acts as a barrier because they remain unconcerned about planning the family.

Since illiteracy is found more among the poorer section of our society, it is seen that women with low education in the lower strata are more reluctant to accept family planning methods. Their contention is that since they have no money to fall back upon, their only hope of survival is their children's income. An average poor Indian couple is not satisfied with less than two or three children.

The encouraging feature is that though the older generation is inclined towards passive helplessness, they want their daughters to have fewer children and adopt birth control methods. In the rural areas, it has been observed that a woman with six children now compels her married daughter to undergo an operation to stop childbirth after her third delivery. In the urban areas, especially with the breakdown of the joint family system, many women in nuclear families face difficulties in bringing up children. Servants are a problem and there is no help from the in-laws or one's own mother. Housing is often a problem and commodities are scarce. No wonder that urban women in the younger age group favour family planning methods which allow them to devote their attention to their careers. Though a large number of women approve of family planning, only half of them actually practise it. Women in the low and middle strata need to be more effectively covered by family planning methods than those who are economically better off.

Measures Suggested to Contain Population Growth

The continuing population explosion in our country calls for some soul searching. The government is aware of the magnitude of the problem and considers the alarming population growth as the biggest challenge facing the nation as well as the government. The following programmes may be suggested to check population growth:

Incentives vs Disincentives

An important question has now been raised by some thinkers pertaining to population policy – that is of cooperation vs coercion, or incentives vs disincentives, or Kerala model vs Chinese model? There are some thinkers who support cooperation while there are others who support coercion. Nobel laureate Professor Amartya Sen, favoured 'cooperation' approach and denounced the use of coercion to bring down the lines of two famous theories of Condorcet (of France) and Malthus (of Britain). He supported Condorcet's approach regarding the problem of population which talked of the emergence of new norms of small family size based on 'the progress of reason'. Condorcet believed that female education would lead people to voluntarily choose smaller families and lower fertility rates. Malthus, however, was skeptical about this view of 'voluntary acceptance of family planning'. In his opinion, 'positive checks' such as economic penury or rise in mortality rate would eventually coerce people to reduce population growth rate. Sen described Condorcet's path of cooperation as unequivocally right and Malthus' path of coercion as undesirable and even counter-productive in checking population growth.

Opposed to the 'Kerala model' is the 'Chinese model' of coercion in population control. Looking at the near catastrophic state of our population scenario, thinkers support this 'coercive model' as the only effective solution of the population problem. These thinkers also point out the vested political interests that are promoting population growth rates of various vote banks to the detriment of the nation. Some thinkers, however, talk of the combination of cooperation and coercion or incentive and disincentives to check India's population growth, but the nature of disincentives has not been identified so far. Would denying the 'benefit of reservation' to people with more than two children prove to be a disincentive? Can denying promotion or admission or a voting right or right to contest election be disincentives? Will such denials not be the violation of fundamental rights? Laying down mechanisms to implement the disincentives in the prevailing socio-political situation in India.

Searching for New Contraceptives

The search for a new, inexpensive, easy to use and harmless contraceptive has not met with dramatic success so far. Though pills have come to be accepted in a big way, it is necessary that Indian herbs should also be thoroughly investigated for their effects. Pursuing vigorous investigation of the health status and dietary habits of some of the tribals in Andaman and Nicobar Islands, among some of whom the fertility rate is found to be extremely low, might provide the needed solution.

Increase in Marriage Age

Raising the statutory marriage age is bound to reduce the family size in other states too. This calls for serious and whole-hearted efforts for creating the necessary public awareness.

Economic Development

Economic development may prove to be the best contraceptive. We have to go for quick population control at any cost on sheer economic principles of supply and demand. To balance any economic equation, we can either increase the supply which depends on both financial and material resources, or reduce the demand which depends on the number of people asking for varied services and commodities.

This approach has another important dimension. If we tackle the problem from the supply side, it will increase the demand *per se* in other sectors. For example, if we increase the number of houses, it would increase demand for cement, bricks, wood material and electrical goods. But if we approach the problem from the demand side and reduce the number of houses needed, the pressure in all sectors will be relieved. With 29 births every minute or about 16 million births every year, the demand for money and materials in sectors like education, transport and welfare, will so enormously increase that in ten years' time the situation will have crossed the point of no return and incalculable and irretrievable damage will have been done to the country and its economy.

While this linkage between population and development is well taken, the nature or mode of 'development' has itself been a somewhat debatable question. There are leading Third World analysts who contend that 'development' (through high technology, mass production, and induced consumerism) as projected by the affluent nations and sold to the Third World tend to aggravate the population problem. Hence, to continue to talk and apply this technology indicates how little people have thought about this problem. What this viewpoint implies is that modern technology generates a largely profit-motivated elite in an industry which is concerned only with its own interests and is indifferent to the poverty and misery of workers. The result is an economic and demographic scenario that is becoming explosive both at the top (due to growing wealth) and at the bottom (due to increasing poverty of the masses). Thus, the feeling is that population problem should not be viewed out of social context. Development which aims at distribution and equality alone can remove poverty and contain population growth.

Role of NGOs

Success of any programme depends on its acceptance by the people. Unless the community is fully involved in the programme and it considers it to be its own programme, it may not be possible to achieve the desired results. This can be achieved in a better way by the non-governmental organizations (NGOs) as these have very intimate relations with the people. Their role in removing deep-rooted beliefs favouring large families and male children, improving female literacy, raising statutory age of girls for marriage, essential newborn care, birth spacing, etc. can be very significant. Such organizations not only have the capacity to reach the remote areas but their activities are cost-effective also. The Department of Family Welfare has launched several schemes over the years to ensure better participation of the NGOs in the family welfare programme. Some of these schemes are: (a) Helping NGOs to the extent of 90 per cent of the cost of the project on promotion of small family norm and population control schemes. (b) Wide publicity by the government to inform voluntary organizations to come forward to undertake these schemes. (c) A large number of regional conferences were held in last four to five years to increase the involvement of the NGOs. (d) Recognizing its larger organizations in Delhi, Mumbai, Kolkata, Chennai and Lucknow as Mother Units for identifying small NGOs in their areas and giving them grants for approval schemes. (e) Setting up State Standing Committees on Voluntary Action, set up under the chairmanship of the Family Welfare Secretary with power to sanction upto ₹ 10 lakh per project. (f) Asking states to identify one institution in the NGO sector for the purpose of providing training to health workers. (g) Arranging study tours for NGOs from states with poor community participation to better performing states.

Conclusion

The population policy of our government should aim not only at controlling the unregulated human growth of numerical strength (population explosion) but also at checking the unregulated movement of population and the increasing concentration of people in the urbanized areas (population implosion), and providing adequate living space and attractive environment to heterogeneous mixture of people (population displosion). These goals have to be jointly linked with the formulation and implementation of policies aimed at population regulation and planning for harnessing both natural and human resources. Thus, only population growth *per se* may not be perceived as a problem but its relation with the availability of resources may be viewed with great concern.

Family planning needs to be salvaged from the morass into which it has drifted. For this, the programme has to look inwards and treat itself as a development input in its own right. In fact, development is the best method for controlling population growth, though the reverse is also true that high population growth is a sure recipe for slow, if not negative development. A variety of measures will have to be introduced to put the family planning campaign back on its feet. Compulsion will not work; only persuasion will succeed. Legal measures may help, but what is urgently required is social awareness and involvement to create responsible parenthood.

What is to be stressed most in achieving a commensurate demographic effect is promoting spacing method instead of overemphasizing on sterilization in the family planning programme. We have to check the phenomenon of 'children producing children'. This could be achieved only by promoting spacing methods and marrying girls after 21 years of age.

In addition to its important role in checking the population growth, family planning will help to improve the general status of women. A woman cannot play any role in the community and the society, unless she is able to limit her family to a reasonable size. Family planning will improve not only family welfare but will also contribute to social prosperity and individual happiness.

References

Banerjee, D., *Family Planning in India: A Critique and a Perspective*, People's Publishing House, New Delhi, 1971.

Bose, Ashish, *Meeting India's Best Needs: The Human Development Index*, Census of India, Delhi, 1996.

Chandrashekhar, S., *India's Population: Fact and Policy,* Indian Institute for Population Studies, Annamalai University, Chidambaram, 1950.

Doron, Harold F., 'World Population Growth', in Philip Houser (ed.), *The Population Dilemma,* Columbia University, New York, 1963.

Handbook of Social Welfare Statistics, Ministry of Social Welfare, New Delhi, 1981.

Kothari, Devendra, *Family Welfare Programme in Rajasthan,* IIHMR, Jaipur, 1989.

Misra, B.D., *Introduction to the Study of Population,* South Asian Publishers, New Delhi, 1980.

Mukherjee, R.K., *Family and Planning in India,* Orient Longmans, Calcutta, 1976.

Nortman, Dorothy L., 'A Longitudinal Analysis of Population Policies in Developing Countries', in R.K. Godwin (ed.), *Comparative Policy Analysis,* D.C. Heath, Lexington, 1975.

Rao, P.S.S. and Inbaraj, S.C., *Journal of Family Welfare,* Vol. XVII, Family Planning Association of India, Mumbai, June, 1970.

The Times of India, 3 July 2020.

United Nations, *Determinants and Consequences of Population Trends,* Vol. 1, New York, 1973.

5

Ageing and Elder Abuse

Facts and Statistics on Elderly (According to Census 2011)

1. There are nearly 104 million elderly persons (aged 60 years or above) in India; 53 million females and 51 million males. The increase in life expectancy over the years has resulted in an increase in the population of the elderly. The number of elderly persons is expected to grow 173 million by 2026.
2. Both the share and size of the elderly population is increasing over time. From 5.6 per cent in 1961, the proportion has increased to 8.3 per cent in 2011. For males, it was marginally lower at 8.2 per cent, while for females it was 9 per cent.
3. Regarding rural and urban areas, 71 per cent of the elderly population resides in rural areas while 29 per cent is in urban areas.
4. The sex ratio among elderly people was as high as 1,028 in 1951 which subsequently dropped but again reached up to 1,033 in 2011.
5. The old-age dependency ratio climbed to 14.2 per cent in 2011 for India as a whole. For females and males, the value of the ratio was 14.9 per cent and 13.6 per cent and the old-age dependency ratios are 15.1 and 12.4 for rural and urban areas respectively.
6. In rural areas, 66 per cent of elderly men and 28 per cent of elderly women were working, while in urban areas only 46 per cent of elderly men and about 11 per cent of elderly women were working. Elderly constitute 8 per cent of the population today and need support from the government for schemes and pensions that will enable them to live a life of dignity. Only 0.032 per cent of GDP is spent on pensions, whereas 1 per cent of the GDP is required for elders' needs and security.

7. The percentage of older persons, 60 years and above, is projected to go up to 19 per cent in 2050, increasing three-fold from around 100 million to 300 million by 2050, according to a population fund's India ageing report 2017.
8. The per cent of literates among elderly persons increased from 27 per cent in 1991 to 44 per cent in 2011. The literacy rates among elderly females (28%) is less than half of the literacy rate among elderly males (59%).

Highlights

1. The cost-norms of an integrated programme for older persons (IPOP) scheme implemented by the Ministry of Social Justice and Empowerment has been revised w.e.f. 1 April 2015. The average increase in cost norm ranges between 70–110 per cent.
2. According to the UNDP, 13 per cent of older Indians sampled, have some type of disability that affects at least one activity of daily living. Most common disability among the aged persons was locomotors disability and visual disability.
3. Prevalence of heart diseases among the elderly population was much higher in urban areas than in rural parts.
4. Old age care will become a big challenge as non-communicable diseases like heart disease and cancer rise and longevity increases.
5. The life expectancy at birth during 2009–13 was 69.3 for females as against 65.8 years for males. At the age of 60 years, average remaining length of life was found to be about 18 years (16.9 for males and 19.0 for females) and that at age 70 was less than 12 years (10.9 for males and 12.3 for females).
6. More than one-quarter of this population is underweight and nearly one-third has undiagnosed hypertension. Nearly 60 per cent live in dwellings lacking access to an improved sewer system.
7. With little old-age income support and few savings, labour force participation remains high among those aged 60 and older, particularly among rural Indian households, surveys suggest.
8. Not only do a large share of the elderly earn an income, they even support their adult children who live in homes and work on farms owned by their parents.

While the Indian government invests significantly on the country's youth, expecting them to contribute to the economy, support for those who are feeble remains abysmal, rue senior or citizens. For instance, the government's Indira Gandhi National Old Age Pension Scheme offers a paltry rupees five hundred per month to those above 65 years of age, living below the poverty line. Employer insurance and pension schemes are available only to as low as nine per cent of rural males and 41.9 per cent of urban males who are in the formal sector; among females, the figures are still lower.

AGEING

Ageing is an ongoing biological process which no human being can escape. It begins at birth or, to be more precise, at conception, and ends with death. In other words, a society ages when there is an increase in its elderly population along with decrease in the rest of the population. It is the result of demographic transition in which a population moves from high to low fertility and mortality rates. This inevitable and irreversible process affects one's physical and psychological well-being. Besides, it is said to have social, economic and cultural implications too. Therefore, the studies on ageing are significant for understanding the problems related to elderly care, which is an urgent need in the 21st century.

Background

A man's life is normally divided into five main stages namely infancy, childhood, adolescence, adulthood and old age. In each of these stages, an individual has to find himself in different situations and face different problems. The old age is also not without problems. In old age, physical strength deteriorates, mental stability and money power diminish, coupled with negligence from the younger generation. Life expectancy has increased from 40 years in 1951 to 67 years today, a person today has 27 years more to live than he would have 50 years back. Old age has never been a problem for India where a value-based, joint family system is supposed to prevail. Indian culture is automatically respectful and supportive of elders. With that background, elder abuse has never been considered a problem in India and has always been thought of as a western problem. However, the coping capacities of the younger and older family members are now being challenged and there is unwanted behaviour by the younger family members, which is experienced as abnormal by the older family members but cannot, however, be labelled.

Main problems as faced by elderly men and women are economic problems, mental health problems, lack of work, lack of facilities for utilization of leisure time and a general feeling of loneliness. The causes of abuse of older people are complex and multifaceted and may encompass physical, psychological, social, medical, legal and environmental. Elderly abuse is a complex phenomenon that results from several different causes, and often has roots in multiple factors.

Defining Ageing/Old Age

Although everyone is familiar with ageing, defining it is not so easy. Elderly or old age consists of age nearing or surpassing the average life span of human beings. The boundary of old age cannot be defined exactly because it does not have the same meaning in all societies. However, despite a number of commonly used definitions of old age, there is no general agreement on the age at which a person becomes old. Though most countries of developed world have accepted the chronological age of 65 years as a definition of 'elderly' or older person, but like many westernized concepts, this does not adapt well to the situation in developing or underdeveloped countries. At the moment, there is no United Nations standard numerical criterion, but its agreed cutoff is 60+ years to refer to the older population.

Lacking an accepted and acceptable definition, in many instances, the age at which a person becomes eligible for statutory and occupational retirement pensions has become the default definition. According to Gorman (2000), 'The ageing process is of course a biological reality which has its own dynamic, largely beyond human control. However, it is also subject to the constructions by which each society makes sense of old age. In the developed world, chronological time plays a paramount role. The age of 60 or 65, roughly equivalent to retirement ages in most developed countries, is said to be the beginning of old age. In many parts of the developing world, chronological age has little or no importance in the meaning of old age. Other socially constructed meanings of age are more significant such as the roles assigned to older people; in some cases it is the loss of roles accompanying physical decline which is significant in defining old age. Thus, in contrast to the chronological milestones which mark life stages in the developed world, old age in many developing countries is seen to begin at the point when active contribution is no longer possible'.

When attention was drawn to older populations in many developing countries, the definition of old age many times followed the same path as that in more developed countries, that is, the government sets the definition by stating a retirement age. Later, results of an international anthropological study conducted in Africa in late 1970s provided a basis for a definition of old age in developing countries (Glascock and Feinman, 1980). Definitions fell into three main categories: (a) chronology; (b) change in social role (i.e. change in work patterns, adult status of children and menopause); and (c) change in capabilities (i.e. invalid status, senility and change in physical characteristics). Results from this cultural analysis of old age suggested that change in social role is the predominant means of defining old age. When the preferred definition was chronological, it was most often accompanied by an additional definition.

While a single definition, such as chronological age or social/cultural/functional markers, is commonly used by, amongst others, demographers, sociologists, anthropologists, economists and researchers, it seems more appropriate to use a combination of chronological, functional and social definitions. However, the challenge of how to incorporate a suitable multidimensional definition into the 'pensionable age' concept remains.

However, despite these problems, there exists, as stated above, many commonly used definitions of 'ageing'.

According to Wikipedia, ageing is a change in an organism over time. It refers to a multidimensional process of physical, psychological and social change (Hultsch and Deutsch, cited in Parikh, 2011). Some dimensions of ageing grow and expand over time, while others decline. Reaction time, for example, may slow with age, while knowledge of world events and wisdom may expand (Schaie, cited in Parikh, 2011). Research shows that even late in life, potential exists for physical, mental and social growth and development. Ageing is an important part of all human societies reflecting not only the biological changes that occur, but also reflecting cultural and societal conventions. Age is usually measured in full years – and months for young children.

Chronological ageing, referred to how old a person is, is arguably the most straightforward definition of ageing and may be distinguished from 'social ageing' (society's expectations of how people should act as they grow older) and 'biological ageing' (an organism's physical state as it ages).

Bhatia (1983, cited in Saluja, 2011) defined the term 'ageing' from three perspectives: biological, psychological and sociocultural. *Biological ageing* refers to bodily changes that occur in the later part of the life of an individual that includes graying of hair, loss of teeth and the diminishing of sight and audibility. *Psychological ageing* is studied in terms of changes in the nervous system and it consists of general decline in the mental abilities that accompany old age. It also includes the attitude and behaviour of others towards them. *Sociocultural ageing* refers to changes in the individual, and changing circumstances as a member of family, community and society. These changes include completion of parental role, retirement from work, reduced income, diseases, disability and need for support.

Mukherji (1972, cited in Saluja, 2011), while defining ageing, distinguishes between biological, sociological and psychological age. According to him, biologically, a person may be old but if he or she possesses a youthful mentality, sociologically and psychologically speaking, he or she should be included in the younger generation.

According to Tibbittis (1960, cited in Saluja, 2011), ageing may be best defined as the survival of a growing number of people who have completed their traditional adult roles of making a living and child rearing and years following the completion of these tasks, represent an 'extension of life'. It is also said that the aged acquire knowledge through experience and so are of much help to young in a number of ways.

In Indian context, the National Policy on Older Persons, 1999 defines 'senior citizen' or 'elderly' as a person who is 60 years of age and above.

Thus, in brief, ageing means deteriorative biological and psychological changes that occur in genetically matured organism. Indeed these changes are irreversible, weaken the organism's ability for survival and adjustment, and eventually cause the organism's death.

Theoretical Framework

The complexity of the problem of elder abuse remains a challenge because there is no theoretical framework that properly explains the causes of elder abuse. Some well-known theories on elder abuse are: learning theory, dependence theory, psychopathology theory, caregiver stress theory, family systems theory, social exchange theory and ecological theory. Ecological theory offers a better explanation of the complexity of the problem of elder abuse and neglect. Pierson and Thomas (2010: 190) and Teeter (2010: 24) claim that ecological theory focuses on the adaptive and mutual relationships, interactions and transactions between people and their environment. In the context of elder abuse, the ecological theorist has a keen interest in the relationships and interactions between the older person and the caregiver, as well as within the caregiving and broader societal context.

Social Exchange Theory

Social exchange theory was developed by the sociologist George C. Homans in the year 1950. The basic principle of this theory is that the individuals in social situations choose behaviours that maximize their likelihood of meeting self-interests in those situations. This theory focuses on the power and exchange relations of the individual within the family. Older people did not have decision making power within the family. The older people are weak in mutual exchanges with other members in the family and are dependent on the family members for their day-to-day activities. All these lead to abuse of the elderly within the family.

Situational Model Theory on Elder Abuse

The situational theory is one of the most widely accepted explanations of elder abuse. According to this perspective, elder abuse occurs when an overburdened caregiver who suffers from the immense stress take out their frustrations on the person requiring care. According to situational theory, there are three important factors which affect the living condition of an individual. The most important among them is the individual related factors, such as physical and emotional dependency, poor health, impaired mental status and a difficult personality. They became physically and emotionally weak and need more support. The second factor that is the structural factors like economic strain, social isolation and environmental problems. Finally, caregiver-related factors such as life crisis, burnout or exhaustion with caregiving and substance abuse. Role conflicts and over-dependency of the elderly on the caregiver make stress on the caregiver and they react negatively towards the elderly. This makes a gap in the relationship between elderly and the caregiver or family members.

Problems Faced by the Aged

In general, the following problems are faced by an elderly person:

(i) *Failing health*: It has been rightly said that 'we start dying the day we are born'. The ageing process is synonymous with failing health. While death in young people in countries such as India is mainly due to infectious diseases, older people are mostly vulnerable to non-communicable diseases. Failing health due to advancing age is complicated by non-availability of good quality and age-sensitive health care for a large proportion of older persons in the country. In addition, poor accessibility and reach, lack of information and knowledge and/or high costs of disease management make reasonable elderly care beyond the reach of older persons, especially those who are poor and disadvantaged.

To address the issue of failing health, it is of prime importance that good quality health care be made available and accessible to the elderly in an age-sensitive manner. Health services should address preventive measures keeping in mind the diseases that affect – or are likely to affect – the communities in a particular geographical region. In addition, effective care and support is required for those elderly, suffering from various diseases through primary, secondary and tertiary health care systems. The cost (to the affected elderly individual or family) of health has to be addressed so that no person is denied necessary health care for financial reasons. Rehabilitation, community or home-based disability support and end-of-life care should also be provided wherever needed, in a holistic manner, to effectively address the issue of failing health among the elderly.

(ii) *Economic insecurity*: The problem of economic insecurity is faced by the elderly when they are unable to sustain themselves financially. Many older persons either lack the opportunity and/or the capacity to be as productive as they were. Increasing competition from younger people, individual, family and societal mind sets, chronic malnutrition and slowing physical and mental faculties, limited access to resources and lack of awareness of their rights and entitlements play significant roles in reducing the ability of the elderly to remain financially productive, and thereby, independent.

Economic security is as relevant for the elderly as it is for those of any other age group. Those who are unable to generate an adequate income should be facilitated to do so. As far as possible, elderly who are capable, should be encouraged, and if necessary, supported to be engaged in some economically productive manner. Others who are incapable of supporting themselves should be provided with partial or full social welfare grants that provide at least for their basic needs. Families and communities may be encouraged to support the elderly living with them through counselling and local self-governance.

(iii) *Isolation*: Isolation, or a deep sense of loneliness, is a common complaint of many elderly. It is the feeling of being isolated. While there are a few who impose it on themselves, isolation is most often imposed purposefully or inadvertently by the families and/or communities where the elderly live. Isolation is a terrible feeling that, if not addressed, leads to tragic deterioration of the quality of life.

It is important that the elderly feel included in the goings-on around them, both in the family as well as in society. Those involved in elder care, especially NGOs in the field, can play a significant role in facilitating this through counselling of the individual and families, sensitization of community leaders and group awareness or group counselling sessions. Activities centred around older persons that involve their time and skills help to inculcate a feeling of inclusion. Some of these could also be useful for the families and the communities.

(iv) *Neglect*: The elderly, especially those who are weak and/or dependent, require physical, mental and emotional care and support. When this is not provided, they suffer from neglect, a problem that occurs when a person is left uncared for and that is often linked with isolation. Changing lifestyles and values, demanding jobs, distractions such as television, a shift to nuclear family structure and redefined priorities have led to increased self-neglect of the elderly by families and communities. This is worsened as the elderly are less likely to demand attention than those of other age groups.

The best way to address neglect of the elderly is to counsel families, sensitize community leaders and address the issue at all levels in different forums, including the print and audio-visual media. Schools and work places offer opportunities where younger generations can be addressed in groups. Government and non-government agencies need to take this issue up seriously at all levels. In extreme situations, legal action and rehabilitation may be required to reduce or prevent the serious consequences of the problem.

(v) *Abuse*: The elderly are highly vulnerable to abuse, where a person is willfully or inadvertently harmed, usually by someone who is part of the family or otherwise close to the victim. It is very important that steps be taken, whenever and wherever possible, to protect people from abuse. Being relatively weak, elderly are vulnerable to physical abuse. Their resources, including financial ones are also often misused. In addition, the elderly may suffer from emotional and mental abuse for various reasons and in different ways. The major forms of abuse are physical, sexual, psychological and economical, which are discussed in detail in the latter part of this chapter.

The best form of protection from abuse is to prevent it. This should be carried out through awareness generation in families and in the communities. In most cases, abuse is carried out as a result of some frustration and the felt need to inflict pain and misery on others. It is also done to emphasize authority. Information and education to groups of people from younger generations is necessary to help prevent abuse. The elderly should also be made aware of their rights in this regard.

Where necessary, legal action needs be taken against those who willfully abuse elders, combined with counselling of such persons so as to rehabilitate them. Elderly who are abused also require to be counselled, and if necessary rehabilitated to ensure that they are able to recover with minimum negative impact.

(vi) *Fear*: Many old people live in fear. Whether rational or irrational, this is a relevant problem faced by the elderly that needs to be carefully and effectively addressed.

Elderly who suffer from fear need to be reassured. Those who consider fear to be irrational need to be counselled and, if necessary, may be treated as per their needs. In the case of those with real or rational fear, the cause and its preventive measures needs to be identified, followed by appropriate action where and when possible.

(vii) *Boredom(Idleness)*: Boredom is a result of being poorly motivated to be useful or productive and occurs when a person is unwilling or unable to do something meaningful with his/her time. The problem occurs due to forced inactivity, withdrawal from responsibilities and lack of personal goals. A person who is not usefully occupied tends to physically and mentally decline and this in turn has a negative emotional impact. Most people who have reached the age of 60 years or more have previously led productive lives and would have gained several skills during their lifetime. Identifying these skills would be a relatively easy task. Motivating them and enabling them to use these skills is a far more challenging process that requires determination and consistent effort by dedicated people working in the same environment as the affected elders.

Many elderly can be trained to carry out productive activities that would be useful to them or benefit their families, communities or environment; activities that others would often be unable or unwilling to do. Being meaningfully occupied, many of the elderly can be taught to keep boredom away. For others, recreational activities can be devised and encouraged at little or no additional cost.

(viii) *Lowered self-esteem*: Lowered self-esteem among older persons has a complex etiology that includes isolation, neglect, reduced responsibilities and decrease in value or worth by oneself, family and/or the society.

To restore self-confidence, one needs to identify and address the cause and remove it. While isolation and neglect have been discussed above, self-worth and value can be improved by encouraging the elderly to take part in family and community activities, learning to use their skills, developing new ones or otherwise keeping themselves productively occupied. In serious situations, individuals may require counselling and/or treatment.

(ix) *Loss of control*: This problem of older persons has many facets. While self-realization and the reality of the situation is acceptable to some, there are others for whom life becomes insecure when they begin to lose control of their resources – physical strength, body systems, finances (income), social or designated status and decision making powers.

Early intervention, through education and awareness generation, is needed to prevent a negative feeling of inevitable loss of control. It is also important for society to learn to respect people for what they are instead of who they are and how much they are worth. When the feeling is severe, individuals and their families may be counselled to deal with this. Improving the health of the elderly through various levels of health care can also help to improve control. Finally, motivating the elderly to use their skills and training them to be productive will help gain respect and appreciation.

(x) *Lack of preparedness for old age*: A large number of people enter 'old age' with little or no awareness of what this entails. While demographically, we acknowledge that a person is considered to be old when (s)he attains the age of 60 years, there is no such clear indicator available to the individual. For each person, there is a turning point after which (s)he feels physiologically or functionally 'old'. This event could take place at any age before or after the age of 60. Unfortunately, in India, there is almost no formal awareness programme – even at higher level institutions or organizations – for people to prepare for old age. For the vast majority of people, old age sets in quietly, but suddenly, and few are prepared to deal with its issues. Most people living busy lives during the young and middle age periods may prefer to turn away from, and not consider, the possible realities of their own impending old age. The majority of Indians are unaware of the rights and entitlements of older persons.

The problem of not being prepared for old age can be prevented. Awareness generation through the work place is a good beginning with HR departments taking an active role in preparing employees to face retirement and facing old age issues. For the majority who have unregulated occupations and for those who are self-employed, including farmers, awareness can be generated through the media and also through government offices and by NGOs in the field. Older people who have faced and addressed these issues can be 'recruited' to address groups at various forums to help people prepare for or cope with old age.

Responses to elder abuse may take a number of forms. These strategies occur at different times and involve different interventions targeting different personal:

1. *Primary prevention*: Focussing on stopping the abuse before it happens, by removing the cause or preventing the development of risk factors. Examples include education and changing ageist perceptions of older people. It is about changing behaviour and building the knowledge and skills of individuals. The structural, cultural and societal contexts in which abuse occurs are also a key focus.
2. *Secondary prevention*: Is the immediate response after abuse has occurred to eliminate the risk and deal with the short-term consequences. This often involves taking steps to ensure safety of the older person.
3. *Tertiary prevention*: It takes place after the abuse has occurred to deal with the lasting consequences. It aims to prevent or minimize the impacts of violence and to prevent perpetrators from re-offending. It can involve minimizing the impacts of abuse and restoring health, wellness, and/or safety as soon as possible.

Certain cultural values, beliefs, and traditions influence family dynamics, intergenerational relationships and ways in which families define their roles and responsibilities and respond to daily challenges. These differences make some situations difficult to distinguish from abuse or neglect. Although definitions of abuse may vary across diverse cultures, it is important not to ignore signs of abuse by attributing the behaviours to cultural differences. Persons working with older people in potentially abusive situations need to be sensitive to cultural differences and intervene accordingly. Formulating culturally sensitive prevention and intervention efforts requires an understanding of roles and responsibilities within the family and help-seeking behaviours.

The first and most important step toward preventing elder abuse is to recognize that no one of whatever age should be subjected to violent, abusive, humiliating or neglectful behaviour. Violence, abuse, and neglect toward older individuals are signs that the people involved need help immediately. Education is the cornerstone of preventing elder abuse. There is a need for a concerted effort to educate the public about the special needs and problems of older adults and the risk factors for abuse. Respite care is especially important for caregivers of people suffering from Alzheimer's disease or other forms of dementia or of older people who are severely disabled. Social contact and support can be a boon to older persons. Isolation of elders increases the probability of abuse, and it may even be a sign that abuse is occurring. Counselling for behavioural or personal problems in the family or for the individual with mental health and/or substance abuse problems can play a significant role in helping people change lifelong patterns of behaviour or find solutions to problems emerging from current stresses. In some cases, a nursing home may be a more appropriate living environment than living with adult children who are not equipped emotionally or physically to handle the responsibility. Elder abuse refers to intentional or neglectful acts by a caregiver or a 'trusted' individual that lead to or may lead to, the harm of a vulnerable elder. Elder abuse may be physical, mental, emotional, or sexual. Neglect can be self-neglect or neglect by a caregiver. A caregiver may be a family member, an in-home paid worker, a staff person of a programme such as an adult day care centre or of a facility such as a nursing home, or any other person. Exploitation means that a person in a position of trust knowingly, by deception and intimidation, obtains and uses or tries to obtain and use a vulnerable person's funds, assets, or property. This includes failure to use the vulnerable person's income and assets to provide for the necessities required for that person's care.

Indian Scenario on Ageing

India is undergoing a demographic transition. While 8 per cent of its population was recorded 60 years and above in 2011 Census, it is expected to increase its share to 12.5 per cent and 20 per cent by 2026 and 2050 respectively. However, this is not without problems. With this kind of an ageing scenario, there is pressure on all aspects of care for the older persons – be it financial, health or shelter. Older people are living longer, households are getting smaller and congested, causing stress in joint and extended families. Even where they are co-residing, marginalization, isolation and insecurity are felt among older persons due to the generation gap and changes in lifestyles. Increase in lifespan also results in chronic functional disabilities creating a need for assistance required by the older person to manage daily chores. With the traditional system of the lady of the house looking after the older family members at home is slowly changing, as the women at home are also participating in activities outside the home and have their own career ambitions, there is a growing realization among older persons that they are more often than not being perceived by their children as a burden.

Apart from the steady rise in the number of elderly, the traditional roles of these people have changed a lot due to reasons such as modernization, urbanization, industrialization, etc. Traditionally, in India, the aged enjoyed honour, respect and legitimate authority within the family and society but in modern times the younger generation has replaced them in strategic positions leaving them in a weakened and functionless situation. Today, they are viewed as non-productive and dependent lots. Thus, there is a need to initiate requisite appropriate programmes and policy interventions on the part of the government to ensure life and dignity for its senior citizens.

Policy and Programme Initiatives for Elderly Welfare

The Ministry of Social Justice and Empowerment, which is the nodal ministry for this purpose focusses on policies and programmes for the senior citizens in close collaboration with state governments, non-governmental organizations and civil society. The programmes aim at their welfare and maintenance, especially for indigent senior citizens, by supporting old age homes, day care centres, mobile medicare units, etc.

Constitutional Provisions

Article 41 of the Constitution provides that the state shall, within the limits of its economic capacity and development, make effective provisions for securing the right to work, to education and to public assistance in cases of unemployment, old age, sickness and disablement, and in other cases of undeserved want.

Further, Article 47 provides that the state shall regard the raising of level of nutrition, standard of living of its people and the improvement of public health among its primary duties.

Legislations

General improvement in the health care facilities over the years is one of the main reasons for continuing increase in proportion of population of senior citizens. Ensuring that they not merely live longer, but lead a secure, dignified and productive life, is a major challenge. The Government of India enacted the Maintenance and Welfare of Parents and Senior Citizens Act in 2007. The main purpose of bringing out this Act was to provide for more effective provisions for the maintenance and welfare of parents and senior citizens, guaranteed and recognized under the Constitution and for matters connected therewith or thereto. In a nutshell, the Act provides for:

1. maintenance of parents/senior citizens by children/relatives made obligatory and justiciable through tribunals;

2. revocation of transfer of property by senior citizens in case of negligence by relatives;
3. penal provision for abandonment of senior citizens;
4. establishment of old age homes for indigent senior citizens; and
5. adequate medical facilities and security for senior citizens.

Section 19 of the Act also envisages a provision of at least old age home for indigent senior citizens with 150 capacities in every district of the country. The Act has to be brought into force by individual state government. As on February 2010, the Act had been notified by 22 states and all UTs. It is however not applicable to the state of Jammu & Kashmir, while Himachal Pradesh has its own Act for senior citizens but citizens of India living abroad will come within its purview.

Rajasthan is among the first states that has notified the Maintenance and Welfare of Parents and Senior Citizens Act, 2007 and made rules thereunder, called Rajasthan Maintenance and Welfare of Parents and Senior Citizens Rules, 2010. Accordingly, parents, grandparents and senior citizens who are unable to maintain themselves from their own income and property are entitled to demand maintenance from their children and specified relatives respectively with sufficient means. The maintenance would include provision for food, clothing, residence, medical attendance and treatment. The maximum amount which may be ordered for maintenance of a senior citizen by the tribunal shall be such as prescribed by the state government which shall not exceed ₹ 10,000 per month.

Rajasthan has also established tribunals at sub-divisional levels with the Sub-Divisional Officer presiding over it to monitor the status of the senior citizens in the area and book the erring wards. The state government has also constituted an appellate authority in each district to hear appeals against the orders of the tribunal. The district magistrate of the concerned district would be the presiding officer of the appellate tribunal. The District Social Welfare Officers of the Social Welfare and Empowerment Department have been designated as the Maintenance Officers (*The Hindu*, 11 June 2010).

National Policy on Older Persons, 1999

The National Policy on Older Persons (NPOP) was announced in January 1999 to reaffirm the commitment to ensure the well-being of the older persons. The policy envisages state support to ensure financial and food security, health care, shelter and other needs of older persons, equitable share in development, protection against abuse and exploitation, and availability of services to improve the quality of their lives. The primary objectives are:

1. to encourage individuals to make provisions for their own as well as their spouse's old age;
2. to encourage families to take care of the older family members;
3. to enable and support voluntary and non-governmental organizations to supplement the care provided by the family;

4. to provide care and protection to the vulnerable elderly people;
5. to provide adequate healthcare facility to the elderly;
6. to promote research and training facilities to train geriatric care givers and organizers of services for the elderly; and
7. to create awareness regarding elderly persons to help them lead productive and independent lives.

The implementation strategy adopted for operationalization of national policy envisages the following:

1. Preparation of plan of action for operationalization of the national policy.
2. Setting up of separate Bureau for Older Persons in Ministry of Social Justice & Empowerment.
3. Setting up of Directorates of Older Persons in the states.
4. Three-Yearly Public Review of implementation of policy.
5. Setting up of a National Council for Older Persons headed by Ministry of Social Justice and Empowerment from Central Ministry, states, non-official members representing NGOs, academic bodies, media and experts as members.
6. Establishment of an autonomous National Association of Older Persons.
7. Encouraging the participation of local self-government.

National Council for Older Persons

In pursuance of the NPOP, a National Council for Older Persons (NCOP) was constituted in 1999 under the chairpersonship of the Minister for Social Justice and Empowerment to oversee implementation of the policy. The NCOP is the highest body to advise the government in the formulation and implementation of policy and programmes for the aged. The Council was re-constituted in 2005 with members comprising central and state governments, representatives of NGOs, citizens' groups, retired persons' associations, and experts in the field of law, social welfare, and medicine.

Inter-Ministerial Committee on Older Persons

An Inter-Ministerial Committee on Older Persons comprising 22 ministries/departments, headed by the Secretary, Ministry of Social Justice and Empowerment is another coordination mechanism in implementation of the NPOP. Action plan on ageing population issues for implementation by various ministries/departments concerned is considered from time-to-time by the committee.

Central Sector Scheme of Integrated Programme for Older Persons

An Integrated Programme for Older Persons (IPOP) is being implemented since 1992 with the objective of improving the quality of life of senior citizens by providing basic amenities like shelter, food, medical care and entertainment opportunities and by encouraging productive and active ageing, through providing support for capacity building of government/ NGOs/PRIs/local bodies and the community at large. Under the scheme, financial assistance up to 90 per cent of the project cost is provided to NGOs for establishing and maintaining old age homes, day care centres and mobile medicare units. The scheme has been made flexible so as to meet the diverse needs of older persons including reinforcement and strengthening of the family, awareness of generation on issues pertaining to older persons, popularization of the concept of lifelong preparation for old age, facilitating productive ageing, etc.

The scheme has been revised from April 2008. Besides increase in amount of financial assistance for existing projects, several innovative projects have been added as being eligible for assistance under the scheme. Some of these are:

1. Maintenance of respite care homes and continuous care homes;
2. Running of day care centres for Alzheimer's disease/Dementia patients;
3. Physiotherapy clinics for older persons;
4. Helplines and counselling centres for older persons;
5. Sensitizing programmes for children, particularly in schools and colleges;
6. Regional Resource and Training Centres for caregivers to the older persons;
7. Awareness generation programmes for older persons and caregivers;
8. Formation of Senior Citizens Associations, etc.

The implications of ageing for India are many and far-reaching. The numbers are increasing, the resources are limited and the priorities lie elsewhere. Hence, the response to this social problem has to be well-orchestrated, multi-sectoral and based on systematic planning. The first step is advocacy, to raise policy makers' awareness of the multiple issues related to ageing in the country. Professionals, politicians, voluntary workers, NGOs and the general public should come forward for this worthy cause.

Rights of the Elderly

Parents cannot be evicted from a house without due process of law if they have been staying there from the beginning. There are three enactments that can be applied:

1. Under Section 125 of the CrPC, a magistrate can order a child to maintain his old parents under the Maintenance of Parents Act.
2. The Hindu Adoptions and Maintenance Act says that an aged parent can demand maintenance from children in the same way that a wife can demand it from her husband.
3. The Domestic Violence Act provide parents with the right to seek relief from any kind of abuse.

A National Policy on Older Persons was announced in January 1999 which identified a number of areas of intervention: financial security, healthcare and nutrition, shelter, education, welfare, protection of life and property for the well-being of older persons in the country. A National Council for Older Persons (NCOP) was constituted by the Ministry of Social Justice and Empowerment to operationalize the National Policy on Older Persons. In the wake of the Shanghai Plan of Action 2002 and the Macau Outcome Document 2007, the government formulated the National Policy on Senior Citizens in 2011. Its recommendations retain familial involvement, bringing in, now, the involvement of the government and private sector towards creating an 'inclusive, barrier-free and age-friendly society'.

Law

But what is even more concerning is that not many are aware of a law that protects senior citizens from abuse and abandonment – Maintenance and Welfare of Parents and Senior Citizens Act, 2007. Section 24 of the Act deals with offences related to abandonment. According to this Section, any person who abandons a senior citizen they are responsible for, can be jailed for up to three months, and/or be made to pay a fine of up to ₹ 5,000.

The Act was enacted 'to provide for more effective provisions for the maintenance and welfare of parents and senior citizens, guaranteed and recognized under the Constitution and for matters connected therewith or incidental thereto'. The Act states that parents and grandparents who are unable to maintain themselves from their own earning can seek maintenance from their children. Childless senior citizens can also demand maintenance from a 'relative' who is the legal heir of the former and is in possession or will inherit their property after their death.

Provisions

If the children or said relatives, neglect or refuse to maintain senior citizens, the maintenance tribunal can order the former to make monthly allowances that shall not exceed ₹ 10,000. 'Maintenance' includes provisions for food, clothing, residence, medical attendance and treatment. Maintenance applications can be made in a tribunal which will have the powers of a civil court. A significant provision in the Act deals with the transfer of property, which can be made void under certain circumstances – like if children/relatives refuse to provide elders with basic amenities and physical needs. This is only applicable in cases where the property was transferred after the commencement of the action in 2007. According to the Act, such a transfer of property 'shall be deemed to have been made by coercion or under undue influence'.

Challenges of Ageing

The speedily ageing population in India is witnessing new challenges. Despite advances in health care, however, many elderly people have chronic, incurable progressive diseases and need assistance with the activities of daily living. The greatest challenge facing us as we age is the prevention of physical disability and the extension of active life expectancy, fortunately, recent studies suggest that healthy ageing is achievable, with sound planning for old age. Illnesses like diabetes, congestive heart failure, and some forms of dementia can be delayed or even prevented. Even loss of muscle strength with ageing is partly preventable. Perhaps most important prevention is a positive attitude which helps us to overcome illness and personal losses while we look forward to the days to come. This demographic shift has moved the focus of researchers, health care providers and policymakers from how to extend the lifespan to ways to improve the quality of our later years. Staying healthy, active and productive are admirable goals for our nation's older adults. To face the challenges of the ageing population, the country needs to be well prepared. Suitable redistributive policies are required. Women issues also are of paramount importance in considering social policies for the elderly population. Appropriate care and support for them is a priority.

According to Population Reference Bureau (PRB) projection, in India, the proportion of those above 65 years will rise from 6 to 13 per cent. The share of the 65 above population will rise from less than one in 10 in 2018 to about one in six. As a result, India will go from being characterized as a country with moderate child dependency at present to one with a high old age dependency by mid-century.

Long Term Palliative Care (LTPC) is an interdisciplinary medical speciality that focuses on preventing and relieving suffering and supporting for elders patients and their families facing serious illness. Family members provide medical care for older adults which often involves medically and ethically complex decision-making, requiring consideration of patients' multiple comorbid conditions. An age-well survey of more than 10,000 respondents across northern, southern, western, eastern, and central India during May–June 2018 revealed that about 62 per cent of the elderly do not get such facilities. In India, according to Census 2011, the 70 plus population was 2.84 crores and the 80 plus was 1.12 crores. Moreover, the proportion of females is more in the older age group. So there is a need that LTPC should be made an important component of primary health care.

Income

After retiring from formal employment, scores of the country's elderly people have money, properties, savings, investments, inheritance and above all supportive children. However, 35 per cent of old people are poor with no source of known income. What is more saddening is that irrespective of their financial status, most old people face abuse in one form or the other.

Lack of Awareness

Due to lack of awareness about their rights in old age, many people are compelled to live in inhuman conditions. With the significant increase in the elderly population, elder abuse has become rampant and a majority of older people have resigned to their circumstances for sake of the well-being of their loved ones and their own peace of mind.

Gender Discrimination

Our society is very orthodox and puts the restriction on women. Older women are more prone to suffer abuse due to factors like gender discrimination, longer lifespan than older men, longer span of widowhood and no source of income as traditionally most of them are housewives. Most elderly women remain within the four walls of their homes and the majority of them are abused by their own family members and are forced to live a life of humiliation, abuses and isolation.

Other Factors

Other factors include comparatively high illiteracy among elderly women, lack of awareness about their rights, social norms and, above all, their higher level of patience and tolerance. Many older adults continue to work, volunteer and act as caregivers. Regular positive interactions with family and friends and being involved in different social networks help older adults to be healthier. Conversely, loneliness has a negative physical and emotional impact. Loneliness is a challenge that many elderly faces. They lack social interaction and can often feel isolated in their age.

People are often classified by age group and not by individual characteristics. This categorization often results in inaccurate stereotypes about ageing and older adults. Most retired individuals aged of 65 and older are referred to as seniors. However, society's view of 'old age' has not always kept up with the reality of being old. Many current beliefs about ageing are based on information that are no longer valid given recent scientific advances. Many people are continuing to work beyond age 65 because they are healthy and productive even up to 80s. Older adults can learn skills in late life, although learning some skills may take longer than in younger adults. For many seniors, this is a period of time prior to their death that they are struggling to keep their heads above water both physically and financially. Healthcare costs are rising, savings are being depleted and income is not keeping pace with inflation. As the number of old persons is rising and the social environment is changing, the proportion of the destitute among them is also increasing. Thus, there is a need for a large number of old-age homes where old people may enjoy the end part of their lives in a group of their own.

Prevention

For the elderly, prevention focuses mainly on the disease, frailty, accidents, iatrogenic complications, psychosocial problems, and maintaining ability to perform activities of daily living. Choice of preventive measures is guided by whether the patient's general condition is healthy, chronically ill or poor health.

Healthy elderly people have minimal or no chronic disease and are functionally independent. Primary and secondary prevention of disease and prevention of frailty are the most beneficial measures for this group. Primary prevention aims to stop the disease before it starts, often by reducing or eliminating risk factors. Secondary prevention aims to detect and treat the disease or its complications at an early stage, before symptoms or functional losses occur, thereby minimizing morbidity and mortality.

Chronically ill people have several non-curable but treatable diseases, are usually functionally independent or minimally dependent, often take several prescription drugs, and occasionally are hospitalized due to exacerbations of their chronic diseases. Secondary and tertiary prevention of disease and prevention of frailty are priorities, as are the primary prevention of disease and prevention of iatrogenic complications and accidents. In tertiary prevention, an existing symptomatic, usually chronic disease is appropriately managed to prevent further functional loss. Patients with the chronic disorders, which are common among the elderly, can potentially benefit from tertiary prevention.

Critically ill people have many severe chronic diseases, are functionally dependent, and have lost their physiologic reserve. They are frequently hospitalized and institutionalized. For them, prevention of accidents and iatrogenic complications is most important. If a patient has multiple unmet needs, especially when coupled with functional decline, can be referred to a specialist.

General Preventive Measures

Some preventive measures that apply to all elderly people include:

1. *Diet and exercise*: A healthy diet and regular exercise help prevent or postpone frailty and many diseases. Other disease prevention measures, exercises can help preserve functional ability and reduce the incidence of accidents.
2. *Screening and prevention*: Healthy elderly people should visit their primary care physician at least annually to ensure timely completion of primary and secondary disease prevention measures.

ELDER ABUSE

Abuse is the term used to describe the mistreatment and/or abuse of an elderly person. Elder abuse is a growing problem. Abuse of an elderly person can occur at home or at other places. Health care providers are also capable of elder abuse. Elder abuse is an unacceptable attack on human dignity and human rights. Ignoring the rights of older people makes the senior citizens vulnerable to the risk of abuse, neglect, exploitation and marginalization.

Elder abuse is recognized as a continually increasing and serious problem in our society. According to World Health Organization (WHO), it is a violation of human rights and is a significant cause of illness, injury, loss of productivity, isolation and despair. Each year, hundreds of thousands of adults over the age of 60 are abused, neglected or financially exploited. In India alone, a majority of older adults are believed to be abused or neglected at various levels. These statistics are likely an underestimate because most of the victims are unable or afraid to tell the police, family or friends about the violence. In other parts of the world too elder abuse occurs with little recognition or response. Until recently, this serious social problem was hidden from the public view and considered mostly a private matter. Though it exists in both developing and developed countries yet it is typically underreported globally. Thus, even today, elder abuse continues to be a taboo, mostly underestimated and ignored by societies across the world. Despite this, its social and moral significance is obvious. As such, it demands a global multifaceted response, one which focusses on protecting the rights of older persons.

Defining Elder Abuse

Elder abuse is defined by the World Health Organization as 'a single, or repeated act, or lack of appropriate action, occurring within any relationship where there is an expectation of trust which causes harm or distress to an older person'.

Like ageing, there is no consistent definition of elder abuse. It is generally defined either in a poor or imprecise way, or specifically to reflect the unique statutes or conditions present in specific locations (e.g., states, counties or cities), or for research purposes. As a result, no universally accepted definition exists. However, several scholars, including Hudson and Johnson (1986) from the US and Stones (1991) from Canada, have attempted to define this phenomenon. The Canadian framework for defining abuse or neglect, for example, contains 71 items grouped into nine categories such as physical assault, excessive restraint, putting health at risk, failure to give care by someone acting as a paid or unpaid caretaker under pressure, humiliating behaviour, abuse in an institution, material (including financial) exploitation and verbal humiliating (Stones, 1995). Based on the World Health Organization (WHO)/International Network for the Prevention of Elder Abuse (World Health Organization 2002), elderly abuse has been classified into three broad categories: first, neglect, including isolation, abandonment and social exclusion; second, violation of human, legal and medical rights; and third, deprivation of choices, decision, status, finances and respect.

In fact, the concept of 'elder abuse and neglect' was developed in an era when older people were identified as a homogenous group based on chronological age, and were marginalized by an understanding of their capacities that was associated with their exclusion from the labour market and with a perception that their roles in society were limited and subject to decline (Neugarten, 1967). Baumann (1989) argues unequivocally that 'elder abuse and neglect' was socially constructed by professional 'experts' as part of the development of gerontology as a discipline. Baumann's perspective is coincident with that of Leroux and Petrunik (1990: 653), for whom the idea of 'elder abuse' as a social phenomena/problem emerged from the 'public perception of old age as a social problem', where 'old age overrides all other statuses and has the most priority in the characterization of the individual'. Based on the perception of old people as frail in mind and body, there is 'an assured need to protect the elderly' through professional intervention. Moreover, this construction 'overrides their status as legally and socially competent adults'.

In brief, it can be stated that a consistent definition is needed to monitor the incidence and examine trends over time. It can also help determine the magnitude of the problem and enables comparisons across locations, which ultimately leads to prevention and intervention efforts. Besides, approaches to define, detect and address elder abuse need to be placed within a cultural context and considered along side culturally specific risk factors. For example, in some traditional societies, older widows are subjected to forced marriages while in others, isolated older women are accused of witchcraft. Similarly, from health and social perspectives, unless both primary health care and social service sectors are well equipped to identify and deal with the problem, elder abuse will continue to be underdiagnosed and overlooked.

Elder abuse can have a devastating impact on the health and well-being of older people. The older people who experience abuse are:

1. Three times more likely to die prematurely.
2. Four times more likely to be admitted to a nursing home.
3. Three times more likely to be admitted to a hospital.
4. More likely to suffer from depression or psychological distress including feelings of helplessness, alienation, guilt, shame, fear or anxiety.

Forms of Elder Abuse

There is a link between elder abuse and a lack of respect for older people. Ageism also contributes to a lack of willingness on the part of older people to report abuse. Ageism can diminish self-esteem and self-worth which increases vulnerability to abuse and prevents older people from reporting abuse. Elder abuse is a single or repeated act and lack of appropriate action occurring within any relationship where there is an expectation of trust which causes harm or distress to an older person. Elderly abuse varies in form and severity. It includes physical, sexual and verbal maltreatment as well as financial exploitation and neglect. Elderly abuse can have several health consequences including an elevated risk of depression, anxiety, self-neglect, physical inactivity and mortality. Instances of elder abuse range from the infliction of physical harm to the use of fraud or coercion to extract financial or material gain from vulnerable seniors. Elder abuse includes physical abuse, emotional abuse, sexual abuse, exploitation, neglect, and abandonment. Besides these extortions, unreasonable confinement, active versus passive neglect and coercion are also identified as forms of elder abuse. Perpetrators include children, other family members, and spouses – as well as staff at nursing homes, assisted living, and other facilities.

There are various types of maltreatment that occur among people over the age of 60. These include:

1. *Physical abuse* occurs when an elder is injured (e.g., scratched, bitten, slapped, pushed, hit, burned, etc.), assaulted or threatened with a weapon (e.g., knife, gun, or other object), or inappropriately restrained.

   Physical abuse means inflicting physical pain or injury on an older adult. Physical abuse (the infliction of physical pain or injury, physical coercion, physical restraint, chemical restraint) can range from slapping or shoving to severe beatings and restraining with ropes or chains. Physical abuse can include hitting, beating, pushing, shoving, kicking, pinching, burning or biting. It also includes the inappropriate use of medications, physical restraints and physical punishment of any kind. Physical signs may include burns, bruises, cuts, sunken eyes or cheeks, malnutrition, soiled clothing, etc. Elders' skin is generally more susceptible to scars, bruising and infection.
2. *Sexual abuse or abusive sexual contact* is any sexual contact against an elder's will. Sexual abuse occurs when an elder is forced into unwanted sexual activity. Sexual abuse means touching, fondling, intercourse, or any other sexual activity with an older adult, when the older adult is unable to understand, unwilling to consent, threatened, or physically forced. Sexual abuse can include inappropriate touching, photographing the person in suggestive poses or any unwanted sexualized behaviour. It also includes rape, sodomy or coerced nudity. Abusive sexual contact is defined as intentional touching (either directly or through the clothing), of the genitalia, anus, groin, breast, mouth, inner thigh, or buttocks.
3. *Psychological or emotional abuse* occurs when an elder experiences trauma after exposure to threatening acts or coercive tactics. Examples include humiliation or embarrassment; controlling behaviour (e.g., prohibiting or limiting access to transportation, telephone, money or other resources); social isolation; disregarding or trivializing needs; or damaging or destroying property.

   Psychological abuse (the infliction of mental anguish) can range from name calling or giving the 'silent treatment' to intimidating and threatening the individual. When a family member or another person behaves in a way that causes fear, mental anguish or emotional pain or distress, that behaviour can be regarded as abusive.

   Emotional abuse means verbal assaults, threats of abuse, harassment, or intimidation. Verbal and emotional abuse can include yelling, swearing and making insulting or disrespectful comments. Elder victims become quiet during this period of abuse because they fear speaking out may result in more harm. Psychological abuse can also include treating the older person like a child and isolating the person from family, friends and regular activities through force, threats or manipulative behaviour.

4. *Neglect* is the failure or refusal of a caregiver or other responsible person to provide for an elder's basic physical, emotional, or social needs, or failure to protect them from harm. Examples include not providing adequate nutrition, hygiene, clothing, shelter, or access to necessary health care; or failure to prevent exposure to unsafe activities and environments.

    Neglect is either active or passive, meaning the caregiver either intentionally withholds care (active) or becomes unable to fulfill his or her responsibilities (passive) for many number of reasons, such as excessive stress or lack of resources. Neglect is the failure to provide a dependent senior citizen with life necessities, such as food, clean water, shelter, personal hygiene, clean clothing, medicine, safety, or basic comfort. Neglect may also contribute to emotional abuse.

    (i) *Active neglect* is refusal or failure to undertake a caretaking obligation, including a conscious and intentional attempt to inflict physical or emotional distress on the older person.
    (ii) *Passive neglect* (refusal or failure to fulfil a caretaking obligation, excluding a conscious and intentional attempt to inflict physical or emotional distress on the older person). Passive neglect is a caregiver's failure to provide an older adult with life's necessities, including, but not limited to food, clothing, shelter, or medical care.

    Self-neglect is the only category of elderly abuse without a perpetrator. Typically, self-neglect occurs when an elderly person threatens his or her own health or safety by failing to provide himself or herself with adequate hygiene, food, water, medications, shelter or safety precautions. The individual is determined to be a mentally competent older person who nevertheless fails to take care of his basic needs. Self-neglect, which does not involve other parties, is identified as a form of abuse for purposes of referring such cases to adult protective services (APS).

5. *Abandonment* is the wilful desertion of an elderly person by caregiver or other responsible person. Abandonment occurs when a designated caretaker or legal guardian leaves an elder person to fend for himself or herself. While it includes elements of neglect, abandonment is the total desertion of an elderly person.

6. *Financial abuse or exploitation* is the unauthorized or improper use of the resources of an elder for monetary or personal benefit. Examples include forgery, misuse or theft of money or possessions; use of coercion or deception to surrender finances or property; or improper use of guardianship or power of attorney.

    Financial abuse covers a broad spectrum of fraud, confidence (or 'con') jobs, outright theft and other methods of extracting financial or material gain from vulnerable senior citizens. Common examples of financial elder abuse include cashing cheques without authorization; forging signatures; stealing or misusing money or possessions; coercing or deceiving an elderly person into signing a document; and improperly using a guardianship, conservatorship or power of attorney. Often the perpetrator of financial elder abuse is an unscrupulous telemarketeer, confidence (or 'con') artist, or any individual who preys on the weaknesses of senior citizens. For example, elderly persons, who are more likely to own their homes outright, sometimes are tricked into signing over the deed of their home in exchange for a future payoff that never comes.

7. *Confinement* means restraining or isolating an older adult, other than for medical reasons.
8. *Willful deprivation* means denying an older adult medication, medical care, shelter, food, a therapeutic device, or other physical assistance, and exposing that person to the risk of physical, mental, or emotional harm – except when the older, competent adult has expressed a desire to go without such care.
9. *Material abuse* means the illegal or improper exploitation and/or use of funds or resources.

Indian Scenario on Elder Abuse

India has an estimated 98 million senior citizens today and their number is expected to increase to 315 million by 2050.

Currently, there are no official statistics available relating to the prevalence of elder abuse in the country. However, it is said that one in three elderly persons is neglected or ill-treated by close relatives. In a HelpAge India survey report (2013) too, it was revealed that the main perpetrator comes from within one's family as more than one-fifth (23%) of elderly across the country experienced abuse at home. Another finding that came was that both daughter-in-laws and sons were the primary perpetrators of abuse, with just a negligible difference (39% and 38% respectively) (*Hindustan Times*, 15 June 2013). This finding is in contradiction to the general belief that in most of the cases of elder abuse the perpetrators are male.

In 2012, the HelpAge India also conducted a similar survey in 20 cities across the country. Here, we present the main findings of the report:

1. 31 per cent of older persons reported facing abuse.
2. More than half of those abused were facing it for more than four years and all these were facing multiple forms of abuse.
3. 24 per cent older people faced abuse almost daily.
4. 75 per cent of those who faced abuse lived with family and 69 per cent were owners of the house in which they were living.
5. The primary abuser was the son in 56 per cent cases, followed by the daughter-in-law with 23 per cent cases.
6. 55 per cent of those abused, did not report it to anyone. More than 80 per cent of these did not report the matter to uphold family honour.
7. 62 per cent older persons suggested that the most effective mechanisms to tackle elder abuse was sensitization of children and strengthening of

intergenerational bonding and 38 per cent stated it to be economic independence.

8. The older persons considered disrespect, neglect and verbal abuse as elder abuse.
9. Six per cent older persons did not know what constitutes elder abuse.
10. 81 per cent older persons thought that elder abuse was prevalent in our society.
11. Only 22 per cent older persons considered the prevalence rate of elder abuse in society to be high; an equal proportion considered it to be low and 56 per cent said it was moderate.
12. Little less than 50 per cent of the older persons had seen cases of elder abuse in their surroundings.
13. Out of those who reported abuse, 49 per cent elders chose a family member for reporting/confiding about it.
14. Police helplines and services were known to majority of the respondents but were never used, probably due to lack of trust or to maintain family honour.
15. Delhi NCR witnessed a rise in abuse from last year, with 29.82 per cent elderly stating they faced abuse, as against 12 per cent the year before. Mumbai (Maharashtra) followed a close second to Delhi NCR with 29.46 per cent.
16. Bhopal (Madhya Pradesh) ranked the highest in elder abuse with 77.12 per cent elders stating they faced abuse, followed closely by Guwahati (Assam) with 60.55 per cent and Lucknow (Uttar Pradesh) with 52 per cent.
17. Other than Bhubaneswar (Odisha) with 23.31 per cent, eastern India on an overall basis had high percentage of elder abuse with Guwahati (Assam) 60.55 per cent and Kolkata (West Bengal) 40.93 per cent.
18. 11 per cent of older women and 6 per cent of older men did not have any knowledge about the currently available reporting and redress mechanisms. None of the respondents knew about all the available mechanisms.
19. 19 per cent older women knew about one mechanism as compared to 17 per cent men, and 21 per cent women knew two or three mechanisms as compared to 25 per cent older men.

Help Age India conducted a survey (2018) on elder abuse in 23 cities in India by interviewing elderly above 60 years of age. Around 60 per cent of elders confirmed that elder abuse is prevalent in our society. Of those, who reported prevalence, 88 per cent of them believed its existence is high. The most common form of abuse they experienced was disrespect (56%), verbal abuse (49%) and neglect (33%). The main abusers were son (57%) and daughter-in-law (38%). Only 18 per cent of elders have confirmed that they have made an attempt to report abuse. And, only 35 per cent of the total reporting was successfully resolved. Around 11 per cent were aware of the Maintenance and Welfare of Parents and Senior Citizens Act, 2007. Thus, action needs to be taken against situations which make life difficult for the elderly. Social security of elderly should be taken care of, they should be given opportunities for income generation, programmes to sensitize children and young adults and involvement of society at large against elder abuse should be initiated.

Preventive Measures

15 June marks the officially recognized 'United Nations World Elder Abuse Awareness Day'. Millions of people around the world organize events to raise awareness about this global injustice. Richard Blewitt, HelpAge CEO said, 'Our rights do not change as we grow older. Sadly, what does change is that older women and men are considered to be inherently less valuable to society'.

As said at the outset, elder abuse spans a broad spectrum. It ranges from physical violence to the neglect of elders, who depend on others for their basic needs. There has always been lack of attention on the part of governments towards this social problem. Actually, older people's rights are protected under international human rights law, but as the existing commitments are not enshrined in human rights treaties, governments have no legal obligation to implement them. Most governments do not see older people as rights holders with responsibilities, but only as recipients of welfare. This attitude needs to be changed. A new UN convention on the rights of older people is necessary to bring about this change. It would provide governments with a legal framework, guidance and support to help them protect older people's rights.

Although little is known about elder abuse in India, the existing literature and accounts by Indian elders and their families suggest that it is a serious and pervasive problem. Over the past few years, both central and state governments across the country have crafted policies and programmes, besides enacting laws, to stop abuse, treat its effects and prevent its recurrence. Besides, the civil society can play a crucial role in prevention of elder abuse from the society. HelpAge is a classic example which is working all over the world for this human cause.

At the most basic level, greater importance must be attached to primary prevention. This requires building a society in which older people are allowed to live out their lives in dignity, adequately provided with the necessities of life and with genuine opportunities for self-fulfillment. For those societies overwhelmed by poverty, the challenge is enormous. Prevention starts with awareness. One important way to raise awareness – both among the public and concerned professionals – is through education and training. Those providing health care and social services at all levels, both in the community and in institutional settings, should receive basic training on the detection of elder abuse. The media is a second powerful tool for raising awareness of the problem and its possible solutions, among the public as well as the authorities.

Programmes in which older people themselves play a leading role in preventing abuse in their homes include:

1. Recruiting and training older people to serve as visitors or companions to other older people who are isolated.
2. Creating support groups for victims of elder abuse.
3. Setting up community programmes to stimulate social interaction and participation among the elderly.
4. Building social networks of older people in villages, neighbourhoods or housing units.
5. Working with older people to create 'self-help' programmes that enable them to be productive.

Preventing elder abuse by helping abusers, particularly adult children, to resolve their own problems is a difficult task. Measures that may be useful include:

1. offering services for the treatment of mental health problems and substance abuse;
2. making jobs and education available; and
3. finding new ways of resolving conflicts.

Much can also be done to prevent abuse of the elderly in institutional settings. Measures that may be useful include:

1. the development and implementation of comprehensive care plans;
2. training for staff;
3. policies and programmes to address work related stress among staff; and
4. the development of policies and programmes to improve the physical and social environment of the institution.

In the words of J. Randal and T. German: 'The problems of ageing and elder abuse cannot be solved if the essential needs of older persons, viz., food, shelter, security and access to health care, are not met. The nations all over the world must create such an environment in which ageing is accepted as a natural part of one's life cycle, where anti-ageing attitudes are discouraged, where older people are given the right to live with dignity – free of abuse and exploitation – and are given opportunities to participate fully in educational, cultural, spiritual and economic activities'.

Suggestions

1. With the number of older persons set to double over the next twenty years, there must be an increased priority and increased funding, given to policies for older persons. There is a need to plan and manage the costs of providing pensions, health and social care services.
2. Governments should ensure an adequate standard of living for older persons, promotion of their physical and mental health, and protection from cruel, inhuman or degrading treatment.

3. The legislation is fundamental to the protection and fulfilment of the rights of older persons in areas such as social security, equality of access to health care, regulation and monitoring of social care services particularly long-stay institutions, preventing elder abuse and regulation of the pension and insurance industry.
4. There will likely be an increase in the number of older persons living in residential and old age homes. There should be strong legislation governing the licensing, monitoring and inspection of old age homes. Old age homes which do not provide an acceptable standard of care should face warnings, the suspension of new admissions until problems are resolved, suspension or cancellation of registration, and ultimately legal proceedings against those that violate the law.
5. Research is needed to achieve a national perspective of the nature and scope of elder abuse, and how it is perceived, in India. This information will guide national policy and programme development and point towards promising approaches for prevention. Data collection methods must be culturally sensitive and appropriate.

The phenomenon of population ageing is becoming a major concern for the policymakers. The changing demographic profile has thrown many new challenges in the social, economic and political domains. There is an emerging need to pay greater attention to ageing related issues and to promote holistic policies and programmes for dealing with ageing society.

References

Baumann, E.A., 'Research Rhetoric and the Social Construction of Elder Abuse', in J. Best (ed.), *Images of Issues: Typifying Contemporary Social Problems*, Aldine de Gruyter, New York, 1989.

Brubaker, T.H. and Powers, E.A., 'The Stereotype of "Old": A Review and Alternative Approach', *Journal of Gerontology*, Vol. 31, No. 4, 1976, pp. 441–47.

Freund, A.M. and Smith, J., 'Self-definition in Old Age (German Abstract)', *Zeitschrift fur Sozialpsychologie*, Vol. 28, Nos. 1–2, 1977, pp. 44–59.

Glascock, A.P. and Feinman, S.L., 'A Holocultural Analysis of Old Age', *Comparative Social Research*, Vol. 3, 1980, pp. 311–32.

Gorman, M., 'Development and the Rights of Older People', in J. Randel et al. (eds), *The Ageing and Development Report: Poverty, Independence and the World's Older People*, Earthscan Publications Ltd., London, 1999, pp. 3–21.

Government of India, *Situation Analysis of the Elderly in India*, Central Statistics Office, Ministry of Statistics & Programme Implementation, 2011.

Hudson, M. and Johnson, T.F., 'Elder Abuse and Neglect: A Review of the Literature', *Annual Review of Gerontology and Geriatrics*, Vol. 6, No. 1, 1986, pp. 81–132.

Johnson, M., 'Is 65+ Old?', *Social Policy*, November/December, 1976, pp. 9–12.

Leroux, T.G. and Petrunik, M., 'The Construction of Elder Abuse and Neglect as a Social Problem: A Canadian Perspective', *International Journal of Health Services*, Vol. 20, No. 4, 1990, pp. 651–63.

Mathew, Amala, 'Theoretical Perspectives on Elder Abuse: A Framework Analysis for Abused Elderly in Kerala'. *IOSR Journal of Humanities and Social Science*, Vol. 22, No. 09, 2017.

McDonald, Lynn and Sharma, K.L., *Ageism and Elder Abuse*, Rawat Publications, Jaipur, 2011, pp. 343–44.

Neugarten, B., 'The Aged in American Society', in H. Becker (ed.), *Social Problems: A Modern Approach*, Wiley, New York, 1967.

Parikh, Varsha, 'Greying Community of India', in Sarjoo Patel and Veena Gandotra (eds), *Ageing: An Interdisciplinary Approach*, Rawat Publications, Jaipur, 2011, p. 158.

Premi, Mahendra K., *Population of India in the New Millennium: Census 2001*, NBT, New Delhi, 2011, p. 85.

Randal, J. and German, T., *The Ageing and Development Report: Poverty, Independence and the World's People*, HelpAge International, London, 1999.

Saluja, Dimple, 'Senile Miseries and Ways for Resolution', in Sarjoo Patel and Veena Gandotra (eds), *Ageing: An Interdisciplinary Approach*, Rawat Publications, Jaipur, 2011, pp. 3–4.

Stones, M., *A Lexicon for Elder Mistreatment*, written for St. John's Provincial Work Committee, Newfoundland, 1991.

Togunu-Bickersteth, F., 'Chronological Definitions and Expectations of Old Age among Young Adults in Nigeria', *Journal of Ageing Studies*, Vol. 1, No. 2, 1987, pp. 113–24.

6

Communalism, Secularism and Regionalism

COMMUNALISM

Meaning of Communalism

Communalism, as we understand it in our country, is blind loyalty to one's own religious group. It is described as a tool to mobilize people for or against, by raising an appeal on communal lines. Communalism is associated with religious fundamentalism and dogmatism.

It is basically an ideology which consists of three elements:

1. A belief that people who follow the same religion have common secular interests, i.e. they have the same political, economic and social interests.
2. A notion that, in a multi-religious society like India, these common secular interests of one religion are dissimilar and divergent from the interests of the follower of another religion.
3. The interests of the followers of the different religions or of different 'communities' are seen to be completely incompatible, antagonist and hostile.

Bipan Chandra holds that communalism is the product of a particular society, economy and polity, which divides people on the basis of religious and economic differences. Thus, communalism is an ideological tool for the propagation of economic and political interests. It is an instrument in the hands of the upper class to concentrate power by dividing people.

The rising trend of communalism and the accompanying violence have created a feeling of insecurity among the religious minorities and ethnic groups. This may just be a fear, but the nation cannot afford to let about one-sixth of the country's population fall victim to panic, suspicion and insecurity. The events between 1984 and 2002 in different parts of the country give ample evidence and taste of the destructive outcome of the communal virus in its varied forms. Muslims, Sikhs and other religious minorities in India are protected by the Constitution which provides for the existence of perfect justice, tolerance, equality and freedom. But in an age in which religious fundamentalism is on the verge of becoming religious bigotry, intolerance and narrow mindedness, the notion of *Ram Rajya* is misinterpreted by Muslims to mean the rule of the Lord Ram, i.e. Hindu rule. The presence of police near the *gurudwaras* to keep an eye on and to check the hide-outs of terrorists in the religious shrines (as in Amritsar in 1985 and in Kashmir in November 1993 and May 1995) is viewed as interference in religious faith. Therefore, to prevent damage to the peace and integrity of the nation, there is a need to analyse and debate on the problem of communalism and communal violence. It has become absolutely important to define 'communalism' today. Also, it is equally pertinent to discover who is 'communal'.

If a Hindu declares with pride that he is a Hindu, does it amount to communalism? If a Muslim says, he is proud of being a Muslim and would give his life to stay a good Muslim, would that be communalism? When a minority community feels (rightly or wrongly) that it has been suppressed by decades of injustice and is being exploited and deprived, and reacts and protests sharply or sometimes even violently, can this be called communalism? If the Christians, the Buddhists and the Parsis lead their personal and private lives in the way they like, according to their own beliefs and creeds, are they communal? Do those Hindus, who accuse Muslims of hurting their religious sentiments and sensibilities by a variety of acts of omission and commission, be permitted to feel that they are above public accountability by dint of sheer superiority in numbers when they themselves commit the same sin of hurting Muslims' sentiments and faith in a systematic fashion? Can those people who fight over one particular place of worship and neglect thousands of temples, mosques, churches, *gurudwaras* and similar holy places, which are crumbling because of lack of repair and maintenance, be called religious leaders? Is a religious leader bigger than the nation? Should the religious leaders be exempted from the definition of communalism? All these factors compel us to precisely define 'communal' and 'communalism'.

Concept of Communalism

Communalism is an ideology which states that society is divided into religious communities whose interests differ and are, at times, even opposed to each other. The antagonism practised by the people of one community against the people of other community and religion can be termed as 'communalism'. This antagonism goes to the extent of falsely accusing, harming and deliberately insulting a particular community and extends to looting, burning down the homes and shops of the helpless and the weak, dishonouring women, and even killing persons.

'Communal persons' are those who practise politics through religion. Among leaders, those religious leaders are 'communal' who run their religious communities like business enterprises and institutions which raise the cries of 'Hinduism, Islam, Sikhism or Christianity in danger', the moment they find that donations into their holy 'corporations' have begin to dwindle, or their leadership has come to be challenged, or their ideology has been questioned. Thus, 'communal' is not one who is 'a man of religion' but 'one who practises politics by linking it with religion'. These power politicians are neither good Hindus nor good Muslims, Sikhs, Christians, Parsis or Buddhists. They can be viewed as dangerous political 'scum'. For them, God and religion are merely instruments to be used to live luxuriously as the 'king parasites' of society and to attain the political goals.

Communalism can be practised in many ways; for example, as political communalism, religious communalism and economic communalism. Political communalism is the product of abiding or lasting political expediency and developing and conserving vote bank, and in which covering up one's wrongs and, at the same time, diverting the attention of the people by a series of 'lid off' exercises to pass the 'communal buck' and shift the blame on one's rivals constitute the familiar game plan. In this political game plan, leaders invariably say what they do not mean and mean what they do not say.

Oommen (1989) has suggested six dimensions of communalism: assimilationist, welfarist, retreatist, retaliatory, separatist, and secessionist. *Assimilationist communalism* is one in which small religious groups are assimilated/integrated into a big religious group. Such communalism claims that scheduled tribes (STs) are Hindus, or that Jains, Sikhs and Buddhists are Hindus and they should be covered by the Hindu Marriage Act. *Welfarist communalism* aims at the welfare of a particular community, say, improving living standard and providing for education and health of Christians by the Christian associations, or Parsi associations working for the upliftment of the Parsis. Such communal mobilization aims at working only for the members of one's own community. *Retreatist communalism* is one in which a small religious community keeps itself away from politics; for example, Bahai community, which proscribes its members from participating in political activities. *Retaliatory communalism* attempts to harm, hurt, injure the members of other religious communities. *Separatist communalism* is one in which a religious or a cultural group wants to maintain its cultural specificity and demands a separate territorial state within the country, for example, the demand of some Bodos in Assam or of Gorkhas for Gorkhaland in West Bengal, or of Vidarbha in Maharashtra. Lastly, *secessionist communalism* is one in which a religious community wants a separate political identity, and demands an independent state. A very small militant section of Sikh population demanding Khalistan or some Muslim militants demanding Azad Kashmir were engaged in practising this type of communalism. Of these six types of communalism, the last three create problems engendering agitations, communal riots, terrorism and insurgency.

Characteristics of Communalism

1. Communalism is an ideological concept.
2. It is a complex process.
3. It has a broader base which encompasses social, economic and political aspects for its manifestation.
4. It causes rivalry, violence and tension among masses.
5. It is used by the higher class people and elites as an instrument for division and exploitation of the communal identities of the poorer sections of their co-religionists.
6. Communalism is simply engineered by opportunistic political and economic interest of contending groups and factions within a political party or by political parties.
7. It strikes at the roots of democracy, secularism and national integration.
8. Its effects are disastrous.

Causes of Communalism

There are a number of causes which are responsible for the prevalence of communalism. Some of the important causes of communalism are discussed below:

1. *The tendency of the minorities*: A few Muslims fail to intermingle in the national mainstream. Some of them do not participate in the secular nationalistic politics and insist on maintaining their separate identity. The elite among the Muslims have failed to generate the appropriate national ethos.
2. *Orthodoxy and obscurantism*: The orthodox members of minorities feel that they have a distinct entity with their own cultural pattern, personal laws and thoughts. There are strong elements of conservatism and fundamentalism among the Muslims. Such feeling has prevented them from accepting the concept of secularism and religious tolerance.
3. *Design of the leaders*: Communalism has flourished in India because the communalist leaders of both Hindu and Muslim communities desire to flourish it in the interest of their communities. The demand for a separate electorate and the organization of Muslim league were the practical manifestations of this line of thought. The British rule which produced the divide and rule policy, separated electorate on the basis of religion, strengthened the basis of communalism in India. Ultimately the partition of the country into India and Pakistan further provided an antagonistic feeling towards each other.
4. *Weak economic status*: A majority of Muslims in India have failed to adopt the scientific and technological education. Due to their educational backwardness, they have not been represented sufficiently in the public service, industry and trade, etc. This causes a feeling of relative deprivation and such feelings contain the seeds of communalism.

5. *Geographical causes*: The territorial settlement of different religious groups especially Hindus, Muslims and Christians causes a wide variation in the mode of life, social standards, and belief system. Most of these patterns are contradictory and this may cause communal tension.
6. *Historical causes*: Many Muslims, all over the subcontinent, are converted from Hinduism, which was facilitated due to the caste-hate relations and under the compulsions of Muslim rulers. The problems of social segregation, illiteracy and poverty that had set apart the low caste people remained unresolved, as the foreign elite that ruled never shared power with them. It caused their alienation. Gradually, elements of communalism entered in the Muslim community. The separatist elements in the Muslim community, from the very start of the national resurgence, had discouraged others of their community from associating themselves with it. As a result, the Muslim League was formed which demanded partition of the country.
7. *Social causes*: The cultural similarity is a powerful factor in fostering amicable relations between any two social groups. But the social institutions, customs and practices of Hindus and Muslims are so divergent that they think themselves to be two distinct communities.
8. *Psychological causes*: Psychological factors play an important role in the development of communalism. The Hindus think that the Muslims are fanatics and fundamentalists. They also believe that Muslims are unpatriotic. On the contrary, the Muslims feel that they are being treated as second-rate citizens in India and their religious beliefs and practices are inferior. These feelings lead to communal ill-feeing.
9. *Provocation of enemy countries*: Some foreign countries try to destabilize our country by setting one community against the other through their agents. Pakistan has played a role in fostering communal feeling among the Muslims of our country. Pakistan has been encouraging and promoting communal riots by instigating the militant sections of Indian Muslim community. Kashmir youths are trained by Pakistan to destabilize India's internal security by spreading communal venom.
10. *The negative impact of mass media*: The messages relating to communal tension or riot in any part of the country is spread through the mass media. This results in further tension and riots between two rival religious groups.

Communalism in India

The pluralistic society of India is composed not only of religious groups such as Hindus (80.50%), Muslims (13.40%), Christians (2.30%), Sikhs (1.90%), Buddhists (0.80%), Jains (0.40%), and so on (Census of India, 2011), but these groups are further divided into various sub-groups. Hindus are divided into sects like Arya Samajis, Shivites, Sanatanis and Vaishnavas, while Muslims are divided into Shias and Sunnis on the one hand, and Ashrafs (aristocrats), Azlafs (weavers, butchers, carpenters, oilmen) and Arzals, on the other. The strained relations between Hindus and Muslims have existed for a long time, whereas some Hindus and Sikhs have also started viewing each other with suspicion, particularly after the Operation Blue Star and assassination of Prime Minister Indira Gandhi and the resultant anti-Sikh riots in Delhi in 1984. We also hear of some conflicts between Hindus and Christians and Muslims and Christians too but, by and large, Christians in India do not feel deprived or exploited by other communities. Among Muslims, Shias and Sunnis too bear prejudicial attitudes towards each other. Here, we will mainly analyse Hindu-Muslim and briefly Hindu-Sikh relations.

Hindu-Muslim Relations

Muslim attacks on India started from the 10th century, but early Muslim conquerors like Mohammad Ghazni and Mohammad Gori were more interested in looting rather than establishing religious dominance. It was when Qutubdin became the first Sultan of Delhi that Islam found a footing in India. Later, it was the Mughals who consolidated their empire and Islam in the process. Some of the policies, proselytization efforts, destruction of Hindu temples and construction of mosques over these temples by Moghul rulers aroused communal bickerings between Hindu and Muslim communities. When the British established their dominance in India via the East India Company, they initially adopted the policy of patronizing Hindus, but after the First War of Independence in 1857 in which Hindus and Muslims fought shoulder to shoulder, the Britishers adopted the policy of 'divide and rule' which resulted in fostering communal clashes deliberately for keeping intact their hegemony. The relations between Hindus and Muslims were further strained when during the freedom struggle, power politics came into play. Thus, though antagonism between Hindus and Muslims is an old issue, Hindu-Muslim relations in India can be described as a legacy of British rule during the freedom struggle. The communalism between these two communities operates today in a significantly changed social and political milieu. It is now perceived as a problem that impedes and warps the process of development of our country. It is the single largest threat to the secular ideals that are enshrined in our Constitution. The sectarian interests keep on fanning the flames of communal hatred.

The slogan of Pakistan was first articulated by the Muslim League in Lahore in 1940. Different sections of the Muslim population had different perceptions of Pakistan. For the Muslim peasant, it meant freedom from the exploitation of the Hindu zamindar; for the Muslim business class, it meant freedom from a well-established Hindu business network; and for the Muslim intelligentsia, it meant better employment opportunities. Later, when the Congress leaders accepted the partition in 1946, it led to the displacement of millions of Hindus, Muslims and Sikhs amid bloodshed and carnage. About 2 lakh persons were estimated to have been killed in the 1947 partition riots and about 6 million Muslims and four and a half million Hindus and Sikhs became refugees. Even after the partition, the Congress failed to come to grips with communalism. It could, therefore, be said that Hindu-Muslim communalism in India had politico-social origins, and religion alone was not the cause of the conflict between Hindus and Muslims. Economic interests and cultural and social mores (such as festivals, social practices and lifestyles) were factors that further divided the two communities.

Today, the Muslims constitute the second largest religious community in India as well as the second largest Muslim minority in the world. Approximately, more than 138 million Muslims are spread out over all parts of our country, and the ratio of Muslim population over Hindu population exceeds the national average (1: 6) in some states like Jammu & Kashmir, Assam and West Bengal. India's Muslims are as varied in language, culture and socio-economic conditions as the Hindus. There is little in common between the Muslims in Uttar Pradesh and the Muslims in Kerala or in Assam or in Jammu & Kashmir. Their unifying factor is religion but the fact is that they do not even have a common language. Though about 13.4 per cent of Indians are Muslims, not even half of them speak Urdu, and all those who speak Urdu are not Muslims.

The Hindu-Muslim antagonism can be ascribed to a complex set of factors. These are: (a) Muslim invasions in which the invaders looted the property and constructed mosques over/near Hindu temples. (b) British encouragement of Muslim separatism for their own ends during their imperial rule. (c) The behaviour of some of the Muslims in India after partition, like hoisting of Pakistani flags when the Pakistani team wins the cricket match and or observing national independence day as a 'black day' after a call given by some Muslim leaders. Such behaviour creates a feeling among the majority community that these Muslims are not patriotic. The stereotyped image of a Muslim which is entrenched in the Indian psyche is that of a bigoted, inward-looking outcaste. A Muslim similarly looks upon a Hindu as a conniving, all-powerful opportunist and he views himself as victimized by him and alienated from the mainstream of the society. (d) A new aggressiveness on the part of the Muslim political parties in an effort to find a place in the country. Reports are rife about some Muslim extremists obtaining 'foreign money', turning into 'foreign agents', indulging in a well-designed plan to soil the secular ideal of the country, and attempting to incite Indian Muslims. (e) A failure on the part of Muslim leaders to unite Muslims and resolve their problems is perhaps due to frustrations because they have been influenced by the wave of Islamic fundamentalism sweeping West Asia and Pakistan. The leaders have only exploited the numerical strength of the Muslims (especially in Kerala, Kashmir and Uttar Pradesh) to strike barter deals, secure a chunk of Muslim seats in the parliament and legislatures and to seek power and pelf for themselves and their friends. (f) The government is also responsible for neglecting the Muslims, large sections of whom feel alienated and consequently become willing victims of selfish leaders. The ruling elite merely preach religious amity and have little understanding of the real problems of the Muslims. The Hindu leadership only deals with those Muslim leaders who toe their line.

The Indian Muslims, not surprisingly, tend to consider their future as a question of 'Us' versus 'They'. When they make their demands known, as any segment of society would do to voice their grievances, it more often than not explodes into an orgy of Hindu-Muslim violence which leads to accusation of foreign incitement. Should the Muslim problem be perceived only as a communal problem? Is it not a fact that the Hindu-Muslim issue is not any different from the anti-Brahmin agitations in Tamil Nadu or the inter-caste conflicts in Uttar Pradesh, Bihar and some other states, or the Bengali-Assamese trouble in Assam, or the Maharashtrian versus non-Maharashtrian conflict in Maharashtra? The problem in reality is one of social and economic change.

The militant Hindus maintain that the Muslims in the country are being pampered. The Ram Janambhumi–Babri Masjid issue in 1992–93 further affected the delicate balance of communal harmony. After the Babri Masjid demolished in 1992, riots erupted in which about 2,000 people were killed and property worth thousands of crores of rupees was destroyed causing communal tensions in the nation.

Ram Janambhumi–Babri Masjid Dispute

On 9 November 2019, the Supreme Court settled the centuries old Hindu-Muslim conflict that lingered in courts for nearly seventy years by handing over entire 2.77 acres of disputed land for construction of Ram Temple and set up a trust for the purpose. The Suni Waqf Board was allocated five acres of land at a prominent alternative location in the temple town. The unanimous verdict was in favour of deity Ram Lalla – one of the three litigans at Ayodhya because Hindu parties could produce better evidence to substantiate their rights. The verdict given after a marathon hearing of 40 days (200 plus hours) without being distracted, making it one of the greatest judicial verdicts in the world. Supreme Court's verdict on one of India's most community sensitive dispute case is a 'victory of the rule of law' which has balanced the interest of all parties. The dispute has been settled through arguments, evidences and records by the Supreme Court. The judgement is based on the evidences, facts and findings of Archaeological Survey of India (ASI).

The verdict is significant not just for its value in providing a sense of resolution and closure on such a ling snoldering issue. It is significant because it is directly related to the shifts that are currently underway in India – state institutions and its changing relationship with faith and customs, identity-based political mobilization and the inter-community dynamics on the ground. The Ayodhya chapter, it seems, has finally closed with the past burying its dead and will prove to be a mile stone and further strengthen India's unity in diversity in the cultural commitment.

Hindu-Sikh Communalism

The Sikhs constitute less than 2 per cent (1.9 crore) of India's population. Though dispersed widely over the entire country and even abroad, their largest concentration is in Punjab, where they form the majority of the state's population. Sikhism started as a reform movement against the dogmas of Hindu religion. After the tenth guru, the tradition of gurus among Sikhs ended and the Granth Sahib was accorded utmost reverence. The Sikh shrines (*gurudwaras*) remained under the control of priests, some of whom misused their position and amassed personal wealth. In the early years of the 20th century, some young Sikhs started a movement against the hegemony of the Sikh *mahants*. These people – called *Akalis* – wanted shrines to be managed by a body of democratically elected representatives. The Shiromani Gurudwara Prabhandak Committee (SGPC), thus, came into existence in 1925 after the Sikhs waged a hard struggle to liberate their *gurudwaras* from the corrupt *mahants*. Since its inception, the SGPC has been a seat of great power.

Another group (sect) called the *Nirankaris* started a movement against the dogmas, rituals and traditions which had crept into Sikhism. Thus, the Nirankari movement was a reformist movement (purely religious in character) against the induction of Hindu religious practices in the Sikh system of worship. It emphasized the elimination of the worship of several deities and revived simplicity, austerity and purity in rituals and ceremonies. The *Nirankaris* remained within the Sikh fold till 1943 after which there arose a conflict. In 1973, the undivided *Akali Dal* under the leadership of Master Tara Singh demanded 'autonomous status' for Punjab dominated by Sikhs. On 17 October 1973, the *Akalis* passed a resolution, now popularly called the 'Anandpur Sahib Resolution', in which they made 45 demands. Later, the *Akalis* came to be divided into extremists and moderates. One militant group led by Jarnail Singh Bhindranwale emerged as a powerful group in the early eighties of the 20th century. Initially, he launched a movement against the *Nirankaris* to purify the Sikh religion but ultimately he started a Sikh separatist movement and began a demand for Khalistan. Though a small section of Sikhs continues to work for this demand, the majority of the *Akalis* are for a state in which the authority of the Centre is to be confined to defence, foreign relations, communications, railways and currency.

The Sikh agitation, which started in Punjab in the early eighties with the murder of a local editor, hijacking of a Srinagar-bound flight, and the issuing of passports for a fictitious nation called Khalistan, began to intensify. The number of killings and firings increased and the Sikh protests became organized, militant and increasingly violent. In 1984, when the military launched Operation Blue Star for seizing weapons and arresting militants from the Golden Temple at Amritsar, the Sikhs reacted violently. In October 1984, when Indira Gandhi was assassinated and thousands of Sikhs were killed in Delhi and other states, and their property was looted, burnt or destroyed, some Sikh militants became so agitated that they killed hundreds of Hindus in trains and buses, destroyed their property and forced many Hindus to leave Punjab. In May 1988, when Operation Black Thunder was launched once again by the military to clear militants from the Golden Temple in Amritsar which remained under their seize for about ten days, the Sikhs retaliated by exploding bombs, killing Hindus and looting banks. The relations between Sikhs and Hindus thus remained strained for about one and a half decade. However, the militancy of extremist Sikhs in Punjab has now been suppressed and from 1993 onwards, there has been considerable improvement in the relations between the people of the two communities. There is goodwill and respect among them for each other's religious beliefs and places of worship.

Ethnic Violence

Besides the Hindu-Muslim conflicts and Hindu-Sikh skirmishes, how do we perceive the relations between different ethnic groups, say between the Sinhalese and the Tamils, or between the Assamese and the non-Assamese? In Assam, for nearly a century and a half, the economic development of the state was fuelled by the labour and enterprise imported from outside the state. Over this period, Assam has been home to generations of the so-called 'outsiders', who have no home, no land other than the soil of Assam itself. Some have indeed grown rich, but most have remained desperately poor. The Assamese have now raised the question of nationality. The All Assam Students' Union (AASU) and the All Assam Gana Sangram Parishad (AGSP) agitation (which fathered the AGP as a political party) confused 'outsiders' with 'foreigners' (including Bengali refugees from the Bangladesh). Fantastic figures were brandished ranging from five million at one stage, six million at another and then seven million at yet another stage as the number of foreigners (*bahiragat*) illegitimately lurking in the state. This issue of ridding Assam of foreigners held the state to ransom for six years – from 1979 till the Assam accord on 15 August 1985. Hatred was stoked up against the Bodos, the Bengalis, the Marwaris and the non-Assam Muslims. This secessionist movement was responsible for thousands of innocent deaths. The massacre of 1,383 women and children and some men in ten villages in and around Nellie in Nowgong district was a part of this ethnic violence. The AGSP which remained in power between 1985 and 1990 could not contain the ethnic tension.

The ULFA militants launched a movement and the President's rule was imposed in the state in November 1990 instead of holding elections due in January 1991. The army and the security forces launched an operation to round up the rebels and recover weapons. The President's rule was lifted on 30 June 1991 when the new Congress government assumed power in the state. But, the ULFA militants jolted new government by kidnapping 14 government servants including eight top ONGC officials from different parts of the state on the very first day of government's tenure. The May 1996 elections also did not prevent the reprisals from the Bodos. The militants are yet to realize that Assam is like all other states in India, and it belongs to all the legitimate citizens of India, whatever language they speak, whatever religion they follow and whatever rites and rituals they practise. The Bodos – a tribe which comprised about 49 per cent of Assam's population in 1947 and about 5.5 per cent in 2011 and which ruled over Assam until around 1825 – are now demanding autonomy. Though an accord was signed by the Assam government and the Bodo leadership represented by the All Bodo Students Union (ABSU) and the Bodo People's Action Committee (BPAC) on 20 February 1993 but the problem still remains unresolved. Later, in February 2003, another accord was signed with provision of Bodoland Autonomous Council (BAC), but the Bodo leaders and the state government have failed to arrive at an agreement on the boundary issue and transfer of about 3,000 villages to the BAC. The Bodos also do not want that Assamese language should be thrust upon indigenous tribals. The Bodo movement in the 1960s, the 1970s and the 1980s took place in fits and starts, but today it has gathered momentum. Bodos now demand a union territory called 'Udayachal'. Violent activities like bomb blast of Brahmputra Mail in Assam on 30 December 1996 (in which 32 persons were killed and 49 injured) and blowing up of the road and railway bridges by the Bodo militants in lower Assam in the last week of December 1996 point out the domestic and 'foreign' aid to the militants and the need for firm action by the government to contain insurgent activities.

The Bodo militants in their attack on non-Bodo settlers indulged in an ethnic carnage against the Santhal tribals in May 1996. The violence had erupted when a Santhal congress leader was killed during the April 1996 polls to the Assam Legislative Assembly by some insurgents and in retaliation, the Santhals killed three Bodo girls. This infuriated the Bodos who burned down several Santhal villages. The death toll was reported to be upwards of 50. One view is that a month prior to the April polls, some Congress candidates in Assam had brought Santhal extremists from Jharkhand in Bihar who had begun attacks on those Bodos who supported PDFB (Peoples Democratic Front of Bodoland) candidates. The Bodo leaders had also claimed that the Congress leaders had brought Santhals from Bihar to neutralize the Bodo claims for statehood. These Santhal tribals had started encroaching upon the Bodo agricultural lands. After the violent attacks of Bodos on Santhals, over one lakh Santhals and Bodos were reported to have vacated the villages in two districts. The government had to open 16 relief camps to look after these refugees of the two tribal groups. Thus, the reasons for the violence were partly political and partly ethnic.

How do we explain the caste carnage in various parts of the country reported almost daily in the mainstream newspapers? Though abolished by law, caste violence is far from having been overcome in real, daily life. Some of these incidents of communal violence started because of the tension between the 'upper castes' and the 'backward castes' while others started over land disputes. Also, the orgies of killing and rape, the incidents of assault, loot and arson are in many ways fanned by political leaders for their own ends.

Despite the death of the major rebel group Liberation Tigers of Tamil Eelam (LTTE) leader Vellupillai Prabhakaran, the ethnic violence in Sri Lanka still rages. On the question of the future of the Tamil majority in the north-eastern province, the LTTE keeps on fighting with the Sinhalese government and troops. In 1987, it refused to heed to the intervention of the IPKF (Indian Peace Keeping Force) and demanded its withdrawal. In the 19th century, the British had taken more than 10 lakh Tamil labourers from different parts of Madras (now Chennai) to Sri Lanka promising alluring terms of employment in the tea and coffee gardens. For over hundred years, these Tamils laboured for the prosperity of Sri Lanka but in 1948–49, the Sinhalese government passed stringent citizenship laws which deprived them of their citizenship. Their representation was reduced to eight seats in the 75-member Sri Lankan parliament. On this issue, discussions continued between the Tamils and the Sri Lankan government and an agreement was signed in 1964 by the governments of India and Sri Lanka (known as Sirimavo-Shastri Pact) which provided that 5,25,000 Tamils would be sent back to India and Sri Lanka would confer citizenship on three lakh Tamils during a period of 15 years. Still there remained one and a half lakh Tamils without citizenship. After some time, there was a further agreement between the two governments that each of them would absorb 50,000 of the stateless Tamils. But since 1976, the Sri Lankan government had been extending the time limit of 15 years provided in the pact. In 1982, India refused to grant any further extension. The hostility of the Sinhalese towards the Tamils and the escalating ethnic violence worsened the situation. Tamils have been claiming mass killings of the people of their community, burning of their factories, hotels and shops and atrocities committed by Sinhalese soldiers on them. In this perspective, the Indo-Sri Lankan accord was signed by the Indian and the Sri Lankan governments on 29 July 1987 and the IPKF was sent to Sri Lanka to maintain peace in that country. In their efforts to restore peace and help, the Sri Lankan government in running of hospitals, power houses and schools, more than 1,100 Indian soldiers and officers were killed and 30,000 were injured. Gradually, however, the new Sri Lankan President asked for the withdrawal of IPKF from Sri Lanka and all IPKF soldiers were ultimately withdrawn in 1990. But, the Tamils continue to fight for their rights and the ethnic violence continues to persist.

COMMUNAL VIOLENCE

The Concept

The problems and characteristics of communal violence are different from those of student agitations, workers' strikes and peasants' movements. At the conceptual level, we have to differentiate between communal violence and agitations, terrorism and insurgency. This difference has been examined at seven levels: mass mobilization, degree of violence, degree of cohesion, target of attack, flare-ups, leadership, and aftermath experiences (Singh, 1993).

The *mass mobilization* in agitations is to register protest and voice grievances and put demands in the form of processions, demonstrations and *gheraos*. In communal violence, the involvement of people is mobilized against another community. The movements here are unpredictable, uncheckable and carry an emotional fury and violent expressions which take the form of rioting.

The *degree of violence* and the methods of executing violence also vary in agitations and communal riots. In terrorism, the support of masses is passive, latent and clandestine. Considering the insurrection impossible, it is a few active armed terrorist groups who use violence systematically. In insurgency, the mass support is mobilized to change a political order as against communal violence in which resentment is expressed against the social order. Insurgency is fought by trained groups whereas people participating in communal riots are untrained. In insurgency, propaganda among masses is against a regime but in communal riots, it is against social discrimination, social neglect and social and religious exploitation.

The *degree of cohesion* also varies in communal violence, agitations, terrorism and insurgency. The high degree of cohesion in a communal riot situation is built around hostility, tensions and polarization of population, while in agitations it is based on rationalization of interest. In terrorism and insurgency, the cohesion is between activists and the leader; in masses it exists relatively at a lesser degree.

The *target of attack* in insurgency and terrorism is the government, in agitations it is the group in power, and in communal violence it is members of the 'enemy' community. Sometimes, violence in both agitations and communal riots is exercised against public property in the form of loot and arson. Anti-social elements are given a free hand to operate in agitations and communal riots but this is not the case in terrorism and insurgency. The weapons used against targets in insurgency and terrorism are more modern and sophisticated than those used in agitations and communal disturbances.

The *flare-ups* in communal disturbances are restricted to particular structures whereas in insurgency and terrorism, the flare-ups are indefinite and uncertain. In agitations, flare-ups do not depend on particular structures but are dependent on perceived deprivations and the organization of people.

The *leadership* in terrorism, insurgency, and agitations is easily identifiable but not always so in communal riots. There is no leadership in communal riots which could control and contain the riot situation. In agitations, terrorism and insurgency on the other hand, actions emanate from leaders' decisions who have effective control over the situation.

Lastly, the *aftermath of communal violence* is intensified animosity, prejudice and mutual suspicions of one community against the other. In agitations, the human loss is comparatively much less though the loss of property is sometimes huge. When agitations are settled, the animosity against government agencies also subsides and the revengeful attitude dies down in the due course. In terrorism, the victims are mostly innocent. They remain passive against terrorists and feel more secure in such passive behaviour. Victims can never think of seeking revenge because of the terrorists' anonymity and their being armed in an organized way with sophisticated weapons. In insurgencies, the victims are mostly the members of the security forces or government servants who help in counter-insurgency measures.

It could, thus, be said that communal violence is based mainly on hatred, enemity and revenge. This brings us to the question of features of communal violence.

Theories of Communal Violence

Communal violence is a collective violence. When large sections of people in the community fail to achieve their collective goals, or feel that they are being discriminated against and deprived of equal opportunities, they feel frustrated and disillusioned and this collective frustration (or what Feierabends and Nesvold have called 'systematic frustration') leads to collective violence. However, it is not the whole community which launches a violent protest. In fact, the action planned by discontented people against the ruling group or the power elite (against whose ways they protest) is often non-violent. It is only a small band of protesters who consider non-violence ineffective and violence essential for the success of the struggle, who snatch every precipitating opportunity to use violence to assert the strength of their ideology.

This sub-group indulging in violent behaviour does not represent the whole community or the total group of discontented people. The behaviour of this sub-group, by and large, is not equivocally supported by the rest of the community. My contention, thus, falls close to the old 'riffraff theory' of violent riot behaviour which holds that the majority of the people disown and oppose the violent/delinquent behaviour of the sub-group by describing it as 'irresponsible' behaviour.

The question is, what causes the 'group of individuals' to be violent. Two of the important theoretical propositions on collective violence are: (a) it is a normal response to provocation, and (b) it is a response that is consistent with norms supporting its use. This calls for the analysis of some of the important existing theories.

Excluding the psycho-pathological theories (because they focus on the aggressors' psychological personality characteristics and pathological disorders as the chief determinants of violence, and I consider these important for explaining individual violence but not collective violence), other theories may be classified into two categories: (a) at the level of the socio-psychological analysis, and (b) at the level of the sociocultural or sociological analysis. In the first group, theories like Frustration-Aggression Theory, Perversion Theory, Motive Attribution Theory and Self-Attitude Theory may be included, while in the second group theories like Social Tension Theory, Anomie Theory, Theory of Sub-culture of Violence, and Social Learning Theory may be included. My contention is that all these theories fail to explain the phenomenon of collective violence in communal riots. My theoretical approach (called Social Barriers Approach) concentrates on the sociological analysis of social-structural conditions.

Social Barriers Theory

The conditions which lead to collective communal violence are: stress, status frustration and crises of various kind. My thesis is that aggressors use violence because they suffer from insecurity and anxiety. The origin of these feelings and anxieties in an individual can be traced to social barriers created by the oppressive social systems, the power elite, as well as the individual's background and upbringing which have probably put up hurdles for him and which serve to aggravate his tendency to irrational and unrealistic attitudes to social norms and social institutions. My theory also takes into account three factors in aggressors' behaviour, namely, adjustment (in status), attachment (to community) and commitment (to values), as well as the social environment (in which individuals/aggressors live) and the socialized personalities of the individuals (aggressors). My theoretical model, thus, gives importance to the social system, the personality structure of individual aggressors, and sub-cultural patterns of the society in which individuals use violence. In social system, I include strains and frustrations which are the result of the functioning of social structures in society; in personality structure, I include adjustment, attachment and commitment of the individual aggressors; and in sub-cultural patterns, I include the values which operate as a means of social control.

My thesis is that maladjustment, non-attachment, and non-commitment of an individual lead to a feeling of relative deprivation. Relative deprivation is the perceived discrepancy between groups' expectations and their capabilities (conditions of life individuals/groups think they are capable of attaining or maintaining, given the proper opportunities and legitimate means). Here the important term is 'perceived' (by the members of the groups); hence different variations in behaviour, or relative deprivations do not always lead to violent behaviour.

Relative deprivation (of a group) occurs when (a) expectations increase while capabilities remain the same or decline, or (b) when expectations remain the same while capabilities decline. Since both expectations and capabilities rest on perception, therefore, value orientations of a group have an important bearing on (a) the way the group will perceive deprivation, (b) the target to which it (relative deprivation) will be directed, and (c) the form in which it will be expressed. Since each group/individual is subjected to different forces, each group/individual will respond differently in terms of violence or participation in collective communal violence.

Among the several cases of collective communal violence – the main issue was the reservation issue, where two groups – the anti-reservationists as well as the pro-reservationists – felt deprived and frustrated. Their frustration was exploited by the political parties for their vested interests and the reservation issue came to be linked with caste and religion. Anti-social elements engaged in bootlegging and thriving on political support were used to spread communal distrust. Even a minor provocation was enough to cause flare-ups in the population which was sharply divided along communal lines.

The Social Barriers Theory is not essentially an elitist theory of violence where a small group, ideologically superior, takes the initiative to spread violence and decides how to use it 'for the good' of the whole frustrated group on whose behalf it violently vocalizes its protest. Further, the small group does not depend upon the widespread collective action of the frustrated masses. In this context, my explanation is opposed to the orthodox Marxist theory because Marx did not envisage this kind of uprising and mass revolution.

Theory of Polarization and Cluster Effect

This conceptual paradigm was developed based on an empirical study of communal riots in Uttar Pradesh to explain the inter- and intra-community violence in India (Singh, 1993). The paradigm is based on three concepts – polarity, cleavage, and cluster. Polarity is 'sense of affinity, affiliation, belongingness, concern and identity which people share with a particular issue'. The issue may be religious, ideological, political, or economic in nature. Polarization is the 'heightened sense of identity and belongingness resulting in emotional, mental or physical mobilization of individuals or groups to cause cohesion'. Cleavage is a phenomenon by which population in a particular place is divided into two different polarities which have conflicting, contrasting or opposite principles or tendencies. Cluster refers to the habitation pattern of the people belonging to one polarity sharing commonness in a given area at a particular time. The paradigm has been built up on the basis of the facts in 'pre-riot', 'riot' and 'post-riot' situations and the analysis of group behaviour of individuals belonging to different social groups (polarities) in animosity with each other. Since the communal disturbances involve two antagonistic social groups, it necessitates a careful analysis of animosity (state of mind and psyche), structural conduciveness (physical situation), and prejudices.

The individual in isolation is weak and insecure. The strength lies in assemblies, collectivities and groups. The individual joins them for his gain and security. Various polarities exist in society at all times. To each individual, these polarities are references in the matter of interpersonal relationships. The polarities are of two types – permanent and temporary. To the former category belong ideology, religion, language, caste, region and sex. These polarities constitute individual's basic identity which lasts with the individual. To the second category belong occupation, profession, functions based on vested interests. Though normally the polarities are not mutually exclusive but they become exclusive when the society undergoes a cleavage phenomenon due to perceived difference and division of the population as a consequence of polarization. When masses in general assign the same closeness to single polarity, it becomes a dominating polarity at that time at that particular place for that particular population. This dominant polarity sets the pattern of inhibitions of the population (cluster formation), that is, the polarity-based clusters determine the demographic living pattern. Such clusters in old cities and towns are based on religion, caste and sect, but in modern cities these are more class-based. When such clustering takes place because of two different polarities (say, of religion/or religious sects), there is a clash.

The social dynamics of living in clusters is that these prove highly conducive to the emergence of a riot-prone situation, as interpersonal relationships deteriorate and build irritants which are often perceived as deliberate insult, deprivation and injury by one to the other. The incidents affect most people in the clusters due to the physical proximity. This prompts people to build contacts among one's own polarity population and also facilitates the building of mass insurrection.

The nature of polarity dominance depends upon five factors: (a) time and space (that is, period, area, location and situation or geographical limits), (b) social structure (that is, caste, community and social group), (c) education (that is awareness of interest), (d) economic interests, and (e) leadership (that is, emotional speeches, promises and policies of the leaders).

On the basis of the above analysis, V.V. Singh (1993) describes the riot-prone (communal) structure as follows:

1. bi-polarity population in identifiable clusters;
2. close proximity;
3. common interest and resultant animosity;
4. potency of polarized population, which is based on numerical strength, economic prosperity, state of possession of arms, cohesion, type of leadership, and the strength of activity; and
5. administrative expediency and inefficiency of district police and public administration.

The flare up (of communal riot) process is explained by him as follows (Diagram 1):

Diagram 1

Process of Flaring Up of Communal Riots

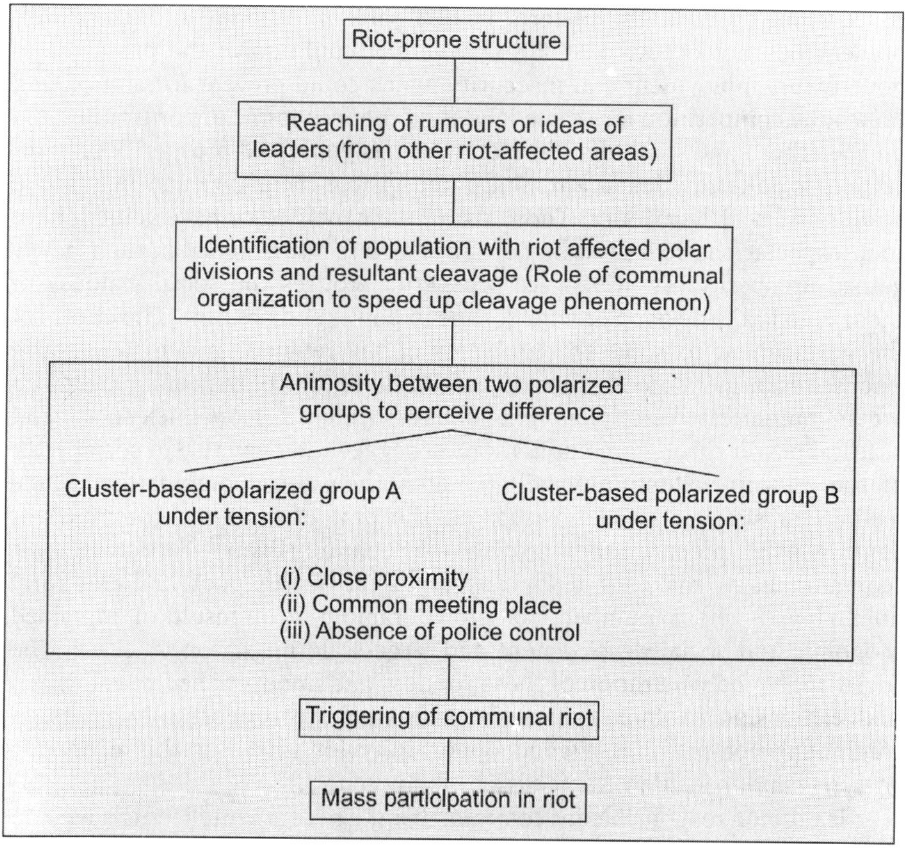

Factors of Communal Violence

Different scholars have approached the problem of communal violence with different perspectives, attributing different causes and suggesting different measures to counter it. The Marxist School relates communalism to economic deprivation and to the class struggle between the haves and the have-nots to secure a monopoly control of the market forces. Political scientists view it as a power struggle. Sociologists see it as a phenomenon of social tensions and relative deprivations. The religious experts perceive it as a diadem of violent fundamentalists and conformists.

The class analysis of communalism requires some attention. The explanation is that the economic, social and political situations in a society sometimes create such problems and crises for the people that even though they try to come to grips with these crises, they fail to do so. Without attempting to grasp the real causes for this failure, they 'perceive' the other community (numerically much stronger than their own) as the cause of their woes. Communalism is thus a social reality which is generated and reflected in a distorted way.

After independence, though our government claimed to follow 'socialistic pattern of economy' but in practice the economic development was based more on capitalist pattern. In this pattern, on one hand, the development has not occurred at a rate where it could solve the problems of poverty, unemployment and insecurity which could prevent frustration and unhealthy competition for scarce jobs and other economic opportunities, and on the other hand, capitalist development has generated prosperity only for certain social strata leading to sharp and visible inequality and new social strains and social anxieties. Those who have benefited or have gained, have their expectations soar even higher. They also feel threatened in their newly gained prosperity. Their relative prosperity arouses the social jealousy of those who fail to develop or who decline in power and prestige. The efforts of the government to solve the problems of the religious minorities arouse intense resentment among those prosperous sections of the community who are in numerical majority and who have achieved economic, social and political power through manipulations. They feel that any rise in social scale of the minority community will threaten their social domination. Thus, feelings of suspicion and hostility on the part of both the communities continuously prepare the growth of communalism. Particularly, it (communalism) makes a ready appeal to the urban poor and the rural unemployed whose number has grown rapidly as a result of lop-sided economic and social development and large-scale migration to cities. The social anger and frustration of these rootless and impoverished people often find expression in spontaneous violence whenever opportunity arises. A communal riot provides a good opportunity for this. But this economic analysis is not considered objective by many scholars.

Is religion responsible for communalism? There are intellectuals who do not believe that religion has any role to play in it. Bipan Chandra (1994), for example, holds that communalism is neither inspired by religion nor is religion an object of communal politics, even though the communalist bases his politics on religious differences, uses religious identity as an organizing principle, and in the mass phases of communalism uses religion to mobilize masses. The religious difference is used to 'mask' non-religious social needs, aspirations and conflicts. However, religiosity, i.e. 'too much religion in one's life' or the intrusion of religion in to areas other than those of personal belief, tends to create a certain receptivity to communal ideology and politics. Moreover, religious obscurantism, narrow-mindedness and bigotry in the name of going back to fundamentals tends to divide people whom life and history have brought together. In this respect, different religions have different elements in their structure, rituals and ideological practices which relate to communalism in different manners. Their analysis and elimination has to be specific to different religions.

Some scholars have proposed a multiple-factor approach in which they give importance to several factors together. Ten major factors have been identified in the etiology of communalism (Surolia, 1987: 62): These are: social, religious, political, economic, legal, psychological, administrative, historical, local, and international. The *social* factors include social traditions, caste and class ego, inequality and religion-based social stratification; the *religious* factors include decline in religious norms and secular values, narrow and dogmatic religious values, use of religion for political gains and communal ideology of religious leaders; the *political* factors include religion-based politics, religion-dominated political organizations, canvassing in elections based on religious considerations, political interference, instigation or support to agitations by politicians for vested interests, political justification of communal violence and failure of political leadership; the *economic* factors include economic exploitation and discrimination of minority religious communities, lop-sided economic development, competitive market, non-expanding economy, displacement and non-absorption of workers and the influence of gulf money in provoking religious conflicts; the *legal* factors include absence of common civil code, special provisions and concessions for some communities in the Constitution, the special status of certain states, reservation policy, and special laws for different communities; the *psychological* factors include social prejudices, stereotyped attitudes, distrust, hostility and apathy against another community, rumour, fear psychosis and the misinformation/misinterpretation/misrepresentation by mass media; the *administrative* factors include lack of coordination between the police and other administrative units, ill-equipped and ill-trained police personnel, inept functioning of intelligence agencies, biased policemen, and police excesses and inaction; the *historical* factors include alien invasions, damage to religious institutions, proselytization efforts, divide and rule policy of colonial rulers, partition trauma, past communal riots, old disputes on land, temples and mosques; the *local* factors include religious processions, slogan raising, rumours, land disputes, local anti-social elements and group rivalries; and the *international* factors include training and financial support from other countries, other countries' mechanizations to disunite and weaken India and then support to communal organizations.

Against these approaches, we need a holistic approach to understand the problem of communalism and communal violence. The emphasis of this approach would be on various factors distinguishing the major from the minor. Like Cyril Burt (1944), we can classify these factors in four sub-groups: most conspicuous, chief cooperating, minor aggravating, and apparently inoperative. Specifically, these factors are communal politics and politicians' support to religious fanatics, prejudices (which lead to discrimination, avoidance, physical attack and extermination), the growth of communal organizations, and conversions and proselytizations. Broadly speaking, attention may be focussed on fanatics, anti-social elements and vested economic interests in creating and fanning violence in the rival communities.

My own thesis is that 'communal violence is instigated by religious fanatics, initiated by anti-social elements, supported by political activists, financed by vested interests and spread by the callousness of the police and the administrators'. While these factors directly cause communal violence, the factor which aids in spreading violence is the ecological layout of a particular city which enables rioters to escape unapprehended. The case studies of Baroda and Ahmedabad communal riots in Gujarat in Western India; Meerut, Aligarh and Moradabad riots in Uttar Pradesh; Jamshedpur in West Bengal; Srinagar in Kashmir in North India; Hyderabad and Kerala riots in South India; and Assam riots in East India vindicate my thesis.

In the holistic approach on communal violence, a few factors need explanation. One is the illogical feeling of discrimination among the Muslims. Muslims comprise 13.40 per cent (138 million) of the total population in the country. According to a survey conducted by the minority ministry of the Government of India, the proportion of Muslims in government services is just 2.5 per cent (*The Free Press Journal,* 14 August 2013). They, thus, feel discriminated against. The fact is that the number of Muslims who compete for these jobs is very low. All said, these excuses hardly accord any validity to the accusations of religious discrimination and nepotism. The feeling of discrimination among Muslims is ludicrous and irrational.

The mass media also sometimes contribute to communal tensions in their own way. Many a time the news items published in papers are based on hearsay, rumours or wrong interpretations. Such news items add fuel to the fire and fan communal feelings. This is what happened in Ahmedabad in the 1969 riots when '*Sevak*' reported that several Hindu women were stripped and raped by Muslims. Although this report was contradicted the next day, the damage had been done. It aroused the feelings of Hindus and created a communal riot.

Muslim Personal Law

One of the issues which has been agitating both Muslims and Hindus in recent years is the Muslim Personal Law. With the decision of the Supreme Court in favour of Shah Bano, and its advice in April 1995 to the government that it should enact a uniform civil code, the Muslims fear that their personal law is being interfered with. The politicians also exploit the situation to keep themselves in power.

Triple Talaq

Triple Talaq is a form of Islamic divorce practiced by Muslim men that allows husband to instantly divorce his wife by stating 'Talaq' thrice continuously in oral, written or electronic form. The Muslim Personal Law (Shariat) Application Act of 1937 had legalised and allowed the practice of Triple Talaq which gave a Muslim husband special privileges over his wife.

In April 1978, a 62 year-old Muslim woman (Shah Bano) filed a petition in court demanding alimony or maintenance from her divorced husband

Mohammed Ahmad Khan, a renowned lawyer from Indore. The Supreme Court (SC) granted Shah Bano the right to alimony from her husband. In August 2017, the SC declared that the Triple Talaq was unconstitutional.

The Muslim Women (Protection of Rights on Marriage) Act, 2019 makes the practice of Triple Talaq a cognizable offence resulting in imprisonment with a maximum jail term of upto three years and a fine.

Arguments in Favour

1. The practice of Triple Talaq is neither mentioned in the Quran nor as per Sharia law.
2. Triple Talaq is banned in more than twenty Islamic countries.
3. It empowers Muslim women and strengthen gender justice.
4. This law has been placed as a deterrent to this social evil.

Arguments Against

1. Divorce is a civil matter and making Triple Talaq a criminal offence is disproportionate to criminal jurisprudence.
2. Since marriage is a civil contract, the procedure should also be of civil nature.
3. Criminal law must be applicable for all communities.
4. Though the arrested person can apply for bail, it will be granted only after a magistrate has heard the aggrieved woman.
5. The Act allows the relatives of woman to file complaints in terms of women rights. The law is arbitrary and it may be used to harass Muslim men.
6. According to law, jailed husband is responsible for providing subsistence allowance to wife and children. How can a jailed husband provide it?

For the government, it was not about religion but about 'justice to women', while for opponents why only Muslim men should be punished when desertion by a husband is rampant in all religions.

Politicians charge the social atmosphere with communal passion by their inflammatory speeches, writings and propaganda. They plant the seeds of distrust in the minds of the Muslims while the Hindus are convinced that they are unjustly coerced into making extraordinary concessions to the Muslims in the economic, social and cultural fields. They also exploit the deep religious traditions of both the communities and highlight the differences in their respective practices and rituals.

Features of Communal Riots

A probe of the major communal riots in the country in the last five decades has revealed that: (a) Communal riots are more politically motivated than fuelled by religion. Even the Madan Commission which looked into communal disturbances in Maharashtra in May 1970 had emphasized that 'the architects and builders of communal tensions are the communalists and a certain class of politicians – those all-India and local leaders out to seize every opportunity to strengthen their political positions, enhance their prestige and enrich their public image by giving a communal colour to every incident and thereby projecting themselves in the public eye as the champions of the religion and the rights of their community'. (b) Besides political interests, economic interests too play a vigorous part in fermenting communal clashes. (c) Communal riots seem to be more common in North India than in South and East India. (d) The probability of recurrence of communal riots in a town where communal riots have already taken place once or twice is stronger than in a town in which riots have never occurred. (e) Most communal riots take place on the occasion of religious festivals. (f) The use of deadly weapons in the riots is on the ascendancy.

Incidents of Communal Riots in India

All these riots point out the weakening of the communal amity in almost every corner of the country. But, the anti-Sikh riots of 1984 in Delhi following the assassination of the then Prime Minister Indira Gandhi by her two Sikh bodyguards and the Gujarat riots of 2002 after the Godhara incident marked the extent of communal hatred. In both the riots hundreds of innocent people were killed and property worth crores of rupees was destroyed.

Infamous Communal Violence in India

Partition of India, 1947

After partition, millions of people were forced to move from both sides of the border. Hindus in Pakistan and Muslims in India were killed in masses, women were raped, and many children lost their parents. There was hatred everywhere, violence did not result in anything except bloodshed. Later, it turned in the problem of refugees and their rehabilitation, and became one of the biggest challenges for independent India.

Anti-Sikh Riots, 1984

This is one of the bloodsheds in India, where Sikhs in large number were massacred by anti-Sikh mob. This massacre took place in response to the assassination of the then Prime Minister Indira Gandhi by her own Sikh bodyguards in response to her actions authorizing the military operation.

Ethnic Cleansing of Kashmiri Hindu Pandits in 1989

Kashmir is known as the heaven of India and was known for its *Kashmiryat*, i.e. the reflection of love, peace, and harmony through brotherhood and unity of Hindu, Muslims and other communities living together. But, the brotherhood saw a serious blow due to Extremist Islamic terrorism in the Kashmir valley, which led to the mass killing and large-scale exodus of Kashmiri Pandits from the valley to the various regions and corners of India, giving them the status of refugee in their own country. Since then, the valley is under the grip of communal violence and the ongoing unrest has become a problem for the development of the people.

Babri Masjid Demolition in Ayodhya, 1992

According to Hindu mythology, Ayodhya is the birthplace of Lord Rama and therefore, it is a sacred place for Hindu religion. But in medieval period Mughal general Mir Baqi built a mosque, named after Mughal ruler Babur. There were disputes since then and riots also took place. But in 1990, due to some political mobilization, there was an atmosphere of protest and in large-scale *car sevak* visited Ayodhya from all parts of India, in support of demolishing Babri Masjid and building Ram temple there. These movements caused a huge amount of bloodshed and since then it is a disputed matter. After this, violence was followed by the Godhra incident in 2002, when *car sevak* returning from Ayodhya in a Sabarmati Express were killed by fire in the coaches of the train. This act was followed by the extended communal violence in Gujarat. That violence is like a black spot in the history of Gujarat and nation too, as people were killed without any mercy. Hindu and Muslim community became an antagonist to each other.

Assam Communal Violence, 2012

Northeastern states are known for their distinguished tribal population and ethnic diversity. Large-scale Bangladeshi immigration has changed the demography of Northeastern states, which often becomes a reason for clashes. In 2012, there were ethnic clashes between Bodos (Tribal, Christian and Hindu faith) and Muslims. Ethnic tensions between Bodos and Bengali-speaking Muslims escalated into a riot in Kokrajhar in July 2012, when unidentified miscreants killed four Bodo youths at Joypur.

Muzaffarnagar Violence, 2013

The cause of this ethnic clash between Jat and Muslim community is very much disputed and has many versions. According to a few, it was started after some suspicious post on a social media platform, Facebook. According to some, it was escalated after the eve teasing case in Shamli. Let the reasons be unknown, but what matters is, the nature and scale of loss to the country with respect to human resource and peace.

Delhi Riots, 2020

Riots are like nucleus events in India's politics. Large parts of the north-east Delhi witnessed widespread violence that started clashes between the supporters and groups protesting against Citizenship Amendment Act. It later turned into full-blown communal riots on 24–26 February 2020, which resulted in burnt streets and scurred landscape, littered with stones, bricks and shattered glasses all over.

The trail of damage included mosques, schools, shops, showrooms, vehicles, commercial buildings and residences. These properties had borne the brunt of arson, vandalism and ransacking by armed mobs. The victims were both Hindus and Muslims. At least 123 houses, 322 shops and over 1,000 vehicles, most of them motorcycles and auto-rikshaws, were gutted or completely damaged. Moreover, four mosques, three factories and two schools were brunt during the violence and at least 53 people died, while 400 sustained grievous injuries. Over 350 empty cartridges were recovered after over 500 rounds of gunfire during the three days of rioting. The government appointed a retired High Court judge to assess the damage caused to the public and private property during the riots. The report submitted to Delhi High Court would determine recovery of damage amount after hearing the parties concerned.

The perpetrators of violence generally belonged to margins of their communities and rarely maintained their religion's commitment and hardly displayed any guilt or shame for their action. Heavy use of unlicensed country-made pistols appeared to be a departure from convention when it comes to communal riots in the country, in which most victims have succumbed to blast force trauma or burnt to death.

Perhaps the erroneous judgments, inadequate deployment and absence of swift decisions on the part of police has led to the riots spreading out of control. One thing that must not be denied to the Delhi riots victims is speedy justice system that in the case of justice has been allowed to slide in so many instances, whether it is Mumbai riots of 1983, the Sikh riots of 1984, the Gujarat riots of 2002, and several others.

Similar to above there are many more incidents which have impacted the common masses and killed people on large scale. Be it large scale terrorist attacks or hundreds of other riots, one thing is common that the majority of victims had nothing to do with communal hatred. In short, perpetrators of violence and victims of violence are different persons.

The main reasons for the involvement of external elements or their role in riots are as follows:

1. To create an atmosphere of instability, so that it becomes socially weak;
2. To hope for gaining sympathy from minorities;
3. To try to weaken the economic structure of a foreign country; and
4. The aim to conceal their own incompetence.

The above communal violence once again reminds us of the urgent and dire need for a law against communal and targeted violence not only against the minorities but also the majority.

Consequences of Communalism

1. A sudden increase in violence against any particular community causes mass exodus and stampede which in turn kills any number of people. With killings in mass, the real sufferers are the poor who lose their house, their family members, their lives, their livelihood, etc.
2. It violates the human rights from all direction. Sometimes children will lose their parents and will become orphans for a lifetime and nobody will be there to look after them.
3. The refugee problem is the other dimension of communalism induced violence, whether its inter-country or intra-country. For example, this was seen in the case of Bangalore in 2012, with respect to people from northeastern states, which was stimulated by a rumour.
4. Apart from having the effect on the society, it is also a threat to Indian constitutional values, which promotes secularism and religious tolerance. In that case, citizens do not fulfil their fundamental duties towards the nation. It becomes a threat to the unity and integrity of the nation as a whole. It promotes only the feeling of hatred in all directions, dividing the society into communal lines.
5. Other than these, minorities are viewed with suspicion by all, including state authorities like police, paramilitary forces, army, intelligence agencies, etc. There have been many instances when people from such community have been harassed and detained and finally, have been released by court orders guilt free. For this, there is no provision of compensation for such victims, about their livelihood incomes forgone, against social stigmas and the emotional trauma of the families.
6. Such things are set back for the society and become a barrier to its development. This is also one of the reasons which is keeping India still under the status of 'developing nation' because such activities occurring frequently do harm the human resource and economy of the country. And then again it takes years for the people and the affected regions to come out of the traumas of such violence, having a deep impact on the minds of those who have faced it. For their whole life, they feel emotionally broken and insecure.
7. Communal violence threatens the secular fabric, unity, integrity and internal security of India and poses a problem of rehabilitation of victims of such violence.

Role of National Integration Council in Containing Communalism

A National Integration Council (NIC), a group of senior politicians and public figures, was established in June 1962, to deal with problems of regionalism and communalism. But this effort was not pursued in the wake of the Chinese aggression which created national solidarity. However, this was a short-lived phenomenon and communal violence erupted in a menacing form, with a vengeance as it were, in the sixties which led to the reconstruction of another NIC in 1968. This time, three committees were set up to deal with communalism, regionalism and educational problems. A Standing Committee was also set up. All these committees produced worthy recommendations focussing on guidelines, legislation and administrative action. In 1980, the second incarnation of the NIC appeared and it met in 1980 and again in 1984. This time also three sub-committees were set up but they too failed to do anything substantial. The next incarnation took place in 1986 which focussed on Punjab. The September 1986 meeting set up a sub-group of five persons to suggest action for the defence of the interests of the minorities and to foster national integration and communal harmony. The report of this group was adopted by the Council which however did not meet for the next three years. In February 1990 came yet another incarnation of the NIC which took up for its agenda the Punjab, Kashmir and Ayodhya issues. This time too, three committees were set up but it was later boycotted by members of the BJP. In November 1991 came the next reincarnation and only Ayodhya issue was discussed in its meeting. A second meeting was called on 31 December 1991 in which the focus was shifted to Jammu & Kashmir and Punjab. After this, a meeting of the NIC was held on 18 July 1993 but no solution has been evolved till date on the burning problem of national integration and creating communal harmony.

Role of the Police

The role of the police in communal violence is to arrest trouble shooters, disperse rioters congregated at one place, protect public property from loot and arson, prevent the spreading of rumours (which instigate people of different communities in other districts and states), and maintain public order. The police cannot perform the role of enforcing law and order without the active cooperation of politicians, bureaucrats, judiciary and the people at large. It is seen that, by and large, the bureaucrats in our country are ritualists, politicians function on the basis of vested interests, judicial officials are traditionalists, and people have no confidence in the police. The police have, thus, to face many constraints in playing the roles expected of them. Controlling riots and preventing communal violence by police have, therefore, to be examined in the background of these constraints.

The prevention of communal violence requires a check on the symptoms of tension building and tension management in riot-prone areas. The police has to identify riot-prone structures in states, districts and cities where communal riots take place frequently and keep a watch on the various polarity-based clusters of population in the city layouts. Keeping a watch on individuals in different clusters and their militant tendencies and *modus operandi* is vital for the police to identify sensitive zones, common meeting places, targets of violence, insecure belts, hide-outs and shelter places at the time of rioting.

The police can no longer afford to allow communal issue to foster in the manner that it has. Adopting corrective measures like keeping the police department free from the politicians' control, strengthening the police intelligence section, restructuring the police force, gearing the police administration to be more sensitive, and reworking the training programme of police officials and enabling them to acquire a secular outlook and making them responsible for their failures could prove to be effective measures to tackle the problem of communal riots. An efficient police organization, enlightened policemen, well equipped and specially trained police wings are bound to yield positive results.

Prescriptive Measures to Meet Communalism/Communal Violence

The canker of communal confrontation is widespread in India. Many cities have been a communal powder keg these last several years. There are a good number of states where communalism has taken deep and seemingly permanent roots and communal politics is in full bloom. The support for communalists has certainly swelled in the last few decades. The number of districts affected by communal violence has grown. People with established criminal records are supporting leaders with communal philosophies and are using them as a shield to protect themselves from police action and as a crutch of respectability.

Measures to meet the challenge of communalism and communal violence can be of two types: long-term and short-term (Bipan Chandra, *Hindustan Times*, 15 August 1994). The long-term remedy lies: *First*, in initiating the process of de-communalizing the people at all levels, say, by bringing home to them that communal assumptions are false, by explaining to them the socio-economic and political roots of communalism, and by telling them that what the communalists project as problems are not the real problems and what they suggest as remedies are not the real remedies. *Second*, communalization of the state and of the political elite in power has to be checked because it leads to inaction against communal violence and covert or overt political and ideological support to communalism by the state apparatuses, including the media under state control. *Third*, the communalization of civil society also needs to be checked because it leads to more communal riots and other forms of communal violence. People with communal ideas and ideologies pressurize the government to act in a manner which is always against the principle of secularism. The secular state, the secular party in power and the secular power elite many a time succumb to the pressures of these communal people. It is here that intellectuals, political parties and voluntary organizations can be most effective. *Fourth*, the role of education, particularly emphasizing on value oriented education both in schools and colleges/universities, is important in preventing communal feelings. *Fifth*, the media can also prove to be significant in preventing communal feelings. Communal press can be banned and legal action can be taken against communal writers. *Sixth*, the ideology that economic development, industrialization, growth of capitalism and the growth of the working class would automatically weaken and ultimately eliminate communalism should not be overplayed. This economic reductionist approach of the left parties and organizations like naxalites only increases communal poison. It is not being suggested that modern economic development is not needed in our society. What is being pointed out is that economic development alone cannot contain communalism. It is not class struggles which eliminate communalism but communalism surely hampers class unity. Communal violence is more prevalent in developed states like Maharashtra, Punjab and Gujarat and in developed cities like Mumbai, Ahmedabad, Jamshedpur and Kanpur.

Some immediate measures are imperative for containing communalism and communal riots: *First*, peace committees can be set up in which individuals belonging to different religious communities can work together to spread goodwill and fellow-feelings and remove feelings of fear and hatred in the riot-affected areas. This will be effective not only in diffusing communal tensions but also in preventing riots from breaking out. *Second*, the state has to plan and use new strategies in dealing with communal violence. India's experience in recent years confirms the utility of this step. Whenever strong and secular administrators have used or threatened the use of strong steps, riots either did not occur or were of short duration. *Third*, the role of media is immensely heightened during the course of communal violence. Newspaper can pour oil over the troubled waters or extinguish raging fire. The fear and hatred can be checked if the press, radio and TV report the events in a way conducive to soothing the frayed nerves of people instead of inflaming the temper further. *Last*, the government in power has to treat the extremist communal outfits as its immediate targets and cripple their capacity to disrupt law and order. The Pandits in Kashmir, the innocent victims of communal riots in Mumbai, Uttar Pradesh, Gujarat and other states, and the sufferers of violence of extremists in Bihar, Assam, etc. look towards the secular state of India for the security of life and property.

If the surging tide of communalism is not reversed, it will swap the country. Before independence, it was easy to argue that communal violence was the result of the British policy of Divide and Rule. Now, the reality is more complex. Religion has come to be politicized and the politics has come to be criminalized. Unless all communities consider themselves a part of one nation, the containing of communal disharmony will remain difficult. A country that prides itself on the secular character of its policies has to be wary of politicians who speak only for their own religious community. It has to expose and alienate the bureaucrats who consider secularism only as a theoretical possibility.

The government has also to take measures for removing the feeling of discrimination and deprivation which do not actually exist. The Minorities Commission set up in 1978 and was recognized as a statutory body in May

1992 with a view to enhancing its effectiveness. The Commission is intended to safeguard the interests of the minorities whether based on religion or language. Its eight-point objectives are as follows:

1. Evaluating the working of various safeguards for the minorities in the Constitution and the laws passed by the union and state governments.
2. Recommending the most effective way to implement the laws pertaining to the minorities.
3. Looking into specific complaints.
4. Conducting studies and research on the question of avoidance of discrimination against minorities.
5. Reviewing union and state government policies towards minorities.
6. Suggesting appropriate legal and welfare measures to be undertaken by the union and state governments.
7. Submitting reports (on minorities) to the government from time to time.
8. Serving as a national clearing house for information in respect of the conditions of the minorities.

Its status was such that nobody took the Commission seriously because both the Centre and the state governments were not bound to follow its suggestions. Over the years, the Commission's annual reports on the plight of the minorities gathered dust. But the statutory status will now change the position. Its role will not only be investigative but also a judicial one. It is expected that with more powers, the Commission would now become a truly effective tool in tackling the deteriorating communal situation in the country and ensuring the welfare of the religious minorities which comprised 20 per cent of the total population of the country.

Symbolic gestures will not suffice. It is necessary to look at the real problems of the religious minorities in terms of employment, literacy and getting them a fair share of representation in every field. Efforts are needed for the development of the minority communities and removing their mass illiteracy and unemployment. Public opinion and mass enlightenment have to be brought about to make secular values functional.

Along with these measures, other measures that should be undertaken by the government to contain communal violence are: (a) Posting of secular-minded district and police officials in riot-prone areas. (b) Setting up of special courts to try communal offences. (c) Providing immediate relief and adequate financial assistance to victims of communal riots for their rehabilitation. (d) Taking severe action against all those who incite communal tensions or take part in violence. Thus, multipronged measures are needed to contain the communal tensions and bring about communal harmony in the country. We have not only to fight religious communalism but have also to contain political communalism which is more degrading and dangerous.

Social scientists and intellectuals have to evince serious interest in controlling the national malaise of communalism and in related issues like religious violence, separatism, secessionism, and terrorism.

Suggestions for the Eradication of Communalism

The following measures may be taken for the eradication of communalism:

1. *Abolition of communal parties*: All the political parties which thrive on religious loyalties should be banned or abolished by the government. Even non-political cultural organizations should always be kept under constant vigil so that they cannot preach communalism.
2. *Transmission of the past heritage*: Feelings of nationalism should be inculcated in the minds of people by reminding them about the glorious moments in history when Hindus, Muslims and Sikhs were combined to safeguard the interest of the country.
3. *Public opinion*: Efforts should be made through mass media for changing the attitude of people towards other communities. People must be aware of the evils of the communalism. Attention should be given for equal development of both the communities.
4. *Inter-religious marriage*: Youth organizations and other types of associations should be formed in every locality to give the opportunity to people of different communities to come closer and know each other. This may help them to practice inter-religious marriages which will lessen the social distance among the members of different religious groups.

The Constitution of India via its Article 355 says that it shall be the duty of the Union to protect every state against external aggression and internal disturbance and to ensure that the government of every state is carried on in accordance with the provisions of Constitution. But this constitutional provision by itself has not been able to check the sporadic events of communal violence in various parts of India.

Both the government and people should make efforts for eradication of communal tension and conflict.

SECULARISM

The word 'secularism' was coined by George Jacob Holyouke in the middle of the nineteenth century based on the latin word 'seculum'. The word 'secular' refers to things which are not religious or spiritual. The concept of 'secular' in fact was first used in Europe where the church had complete control over all types of properties and nobody could use property without the consent of the church. Some intellectuals raised their voice against this practice. These people came to be known as 'secular' which meant 'separate from church' or 'against church'. In India, this term was used in a different context after independence. After the partition of the country, the politicians wanted to assure the minority communities, particularly the Muslims, that they would not be discriminated against in any way. Hence, the new Constitution provided that India would remain 'secular' in the Constitution, which meant that: (a) each citizen would be guaranteed full freedom to practise and preach his religion, (b) state will have no religion, and (c) all citizens, irrespective of their religious faith, will be equal. In this way, even the agnostics were given the same rights as believers. This indicates that a secular state or society is not an irreligious society. Religions exist, their followers continue to believe in and practise the religious principles enshrined in their holy books, and no outside agency, including the state, interferes in the legitimate religious affairs. In other words, two important ingredients of a secular society are: (a) complete separation of state and religion, and (b) full liberty for the followers of all religions as well as atheists and agnostics to follow their respective faiths. In a secular society, the leaders and followers of various religious communities are expected not to use their religion for political purposes.

Secularism in India

India has been declared a secular state by its written Constitution and it is every Indian's duty to stand by and believe in this declaration. The concept of secularism plays an important role in India. Secularism in India is a positive, revolutionary and comprehensive concept which takes within its sweep all the communities in India following several religions. It is not negative in nature, it is not anti-God. Indian secularism recognizes the importance of religion in human life. Secularism refers to the official attitude of the state which is pledged to equal protection of all its citizens irrespective of religion, caste or creed and to equal distribution of all the facilities of life to them.

The most important component of secularism in India is to be found in Articles 14, 15(2) and 16(2). These Articles compel equality of all citizens before the law and entitle them to equal protection of the laws. Another facet of it was in Article 19(1) which granted freedom of speech and expression and Article 25 which preserved the total freedom of conscience and the right freely to profess, practice and propagate religion.

Indian secularism took on a distinct form as a result of an interaction between what already existed in a society that had religious diversity and the ideas that came from the west. It resulted in an equal focus on intra-religious and inter-religious domination. Indian secularism equally opposed the oppression of Dalits and women within Hinduism. It also opposes the discrimination against women within Islam or Christianity and the possible threats that a majority community might pose to the rights of the minority religious communities. Indian secularism deals not only with the religious freedom of individuals but also with the religious freedom of minority communities, i.e. an individual has the right to profess the religion of his/her choice. Likewise, religious minority also have a right to exist and to maintain their own cultural and educational institutions.

Importance of Secularism in India

Secularism and democracy are two remarkable achievements of independent India. These two achievements have stood the test of time and set the goal of the nation on religious and political fronts. The state, remaining free from religious obligations, can take a tolerant attitude towards every religion and can pursue the idea of achieving the well-being of the people, irrespective of caste, creed, religion, etc. The concept of secularism has a firm root in India. The whole world recognizes this fact.

Comparison between Secular and Communal

	Secular	*Communal*
Definition	It is philosophy which forms its ethics without any religious influence.	It is a principle of living together and sharing.
Promotion	It promotes development of human arts and science.	It promotes the principle of common sharing.
Beliefs	It does not consider religious beliefs.	It considers religion as a part.
Dependence	It is independent of religion.	It can be dependent on religion.
Living	It practices individual living.	It practices community living.

Citizenship Amendment Act (CAA), 2019

The CAA amends Citizenship Act, 1955 to facilitate Indian Citizenship to non-Muslim immigrants Hindus, Christians, Buddhists, Sikhs, Parsis and Jains facing 'persecution' in Pakistan, Bangladesh and Afghanistan, who entered in the country on or before 31 December 2014. CAA also relaxes provisions for citizenship by naturalization – immigrants can become Indian Citizens after residing in the country for six years instead of eleven years.

In Chapter 2 of the Constitution, Article 5 and Article 11 specify that there are two bases for citizenship – geographical and one relating to blood. The Citizenship Act added two additional bases – registration and naturalization. The 1955 Act has been amended in 1957, 1960, 1985, 1986, 1992, 2003, 2005 and 2015 without causing much furore. The issue with the current Act is that it is unconstitutional on the ground that in a secular nation, religion cannot be the basis of citizenship whether territorial or extra-territorial. It is also a violation of Article 14 of the Constitution which guarantees the right to equality.

Features

1. The Citizenship Amendment Act, 2019 aims to make changes in the Citizenship Act, the Passport Act and the Foreigners Act and will grant the illegal non-Muslims migrants from three countries, the status of legal migrants.
2. The Act does not apply to the tribal areas of Tripura, Mizoram, Assam and Meghalaya because they are included in the Sixth Schedule of the Constitution.

3. The states and areas under the Inner Line Permit (ILP) system have also been excluded. The ILP is a special mandatory for citizens from other parts of India to enter Arunachal Pradesh, Mizoram and Nagaland.

Arguments in Favour of CAA

1. It is against the infiltrators.
2. Citizenship Amendment Act, 2019 is a way of correcting historical mistake that was done during India's partition.
3. The Act only extends citizenship, but does not take away anyone's citizenship. The Act (CAA) just expedites acquiring citizenship to prosecuted minorities. It does not change the basic structure of the Constitution.
4. Most of the opposition to CAA is crassly political and ignorance of a large section of society.
5. CAA only gives priority to most persecuted amongst the lot, seeking refuge in India.
6. Muslims in India do not have to worry as this Act concern only migrants.

Arguments Against CAA

1. This Act is against the spirit and values of Constitution.
2. This law is violative of the basic principles of the Constitution, which never put religion as a criteria for obtaining Indian Citizenship.
3. Religion as an instrument of determining citizenship was rejected by the constituent assembly.
4. The Act points out the demography and linguistic uniqueness of North-eastern states.
5. Citizenship can not be determined or linked to religion.
6. CAA is discriminatory against Muslims. Religion cannot be the basis of discrimination. It puts the Muslim Community under a glare of mistrust and alienation. The cut off date (31 December 2014) is arbitrary.
7. There is no clarity in the Act on which criteria is to be applied on determining the scale of persecution.
8. CAA is ambitious, unnecessary, deceptive and unconstitutional.

Protests and demonstrations against the CAA first erupted in the Northeast and then spread across the country. People of all communities are involved in the protests. General opinion was that the implication of the CAA has not been fully thought through. It is a bundle that undermines Indian ethos, values, citizen rights, foreign relations and international image. However, the implementation of the CAA will be dependent upon the ruling of the Supreme Court. On the issue the Apex Court has an opportunity to pass a judgement that is pragmatic, constitutional and restore peace in society at large.

REGIONALISM

Regionalism is a strong attachment to one's own region. India is a country with wide diversity and plurality. No other country in the world had existed with a broad unity, peace and tolerance as India does. Despite this unity, there are sources of regional conflict. The factors that cause regionalism are as follows:

1. *Geographical factors*:
   (i) As a result of geographical differences, there is a huge variation in climate.
   (ii) These differences in climate cause changes in lifestyle and food habits.
   (iii) People living in forests depend on it for food, shelter and other needs. Thus they have a lifestyle that is significantly different from the rest of the population.
2. *Historical factors*: During the ancient phase of history, it was only during the time of Ashoka's rule, India became a single political entity. During medieval India, India was ruled by kings who belonged to various sections of Islam. It was only during Akbar's rule, India again became united. India again becomes politically united during the British rule. The British, however, due to their policy of divide and rule, encouraged the regional differences. This prevented the formation of a unified country.
3. *Linguistic factors*: India has 22 official languages that are recognized by the Constitution. There are 29 languages with more than 10 lakh native speakers. The mother tongue of a person creates a profound attachment to his own language and hence, the identity of belonging also develops. This linguistic unity has been a major factor in the formation of states during post-independent India. Residing and settling in any part of India is a fundamental right enshrined in the Constitution but linguistic differences create discomfort and confusion for taking up jobs and make a living.
4. *Religious factors*: Regionalism in India also has a religious dimension.
5. *Political factors*: India's politics and its political parties showcase the regionalism present in our country. They are broadly divided into:
   (i) National parties have a stronghold in many states. They work based on an all India agenda.
   (ii) Regional parties are mostly confined to a single state. They work based on the interest of the political aspirations of state leaders and remains a major source of regionalism. Many regions want political autonomy, ranging from complete secession to autonomy within the confines of Constitution.
6. *Economic factors*: Economic factors also contribute to the development of regionalism. These economic factors cause problems between regions. Regionalism against loss of economic opportunities and exploitation of resources by an outsider gives a feeling to the people of the particular region that others are benefitting whereas, they are losing.

7. *Cultural factors*: The culture of Indian population varies with respect to the region. When a citizen from other cultural group offends these traditions or shows cultural insensitivity, there arise the seeds of conflict.

Caste system: Caste system attributed differing social status to different sections of the population. It has also promoted regional aspirations.

Rituals and Festivals: Festivals of both religious and secular nature are numerous and vary according to the region.

Hinduism is followed by a majority of people in India. Even within Hinduism, festivals and rituals vary widely based on region. There are numerous tribal festivals that showcase the tribal way of life.

The Effects of Regionalism

Regionalism has both positive and negative effects on the nation, but negative effects are more.

1. On the positive side, it helps in strengthening the nation. Creation of new states has helped the nation as these have removed the fissures which would have continued to exist and may have become fatal.
2. It has brought imbalanced regional development and regional issues to focus and opportunity to solve them at the same time regionalism affects negatively as:
    (i) It hampers the economic growth. The instability created by it erodes the faith of investors.
    (ii) It created serious internal security challenges which can be exploited by forces not favourable to India.
    (iii) It affects the politics of the country, as regional demands become national demands. It has many times resulted in an extra burden on the exchequer in the form of grants, special packages, etc.

Solutions to Contain Regionalism

1. Political parties should try to avoid partisanship. They should aim at bringing a national unity besides all sectarian interests.
2. Economic development of our country must be uniform and measures must be taken to ensure it. The development of underdeveloped, backward regions and Naxal hit areas must become a priority to avoid discontent of people.
3. The role of National Integration council must be revamped to solve conflicting regional aspirations.
4. The existing mechanisms like zonal councils, interstate council, national development council, etc. can be strengthened.
5. Creating strong interdependence among states. Each state must see other as a partner in development. This will help in ensuring all-round development of the state.
6. New institutional structures like NITI Aayog can be utilized to find out the solutions to the problems of the state.

7. Uniform development of all regions should be taken up so that no region feels isolated and left behind.

Problems of people must be solved in a peaceful and constitutional manner. Politicians must not be allowed to misuse the issue of regional demands. India is a highly diverse pluralistic society and a federal state whose social dynamics in the last 70 years needs to be understood and analysed rationally. At the time of independence, it was a smaller nation both quantitatively and qualitatively. Since then, not only its population has increased from 340 million to about 1,210 million (in 2011) but economically, educationally, socially and politically too it has matured. The resurgence of regionalism in various parts of the country has emerged as such a serious problem that it literally threatens to divide the country. The creation of new states like Jharkhand, Uttaranchal (Uttarakhand) and Chhattisgarh is, in fact, the expression of territorial regionalism. Again, the demand for Bodoland, Vidarbha, Gorkhaland, etc. cannot be traced in the earnest desire of the people to have their regional identity, which results from regional imbalances. In fact, it is the natural desire of the people in a region or territory to make rapid social and economic development so that they may live happily. Besides, the local leadership is to be held equally responsible, which fails to reconcile with the aspirations of the people. Thus, the need of the hour is to develop a realistic perception of regionalism at the conceptual level focussing on righteousness and judicious outlook on the part of the political parties.

There have been arguments both for and against this regionalization and creation of states. One school finds nothing wrong in this regionalization (division of geographical territory with definite boundaries) because it fulfils democratic urges, facilitates political management, smoothens development, provides for greater access to and participation in the decision-making process, enhances local accountability and increases national unity. The other school describes regionalization as a process of balkanization of the country which divides people raising slogans like 'Maharashtra for Maharashtrians' or 'Assam for Assamese only', and creates agitations and violence. Some people are worried about the demand for greater autonomy for states like Jammu & Kashmir which may catalyse such demands for more autonomous regions. Each act of fragmentation is thus seen as encouraging further fragmentation. The questions is: Whether optimism of the first school logical or is the pessimism of the second school mistaken? It is true that at times feelings of regionalism and regionalization become so strong that states do not want to share even the river water (like Kaveri water by Karnataka and Tamil Nadu) or electricity (like Punjab and Delhi) with their neighbour states. States like Assam claim that in spite of their great contribution to national economic growth through oil and jute, they are totally neglected in development schemes, while states like Jammu & Kashmir hold that being a Muslim-dominated state, it is discriminated in industrial development schemes. While economic backwardness of certain regions is at the root of the unrest there (i.e. Gorkhaland in West Bengal, Bodoland in Assam), some demands for new states are purely politically motivated (like Harit Pradesh bifurcating Uttar Pradesh). With increasing social and political awareness among all levels of people, it is not difficult to mobilize masses for demanding a place in the sun. If people's protests are ignored, law and order problems are bound to escalate. Such problems cannot be suppressed for long or put down with a firm hand. It will compel people to take to violence. The gulf between 'them' and 'us' has to be bridged through accommodation and compromises. The growing population in many states will be difficult to manage. Uttar Pradesh, Madhya Pradesh, Bihar and Maharashtra are such states. While in 1947, there were 300 districts in the country, today there are about 700 districts. Several districts are or may even become larger in area and population than many members of the United Nations. Hence, the rationale of new smaller states need not necessarily be perceived as balkanization or growth of regionalism and regionalization. If number of states increase to 50 and number of districts increases to 800, administrative management may be more efficient, accountability may improve, and democratic participation may increase, provided of course the new states are economically viable. National integrity will not be imperiled only by creating new political or administrative units. Regionalization, if sensibly handled, will not disintegrate India. Ethnic sentiments and linguistic homogeneity, however, may not be desirable as considerations calling for the creation of new states. There is the severe resources crunch. There is also the problem created by militancy in certain parts of the country. Dangers, both internal and external, loom large. As such, the demand for new states has to be effectively scotched and conceded only after careful scrutiny of each case on the basis of economic development and administrative convenience.

References

Chandra, Bipan, *Communalism in Modern India*, Vikas, New Delhi, 1984.

——, *Ideology and Politics in Modern India*, Har Anand Publications, Delhi, 1994.

Das, Veena (ed.), *Mirrors of Violence: Communities, Riots and Survivors in South Asia*, Oxford University Press, Delhi, 1990.

Engineer, Asghar Ali (ed.), *Communal Riots in Post-independent India*, Sangam Books, Delhi, 1984.

Engineer, Asghar Ali, *Meerut Riots: Analysis, Compilation and Documentation*, Ajanta Publications, Delhi, 1988.

Frontline, Madras, 2–15 April 1988, pp. 99–104.

Ghosh, S.K., *Riots: Prevention and Control*, Eastern Law House, Calcutta, 1971.

Gopal, Servepalli (ed.), *Anatomy of a Confrontation*, Penguin Books, New Delhi, 1991.

Hasan, Mushirul, *Nationalism and Communal Politics in India*, Manohar Publications, New Delhi, 1991.

Hindustan Times, Delhi, 21 August 1986; 17 March 1988, 10 June 1996 and 8 December 2019.

Kapur, Rajiv A., *Sikh Separatism: The Politics of Faith*, Vikas Publishing House, Delhi, 1987.

Krishna, Gopal, 'Communal Violence in India: A Study of Communal Disturbance in Delhi', *Economic and Political Weekly*, Vol. XX, No. 2, 1985, pp. 61–74.

Naqvi, Saba and Koppikar, Smruti, 'Gujarat Riots: A Beast Asleep?', outlookindia.com e-magazine, 5 March 2012.

Oommen, T.K., *Hindustan Times*, Delhi, 8 August 1989.

Singh, V.V., *Communal Riots*, Rawat Publications, Jaipur, 1993.

Surolia, Shankar, *Indian Police: Issues and Perspectives*, Gaurav Publishers, Jaipur, 1987.

7

Backward Castes, Tribes and Classes

Some Important Statistics

According to a 2014 report to the Ministry of Minority Affairs, over 44.8 per cent of the scheduled tribe (ST) and 33.8 per cent of scheduled caste (SC) populations in rural India are living below the poverty line. Some Dalits achieved affluence, although most remain poor.

According to Socio-Economic and Caste Census 2011, nearly 79 per cent of rural *adivasi* households and 73 per cent of Dalit households are most deprived among rural households in India. While 45 per cent of scheduled caste households are landless and earn by manual casual labour for their living, the same is for 30 per cent of *adivasis*. Dalits contribute to about 25 per cent of India's population.

The amelioration of the lot of the underprivileged people in India, particularly of the tribes and those castes and classes which are given an inferior status due to the accident of birth, has to be an important aim of any government committed to democracy.

The Constitution of India prescribes protection and safeguards for the scheduled castes (SCs or Dalits) and scheduled tribes (STs). Initially in 1950 Constitution provided reservation of 12.5 per cent for the SCs and 5 per cent for the STs but these percentages were subsequently enhanced in 1970 to 15 per cent and 7.5 per cent for SCs and STs respectively. And now even for other backward classes (OBCs) with the object of removing their social disabilities and promoting their varied interests. The reservation was provided in jobs, admission to colleges and universities, and the central and state legislative assemblies. The main safeguards are: abolition of untouchability, protection from social injustice and various forms of exploitation, throwing open religious institutions of public character to all sections, removal of restrictions on access to shops, restaurants, wells, tanks, and roads, giving them the right to move freely and acquire property, giving them the right of admission to educational institutions and receiving grants out of state funds, permitting the state to make reservation for them in services, giving them special representation in the Lok Sabha and Vidhan Sabhas, setting up separate departments and advisory councils to promote their welfare and safeguard their interests.

Provisions in the Indian Constitution

For the welfare of the backward classes, scheduled castes and scheduled tribes also the Anglo-Indians, some special rights have been given by the Constitution. The Constitution also provides for the appointment of commission 'to investigate the conditions of the backward classes'.

First, three specific provisions in the Constitution of India ensure that persons belonging to such categories are in no way discriminated against. Not only that, care has been taken to see that special privileges created for their upliftment are not struck down as being discriminatory against others.

Provision in Regards with Rights of Scheduled Tribes

Maharashtra is the only state where they (Dalits, SCs and STs) are in good position as others (high caste people) are. It is the only state where people face less discrimination compared to other Dalits living in India. Dalits in the states like UP, Bihar, Tamil Nadu, Kerala are still being suppressed and not given the chance to rise. This is the reason why Dalits are still poor among all the communities even after more than 70 years of independence.

Article 13 forbids discrimination against any citizen on grounds of race, religion, caste, etc. but special provisions have been made by the state for the advancement of socially or educationally backward classes, i.e. the scheduled castes and scheduled tribes. In other words, special benefits to scheduled castes and scheduled tribes cannot be struck down by the courts as being volatile of the right to equality.

Article 15(4) on promotion of social, economic and educational interests: This article empowers the state to make any special provision for the advancement of socially and educationally backward classes of citizens or for the scheduled castes and scheduled tribes. This clause has been especially incorporated to prevent any special provision made by a state for the advancement of socially or educationally backward classes of citizens from being challenged in the courts of law on the ground of discrimination.

Article 16 of the Indian Constitution confers on citizens' equal right in matters of employment under the state. But the state is fully within its rights to make special provisions for the employment of persons belonging to scheduled castes and scheduled tribes.

Article 19 (5) on safeguard of tribal interests: While the rights of free movement and residence throughout the territory of India and of acquisition and disposition of property are guaranteed to every citizen, special restrictions may be imposed by the state for the protection of the interests of any scheduled tribe.

Article 23 human trafficking: Traffic in human beings, *begar* and other similar forms of forced labour are prohibited. This is a very significant provision as far as scheduled tribes are concerned.

Article 29 cultural and educational rights: According to this article, a cultural or linguistic minority has the right to conserve its language or culture. The state shall not impose upon it any culture other than the community's own culture. But this does not prevent the state from making special provisions for the admissions of students belonging to the backward classes, i.e. the scheduled castes and scheduled tribes.

Article 164 provides for a minister-in-charge of tribal welfare in the states of MP, Chhattisgarh, Odisha, and Jharkhand. These states have a substantial tribal population and special provision of a Minister looking after tribal welfare is an evidence of the concern of the framers of the Constitution for safeguarding the interests of scheduled tribes.

Reservation: Over and above these, the Constitution contains special provisions for reservation of some seats for the members of the scheduled castes and scheduled tribes both in the Lok Sabha and in the State Legislative Assemblies. Further, if the President is satisfied that the Anglo-Indian community is not adequately represented, in the house of people, he may nominate two members of that community to the Lok Sabha. The governor of a state has similar power to nominate one member of the Anglo-Indian community to the State Legislative Assembly.

Article 335 provides that consistent with the efficiency of the services, members of the scheduled castes and scheduled tribes shall be appointed in the services of the union and the state governments. Indeed seats are often kept reserved for such candidates.

The President is empowered to appoint a special officer to keep vigil over the interests of the scheduled castes and scheduled tribes. The central government has the power to issue directives to the states for the execution of schemes beneficial to the scheduled castes and scheduled tribes.

The Constitution of India further enjoins that the ministers of certain specific states must have a minister in charges of the welfare of the scheduled castes and scheduled tribes. Again, though every Indian may move freely and acquire property anywhere in India, restrictions may be imposed by the state to prevent alienation of tribal property. In a bid to abolish untouchability, Hindu religious establishments have been thrown open to all Hindus. Besides enjoying the rights that all citizens and minorities have, the member of the scheduled tribes have been provided with special safeguards as follows:

Protective Safeguards

1. Educational safeguards – Article 15(4) and 29.
2. Safeguards for employment – Articles 16(4), 320(4) and 333.

3. Economic safeguards – Article 19.
4. Abolition of bonded labour – Article 23.
5. Protection from social injustice and all forms of exploitation – Article 46.

Political Safeguards

1. Reservation of seats for ST in Lok Sabha and assemblies – Article 330, 332 and 164.
2. Appointment of a Minister in charge of tribal welfare.
3. Special provisions in respect of Nagaland, Assam and Manipur – Articles 371(a), 371(b) and 371.

Developmental Safeguards

1. Promoting educational and economic interests of the scheduled tribes – Articles 46.
2. Grants from central government to the states for the welfare of scheduled tribes and raising the level of administration of Scheduled Areas – Article 75.

The machinery for safeguarding the interests of SCs and STs was created in the form of setting up a Commission for Scheduled Castes and Scheduled Tribes. This was later on renamed as National Commission for Scheduled Castes and Scheduled Tribes and was given constitutional status on 12 March 1992.

At present, there exists two separate commissions for SCs and STs. It was later on brought to the notice of the government that not only geographically and culturally, the STs were different from the SCs but their problems were also different from those of the problems of the SCs. In recognition of this public perception, a new Ministry of Tribal Affairs was created in October 1999 to provide a sharp focus to the welfare and development of STs. It was felt necessary that the Ministry of Tribal Affairs should coordinate all activities relating to the STs, as it would not be administratively feasible for the Ministry of Social Justice & Empowerment to perform this role. It was also felt necessary that a separate National Commission for Scheduled Tribes (NCST) also be set up to safeguard the interests of STs more effectively by bifurcating the existing National Commission for the Scheduled Castes and Scheduled Tribes. The NCST is the outcome of this realization which was set up in February 2004 to monitor all matters relating to the welfare of STs.

For the welfare of SCs, the National Commission for Scheduled Castes (NCSC) is committed to the full implementation of various acts like the PCR Act, 1955 and SC and ST (POA) Act, 1989. It endeavours to ensure that the economic development schemes for SCs are implemented as per guidelines and every penny of the government is spent appropriately and exclusively for their benefit. It also endeavours to ensure that reservations are implemented at every level, strictly as per government rules and regulations. The important functions of the NCSC are:

1. To investigate and monitor all matters relating to the safeguards provided for the SCs under the Constitution of India or any other law in force or under any order of the government and to evaluate the working of such safeguards.
2. To inquire into specific complaints with respect to the deprivation of rights and safeguards of the SCs.
3. To participate and advise on the planning process of socio-economic development of the SCs and to evaluate the progress of their development under the Union and any State.
4. To present to the President, annually and at such other times as the Commission may deem fit, reports upon the working of those safeguards.
5. To make in such reports/recommendations as to the measures that should be taken by the Union or any State for the effective implementation of those safeguards and other measures for the protection, welfare and socio-economic development of the SCs.
6. To discharge such other functions in relation to the protection, welfare and development and advancement of the SCs as the President may, subject to the provisions of any law made by parliament, specify.

The functions of the NCST are almost the same as those of NCSC.

The state governments have separate departments to look after the welfare of SCs, STs and OBCs. Their administrative set-up, however, varies from state to state. A number of voluntary organizations also promote the welfare of Dalits and tribals.

Some of the important centrally sponsored schemes are: (a) coaching and training for various competitive examinations (IAS, IPS, etc.) in order to improve the representation of SCs and STs in various services, (b) providing post-matric scholarships to students for higher education, (c) launching vocational training in tribal areas and educational complexes in low literacy pockets for promotion of female literacy in tribal areas, (d) construction of hostels for providing residential facilities to SC and ST girls studying in schools, colleges and universities, (e) financial assistance to reputed social science research institutions for research in development and problems of SCs and STs, (f) providing textbooks to SC and ST students of medical/engineering courses, and (g) scholarships and passage grants for higher education abroad.

Besides the above measures to bring about their speedy development, the Constitution has also provided for adequate representation in the legislative organs at different levels as well as reservation in services and educational institutions. The reservation is 15 per cent for the SCs and 7.5 per cent for the STs. This limit has been exceeded in several states. For example, in the states in the north-east, the reservation for STs has reached the level of 85 per cent. There are moves in some states in the north-east to increase this percentage to 95. Other states like Tamil Nadu, Karnataka, Uttar Pradesh, and Bihar are not far behind in this regard.

Though the principle of separate electorate was not accepted but the constituencies are earmarked from time to time from which persons belonging only to either SCs or STs can seek election. The number of reserved seats reflects their proportion in the population.

In government services, special quotas are allotted to them. The reservations are not only confined to recruitments but they are also extended to promotions for higher positions. To facilitate their adequate representation, concessions such as relaxation of age limit, relaxation in the standards of suitability, relaxation of the qualification and experience, have also been provided to them.

SCHEDULED TRIBES

In Indian context, T.B. Naik (1960) raises the problem in proper perspective by talking about the criteria and indices of the tribal life specifically in the Indian setting. Naik goes on to present his own criteria for a tribe which is, 'a tribe to be a "tribe" should have the least functional interdependence within the community'. The Hindu caste system is an example of high interdependence. A tribe should to be economically backward, which means:

1. The full import of monetary economics should not be understood by its members.
2. Primitive means of exploiting natural resources should be used.
3. The tribe's economy should be at an underdeveloped stage.
4. It should have multifarious economic pursuits.
5. There should be a comparative geographic isolation of its people from others.
6. Culturally, members of a tribe should have a common dialect which may be subject to regional variations.
7. A tribe should be politically organized and its community panchayat should be an influential institution.
8. The tribe's members should have the least desire to change. They should have a sort of psychological conservatism making them stick to their age-old customs.
9. A tribe should have customary laws and its members might have to suffer in a law court because of these laws.

Naik further elaborates that a community to be a 'tribe' must have all these attributes.

The principal criteria for specifying communities as the scheduled tribes include: (a) relative geographical isolation (b) distinctive culture (c) traditional occupation of a definite geographical area (d) 'primitive traits' depicting occupational pattern, economy, etc. (e) relatively lower level of techno-economic development.

The term 'scheduled tribes' first appeared in the Constitution of India. Article 366 (25) defined scheduled tribes as 'such tribes or tribal communities or parts of or groups within such tribes or tribal communities as are deemed under Article 342 to be scheduled tribes for the purposes of this Constitution'.

A Tribe is a group of distinct people, dependent on their land for their livelihood, who are largely self-sufficient and not integrated into the national society. The reason why they are called 'scheduled' is that they are included in one of the Schedules of the Constitution of India. Our Constitution has 12 Schedules. According to Hindu mythology, this is the fifth category in the varna system. The scheduled tribe's people are generally called as *adivasi* in the pre-independence records, official gazetteers, and texts. *Adivasis* being referred to as aboriginals. The *adivasi* or indigenous people have been exploited, and continue to be exploited to the maximum in all respects.

The essential characteristics of these communities are:

1. Distinguishable historical background
2. Geographical isolation
3. Ancestral traits and customary laws
4. Kinship as an instrument of social bonds
5. The absence of strong, complex, formal organization
6. Economically backward
7. A lack of hierarchy among men and groups
8. The communitarian basis of landholding
9. Segmentary character
10. Little value on surplus accumulation on the use of capital and on market trading
11. Lack of distinction between form and substance of religion
12. A distinct psychological bent for enjoying life

Some of the important features of the tribals are: most of them live in isolated terrains; the main sources of their livelihood are agriculture and gathering of forest produce; they do not cultivate for profit; they still largely rely on barter system; they spend a greater part of their earnings on social and religious ceremonies; and a large number of them are illiterate and are victimized by unscrupulous forest contractors and moneylenders.

Tribal communities live in various ecological and geo-climatic conditions ranging from plains and forests to hills and inaccessible areas. Tribal groups are at different stages of social, economic and educational development.

Tribal Territories of India

Tribals in India live in the following five territories:

1. *The Himalayan Belt*: Assam, Meghalaya, Arunachal Pradesh, Nagaland, Manipur, Mizoram, Tripura, hills of Uttar Pradesh and Himachal Pradesh.
2. *Central India*: Bihar, West Bengal, Orissa, and Madhya Pradesh. Fifty-five per cent of the total tribal population of India lives in this belt.

3. *Western India*: Rajasthan, Maharashtra, Gujarat, Goa, Dadra and Nagar Haveli.
4. *The Dravidian Region*: Karnataka, Andhra Pradesh, Kerala and Tamil Nadu.
5. Andaman, Nicobar and Lakshadweep islands.

The scheduled tribes are notified in 30 States/UTs and the number of individual ethnic groups notified as scheduled tribes is 705. The tribal population of the country, as per 2011 Census, is 10.43 crore, constituting 8.6 per cent of the total population. Out of which, 89.97 per cent of them live in rural areas and 10.03 per cent in urban areas. The decadal population growth of the tribal's from Census 2001 to 2011 has been 23.66 per cent against 17.69 per cent of the entire population. The sex ratio for the overall population is 940 females per 1,000 males and that of scheduled tribes 990 females per thousand males. According to 2011 Census of India, *Bhil* is the most popular tribe with a total population of 4,618,068 constituting 37.7 per cent of the total ST population. *Gond* is the second-largest tribe, with a population of 4,357, constituting of 35.6 per cent. Madhya Pradesh has more than 1.6 crore ST population (21% of the state population.).

The scheduled tribes are more unevenly divided across states than the remaining social groups. These groups had been very poor at independence and happened to be outside the mainstream of the economy, states with high proportions of ST population may be at a disadvantage in combatting poverty. From this perspective, the four southern states enjoy a clear advantage: Kerala and Tamil Nadu have virtually no tribal populations while Andhra Pradesh and Karnataka have proportionately smaller tribal populations (5% and 9% of the total, respectively) than some of the northern states which had high concentrations. Among the large states, Madhya Pradesh, Gujarat, and Rajasthan have proportionately the largest concentrations of ST populations. The ST constitute 21 per cent, 17 per cent, and 14 per cent of their respective populations. Some of the medium-size states, of course, have proportionately even larger concentrations. These include Chhattisgarh, Jharkhand, and Orissa with the ST forming 30 per cent, 29 per cent, and 22 per cent of their populations, respectively.

Exploitation and Unrest

For ages, tribals were considered a primitive segment of Indian society. They lived in forests and hills without having more than a casual contact with the so-called civilized and advanced neighbours. There being no population pressures, there was no attempt to penetrate their areas and impose alien values and beliefs on the tribals. But, when the British consolidated their position in the country, their colonial aspirations and administrative needs necessitated to 'open up' the entire country through an effective communication system. The British introduced the system of land ownership and revenue. Annual tax was trebled which was beyond the paying capacity of tribal cultivators. Under the increasing pressure of population, many outsiders also started settling in tribal regions. With their money power, they offered credit facilities at the doorstep. Initially, it provided relief to tribals but gradually the system became exploitative. Newly established courts of law helped the exploiters. This economic, and later social and cultural exploitation aroused the tribal leaders to mobilize the tribals and start agitations. With the increasing feelings of deprivation, mass agitations, struggles and movements also increased. Initially, they were against the blood suckers and usurpers of their rights but ultimately they turned against the government or the rulers.

Tribal unrest and discontent, thus, may be described as the cumulative result of a number of contributory factors. The main factors were:

1. Lethargy, indifference, and lack of sympathy from administrators and bureaucrats in dealing with tribal grievances.
2. Harshness of forest laws and regulations.
3. Lack of legislation to prevent the passing of tribal lands into the hands of non-tribals.
4. Lack of credit facilities.
5. Ineffective government measures to rehabilitate tribal population.
6. Lack of interest and dynamism among the political elite to solve tribal problems.
7. Delay in the implementation of recommendations made by high level bodies.
8. Discrimination in implementation of reformatory measures.

In short, the causes of tribal unrest may be described as economic, social and political.

National Committee Report on Tribal People

The High-Level Committee on Socio-Economic, Health and Educational Status of Tribal Communities of India, submitted its report to the Government of India in 2014. This is one of the most exhaustive reports on tribal societies in India, providing well-analysed data on the different indices of their social and cultural life. Followed by a set of recommendations that the state and the institutions of civil society may judge. An important point, the report makes, is that the state has paid a lot of attention to issues of development in tribal areas without caring for protecting them from the elements which have been exploiting them.

Problems of Tribal Communities

Land Alienation

The expansion of the railway in India, heavily devastated the forest resources. The government started reserving teak, sal and deodar forests for the manufacture of railway sleepers. Forest land and its resources provide the best means of livelihood for the tribal people and many tribes including the women engage in agriculture, food gathering and hunting. They are heavily dependent on the products of the forest. Therefore, when outsiders exploit the tribe's land and its resources, the natural life cycle of tribal ecology and tribal life is greatly disturbed.

Poverty and Indebtedness

Most of the occupation falls into the primary occupations such as hunting, gathering, and agriculture. The technology they use for these purposes belong to the most primitive kind. Hence their per capita income is very meagre, much lesser than the Indian average. Most of them live in abject poverty and are in debt. In order to repay, they often mortgage or sell their land. Indebtedness is almost inevitable since heavy interest is to be paid to these moneylenders.

Health and Nutrition

Because of the economic backwardness and insecure livelihood, the tribals face health problems, such as the prevalence of diseases like malaria, cholera, tuberculosis, diarrhoea and jaundice, problems associated with malnutrition like iron deficiency and anaemia, high infant mortality rates, low levels of life expectancy, etc. In many parts of India, tribal population suffers from chronic infections and diseases out of which water-borne diseases are life-threatening. They suffer from goitre due to lack of iodine. Malnutrition is common and has affected the general health of the tribal children as it lowers the ability to resist infection, and leads to chronic illness.

Education

Formal education has made a very little impact on tribal groups, as it is not considered necessary to discharge their social obligations. Superstitions and myths play an important role in rejecting education. Most of the tribes are located in the interior and remote areas. It is not easy for them to send their children to schools although it cannot be denied that education can act as the instrument for the betterment of the tribals ensuring greater participation for them in the development process, still, there are certain factors which inhibit the tribals from taking to education.

Cultural Problems

Due to contact with other cultures, the tribal culture is undergoing a revolutionary change. Due to the influence of Christian missionaries, the problem of bilingualism has developed which led to indifference towards tribal language. The tribal people are imitating western culture in different aspects of their social life, leaving their own culture. It has led to the degeneration of tribal life and tribal arts such as dance, music and different types of craft.

Loss of Control Over Natural Resources

Before coming of the British, the tribals enjoyed unhindered rights of ownership and management over natural resources like land, forests, wildlife, water, soil, fish, etc. With the advent of industrialization in India and the discovery of mineral and other resources in tribal inhabited areas, pressure on land and forests increased and state control replaced tribal control. Moreover, with the concepts of protected forests and national forests, the tribals lost their ownership rights over land. The ecological imbalance like cutting of trees has increased the distances between villages and the forest areas, thus, forcing tribal women to walk long distances in search of forest produce and firewood.

Migration and Rehabilitation

After independence, the focus of the development process was on heavy industries and the core sector. As a result, huge steel plants, power projects and large dams came up – most of them in the tribal inhabited areas. The mining activities were also accelerated in these areas. Acquisition of tribal land by the government for these projects led to large-scale displacement of the tribal population. Many tribal concentration regions and states have also been experiencing the problem of heavy migration of non-tribals in response to the pressures of development. The industrial areas of Jharkhand have suffered dilution of the tribal share of the population. These processes continue to prevail and have become even more powerful since the 1990s, when the country was opened up for liberalization. The huge agitations in Maharashtra against Jaitapur nuclear power plant and mining giant Vedanta in Niyamgiri in Orissa are the examples of reactionary movements against the policy of alienation and exploitation of the tribals. The cash compensation provided by the government was frittered away on wasteful expenditure. No settlements were provided for the displaced tribals within the industrial areas, who were forced to live in peripheries in slums or to migrate to adjoining states to work as unskilled workers in conditions of poverty. The migration of these tribals to the urban areas causes psychological problems for them as they are not able to adjust well to the urban lifestyle and values.

Gender Issues

The degradation of the natural environment, particularly through the destruction of forests and a rapidly shrinking resource base, has had its impact on the status of women. The opening of the tribal belts to mining, industries and commercialization has exposed tribal men and women to the ruthless operations of the market economy, giving rise to consumerism and commoditization of women.

Erosion of Identity

Increasingly, the traditional institutions and laws of tribals are coming into conflict with modern institutions which create apprehensions among the tribals about preserving their identity. Extinction of tribal dialects and languages is another cause of concern, as it indicates an erosion of tribal identity in certain areas. These factors include tribal superstitions and prejudices, extreme poverty, nomadic lifestyle of certain tribes, lack of interest in alien subjects taught through an alien language and a lack of suitable teachers and other facilities in the tribal areas.

The Concept of Private Property

The advent of the concept of private property in land has also adversely affected tribals whose community-based forms of collective ownership were placed at a disadvantage in the new system. Scheduled Tribes and Other Traditional Forest Dwellers (Recognition of Forest Rights) Act 2006 popularly known as Forest Rights Act, 2006 tried to restore this status quo and ownership of the tribals but its implementation is not up to the mark.

The Problem of Separatism

The divide and rule policy adopted by the British did a lot of damage to the tribal community of India. The British superimposed their own administrative patterns in the tribal areas and deprived the tribals of their traditional methods of interacting with the people. The Criminal Tribes Act, which the British introduced, gave an impression that the tribals were either criminals or anti-social. The tribal groups such as Kolis, Mundas, Khasis, and Sandals who fought against the British were branded as dacoits and robbers. The British also promoted missionary activities, especially in the central and north-eastern hills. All these activities alienated tribals which continued even in the post-independent India, but this brought increasing destitution and displacement. After the British came to power, the forest policy of the British government was more inclined towards commercial considerations rather than human. Some forests were declared as reserved ones, where only authorized contractors were allowed to cut the timber and the forest-dwellers were kept isolated deliberately within their habitat without any effort to ameliorate their economic and educational standards. The expansion of the railway in India heavily devastated the forest resources in India. The government started reserving teak, sal and deodar forests for the manufacture of railway sleepers. Forest land and its resources provide the best means of livelihood for the tribal people and many tribes including the women engage in agriculture, food gathering and hunting and they are heavily dependent on the products of the forest. Therefore, when outsiders exploit the tribe's land and its resources the natural life cycle of tribal ecology and tribal life is greatly disturbed.

The other problems the tribals face are:

1. They possess small and uneconomical land holdings because of which their crop yield is less and hence they remain chronically indebted.
2. Only a small percentage of the population participates in occupational activities in the secondary and tertiary sectors.
3. A good portion of the land in tribal areas has been legally transferred to non-tribals. Tribals demand that this land should be returned to them. In fact, the tribals had earlier enjoyed considerable freedom to use the forest and hunt the animals. Forests not only provide them materials to build

their homes but also give them fuel, herbal medicines for curing diseases, fruits, wild games, etc. Their religion makes them believe that many of their spirits live in trees and forests. Their folk tales often speak about the relations of human beings and the spirits. Because of such physical and emotional attachment to forest, the tribals have reacted sharply to restrictions imposed by the government on their traditional rights.

4. Tribal development programmes have not significantly helped the tribals in raising their economic status. The British policy had led to ruthless exploitation of the tribals in various ways as it favoured the *zamindars*, landlords, moneylenders, forest contractors, and excise, revenue and police officials.
5. Banking facilities in the tribal areas are so inadequate that the tribals have to depend mainly on the moneylenders. Being miserably bogged down in indebtedness, the tribals, therefore, demand that Agricultural Indebtedness Relief Acts should be enacted so that they may get back their mortgaged land.
6. About 90 per cent of the tribals are engaged in cultivation and most of them are landless and practise shifting cultivation. They need to be helped in adopting new methods of cultivation.
7. The unemployed and the underemployed want help in finding secondary sources of earning by developing animal husbandry, poultry farming, handloom weaving and the handicrafts sector.
8. Most of the tribals live in sparsely populated hills and communication in the tribal areas remains tough. The tribals, therefore, need to be protected from leading an isolated life, away from towns and cities, through the network of new roads.
9. The tribals are exploited by Christian missionaries. In several tribal areas, mass conversion to Christianity had taken place during the British period. While the missionaries have been the pioneers in education and opened hospitals in tribal areas, they have also been responsible for alienating the tribals from their culture. Christian missionaries are said to have many a time instigated the tribals to revolt against the Indian government.

Relations between the tribals and non-tribals are worsening and non-tribal residents are increasingly depending for protection on the para-military forces. The demand for separate states for tribals has taken the shape of insurgency in Mizoram, Nagaland, Meghalaya, Bihar, Manipur, Arunachal Pradesh and Tripura. Neighbouring countries, unfriendly to India, are active in exploiting these anti-Indian sentiments. Infiltration of foreign nationals, gun-running, trafficking in narcotics and smuggling are very serious problems in these states surrounded by tribal belts.

In short, the main problems of the tribals are poverty, indebtedness, illiteracy, bondage, exploitation, disease and unemployment.

Tribal Struggles

Numerous uprisings of the tribals have taken place beginning with the one in Bihar in 1772, followed by many revolts in Andhra Pradesh, Andaman and Nicobar Islands, Arunachal Pradesh, Assam, Mizoram and Nagaland. The important tribes involved in revolt in the nineteenth century were Mizos (1810), Kols (1795 and 1831), Mundas (1889), Daflas (1875), Khasi and Garo (1829), Kacharis (1839), Santhals (1853), Muria Gonds (1886), Nagas (1844 and 1879), Bhuiyas (1868) and Kondhs (1817).

After independence, the tribal struggles may be classified into three groups: (a) struggles due to exploitation by outsiders (like those of the Santhals and the Mundas), (b) struggles due to economic deprivation (like those of the Gonds in Madhya Pradesh and the Mahars in Andhra Pradesh), and (c) struggles due to separatist tendencies (like those of the Nagas and Mizos).

The tribal movements may also be classified on the basis of their orientation into four types: (a) movements seeking political autonomy and formation of a state (Nagas, Mizos, Jharkhand), (b) agrarian movements, (c) forest-based movements, and (d) socio-religious or sociocultural movements (the Bhagat movement among Bhils of Rajasthan and Madhya Pradesh, movement among tribals of south Gujarat or the Raghunath Murmu's movement among the Santhals).

If we take into consideration all the tribal movements, it could be said that the tribal unrest and the resultant movements were mainly the movements launched for liberation from (a) oppression and discrimination, (b) neglect and backwardness, and (c) a government which was callous to the tribals' plight of poverty, hunger, unemployment and exploitation.

When the law does not help them, the government remains callous, and the police fails to protect them, and also harasses them, they take up arms against the exploiters. These struggles and movements indicate that the tribals adopted two paths of achieving goals: (a) non-violent path of bargaining and negotiating with the government and using a variety of pressure tactics without resorting to violence/revolts, and (b) militant path of revolts or mass struggles based on developing the fighting power of the exploited/oppressed tribal strata. The consequences of both these paths are different. One indicates struggle oriented to reforms, while the other indicates structural transformation of the community. The fact that tribals continue to be faced with problems and also continue to feel discontented and deprived, brings to the fore the conclusion that both the paths have not helped them to achieve their goals.

Crime Against Scheduled Tribes

Since 2014, crimes against STs have seen an overall decrease of 3.8 per cent, with a significant drop of 8 per cent in 2015. However, there was a rise of 4.6 per cent in 2016. According to 2016 statistics, Madhya Pradesh accounts for a large proportion of crimes against SC/STs in 2016 (27.8%), followed by

Rajasthan (18.2%) and Odisha (10.4%). States with high number of crimes against STs like Madhya Pradesh show a low number of crimes in metropolitan cities such as Indore, which reports only 0.3 per cent of total crimes against STs in the state. Strikingly, Jaipur accounts for over half the number of crimes in metropolitan cities (55.3%). It is followed by Hyderabad with a proportion of 13.2 per cent.

Status of Women in Tribal Communities

Tribals or *adivasis,* are popularly known as a symbol of self-assertion. The status of tribal women usually depends on the economic roles they play. The position of a woman to a large extent depends on the kind of family one is placed in. In a joint family system, the eldest woman usually enjoys a prerogative in the decision-making process. Since women in the tribal communities toil hard, they are considered to be assets. The practice of bride price during marriages is quite common among them. In recent years, as the capitalist economy is setting in and women are being deprived of their traditional role, their economic value is decreasing and the practice of 'bride-price' is giving way to the system of dowry as witnessed in the general society. Tribal women generally inherit the ornaments from the mother. The customary laws do not permit them to own land. Women among some of the tribes of the north-east are very proficient in doing business and were famous for their weaving skills. The tribal women in India have virtually no role to play in the social and political spheres.

Development Programmes for STs

The British had superimposed their own administrative patterns in tribal areas and deprived the tribals of their traditional methods of interacting with people. The tribals have no written laws but the sanction of the community has a force which none dares to violate. Every able-bodied person is ready to lay down his life in defence of his village in the event of a crisis. A tribal village had been an autonomous unit and, barring areas such as the Mizo and Khasi Hills where the administration of number of villages was sometimes coordinated under a chief, assisted by a council of elders, a village remained independent for all intents and purposes. The isolation helped the tribals to retain the shape and strength of their social institutions and social structures.

After independence, the Constituent Assembly appointed a sub-committee under the chairmanship of A.V. Thakkar, after whose recommendations the development of tribal areas became an integral part of development of the Indian people as a whole.

The bonded labour in tribal areas was prohibited under the Constitution of India. In practice, however, it continues to exist in one form or the other in tribal areas of most of the states. In 1976, when the Bonded Labour System (Abolition) Act was passed, it was found that 80 per cent of the bonded labourers in the country belonged to SCs and STs. To loosen the grip of the moneylenders and the *mahajans* on the tribals, the government organized

Large Area Multi-Purpose Societies (LAMPS). However, their performance has been reported to be poor. There have been a large number of instances when the tribals have been cheated into signing bank loans. The cooperative societies failed to extend adequate credit for productive purposes, to purchase agricultural and minor forest produce from the tribals and fair price shops of essential consumer goods.

The sources of funds made available are:

1. State plan
2. Special central assistance
3. Sectoral programmes of central ministries/departments
4. Institutional finance.

The state governments are required to quantify the funds from a state plan for tribal area development in proportion to the percentage of the tribal population in the states.

Grant-in-Aid to Voluntary Organizations

Various projects with a focus on tribal education, literacy, medical and healthcare, vocational training in agriculture, horticulture, craftsmanship, etc. are being supported by the ministry under this scheme through registered non-governmental organizations.

Research and Training Scheme

Under the scheme 'Research and Training', the ministry provides financial assistance under grants to tribal research institutes on 50:50 sharing basis for conducting research and evaluation studies, seminars, and workshops, etc. Award of Research Fellowship to tribal students on 100 per cent basis registered in Indian universities. Supporting projects of All-India or Inter-State nature on 100 per cent basis to NGOs/universities, etc. for conducting research on tribal matters, travel grants and for publication of books on tribals.

Development of Primitive Tribal Groups

Under this scheme, 100 per cent assistance is provided to NGOs and other institutions for undertaking projects on the development of activities mainly focussing on their food security, literacy, agriculture technology upgradation, etc.

Tribal Advisory Council (TAC)

Eight states having Scheduled Areas, namely, Andhra Pradesh, Bihar (now Bihar and Chhattisgarh), Gujarat, Himachal Pradesh, Maharashtra, Madhya Pradesh (now Madhya Pradesh and Chhattisgarh), Orissa and Rajasthan and two non-Scheduled Areas. The governor of the state may refer matters concerning to administration of welfare of tribals to the TAC for recommendations. The ministry issues guidelines for TAC.

Point 11(b) of the 20-Point Programme

The point 11(b) of the 20-point programme is to provide economic assistance to the scheduled tribe families to enable them to rise above the poverty line. The ST families are assisted through various schemes implemented by departments of agriculture, rural development, horticulture, animal husbandry, sericulture, forestry, small and cottage industries, etc.

Tribal development has been based on a two-pronged approach: (a) promotion of development activities to raise the level of living of the scheduled tribes, and (b) protection of their interests through legal and administrative support. The tribal sub-plans (TSP) evolved for the tribal development projects during the Fifth Five-Year Plan (1974–79). The TSP is mainly an area development plan. The financial resources for the sub-plans are drawn from state plans, special central assistance (by the Ministry of Welfare), central ministries' programmes, and institutional finance.

The 20-point Programme, too, focussed attention on the development of STs, including assisting the tribal families economically to enable them to cross the poverty line.

The Tribal Research Institutes (TRIs) also play a useful role not only in the research and training of the tribals but also in the formulation of tribal sub-plans, project reports and their evaluation. For marketing the tribal produce, the Tribal Cooperative Marketing Development Federation of India (TRIFED) has been set up. It also works for eliminating exploitation of the tribals and for the realization of better prices.

SCHEDULED CASTES

Provisions in the Indian Constitution

Article 366(24) of the Constitution of India

Scheduled caste means such castes, races or tribes or parts of or groups within such castes, races or tribes as are deemed under Article 341 to be scheduled castes for the purposes of this Constitution.

Article 341 of the Constitution of India, 1949

1. The President may with respect to any state or union territory, and where it is a state after consultation with the governor thereof, by public notification, specify the castes, races or tribes or parts of or groups within castes, races or tribes which shall for the purposes of this Constitution be deemed to be scheduled castes in relation to that State or Union Territory, as the case may be.
2. Parliament may by law include in or exclude from the list of scheduled castes specified in a notification issued under clause (1) any caste, race or tribe or part of or group within any caste, race or tribe, but save as aforesaid a notification issued under the said clause shall not be varied by any subsequent notification.

The scheduled castes (SC) and scheduled tribes (ST) constitute the backward classes in India. In terms of Articles 341 and 342 of the Constitution, the President in consultation with the governor of a state specifies the castes or, tribes to be included in the schedule, or, list of backward castes. Unlike the tribes, they did not have a history of isolation. Whereas the tribal people are concentrated in specific geographical regions, the scheduled castes are scattered throughout the country. The chief features of scheduled castes reflect their problems:

1. The scheduled castes constitute the lowest strata of Indian society.
2. They had been subjected to a variety of disabilities, deprivations, and oppression under the traditional system.
3. They were placed outside and down below in social and ritual hierarchy under the *varna* model of society.
4 They were engaged in manual tasks which were considered impure and unclean. They were considered untouchables.
5. Generally, they lived near the outskirts of the village in poor housing conditions.

The Strength

There are altogether 1,241 ethnic groups, etc. which are notified as scheduled castes (SCs; also called as Dalits) in the country. Their total population, according to 2011 Census, is 201.40 million and comprised 16.60 per cent of the country's total population. In the period 2001–2011, the SCs grew by 20.80 per cent whereas the total population has witnessed a decadal increase of 17.64 per cent to touch 1.21 billion.

Development Strategies for the Scheduled Castes

A comprehensive three-pronged strategy was evolved for the development of the SCs during the Sixth Five-Year Plan (1980–85). This was a combination of three schemes: (i) Special Component Plans (SCPs) of the central ministries and state governments, (ii) Special Central Assistance (SCA) to SCPs for the SCs of the states, and (iii) Scheduled Caste Development Corporations (SCDCs) in the states.

The SCPs envisage identification of schemes of development which would benefit SCs, quantification of funds from all divisible programmes, and determination of specific targets as to the number of families to be benefited from these programmes. The overall objective is to assist SC families to substantially improve their income. The provision of basic services and facilities and of access to opportunities for social and educational development are also to be brought under the purview of the SCPs.

The Special Central Assistance (SCA) to the SCPs for SCs is an addition to the state plans and programmes for SCs. It does not follow the systematic pattern for special schemes. The states use this additional assistance from the Centre for income-generating economic development schemes in conjunction with the outlays in their SCPs so as to assist the economic advancement of the maximum possible number of SCs families living below the poverty line.

At present, the Special Central Assistance (SCA) to Scheduled Castes Sub-Plan (SCSP) is a central scheme under which 100 per cent grant is given to the states/UTs as an additive to their own SCSP. The main objective is to give a thrust to family-oriented schemes of economic development of SCs below the poverty line, by providing resources for filling the critical gaps and for providing missing vital inputs so that the schemes can be more meaningful. Since the schemes/programmes for SCs may be depending upon the local occupational pattern and the economic activities available, the states/UTs have been given full flexibility in utilizing SCA with the only condition that it should be utilized in conjunction with SCP and other resources available from other sources like various corporations, financial institutions, etc. State governments have also been given flexibility in choice of schemes to be implemented out of SCA, within the overall framework of the scheme.

The Scheduled Caste Development Corporations (SCDCs) in the states are envisaged to interface between the SC families and financial institutions in respect of bankable schemes of economic development. The corporations provide money, loan assistance to these families, thereby helping to increase the flow of funds from financial institutions to SC families. At present, such corporations are working in 36 states/union territories. Grants are given by the central government to the state governments for investment in the share capital of the corporations in the ratio of 49:51. The SCDCs finance the employment-oriented schemes covering diverse areas of economic activities, which inter-alia include: (a) agriculture and allied activities including minor irrigation; (b) small-scale industries; (c) transport; and (d) trade and service sector. According the Ministry of Social Justice and Empowerment, Government of India, the share capital assistance provided to the SCDCs during the last five years and the number of beneficiaries are as under:

Venture Capital Fund for Scheduled Castes: The objective of the fund is to promote entrepreneurship amongst the scheduled castes who are oriented towards innovation and growth technologies and to provide concessional finance to the scheduled caste entrepreneurs. Industrial Finance Corporation of India Ltd. is a Nodal agency to implement it.

Credit Enhancement Guarantee Scheme for Scheduled Castes: The objective of this Scheme is to provide credit guarantee facility to young and start-up entrepreneurs, belonging to scheduled castes, who aspire to be part of neo middle-class category, with an objective to encourage entrepreneurship in the lower strata of the society resulting in job creation besides creating confidence in scheduled castes.

In 1989, the Government of India set up the National Scheduled Castes and Scheduled Tribes Finance and Development Corporation (NSCSTFDC) under the Companies Act, 1956. Later, the Government of India declared bifurcation of the NSFDC into two separate corporations (one each for SCs and STs) but with effect from April 2001, the NSFDC is functioning exclusively for the development of the SCs. NSFDC is the apex institution for financing, facilitating and mobilizing funds from other sources and promoting the economic development activities of the persons belonging to the SCs living below double the poverty line. Its main functions are:

1. Financing income generating schemes for the SCs through the State Channelizing Agencies (SCAs) and other recognized institutions nominated by the respective state/UT governments.
2. Providing micro-credit finance to the target group through the SCAs.
3. Providing educational loan to the eligible SC students for pursuing full-time professional/technical educational courses in India or abroad.
4. Providing grants for skill development programmes through the SCAs.
5. Providing advisory services to target group and SCAs.
6. Upgrading the skill levels of the SCAs.

Crimes Against Scheduled Castes

The reports of the National Commission on Scheduled Castes have every year reflected an increase in the number of crimes against the SCs. Most of the SC women are the victims of rape by upper caste men. The SC men, on the other hand, are exploited by upper castes by usurping their lands, giving them low wages, using them as bonded labour, and so forth. For checking this exploitation, a set of comprehensive guidelines covering preventive measures have been formulated and communicated by the central government to the states for necessary action. Some of the measures taken by the states in this connection are:

1. Gearing up machinery for apprising the government of disputes of land, wages, etc. concerning the SCs.
2. Helping the SCs in getting possession of lands belonging to them or allotted to them.
3. Specially instructing police authorities to intervene in instances of criminal trespass into lands belonging to SCs. The police is instructed to treat cases of crime against SCs as special report cases and arrange for quick trial and prosecution.
4. Helping agricultural labourers in getting statutory minimum wages.
5. Setting up special courts (in some states) for ensuring quick disposal of cases pertaining to SCs.
6. Instructing officers to spend a part of their time, when on a tour, in residential areas of SCs.
7. Setting up special Scheduled Caste Cells under DIG Police to ensure that crimes against SCs are properly registered, promptly investigated and expeditiously prosecuted.

8. Setting up state level committees under the chairmanship of the Chief Ministers to look after various aspects concerning welfare of SCs.

Official statistics stated that more than 40,000 crimes against scheduled castes were reported in 2016. Several incidents were reported of members of dominant castes attacking Dalits for accessing public and social spaces or for perceived caste transgressions.

Since 2014, crimes against SCs have increased one per cent overall, although there was a steep rise of 5.5 per cent in 2016. As per 2016 statistics, Uttar Pradesh accounts for over a quarter (25.6%) of these crimes in 2016, followed by Bihar and Rajasthan. This is further reflected in the fact that their respective capital cities constitute almost 45 per cent of the total crimes against SCs among all 19 metropolitan cities. States with a low prevalence of violence include West Bengal (0.3%), Jharkhand (1.3%) and Kerala (2%). Coimbatore and Chennai have emerged with the lowest prevalence of violence against SCs amongst all metropolitan cities, with 0.2 per cent and 0.6 per cent respectively.

Evaluation of Welfare Schemes

It is believed that in spite of a large number of welfare schemes for SC people, only a little progress has been in the last seven decades. There has been a quality of ritualistic formalism about many welfare and development schemes formulated for these people.

The polity of our country has realized the significance of the development of weaker sections specially the scheduled castes since independence. Consequently, planned efforts have been made for their upliftment by the government. Based on secondary data, it has been found that no doubt, a positive change on various socio-economic parameters has been recorded but, that change has touched merely less than half of their population. Further, the gap between the mainstream and scheduled caste population still persists significantly in our traditional society. Therefore, there is an urgent need to reorient and focus the strategy in order to support the lesser privileged by providing qualitative education and infusing among them the individualistic and moralistic values of self-denial, temperance, forethought, thrift, sobriety and self-reliance essential to bring these downtrodden into the national mainstream.

OTHER BACKWARD CLASSES

On the basis of certain elements of backwardness such as illiteracy and lack of education, poverty, exploitation of labour, non-representation in services and untouchability, scheduled castes and scheduled tribes are listed in the Constitution, while the third group, i.e. other backward class (OBC) is unlisted. Instead, it is loosely defined. As a result of the absence of a clear definition, the problem of other backward classes is very complicated and very difficult to deal with. The Backward Class Commission was appointed in 1953 with Kaka Kelkar as the chairman according to the Article 340 of the Constitution. The Commission was asked to determine the criteria to be adopted to provide concessions to 'socially and educationally backward classes' besides the scheduled castes and scheduled tribes. The commission prepared a list of about 2,400 castes. List prepared for backward classes deemed to have been made in terms of castes and the term 'backward classes' has been used to describe and include 'backward castes'. The 'backward class' does not constitute one single whole but a multitude of social groups with varying positions and socio-economic standing in the social hierarchy of Indian society.

The other backward classes are entitled to special provisions in education and employment. Unlike the scheduled castes and the scheduled tribes, they are not given the privilege of political representation through reserved constituencies. The OBC is not identified as a separate group in the censuses so that their proportion can be obtained from the National Sample Survey Office (NSSO) surveys only. The Socio-Economic and Caste Census 2011 was conducted whose first findings were revealed on 3 July 2015. Mandal Commission report of 1980 quoted OBC population at 52 per cent, though the National Sample Survey Office (NSSO) survey of 2006 quoted OBC population at 41 per cent. The figure has varied from 36 per cent to 42 per cent across the three quinquennial expenditure surveys since the OBC began to be recorded as a separate group.

Mandal Commission

The second backward class commission was established on 1 January 1979, with B.P. Manual as its chairperson. The commission submitted its report in December 1980, which included both Hindus and non-Hindus consisting of around 52 per cent of the total population. Mandal commission recommended 27 per cent reservation, as the Supreme Court (SC) had set the bar for reservation to not extend 50 per cent in any case. The recommendation included reserving 27 per cent of seats for OBC in education and government jobs, relaxation in upper age limit for jobs, separate hostel for OBC students, vocal training for OBC youth. The government accepted the mentioned recommendations in 1989 and established OBC category with extra added reservation policy. By 1993 government introduced creamy layer with 1 lakh income cap which has been revised many times.

What were the criteria used by the Mandal Commission for identifying a specific caste/class as 'backward'? The Commission used three indicators: social, educational, and economic. With regard to social indicators there were four criteria, for the educational indicators there were three criteria, and for the economic indicators there were four criteria. Thus, in all, there were 11 criteria.

The four social criteria were: (a) castes/classes which are considered as socially backward by others, (b) castes/classes which mainly depend on manual labour for their livelihood, (c) castes/classes where at least 25 per cent females and 10 per cent males above the state average get married at 17 years in rural areas and at least 10 per cent females and 5 per cent males do so in urban areas, and (d) castes/classes where participation of females in work is at least 25 per cent above the state average.

The three educational criteria were: (a) castes/classes where the number of children in the age group of 5–15 years who never attended school is at least 25 per cent above the state average, (b) castes/classes where the rate of student dropouts in the age group of 5–15 years is at least 25 per cent above the state average, and (c) castes/classes amongst whom the proportion of non-matriculates is at least 25 per cent above the state average.

The four economic criteria were: (a) castes/classes where the average value of family assets is at least 25 per cent below the state average, (b) castes/classes where the number of families living in *kutcha* houses is at least 25 per cent above the state average, (c) castes/classes where the source of drinking water is beyond half a kilometre for more than 50 per cent of households, and (d) castes/classes where the number of households having taken loan is at least 25 per cent above the state average.

The weightage that was given to each indicator was arbitrary and illogical. The social indicators were given a weightage of three points, the educational indicators two points and the economic indicators were accorded one point. The total value was 22 points. Castes which secured the score of 50 per cent, that is, 11 points or above, were listed as 'backward'.

The government's decision to implement the Mandal Commission's report on reservations for the backward castes provoked widespread resentment among students. Spontaneous agitations erupted all over the country. Most families endure hardship and sacrifice to educate their children. The prospects of gainful employment already remain bleak because of the vast unemployment in our country. Most students are haunted by the nightmare of unemployment or of underemployment. In such a situation the government's 'electoral' decision to reserve jobs on the basis of caste for an additional 27 per cent to the existing quota of reservation of 22.5 per cent for SCs and STs, was bound to create frustration among the youth.

Arguments in Favour of Mandal Report

The following arguments were given in favour of the Mandal Commission's recommendations:

1. These fulfil the mandatory requirement of the Constitution (Articles 15, 16 and 46) of satisfying those sections of society who have been simmering with discontent for decades.
2. It is our moral and social duty to ensure that the oppressed and the suppressed people are at par with the affluent people in society. The underprivileged people need to be instilled with a sense of confidence.

3. The reservation will be only for the central government services (the state governments have their separate laws) and not more than 1 per cent of the total population of the country are in these services. Of that 1 per cent, 27 per cent has been reserved for the backward classes. Therefore, the reservation will not adversely affect mass people.
4. The recommendations are not based on caste as is wrongly believed by most people. For example, the Rajputs in Bihar are not included in the list but the Rajputs in Gujarat are included; the Patels of Bihar are in the list but Patels of Gujarat are not; and the Yadavas of Uttar Pradesh and Bihar are included but Yadavas in Haryana are not. Thus, the basis is the situation of a particular caste in each state.
5. Nation's SC, ST and OBC population with 52 per cent strength has altogether a mere 4 per cent representation in Class I government and public sector employment. This is utter injustice to the weaker sections which needs to be corrected.
6. One argument given by the anti-reservationists against increasing reservation is based on the question of 'merit'. Here, the assumption is that merit resides with the high castes who, therefore, must be allowed according to the colonial fashion, to continue to bear the burden both of running the state and its services and of civilizing the low castes. Is this argument valid and justified? Is this not the argument supported by the British government while giving higher posts to the Britishers and lower posts to the Indians? Was not the Britishers' reluctance to grant self-government to India based on a similar argument? Did we accept that? If we had described that argument as fallacious at that time, how can we accept a similar argument against the lower castes and classes today? Further, if it is argued that employment in this country has all along taken place on the basis of 'merit', have we offered concrete opportunities to the deprived low castes to acquire merit? If our state places every citizen on an equal footing, denying equal opportunity to the backward groups is nothing but continuing dominance of the oppressed. Extending reservations to these oppressed and the underprivileged people, therefore, calls for much soul-searching, something that many of us seem instinctively to resist.

Arguments Against Mandal Report

The Mandal Commission's report elicited severe criticism from several quarters on various scores. Five major arguments against it were: (a) the criteria used for defining the other backward castes/classes, (b) using very old census data for making population projections on the basis of an assumed constant rate of population growth, (c) bungling of facts and figures related to the identification of the other backward castes/classes, (d) non-objective sampling procedure and lacunae in the data collected, and (e) the terminological discrepancies specifically with reference to the use of terms like 'caste' and 'class'.

The arguments given against the Mandal Commission's report were:

1. The manner of its implementation was too hasty. The people should have been prepared for its implementation as it was likely to give a feeling of deprivation to some sections. The report was, thus, implemented without any consensus.
2. The administrative efficiency has been imperiled in the name of concessions to backward classes. Even the Constitution maintains that the reservation shall be consistent with and not subversive to the maintenance of efficiency of the administration.
3. Reservation should have been valid only for one generation.

Thus, an unscientific study based on assumptions, fallacies, paucity of relevant data, loopholes in information, arbitrariness, subjectivity, anomalies, a high degree of generalization, and which goes against the expert social scientists' advice, needs to be treated with extreme caution.

The reservation issue, based on government's notification of 12 August 1990 and of 25 September 1991 was referred to the Supreme Court which gave its verdict on 15 November 1992. The majority judgement (of six justices against the minority judgement of three justices) held that reservations in government service on the basis of caste are permissible (though discrimination against any citizen on the ground of caste in respect of any employment is prohibited). The apex court accepted the policy of 27 per cent reservation for the backward castes/classes, though it gave certain directions for change in this policy. One, that 'creamy layer' of backward castes/classes should be excluded. Two, armed forces and sensitive higher civilian posts (like scientists, university professors, pilots, etc.) should be kept outside the purview of caste reservations. Three, while Mandal Commission had identified 3,743 backward castes/classes (OBCs), the Supreme Court recognized only half this number as OBCs, as identified earlier by various state governments. It also held that those castes which were adequately represented in government jobs should be excluded from the list (of OBCs). Four, while Mandal Commission wanted to carry forward such vacancies which remained unfulfilled, the Supreme Court gave direction for treating such vacancies as unreserved. The Court thus, emphasized on maintaining 'minimum standard' in filling the posts. Five, while Mandal Commission was in favour of reservation in 'promotions' too, the Supreme Court recommended reservations only in original appointments. Six, the Supreme Court declared the reservation of 10 per cent seats for the weaker sections in the higher castes as unconstitutional. Lastly, the Supreme Court directed that the reservation quota should not go beyond 50 per cent.

Besides these directions, the Supreme Court also gave following four directions to the central government: (a) the Government of India should specify within four months the basis of exclusion of the 'creamy layer'; (b) the inclusion or exclusion of a caste or a section of a caste would have to be periodically reviewed to take care of changing circumstances; (c) permanent commissions should be appointed within four months by the central government as well as state governments to decide regularly the cases which should arise involving questions whether a particular caste or a section of a caste was rightly included or excluded.

Accepting the Supreme Court's verdict, the union government implemented from 8 September 1993 the reservation of 27 per cent quota for 1,238 backward castes/classes in central services and public undertakings. The first appointment of an OBC candidate was made on 20 February 1994.

In a notification issued by the government on 22 October 1993, it was stated that the 'concessions' permitted to SCs/STs are not 'admissible' to the OBCs. These concessions are; relaxation of minimum standards, upper age limit, permitted number of attempts, and stipulated experience. This is expected to safeguard merit in the government service. Further, a candidate seeking employment under the OBC quota has to produce a certificate from a gazetted officer that he does not belong to the creamy layer. The certificate is issued on the basis of the candidate's answers to a detailed questionnaire which goes into all the criteria laid down for identifying the creamy layer. The certificate also has to show that the candidate belongs to one of the 1,238 OBCs short-listed by the Centre in a notification. These names are common to the Mandal Commission's report and list of the fourteen states where OBC reservations have been in existence. The October 1993 notification, however, says that the 'carry forward' facility will continue (*India Today*, 15 December 1993).

No time limit of reservation (like 10 or 20 years) for OBCs has been fixed in the union government's declaration, as it is fixed or extended for SCs/STs from time to time. The National Backward Classes Commission was constituted on 14 August 1993. The commission has been granted the status of a constitutional authority in 2018. The commission is also crucial to the process of evaluating claims of groups demanding reservation under OBC status. Such commissions have been established by state governments also. The National Backward Classes Finance and Development Corporation was also set up on 13 June 1992 with a share capital of ₹ 2,000 crore for giving loans to OBC members below the poverty line.

The reservation quota system is, thus, being abused in a number of ways. For example, (a) SC/ST lists have been lengthened by the Centre on 20 occasions. (b) At least two states have exceeded the 50 per cent limit of total reservations fixed by the Supreme Court and more threaten to follow suit. (c) Creamy layer rule mandated for OBC reservations is being disregarded by the states. (d) Reservations have been extended even to some advanced castes (for example, Vokkaligas and Lingayats in Karnataka). (e) Some states (like Madhya Pradesh) have scrapped cut-off marks for SCs and STs in entrance tests to professional courses. (f) Officials in some states (like Uttar Pradesh and Bihar) manipulate recruitment processes to favour OBCs or Dalits. (g) Some intermediate castes have been given the status of tribes and scheduled castes to achieve political benefits.

Thus, being abused by politicians, reservation system has been perverted and often it works against and hurts those they were intended to help.

Economically Backward Class (EBC)

The term Economically Backward Class was coined for the first time in 2014–15. Indian citizens belonging to the general category with an income equal to or less than ₹ 1 lakh per annum are classified as economically backward (EB). There is a commission for economically backward classes under the ministry of social justice and empowerment. Its objective is to collect the views of all the state governments/UTs on the subject of EBC, develop criteria to identify EBC and suggest methods for the welfare of the economically backward classes, the required legal, constitutional and administrative changes to the EBC to uplift the people belonging to the EB Category.

The Reservation Policy

Implementation of Mandal Commission's recommendations in August 1990, the Supreme Court's judgement on this issue in November 1992, raising of reservation quota to 69 per cent and even to 80 per cent in some states in 1994, and the amendment of Constitution by the parliament in May 1995 to extend reservation even to 'promotion' cases (against the directions of the Supreme Court) will always be sadly referred to by the future historians as failing to establish an egalitarian system in India. All these measures have resulted into such situations whose consequences are bound to be disastrous. A few important effects have been: (a) Casteism has been granted a fresh lease of life. (b) Merit and calibre have been replaced by mediocrity. (c) Politicians' definition of 'creamy layer', excluding political posts from this category, and the attempts to include more and more castes/classes in the list of OBCs, have changed the social and economic landscape beyond recognition. (d) Tremors let off in some states for anti-reservation agitation have increased violence in the society. (e) Migration of students and other people to those regions where they have greater possibilities of getting job reservation benefits has increased. (f) There is increase in discontent among people of advanced castes. Surprisingly, the Supreme Court also accepted the idea of reservations in government service on caste basis. Is the idea of reservation on caste basis not erroneous for our country? Will it not leave the nation into two categories of people – forward and backward – and open up new vistas for mutually destructive conflicts and fissiparous forces and make backwardness a vested interest? Will it ensure real social justice in society? Will it create an egalitarian system? Will it develop a cohesive and an integrated society?

The demand for special concessions and privileges to the underprivileged are matters of right and not of charity or philanthropy. All the commissions and the committees have examined this issue. The question to be discussed today, therefore, is: Is reservation policy, or protective discrimination, a logical and useful strategy for ensuring justice and equal opportunity to the economically exploited and socially oppressed groups?

The first argument is that reservation in educational institutions and government jobs, by itself cannot achieve much. In fact, if extended to larger sections of the population, they can be counter productive too. At best, reservations are 'palliatives' and no decisive transformations can take place unless such a measure is accompanied by structural changes in the nation's production relations, and most crucially, until land reforms become a reality, and educational support systems are so buttressed that candidates from all social groups are available for higher level jobs.

The second argument is that our country is already divided into various groups. Reservation will further divide the population artificially. Earlier, reservations were accepted under special conditions for a period of fifteen years only, but continuing them for ever will produce vested interests and separatism, and will lead to a caste-war and the disintegration of the country. Sometime back, it was ordered that caste will not be mentioned in applications for jobs. But if the reservation policy is to be continued for SCs, STs and OBCs, the applicants will have to mention their caste, otherwise how will they be known? This will fragment the Hindu society into pieces.

The third argument is that when the reservation policy was implemented after the independence, there were only a few SC and ST people in the administrative set-up. It is time that the beneficiaries and society reconsider the issue of reservations. The society should immediately think of bringing about conditions where all jobs and admissions are decided only on merit in an open competition, in which all aspirants are assured of a fair chance.

The fourth argument is that our experience in the last 65 years has shown that the reservation policy has not delivered the desired results. A large number of SC and ST representatives in Lok Sabha and Vidhan Sabhas have not been able to adequately articulate the grievances and needs of people of their constituencies. Reservation in jobs and in educational institutions has benefited only a few tribes and castes. The reservations have also generated conflicts and tensions.

There is one school of thought which favours reservations. The supporters of this school maintain that there is a wide gulf between the social order that people of India were promised by a political party led by Gandhiji, and the one that has actually been established since Independence. The oppression of the weaker sections of society (including lower and backward castes and tribes) by the stronger (upper castes) sections has not ended. In fact, it has been aggravated. A new era of social justice and equality still remains a dream to be achieved. The benefits of development have been appropriated by about 20 per cent of the population at the top. The English-speaking educated middle class has come to control and operate levers of state power. It has emerged as the ruling class of the country. By accepting the reservation policy, the government will only be working for the establishment of a new social order that would secure social justice to the underprivileged sectors of our society and provide equality of opportunity to rise in the social scale.

There is another school of thought which favours reservations but wants economic needs and not caste as the basis of reservation. Almost all political parties, implicitly or overtly have supported this idea of reservation on the economic-need basis. They hold that this will help the deserving poor of all classes and castes to rise in society. The disadvantaged groups do need protection but it cannot be extended en masse and for all time to come. The poor should get special weightage but a watchdog body should keep an eye on their progress. As soon as it is found that they no longer need the crutches of reservations, all jobs should be declared open to all.

Even intellectuals like B.R. Ambedkar were against the caste politics. In Ambedkar's words: 'Fraternity means a sense of common brotherhood of all Indians, of Indians being one people. Castes are anti-national. They bring about separation in social life and generate jealousy and antipathy between caste and caste. If we wish to become a nation in reality, we must oppose caste feelings'. Pandit Jawaharlal Nehru too had written a letter to Chief Ministers on 27 June 1961 saying, 'I dislike any kind of reservation, more particularly in service as it will lead to inefficiency and second-rate standards. The only real way to help a backward group is to give opportunities for good education'.

It will not be out of place here to refer to the desperate tale of a forward caste woman in Kerala who, merely with a view to gain admission for her son in a medical college, deposed before a magistrate in the presence of her husband that the son was her illegitimate offspring by a *Harijan*. Such ideas and actions will result into disaster for the country. Public opinion needs to be mobilized against the policy of reservation, and the government and the politicians have to be made to realize that it is not in the national interest to continue the system of caste quotas. A political party may get a few votes by pursuing populist policies like caste reservation but such policies will only replant the poisonous weed of casteism which will harm the country for hundred years to come.

Reservation among the SCs, STs and OBCs has led to the emergence of the elite class which has been cornering the benefits of reservation for itself and has become self-perpetuating. Time has come to introduce some changes in the reservation policy. Some of these changes could be as follows:

1. Safeguarding the true meaning of 'reverse discrimination' and applying the principle in such a manner that the really deserving get the benefits and the SCs, STs and OBCs are protected from their own self-serving leaders.
2. No state should be allowed to cross the limit of 50 per cent reservation. Those states which have fixed a quota more than this should be given a time-limit of two-three years to fall in line and bring reservation quota to 50 per cent.
3. We should incorporate the principle of limiting the benefit of reservations to one generation only, i.e. if a person has taken advantage of

reservations to get a job, his children will not be entitled to the benefit of reservation.

4. There should be no reservation in 'promotions'. This would avoid conflicts between junior reserved category employees and senior general category employees and check heartburn and demoralization of people in the later category.
5. All organizations must set minimum standards for recruitment at all levels. In no case should the minimum standards be compromised.

Reservation is a form of quota-based affirmative action and is governed by constitutional laws, statutory laws, and local rules and regulations.

Advantages and Disadvantages of Reservation

There are advantages and disadvantages of reservation for STs, SCs, and OBCs in the field of education and politics.

In India, reservation is provided for historically backward and suppressed classes of Hindu society. These include the scheduled caste (SC), scheduled tribe (ST) and other backward classes (OBC). The reservation is provided in the fields of education as lower cut-off marks for entry into educational institutes, reserving parliament or legislative assembly seats and reserving job vacancies.

The advantage of these reservations is that they allow these backward classes a chance at improving their lives and status in society and getting meaningful employment. They also get representation in various aspects of society and decision making, something that has been denied to them for a long time. It has encouraged the people to fight for justice whenever there is a violation of their human rights. The reservation has slowed down the process of forward becoming richer and backward becoming poorer.

The disadvantage of the reservation is that it suppresses meritocracy, that is, the availability of options to the most capable and deserving person. So, even though the system may have some merits, it should be used with caution and not indiscriminately. Though the reservation system works in favour of the backward castes of the society, at the same time, it has brewed up some controversies in the country too. It is believed that the system supersedes merit in certain circumstances when meritorious candidates are deprived of the jobs or admissions so that candidates of backward classes can be accommodated as per the reservation system. It is the biggest enemy of meritocracy. It is resulting in the degradation of quality of students and workers enrolled in different institutions. Moreover, the system is confined to government institutions and firms, while those in the private sector are still beyond the reach of people belonging to the backward classes, either because they lack the skills needed to enter these firms or institutions or they are not financially sound enough to afford them. Beneficiaries of reservation are largely from dominant class in backward castes. The marginalized section still remains marginalized. Some believe that the reservation system has an overall negative impact on the productive workforce of the country by ignoring the people with true potential and giving people opportunities on the basis of caste rather than merit. It's propagating the notion of caste-based society instead of eliminating it. It is a form of ethnic discrimination.

Criticism of Reservation in India

Reservation has been criticized by various groups and people (usually from general category) from time to time, that reservation is against the Constitution of India which says 'no discrimination on the basis of caste, religion or sex'. The main reason given by these groups is that reservation was intended for 10 years only and now it has been more than 70 years since the policy was implemented. The government is increasing reservations through various amendments.

Arguments against Reservation

1. It is dividing India into caste lines which our freedom fighters and social reformers fought so hard to eliminate.
2. It is against the fundamental right to equality as safeguarded by the Constitution of India. It violates the very spirit of democracy.
3. The benefits of reservation have been denied to really deserving people by the rich and powerful in their own classes.
4. Reservation is just a populist measure used by politicians for electoral gains.
5. As a consequence of legislating to provide reservations on the basis of religion, religious minorities in all government education institutions will be introduced which is contrary to the ideas of secularism and is a form of anti-discrimination on the basis of religion.
6. Most of the times, only economically sound people from the so-called lower castes will make use of most of the reserved seats, thus, counteracting the spirit of reservations.
7. The quality of the elite institutes may go down because merit is severely being compromised by reserving seats for certain caste-based communities.
8. The reservation policy is creating huge unrest in the society. Providing quotas on the basis of caste and not on the basis of merit will deter the determination of many educated and deserving students of India.

The arguments both in justification and also in criticism of the reservation have values. There is no immediate solution either in retaining or in terminating the policy of reservation. The Supreme Court also is in favour of retaining the policy. The decision that the 'creamy layer' should be denied the benefit of reservation is a justified one. Otherwise, a section of the weaker class will get the benefit of reservations while the deprivation will continue for others. Time has come for the policymakers, to think over it.

Scheduled castes (SCs) and scheduled tribes (STs) are among the most disadvantaged socio-economic groups in India. The SCs are one of the most oppressed and backward communities in Indian society. The scheduled tribes on the other hand, comprise of social groups, the nature of whose marginalization and deprivation is primarily due to geographical and spatial isolation.

Reservation Must be Given to the Needy People

The rich persons in SC/ST community must not enjoy the fruits of reservation. The benefit of reservation must be given for the first two children. Financially poor persons must be given priority. Now-a-days, politicians are playing a major role in reservation policy. The reservation policy was only for 10 years after the independence, for the upliftment of SC and ST but till now it continues and no one has taken any step to amend it or revise it or change it. The reason behind this is the population of SC and ST in the country. Nearly 33 per cent voting is done by SC and ST so, if they make any change in the reservation policy against the SC and ST then, they have to suffer a lot for the same. Hence, they are not taking any steps against the reservation policy.

While framing the Constitution of India, Ambedkar had suggested three propositions: (a) there should be equality of opportunity for all citizens; (b) there ought to be no reservations of any sort for any class or community at all, i.e. all qualified persons should be placed on the same footing or equality so far as the public services are concerned; and (c) there should be reservations for a limited period in favour of certain communities which have so far been outside the administration. These three seem to be the workable propositions even today for our society, for social justice will be combined with some semblance of merit. It is time that we tackle all problems of reservation with sanity and rationality.

What are the youth to do then? The youth in India have to realize that reservation of OBCs is not the only crucial problem to fight for or against. The real problem is India's political elite who work only for vested interests and whose attitudes and obscurantist notions have corrupted the thinking of our society and brought the country to its present critical condition. If they want to protect their future, if they want to be the future elite of the nation, they have to widen their perspective to encompass the crucial problems of our society instead of focussing on one aspect of reservation for backward castes/classes, etc. Instead of raising the issue of forward versus backward castes, they should raise the issue of vested interests of the political parties and leaders versus the logical interests of society in general and youth in particular. They can propose certain amendments in the reservation policy to ensure that instead of benefit being drawn only by a few tribes, castes and OBC families, it should benefit a large number of deserving people belonging to both the forward and the backward castes. Second, there should be no compromise on quality and efficiency. Third, they have to take the youth of the backward castes/classes with them on this issue and be able to convince them of their stance.

It may be suggested that benefit may be given to only those who really deserve help.

1. Income, not only caste should be given importance in determining backwardness.
2. The concept of the creamy layer should be applied to SCs and STs also.
3. Reservation should be restricted only to the first generation beneficiaries. The candidates whose parents have already availed reservation facilities in securing a job should not be given the facility again.
4. Concession of scholarship may be provided to SC, ST and OBC students securing more than the specified percentage of marks for getting a quality education.

The government has used a two-fold strategy for the empowerment of the SC/STs, which includes the following: first, the provision of legal safeguards against discrimination and second, pro-active measures in the form of the reservation policy for the public sector and state-supported sectors. Reservations for the SC/STs in the government services, educational institutions, and political bodies like the Central and the state legislatures also fall under pro-active measures. These measures have been incorporated to ensure the proportional participation of the SC/STs in the public domain democratic decision-making bodies. It is equally important to understand that the reservation policy is confined to the State-run and supported sectors. The private sector, wherein, more than 90 per cent of the SC/ST workers are engaged is excluded and therefore, remains outside the purview of the reservation policy and open to possible discrimination.

Suggested Strategies

1. Create an enabling environment that is conducive for the SCs, STs, OBCs, and minorities to exercise their rights freely, enjoy their privileges and be able to lead a life with confidence and dignity.
2. Adopt a three pronged strategy of (a) Social Empowerment; (b) Economic Empowerment; and (c) Social Justice, in empowering these disadvantaged groups.
3. Ensure removal of disparities, eliminate exploitations and suppression and provide protection to the disadvantaged groups.
4. Ensure the developmental benefits to 'Reach the Unreached' through equitable distribution and social justice.
5. Ensure participation of the Social Disadvantaged Groups in the process of planning not merely as the beneficiaries but to take part effectively in the formulation of the need-based programmes/project, their implementation, supervision, and monitoring.
6. Accelerate the ongoing process of improving the socio-economic status of the disadvantaged groups through effective implementation of various policies and programmes and thus bring them on par with the rest of the society.

Conclusion

If weaker sections in India are to rise in revolt because they feel that only violence facilitates their voice to be heard, the nation will have to pay a very heavy price for this. Our government and our people have to give these docile people the chance of a fair deal to live with honour and self-respect. Similarly, little will be achieved by a debate on the pros and cons of reservations. It will only aggravate the problem and lead to fragmentation of the country. The power elite, the government, political parties and people have to delve deeper into the very reasons why reservation has seemingly become necessary and what needs to be done to eliminate this pernicious practice.

References

Goswami, B., *Constitutional Safeguards for Scheduled Castes and Scheduled Tribes*, Rawat Publications, Jaipur, 2003.

Guru Chandra, Mahesh et al., SC/ST development in India, *EPRA International Journal of Economic Business Review*, Vol. 43, Issue 10, October 2015.

Maheshwari, S.R., Reservation Policy in India: Theory and Practice, *Indian Journal of Public Administration*, Vol. 43, Issue 3, 1997.

Shourie, Arun, *Falling Over Backwards: An Essay on Reservations and Judicial Populism*, HarperCollins Publishers, New Delhi, 2012.

8

Youth Unrest and Agitations

Along with caste, religious and linguistic stereotypes, there exists many other stereotyped images in our country. One such image is about our youth. The stereotyped image is that youth are militant, rebellious, revolutionary, irrational and undisciplined. It is true that the youth is vulnerable to outside influences and imitate others but this does not mean that the youth believes only in destruction, killing, assault and terrorism. When there is a total disillusionment in society with the existing social structures and institutions, with the contradictions in the social system, with the politics and the politicians, with the decisions and decision-makers, and when everybody is conscious of the falling standards in all walks of life, social discrimination, prevailing corruption, and the search for quick monetary gains through illegitimate means, why should the youth alone be expected to conform to traditional moral values and lofty ideals? How can they look up to self-proclaimed political, religious and social leaders for inspiration?

The youth tend to become angry when they notice the widening chasm between what the leaders preach and what they practise; when the leaders call for sacrifice but they themselves loll in luxury; when the leaders talk of morality but they themselves maintain liaison with smugglers, criminals and anti-social elements; when they appeal for peace and harmony but they themselves revel in factional squabbles, when they shed crocodile tears for the poor but always live with and support the rich. Disappointed and disillusioned by this, the frustrated youth start some agitation to lodge a social protest. Some politicians start taking an interest in these agitations and in some cases, they use the help of anti-social elements to keep these agitations alive. When these anti-social elements indulge in loot and arson, it is the youth who come to be blamed for these destructive activities. The frustrated youth, thus, become more frustrated and the unrest among them further increases.

Concept of Youth Unrest

What is unrest? What is social unrest? What is youth unrest? 'Unrest' means 'disturbed condition'. It is 'the state of disillusionment and dissatisfaction'. 'Youth unrest' is often described as 'student revolt', 'student power' and 'student activism'. The last three decades have witnessed innumerable outbursts of the youth unrest in many nations of the world. The youth seems to have an anti-establishment and a revolutionary tone. Social unrest is the manifestation of collective disillusionment, discontentment and frustration of the group, community or society. If there is unrest among the students of one university, it is not perceived as the problem of 'student unrest' as such. It is only when students all over the country feel frustrated on common issues like admissions, content of courses, the examination system and the representations in academic bodies, can we say that there exists the problem of student unrest in our society. Similarly, it is not the unrest among the workers of one industry that is termed 'industrial unrest' but it is the collective discontentment among all workers in different industries in the country on issues of minimum wages, safety measures, security of employment, and certain intra-mural and extra-mural facilities that is referred to as the problem of 'industrial unrest'. The same is true for the peasant unrest, tribal unrest and women unrest. The emphasis in the concept of social unrest is on 'collective frustration and disillusionment on common issues of the groups in the society'.

On this basis, youth unrest may be defined as the 'manifestation of collective frustration of the youth in the society'. It is manifested when the existing norms in the society are perceived by the youth as ineffective or harmful to the extent that they offend them, and they feel so disillusioned and disgusted that they recognize the need for changing these norms.

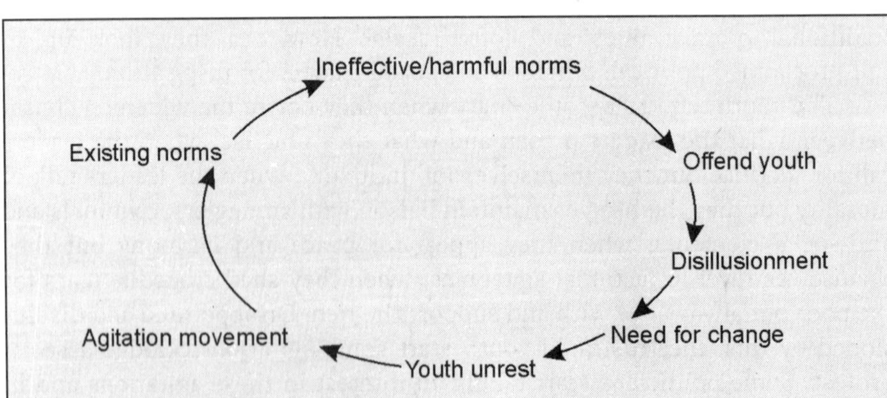

Characteristics of Youth Unrest

On the basis of the above definition, it may be said that youth unrest is characterized by: (a) collective discontent, (b) dysfunctional conditions, (c) public concern, and (d) the need for change in the existing norms.

Youth agitation, on the other hand, is characterized by: (a) action based on the feeling of injustice, (b) growth and spread of a generalized belief among the youth which identifies the source of discontent, frustration and deprivation, (c) emergence of leadership and mobilization for action, and (d) collective reaction to stimuli.

It will not be out of place to explain the concept of student indiscipline at this stage. Indiscipline is disobedience to authority, or disrespect to elders, or deviation from norms, or refusing to accept control, or rejecting goals and/or means. Student indiscipline leads to the 'use' of 'undesirable methods' by students. A committee appointed by the University Grants Commission (UGC) in 1960 included three types of behaviour in student indiscipline: (a) disrespect for teachers, (b) misbehaviour with girls, and (c) destroying property. Further, it included the indiscipline of not a few students but of a large group of students. Some scholars describe this definition as faulty. They maintain that three situations create indiscipline among students: (a) Students lose interest in the goals of the (educational) institution. In such a situation, they remain members (of the institution) but do not follow its norms. (b) Students accept the goals but doubt whether the institution can achieve them. They, therefore, try to 'improve' the institution by deviating from its norms. (c) Norms of institutions fail to achieve goals and students, therefore, want a change in norms.

Youth unrest may be viewed from three perspectives: (a) unrest among youth, (b) unrest due to the youth, and (c) social unrest in the country and its effect on the youth.

The important functions of youth agitations are:

1. To create collective consciousness and group solidarity,
2. To organize the youth to work for new programmes and new plans, and
3. To provide opportunities to young individuals to express their feelings and make some impact on the course of social change.

Types of Youth Unrest

Youth unrest has assumed different forms. In no country, the youth unrest takes place for the same reason and assumes the same form all the time. The nature of youth unrest is that it is unsteady, irregular and sometimes happens spontaneously. Myron Weiner has classified the youth unrest into four types.

Myron Weiner's Classification of Youth Unrest

According to Myron Weiner, the so-called student indiscipline or students unrest assumes four forms. They are as follows:

1. *Political activities and movements*: In some instances, youth unrest is associated with the larger political movements. Students often take up political issues and join hands with other non-youth organizations and

political parties and fight for them. Students have participated in various political movements launched for issues such as border disputes, steel plant location, price rise, water dispute, anti-Hindi and anti-English agitations, emergency; postponement of elections, dismissal of ministers, etc. They have taken out processions, staged demonstrations, *gheraoed* ministers, resorted to violence and conflicted with police authorities.

2. *Student agitations for educational causes*: Students have agitated for educational causes also. Students have agitated demanding the appointment of lecturers, enough supply of laboratory equipments and library books, cancellation of donation and capitation fees, reforms in examination system and type of question papers, retainment of carryover system, recognition of the student union, participation of students in university administrative bodies such as senate, syndicate, academic councils, postponement of examination, etc.
3. *Agitations against non-university authorities*: Students have agitated for non-educational and non-political causes also. For example, they have agitated demanding special concessions for travelling on buses and trains, concessions in commercial recreational centres, etc.
4. *Spontaneous student agitations*: Sometimes, students do agitate suddenly in an unexpected manner. They may quarrel with bus conductors, auto-rickshaw drivers, hotel owners, police and public servants, and may even go on strike against them. These agitations can be treated as spontaneous outbursts of youth force. If these agitations are not handled carefully they may be intensified and prolonged in an even worse way.

Youth Protests, Agitations and Movements

Social protest is an expression of disapproval to something a person is powerless to prevent or avoid. It is a mode of communicating discontentment rather than direct action. It is an expression of outrage against injustice. The important elements of social protest are: (i) action expresses grievance, (ii) it points out to a conviction of injustice, (iii) protesters are unable to correct the condition directly by their own effort, (iv) action is meant to provoke ameliorative steps by the target group, and (v) protesters bank upon the combination of coercion, persuasion, sympathy and fear to move the target group.

The difference between an agitation and a social movement is that social movement may take the form of agitation but every movement does not do so. Many movements are peaceful, for example, women's liberation movement, the prohibition movement or the anti-nuclear movement. These peaceful movements are the result of cultural drift. Youth agitation is the behaviour of the youth whose goal is neither injury to a person nor destruction of public property but social protest. It is neither the result of innate destructive drive nor it is an inborn reaction to frustrations. It is a learned behaviour.

If the protesters indulge in looting, it is not to acquire property; if they indulge in breaking windows, it is not to seek vengeance; if they shout slogans against a person, it is not to insult him. All these methods are resorted merely to express resentment against their unfulfilled demands and towards the callous attitude adopted by the powers that are in relation to their grievances.

Youth Agitations

India has witnessed youth agitation in different parts and in different forms. Youth agitation helps in remedying the discrepancies in administration. It also helps in pushing the administration not to delay the work of the students which usually leads to a lot of adversity on the students. Youth agitation on a large scale can also help in shaking the governments so as to ensure better administration. However, there exists another side to this coin. Youth agitation, which takes the form of violence, can lead to unnecessary strikes and complete shutdown of administration. Youth agitation for unreasonable demands is also vague and hinders the progress of the university or institution. Various forms of youth agitations are demonstrations, slogan shouting, strikes, hunger strikes, roadblocks (*rasta roko*), *gheraos*, and boycott of examinations.

Social protests may lead to aggression, agitation and movement. Aggression is a hostile act intended to harm or object, often the result of frustration. It is an unprovoked attack. It is directed at the source of individual's frustration. Myres (1988: 395) defines aggression as 'physical or verbal behaviour that hurts, harms or destroys'. This excludes accidental hurts or unintentional hitting; but it certainly includes gossipy 'digs' about a person which hurts him. Feshbach (1970) has given two types of aggressions – hostile aggression and instrumental aggression. The former springs from anger and its goal is to injure. It is resorted to as an end in itself. The latter also aims at hurting but only as a means to some other end. The term 'aggression' is used more in wars, while the term 'agitation' fits in more with the youth's collective behaviour, causing anxiety to persons, their minds or feelings.

Agitation is 'to bring grievance and injustice to the notice of people in power'. It is to shake up, to move, to stir up, to cause anxiety, and to disturb the power holders. Social movement is the activity of diffused collectivity oriented towards changing the social order. According to Turner and Killian (1972: 246), social movement is a collective behaviour based on some continuity to promote or resist change in society or group of which it is a part. It is characterized by: (a) collective action which is initiated, organized and sustained, (b) ideology, and (c) orientation towards social change. A pressure group is one that attempts to influence decision-makers or 'governing elite' for its own interests or the interests of a larger group that it represents. It wants the existing norms to be interpreted to benefit it. In an agitation, there is always a pressure group tactics but in a social movement, it may or may not be there. The difference between an agitation and a social movement is that social movement may take the form of agitation but every movement does not do so. Many movements are peaceful, for example, women's liberty movement, the prohibition movement or the anti-nuclear movement. These peaceful movements are the result of cultural drift.

Youth agitation is the behaviour of the youth whose goal is neither injury to a person nor destruction of public property but a social protest. It is neither the result of innate destructive drive nor it is an inborn reaction to frustrations. It is a learned behaviour. Various forms of youth agitations are: demonstrations, slogan shouting, strikes, hunger strikes, road blocks (*rasta roko*), *gheraos* and boycott of examinations. The preconditions for youth agitations are: (a) structural strain, (b) identifying the source of strain, (c) precipitating factor in initiative action, and (d) mobilization of force for action by a leader. The important functions of youth agitations are: (a) to create collective consciousness and group solidarity, (b) to organize the youth to work for new programmes and new plans, and (c) to provide opportunities to young individuals to express their feelings and make some impact in the course of social change.

Majority of the modern Indian youth are not interested to be bound by the traditional norms and values. They are interested to adopt the secular lifestyle and a rational outlook. These causes conflict which at some later stage leads to alienation. Youth in recent time are trying to define their own identity in order to obtain the resources for survival and try to get a place in the existing social order. The educated students have come to believe that (a) In the present set up, the government policies have ignored merits and abilities. (b) The other important cause of student unrest has been the interference of political parties with student union or organizations. Several studies have supported the views that the association of various political parties through the student wings in many ways are responsible for the outbreak of violence. The national political parties and their local bodies tend to use the students as their strength for upcoming elections. (c) The third contributing factor to unrest is unemployment. It is a well-known fact that the present day education system in the country does not guarantee suitable employment. Therefore the future programmes, that is, educational policies, must be flexible and more sensitive than at present towards regional and local traditions. Further, the youth are most affected by the erroneous process of development. As such future educational planning should take particular account of the situation and prospects of the employment including linking work with study.

Students' Agitations

Students' agitations may be classified as: (a) student-oriented agitations, and (b) society-oriented agitations. The former includes problems at college/university level and at the national level while the latter refers to taking interest in state/country's politics and policies and programmes. Student-oriented agitations are generally discontinuous and problem-oriented rather than value-oriented. For example, students will agitate for the removal of a particular vice-chancellor of a university but they will never fight for a change in the system of selecting vice-chancellors in universities in India. Similarly, they will fight to postpone examinations for a particular year but they will not agitate for restructuring the examination system as such.

A few student's agitations are described below:

The University of Hyderabad: Caste Tensions

A 26-year-old doctoral student at the University of Hyderabad was found dead after he was suspended from the university. He was one of five students, all from India's Dalit caste, to be suspended after being accused of assaulting the head of a student political group. A complaint was filed that he had indulged in anti-national activities. His mother defended him and rejected all accusations. His death prompted protests in Hyderabad and other parts of the country.

IIT Roorkee: Poor Academic Performance

In July 2015, 73 students from the prestigious IIT Roorkee were expelled due to poor academic performance. Though they were taken back, what made the protests against this move of the institution significant was that of the expelled students, 90 per cent of them were from the reserved category, and it is unclear whether 'marks' were the only reason behind the expulsions.

Jadavpur University: Molestation Case

In January 2015, the spark to the fire was added by a molestation case on campus, which was overlooked by the Vice-Chancellor. Students forced their Vice Chancellor to resign. Students went on a hunger strike and two rallies were held in Kolkata in support of the cause. It culminated with nearly 100 students refusing to take their degrees during the Convocation. After four months of continued agitation, the VC of Jadavpur University resigned.

FDDI Agitation: Recognition of Degree

The Footwear Development and Design Institute (FDDI) is a government institute. Students who had enrolled post-2012 had been promised degrees from Mewar University in Rajasthan, whereas the campuses of the institute were located outside Rajasthan. In May 2015, there was a rumour in the media that the degrees of students were invalid. On filing RTIs, the students discovered that this was true and that the UGC had already raised questions against the MoU between FDDI and Mewar University. Students at FDDI went on a strike demanding an INI status for the University. Only after discussion in the Ministry of Commerce and Industry that is in charge of the University, it was decided that the students should be awarded a degree from IGNOU.

Jamia Millia Islamia (JMI) Agitation

JMI, about a 100 years old institution, was set up with a clear objective to promote secular and multicultural values. It was established as a past of the non-cooperation movement of 1920 led by Mahatama Gandhi. The Citizenship Amendment Act (Bill) protests, also known as CAA Protest or CAB Protest, occurred after the CAA was enacted by Government of India on 12 December 2019. The law was believed to be discriminatory on the grounds of making an exception for non-Muslim minorities from Pakistan, Bangladesh and Afghanistan in the granting of Indian Citizenship.

On 15 December 2019 locals around JMI called a peaceful march against CAA. The university students joined them. Mob of unidentified people also joined the peaceful protests. The police alleged that some protestors set two DTC buses and a motorcycle on fire. The police moved in the campus because many unruly protestors had entered there. The police entered the campus without permission, acted brutally, vandalised the library, hit the students with batons. Even guards suffered head wounds and body injuries.

The students wanted social peace and harmony, equity and divisiveness and not the police discrimination on the basis of religion. The police action has raised protests. University Grant Commission's 2016, guidelines an off-campus safety do not mention any restriction on police from entering in university campus. The convention of police seeking permission is merely an understanding between the local police and the university. The action of police is being slammed for provoking violence.

Aligarh Muslim University (AMU) Clashes

Aligarh Muslim University (AMU) witnessed clashes between police and protesters on 15 December 2019, after protests against CAA turned violent at Jamia Millia Islamia, New Delhi. Hundreds of students of the university were protesting against the amended Citizenship Act when they clashed with the police. Dozen of policemen stormed into the AMU campus chasing students into their hostel and other buildings, firing tear gas and stun grenades and launching a baton attack on them as they ran for cover. Police said the students broke down the police cordon. Police denied the allegations saying that they entered the campus on the request of AMU authorities and followed standard operating procedure. On the morning of the 16 December, the university announced the postponement of all the semester exams and advanced the winter vacation that were actually scheduled from 23 December. All of hostel students were asked to pack their bags and leave within hours of the violence. This was unprecedented in the university. In the aftermath of the violence, AMU authorities tried to bridge the trust deficit with angry students. Meanwhile, the police were at pains to prove their proportional and justified action. A case has been registered against unidentified students of AMU in connection with the violence which broke out during the protest.

JNU Campus Face Off

The whole problem started with UGC stopping funds to the university, citing it to be an autonomous body. Students of have been protesting since November 2019 against the Draft Hostel Manual, which has provisions for hostel fee hike. The JNU Students' Union (JNUSU) has demanded a complete rollback of the hostel manual.

The JNU administration's rationale for the hike is that the fee has not been revised for nearly nineteen years. While the JNUSU has cited the university's annual reports to suggest that more than 40 per cent of the students come from lower-income groups who cannot afford this hike. The new hostel charges require students to pay a service charge of ₹ 1,700 per month which previously did not exist.

Students argued that JNU will be the costliest central university if the fee hike is implemented. A high powered committee was set up to look into the matter and certain mutually agreeable agreements were arrived at, such as students were not been asked to bear the cost of service and utility charges proposed for the winter session. The revised hostel room charges, however, will remain applicable with 50 per cent concession for BPL students.

Once again, JNU has been on the boil since 5 January 2020, when a group of masked miscreants intruded into the campus and assaulted students in Sabarmati hostel with sticks and metal rods and damaged property on the campus, prompting the administration to call in the police. The police reached there after the mob has dispersed after running a mock. At least 35 students including President of the Student's Union were injured in the violence. The two groups accused each other for the violence that continued for nearly two hours. The incident did not take long for national and social media to spark a wave of anger and condemnation. A tusnami of outrage against the hooliganism at JNU rose from some of the country's top campuses on next day and swept through several cities and towns.

In India, the campus face-off is not new, a reason why every political party has assured, it has a youth outfit to carry its flag among students. Campuses have been the frontline of ideological battles. The shouting of anti-national slogans at some universities by outsiders also indicates that extremism and Naxalism have found their way into the campuses. The recent turn of events in campuses of JNU, AMU and Jamia Millia also show that. Today, the students are brilliant and hardworking. They seek independence and make choices for their future. They believe, they can be a part of nation-building and take part in academic as well as national and social issues, along with the opportunity to learn and build their future.

Process of Growth of Agitation Due to Youth Unrest

A lifecycle which many youth agitations follow can be explained. The stages include: (a) the discontent stage, which is the stage of dissatisfaction and growing confusion with the existing conditions; (b) the initiation stage, in which a leader emerges, the causes of discontent are identified, excitement increases and proposals for action are debated; (c) the formalization stage, in which programmes are developed, alliances are forged, and support is also sought of some crusaders; (d) the public support stage, in which youth trouble is transferred into public trouble. This not only creates awareness among public but also seeks public support on the concerned issue. Initially, the action starts in one area but then it spreads in other areas. The youth fail to get the public support where (i) the claim is too vague, (ii) the issue is incorrectly focussed, (iii) the issue is not powerful to gain attention, (iv) ineffective strategies are adopted by the youth for pressing claims, and (v) there is opposition from other groups; and (e) official action stage in which the agencies in power realize the importance of the issue, officially acknowledge the discontentment and agree to adopt strategies to solve the issue. Sometimes, the strategy adopted by the group in power is rejected by the youth leaders and the youth start a movement to counter the strategies of people in power.

Important Youth Agitations in India

Gujarat Agitation

The anti-reservation youth agitation in Gujarat in 1985 had started when, following the recommendations of the Rane Commission (which was appointed in April 1981 and had given its recommendations in October 1983), the Government of Gujarat hastily enhanced the reservation quota in March 1985, just before the Assembly elections, for the students of the Socially and Educationally Backward Classes (SEBCs). The quota was increased from 10 per cent to 28 per cent, the maximum allowed by the Rane Commission. The Rane Commission had laid emphasis on income and occupation rather than caste as a criterion for backwardness, using ₹ 10,000 a year as a yardstick. The Gujarat government had already reserved 14 per cent seats for the STs, 7 per cent for the SCs, 3 per cent for the handicapped, 1 per cent for the children of the ex-servicemen and 10 per cent for the SEBCs. The increase of 18 per cent more seats for the SEBCs meant a total reservation of 53 per cent seats in colleges. Since 70 per cent of the state's population (of 3.4 crore) was covered by the reservation (of 53% seats), it meant that only 47 per cent seats were open to the 30 per cent population of the state. Further, out of every 100 seats in colleges, 30 seats were reserved for other states. Adding these 30 seats to the 39 reserved seats for STs, SCs and the SEBCs (out of every 100 seats) meant that only 31 seats were available to rest of the students. Naturally, the students reacted, and started an anti-reservation agitation. Unfortunately, the peaceful Gujarat bandh organized by the students on 18 March 1985, was followed by Hindu-Muslim clashes on 19 March 1985 when the Muslims refused to join the anti-reservationists against the Dalits. When six student leaders were arrested under the National Security Act (NSA), the agitationists intensified their stir. They were joined by government doctors which forced the government to suspend some striking doctors. The suspension of the doctors added fuel to the fire and the agitation flared up.

The students were now joined by their parents who formed a small body in Ahmedabad and decided to work shoulder to shoulder with their wards in their efforts to get the reservation policy scrapped. For calming down the communal riots which had simultaneously started, the police beat up people indiscriminately in some lower middle class residential areas in Ahmedabad. Soon the government started talks with student leaders, opposition leaders, and leaders of the parents' body and accepted all demands put up by the agitationists. It also agreed to review the policy of reservation. With the release of student leaders and the reinstatement of the suspended doctors, another round of violence by the agitationists started. The stir gained momentum in other parts of the state too. Several persons died and many were injured and arrested in the violence. When the agitating students killed one constable (on 22 April 1985), the constabulary revolted and stopped work. In an unexpected move, the constables in the funeral procession of the constable killed, attacked the journalists covering the incident. They also set fire to a building of a Gujarati daily. Many shops, houses, banks, vehicles and public offices were set aflame by the agitationists. The opportunist politicians clamouring for power not only instigated the agitationists but also demanded the resignation of the Chief Minister. Thus, what had started as an anti-reservation agitation by students soon took the shape of Hindu–Muslim antagonism and strife, Dalit versus upper caste communal clashes and political bickering. The stir continued for two months till the government retreated and promised to review the reservation policy.

Similarly, we may take the case of the anti-reservation agitation by the youth in Madhya Pradesh in 1985. In this state, 23 per cent seats were reserved for STs, 14 per cent for the SCs, 25 per cent for the backward classes, 3 per cent for the defence personnel and ex-servicemen, 5 per cent for the freedom fighters, 4 per cent for the poor candidates and 3 per cent for the candidates with a technical degree. Thus, since 77 per cent seats were reserved for various groups, only 23 per cent seats remained for other persons. When students agitated, the Chief Minister appealed to them to 'appreciate' the government's reservation policy of providing crutches to weaker sections of the society. The students described it as a ludicrous appeal and continued their agitation. The government did not take sufficient care to calm down the hostility simmering among the 'meritorious' upper caste students. It only agreed to discuss the issue with the students after the election. No wonder, the state remained traumatized by violent incidents between different sections of its populace for quite some time.

Assam Agitation

The youth of Assam started agitation in 1983–84 on the issue of refugees from East Bengal and ultimately were joined by a majority of the population in the state. The agitation culminated in the student community winning the assembly elections in 1985 and forming the government. For the first time in the history of the country, the students became political rulers.

However, the state government continued to feel the pinch of being neglected by the central government. The youth felt so agitated that United Liberation Front of Assam (ULFA) came into existence. The ULFA activists not only challenged the state authority but sowed seeds of separation, silenced opposition at gun-point, extorted money and erected a parallel government in the state.

Anti-Mandal Agitation

The agitation and self-immolation cases of the youth in 1990 is something that cannot be easily forgotten. Challenging the true purpose of the government in accepting the Mandal Commission's report, the students went on a rampage and took to agitations and immolations. A large number chose to set themselves on fire in full public view while some took poison or quietly burnt themselves to death. In almost all the cases, the victims came from the lower-middle class families. The elite and the poor were, however, not hit by the anti-Mandal wave. In all cases, the students left behind melodramatic and vitriolic suicide notes. Some students were killed in police firing at various places; many were injured, while thousands were arrested. The students also damaged thousands of government vehicles, private buses, cars and trains. The total loss was estimated to be worth several crores of rupees. There was a sense of frustration and anger at the system, a feeling that the system had given them the false hope that education would give them better jobs, and thus, a better future.

Role of Youth in Other Agitations

Navnirman Andolan (Re-invention or Re-construction movement) was a socio-political movement in 1974 in Gujarat by students and middle-class people against economic crisis and corruption in public life. It is the only successful agitation in the history of post-independence India that resulted in the dissolution of an elected government of the state. The militants' agitation for Khalistan in Punjab and for an independent Kashmir in Jammu & Kashmir and the tribals' demand for a Jharkhand state in Bihar have also to be explained in terms of the frustrations of the youth in the respective states.

In Punjab, the figures compiled by the Directorate of Employment point out that till December 1984, as many as 59,360 persons were registered in the Employment Exchanges in Amritsar and 65,619 in Gurdaspur. Adding figures of other cities to the registered cases, one gets the idea of the prevalent unemployment among the youth. Large-scale unemployment has surely helped in the growth of extremism. Even the political leaders have confessed that the problem of extremism in Punjab has its roots in the economic hardships faced by the youth. It was on this basis that at least two governors of Punjab insisted, between 1985 and 1987, on focussing on the solution of the unemployment problem of the youth in the state along with concentrating on the political solution of the problem.

In Kashmir also, the real power now rests with the young men. Many persons arrested by the police for getting training in Pakistan are young persons in the 18–25 age group. A lot of Kashmiris asking for independence are angry young men, who have sworn vengeance, and there is no method in their madness.

The movement of the tribals of Chotanagpur and the Santhal Pargana areas of Bihar, popularly called the Jharkhand movement, for a separate state entered a new phase with All Jharkhand Students Union (AJSU) organizing a successful 72-hour economic blockade in February 1991, by disrupting the movement of minerals from south Bihar. The Centre appeared to be prepared to concede an autonomous council on the Gorkhaland pattern but the Jharkhandis were insisting on nothing less than a separate state for preserving their cultural heritage and distinct identity. The tribal youth believed that the Hinduization (because of settlement of outside low caste Hindus in the interior areas) and the spread of Christianity have had a deleterious effect on their centuries-old social cohesiveness. They thought that the emerging cross-cultural milieu (because of the urbanization and industrialization processes) had only exposed them to assimilation.

The Chotanagpur tribals have been resisting the iniquitous system of dams, factories and exploitation of mineral wealth. The State Reorganization Commission had dismissed the demand for Jharkhand as impractical and ill-founded but the Adivasi Mahasabha, the precursor of the Jharkhand party, used this slogan of separate state and captured all the tribal majority seats in the area in 1991 elections. Since then, the movement gained momentum, though the lack of proper leadership and a united organization was the main drawback of the movement. The AJSU formed a United Jharkhand Party (UJP) on the AASU pattern in Assam. The tribal youth, then, seemed to be determined to prove their strength and could succeed in getting their demand for a separate Jharkhand state in 2000 fulfilled.

Taking all these youth agitations into consideration, it appears that most Indian youth was so frustrated and pessimistic that they started believing that it would not be possible to improve the lot of the people in the country even after making a large number of policies and programmes by the government. According to an all-India survey done of a sample of 2,100 youth in 38 towns across the country by the Operation Research Group (ORG), a multidisciplinary research organization, in April 1988, on youth perceptions, the youth voiced their concern at the dwindling job opportunities (*Hindustan Times*, 15 May 1988). More than 62 per cent respondents said that the employment situation had worsened. About 52.2 per cent were convinced that India was not set on the right track for progress and development. Another 36.7 per cent felt that there would be no improvement in the lot of Indians even ten years hence. About 26 per cent thought that the conditions would, in fact, worsen. The survey also revealed a mixed response to the government's new education policy. Less than 37 per cent felt the policy was good or necessary for the country. In contrast, more than 27 per cent asserted that the policy would be of little consequence.

But, of late two agitations – Anna Hazare's anti-corruption movement (2011) and the one for demanding justice for the victim of Delhi gangrape case (2012) – have not only offered a ray of hope but also set a new trend of cause-driven youth agitations in India. Till now, we have been witnessing two types of youths in India – one who is pro-government and the other who is anti-government. But, during these agitations, we have seen the birth of a 'new' youth who did not believe in *'sab chalta hai'* dictum and wants immediate change in the system. These are the people who are now agitating across the country and are also achieving satisfactory results. The main reasons for this are social media, system failure and the paralysis of our political system.

Anna's movement against corruption inspired youth in a big way. In contrast to the massive hired crowds generally seen at political rallies, those who came to meetings were mostly the young people for whom Anna was a combination of both Gandhi and a rockstar. These demonstrations were also different in a way that they were mostly attended by youth of the country, just expressing their concern about corruption. Thus, it was the active participation of youth that made Anna's movement a great success.

Similarly, the gang-rape of a 23-year-old paramedical intern (who later died after 13 days in a Singapore hospital) by six persons in a moving bus in the capital city on the night of 16 December 2012 also disenchanted the country's youth in a big way. In the protests following the incident in different parts of the country, especially Delhi, the participation of youth was tremendous. Even the police action against the protesters could not dampen their spirits, demanding justice for the girl. In Delhi, the protests were mainly held at India Gate where thousands of young demonstrators were lathi-charged, shot with water cannons and tear gas shells, and arrested by police. In similar protests held in other parts of the country mostly young people took part. The issue was highly sensitized both in print media and social media. Lakhs of youths also signed an online petition protesting the incident. It was the result of these widespread protests that governments at the centre and in various states announced several steps to ensure the safety of women. The important thing that was noticed during both the movements was their being non-violent in character.

Types of Youth Agitations

Youth agitations are not always violent or coercive. Many a time they use persuasive technique too. We may classify youth agitations into the following groups:

1. *Persuasive agitations*: In these agitations, the youth attempts to change the attitude of the powers by discussing their problems with them across the table and making them accept their viewpoint. These agitations range from the relatively trivial issues (postponing the examinations, extending the admission date) to significant issues (increasing the number of seats) to really serious issues (giving representation in academic bodies, associating students with decision-making processes). Protest demonstrations, shouting of slogans, persuading the power holders to meet the representatives of the students/youth to try and understand their views and demands are some of the methods used in this kind of agitation. The anger and injustice expressed through this method not only serves to arouse and mobilize popular support of passive students/youth but also helps drain off discontent into 'harmless' emotional outlets.
2. *Resistance agitations*: The main object in these types of agitations are to keep the power holders in their place. Many changes intended to be introduced by the authorities appear to be disturbing to students/youth who feel that either their precious years are being wasted or that legitimate opportunities are being denied to them or their careers are going to be adversely affected. For example, the decision of one university to show reduced marks on the marks sheet, when on revaluation the candidate's marks are reduced, was resisted by the students through agitations which ultimately forced the academic council of the university to decide that marks would not be reduced on revaluation. Or say, a university decides to introduce semester scheme or internal assessment scheme or scheme of making 75 per cent attendance compulsory. Students may resist these measures. Resistance agitations express the dismay and concern of the students at the direction in which the university is moving.
3. *Revolutionary agitations*: These agitations aim at bringing sudden sweeping changes in the educational or the social systems. For example, forcing the authorities to decide that no student will be declared as failed but will be promoted to higher class and given the opportunity to appear in the failed paper/subject till he clears it. Revolutionary leaders see basic change possible only after the existing system is overthrown and a new system is introduced in one go. Instances of revolutionary agitations can be illustrated by the youth agitation, such as the All Assam Student's Union (AASU) agitation in Assam in 1984, Uttarakhand agitation in Uttar Pradesh in 1994 and Bodo agitation in Assam during 1989–96. The last agitation is characterized by a growing discontent, increasing disorder, an attempt to overthrow the government, militant activities of the extremists, a reign of terror, and an attempt to smuggle weapons from abroad.

Youth Receptive to Agitations

Five types of youth who take to agitational activities have been identified:

1. *Socially isolated*: Youth who feel alienated and cut off from the larger society.
2. *Personally maladjusted*: Youth who have failed to find a satisfying life role, for example, those who have not developed an adequate interest in studies, are unemployed or underemployed or unsuccessful. They join agitations because of an emotional need to fill the void in their lives.
3. *Unattached to family*: Youth who lack intimate ties with their families are encouraged to participate in agitations. Young persons with warm and satisfying family ties have no emotional need to join agitations.
4. *Marginals*: Youth who are not fully accepted and integrated with their caste/religious/linguistic group feel uneasy, insecure and resentful. They find it difficult to resolve the discrepancy in self-image and public image which necessitates them to join agitations to get some recognition.
5. *Mobile/migrants*: Migrants have little chance of getting integrated into the larger community. Joining agitations acts as refuge for them.

Shah (1968: 57–63) conducted a study of university students in Gujarat. He classified students on the basis of their social status into four groups to point out the type of students who are more undisciplined or in whom we find more unrest:

1. *High status, high ability*: These are students who are eligible for admission in any course, who have full confidence in self, who can adjust to any situation and who take keen interest in studies. They remain confident of achieving goals because of their abilities, work hard, do not create any problems and remain away from strikes and demonstrations.
2. *Low status, high ability:* These are students who have high ability and are mature, who try to differentiate between right and wrong, work hard, aim at good percentages and grades, remain away from activities which harm them since they have to depend on themselves for getting jobs and promotions and do not participate in strikes and demonstrations. However, there are some youth in this group who in spite of their abilities fail to get recognition as they belong to poor class or to the SCs, STs or OBCs. These students participate in agitations because of their frustrations.
3. *High status, low ability*: These are students who can get admission in the desired course because of their influence. However, they cannot compete with good students of high academic standards because of their low ability and, therefore, develop new non-academic values and behaviour patterns. For example, they find nothing wrong in using unfair means, remaining absent from class, creating noise in the classroom, spending more time in college canteens, using pressure

tactics on teachers, attempting to bribe examiners and participating in agitations and instigating others to indulge in such activities.

4. *Low status, low ability*: These are students some of whom take interest in agitations but some keep themselves aloof from such activities. It depends on their peer group as well as their personal aspirations. Thus, more unrest is found among students of second and third categories.

It may, therefore, be concluded that important things in students' unrest and agitations are: students' family background, students' abilities, availability of opportunities to earn livelihood, and educational system, that is, teachers' abilities, teaching techniques, the content of courses (whether these courses are job-oriented or otherwise) and administrators' interest in solving students' legitimate grievances. Lipset gives importance to one more factor, namely, the number of years a student has spent in college/university. The more the years spent, the more is participation in agitations.

Limitations of Youth Agitations

However rational or irrational a youth agitation may be, it is limited by at least four considerations: (a) number of persons participating, (b) feelings of agitators, (c) leadership, and (d) the external controls.

If the number of persons who have joined the agitation is small, it may not last long, but if the number is large and adequate enough to attract the attention of the power holders, it may get some stability and also arouse enthusiasm and dedication of the youths.

Second, the feelings, resentments and prejudices of the agitating members also provide stimulus to agitation. If the members are volatile, they will express their hostility without much restraint, but if they are more passive, they will refrain from expressing their emotions and impulses. Young people in agitations can be vocal without guilt feelings. At the same time, they can also be less responsive and can respond unenthusiastically to a good leader/speaker. If a large number of members of the aggressive group share common feelings, the group is likely to edge forward, but if only a few members share common emotions, the group is likely to progress slowly.

The mores of the agitators equally affect their behaviour. Will students shout slogans against the teachers? Will they destroy the university property? Will they bodily harm the vice-chancellor? Will they seek the help of anti-social elements? Will they use coercive methods in getting donations from the public? All this will be decided by the mores and the moral values of the agitators.

Third, the function of the leader of the agitating group is not to paralyse the moral judgements of the agitating members but to neutralize and isolate their moral judgements. The youth leader also affects the intensity and the direction of agitation. Given a group of frustrated, discontented and resentful young people, a skilful leader can convert them and direct their aggression at any 'enemy' whom they already hate. Likewise, a leader can also divert the agitation by a strategic suggestion or command. Since most youth agitations are unstructured with no designated leaders, the leadership position is 'up for grabs'. Anyone may become a leader by simply displaying capacity for giving suggestions in an authoritative manner.

Lastly, an agitation faces certain limitations because of the external controls. The vice-chancellor may call the police in the campus but only a few policemen may be sent. The agitators in such a situation will not face many constraints. But when the youth agitators in the city are surrounded by large number of policemen or policemen with *lathis* and guns in their hands, they may have to face defeat. Similarly, cold weather, rains, heat and unsympathetic onlookers near the place of agitation, may prevent the agitators from vigorously and successfully pursuing their efforts.

Causes of Youth Unrest and Agitations

The youth of today are in a grave situation. One cause of youth unrest could be dissatisfaction among young people with the status quo and a desire to change it. There is unrest among them because they are facing numerous problems like ambition, anxiety, identity, etc. They perceive that their futures are out of their control and that decisions are made without taking their interests into account. There is the deep divide between the urban youth and the rural one. The former is in a state of defiance against the old order. They find it difficult to adjust themselves in the present set up and thus, they become victims of alienation or estrangement. Deprived of the opportunity to develop intellectually, many suffer from the problem of subjective isolation and self-estrangement. The life of modern youth is centred on one question: how to make money? They equate success, happiness, fame everything with money and they are looking for the fastest route to go there. The rural youth, on the contrary, generally comes to towns and cities in bulk, in search of employment after completing their studies. On one hand, they find themselves free from traditional institutions of rural life, while on the other, they have to adjust themselves with the youth of urban background.

The UGC Committee of 1960 pointed out the following reasons for student agitations: (a) economic causes, like demands for reducing fees, increasing scholarship, (b) demands for changes in existing norms pertaining to admissions, examinations, and teaching, (c) poor functioning of colleges/universities with non-purchase of chemicals and instruments for laboratories, or books and journals for libraries, (d) conflicting relations between students and teachers (teachers being accused of frequently cutting classes and remaining non-committed to teaching), (e) inadequate facilities in the campus, like inadequate hostels, poor food in hostels, lack of canteens and poor drinking water facilities, and (f) leaders being instigated by politicians.

Dibona Joseph studied agitations in one university in Uttar Pradesh and gave three causes of student agitations: (a) *economic causes*, which included a sense of insecurity for the future and gap between economic needs of the country and the educational system, that is, education being viewed as non-job-oriented; (b) *socio-psychological causes*, which included defective educational system, gap between aspiration and achievement (getting 80% marks and yet failing to get admission in college of one's interest), social distance between teacher and students, non-committed teachers, policy of status quo, corruption and inefficiency, and large number of students in the class or inadequate number of sections in the department/college; and (c) *political causes*, which included, political interference, and instigation by political leaders. All these factors indicate that the main cause of student unrest and agitations in particular and youth agitations in general lies in social system rather than the personality of the youth.

Various factors have contributed to the problems of youth unrest. Some of them may be noted here:

1. *Improper socialization and family problems*: The failure on the part of parents to bring up their children, in accordance with the cultural expectations of the society has made the youth to go astray. The immoral habits and bad qualities of the parents also have a harmful effect on the personal growth of the children. The family problems spoil the mental peace and the emotionality of the growing children.
2. *Political, social and economic inequalities*: The young people are more sensitive to the political, economic and social inequalities and exploitation. They have contempt for the existing 'system'. They are disillusioned with what they are having and are pessimistic about the future.
3. *Defective educational system*: The students do not have any respect for the present defective educational system. The outdated, uninspiring, unintegrated and irrelevant educational system cannot make the students become disciplined and responsible.
4. *Unemployment*: Unemployment of the educated youths is on the increase. The education that they receive does not enable them to become economically self-reliant. On the other hand, the government is not in a position to provide employment to all the educated youth. As a result, the youth are losing confidence in themselves and are becoming more and more restless.
5. *Corrupt and discredited authority*: The youth are disappointed with the corrupt and discredited authority. Corruption, craziness for power, moral lapses, opportunism, nepotism, discrimination, etc. found among the political and social leaders have made the youth to have nothing but contempt for them. The leadership has failed to set a good model for the students to emulate.
6. *Misuse of student power by the politicians*: The corrupt and unscrupulous politicians, who are making use of student power to further their partisan political interests, are also contributing to the problem. Students are becoming puppets in the hands of some disgruntled politicians to serve their selfish ends.

7. *Administrative failures:* Youth unrest is often caused by administrative errors and miscalculations. The indifference and lack of sympathy for the students' demand on the part of the administrations (of the university as well as the government) many times force the students, to resort to strikes.
8. *Communication gap*: Lack of understanding and lack of proper communication between the students and teachers, on the one hand and parents and children, on the other, also cause youth unrest. The failure on the part of the parents to understand the aspirations of their young children also adds to the problem.
9. *Value differences and conflict of values*: The value differences in society, the changes and conflicts of values also contribute to youth unrest:
   (a) Some of the old values are at conflict now, the traditional beliefs, practices, ideas, ideals and values appear to be outmoded, unscientific, irrelevant and irrational for the modern youths.
   (b) The youths are becoming more and more rationalistic. They are impressed by the modern values based on science and rationalism. Still, they are not in a position to give up the traditional values completely. They are in a state of confusion. They can neither accept the new completely nor do away with the old once and for all. This has made them restless.
   (c) The youth is influenced by values of individualism and democracy. Hence, they are revolting against the old traditional order.
   (d) The youths feel they are also mature, responsible and sensible. They resent their elders treating them as 'immature' and 'irresponsible lot'. They feel annoyed and embarrassed to find themselves in a helpless situation. They do not want to remain dumb witnesses to all the unfortunate and unwanted events that happen in society.
   (e) Some of the youths are carried away by the hedonistic values or pleasure philosophy. They want to take the maximum benefit out of the disturbed social situations. They have no respect for any values for they have lost faith in them.
10. *Lack of opportunities*: The youths do not get proper opportunities, to express their talents, cultivate their interests and develop their personality. This has contributed to their dissatisfaction.
11. *The gap between the aspirations and achievement*: The youths are likely to have their own aspirations and ambitions. They will be dreaming about it all the while. But the reality of life makes them become disgusted. The youths with unfulfilled desires and aspirations can hardly be at rest.
12. *Lack of determination and self-responsibility*: Some of the youths lack willpower and self-determination. They depend more on others rather than on their intrinsic abilities and talents. They apishly imitate others and fail to develop the spirit of self-reliance. They are hesitant

to assume responsibilities. Such youths are highly vulnerable to any kind of use.

13. *Influence of movies*: The modern movies which mostly portray violence, arson, loot, rape, murder, immorality, crimes, etc. have a great demoralising effect on the modern youths. Students in particular, imitate their pet film actors and actresses with all their frailties. Scant respect for their cultural values and the apish imitation of the western tendencies has further contributed to the problem.

Remedies for Youth Unrest

The problem of the youth must be understood in connection with the relationships of the students with parents, teachers, politicians, police authorities, student union leaders, university authorities, and the values, traditions, needs, motivations and aspirations of the students. These variables are found to be associated with the tension in the college-going youth. A few suggestions may be made here to minimise the youth unrest.

1. *The system of education*: A thorough overhauling of our education system is necessary to help the students to face the problems and challenges of life. No hotch-potch change in education would suffice. But education requires a comprehensive planning and an integral approach. This would bridge the gap between what the students actually experience and what is taught to them in schools and colleges. Colleges and universities should make proper provision for (a) adequate boarding and lodging facilities, (b) better libraries and reading rooms and laboratories, (c) enough facilities for recreation and extra-curricular activities (d) seminar and tutorial system.
2. *Employment opportunities*: Efforts should be made to provide opportunities for the students to offer courses in agriculture, engineering, business management, commerce, medicine, etc. The spirit of self-reliance must be created and the students should be encouraged to set up business and cottage industries of their own.
3. *Provision for leisure-time activities*: Students should not be allowed to idle their time. Hobby clubs and workshops catering to painting, music, photography, stamp collection, swimming, etc. should be established in colleges. Indoor games, dramatic performances, excursions and picnics, functions catering to the interest of fine arts and literature must be encouraged among them.
4. *Economic difficulties*: Poor and needy students should be given financial help through scholarships, freeships, loan scholarships, free hostel facilities, stipends, etc. so that they do not drop out of schools and colleges. The programme of 'earn while you learn' needs to be well organized.
5. *Discipline:* Students should be assisted in developing self-discipline for it is long lasting than the imposed discipline. Acts of indiscipline should

be dealt with sternly, but of course, humanistically. The teachers must play an important role in this respect.

6. *Able leadership*: Students very badly need able and efficient leadership. In any democratic set-up, leadership is very important. Leadership training programmes under supervision should be introduced in colleges. Politicians must not be allowed to misguide the students.
7. *Role of political parties*: Political parties should be kept out of the college campuses. The students should have political awareness, but their active participation in politics would spoil the peaceful atmosphere of the campus. The student leaders, teachers and university authorities must make a joint venture to save education and campus from power politics.
8. *Students' participation*: As Dr V.K. Rao, ex-Union Minister for Education had suggested 'students the world over have become restive and are demanding a voice in the affairs of universities and a fair share in running the machine and in decision-making'. This demand cannot be evaded for long except at great peril. In brief, the students should be given ample opportunities to take part in the administrative bodies of the university. The communication gap between the students and teachers should be bridged. The teacher must not look at the students with suspicion. They must have confidence in their students. They must act as their friend, guide and philosopher. The teacher-student ratio must be reduced. Every student must get due attention of the teacher. More than this, basically the teacher must change their attitude towards the students and the profession.

Theories on the Causes of Youth Agitations

Two kinds of theories may be suggested to explain youth agitations: psychological and sociological. The former emphasizes on the personality of the individual and the latter on the society. The two important psychological theories are: (a) discontent theory, and (b) personal maladjustment theory, while the two important sociological theories are: (a) relative deprivation theory, and (b) resource mobilization theory.

The *Discontent Theory* holds that agitations are rooted in discontent. Youth who have either no high aspirations or are contented and comfortable with what they have or what they are likely to have will have no interest in agitations. But, the angry youth who feel victimized by outrageous injustice, or those who feel even mildly annoyed with existing structures and opportunities will collectively act to pressurize the power holders to bring some change (Figure 1).

It is probably true that without discontent amongst the youth, there will be no youth agitations. But 'discontent' is not an adequate explanation. There is no convincing evidence of any close association between the level of grievance and discontent amongst the youth and its level of agitational activity. Young people may endure great discontent and refrain from

Figure 1
Discontent Approach in Youth Agitations

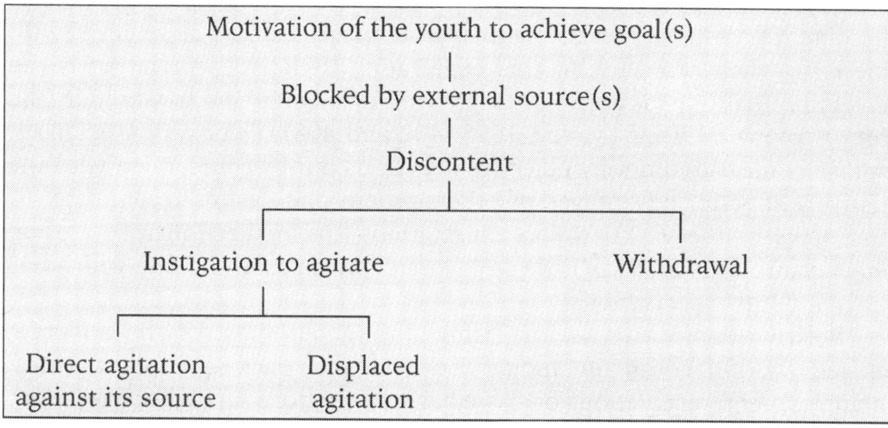

agitating. Since independence, youth in India have endured corruption, inequality, exploitation, political manipulations, police brutality, bureaucratic callousness, religious fanaticism without serious social protest. In fact, all modern societies always have enough discontent to fuel many agitations and movements (Turner and Killian, 1972: 271). Discontent may be a necessary condition but not a sufficient condition for youth agitations.

The *Personal Maladjustment Theory* sees agitations as a refuge from personal failure. Agitators find their supporters among the unhappy, frustrated young persons whose lives lack meaning and fulfilment. Huffer (1951) has also said that the kinds of people who are drawn to agitations and social movements are the bored, the misfits, the creative who cannot create, the guilty, the downwardly mobile, and those who are seriously dissatisfied with their lives. They add meaning and purpose to their empty lives through agitational activity. Horton and Hunt (1984: 500) have also said that it is plausible that young people who feel unfulfilled and maladjusted should be more attracted to agitational activities than those who are complacent and feel adjusted. Those who find their personal lives absorbing and fulfilling are less in need of something to give them feelings of personal worth and accomplishment, for they already have these. The agitation supporters are mainly the frustrated misfits of society.

Even though, the misfit theory is plausible, it is not well substantiated. It is difficult to measure a person's sense of non-fulfilment. All student agitations in universities and colleges cannot be explained simply in terms of personal failures of student leaders and activists. Youth agitations in different parts of the country on the occasion of implementing Mandal Commission's report in August 1990 cannot be described in terms of young persons' personal maladjustment.

The *Relative Deprivation Theory* was propounded by Samuel Stouffer in 1949 (*The American Soldier*, Princeton University Press, Princeton, 1950) It can be properly explained by distinguishing between discontent, deprivation and relative deprivation. A group feels 'deprived' if it is prevented from using or enjoying a goal/object it regards as attractive or desirable, but it feels 'discontented' when it had been anticipating the pleasure to be achieved with object and then cannot fulfil this expectation. Relative deprivation is the perception that one (as a group) is less well-off than others to whom it (the group) compared itself (Myres, 1988: 402 and 408). Deprivation or disadvantage is measured not by objective standards but by comparison with the relatively superior advantages of others whom one desires to emulate. It, thus, talks of the gap between expectations and realizations. The group which wants little and has little feels less deprived than the one which has much but still expects more.

Relative deprivation is increasing throughout most of the underdeveloped world. Youth in India also feel that lack of opportunities, unemployment, reservations on caste basis, limitations on higher education, particularly technical and professional education, adversely affect intellectual ability, and as such are avoidable. They long for better jobs, economic security, promotional opportunities, social mobility and all those things that many others enjoy. They long for these treasures but have little real understanding of what it takes to produce them. Even where the youth are beginning to get some of the things they covet or eagerly desire, these satisfactions come with an unbearable slowness. A weakening of traditional controls accompanies this enormous inflation of desires. The existing social structures and the power elite have little hope of keeping up with the youth's expectations. Thus, when young people become most miserable, agitations seem most likely to occur. Davies (1962) and Geschwender (1968) have also maintained that the outbreak of agitations most often happens after a downturn has interrupted a period of improvement, creating an intolerable gap between rising expectations and falling realizations.

The *Relative Deprivation Theory* is plausible but not substantiated. Feelings of deprivation in youth are easy to infer but difficult to measure and still more difficult to plot over a period of time. It may, therefore, be said that relative deprivation of youth, even when unmistakably severe, is only one of the many factors in youth agitations.

The *Resource Mobilization Theory* stresses techniques rather than causes of (youth) agitations. It attributes importance to the effective use of resources in promoting agitations, since a successful agitation demands effective organization and sage tactic. Resource mobilization theorists see (youth) leadership, organization and tactics as major determinants of the success or failure of (youth) agitations. These scholars concede that without grievances and discontent, there would be few agitations but add that mobilization is needed to direct this discontent into an effective agitation.

The resources to be mobilized include: support of the masses, help of rules/laws that can provide leverage, cooperation of organizations and officials that can be helpful, and assistance of target groups whom these benefits might attract. These are weighed against costs of agitational activity, opposition to be anticipated, difficulties to be overcome, and tactics of operation to be developed.

The *Resource Mobilization Theory* does not explain all kinds of youth agitations. If we classify agitations as persuasive, revolutionary and resistance agitations, the resource mobilization theory does not fit into resistance agitations. These agitations succeed without organization and tactics. Further, evidence for resource mobilization theory is largely descriptive and is challenged by scholars like Goldstone (1980).

It may be concluded that it is likely that discontent, personal maladjustment, relative deprivation, and resource mobilization are all involved in youth agitations but in undetermined proportions. Each theory is, thus, plausible but each lacks clear proof and evidence. Many variables are involved in youth agitations that possibly no one theory can ever be conclusively established.

Youth Leadership

The leadership profoundly affects the intensity and direction of youth agitations and movements. The important functions of a youth leader are: (a) establishing a responsive, trusting, attentive relationship with the members of his group. He senses their feelings and speaks their language; (b) building an emotional rapport with the members by an impassioned reminder of their problems and grievances. He stimulates them to direct activity from one objective to another; and (c) suggesting action to achieve goal(s). It could take the form of demonstrations, road blocks, *gheraos*, strikes or even boycott of classes. These functions could be successfully performed only by leaders who have certain qualities and background. Sarkar's (1960) study of the office-holders and the king-makers of student unions in different universities has revealed that union leaders are mainly those: (a) who have money, (b) who do not have high academic aspirations, (c) who have some political backing, (d) who are good orators, and (5) who are manipulators.

Youth leadership is important for the future of the community and the country. Without youth leadership, there will never be the next leaders in line and there will be no one to pass on the torch of the community.

Role of Police in Youth Agitations

The role of the police in youth agitations starts when the youth indulge in violence, destroy public property, *gherao* administrative officer(s), declare *bandh* and force shopkeepers to close market, sit on hunger strike, or block the road and stop movement of the traffic.

The traditional methods which are usually adopted by the police in such situations are: arresting the trouble-makers, ordering onlookers to move on, using tear-gas and lathi-charge, bringing enough police and creating fear, isolating riot-area by throwing a police cordon around it, and diminishing the crowd by directing persons to disperse, thus, depriving the core (of agitated group) of its mass support. Generally, the police succeeds in containing youth agitation by these methods. If it fails, it is only because of its own indecision and hesitation, or because it covertly sympathizes with rioters, or because it is not able to arrest the real trouble-makers because of the political or bureaucratic interference.

What the policemen need is: (a) to secure a preliminary tuning with agitators. On their arrival at the agitation spot, they need not immediately threaten the agitators or start beating them. On the contrary, they should give a feeling that they are there only to maintain law and order and not to punish the agitators; (b) to establish a rapport with the agitationists either by talking to the leader or the activist members; (c) to break 'one-to-all' relationship, that is, relationship between the leader and the followers; and (d) neither to use logic nor appeal to the intellect of the agitators but to appeal to their emotions.

All this can be made possible by either (a) manipulating the situation, or (b) manipulating the individuals (agitators). The manipulation could be positive or negative as shown in the following figure:

Figure 2

Handling Agitational Situation (Manipulation) by Police

Type of manipulation	*Manipulation of situation*	*Manipulation of individuals' (agitators') intentions*
Positive	Inducement	Persuasion
Negative	Coercion	Activation of commitment

The police can adopt measures like this only if it believes in neutrality, loyalty, moral duty, and accountability. The decision of the decision-maker (police) in a decision-making situation depends upon: (i) degree of involvement of self in solving the problem and (ii) perception of uncertainty to handle the situation (agitation) by following precedents (used earlier by other officers) or by using new approaches. Low degree of involvement of self (LIS) and high perception of uncertainty (HPU) lead to poor decision (PD) on the part of the decision-maker (police), while high involvement of self (HIS) and low perception of uncertainty (LPU) lead to correct or adequate decision (AD).

$$PD = LIS + HPU$$
$$AD = HIS + LPU$$

That police officer will have a low involvement of self in solving problem or containing an agitation who takes decisions not on the basis of his moral convictions or values but by external pressures, who depends on others for evaluating his decision, who feels satisfied with his own decision only if others feel satisfied, who considers agitation as a routine task and not as a challenge, who has low personal stake in containing the agitation or solving the problem, and who avoids certain decisions for fear of their consequences.

The perception of uncertainty by the decision-maker (police officer) in the decision-making situation may also be because of his lack of past experience, that is, he may not have met with such a situation earlier, or he may have been unable to get the right amount of information, that is, there may be too little information about the decision-making situation, or the situation itself may be poorly defined in terms of objectives, time and direction, or the police officer may lack the ability to evaluate situation as well as the decision choices.

Our ruling political elite have never given proper attention to revamping the police system. What is needed more today is more professionalism in this field (Sharma, 1977) which is characterized by decentralization (a separation of administration of law-violence from administration of preserving order, as these two kinds of jobs are not similar), autonomy (preventing the undesirable intervention of political leaders and bureaucratic executives), specialization (having separate police for dealing with agitations, juvenile delinquency, communal riots, and so forth), modernization (equipping police with modern technology) as well as developing modem ideology (correctional and protective rather than bossist), and accountability (to the public, to ideology, to law rather than the politicians in power).

Controlling Youth Agitations

The forces producing unrest and agitations cannot be eliminated easily. Youth agitations may be minimized by making efforts and taking actions at the right time.

Few ways are suggested below:

1. An average young man is individualistic, imaginative and competitive. He only wants guidance so that his enthusiasm and zest could be properly channelized. Youngsters should be taught to vent their anger. If a person bottles up his rage, he has to find an outlet which may give him an opportunity to let off the stored steam. In psychiatric terminology, this means that one's accumulated aggressive energy, be it from frustrations or from the building up of instinctual impulses, needs a release. Parents should also encourage their children's release of emotional tension in various kinds of activities.
2. The adult world has to accept the fact that youth problems cannot be solved for them but with them. Therefore, co-operation of students/youths need to be sought by parents, teachers and administrators. Youth/students, parents, teachers, educational administrators, politicians and political parties should cooperate in understanding problems/grievances of the youth and giving them logical guidelines.
3. Efforts should be taken to remove minor irritants in students'/youths' day-to-day contacts with teachers and educational administrators. Each educational institution must have an efficient machinery to identify and settle student grievances. Such arrangements must not only start tackling

problems after they flare up but must continuously strive to prevent incidents which lead to complications. Such bodies (students/teachers, etc.) should be continuously in session. The effective measures for the redressal of the grievances could be: (a) accessibility to senior functionaries, (b) ensuring action on grievance in shortest possible time or within definite time-frame, (c) establishing monitoring system and getting regular reports from teachers and subordinate administrative staff, and (d) sudden check-up by vice-chancellor or dean or person-in-power.

4. All political parties have to agree on a common code of conduct regarding students' participation in politics. It will prepare them for shouldering responsibilities in future for national development. There is no point in exhorting students to keep away from politics and yet expect them to get enthusiastically involved in the process of building up our society.
5. The question of the extent and pattern of student participation in the process of educational administration will have to be decided at the earliest.
6. Definite rules should be framed regarding police intervention in educational institutions. We can think of instituting a special University Police Force. We can also have specially trained police personnel for dealing with students in particular and youth in general.

It is high time that the vast youth power, which hitherto has been neglected and ignored, is harnessed for development, removal of social injustice and achieving national collective goals. The need for creating a climate of hope, confidence and trust rather than coercion and confrontation has to be realized and this initiative has to be taken for mobilizing the young.

A student movement is distinguished from the youth movement. Student movements are mostly built around ideal issues. All people belonging to a certain age group (15–30) are youths. But all youths are not students. School, college and university students form a fraction of the total youth population of a country. Students occupy a very important place in the youth population of the country. The main features of student movements are as follows: First, student movements deal with ideal issues. Second, student movements are elitist in character because students comprise only a microscopic minority of the total population.

Role of Students in Indian National Movement

The youth unrest in India started at the beginning of the 20th century. Unorganized youth movements were taking place here and there, most of them were directed against the British rule in India. The youth joined hands with the people in launching protest movements against the British. They played an important role in the freedom struggle. The students took part in the Indian freedom struggle on a very wide scale for the first time when Lord Curzon partitioned Bengal in 1905. Since then, the students have been taking part in all the major national struggles. The youths were mainly behind the Indian National Congress at that time. When the Congress was split into two groups of extremists and moderates in its Lahore session in 1907, the students also got distributed between these groups. They rallied around the leadership of Bal Gangadhar and later on, of Mahatma Gandhi. Under the leadership and guidance of Gandhiji, the students became a formidable force in India.

Role of Gandhi

After his return from South Africa, Gandhiji entered politics, i.e. the freedom struggle in 1919, on the advice of his 'political guru' Gopalakrishna Gokhale. Gandhiji launched his campaign against Rowlatt Act (1919), the Jallianwalla Bagh atrocities in 1919 in which the students had taken part in a big number. Gandhiji called the nation to wage a passive resistance movement against the government; to boycott all things British, break links with the government, resign from posts, surrender titles and offices, and withdraw from schools and colleges. The nation responded promptly and students in a very big number boycotted schools and colleges. For the first time, the student force was organized and mobilized against the British rule. In 1920, the First All-India Students' Conference was held in Nagpur under the presidentship of Lala Lajpat Rai. Students could now get the support and guidance of leaders like, Subhas Chandra Bose and others. Students took an active part in various campaigns launched by Gandhiji against the British such as the 'No Tax' Campaign 1921, the Civil Disobedience Movement, the Dandy Satyagraha of 1930, etc. They also took interest in Gandhiji's constructive programmes such as – removal of untouchability and casteism, adult education, popularizing the *Swadeshi* articles and the use of *Khadi*, cleaning of the villages, promotion of communal harmony, and so on. In 1936, the All-India Students' Federation, the first student organization of India, was born in order to support the Indian National Congress in its struggles. The followers of Gandhiji and also the communists supported this organization in the beginning. Due to the clash of personalities and differences of opinion regarding its principles, the Students' Federation was divided into two factions (in 1938) such as – the All-India Youth Congress and All-India Students' Federation (AISF). The socialists within the Congress and the Gandhians supported the former, while the communists who wanted to follow the violent methods took into their hands the latter. Since then, the AISF is in the hands of the communists.

Role of Students in the Quit India Movement of 1942

The 'Quit India' Movement launched by the Indian National Congress under the leadership of Gandhiji was an important event in the Indian freedom struggle. M.K. Gandhi exhorted the students to give up their studies and join the movement to drive the aliens out of the country. Students' participation in the freedom struggle took a new dimension in this movement. It was almost the climax of the youth movement. Students in every nook and corner of India took part in it. They came out of the schools, colleges and universities, and boycotted the educational institutions. They organized mass processions and rallies in the towns and cities. They educated the uneducated and ignorant masses to fight for the cause of the nation. The students took to some violent actions to paralyse the British administration. They resorted to such methods as cutting telephone wires, blocking transport routes, destroying public property, disturbing postal, police, banking and other services. They ransacked government offices, burnt official documents and gheraoed police stations. They brought the government machinery to a standstill. They also kept in touch with the underground leaders and carried on the tempo of agitation. The British Government resorted to suppressive measures. The police lathi-charged on student gatherings, arrested and imprisoned a number of them and gave physical harassment to many of them. Some of them were killed in police firings also. The students made a considerable sacrifice in this movement and demonstrated that the youth of India were not lagging behind in the national struggle. They continued their struggle with the same spirit even up to 1947, that is, till India got the independence.

It is true that student movement was very much associated with politics before independence, but the student energy was spent for a national cause. From the political point of view, the youth movement in India before independence performed two important political functions: first, the youth supported the national freedom struggle and joined hands particularly with the Congress to disrupt the British institutions and paralyse the government. Second, the youth organizations and movements served as recruitment centres for the political parties. The then existing political parties (such as the Congress, Muslim League, Hindu Mahasabha) were looking forward with eagerness to catch young and dynamic persons for their parties from these movements and organizations.

Conclusion

It is true that there is youth unrest, but it is a part of the national malady. The students as a class can play a vital role in any attempt to change the national scene. Student activism is positively anti-establishment. Asking the students to behave, without the authorities doing anything to solve their problems, is not only unjust to the students but will further alienate them from the authorities. The student is a force. They are not a citizen of tomorrow, but they are very much a citizen of today. They have a participatory role to play in the task of nation-building. What they want is not a dozen advice but they want to see the models to be emulated by them. In the changing society where the authority stands discredited, the youth shall triumph and usher in an era of social change. The student power has shown that it is a potential factor that can bring about vast socio-political changes.

References

Altbach, Philip, 'Students and Politics', in S.M. Lipset (ed.), *Student Politics,* Basic Books, New York, 1967.

——, *Turmoil and Transition: Higher Education and Students' Politics in India,* Lalvani Publishing House, Bombay, 1968.

Bansod, Pushpa, 'Crisis on the Campus', *Seminar,* Vol. 44, April, 1963.

Berkowitz, L. (ed.), *Advances in Experimental Social Psychology,* Vol. 10, Academic Press, New York, 1979.

Blumer, Herbert, 'Collective Behaviour', in Alfred McClung Lee (ed.), *Principles of Sociology,* Barnes & Noble, New York, 1969.

Dibona, Joseph, 'Indiscipline and Student Leadership in an Indian University', in S.M. Lipset, *Student Politics,* Basic Books, New York, 1967.

Dollard, J., Doob, L., Miller, N., Mowrer, O.H. and Sears, R., *Frustration and Aggression,* Yale University Press, New Haven, 1939.

Feshbach, S., 'Aggression', in David Myres (ed.), *Social Psychology,* McGraw Hill Book Co., New York, 1970.

Geen, R.G. and Quanty, M.B., 'The Catharsis of Aggression: An Evaluation of a Hypothesis', in L. Berkowitz (ed.), *Advances in Experimental Social Psychology,* Vol. 10, Academic Press, New York, 1977.

Gore, M.S., *Education and Modernisation in India,* Rawat Publications, Jaipur, 1982.

Horton, Paul B. and Hunt, Chester L., *Sociology* (6th edn), McGraw Hill International Book Company, Singapore, 1984.

Huffer, Eric, *The True Believer,* Harper & Row, New York, 1951.

Myres, David G., *Social Psychology* (6th edn), McGraw Hill, New York, 1988.

Report of the UGC Committee on *The Problem of Student Indiscipline in India,* UGC, Delhi, 1960.

Sarkar, Chanchal, *The Unquiet Campus: Indian Universities Today,* The Statesman Press, New Delhi, 1960.

Shah, B.V., 'Students' Unrest: A Sociological Hypothesis', *Sociological Bulletin,* Vol. 18, Bombay, March, 1968.

Sharma, P.D., *Indian Police: A Development Approach,* Uppal Publishing House, Delhi, 1977.

Shaw, Robert C., 'Student Politics and Student Leadership in an Indian University: The Case of Osmania', in P.G. Altbach (ed.), *Turmoil and Transition,* Basic Books, New York, 1968.

Shils, Edward, 'Indian Students: Rather Sadhus than Philistines', *Encounter,* Vol. 17, September, 1961.

Stouffer, S.A., *The American Soldier: Adjustment During Army Life,* Vol. 1, Princeton University Press, Princeton, 1950.

Turner, Ralph H. and Killian, Lewis M., *Collective Behaviour,* Prentice Hall, Englewood Cliffs, New Jersey, 1972.

Walsh, Edward J., 'Resource Mobilisation and Citizen Protest in Communities', *Social Problems,* Vol. 29, October, 1981.

9

Child Labour and Child Abuse

Facts and Statistics on the Issue of Child Labour in India

1. One in every 11 children in India is working.
2. 80 per cent of working children live in India's villages, where most of them work in agriculture. Some of them also work in household industries and are employed in home-based businesses.
3. More than half of the 5.5 million working children in India are concentrated in five states – Bihar, Uttar Pradesh, Rajasthan, Madhya Pradesh and Maharashtra.
4. Adolescents doing hazardous work form 20.7 per cent of those employed in this age group, while almost 25 per cent of adults work in hazardous conditions.
5. Children between 14–17 years engaged in hazardous work account for 62.8 per cent of India's child labour workforce.
6. Nearly 10 per cent of adolescents working in hazardous conditions are working in family enterprises.
7. 56 per cent of the working adolescents are no longer studying.
8. More boys (38.7 million) than girls (8.8 million) are involved in hazardous work.
9. In 2018–19, out of 35,000 child labour complaints received nationwide, begging constituted the highest (45%), followed by employment in restaurants and *dhabhas* (23%).

Despite hectic planning, welfare programmes, legislation and administrative action in the past seven decades, a large majority of the Indian children continue to remain in distress and turmoil. In most families, the parents neglect them, caretakers batter them and in workplaces employers sexually abuse them. Though this problem of emotional, physical and sexual abuse of children in India is increasing, it has failed to capture the attention of sociologists and psychiatrists in our country. The public and the government also are yet to recognize it as a serious problem. Public indignation and professional concern is yet to be translated into positive and realistic action.

CHILD LABOUR

Child Labour typically means the employment of children in any manual work with or without payment. UNICEF has categorized child work into three categories:

1. *Within the family*: children are engaged in domestic household tasks without pay.
2. *Within the family but outside the home*: example: agricultural labourers, domestic maids, migrant labourers, etc.
3. *Outside the family*: example: commercial shops in restaurants and jobs, prostitution, etc.

Child labourers are exploited, exposed to hazardous work conditions and paid a pittance for their long hours of work. Forced to forego education, shouldering responsibilities far beyond their years, becoming worldly-wise when their peers have yet to leave the cocoons of parental protection, these children never know what childhood is. The Indian Constitution enshrines that:

1. No child below the age of 14 years shall be employed to work in any factory or in any hazardous employment (Article 24).
2. Childhood and youth are to be protected against exploitation and against moral and material abandonment (Article 39(f)).
3. The state shall endeavour to provide within a period of 10 years from the commencement of the Constitution free and compulsory education for all children until they complete the age of 14 years (Article 45).

The worst effects of child labour are:

1. mentally, physically, socially or morally dangerous and harmful to children;
2. interferes with their schooling;
3. depriving them of the opportunity to attend school;
4. obliging them to leave school prematurely; and
5. requiring them to attempt to combine school attendance with excessively long and heavy work hours.

In its most extreme forms, child labour involves children being enslaved, separated from their families, exposed to serious hazards and illnesses and/or left to fend for themselves on the streets of large cities – often at a very early age. Whether or not particular forms of 'work' can be called 'child labour' depends on the child's age, the type and hours of work performed, the conditions under which it is performed.

The agriculture sector comprises activities in agriculture, hunting, forestry, and fishing. The industry sector includes mining and quarrying, manufacturing, construction, and public utilities. Thousands of children still spend gruelling shifts in labour-intensive professions like farming, stone cutting sector, mining industry, and *zari* and embroidery. Ten million bonded children in India are working in professions like *beedi*-rolling, brick kilns, farming, stone cutting sector, mining industry, and *zari* and embroidery, construction, fireworks, hotels, hybrid cotton-seed production, leather, quarries, silk, synthetic gems, etc.

The service sector consists of wholesale and retail trade; restaurants and hotels; transport, storage, and communications; finance, insurance, real estate, and business services; and community as well as social personal services.

While child labour takes many different forms, a priority is to eliminate without delay the worst forms of child labour as defined by Article 3 of ILO Convention No. 182:

1. All forms of slavery or practices similar to slavery, such as the sale and trafficking of children, debt bondage, and serfdom and forced or compulsory labour, including forced or compulsory recruitment of children for use in armed conflict;
2. The use, procuring or offering of a child for prostitution, for the production of pornography or for pornographic performances;
3. The use, procuring or offering of a child for illicit activities, in particular for the production and trafficking of drugs as defined in the relevant international treaties;
4. Work which, by its nature or the circumstances in which it is carried out, is likely to harm the health, safety or morals of children.

Labour that jeopardises the physical, mental or moral well-being of a child, either because of its nature or because of the conditions in which it is carried out, is known as 'hazardous work'. Currently, as the law stands, children under the age of 14 are not allowed to work in only 18 occupations and 65 processes that are deemed to be hazardous. Child labour continues to proliferate across India's cities, slums, and villages despite decades of social reform. Children are not only led to labour due to poor school infrastructure but also find themselves 'caught in the crossfire' of India's poverty problem. In many cases, it is parents and relatives who force children into labour. Child labour also becomes a means of survival for children who find themselves homeless or abandoned as a result of adverse circumstances. There are many circumstances which push children into a lifestyle that takes away their childhood and formative years of education and life skills. These causes must be understood, by India's activists, non-governmental organization programmes and civil society to unite and fight this evil.

The working children in India are mostly engaged in hotels, building sites, factories and in houses as domestic servants. The manufacturing centres, coal mining industry, lock-making factories, carpet weaving concerns, match industry, diamond polishing industry, glass industry, etc. provide a great bulk of the total population of the working children in India. Child victims are more likely to be children from marginalized groups, such as low-caste Hindus, members of tribal communities, and religious minorities. Children from marginalized groups also face barriers to accessing education.

Nature of Child Work

Thus, India has the largest number of child workers in the world. India's 2011 Census found over 40 lakh labourers aged between five and fourteen. They are employed in many industries and trades, including garments, footwear, brick kilns, stainless steel, hotels and textile shops. Many work in export-oriented hazardous industries like carpet weaving, gem polishing, glass blowing, firecrackers units, match works, brassware, electro-plating, lead mining, stone quarrying, lock-making and *beedi*-rolling, and in tea gardens. In addition, nearly 85 per cent of child labourers in India are hard-to-reach, invisible and excluded, as they work largely in the unorganized sector, both rural and urban, within the family or in household-based units, which are generally out of the purview of labour laws.

According to data based on 2001 Census, the distribution of total workforce aged 5–14 years in different industry categories at all-India level shows that the maximum number of children (i.e. 48%) are employed in manufacturing sector, followed by agriculture, hunting, forestry and fishing (i.e. 20%), and wholesale/retail trade (i.e. 10%). The number of children in urban areas, who work in restaurants and canteens, or those engaged in picking rags and hawking goods, is vast but unrecorded and, among the more unfortunate ones are those who are employed in hazardous industries like fireworks and match box units. According to a study conducted by the National Commission for Protection of Children Rights (2013), approximately 70 per cent firecrackers and matches produced in India are from Sivakasi. In 2011, Sivakasi was home to over 9,500 firecracker factories and produced almost 90 per cent of total fireworks and 500 match factories fulfilling 75 per cent demand of matches in the country.

Tamil Nadu has been in limelight for long in terms for its child labour problem where innocent children fall prey to the exploitative labour in firecrackers and match industries. Every year, there occur many fire accidents in these units in which a number of labourers, including children, die.

Mostly children in the age group of 5–15 work for more than 12 hours a day and earn paltry sum as wages. They are generally paid on a piece rate basis, which is very low and thus they are indirectly forced to work faster and longer affecting their health and nutrition. Most of the children are found ignorant of the benefits of education which include decent living without any damage to their health and development. There are also health consequences. Asthma, eye infection and TB are prevalent among 90 per cent of children who are involved in gun powder filling and are directly in contact with the chemical ingredients of crackers and matches. These workers usually do not wear any protective clothes and their whole skins are normally covered with the chemicals such as sulphur, aluminium powder and gun powder.

Similarly, in a study report on children in Indian carpet industry, commissioned by the International Labour Rights Fund, it is found that children account for 7.13 per cent of the total workforce. Most of the children (82%) working on looms are boys, and the majority (58%) of them belong to the labour families. Not only this, the proportion of child labour to the total workforce is higher in the Persian variety of carpets. Though, according to the study, compared to the 1990s, there has been a decline in the magnitude of child labour in the carpet industry, but this is not to the extent of claims made by the government and industry sources.

A study conducted in Tamil Nadu's brick kiln industry demonstrates that child labour is extremely common in this sector. In the interlinked credit-labour market, employers do not directly employ children, but they have implemented a system that compels parents to use their children in order to improve productivity. In such an environment, parents use child labour to improve their own bargaining power.

The surveys of the metropolitan and mega cities make shocking revelations. Mumbai has the largest number of child labourers. Even in Delhi, more than one lakh children work in *dhabas*, tea stalls and restaurants on a daily wage of ₹ 50 or ₹ 100. In the mining sector, about half the workers are children below 15. In most cases, children are favoured as they are docile and hence can be exploited.

Child labour is inextricably linked to bonded labour. In Andhra Pradesh, 21 per cent of the bonded labourers are under sixteen. In Karnataka, 10.3 per cent and in Tamil Nadu 8.7 per cent belong to this age group. A study shows that at the time of entering bondage, many labourers are as young as five years old. In Odisha, one common way of clearing debt is to sell daughters, 8 to 10 years old, as maid servants, to the creditor. In several parts of the country, bonded fathers, over 40 years old, free themselves by deputing their sons into bondage.

In the tea gardens of Assam, where employment of children below 12 years is prohibited, girls who bring food to their working mothers are encouraged to stay back and help with the work. Children, mostly boys, have an important role to play in mining operations. While men do the digging inside the pits, boys carry coal to the surface. Children below 12 are preferred because their height allows them to walk without bending in the tunnels. Preference for child workers is most common in the unorganized sector because here it is relatively easy for employers to circumvent laws. Children are concealed from factory inspectors during inspection, their ages are raised arbitrarily to make them eligible for employment, or those eligible for adult wages are denied their legitimate share because the employers lower their age in the forms.

Causes of Child Labour

1. Children work for a variety of reasons. The most important is poverty. When a family is poor, it is impossible to control child labour as

children have been considered as helping hand to feed their families. Children work to ensure the survival of their family and themselves. Though children are not well paid, they still serve as major contributors to family income. Children are often prompted to work by their parents.

2. Rapid rural-urban migration is the cause for the increasing rate of child labour in urban areas. Families leave the severity of agricultural working conditions for cities in order to search for economic opportunities that often do not exist. The migrant families and their children are forced to work for survival and economic opportunities. In the last 40 years, this movement has been drastic.
3. Due to unemployment, parents are unable to bear the burden of feeding their children and to run their families. So, poor parents send their children for work in inhuman conditions at lower wages. They send their small children to work in factories, homes, and shops.
4. Due to poverty, parents cannot afford the studies of their children and make them earn their wages from a tender age. Children are forced to live without studying. Sometimes the lack of affordable school for the education of poor children leaves them illiterate and helpless. Schooling problems also contribute to child labour. Many times, children seek employment simply because there is no access to schools (distance or no school at all). When there is access, the low quality of the education often makes attendance a waste of time for the students. Illiterate people are not even aware of the evil effects of child labour.
5. In many families, due to addiction, disease or disability, there is no earning, and the child's wages are the sole means of family's sustenance. The children are forced to work in order to support themselves and their families.
6. In modern society, laws stipulate that citizens have the right to receive good education, avail good health services and take care of their health. But in the absence of proper compliance with the laws, child labour is continuing. It can be prohibited only by strict adherence to the related laws.
7. In the greed of cheap labour, some shopkeepers, companies and factory owners employ children so that they have to pay less. In the case of child labour, there is less chance for theft, greed or misappropriation of money too. With the development of globalization, privatization, and consumerist culture, the need for cheap labour and its linkage with the economic needs of poor families have encouraged child labour.
8. The culture and traditional family values play their role in increasing the problem of child labour at the voluntary level. Different cultures of many societies make children start work at a very young age which are related to traditions and cultural factors. They assumed that children need to learn skills that can be good for their future.
9. The poor economic conditions of people force them to borrow money. Due to the insufficiency of income, debtors find it very difficult to pay

back the debt and the interest. This vicious circle of poverty drags them to put their children in assisting them so that the debts could be paid off.

10. There are some industries such as the 'bangle making' industry, where delicate hands and little fingers are needed to do very minute work with extreme excellence and precision, so they require children to work for them and do such a dangerous work with glass.

In a country like India where one in five persons is living, below poverty line, child labour is a complex issue. Children work out of necessity and without their earnings (however meagre they may be), a family cannot survive. A large number of them do not even have families or cannot count on them for support. In these circumstances, the alternative to work may be idleness, destitution, or worse, crime.

Employers give certain justifications for employing children to suppress their guilt feelings. They say that the work keeps children away from starvation. They are prevented from committing crimes which they would have indulged in if they had no jobs. The bureaucrats hold that the total eradication of child labour is not feasible because the government cannot provide substantial alternative employment to them.

Consequences of Child Labour in India

The picture that emerges is dark. Children are working in hazardous export-oriented industries like fireworks, match works, electroplating, *beedi* rolling, glass blowing, brassware, lock making, lead mining and stone quarrying amongst several others. Handling dangerous tools and machines, using pesticides, etc. can cause physical causality and as well as many severe disease to the children. According to WHO, one-eighth of the cases of child labour are of worst forms, which includes physical, mental or even moral well-being. The child labour is viral in various sectors, but the agriculture sector has the maximum (70%) involvement of child labour.

Health Issues

Child labour can also lead to health complications due to undernourishment and poor working conditions. It is highly unlikely that people who employ children, also have the moral capacity to ensure that they have good working conditions. Working in places such as mines and badly conditioned factories may result in lifetime health issues for children employed to work in these places. A child assigned to physically demanding duties may suffer physical trauma that may scar him or her for life.

Harassment and Child Abuse

These days child abuse and harassment cases are also been seen in child labour. According to a study by the Indian government released in 2007, about 20 per cent of children in labour has faced sexual abuse. Most of the cases of sexual abuse occur with the girls below 15.

Indulgence into Crime Field

Uneducated/unguided children who work in society sometimes get influenced by the criminal activities and commit crime at a young age. Some cases of juvenile criminals have been reported in India and its increase is also observed in India.

Loss of Quality Childhood

It is important for human beings to enjoy every stage of their development. A child should play with friends and make memories for a lifetime. Youths should explore life and form strong foundations that would define their adult lives. Child labour, therefore, leads to loss of quality childhood as children will be deprived of the opportunity to enjoy the amazing experiences that come with being young. Children are often encouraged to play because it helps in their growth and development. A child forced to work will miss many of the good things associated with childhood.

Mental Trauma

It is not a pleasant experience to be kept working as a child while your age-mates are out, playing and going to school. Children also lack the ability to shield themselves from most of the challenges that occur in the workplace. Issues such as bullying, sexual exploitation, and unfavourable working hours may result in mental trauma in these children. They will find it hard to forget the past and may become societal misfits because of bad childhood experiences. Child labour may also result in the lack of emotional growth and thus, insensitivity.

Illiteracy

Children that are employed do not have the time to go to school. They spend a lot of time in their workstations as the days and years go by. The lack of education and illiteracy makes them individuals with limited opportunities as far as employment is concerned. Education also prepares a person for several challenges in the society and without it, one may turn out to lack the basic skills required to overcome many of life's problems. An individual who has gone to school may be aware of how to approach certain situations in life without resorting to brute force. An illiterate person, on the other hand, considers force to be the only answer to nearly all of the challenges experienced.

Working Conditions of Child Labourers

Children work in dangerously polluted factories whose brick walls are scarred with soot (black powder in smoke) and there is an oppressive smell in the air. They work near furnaces which burn at a temperature of 1,400° centigrade. They handle dangerous chemicals like arsenic and potassium.

They work in glass blowing units where the work exerts their lungs and creates diseases like tuberculosis.

A large number of the child workers are virtually confined in small rooms under inhuman conditions and in the most unhygienic surroundings. Most of these children come from extremely poor households. They are either school drop-outs or have not seen any school at all. They earn a very meagre wage and work in most unsafe conditions. The hazardous conditions take their toll. Children suffer from lung diseases, tuberculosis, eye diseases, asthma, bronchitis and backaches. Some are injured in fire accidents. Many become unemployable even at the age of 20. If injured or incapacitated, they are discarded mercilessly by their employers.

Ameliorating Child Labour in India

The problem of child labour continues to pose a big challenge before the nation. The government has been taking various pro-active measures to tackle this problem. However, considering the magnitude and extent of the problem and that it is essentially a socio-economic problem, inextricably linked to poverty and illiteracy, it requires concerted efforts from all sections of the society to make a dent in the problem.

There are approximately 12 lakh children working in the hazardous occupations/processes which are covered under the Child Labour (Prohibition & Regulation) Act, i.e. 18 occupations and 65 processes. However, as per survey conducted by National Sample Survey Office (NSSO) in 2004–05, the number of working children is estimated at 90.75 lakh. It shows that the efforts of the government have borne the desired fruits.

Over the years, the Government of India has multiplied its efforts to address the needs and rights of exploited children. Way back in 1979, the Central Government formed the first committee called Gurupadaswamy Committee to study the issue of child labour and to suggest measures to tackle it. The Committee examined the problem in detail and made some far-reaching recommendations. It observed that as long as poverty continued, it would be difficult to totally eliminate child labour and hence, any attempt to abolish it through legal recourse would not be a practical proposition. The Committee felt that in the circumstances, the only alternative left was to ban child labour in hazardous areas and to regulate and ameliorate the conditions of work in other areas. It recommended that a multiple policy approach was required in dealing with the problems of working children.

Based on the recommendations of Gurupadaswamy Committee, the Child Labour (Prohibition and Regulation) Act was enacted in 1986. The Act prohibits employment of children in certain specified hazardous occupations and processes and regulates the working conditions in others. The list of hazardous occupations and processes is progressively being expanded on the recommendation of Child Labour Technical Advisory Committee constituted under the Act.

In consonance with the above approach, a National Policy on Child Labour was formulated in 1987. The policy seeks to adopt a gradual and sequential approach with a focus on rehabilitation of children working in hazardous occupations and processes in the first instance. The Action Plan outlined in the policy for tackling this problem is as follows:

1. Legislative action plan for strict enforcement of Child Labour Act and other labour laws to ensure that children are not employed in hazardous employments, and that the working conditions of children working in non-hazardous areas are regulated in accordance with the provisions of the Child Labour Act. It also entails further identification of additional occupations and processes, which are detrimental to the health and safety of the children.
2. Focussing on general developmental programmes for benefiting child labour: As poverty is the root cause of child labour, the action plan emphasizes the need to cover these children and their families also under various poverty alleviation and employment generation schemes of the government.
3. Project-based plan of action envisages starting of projects in areas of high concentration of child labour. Pursuant to this, in 1988, the National Child Labour Project (NCLP) scheme was launched in nine districts of high child labour endemicity in the country. The scheme envisages running of special schools for child labour withdrawn from work. In the special schools, these children are provided formal/ non-formal education along with vocational training, a stipend of ₹ 150 per month, supplementary nutrition and regular health check ups so as to prepare them to join regular mainstream schools. Under the scheme, funds are given to the District Collectors for running special schools for child labour. Most of these schools are run by the NGOs in the district.

Thus, the governments have accordingly been taking proactive steps to tackle this problem through strict enforcement of legislative provisions along with simultaneous rehabilitative measures. State governments, which are the appropriate implementing authorities, have been conducting regular inspections and raids to detect cases of violations. Since poverty is the root cause of this problem, and enforcement alone cannot help solve it, the governments have been laying a lot of emphasis on the rehabilitation of these children and on improving the economic conditions of their families.

The negative effects or major disadvantages of child labour include:

1. Child labour is an inhuman practice. The mental growth of the children engaged in child labour is hampered.
2. Children get less time and opportunity to go to school. They are unable to participate fully in education. They are deprived of education which makes them illiterate and mental growth is hindered.
3. Child labour obstructs personal growth. The standard of living of people remains low.

4. Child labour destroys their childhood. Child labour does not only limit children's ability to grow emotionally and to relish a period of carefree innocence before they are launched into adulthood. Child labour deprives children of the ability to play, to make friends, to daydream, to relax, and to enjoy all of the key aspects of a normal childhood.
5. The environments in which such species of humanity are nurtured, lead them inevitably to the addiction to country liquor, tobacco, etc. to ward off fatigue.
6. Children who work, often face serious health problems because of working incessantly in perilous conditions. Often the employers do not care at all about underage children who are almost always malnourished and continue to work for long hours with little or no respite.
7. Their mental health also takes a beating owing to this severe form of exploitation. These children often face severe mental trauma when they attain adulthood, owing to the constant threats and ill-treatment they received toiling away as labourers. Being ill-fed and ill-clad, they fall victims to various diseases such as asthma, tuberculosis, etc.
8. Children are the future pillars of the economy and involving them into child labour will only make those pillars weak. Ultimately, child labour affects the country's growth.

Effects of Child Labour

1. Children who cannot find work to feed large families resort to begging on the streets, and in many cases, also fall prey to prostitution. At other times, they even turn into thieves just to make a quick buck on which the family's survival depends.
2. It also has a negative impact on the welfare of the nation. Since these children do not receive any education, it increases illiteracy, hampering the overall economic growth of the country, reflecting poor human development.
3. Lack of education as children, also means that when they turn into adults, finding jobs becomes tough since these children do not possess necessary skills and training. This leads to a sharp hike in unemployment.
4. Such children are always underpaid, and that lowers the country's per capita income, putting long-term economic development in peril. To put an end to this socio-economic problem, the government must target the root causes, namely poverty, unemployment among adults, and take measures to control population growth. Steps must be taken to educate ignorant people from poorer sections about the benefits of education so that children are not deprived of their right to go to school, and they can turn into civilized adults, get suitable jobs, and contribute to the economic growth of the nation. Child employment or under-age labour is a social evil that needs to be abolished. We as a society must work together so children are freed from the evil clutches of this malpractice and lead a happy, healthy life.

Child Labour Laws

The Indian parliament time and again has passed laws and Acts to ensure the protection of children from child labour. The fundamental rights enshrined in our Constitution prohibit child labour below the age of 14 years in any factory or mine or engaged in any hazardous employment under Article 24. Apart from this, it is also provided under Article 21–A that state shall provide infrastructure and resources for free and compulsory education for children of the age of six up to 14 years.

The first Act to regulate the employment of children and their hours of work was the Factory Act of 1881. A commission was appointed in 1929 to fix the minimum age of child employment. On its recommendation, the Child Labour Act, 1933 was passed prohibiting employment of children below 14 years of age.

There exists a set of laws which under the Constitution govern the protection of children from child labour. There are sufficient statutes condemning and prohibiting child labour such as:

Factories Act of 1948: The Factories Act of 1948 provided some safeguards to child labourers. The act prohibits employment of children below the age of 14 years in any factory. The law also placed rules on who, when and how long can pre-adults aged 15–18 years be employed in any factory.

Mines Act of 1952: The Act prohibits employment of children below 18 years of age in a mine. Mining is one of the most dangerous occupations, which in the past has led to many major accidents. Taking life of children from them is completely banned.

Child Labour (Prohibition and Regulation) Act of 1986: The central legislature of India had promulgated a legislation Child and Adolescent Labour (Prohibition and Regulation) Act, 1986 (CL Act) to regulate the child labour practices in India. The act prohibits employment of children below the age of 14 years in hazardous occupations identified in a list by the law. The list was expanded in 2006, and again in 2008.

Juvenile Justice (Care and Protection) of Children Act of 2000: In 1986, the parliament enacted the Child Labour Act (Regulation and Prohibition), prohibiting the employment of children in certain jobs and regulating the conditions of work in hazardous occupations. The Juvenile Justice Act, 1986 which superseded the existing Children's Acts in different states and union territories and came into force from 2 October 1987, provides for the creation of Advisory Boards and the establishment of State Children Funds for preventing the abuse of children, for the protection and care of children, for the mobilization of resources and for the provision of facilities for education, training and rehabilitation of the neglected children. But, in spite of all these measures, children continue to be employed, harassed and abused. This law made it a crime, punishable with a prison term, for anyone to procure or employ a child in any hazardous employment or in bondage. This act provides punishment to those who act in contravention to the previous acts by employing children to work.

Right of Children to Free and Compulsory Education Act of 2009: The law mandates free and compulsory education to all children aged 6 to 14 years. This legislation also mandated that 25 per cent of seats in every private school must be allocated for children from disadvantaged groups and physically challenged children.

In 2016, India made a moderate advancement in efforts to eliminate the worst forms of child labour. The government adopted The Child Labour (Prohibition and Regulation) Amendment Act, which set the minimum age for work at 14 and raised the minimum age for hazardous work to 18, bringing India into compliance with the international standards. The government also increased the financial assistance available under the rehabilitation of bonded labour scheme for children rescued from human trafficking and sexual exploitation.

The National Commission for Protection of Child Rights is another quasi-legal body that aims to safeguard children against miserable slavery. The Commission's mandate is to ensure that all laws, policies, programmes and administrative mechanism are in consonance with the child rights perspective as enshrined in the Constitution of India and also the UN Convention on the Rights of the Child.

Ironically, despite this huge array of laws, there seems to be no improvement in the working conditions of the child labourers and employers also freely flout the provisions of the act covering the prohibition of child labour.

An Evaluation

Despite the aroused hope for some improvement in the lot of the child workers, the enactment of the Child Labour (Prohibition and Regulation) Act, 1986, has not goaded either the state governments or the Centre to any sort of purposive action even on a limited front. Nothing illustrates this apathy as the fate of the plan of action announced by the Labour Ministry in August, 1987 as an essential component of the National Policy on Child Labour. Of the ten projects drawn up under the plan to enforce the Act and provide welfare inputs in such vulnerable areas as the glass industry in Firozabad, carpet weaving industry in Mirzapur, diamond polishing industry in Surat and match industry in Sivakasi, only one has been taken up on an experimental basis. Considering that this lone project in the match industry is an ongoing one that has since been dovetailed into the action plan, the enunciation of the policy as such has achieved nothing beyond delineating the responsibility of the states and the Centre. If this is the fate of a pilot scheme devised to benefit just 30,000 of the 17 million child labour force, the lot of the rest covered by the Act will be no better than that of the vastly greater numbers slogging for a pittance in the unorganized sector, who are outside the purview of the Act. The idea behind formulating the action plan apparently was to make a beginning with the implementation of the new law and related provisions of other legislations affecting children in such sectors where the incidence of child labour is quite endemic. The failure of the projects to take off inspires no hope about the success of the plan to shift the thrust of the anti-poverty programmes to those segments of society that contribute the bulk of child workers.

To this extent, the enactment of the legislation may have proved ineffective in affording a measure of protection for children forced to earn a living because of the rising rural impoverishment and the struggle for existence in urban areas. The legislation was drafted on the sound premise that since the root cause of poverty cannot be eliminated overnight, the pragmatic approach was to regulate the practice of child labour. Accordingly, the employment of children below 14 years has been allowed in selected areas of the non-hazardous organized sector, with suitable safeguards against their exploitation and provision for educational and recreational facilities. But a serious omission in the legislation relates to the enforcement machinery, the laxity of which has enabled employers to circumvent the provisions of the law with impunity. Even if punishment for the violation of the new law has been made stiffer, the cheap, flexible and non-complaining labour provided by children creates a vested interest in perpetuating the practice. In the absence of an efficient and rigorous inspection machinery, nothing prevents the employers from flouting the legal provisions in the full knowledge that the child workers themselves will become willing accomplices in covering it up. Another lacuna in the Act is the failure to define what constitutes hazardous jobs, while the committee set up to identify permissible jobs has not made much progress.

The only way to ensure compliance with the Act is to make punishment for violations more stringent and incorporate a provision for surprise checks and establish a separate vigilance cell. With regard to the workers' interest, it should be made mandatory for all employers to take steps for the intellectual, vocational and educational well-being and upliftment of a child worker, whether one is employed as a factory hand, a domestic servant or a shop assistant.

In this context, the impact of policies which may not be specifically addressed to children but which try to alleviate poverty and inequality can have a significant and even decisive impact. Such policies may include agrarian reforms, employment generation schemes, dissemination of improved technology among the poor, promotion of the informal sector and creation of cooperatives and social security programmes. Laws and regulations must be backed by effective enforcement machinery. This calls for the strengthening of labour inspection and related services. In order to facilitate the verification of age, an effective system of birth registration should be maintained by the public authorities. It should be made mandatory for employers to maintain registers and documents indicating the names and age of all the employed children.

Children have to work is sad, but that they should work in conditions dangerous to their health and safety is totally unacceptable. Nor can the problem of child labour be left untackled until economic conditions and social structures are fundamentally improved.

Toiling long hours for a pittance, these little breadwinners accept exploitation as a way of life. They only know their sorrows. Each day adds more to their growing numbers. Though it is true that labour helps children in their survival, should the children be made to pay for the government's inability to provide alternative employment or inability to curb poverty? Should they be forced to inhabit an adult world, bear adult responsibilities, and suffer abysmal exploitation?

The child workers have no shelter, no food and no education. They run the risk of contracting various ailments and skin diseases. They are vulnerable to exploitation by almost anyone – the employer, the parents, the cops, and even the common man. They become easy targets of drug pushers. They are even sexually abused. Certain principles of policy are, therefore, to be followed by the state so that children get opportunities to develop in a healthy manner and in conditions of freedom and dignity and the childhood and youth are protected against exploitation and moral and material abandonment. Let us hope, by the orders and the directions of the Supreme Court in December 1996, and the measures taken by the state, the child of the 21st century will find himself/herself into the 'heaven of freedom'.

Steps to Overcome the Problem

Child Labour Laws

The Indian government has done a great job in an attempt to overcome child labour. Factory Act, Mines Act, Child Labour (Prohibition and Regulation) Act, Right To Free and Compulsory Education Act were framed to safeguard children from labourious tasks and helping them to rise. The government has implemented new rules for employers of child labourers. These employers can deploy children only in non-hazardous work. They have to ensure that all underage workers are sent to night schools in efforts to eradicate child labour. Amendments made to the Scheduled Castes and Scheduled Tribes (Prevention of Atrocities) Act prescribes severe punishment for people found guilty of retaining bonded labour. The amendment stipulates rigorous imprisonment for those who force children to beg, handle or carry human waste and animal carcasses.

Awareness

Parents must be given awareness about child abuse and bad effects of child labour. This will bring change in the society and minimize the cases of child labour. Many NGOs and agencies like *Bachpan Bachao Andolan*, CARE India, Child Rights and You, Global march against child labour, RIDE India, Childline, etc. have been working to eradicate child labour in India and need support from government to make more people aware specifically the poor people living in villages or slum areas.

Social Alertness

Society must pay attention to the child labour going on in cities, factories or shops. They must report the cases to the police. It is a social etiquette to stop child labour running in your society and supporting those children toward education field.

Solutions

How can child labour be reduced or completely eradicated? Every child born has the right to have dreams and pursue those dreams. Even though the realization of some of these aspirations may be limited by several challenges. It is still possible to overcome them and achieve the highest levels of success. There is a need to involve various stakeholders to realize this objective. These are some of the ways in which the problem of child labour can be addressed:

1. *Free education*: Free education holds the key to eliminating child labour. Parents, who do not have money for school fees, can use this as an opportunity to provide their children with education. It has already proved to be a success in many places around the globe and with more effort, the cases of child labour will greatly reduce. Mid-day meal schemes can also be used as a motivating factor for children whose parents can barely afford a meal to earn. Even if they will be attending school because of the free meals, they will still be able to learn and create a good educational foundation for themselves.
2. *Moral policing*: Child labour should not be entertained at all. It is legally and morally wrong. Children should not be allowed to provide labour at the expense of getting an education and enjoying their childhood. Factory owners, shopkeepers, and industries among others should not employ children. The society should be educated on the negative impacts of child labour so that it becomes an issue that is frowned upon whenever it occurs. This type of moral policing would act as a deterrent to people who intend to employ children and use them as a source of cheap labour. Many of the ills that go on in the society do so because people turn a blind eye or fail to consider their moral impacts. With this kind of approach, cases of child labour will greatly fall among our communities.
3. *Create demand for skilled and trained workers*: The employers should take steps towards replacing child workers with adult workers. It will benefit not only the society, but the country at large. By creating the demand for skilled and trained workers, child labour cases will reduce since almost all child labourers fall under the unskilled worker category. It will lead to adult employment as the demand for skilled labour rises. Establishing skill-based learning centres, vocational training centres, and technical training institutions, improve literacy and contribute to the availability of skilled and trained workers in the job market. Creation of job opportunities by the government is also another way in which cases

of unemployment can be reduced and household income for the population increased. Such government policies improve living standards and eliminate the need for children to seek work in order to support their families.

4. *Awareness*: Creating awareness about the illegality of child labour can also help in stemming the practice. Parents should be made aware that sending their children to work has legal ramifications and the law would take its course if they are found to be aiding and abetting this vice. It is the ignorance among many parents and members of the society that makes them participate in child labour practices. Conducting a campaign to create awareness about its harmful effects would eliminate the practice. The government, together with non-governmental organizations and the civil society, can create a strategy to make such an initiative a success. The solution lies in the social awakening coupled with the honest bid of the government to translate the intended measures into reality.
5. *Empowerment of poor people*: Poor people are the most affected by child labour. The poor living standards and financial constraints sometimes make them unwilling participants in this vice. Empowering poor people through knowledge and income generating projects would go a long way in reducing cases of child labour. Parental literacy also plays an important role in ensuring that the rights of children are upheld, and minors are not used as a source of labour. Empowering parents with this kind of knowledge can create a positive change in the society and encourage the shunning of child labour practices in communities.
6. *Enforcement of labour laws*: Present laws are not sufficient to counter the prevailing plight of the working children. It is because mere legislation, without the simultaneous measures to implement them, does not work. The government will have to take more steps towards proper enforcement of labour laws. Child labour is an extremely sad and worrying phenomenon that unfortunately still needs to be eradicated in many parts of the world, including India.

Conclusion

Child labour is not just an affront to the rights of a child but also a symbol of a society that has lost its way. We should, therefore, all strive to ensure that the fundamental rights of children are protected and that they are accorded the opportunity to go after their dreams and aspirations. The future is much brighter when the younger generation has a good foundation for success. The innocence of a child should never be taken away for the purpose of making the lives of adults easier. It is both unfair and morally unacceptable. Child labour is a menace and an obstacle to India's development. The new generation is the base of development of a developing country and as India is going on a wrong path, it must be directed to the right one. This is possible only with the co-operation of all sections of the society and the law enforcement agencies and by removing or minimizing the causes of child labour.

CHILD ABUSE

One of the biggest social stigmas attached to a society is that of child abuse. Child abuse and neglect include any recent act or failure to act on the part of a parent or caretaker which results in death, serious physical or emotional harm, sexual abuse or exploitation. A child can be abused physically, sexually or mentally. It can be in the form of injury, neglect or negligent treatment, blaming, forced sexual stimulation and activity, incest, exploitation and sexual abuse. Child abuse can take place in homes, schools, orphanages, residential care facilities, on the streets, in the workplace, in prisons and in places of detention. Child abuse results in actual or potential harm to the child's health, survival, development, and dignity. In fact, child abuse is a violation of the basic human rights of a child.

Why does Child Abuse Occur?

There are many different underlying causes of child abuse, ranging from individual factors such as low self-esteem or isolation, to societal factors such as community violence or the stresses of poverty. Depending on the type of maltreatment and the individual circumstances of a perpetrator, the 'causes' will vary. Child abuse is, however, more likely to occur with individuals who have low levels of tolerance for frustration, inappropriately developed coping skills, and misconceptions about what it means to be a parent or caretaker. Child abuse cuts across all boundaries of economic level, race, ethnic heritage, and religious faith. Unfortunately, child abuse occurs in all segments of our society, but the risk factors are greater in families where parents:

1. seem to be having economic, housing or personal problems;
2. are isolated from their family or community;
3. have difficulty controlling anger or stress;
4. are dealing with physical or mental health issues.

Concept and Types

Some studies limit the term 'child abuse' to children who have received serious physical injury caused wilfully rather than by accident. This definition has not been accepted by the social scientists because of the ambiguities in the word 'serious' and diversities in 'physical injury'. Kempe and Kempe (1978) have defined child abuse as 'a condition having to do with those who have been deliberately injured by physical assault'. This definition is limited in scope as it restricts abuse only to those acts of physical violence which produce a diagnostic injury. Thus, acts of neglect and maltreatment of children which do not produce an injury but are equally harmful cannot be included in this definition. No definition of child abuse can be considered valid unless it includes non-physical acts like mental injury and neglect and ill-treatment of a child. Burgess (1979: 143) has given a wider definition of child abuse. According to him, child abuse refers to 'any child who receives non-accidental physical and psychological injury as a result of acts and omissions on the part of his parents or guardians or employers …'. Verbal abuse, threats of physical violence, and excessive physical punishment which do not require medical attention are also included in the definition of child abuse.

Child abuse is usually classified into three major types: physical, sexual and emotional. Each has recognizable characteristics. The indicators of *physical abuse* in the child described by Sloan (1983: 2–3) are: bruises, burns, fractures, lacerations and abrasions, abdominal injuries, and human-bite marks. The behavioural indicators of physical abuse are: the abused child is wary of contact with adults, becomes apprehensive when other children cry, show aggressiveness in behaviour, seems frightened of the parents/ caretakers, and is afraid to go home or cries when it is time to go home.

Child sexual abuse has been defined as 'the involvement of dependent and immature children in sexual activities they do not fully comprehend, to which they are unable to give informed consent' (Kempe and Kempe, 1978: 127). The Juvenile Justice Act, 1986 defines child sexual abuse as 'interaction between a child (under the age of 18 for girls and 16 for boys) and an adult (who is significantly older than the victim and is in a position of power or control over the child, or may even be an acquaintance or an unknown person) in which the child is being used for the sexual stimulation of the perpetrator or another person'. Sexual abuse is not often identified through physical indicators alone. Frequently, a child confides in a trusted person (mother, friend, neighbour, kin or sister) that she/he has been sexually assaulted. There are, however, some physical signs of sexual abuse. These are, difficulty in walking or sitting, torn, stained or bloody underclothes, complaints of pain or itching, bruises or bleeding, venereal disease, and pregnancy (in early adolescence) (Sloan, 1983: 6). There are some behavioural indicators too of sexual abuse. The sexually abused child may appear withdrawn or retarded, may have poor peer relationships, may be unwilling to participate in activities, may indulge in delinquent behaviour, may run away, or may display bizarre or unusual sexual knowledge.

Emotional abuse is the neglect or maltreatment of children. 'Neglect' is difficult to define exactly, since it may involve a disregard of the physical, emotional, moral or social needs of the children. Physical neglect has been defined as 'failure to provide the essentials for normal life, such as food, clothing, shelter, care and supervision, and protection from assault'. Emotional neglect includes both the lack of expressed love and affection and the deliberate withholding of contact and approval. Moral neglect includes exposure to situations (alcoholism, obscenity, illicit sex relations) that present a pattern of moral conduct at variance with the norms of society. Social neglect includes failure to train or discipline a child (Kratcoski, 1979: 120). Thus, emotional neglect or 'maltreatment' may be described as 'negligent treatment of a child under the specific age prescribed for the children by the given society (18 for girls and 16 for boys in India) by a person who is responsible for the child's upbringing, care and welfare under circumstances which indicate that the child's health or welfare is harmed or threatened thereby'. This definition characterizes 'omission' and not 'commission' as abuse. Emotional maltreatment of the child includes blaming, belittling, rejecting, constantly treating siblings unequally, and persistent lack of concern by the parent/caretaker for the child's welfare. Emotional maltreatment is rarely manifest in physical signs. A few physical indicators of emotional maltreatment are speech disorders, lag in physical development and failure-to-thrive syndrome (Sloan, 1983: 7). The behavioural characteristics of emotional maltreatment are: habit disorders (biting, thumb sucking), conduct disorders (destructiveness, cruelty, stealing), neurotic traits (sleep disorders, inhibition of play), psycho-neurotic reaction (hysteria, phobias, obsession), behaviour extremes (appearing overly complainant, extremely passive or aggressive, very demanding or undemanding), lag in emotional and intellectual development, and attempted suicide (Denver, 1961: 6–7).

Besides above mentioned three types of child abuse, we can also refer to *social abuse* of children, like kidnapping children and forcing them to beg on streets. We read about such cases in newspapers. In January 1997, for example, 76 children, most of them girls, between the age group of 5 and 12 years were deported from Saudi Arabia to India. These children languished for some time in remand homes in Mumbai. Since they could not be kept indefinitely in these homes as they had not committed any crime, they were sent to their parents or were let off on the streets of Mumbai to beg as they were begging in Saudi Arabia. Some of them might even resort to crime in order to sustain themselves. What is important in a case like this is how did they reach Saudi Arabia from India? If they were allowed out legally, who had applied for their passage? Were they sold by their parents? The children had certain tattoo marks on their arms and these could be some sort of 'branding'. Could flesh running syndicates or begging syndicate be involved in this grim trade of exporting children abroad? Were they used for sexual gratification? Were they used for gold smuggling or Hawala operations? This type of child abuse calls for deep scrutiny.

And, in recent times, *online abuse* has become so commonplace that half of children in Britain accept that it is a part of their daily life, according to a poll carried out by the Anti-Bullying Alliance. Not only this, four in ten parents are unable to help (*Times of India*, 22 October 2013). In India, more or less the same situation exists. In the past two years or so, there has been a spate of incidences involving children and the darker side of the internet, be it pornography, cyber bullying, or online games, such as the Momo Challenge that includes a variety of self-harming dares which culminates with a suicide challenge. The effects of such violence have long-lasting effects on the physical and mental health of the young victims.

Psychological abuse is a pattern of intentional verbal or behavioural actions or lack of actions that convey to a child the message that he or she is worthless, flawed, unloved, unwanted, endangered, or only of value to meet someone else's needs. Withholding isolation, or terrorizing a child are forms of psychological abuse. Domestic violence that is witnessed by a child is also considered a form of psychological abuse.

Key Studies of Child Abuse

1. The study conducted by Pagare (2003) investigated the maltreatment histories of 72 boys in an Observation Home in Delhi, which is one of over 700 juvenile justice homes in India. In the study, 38.1 per cent of the boys disclosed a history of sexual abuse, with most perpetrators unknown to the victims. Signs of physical abuse were observed in 23.8 per cent of the sample, and behavioural and emotional challenges were evident in 16.3 per cent of the boys.
2. The study conducted by Chatterjee, Chakraborty, Srivastava, and Deb (2006) in Kolkata examined characteristics of sexually trafficked children. The researchers found that these children experienced a host of mental, physical, and social challenges. Specifically, depression, loss of interest in daily living, and loneliness were noted. Furthermore, 14.6 per cent of the children in the study had HIV/AIDS. Many children faced rejection by their family members and communities.
3. The National Study on Child Abuse India 2007 (Kacker, Varadan, and Kumar 2007; Kacker and Kumar 2008), was supported by the Government of India and initiated so that a more accurate and comprehensive understanding of child abuse and neglect could be gained. Various forms of abuse, including child sexual abuse, were examined in two states from each of the major geographic regions of India (North, South, East, West, Central and Northeast, as well as the city of Mumbai). The study included children (5–18 years) and young adults (18–24 years). This report provides a great deal of specific descriptive information about various forms and expressions of sexual abuse among children and youth in India. Eight significant findings of child abuse and neglect emerged from the Study on Child Abuse in India. (a) The youngest children in the sample (ages 5 to 12) reported the highest levels of abuse; (b) there were no differences in the incidence of physical abuse in boys as compared to girls; (c) persons who committed sexual abuse were frequently trusted individuals who held positions of authority; (d) 70 per cent of victims of CSA never disclosed their abuse; (e) nearly half (53.2%) of the sample had experienced CSA; (f) 20 per cent of the children had experienced what was termed severe CSA; (g) the most vulnerable children for CSA included street children and working children, and (h) Andhra Pradesh, Assam, Bihar and Delhi reported the highest incidences of CSA overall. The findings are important as they may lead to '... the formulation of appropriate policies and programs meant to effectively curb and control the problem of child abuse' (Kacker and Kumar, 2008: 98).

4. Sahay (2010) investigated the experiences of sexually abused girls and their families in Western Madhya Pradesh. The researcher reported that the reactions of the girls' families often caused re-traumatization and hindered their healing process. Many families, wanting to avoid the stigma of sexual abuse, forced the girls to remain silent about their experiences. Furthermore, girls were expected to deny their need for medical or mental health services. Even if legal actions were taken against the perpetrators by law enforcement, families still expected their daughters to forgive the offender and 'forget' the abuse. Yet, according to Sahay, the girls in the study felt it was impossible to 'forgive and forget'. This study highlighted the complex familial and social factors that influence the well-being and healing process of female victims of child sexual abuse.
5. The study conducted by Deb and Mukherjee (2011) examined the psychological, social and emotional adjustment of 120 sexually abused girls (ages 13–18) in Kolkata, West Bengal who were living in either Observation or Rehabilitation Homes. Amongst the girls in the study, 93 per cent were from families living in rural poverty with little education. The majority (73.3%) of the girls left their homes believing they were going to be married or provided with a job. Only two girls in the study reported their sexual abuse to law enforcement, which resulted in no protection or conviction of the perpetrators. The experience of abuse correlated with violence in the home, substance abuse, and maternal employment status (not working). Over half of the girls no longer had communication with their families. Many of the girls' families wanted them to return home upon finding them, yet the majority of girls stated that they did not want to return home. Mental health inventories indicated high levels of depression and anxiety as well as low self esteem in the sample. Yet, many of the girls believed that counselling was helpful. The authors asserted that every rehabilitation and observation home necessitates counsellors with specialized training in childhood trauma, including sexual abuse. Additionally, programmes must provide children with the tools needed for a successful future including vocational and social skills training.
6. A research study conducted by Tulir and Save the Children among Child Domestic Workers of West Bengal also gathered data on emotional abuse. The study reported that the problem of emotional abuse of child domestic workers seems to be near universal in character, with 441 out of a total of 513 participants saying that they have faced emotional abuse.
7. A study conducted by Bala D. et al., among different age groups of child respondents revealed that 61.69 per cent of respondents reported physical abuse, 17.41 per cent major sexual abuse and 55.22 per cent another form of sexual abuse. Out of the total child respondents 30.85 per cent children reported emotional abuse of one form or the other and 61.47 per cent of respondents feeling gender differences in the family.

Incidence of Child Abuse

In the absence of public and government interest in the problem of child abuse, no formal statistics have been compiled in India to indicate the incidence of abuse. However, studies are conducted by various organizations/agencies from time to time. For example, at the behest of the UNICEF and Save the Children, the Ministry of Women and Child Development, Government of India has recently conducted a study to develop a dependable and comprehensive understanding of the phenomenon of child abuse, and also formulation of policies and programmes meant to effectively curb and control the problem of child abuse in the country. The findings of the study reveal that children are abused not only physically but also sexually and emotionally. Across different forms of abuse, and across different evidence groups, the younger children (5–12 years of age) have reported higher levels of abuse. Boys, as compared to girls, are equally at risk of abuse. Persons in trust and authority are major abusers. And, 70 per cent of abused children never reported the matter to anyone.

So far as the physical abuse of the children is concerned, it was found that:

1. Two out of every three children are physically abused.
2. Out of 69 per cent children physically abused in 13 sample states, 54.68 per cent were boys.
3. Over 50 per cent children in all the 13 sample states were being subjected to one or the other form of physical abuse.
4. Out of those children physically abused in family situations, 88.6 per cent were physically abused by parents.
5. 65 per cent of school going children reported facing corporal punishment, i.e. two out of three children were victims of corporal punishment.
6. The states of Andhra Pradesh, Assam, Bihar and Delhi have almost consistently reported higher rates of abuse in all forms as compared to other states.
7. Most children did not report the matter to anyone.
8. 50.2 per cent children worked seven days a week.

   Regarding the sexual abuse of the children, the study revealed that:

   (i) 53.22 per cent children reported having faced one or more forms of sexual abuse.
   (ii) Andhra Pradesh, Assam, Bihar and Delhi reported the highest percentage of sexual abuse among both boys and girls.
   (iii) 21.90 per cent child respondents reported facing severe forms of sexual abuse and 50.76 per cent other forms of sexual abuse.
   (iv) Out of the child respondents, 5.69 per cent reported being sexually assaulted.
   (v) Children in Assam, Andhra Pradesh, Bihar and Delhi reported the highest incidence of sexual assault.
   (vi) Children on street, children at work and children in institutional care reported the highest incidence of sexual assault.

(vii) 50 per cent abuses are persons known to the child or in a position of trust and responsibility.
(viii) Most children did not report the matter to anyone.

With regard to the emotional abuse of the children, the study found that:

1. Every second child reported facing emotional abuse.
2. Equal percentage of both girls and boys reported facing emotional abuse.
3. In 83 per cent of the cases parents were the abusers.
4. 48.4 per cent of girls wished they were boys.

The gravity of the situation, thus, demands that the issue of child abuse be placed on the national agenda. The government on its part has taken measures such as the enabling legislation to establish the National and State Commissions for Protection of Rights of the Child, the Integrated Child Protection Scheme, Offences against Children Bill, etc. These are a few important steps to ensure protection of children of the country. But clearly, this will not be enough, and the government, civil society and communities need to complement each other and work towards creating a protective environment for children.

Theoretical Explanations of Child Abuse

A number of explanations have been given by scholars to explain the motivational factors in child abuse. Of these, the important ones are: (a) psychiatric explanation; (b) sociocultural explanation which includes (i) social situational explanation, (ii) social habitability explanation, and (iii) social control explanation; (c) resource explanation; (d) social interactional explanation; and (e) social learning explanation.

The *psychiatric explanation* was propounded by scholars like Kempe (1972), Steele and Pollock (1968), Gelles (1973) and Park and Collmer (1975). It links with child abuse factors such as mental illness and personality defects or intra-individual abnormalities. It also links abusive parents' own childhood experiences to the individuals' weak personality development and poor self-control. The thesis that personality disorder is responsible for child abuse was further advanced by reports that abusers often had a propensity for impulsive and/or anti-social acts that extended beyond the preventing role. A parent, according to this explanation, may abuse his/her child due to unmet emotional needs (that signify discontentment, anger or irritability), an inability to balance the child's needs and capabilities with own (parental) expectations, or emotional scars from their own abusive or deprived family background affecting their ability to care for their own offspring (Wolfe, 1987: 45).

This explanation initially drew support from many fields, including law makers and public interest groups because it directed most of the responsibility for abusive behaviour squarely at the individual involved, and absolved society from blame in contributing to the risk of child abuse through lack of education, adequate housing, family support programmes, employment opportunities, and so on. However, recent researches have disproved the role of psychopathology in child abuse.

The *sociocultural explanation*, given in the 1970s, maintained that external forces or socio-demographic variables within the society caused child abuse. This explanation includes three sub-explanations: social-situational, social habitability and social control.

The *social-situational explanation* proposes that abuse and violence arise out of two factors: structural stress and cultural norms. As the social structure in which a parent lives becomes more stress ridden (or is perceived as more stressful), the greater becomes the possibility that family violence will surface as an attempt to gain control over irritating, tense events. Cultural sanctioning of violence as an appropriate conflict resolution technique further provides a foundation for the use of corporal punishment in child rearing. If a parent was frequently exposed to harsh physical punishment as a child, he/she may have greater propensity toward viewing such behaviour as normative and inhibition against physical force may be lessened (Bandura, 1973). Steinmetz and Straus (1974) have maintained that factors such as low income, unemployment, isolation, unwanted pregnancy and conflict with spouse/in-laws, cause structural stresses which, combined with the cultural acceptance for violence to resolve conflict, lead to the use of force and violence against children at home. Talking of social factors which cause stress, Gil (1970) has referred to social class and family size, Light (1973: 556–98) has referred to unemployment, and Garbarino (1977: 721–35) has referred to social isolation.

The major problem in this explanation according to Fieldman (1982) is that it is unable to account for the finding that, given the same set of deprivation or adverse conditions, many parents do and others do not abuse their children.

The *social habitability explanation* was proposed by James Garbarino in 1977. According to him, the nature of child maltreatment depends upon the quality of the environment in which the person and family live, or the level of family support in the environment. The lesser the family support the greater the risk of maltreatment of children.

The *social control explanation* was propounded by Gelles in 1973. According to him, parents use violence against their children because they have no fear of being hit back, nor of being arrested (unless some neighbour lodges a complaint with the police). Thus, violence is used when (i) the cost of being violent is lesser than the rewards, (ii) the absence of effective social control over family relations decreases the cost (of one member being violent towards another), and (iii) family structures reduce social control in family relations and, therefore, reduce the costs and increase the rewards of being violent (Gelles and Cornell, 1985: 121). Laslett (1978: 480) has also said that (a) inequality in home reduces both social control and the costs of being violent, and (b) the privacy in the family serves to reduce the degree of social control exercised over family relations. Gelles (1973) has maintained that certain types of children – like the handicapped, ugly, demanding, premature – are at a greater risk of being abused by their parents. This is because either they make great demands (economically, socially or psychologically) on their parents or they are perceived as not providing sufficient gratification in return for the parents' investment of time and energy. Thus, when a parent perceives the costs of parenthood to outweigh the rewards, he uses violence against his children. Ivan Nye (1979) like Gelles, had also earlier accepted the application of Peter Blau's theory, in explaining child abuse. He has proposed that child beating is less common in families that have relatives and/or friends nearby. Recasting Nye's proposition, Gelles and Cornell (1985) have proposed that child beating is more common when relatives, friends and neighbours (that is, non-family members) are unavailable, unable or unwilling to be part of the daily system of family interaction, and thus unable to serve as agents of formal and informal social control. Gelles has further maintained that the greater the disparity between perceived investment in a family relationship (that is, parenting) and the perceived returns on the investment, the greater the likelihood that there will be violence. This also explains why children of five to seven years of age are more likely victims of child abuse than children of 14 to 16 years of age. Parents of younger children perceive a rather large investment in their children and feel that they get little in the way of actual return than parents of older children.

This explanation has been criticized on the following grounds: (a) It is preposterous to assume that relations between parents and children are based on reciprocity and that parents' treatment of children is determined in terms of calculations of rewards and costs. (b) Assuming it is so, why do all the parents not make such calculations and only a few do it, that is, why do all the parents not beat their children and only some parents indulge in child-beating? Does this not ignore the personality factor in the use of violence? (c) Why are children who work and earn also beaten by their parents (like non-working children) when there is some 'return' of 'parenting'?

The *resource explanation* was given by William Goode in 1971. According to it, the use of force by an individual depends upon the extent to which he can command or master the resources – social, personal and economic. The more resources a person has, the less he will use force in an open manner. Thus, a father who wants to be a dominant person in the family but has little education, low prestige job, low income and lacks interpersonal skills, may choose to use violence against his children to maintain the dominant position.

The *social interactional explanation* was given by R.L. Burgess in 1979. It approaches the etiology of child abuse in terms of the interplay between individual family and social factors in relation to both past (for example, exposure to abuse as a child) and present (for example, a demanding child) events. The parents' learning history, interpersonal experiences, and intrinsic capabilities are regarded as predisposing characteristics presumed to be important contributors to an abusive pattern. In this explanation, the potential role of a child in provoking abuse is also acknowledged. The conditions under which a child is reared and the methods used by the parents, particularly their punitive methods, may help to explain why some adults are predisposed to abusive behaviour, given certain setting conditions.

Although this explanation is primarily concerned with the current behaviour of the abusive parent in the context of the family or community, psychological mechanisms such as perceptions and interpretations of events, are also recognized as important factors in influencing the parent-child interactions (Wolfe, 1987: 49). The interactional explanation, thus, is not necessarily limited to observable behaviour alone (like parental criticisms or displays of anger, etc.) but includes cognitive and effective processes too (like intelligence, attitudes, etc.) that may mediate behavioural changes.

The *social learning explanation* lays emphasis on the learned nature of parenting and the fact that many parents have insufficient knowledge and skill to equip them to carry out the highly complex task of child rearing. They not only lack fundamental skills (of rearing children) but there may also be an absence of coping strategies to deal with stress, giving rise to a spiralling effect of increased stress and less effective coping.

The Victims of Abuse

An empirical study was conducted in Rajasthan in 1990 on child abuse by G.S. Kewalramani to assess the nature, extent, patterns and causes of abuse, to delineate the characteristics of perpetrators and victims of abuse, and to analyse the effect of abuse on a child's role performance and his/her development. The study was focussed on 167 children in the age group of 10–16 years. Of the 167 cases studied, 124 were cases of physical abuse, 23 of sexual abuse and 103 of emotional abuse (the total is more than the cases studies because many children were victims of multiple abuse). Further, of the total cases studied, 61.7 per cent were boys and 38.3 per cent were girls. Amongst boys, 42.7 per cent were working and 57.3 per cent were non-working, while amongst girls, 46.9 per cent were working and 53.1 per cent were non-working. The age groups of the interviewed children were: 10–11 years – 20.4 per cent, 12–13 years – 25.7 per cent, 14–15 years – 24.6 per cent, and 16 years – 29.3 per cent.

The important findings of this study on the three types of child abuse, namely, physical, sexual and emotional, were as follows:

Physical Abuse on Victims

Physical abuse is the inflicting of physical injury upon a child. This may include burning, hitting, punching, shaking, kicking, beating or otherwise harming a child. The parent or caretaker may not have intended to hurt the child. It may, however, be the result of over-discipline or physical punishment that is inappropriate to the child's age.

(a) Boys are more battered than girls (ratio being 1.3:1). (b) School-going children run greater risk of being physically abused than those who do not go to school. (c) Older children (14–16 years) are more abused physically than younger children (10–13 years). (d) Non-working children are beaten more than the working children. (e) The ratio of children who are occasionally abused (twice or thrice a month) to those who are frequently abused (once or twice a week), or very frequently abused (three or four times a week) is 1:5½. (f) A large number of the abused children (about 60%) belong to poor families. Only a small number (about 2%) belong to well-to-do families. This shows that there is a significant relationship between poverty and physical abuse. (g) In a very large number of cases (93%), the perpetrators of physical abuse are members of the family (father, mother, sibling). (h) Perpetrators of either sex, abuse children of their own sex more than that of the opposite sex. (i) Mothers abuse children physically more (60%) than the fathers (40%). However, males abuse children more severely than females. (j) A great majority of the abuser parents are in their thirties and forties, while the siblings are mostly in their teens. (k) The main modes of battering children are slapping and beating with fists (40%), hitting with different objects (35%), kicking (19%), choking and/or strangulating (10%), binding with rope (3%), and tearing hair (2%). (l) In most of the cases (85%), the beating does not cause an injury to the child. (m) The physical violence against children is of various types. Routine beating is different from the non-routine beating. The former is one which the parents believe their children 'deserve', and the children also believe that they 'asked for it'. The latter is one which is instigated by the child. Secondary violence is one which one parent believes is just and legitimate but the other parent believes is unjust.

Non-routine violence has been sub-categorized as volcanic violence, alcohol-related violence, sex-related or jealousy-oriented violence, expressive violence, power-oriented or instrumental violence, and victim-precipitated violence. Volcanic violence is one which is used neither for achieving a desired end nor for legitimizing the act. It occurs when the victimizer (parent, employer, etc.) has run out of patience as the result of externally caused stress, such as losing the job or being insulted by somebody or incurring a loss. Alcohol-related violence is one where violence is the result of alcohol consumption. Alcohol releases aggression as well as makes a person irrational and serves as a disinhibitory agent that releases violence impulses. This type of violence is exclusively male violence. Jealousy-oriented or sex-related violence is one in which the parent of one sex beats the child of the other sex out of jealousy. Stepfather beating his daughter, or stepmother beating her son are examples of this type of violence.

Expressive violence is one in which the use of physical force is an end in itself. Instrumental or power-oriented violence is one in which violence is intended not only as a means of inducing the child to alter his behaviour but also to establish parental authority. Child precipitated violence is one in which the victims of violence contribute to their own victimization either through actions defined as deviant by the aggressor parent or through provoking their (parents) antagonism.

Sexual Abuse on Victims

Sexual abuse is inappropriate sexual behaviour with a child. Child sexual abuse is the involvement of a child in sexual activity that he or she does not fully comprehend, is unable to give informed consent to, or that violates the laws or social taboos of society. Poverty, age, gender, caste, lack of safe spaces, lack of schools, lack of proper institutional care for children without functional families, etc. make the child prone to sexual abuse.

(a) Girls are more victims of sexual abuse than boys (the ratio being 2.3:1). (b) A high proportion of children become victims of sexual abuse when they are 14 or above 14 years of age. The ratio of victims below 14 years to victims above 14 years is about 1:5. (c) There is a strong association between sex and the number of abusers. Males are usually abused sexually by one person while girls are generally assaulted by more than one person. (d) There is rarely an application of force or bodily harm. Victims are usually psychologically enticed by the assaulters by loyalty to, affection for, and the dependence on them (abusers). (e) The victims of sexual abuse are generally from the lower socio-economic families. (f) Sexual abuse of children does not demonstrate a relationship with religion and caste membership. There is some evidence that the low caste women are more frequent victims of sexual assault than the high caste women but this refers more to rape cases than childhood sexual abuse. (g) Whereas the victims' age distribution is more homogeneous, the assaulters' age distribution is more heterogeneous (very young, young, early middle age, late middle age). (h) In about two-third cases (66.7%), the perpetrators have secondary relationship with the victims (employers, co-workers, teachers, tenants, and acquaintances). Persons having blood relationships constitute a small category of perpetrators. In other words, a significant percentage of child sexual abuse (93%) occurs outside the family. (i) Boys are generally the victims of 'employment-related' abuse while girls are generally the victims of 'acquaintance-related' abuse. (j) Of the 'employment-related' sexual abuse, two-thirds is by the co-workers and one-third is by the employers.

The data compiled by the National Crime Record Bureau (NCRB) from all states show that 2018 saw a significant increase in crimes under protection of children from sexual offence. Of the 7,684 child sexual abuses reported to Childline nationwide, 35 per cent of them were neighbours, known persons, including friends, relatives and caretakers.

Emotional Abuse on Victims

Emotional abuse is also known as verbal abuse, mental abuse, and psychological maltreatment. Emotional abuse includes the failure to provide a developmentally appropriate, supportive environment so that the child can develop a stable and full range of emotional and social competencies. Acts include restriction of movement, patterns of belittling, and denigrating, threatening, scaring, discriminating, ridiculing or other non-physical forms of hostile or rejecting treatment.

(a) Boys are more emotionally maltreated than girls, the ratio being 1.3:1. (b) Working children are as much neglected as non-working children. (c) School-going children are a little more maltreated than non-school-going children. (d) Of the various forms of emotional abuse, constant lack of supervision is as high as 62 per cent. Belittling is found in 50 per cent cases, false blaming among 33 per cent, lack of concern for studies and welfare in 28 per cent, rejection among 18 per cent and unequal treatment with siblings in 17 per cent cases. (e) The ratio of parents taking 'no' interest, 'less' interest and 'average' interest in children is about 5: 3: 1. (f) In a large number of cases (76%), the parents who neglect the child are those whose income is low and liabilities are many; who are middle aged, illiterate or less educated; and who are engaged in low-status jobs. (g) A large number of parents who ill-treat their children are those who are aggressive, irritable and domineering in their behavioural characteristics; fickle-minded, inflexible and less tolerant in their emotional characteristics; and have low esteem, feeling of alienation, and lack of ability to empathize in social characteristics.

Causes of Child Abuse

The major cause of child abuse is adaptational failure or environmental maladjustment (both in family and workplace) mostly on the part of the adult perpetrators (parents, employers, etc.) but to some extent on the part of adults responsible for family socialization as well (Kewalramani, 1992: 152). Before discussing this thesis, let us first analyse the causes of three different types of child abuse separately.

Physical Abuse

Different scholars have suggested different causes of physical abuse. Some consider the psycho-pathology of the individual perpetrators as the primary cause, others view the psycho-social pathology of family interaction as the main cause, and still others put major emphasis on situations of acute stress. The empirical study of Kewalramani conducted in Rajasthan, however, revealed that stress factors associated with families give a sufficient causal explanation for child abuse. The situational stresses pointed out four models of dominant causes of a child's physical abuse: (a) relations between spouses, (b) relations between parents and children, (c) structural stresses, and (d) child-produced stress.

Sexual Abuse

The four causes of sexual abuse mostly given are: adjustment problems of the perpetrators, family disorganization, victim's characteristics, and the psychological disorders of the abusers. Kewalramani's study (1992: 78) on child abuse, however, approached the problem of sexual abuse with a 'systems model' and perceived it as behaviour influenced by factors at several different levels, that is, a behaviour which is the result of cumulative influence of a set of factors. In fact, this study used the systems approach not to study sexual abuse but also physical and emotional abuse. The four variables related to sexual abuse were: family environment, family structure, individual predispositions and situational factors.

The analysis of family environment revealed that congestion in family was not related to sexual abuse but conflict between parents and weakening of inhibitions leading to neglect of the children, absence of affectionate parent-child relationship within the family, that fails to give support and protection to child, alcoholism of the earning male member, his lack of accountability, lack of adequate control on the children, illicit relations of the mother with some man and paramour's hold on his mistress, dominance of stepfather, and social isolation of the family (that is, family not participating in social networks or community activities) were factors which were more important in sexual abuse.

The environment in the workplace also contributes to sexual molestation. Several cases of assault by employers and molestation by co-workers of the young victims when they were all alone in the house/workplace/school were found in Kewalramani's study. The loneliness of young girls make them more vulnerable to the overtures of the perpetrators.

Emotional Abuse

Four important causes of emotional abuse can be identified: poverty, 'deficient' parental control and non-cordial relations within family, maltreatment faced by parents in their own childhood or intergenerational transmission of child maltreatment, and alcoholism of parents. Kewalramani also found these factors important in emotional abuse. More than half of the abuser parents (55%) had low income and 5–12 family members to support. Strauss (1979) and Deschner (1984) have also pointed out the effect of poverty on child abuse. However, it has now come to be believed that child abuse is not exclusively a lower SES (socio-economic status) situation, though it is predominantly a lower SES problem. 'Deficient' parental control was found by Kewalramani in 52 per cent cases and intergenerational transmission of maltreatment was discovered in 79 per cent cases. Pagelow (1984) has also referred to the role of inter-generational transmission in child maltreatment. However, Burgess and Youngblade (1985) have questioned this belief. Lastly, Kewalramani did not find alcohol as an important factor in child abuse. He found only 26 per cent parents (fathers) as alcoholic of whom 44 per cent consumed alcohol every day, that is, were addicts. Matlins (1981) has, however, described the alcoholic parent as having an important role in child abuse.

Effects of Abuse on Children

What are the effects of abuse – physical, sexual, social and emotional – on children. Bolton and Bolton (1987: 93–113) have identified eight possible effects of abuse on children, namely, self-devaluation, dependency, mistrust, revictimization, withdrawal from people, emotional trauma, deviant behaviour, and interpersonal problems.

Kewalramani's study of child abuse lays down the effect of abuse on children in five significant areas. The first is the loss of self-esteem. Abused children develop a negative view of themselves. Elmer (1967) has called it 'self-devaluation' while Egeland, Sroufe and Erickson (1983: 460) have called it 'low self-esteem'. Kinard (1980: 686–696) has mentioned it as 'poor self-concept' and Hjorth and Ostrov (1982: 71–72) as 'poor self-image'. Children have no choice but to accept the perpetrators' abuse. The individual who maltreats them is their own parent so they cannot run away. Similarly, they have to tolerate their caretakers' and employers' hostility because of their poverty and their dependence on them.

Kewalramani used three indicators to test his hypothesis (1992: 114) that child's self-esteem is devalued by his abuse. These indicators were: child's own evaluation of his/her performance at school (in the case of the school-going children), evaluation as worker (in the case of the working children), and evaluation as a helper at home. He framed five questions pertaining to these indicators and found that: (a) A high percentage of children (75%) who were physically/emotionally abused felt that they were weak at studies and/or had to make more than one attempt to pass the examination. (b) A high percentage (81%) considered themselves to be indifferent towards their work and/or felt dissatisfied with the work they were engaged in. (c) An equally high percentage (86%) thought of themselves as shirkers than as helpers to their parents/caretakers in the routine household chores. From these, it may be inferred that abuse always devalues a child's self-esteem.

The second effect is on dependency. It was found that a child's dependency is shifted from parents/caretakers to teachers for the gratification of all his/her needs. The three indicators to operationalize dependency were: gratification of physical needs (food, clothes and medicare), emotional and social support, and need of working somewhere to earn money. It was found that (a) a good number of child victims (50%) had a feeling that their physical needs were not being met to their satisfaction; (b) a high percentage of victims (55%) found themselves dependent on others for their emotional and social support; and (c) a still higher percentage (63%) of abused children were forced to take up a job to meet their needs. However, significantly, despite the abuse, a good number of victimized children continued to depend on their parents/caretakers than on others.

The third effect is on deviant behaviour. It was found that abuse had a great effect on a child's conformity to sociocultural expectations and a large number of the victimized children were compelled to indulge in activities that violated the social norms or which are labelled as 'deviance'. The five indicators used by Kewalramani (1992: 128) to study the effect of child abuse on deviance were: absence from school, absence from work, drug addiction, stealing money, and hostile reactions towards perpetrators. The study revealed that (a) A high percentage of emotionally and sexually abused victims (58% to 80%) missed their school frequently. (b) About three-fourth of the victims (74% to 77%) frequently remained absent from work. (c) About one-tenth of the victims (8% to 10%) had either become drug addicts or had started smoking or taking tobacco or consuming alcohol. (d) About one-fifth of the victims (18%) had started stealing money. (e) A large number of the victims (48% to 78%) had developed hostility and aggressiveness towards the perpetrators. From all this, it may be inferred that child abuse causes deviance amongst the victims which varies with regard to its magnitude and type.

The fourth effect is on social and interpersonal problems. The study (1992: 136) revealed that child abuse results in poor communication and coping ability, failure in developing intimacy and social relationships, mistrust, isolation and withdrawal from interactional settings. For verifying these effects, the questions asked from the victims are related to their free time activities, relations with parents and siblings, what constitutes embarrassing situations, their confiding in friends in times of stress and their desire to abandon their families. It was found that: (a) Most of the victims (68% to 83%) avoided situations in which interaction would have been expected, that is, they preferred to live in solitude and passed their leisure time all alone. (b) Only a low percentage of the victims wanted to dissociate themselves from or abandon the family. (c) A high percentage of the victims (76%) had indifferent or antagonistic relations with their parents/caretakers and/or siblings. (d) Only a small number of the victims (24%) had a friend/relative whom they could trust and share their sorrows with. (e) Abuse caused embarrassment but its range differed in relation to the type of abuse. All these observations point out that victims of child abuse always develop certain types of social and interpersonal problems.

The last effect (of child abuse) is on revictimization, that is, the child once abused will essentially be abused time and again. The three indicators used in this context were: frequency of abuse, number of abusing perpetrators, and number of ways or forms of child abuse. The three questions related to these three indicators were how frequently was the victim abused, whether he was abused by one or more persons, and whether he was abused in one way or in more than one way.

The study revealed that (a) a high percentage of children (65% to 84%) were abused regularly or frequently, (b) a large number of victims (53% to 58%) of physical and emotional abuse (but not sexual) were abused by more than one person, and (c) a large number of victims of physical and emotional abuse (66% to 80%) were victimized in more than one way. From all this, it may be inferred that a child who is a victim of abuse once is not only abused frequently and by more than one person, but is also at a greater risk of being victimized in more than one way, that is, physically, emotionally and sexually.

Integrated Model of the Causes of Child Abuse

The major premise of this model is the interdependence between parent, child and situation. This model focusses on four factors in child abuse: (a) family environment, (b) structural stresses, (c) individual characteristics of parents, and (d) sub-cultural learning. The model requires knowledge in five different areas: (a) child development, (b) socialization processes, (c) family interactions, (d) learning principles, and (e) sources of arousing anger, aggression, hatred, and so forth.

These areas point out that:

1. Child abuse can be viewed in terms of the degree to which a parent uses negative or inappropriate control strategies with his/her child. Employing 'normal' methods (meeting all the child's needs, adequate control, positive disciplining, and clear communication) contributes to a child's (social, emotional and intellectual) development, whereas taking recourse to 'abnormal' methods (neglecting child's needs, inadequate control, negative disciplining, unclear communication, and over-reliance on coercion) in child rearing inhibits a child's development and causes child abuse.

   Authoritative parenting (the commanding type of parents), authoritarian parenting (requiring complete obedience to their authority), indulgent parenting (gratifying all desires/fancies), and negligent parenting (being indifferent and unresponsive and not paying due attention) influence a child's characteristics and behaviour. The authoritarian parental style is most harmful and is conducive to child abuse.
2. Stresses also give rise to maladaptive coping responses, since abusive parents are clearly not violent under all circumstances. Factors like unemployment and dissatisfaction with job affect an individual's behaviour which lead to child abuse.
3. Individual characteristics of parents like inherent traits (irritable nature, self-centredness, rigidness, etc.), lack of parenting skill, and lack of resources (low prestige, little education and low income) also cause child abuse.
4. The sub-cultural learning, that is, socialization in a violent home, or experiencing violence in childhood, is yet another cause of child abuse.

All these factors together explain how they affect the behaviour of the perpetrators which ultimately leads to child abuse.

Reasons to Prevent Child Abuse

1. Child abuse can be fatal.
2. It can stymie a child's normal growth and development.

3. Child abuse costs continue to multiply over time.
4. The victims may repeat the violent acts that they experienced, on their own children.
5. Treatment services, while critical, are often ineffective in permanently altering parental behaviours.
6. Prevention programmes targeted at children can improve a child's awareness of how best to avoid child abuse and other unsafe practices.
7. Child abuse prevention efforts serve as a way to combat other social problems of concern to the public and to policymakers.
8. Child abuse prevention creates a more compassionate society.

Prevention of Abuse

There are two types of prevention: primary and secondary. When applied to the problems of child abuse, *Primary Prevention* refers to an action which is taken to ensure child abuse will not occur. On the other hand, *Secondary Prevention* is those steps which are taken after child abuse or neglect has already happened. It is believed that by providing treatment once abuse or neglect has occurred, it will be prevented from recurring. It seems that society has placed more emphasis on treating child abuse after it has occurred (secondary prevention) than on programs to prevent its occurrence.

Child Abuse Laws in India

The Protection of Children Against Sexual Offences (POCSO) Act was passed in 2012 in response to a widely publicised instance of abuse in an Indian orphanage. The Indian parliament also passed the Juvenile Justice (Care and Protection of Children) Act in 2015 to replace a previous 2000 iteration of the law. The 2015 version of the Act includes components such as plans to introduce foster care in India and mandating registration of all institutions housing children in the need of care and protection.

POCSO Act (Amendment) includes the death penalty for aggravated sexual assault on children, besides providing stringent punishments for other crimes against minors.

Conclusion

Child labour refers to exploiting children in such a way so as to deprive them of their childhood. It interferes with their ability to acquire education and it ruins their health. It can take various forms such as involuntary servitude, child slavery, sale by parents, etc. Child abuse also comes in many forms, including sexual, physical, emotional, mental, and neglect. Anytime a child is subjected to physically, emotionally, or mentally harmful behaviour, it is child abuse. Child labour and abuse lead to underdevelopment, incomplete mental and physical development, which in turn results in retarded growth of children. Apart from rescuing the children, the real challenge is proper rehabilitation, else it becomes a vicious cycle where minors are rescued but they again get into labour. Every individual must understand how important it is for the children to grow and study, as they are the ones who will shape the future of the nation.

References

Bandura, A., *Aggression: A Social Learning Analysis*, Prentice Hall, New Jersey, 1973.

Bhukuth, Augendra, 'Child Labour and Debt Bondage: A Case Study of Brick Kiln Workers in Southeast India', *Journal of Asian and African Studies*, 40(4): 287–302, 2005.

Bolton, F.G. and Bolton, S.R., *Working with Violent Families*, Sage Publications, New York, 1987.

Burgess, R.L., 'Child Abuse: A Social Interactional Analysis', in Ben Lahey and Alan Kazdin (eds), *Advances in Clinical Child Psychology*, Vol. 2, Plenum Press, New York, 1979.

Crime in India, National Crime Records Bureau, New Delhi, 2012.

Egeland, B. et al., 'The Developmental Consequence of Different Patterns of Maltreatment', *Child Abuse and Neglect*, Vol. 7, No. 4, 1983.

Elmer, E., *Children in Jeopardy: A Study of Abused Minors and their Families*, University of Pittsburgh Press, Pittsburgh, 1967.

Garbarino, J., 'The Human Ecology of Child Maltreatment: A Conceptual Model for Research', *Journal of Marriage and Family*, 39: 721–35, 1977.

Gelles, R.J. and Cornell, C.P., *Intimate Violence in Families*, Sage Publications, Beverly Hills, 1985.

Gelles, R.J., 'Child Abuse as Psychopathology: A Sociological Critique and Reformulation', *American Journal of Ortho. Psychiatry*, Vol. 43, July, 1973.

Gil, D., *Violence against Children: Physical Child Abuse in the United States*, Harvard University Press, Cambridge, 1970.

Goode, William, 'Force and Violence in the Family', *Journal of Marriage and Family*, Vol. 33, November, 1971.

Hjorth, C.W. and Ostrov, E., 'The Self-image of Physically Abused Adolescents', *Journal of Youth and Adolescence*, Vol. 11, No. 2, 1982.

Joshi, Uma, 'Child Abuse: A Disgrace in Our Society', *Hindustan Times*, 25 June, 1986.

Kacker L., Srinivas Varadan, Pravesh Kumar, 'Study on Child Abuse: India 2007', Report by the Ministry of Women and Child Development – Government India.

Kempe, R.S. and Kempe, C.H., *Child Abuse*, Fontana, London, 1978.

Kewalramani, G.S., *Child Abuse*, Rawat Publications, Jaipur, 1992.

Khatu, K.K., *Working Children in India*, Operations Research Group, Baroda, 1983.

Kinard, E.M., 'Emotional Development in Physically Abused Children', *American Journal of Ortho. Psychiatry*, Vol. 50, 1980.

Light, R. 'Abused and Neglected Children in America: A Study of Alternative Policies'. *Harvard Educational Review*, 1973, 556–98.

Maji, B., Satapathy J., Routray, R.K., 'Prevalence of Child Abuse in Eastern India: A Tip of the Iceberg'. *Int J Contemp Pediatr*, 2: 353–5, 2015.

Maxwild, Denver, 'Protective Services and Emotional Neglect', quoted by Irving Sloan, 1961.

Pagare, D., 'Study of Physical and Sexual Abuse and Behavioural Problems Amongst Boys from an Observation Home in Delhi'. Unpublished Doctoral Dissertation in Community Medicine, University of Delhi, 2003.

Park, R. and Collmer, C., *Child Abuse: An Interdisciplinary Analysis*, The University of Chicago Press, Chicago, 1975.

Premi, Mahendra K., *Population of India in the New Millennium: Census 2011* (2nd edn), NBT, New Delhi, 2011.

Shard, Neel K., *The Legal, Economic and Social Status of the Indian Child*, National Book Organization, New Delhi, 1988.

Sloan, Irving, *Child Abuse: Governing Law and Legislation*, Oceana Publications, New York, 1983.

Strauss, M.A., 'Family Patterns and Child Abuse', *Child Abuse and Neglect*, Vol. 3, 1979.

Wolfe, D.A., *Child Abuse*, Sage Publications, Beverly Hills, 1987.

10

Violence Against Women

Women are getting affected by various kinds of violence almost every day, which is disrupting the society. Women are increasingly becoming victims of violence because of increasing crimes against women. The year 2016 saw the lowest conviction rate (18.9%) in which trials were completed by the courts for crimes against women in a decade. According to National Crime Records Bureau report 2018:

1. The number of crimes committed against women increased in 2017 by six per cent as compared to 2016 figures and by nine per cent compared to 2015 figures.
2. Women reported almost 34,000 rapes in India. One woman reported a rape every 15 minutes.
3. 'Cruelty by husband or relatives' was the most reported crime against women, accounting for 33 per cent of all crimes, followed by assault on woman with intent to outrage her modesty, kidnapping and rape.

Few topics today draw the attention of researchers in social sciences, government, planning groups, social workers and reformers as the problems of women do. Approaches to the study of women's problems range from the study of gerontology to psychiatry and criminology. But one important problem relating to women which has been greatly ignored and shunned is the problem of crime against women.

Women's Harassment

The problem of crime against women is not new. Women in the Indian society have been victims of humiliation, torture and exploitation for as long as we have written records of social organization and family life. Today, women are being gradually recognized as important, powerful and meaningful contributors to the life of men; but till a few decades back, their condition was pitiable. Ideologies, institutional practices and the existing norms in society have contributed much to their harassment. Some of these behavioural practices thrive even today. In spite of the legislative measures adopted in favour of women in our society after independence, the spread of education and women's gradual economic independence, countless women still continue to be victims of violence. They are beaten, kidnapped, raped, burnt and murdered. The latest statistics as released by the National Crime Records Bureau (NCRB) shows that nationwide crimes against women in our country have increased by 7.1 per cent since 2010.

The semantic meaning of 'crime against women' is direct or indirect, physical or mental cruelty to women. Crimes direct or indirect, physical or mental cruelty against women and in which only women are victims and which are directed specifically against them are characterized as 'crime against women'. Various kinds of violence against women are eve-teasing, molestation, bigamy, fraudulent marriage, adultery and enticement of married women, abduction and kidnapping, rape, harassment of women at working place, wife beating, dowry death, female child abuse and abuse of elderly female, etc. Almost every woman has experienced the feeling of being mistreated, kept out, put down, ignored, assaulted, laughed at or discriminated against because of her gender. Although, women may be victims of all kinds of crime, be it cheating, murder, robbery, etc. yet the crimes in which only women are victims are broadly characterized as, crimes against women. These are classified under two categories:

1. Crimes under the Indian penal code (IPC), which include seven crimes: (a) rape, (b) kidnapping and abduction, (c) dowry deaths, (d) torture physical and mental (including wife battering), (e) molestation, and (f) sexual harassment, and (g) importation of girls.
2. Crimes under special and local laws (SLL), which include seventeen crimes, of which the important ones are: (a) Immoral Traffic (1956 and 1978 Act), (b) Dowry Prohibition (1961 Act), (c) Committing Sati (1987 Act), and (d) Indecent Representation of Women (1986 Act).

It is important to clarify here the concept of 'crime(s) against women'. The term 'crime' does not, in modern times, have any simple or universal definition. However, the new *Oxford Advanced Learner's Dictionary* (7th edn., 2005) has defined it as an illegal act or activity that can be punished by law or that one thinks is immoral or is a big mistake.

The Indian Penal Code (IPC), 1860 uses the word 'offence' in place of 'crime'. Section 40 of the IPC defines 'offence' as an act made punishable by the Code. An offence takes place in two ways – either by commission of an act or by omission of an act. Thus, crimes which are 'directed specifically against women' and in which 'only women are victims' are characterized as 'crimes against women' (Singh, 2012). Rape, kidnapping, murder, wife battering, sexual abuse, eve teasing are all examples of crimes against women.

The Police Research Bureau, Delhi has referred to 'crime against women' under two categories: (a) crimes under the Indian Penal Code, and

(b) crimes under the local and special laws (see *Crime in India,* National Crime Records Bureau, Delhi, 1994: 209). The Bureau has identified seven crimes in the first category and four in the second category of crimes. The seven crimes under the IPC are: rape, kidnapping and abduction, homicide for dowry, torture (physical and mental), molestation, eve teasing and importation of girls upto 21 years of age, while the four crimes under the local and special laws are: commission of *sati,* dowry prohibition, immoral traffic, and indecent representation of women.

Laws Protecting Women's Rights in India

The definition of crimes against women listed under the Indian Penal Code (IPC) serves to provide us with a bird's eye view of the legal stance on crime against women in India. The list is as follows:

1. Rape (Section 376 IPC).
2. Attempt to commit rape (Section 376/511 IPC).
3. Kidnapping and abduction of women (K&A) (Section 363, 364, 364A, 366 IPC) – in order to murder, for ransom, to compel her for marriage and other purposes.
4. Dowry deaths (Section 304B IPC).
5. Assault on a woman with intent to outrage her modesty (Section 354 IPC) – including sexual harassment, voyeurism and other forms of sexual violence.
6. Insult to the modesty of women (Section 509 IPC) – including at work and in public transport.
7. Cruelty by husband or his relatives (Section 98A IPC).
8. Importation of girl from a foreign country (up to 21 years of age) (Section 366 B IPC).
9. Abetment of suicide of women (Section 306 IPC).

The gender-specific laws in the country:

1. The Dowry Prohibition Act, 1961.
2. The Indecent Representation of Women (Prohibition) Act, 1986.
3. The Commission of Sati Prevention Act, 1987.
4. The Protection of Women from Domestic Violence Act, 2005.
5. The Immoral Traffic (Prevention) Act, 1956.

Cruelty by husbands and relatives under Section 498–A of Indian Penal Code (IPC) is the major crime committed against women across the country. Kidnapping and abduction of women is the third-most-reported crime followed by rape, an insult to the modesty of women and dowry death. Three more heads under which cases of crime against women have been reported include an attempt to commit rape, abetment of suicide of women under Section 306 IPC and protection of women from domestic violence.

Who are the women who are victimized? Who are their victimizers or the perpetrators of violence? Where do the seeds of violence against women lie? Some scholars who have studied some of these aspects in western society have used the 'personality' approach and the 'situational' approach to explain this problem. But both types of approaches have, however, been criticized on varied counts.

Nature, Extent and Characteristics of Crime

Crime against women may be categorized as:

1. Criminal violence – rape, abduction, murder, etc.
2. Domestic violence – dowry deaths, wife battering, sexual abuse, maltreatment of widows and/or elderly women, etc.
3. Social violence – forcing the wife/daughter-in-law to go for female foeticide, eve teasing, refusing to give a share to women in property, forcing a young widow to commit *sati*, harassing the daughter-in-law to bring more dowry, etc.

If we analyse the data given by various agencies, we find that crimes against women have been constantly increasing every year.

The cases went up not necessarily because of increased reporting but it only indicates an increased awareness about gender parity and women's rights, the confidence of the victims in the new laws for their protection, and because of institutions such as Mahila Courts, Family Courts, and NGOs working for women. But we know that all cases are not reported and recorded for various reasons. The cases of domestic violence like wife battering and forced incest with the women of the household are never reported at all. But by referring to the compiled cases, we get some ideas of the nature and extent of violence against women. We analyse the extent and characteristics of six types of violence below.

Rape

Until a few years ago, the problem of rape in India was not considered as serious as in the western countries, particularly in view of its low prevalence rate in comparison to other countries (i.e. 0.5 per lakh of population in comparison to 26 in the United States, 8 in Canada and about 5.5 in the UK). But now India is considered to be the 'rape capital' of the world.

It is not only the poor girls who become rape victims but even the employees belonging to the middle class are sexually humiliated by their employers. Women patients by hospital personnel, and maid-servants by their masters. Even deaf and dumb, lunatic and blind, and women beggars are not spared. Women who come from the lower-middle class and who are the main bread winners of their families bear sexual abuse quietly and without protest. The victims face social stigma and disgrace and suffer serious guilt-pangs and personality disorders if they register protest.

India does not recognize marital rapes as a criminal offence. According to the 2015–16 National Family and Health Survey, around 6 per cent of Indian women aged 15–49 have experienced sexual violence at least once in their lifetime. National Crime Records Bureau statistics for 2012 to 2016 show that approximately 40 per cent of female reported rape victims were minors and 95 per cent knew the rapist. The rapists belonged to the 'circle of trust' of extended family and friends. Rape is not just the act of individual man against a woman but also a show of patriarchal mindset. It has become an instrument and weapon to prevent women from raising their voice against atrocities.

Kidnapping and Abduction

Kidnapping is taking away or enticing of a minor (female of less than 18 years and a male of less than 16 years of age) without the consent of the lawful guardian. Abduction is forcibly, fraudulently or deceitfully taking away of a woman with an intent of seducing her to illicit sex or compelling her to marry a person against her will. In kidnapping, the victim's consent is immaterial but in abduction, the victim's voluntary consent condones the crime.

The important characteristics of kidnapping/abduction as revealed by my own study are: (a) unmarried girls are more likely to be victims of abduction than married women; (b) abductors and victims are acquainted with each other in a large number of cases; (c) the initial contact between the abductor and his victim frequently occurs in their own homes or neighbourhood than in public places; (d) most often only one person is involved in abduction. As such, a threat on the part of the offender and resistance on the part of the victim is not very common in abduction; (e) the two most important motives of abduction are sex and marriage. Abduction with an economic motive constitutes hardly one-tenth of the total abduction; (f) sexual assaults go with abduction in more than 80 per cent of the cases; and (g) the absence of parental control and disaffectionate relations in the family are crucial factors in contacts between the abductor and the victim and girl's (victim's) running away from the home with some acquainted person (labelled later as abductor under pressure) (Ahuja, 1966).

Dowry Deaths

Dowry deaths either by way of suicide by a harassed wife or murder by the greedy husband and in-laws have indeed become a cause of great concern for parents, legislators, police, courts and society as a whole. Not a day passes when one does not read about a girl being harassed, tortured, killed or driven to suicide because of dowry, and yet how many of the accused are punished? Few killers in bride burning cases are arrested, fewer are prosecuted and fewest finally sentenced.

Traditionally, dowry deaths (homicidal and suicidal) occurred through immolation. Indeed, even though in recent years dowry-related deaths as a result of poisoning or hanging may have been increasing. The Indian Penal Code (IPC) was amended specifically to deal with dowry-related violence, cruelty and dowry deaths in 1983. Unnatural death of a woman within seven years of marriage attracts penal provisions of section 304B IPC. This section defines dowry death as the unnatural death of a woman following harassment or cruelty by her husband or his relatives in connection with a demand for dowry.

Though the Dowry Prohibition Act, 1961 has banned the practice of dowry but in reality all that the law does is to recognize that the problem exists. It is virtually unheard of for a husband or his family to be sued for insisting on taking a dowry. If anything, the demands for dowry have escalated over the years along with dowry deaths. As a modest estimate, the figure of deaths in India due to non-payment or partial payment of dowry could be placed around 9,000 for one year. Most dowry deaths occur in the privacy of the husband's house and with the collusion of the family members. Courts, therefore, admit their inability to convict any one for lack of evidence. Sometimes, the police are so callous in conducting investigations that even the courts question the efficiency and integrity of the police authorities.

The important characteristics of dowry deaths as identified by my own study (1966) are:

1. middle-class women suffer a higher rate of victimization than lower-class or upper-class women;
2. about 70 per cent victims belong to 21–24 years age group, that is, they are mature not only physically but socially and emotionally also;
3. the problem is more an upper-caste phenomenon than a lower-caste problem;
4. before an actual murder, several forms of harassment/humiliation are used against the young brides which show the chaotic pattern of social behaviour of the members of the victim's family;
5. the most important sociological factor in the causation of dowry death is the offender's environmental stress or social tensions caused by factors endogeneous and exogenous to his family, and the important psychological factor is the killer's authoritarian personality, dominant nature, and his personality maladjustment;
6. no correlation exists between the level of education of the girl and her murder committed for dowry; and
7. the composition of a family plays a crucial role in bride burning cases.

Dowry-related domestic abuse of women is still widely prevalent in India. A study by the University of Portsmouth's School of Languages and Area Studies found that giving a dowry is still regularly practised in parts of the country, leading to gender inequalities on a wide scale. The research carried out in Kerala also showed that mothers-in-law were the main harassers and perpetrators of violence against young women, nearly 50 per cent of the time.

Dowry death is a murder or suicide of a married woman caused by a dispute over her dowry in some cases, husbands and in-laws will attempt to extort a greater dowry through continuous harassment and torture which sometimes result in the wife committing suicide.

The majority of these suicides are done through hanging, poisoning or self-immolation. When a dowry death is done by setting the woman on fire, it is called bride burning. Bride burning murder is often set up to appear to be a suicide or accident. Dowry is illegal in India, but it is still a common practice to give expensive gifts to the groom and his relatives at weddings, which are hosted by the family of the bride. Women are not always the only primary victims of dowry deaths. In some cases, children are also killed alongside their mothers.

Wife Battering

Violence towards women in the context of marriage becomes more significant when a husband who is supposed to love and protect his wife beats her. For a woman, being battered by a man whom she trusted most becomes a shattering experience. The violence can range from slaps and kicks to broken bones, torture, and attempted murder and even murder itself. Sometimes, the violence may be related to drunkenness but not always. Bred in Indian culture, a wife rarely thinks in terms of reporting a case of battering to the police. She suffers humiliation in silence and takes it as her destiny. Even if she wants to revolt, she cannot do it because of the fear that her own parents would refuse to keep her in their house permanently after the marital break down.

The important characteristics of wife battering pointed out by my own study (1966) are:

1. wives under 25 years of age have higher victimization rates;
2. wives younger to their husbands by more than five years run a greater risk of being battered by their husbands;
3. low-income women are more victimized, though family income is more difficult to associate with victimization;
4. family size and family composition have little correlation with wife beating;
5. assaults by husbands generally do not involve severe injury;
6. the important causes of wife battering are sexual maladjustment, emotional disturbances, husband's inflated ego or inferiority complex, husband's alcoholism, jealousy, and wife's passive timidity;
7. exposure to violence of the assaulter in his childhood is an important factor in wife battering;
8. though illiterate wives are more vulnerable to husband's beating than the educated wives, there is no significant relationship between beating and the educational level of the victims; and
9. though wives with alcoholic husbands have higher rates of victimization, it has been observed that most of the husbands beat their wives not in a state of drunkenness but while they are sober.

Jejeebhoy (1998) is of the view that not only wife beating is deeply entrenched, but also people justify it. Thus, domestic violence is simply not a personal abnormality but rather its roots are in the cultural norms of the family and society. Again, looking from another angle, it is found that many of the victims of domestic violence have either refused to name the perpetrator of the assault or attributed the injuries to other reasons (Daga et al., 1999).

Acid Attacks

Acid attack is a form of violent assault. It is defined as the premeditated act of throwing acid onto the body of a person 'with the intention to disfigure, maim, torture, or kill'. The most common types of acid used in these attacks are sulfuric, nitric, or hydrochloric acid. The long-term consequences of these attacks include blindness and permanent scarring of the face and body, along with far-reaching social, psychological and economic difficulties.

Acid attacks have their roots in hatred. While there are many villains in such incidents, from spurned lovers and angry mistresses to estranged partners or irate moneylenders, the victim is always a woman.

The most notable effect of an acid attack is the lifelong bodily disfigurement. Consequently, the victim is faced with physical challenges, which require long-term surgical treatment, as well as psychological challenges, which require in-depth intervention from psychologists and counsellors at each stage of physical recovery. These far-reaching effects on their lives impact their psychological, social and economic viability in communities.

Acid assault survivors also face many mental health issues upon recovery. These include anxiety, depression, distress and low self-esteem. For a survivor, an acid attack starts a life littered with obstacles, heartbeaks and isolation. It is tough that many choose to shut out a world which they once dreamt of conquering. Even if these women try and rebuilt their lives, society and the legal system ensure that nothing comes easy.

In addition to the above, many social implications exist for acid survivors, especially women. For example, such attacks usually leave victims handicapped in some way, rendering them dependent on either their spouse or family for everyday activities, such as eating and running errands. This dependency is increased by the fact that many acid survivors are not able to find work, due to impaired vision and range of motion. This negatively impacts their economic viability, causing hardships on the families/spouses that care for them. Moreover, acid survivors who are single when attacked almost certainly become ostracized from society, effectively ruining marriage prospects.

India is one of the countries where cases of acid throwing or attacks are most prevalent. It is estimated that there are as many as 1,000 acid attacks a year in India. But, unfortunately, legal apathy is the most disheartening factor in women's struggle against this growing threat. The latest ordinance amending certain sections of the Indian Penal Code also included identifying acid attacks as a standalone criminal offence. Under the new provision, a person shall be punished with life imprisonment if found guilty of an acid attack. The minimum sentence of 10 years and a fine of ₹ 10 lakh has also been prescribed in the amendment (*Hindustan Times*, 7 February 2013).

In a bid to curb acid attacks, especially on women, various governments – both at the central and state levels – have taken several measures from time to time.

A bench headed by Justice R.M. Lodha gave these directions to states and union territories to frame rules to regulate sale of acids and other corrosive substances within three months. The court said that a photo identity card, containing residential address, issued by authorities concerned, would be required for purchasing such substances which in any case cannot be sold to a person who is below the age of 18 years. Illegal sale and purchase of acid is to be a non-bailable offence. Undisclosed stock to be confiscated, the seller will be fined ₹ 50,000 (*Hindustan Times*, 19 July 2013). It is hoped that the judgement of apex court might go a long way in saving girls from becoming victims of this heinous crime.

For poor women who face financial hardship after a dehumanizing sexual assault or a severe trauma like an acid attack, the National Legal Services Authority (NALSA) in consultation with the centre has drawn up a relief policy offering a minimum amount of ₹ 5 lakh. The scheme is binding on all states.

Persons with Disabilities Act was revised in 2016 to include acid attack survivors as physically disabled. That provides access to education and employment, with 3 per cent of government jobs reserved for acid attack survivors.

To conclude, research has prompted many solutions to the increasing incidence of acid attacks in the world. Many countries look to Bangladesh, whose rates of attacks have been decreasing, as a model, following their lead in many legislative reforms. However, several reports highlighted the need for an increased, legal role of NGOs to offer rehabilitation support to acid survivors. Additionally, nearly all research stressed the need for stricter regulation of acid sales in order to combat this social issue.

Stalking

There is no legal definition of stalking. However, it is generally accepted that it includes repeated attempts to impose unwanted communications and/or contacts on another in a manner that could be expected to cause distress and/or fear in any reasonable person. Stalking is harassment of or threatening another person, especially in a way that haunts the person physically or emotionally in a repetitive and devious manner. Stalking can take place at or near the victim's home, near or in their workplace, on the way to the store or any destination, or on the Internet (cyberstalking). Stalking can be on the phone, in person, or online. Stalkers may never show their face, or they may be everywhere, in person. The stalker may engage in a number of associated behaviours including ordering or cancelling goods/services, making unwarranted complaints (to legitimate bodies), threats, property damage and violence. Stalkers frequently threaten their victims, either directly or indirectly. Examples of indirect threats include sending wreaths or violent images to the victim (often anonymously).

Honour Killings

An honour killing is the murder of a member of a family/social group by other members, due to the belief of the perpetrator(s) that the victim has brought dishonour or shame upon the family/group by his/her act. The apparent dishonour or shame could be caused for having a relationship that the family/group considers to be inappropriate, having sex outside marriage, dressing in ways which are deemed inappropriate, etc. Honour killings are rooted in tradition and cannot be justified by any major world religion because none of the major world religions condones honour-related crimes. The most prominent areas where honour killings occur in India are northern regions. Honour killings are especially seen in Haryana, Bihar, Uttar Pradesh, Rajasthan, Jharkhand, Himachal Pradesh, and Madhya Pradesh. Honour killings have notably increased in some Indian states which have led to the supreme court of India, issuing notices to both the Indian central government and six states to take preventative measures against honour killings.

Honour killing is different from the dowry deaths that are also a very common practice in India as, in the case of dowry deaths, the perpetrators of that action claim that they have not been given enough material rewards for accepting the woman into the family. In that case there is a lot of harassment from the in-laws and many times, it has been noted that the wife commits suicide rather than being killed by the in-laws, though it has to be said that she has been mentally killed, if not physically.

In India, according to a report, more than 1,000 young people die every year owing to honour killings linked to forced marriages. Such killings have been reported from those areas the most where the Khap Panchayats are active. These include Jhajjhar, Jind, Fatehabad and Rohtak districts in Haryana and Meerut, Baghpat and Muzaffarnagar in Uttar Pradesh. These groups, though not directly involved in the crime, have provided the catalytic support to this heinous crime.

In today's scenario, if a young couple wishes to marry outside their caste and community, their endeavour does not receive active support from the state. The procedural requirements of the Special Marriages Act continue to pose difficulties for the consenting adults as a minimum waiting period of one month is required before they can marry. Instances of non-intervention by the police in providing protection to young couples continue to occur with impunity. However, in our country, honour killing has been made a separate provision having severe punishment.

As is evident, honour killings are directed mostly against women and girls. The large number of such killings in the country in recent years has prompted both the government and society to think about this social menace and take measures to prevent it from happening further. First of all, the mentality of the people needs to be changed. It means that parents should always accept their children's wishes regarding marriage as it is they who have to lead a life with their life partners and if they are not satisfied they will lead a horrible married life which might even end in suicide. Second, we need to have stricter laws to tackle these kinds of killings as this is a crime which cannot be pardoned and if need be the Hindu Marriage Act can be amended.

According to the latest National Crime Record Bureau statistics, honour killings in India have grown. This spike could be a result of more vigilant reporting of these crimes, which earlier largely went unreported. A Supreme Court 2006 judgment on such killings has called it 'barbaric'. 'There is nothing honourable in such killings, and in fact, they are nothing but barbaric and shameful acts of murder committed by brutal, feudal-minded persons who deserve harsh punishment'. There is no separate law to punish those found guilty of such murders, and prosecutions are usually among various sections of the Indian Penal Code for homicide and culpable homicide not amounting to murder. Several efforts have been made to create a separate law dealing with honour killings but they have been unsuccessful so far.

Violence Against Widows

All widows do not face similar problems. A widow may be one who has no issue and who has been widowed one or two years after her marriage; or she may be one who becomes a widow after a period of 5 to 10 years and has one or two small children to support, or she may be one who is above 50 years of age. Though all these three categories of widows have to face the problems of social, economic and emotional adjustment, the first and the third categories of widows have no liabilities while the second type of widows have to perform the role of a father for their children. The first two categories of widows have also to face the problem of biological adjustment. These two types are not as welcome in their husband's family as the third type. In fact, while the family members try to get rid of the first two types of widows, the third type of widow becomes a key person in the son's family as she is made responsible for caring for her son's children and cooking food in the absence of her working daughter-in-law. The self-image and the self-esteem of the three categories of widows also vary. A widow's economic dependence is a severe threat to her self-esteem and her sense of identity. The low status accorded to them by their in-laws and others in the family roles lowers their self-esteem. The stigma of widowhood itself negatively affects a woman and she falls in her own esteem.

If we take all types of widows together, we could say that violence against widows includes physical battering, emotional neglect/torture, verbal abuse, sexual abuse, deprivation of legitimate share in property, and abuse of their children. The important characteristics of violence against widows are: (a) young widows are more humiliated, harassed, exploited or victimized than the middle-aged widows; (b) ordinarily, widows know little about their husband's business, accounts, certificates, insurance policies, and bonds, and become easy victims of fraudulent schemes fostered by unscrupulous members of their family (of procreation) who try to acquire their inherited property or life-insurance benefits; (c) perpetrators of violence are mostly the members of the husband's family; (d) of the three most important motives of victimization – power, property and sex – property is a crucial factor in victimization in middle-class widows, sex in the lower class widows, and power in both the middle class and the lower-class widows; (e) though the authoritarian personality of the mother-in-law and the maladjustment of siblings-in-law are important etiological factors in the widow's victimization, the most important factor is widow's passive timidity; and (f) age, education, and class appear to be significantly correlated to the exploitation of the widows but family composition and family size have little correlation with it.

Sexual Violence

Sexual violence can occur in intimate partner and family contexts, in workplaces, and in many other circumstances. Sexual violence can include:

1. Sexual harassment, e.g. verbal street harassment, catcalling, staring, following someone, making unwanted/repeated requests for sex.
2. Sexualized bullying, e.g. sending unwanted pornographic images to threaten or intimidate someone, threatening to share nude photos, making threats to rape.
3. Sexual pressure and coercion, e.g. making threats to break up, playing mind games to trick someone into unwanted sexual acts.

Online Violence Against Women

Revenge porn – someone with a grudge, like an ex-partner, posts nude or semi-nude videos or photos of a person online to get back at them. Sometimes, current partners will threaten to do this to prevent them from breaking up.

1. *Creepshots* – taking creepy photos of someone (e.g. when they're bending over or in a change-room) and posting the images without permission.
2. *Malicious impersonation* – impersonating others online and posting comments or photos, trying to ruin their reputation (e.g. inserting their face into an image of a porn star or a victim of violence).

Among the top 20 countries in internet usage worldwide, India has the highest yearly growth rate of internet users. Easy access to the internet has enabled many people, especially women and other marginalized groups, to overcome traditional barriers and participate in the public sphere. However, the violence women face in these virtual spaces has in many ways left them feeling vulnerable, not empowered. Online violence against women – that is, violence directed at women by virtue of their gender – violates their human rights and is thus, imminent to the attainment of gender equality. Online violence needs to be taken seriously and it often has the potential to spill into physical abuse and violence. Abuse against women on Twitter and other platforms can also include 'doxxing' which involves revealing personal information or identifying documents or details about someone, on an online platform, without their consent. India already has laws that while flawed – can be used to deal with online abuse. What needs attention is a better implementation of the same.

Victims of Violence

If we take all the cases of violence against women into consideration, we find that the victims of violence are generally those:

1. who feel helpless, depressed, have a poor self-image and suffer from self-devaluation, or those who are 'emotionally consumed' by the perpetrators of violence, or who suffer from 'altruistic powerlessness';
2. who live in stressful family situations, or who live in families which, in sociological terms, cannot be called 'normal' families, that is, families which are structurally complete (both parents being alive and living together), economically secure (satisfying basic and subsidiary needs of members, functionally adequate (have rare quarrels) and morally conformists;
3. who lack social maturity or social interpersonal skills because of which they face behavioural problems;
4. whose husbands/in-laws have pathological personalities; and
5. whose husbands are alcoholic.

Perpetrators of Violence

The perpetrators might isolate their partner from friends and family. They can do this in a number of ways, some examples are:

1. The perpetrator might behave rudely in front of their partner's friends to discourage them from hanging out in the future.
2. The perpetrator might get angry when their partner goes out with other friends without them.

Controlling and coercive behaviour can take other forms like:

1. Criticizing how their partner dresses.
2. Checking their text messages and emails to see who they speak to.
3. Making threats to share intimate details.
4. Putting them down in front of other people.

Perpetrators use all sorts of ways to control their partners and justify their violent behaviour. It doesn't matter how small the act seems, if it makes the other person feel frightened or intimidated.

Women are generally abused and attacked by men they know. This is proved by one study even in England (University of Warwick: Joanna Liddle), which has pointed out that 61 per cent of women are abused by their own family members and only 39 per cent by strangers. In the former category, 72 per cent face violence at the hands of their husbands, by men they know well, and that too in places they would consider as safe. In India also, the crimes of marital violence reported to police in different states indicate that the marital home is not always a safe place for a woman (which also does not mean that a woman is safer outside her home than in it). Males argue that today a woman does not adhere to the conventional parameters expected of a wife. Does this reflect that a woman refusing to conform and asking for some freedom and some independence needs violence – whether physical, psychological or emotional – to ensure that conformity? Can we accept this type of 'patriarchal consensus' in this age?

Men are more likely to perpetrate violence if they have low education, a history of child maltreatment, exposure to domestic violence against their mothers, harmful use of alcohol, unequal gender norms including attitudes accepting of violence, and a sense of entitlement over women.

Seven types of victimizers of women may be identified. They are those who:

1. have depression, inferiority complex and low self-esteem;
2. have personality disorders and are psychopaths;
3. lack resources, skills, and talents and have sociopathic personality;
4. have possessive, suspicious and dominant nature;
5. face stressful situations in family life;
6. are victims of violence in childhood; and
7. are frequent users of alcohol.

Types of Violence

If we were to develop a typology of violence against women, we may give six types of violence:

1. violence which is money-oriented;
2. violence which seeks power over the weak;
3. violence which aims at pleasure-seeking;
4. violence which is the result of the perpetrator's pathology;
5. violence which is the result of stressful family situations; and
6. violence which is victim-precipitated.

Motivation in Violence

Violence against women may be explained on the basis of three factors: (a) situations which bring about violent behaviour, (b) characteristics of victims, and (c) characteristics of victimizers. Four causes may be identified in violence against women: (i) victim's provocation, (ii) intoxication, (iii) hostility towards women, and (iv) situational urge.

Victim's Provocation

Sometimes the victim of violence by her behaviour, which is often unconscious, creates the situation of her own victimization. The victim either generates or triggers off the violent behaviour of the offender. Her actions transform him into an assaulter/aggressor making him direct his criminal intentions against her. In my own survey of rape, wife-battering, abduction, ill-treatment of widows, and murders, the focus was on victims, yet some offenders/assaulters/aggressors were also interviewed. Surprisingly, only a few seemed to suffer from any feelings of shame or anxiety. A large number did not suffer from any emotional turmoil or from what psychologists call the problem of 'troubled masculinity'. The assaulters in wife battering cases instead accused their wives of back-biting, talking to person(s) they disliked, ill-treating their sisters or parents or brothers, neglecting their home, talking rudely to relatives, having illicit relations with some person, refusing to obey their in-laws, irritating them with their quarrelsome or nagging nature, or interfering too much in their affairs. Similarly, in criminal assault (rape) cases, there were assaulters who described the behaviour of the victim as a direct invitation to sexual relations or a sign that she would be available if he persisted. It is significant to determine whether the victim actually intended to invite such behaviour or not or whether it was merely the victimizer's own interpretation/perception that led him to exploit her. This may be called an 'act of omission' (failing to react strongly) on the part of the victim, if not an 'act of commission'.

Thus, the 'passive' victim contributes to the commission of violent act to the same extent as the 'active' victim. In murder cases too, we came across a few cases where, according to the assaulters, the homicide situation started when in arguments and altercations, the victims precipitated such circumstances which motivated them to attack them. In abduction cases too, some abductors pointed out that their 'victims' had willingly agreed to run away with them and marry but, when they were arrested on the complaint of parents, the 'victim' on being coerced by their parents had accused them of abduction. On an average, 39 per cent cases were found willing abductions, 24 per cent were forced abductions, 17 per cent accessory abductions (in which victims neither gave their. consent of going with the 'accused person' nor opposed it but succumbed to the relationship of 'power' of the accused over her), and 20 per cent were stress abductions (in which the victim initially agreed to leave the house willingly but later on repented when the 'offender' raped her or sold her ornaments or left her in the hotel).

This analysis enables us to classify victims as active, passive and accidental. At least two kinds of victims create a situation in which the 'offender' becomes 'victim' of the situation and/or compulsion and behaves with the 'victim' (female) in such a way that he comes to be labelled as the 'assaulter' or 'victimizer'.

Intoxication

Some cases of violence occur when the aggressors are intoxicated and in a wildly excited and belligerent state of mind, scarcely comprehending the likely fallout of their actions. For example, in a few cases of rape, the offenders assaulted the victims when they had taken so much alcohol that they were in a state of inebriation and emotional excitement. Their normal restraints had disappeared and their aggressive fantasies were intimately intermingled with sexual lust which then took the shape of irresponsible actions. Alcohol-related sex crimes illustrate a reckless disregard of time, space and circumstances.

A similar relationship between alcoholism and violence was demonstrated in a few cases of wife battering and murder. While in my own study, I had found that wife battering was accompanied by the use of alcohol in 31.7 per cent of the cases Ahuja (1987: 130), Hilberman and Munson (1978: 460–71) had found it in 93 per cent of the cases, Wolfgang (1978) in 67 per cent cases, and Tinkleberg (1973) in 71 per cent cases.

We must admit that when we interrelate violence with alcoholism, we rely only on the reported use of alcohol rather than on the measurements of alcohol levels in the blood. In fact, it is the blood alcohol concentration (BAC) which ought to be the basis of associating battering with the influence of alcohol. A very high BAC reduces the capability of the subject to cause bodily harm to others. However, we assume that the level of BAC must be such that the offender loses control over himself only to the extent that he fails to think of the consequences of his actions. It is only in this state of mind that he becomes violent.

It is not clear whether alcohol induces violent behaviour directly or whether it acts primarily as a disinhibitor of pre-existing aggressive tendencies. The latter hypothesis is perhaps supported by the notion (Blumer, 1973: 73–87) that some perpetrators of violence drink for courage prior to using violence against persons, but not a single case was reported in my study in which the assaulter became intoxicated for the specific purpose of assaulting his victim. However, we cannot provide any proof that the ingest of alcohol alone elicits violent behaviour. There are many people who take alcohol yet they hardly ever become violent. The use of alcohol in violence against women may, therefore, be accepted as a 'cooperative' factor rather than the 'chief' factor.

Hostility towards Women

Some of the reported cases of violence against women are of a nature that no amount of rationalization could convert the aggressors into doing anything other than hostile acts of a cruel kind. A few of them had deeply entrenched feelings of hate and hostility for women that their violent act could be said to be primarily directed towards the humiliation of the victim. If the mere situation had been the motivating factor, it is hard to see why a violent act should have been necessary, considering the fact that most of the 'offenders' are described as 'normal' persons. Perhaps a desire to gloat over the victim's humiliation was far stronger.

Situational Urge

In this category, those cases may be included where the crime is committed neither because of the victim's behaviour nor because of the offender's psychopathological personality but rather because of the chance factors which create such situations which lead to violence. For example, in a wife-battering case, it may be that conflict over money matters or on the ill-treatment of husband's parent(s) may provoke the husband to assault his wife; or in a rape case, a man accidentally meets a female acquaintance from his neighbouring village in a field and begins a conversation, ultimately attempting to have his way with her; or the male employer taking advantage of his young female employee finding her alone in his office/factory in the late hours of the evening; or a young girl runs away from her father's house and accepts a lift in a truck and the truck driver takes advantage of the situation and criminally assaults her. In all these cases, the 'offenders' had not planned the violent acts but when they found the situation conducive or provocative, they used violence. Apart from these violent acts, these offenders had not been living a life of deviant behaviour.

Personality Traits

Some identifying traits of the violence-prone personalities are: extremely suspicious, passionate, dominant, irrational, immoral, easily emotionally upset, jealous, possessive and unjust. Traits developed in the early life affect the aggressive behaviour of a person in adulthood. The aggressor having being abused as a child, and/or his exposure to violence during childhood, therefore, must be examined to delve into his violent behaviour. For example, in the case of some wife-batterers, their childhood, adolescence and early adulthood experiences reveal that they learnt to respond to all emotionally distressing cues with angry and violent behaviour. Unhappy family life amounting to exposure to physical brutality or severe emotional rejection has been found to be the rule in the case of most of the aggressors. Some adult aggressors have faced such situations in their family in their childhood/adolescence where they always found their parents screaming and getting at each other, and their father beating them (children) on the slightest pretext. Often, their fathers would come home drunk and would charge around the house shouting and breaking things. Growing up in a violent home inevitably leads to violent behaviour in individuals, who become aggressive persons in their adult life. Alfaro (1978), Potts, Henberger and Holland (1979), and Fagon, Stewart and Ilansen (1981) have also pointed out a similar correlation in their empirical studies on violent men and their children. Thus, we can say that a good number of aggressors are victims of child abuse and familial violence, and exposure to violence as a child strongly influences the probability of one being generally violent as an adult.

Theoretical Explanation of Violent Behaviour

We have already presented a theoretical explanation of deviant/violent behaviour in one of the earlier chapters (Chapter 9 on 'Child Abuse') by examining the different schools of thought as well as by expounding our own conceptual framework. The theoretical propositions on violence typically encountered, whether violence is a normal response of provocation, or whether it involves the acting out of some psychopathology, or whether it acts as an instrument to obtaining some end or reward, or whether it is a response consistent with norms supporting its use, are explained. Our own conceptual framework is based on a holistic approach and is presented as the 'Social Barrier Theory' which explains violent behaviour to a large extent.

The psychiatric or psychopathological school focusses on the aggressor's personality characteristics as the chief determinant of criminal violent behaviour. The socio-psychological school assumes that criminal violence can best be understood by analysing the external environmental factors that exercise an impact on the individual aggressor. This model also examines the types of everyday interactions (say, stressful situations or family interactional patterns) which are precursors to violence. Theories such as the Frustration-Aggression Theory, the Perversion Theory, the Self Attitude Theory, and the Motive Attribution Theory also fall within the purview of socio-psychological level of analysis. The sociological school provides a macro level analysis of criminal violence. Besides these, the Theory of Subculture of Violence, the Learning Theory, the Anomie Theory and the Resource Theory also fall under the sociocultural analysis.

For developing a new theoretical approach in my empirical study on violence (crimes) against women, I had two alternatives before me: either to take 'intrafamily violence' and 'violence exogenous to family' separately or combine all types of violence together and develop one theory on 'violence against women'. I used the latter approach borrowing certain concepts from sociologists and criminologists like Hirschi, Schultz, etc.

Violence against a person is necessarily 'violence by somebody' and 'violence against somebody'. As such, violence against women has to be understood as 'violence by an individual against an individual' in contrast to 'violence by a group against an individual' or 'violence by a group against a group'. In violence by an individual, its origin or form must be determined in the individual himself and the situation around him. In this approach, not only individual's innate behaviour but also his acquired behaviour has to be taken into account. Our 'Social Bond Approach' takes into consideration both types of behaviour as well as the social structural conditions.

My contention is that causes of violence against women are found to be related mainly to five factors: (a) structure of the situation in which violence is committed, (b) situational facilities which enable the use of violence, (c) precipitating factor(s) that lead to violence, (d) strains experienced by the perpetrator of violence, i.e. his individual problems, and (e) victim's behaviour with the user of violence much before violence is used against her.

A holistic approach to the combination of these factors alone will give us the correct causes of use of violence against women.

Specifically, three factors seem to play a major role in prompting a man to use violence against a woman: (a) perpetrator's history of abuse as a child (like unhappy upbringing, physical beating by parents, and emotional rejection); (b) stressful situations in the family; (c) status frustrations. The first factor points out that the perpetrator's violent behaviour is mostly learnt from childhood and adolescence experiences of emotional distresses. This posits the thesis of the 'Generational Theory' that growing up in a violent home increases the likelihood of an individual becoming violent as an adult. The fact that a very large number of offenders (78%) in my study on 'Crimes Against Women' were the victims of violence in childhood shows that my data supports this theory. The data also supports the 'Social Learning Theory' according to which indulging in violent (deviant) behaviour as a method of conflict resolution or as a coping mechanism is learnt behaviour. Women's tolerance of violence is explained in terms of 'Learned Helplessness Theory' and 'Traditional Socialization Theory'. The latter theory refers to woman's imbibing traditional values and 'sex role ideology' through socialization process that man is superior to woman and that woman has no right to protest. The former theory maintains that some events occur in a woman's life with sufficient regularity because of which she acquires feelings of depression, helplessness and poor self-image and comes to believe that she cannot escape abuse.

Using a holistic approach, I have proposed a new theoretical model (see Ahuja, 1996: 193–95) for understanding violence against women or women's exploitation. My model focusses on the linkage between a woman's (victim's) personality traits and social environment in which she lives and functions. It assumes that woman's exploitation (rape, molestation, beating, harassment for dowry, kidnapping for leading a life of a prostitute) is the result of interaction between a woman's personality (including imbibed feelings of helplessness, timidity, etc.) and her environment. Each woman lives in a social environment composed of different persons with varied perceptions and expectations. A woman's exploitation will depend on her subjective perception of her status and role and her will, ability, and efforts to challenge it (exploitation) with courage. In other words, a woman's exploitation is dependent on five things: (a) social background (which refers to her age, education and training), (b) level of support (which depends on the support of her parents, in-laws, peers and others), (c) expectations of others (including her husband, parents, in-laws, children, kin, working colleagues, peers, etc.), (d) economic base (i.e. whether she belongs to low, middle or upper income group), and (e) self-image (whether she considers herself timid, bold, helpless, weak, strong, etc.). My thesis is that the structural conditions of a person (family crises, role frustrations, unfortunate incidents in life, inappropriate upbringing) create anxieties and stresses in him because of which he fails to adjust himself according to his social status, to attach himself strongly with other persons and groups, and to commit himself to roles and obligations to follow a particular course of action. The resultant frustrations determine his attitude towards others, including the weaker sex or women. Depending on his personality traits and the resistance potential of the victim, a man will use violence against a woman. My theory is thus based on a conjunctive approach which takes into account social factors like stressful situations, endogenous and exogenous to a family, personality traits of perpetrators of violence and victims, and cultural milieu, like normative pressures and ambiguities.

Self-Image, Self-Esteem and Adjustment of Victims

Self-image and role evaluation are two important aspects of behaviour. Every individual when playing a particular role according to certain social expectations is judged by society in accordance with his/her fulfillment of these expectations. A woman too, as a victim of violence evaluates herself which in turn helps/hinders her in performing the expected roles. It was also found that like self-image, self-esteem of the victims too depended on emotional support they got from different sources. Self-image and self-esteem were also found to be correlated with adjustment in family and society. High self-esteem is positive personality dimension and reduces dependency syndrome despite the sociocultural stigma attached to being sexually assaulted, kidnapped, battered, and humiliated. It leads to adequate familial adjustment owing to equalitarian mode of relationship.

Following Mukesh Ahuja's empirical study (1996: 137–38), the following important sociological facts may be pointed out about the female victims of violence and exploitation:

1. *Structures as source of problems*: The problems of females who are victims of violence arise from the functioning of social structures in which they live and work, and the stresses caused by family interactions and support systems.
2. *Tradition of barriers to assertion*: The involvement of victims in social roles and relationships after being victimized is dependent less on their own initiative and self-confidence and more on the will of heads of families (of procreation and orientation) and social pressures, i.e. traditional culture discourages female victims from taking up assertive social engagements outside the home.
3. *Resource deprivation and suffering of self*: Resources like higher education and work with wages increase victim's self-image and self-esteem which considerably changes her relations with others, and also enable her to face the strain of transition to life and 'recovery' and adjust herself in family and society.
4. *Attachment*: A large number of victims of violence overcome their feelings of being isolated and condemned by attaching themselves to some love object, social service, religious commitments, etc.

5. *Structural suffocation*: Factors which prevent victims of violence from renewing, redeeming, restoring, reviving, and revitalizing their lives lie more in social structures than in their personalities.
6. *Negation of revolt*: A few young and independent victims have a secret desire of rebelling and adopting modern methods of adjustment but they fail to rebel for the fear that their husbands, in-laws and parents might sever ties with them. They are also scared of being shunned and ostracized by their kin and friends.
7. *Self-esteem situation*: Victims with soppy emotions lead a suppressed life but victims with courage of conviction, character and consciousness chart their own course in their (working) life.

Adjustment Phases

The adjustment of victims after being stigmatized (i.e. raped, molested, kidnapped, beaten) to new life and their taking up new roles involves several phases, although there is much intermeshing of these phases. The phases seem to follow a sequence. Bowlby (in *Journal of Social Issues*, Vol. 44, No. 3, 1988: 45–46) has identified four phases of recovery from shock and a long interval of adaptation. Following Bowlby (1988) and Ahuja (1996: 139), we may identify the following four phases in female victims' adjustment to life after stigmatization: (a) shock and pain, (b) removing pain, (c) avoidance and humiliation, and (d) adaptation (see Figure 1). However, all victims do not experience the same level of shock and pain, the same level of humiliation and avoidance, and the same problems of finding substitute sources of adjustment.

Figure 1

Phases of Adjustment to New Life by Female Victims of Violence

Phase I	Shock and pain depends on nature of violence against her and also factors like: • Age • Education • Employment • Emotional attachment
Phase II	Removing pain depends on: • Support • Security
Phase III	Avoidance/Humiliation by: • Family • Kin • Friends • Acquaintances
Phase IV	Adaptation through: • Religious consolation • Accepting social challenge • Neutralization • Attachment and identity change

The Depersonalization Trauma and Humanistic Approach

The two important questions are: what has been done to punish perpetrators of violence against women and what measures should be adopted to prevent women's abuse? Besides the enacting of Anti-Dowry Act, 1961, some amendments were made in the existing laws also. One section was inserted in the Indian Penal Code in 1983 against cruelty and harassment for dowry, while another section was inserted in 1986 Act pertaining to causing dowry death. Amendments were also made in the Evidence Act by inserting a section which deals with presumption as to abatement of suicide by a married woman within a period of seven years of marriage and another section which makes the presumption with respect to dowry death once it is shown that the accused had subjected the deceased woman to cruelty or harassment for or in connection with any demand for dowry. Despite these strict laws, a large number of the accused persons are not convicted on charge of murder and harassment for dowry because of many inbuilt loopholes in the investigative process, connivance of unscrupulous forces, interference of so-called 'high people', and many more extraneous factors. All these factors dilute the efficacy and stringency of many provisions in the laws. Unless courts set examples in rigidly dealing with release on bail and in interpreting the evidence produced, it is doubtful that law can reduce this type of crime.

Can social measures help in reducing violence against women? The suggestion that improving the general status of women through education, effective legislative measures, providing training and employment opportunities will reduce violence against women may be valid and logical to some extent but all the same, it is too broad a suggestion. Similarly, it is suggested that too much prominence should not be given to cases of violence against women in the mass media. Although, there are ethical and humanitarian reasons for censoring violence against women in the mass media, we have no evidence that such a move will necessarily lead to reduction in violence. The same is true of providing deterrent punishment to perpetrators and social ostracization by one's kin, neighbours and friends. These measures may be desirable for their social effects, but we cannot be certain that they will lessen the exploitation of women to any extent. While there is lack of evidence to identify which general policies deserve priority, there are nevertheless a number of measures which could be adopted to contain women's harassment.

First, we take up the issue that is already receiving attention from many women's organizations as well as government and private/public institutions. This is to meet the needs of protection, support and advice of the victims. What some, if not all, women need most is a shelter. Women living with authoritarian in-laws and alcoholic husbands would leave their homes, temporarily or permanently, if some shelter is available to them. Voluntary organizations providing such accommodation to women have to publicize their schemes. It has to be borne in mind that even the existing Homes for Women – single and/or married – are not able to meet the required demands. They are often overcrowded, lack financial support and fail to meet safety regulations. Providing short-term accommodation to women, particularly married women who are in distress, or victims of violence like rape, abduction, attempt to murder, and ultimately helping them find a permanent place by the women's organizations will contribute to the alleviation of the distress suffered by many women. There is an urgent need to evaluate and compare the different types of short-term accommodation that could be provided to the victimized women, including widows.

Second, assistance in finding employment and childcare facilities and immediate financial support is also the need of the suffering women. Advisory centres for this purpose could be located centrally but away from the Women Homes so that they can be well advertised without affecting the safety of the residents in the Homes.

Third, establishment of cheaper and less formal courts could also be a measure to help women who are victims of exploitation. It is not being suggested that these courts will handle only the female cases. Their scope has to be wider. We have at present the system of Family Courts in some states in our country. But these courts are mainly concerned with preventing the breakup of the marriages. The scope of these courts could be extended to deal with all types of domestic and non-domestic problems of women. The establishment of courts with judges, magistrates and lawyers chosen for their knowledge and interest in female matters would be an improvement and it will increase the number of women entering the legal profession. To many women, the courts and the laws would seem less frightening and more sympathetic and approachable, if they are less dominated by men. Female judges and lawyers may not differ significantly from their male counterparts in their attitudes and beliefs and in their interpretation of laws, but female victims might be happier to appear before other females in the expectation that they would be more understanding about the problems faced by women.

Fourth, strengthening and increasing voluntary organizations which could take up individual women's problems with their in-laws or the police or the courts or the concerned individuals is equally necessary. This is because the voice of an individual woman carries no weight. In fact, she is accused of being outspoken if she demands her rights or holds radical views or expresses her views and releases her frustrations, but if a group of women join together and raise their voice against woman's suffering, they can assert their views and make an impact.

Fifth, publicity has to be given to those organizations which provide free legal aid to women so that the needy women could approach them and seek their help.

Last, a change in parents' attitudes is also necessary in women's cases. Why do parents force their daughters – married or widowed – who are frequently beaten by their husbands or ill-treated by their in-laws to live in their husbands' house against their own wishes? When parents come to know of their daughter's harassment, why should they not permit their daughters to live with them for a short time till they are able to fend for themselves? Why should they remain so concerned about the social stigma and sacrifice their daughters for the sake of their family?

Why should women submit to oppression? Why do they not realize that they have the potential to look after themselves and their children? Why do they not understand that their torture creates an emotional trauma for their children also? Women have to learn to be assertive and accept new roles for themselves. They have to develop an optimistic and hopeful approach to life.

The passage of the Criminal Law (Amendment) Act, in April 2013, is a milestone for anti-rape laws in the country. Not only this, the judiciary also taken a step forward by establishing fast-track courts to ensure speedy trial for women who have been a victim of any kind of sexual offence. But, in view of the constant increase in the number of cases, it underlines that a mere law cannot change the society by itself. Violence against women reflects larger societal and institutional prejudices and making India safer for women involves a battle to change this culture.

Conclusion

'Violence' must be recognized as a human phenomenon in as much as it consists of an act of one person which encroaches upon the freedom of another. Thus, rape, abduction, kidnapping, murder (all cases of criminal violence), dowry death, wife battering, sexual abuse, maltreatment of a widow and/or an elderly woman (all cases of domestic violence) and eve-teasing, forcing wife/daughter-in-law to go for feticide, forcing a young widow to commit *sati* (all cases of social violence), are issues which affect a large section of society. Crimes against women have more than doubled over the past ten years. Rape is the fastest growing crime in the country today. Over the last few months, cases of rapes and assault have made it to the headlines with alarming frequency. Equally horrific are news reports of foreign tourists being sexually assaulted. It looks like India as a nation has ceased to know how to treat women as human beings, who have a right to dignity and safety. Society is changing and the government is forced to take action as it has run out of excuses such as society's mindset or class divide. Violence against women in India is on the rise. Despite the incredible social changes achieved by the country, the girl child has to remain brave and vigilant to overcome sexual defilement. The law enforcing machinery must be trained and made sensitive to the issue. Women must organize themselves into groups and raise a collective voice against a system that turns a blind eye towards violent acts against women. United efforts can create a public opinion and outcry against humiliations against women done by men. Women have to be aware of their rights and stand up to them. Women must help themselves and each other in the fight against violence. Attitudinal change is required right from the home, to be able for women to stand with dignity in this world.

In a country with gender discrimination operating at so many levels and in so many ways, bringing about the needed change requires dedicated and combined efforts of multiple agencies.

Violence against women is one of the most pervasive human rights violations. It devastates lives, fractures communities, and stalls development. To combat the rising phenomenon of violence against women and girls, those committing the crimes must be prosecuted. The survivors have little hope of seeing their perpetrators pay for their crimes, and so the violence perpetuate. States must ensure, that the economic and social rights of the victims are protected. But laws alone are not enough; for perpetrators to be brought to justice, women and girls must be empowered to report violence before it costs them their lives. According to the United Nations Development Programme (UNDP), violence against women stifles a country's development.

References

Ahuja, Mukesh, *Widows*, New Age Publishers, Delhi, 1996.

Ahuja, Ram, *Crime against Women*, Rawat Publications, Jaipur, 1987.

——, *Sociological Criminology*, New Age Publishers, New Delhi, 1966.

Blumer, D., *Neuro-psychiatric Aspects of Violent Behaviour*, University of Toronto, Canada, 1973.

Borland, Marie (ed.), *Violence in the Family*, Manchester University Press, Manchester, 1976.

Chapman, J.K. and Gates, Margaret (eds), *The Victimization of Women*, Sage Publications, Beverly Hills, California, 1976.

Crime in India, National Crime Records Bureau, New Delhi, 2012, 2016.

Curtis, Lynn A., *Criminal Violence*, Luxington Books, Kentucky, 1974.

Daga, A.S., Jejeebhoy, S.J. and Rajgopal, S., *Domestic Violence Against Women: An Investigation of Hospital Casualty Records*, Mumbai, 1999.

Finkelhor, David, Gelles, Richard, Hotaling, Gerald and Straus, Murraya, *The Dark Side of Families*, Sage Publications, Beverly Hills, California, 1983.

Hilberman, E. and Munson, M., 'Sixty Battered Women', *Victimology: An International Journal*, Vol. 2, 1979–78.

Jejeebhoy, Shireen, 'Wife Beating in Rural India: A Husband's Right? Evidence from Survey Data'. *Economic and Political Weekly*, 33(15): 855–862, 1998.

Leonard, E.B., *Women, Crime and Society*, Longman, New York, 1982.

National Crime Records Bureau: Crime in India, 2016.

Pagelow, M.D., *Family Violence*, Praeger Scientific, New York, 1984.

Roy, Maria (ed.), *Battered Women: A Psycho-Sociological Study of Domestic Violence*, Van Nostrand Reinhold, New York, 1977.

Singh, Awadhesh Kumar, *Violence against Women and Children*, Serials Publications, New Delhi, 2012.

Steinmetz, S.K. and Straus, M.A. (eds), *Violence in the Family*, Harper and Row, New York, 1974.

Tinkleberg, J.R., 'Alcohol and Violence', in P.G. Bourne and R.E. Fox (eds), *Alcoholism: Progress in Research and Treatment*, Academic Press, New York, 1973.

Wilson, Elizabeth, *What is to be Done about Violence against Women*, Penguin, Hammondsworth, 1983.

Wolfgang, M.E., 'Violence in the Family', in I.L. Kutash et al. (eds), *Perspectives in Murder and Aggression*, John Wiley, New York, 1978.

11

Illiteracy

Facts about Illiteracy in India

1. The basic definition of literacy is having the ability to read and write.
2. 47.78 per cent of school children are girls. In the next census, they will be calculated as illiterate women, which would then have a ripple effect on the education of their children.
3. Bihar, Jharkhand and Uttar Pradesh are amongst the bottom five states in terms of literacy of Dalits.
4. India's literacy rate has increased six times since the end of the British rule from 12 per cent to 74 per cent in 2011, yet, India has the world's largest population of illiterates.
5. The literacy rate of female Dalits in Bihar is 38.5 per cent in 2011. It is far behind India's progress trend.
6. 60 lakh children in India are still out-of-school.
7. India has rolled-out the Right to Education Act but is yet to witness its complete and proper implementation. Only 0.92 per cent of government schools are yet to fully implement the Right to Education (RTE) Act, 2009.
8. India is ranked 123rd out of 135 countries in female literacy rate.
9. In the South Asian region, India ranks fourth, behind Sri Lanka with a female-male ratio of 0.97 and Bangladesh with a female-male ratio of 0.85.
10. The percentage of women to the total number of school teachers has gone up from 29.3 per cent in 1991 to 47.16 per cent in 2013–14.
11. Despite government programmes, India's literacy rate increased only 'sluggishly'.
12. There is a wide gender disparity in the literacy rate in India – effective literacy rates (age 7 and above) in 2011 were 80.9 per cent for men and 64.60 per cent for women.

Map 1
Literacy Rate Map of India, 2011

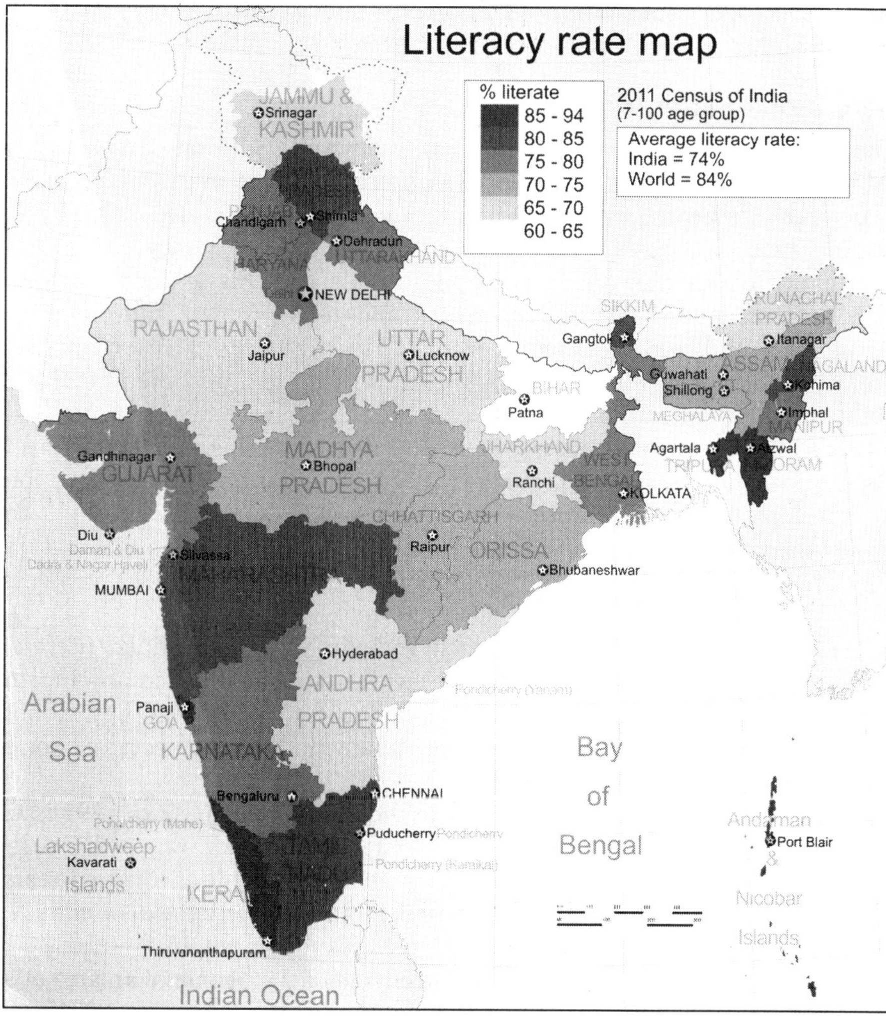

13. The low female literacy rate has had a dramatically negative impact on family planning and population stabilization efforts in India.
14. The census provided a positive indication that growth in female literacy rates (11.8%) was substantially faster than in male literacy rates (6.9%) in the 2001–2011 decadal period, which means the gender gap appears to be narrowing.

After independence, India inherited a system of education that was characterized by large-scale and intra-regional imbalances. The system educated a select few, leaving a wide gap between the educated and the illiterate. The country literacy rate in 1947 was only 14 per cent and female literacy was abysmally low at 8 per cent. It is thus commonly believed that without substantially eliminating illiteracy, India cannot become a cohesive nation and give to all its citizens the quality of life they have long yearned for. No wonder that education in general and literacy in particular have been accorded a high priority in the country's development process.

Definition of Literacy

The United Nations Educational, Scientific and Cultural Organization (UNESCO) has drafted a definition of literacy as the 'ability to identify, understand, interpret, create, communicate, compute and use printed and written materials associated with varying contexts. Literacy involves a continuum of learning in enabling individuals to achieve their goals, to develop their knowledge and potential, and to participate fully in their community and wider society'. The National Literacy Mission defines literacy as acquiring the skills of reading, writing and arithmetic and the ability to apply them to one's day-to-day life. The achievement of functional literacy implies (a) self-reliance in 3 R's, (b) awareness of the causes of deprivation and the ability to move towards amelioration of their condition by participating in the process of development, (c) acquiring skills to improve economic status and general well being, and (d) imbibing values such as national integration, conservation of environment, women's equality, and observance of small family norms.

Following UNESCO, the Census in India in 1991 also defined 'literate' person as one who can read and write 'with understanding' in any Indian language, and not merely read and write. Those who can read but cannot write are not literate. Formal education in a school is not necessary for a person to be considered as literate.

The working definition of literacy in the Indian Census since 1991 is as follows: literacy rate, also called the 'effective literacy rate', the total percentage of the population of an area at a particular time aged seven years or above, who can read and write with understanding. Here the denominator is the population aged seven years or more.

'Crude literacy rate' is the total percentage of the people of an area at a particular time who can read and write with understanding, taking the total population of the area (including below seven years of age) as the denominator.

Literacy is an evolving concept which not only entails the grasping abilities of printed text but also the abilities to adapt visual entities and technological awareness as well. It happens to be a multi-dimensional concept which keeps on adding new parameters to it with respect to the developments that are taking place in a globalized world. Literacy involves a continuum of learning in enabling individuals to achieve their goals to develop their knowledge and potential and to participate fully in their community and wider society. A higher literacy rate is an essential requirement for any nation to bring it at par on a global platform with other nations. No nation is considered as a promising nation if it has a stable economic growth rate but poor literacy rates. It is one of the most dangerous obstacles to the economy's growth. Education after all, is a fundamental right which is ensured to the citizens.

In a resolution on National Policy on Education adopted in 1968, radical reconstruction of education was proposed so that it could involve: (a) a transformation of the system to relate it more closely to the life of the people, (b) a continuous effort to expand educational opportunity, (c) a sustained effort to raise the quality of education at all stages, (d) an emphasis on the development of science and technology, and (e) cultivation of moral and social values. In 1986 policy, stress was laid on providing equal opportunities of education to all classes. The 1986 policy was modified in 1992. It envisaged conduct of a common entrance examination for various professional courses. In 2005, the government adopted a new policy which mainly focussed on higher education.

Literacy in India is a key for socio-economic progress, and the Indian literacy rate has grown to 73 per cent (2011 Census figure) with recent reports of 80 per cent literacy. The literacy rate at the end of British rule in 1947 was around 17 per cent. Although, this was greater than six-old improvement, the level is below the world average literacy rate of 84 per cent. Despite government programmes, India's literacy rate increased 'sluggishly'. The 2011 Census, indicated a 2001–2011 decadal literacy growth of 9.2 per cent, which is slower than the growth as seen during the previous decade. A 1990 study estimated that it would take until 2060 for India to achieve universal literacy at then-current rate of progress.

There is a wide gender disparity in the literacy rate in India: effective literacy rates (age 7 and above) in 2011 were 80.9 per cent for men and 64.60 per cent for women. The low female literacy rate has had a dramatically negative impact on family planning and population stabilization efforts in India. Studies have indicated that female literacy is a strong predictor of the use of contraception among married Indian couples, even when women do not otherwise have economic independence. The census provided a positive indication that growth in female literacy rates (11.8%) was substantially faster than in male literacy rates (6.9%) in the 2001–2011 decadal period, which means the gender gap appears to be narrowing.

Literacy Rate Variations between States

India's literacy rate is at 74.04 per cent. Kerala has achieved a literacy rate of 93.91 per cent. Bihar is the least literate state in India, with a literacy of 63.82 per cent. Several other social indicators of the two states are correlated with these rates, such as life expectancy at birth (71.61 for males and 75 for females in Kerala, 65.66 for males and 64.79 for females in Bihar), infant mortality per 1,000 live births (10 in Kerala, 61 in Bihar), birth rate per 1,000 people (16.9 in Kerala, 30.9 in Bihar) and death rate per 1,000 people (6.4 in Kerala, 7.9 in Bihar). Every census since 1881 had indicated rising literacy in the country, but the population growth rate had been high enough that the absolute number of illiterates rose with every decade. The 2001–2011 decade is the second Census period (after the 1991–2001 Census period) when the absolute number of Indian illiterates declined (by 3,11,96,847 people), indicating that the literacy growth rate is now outstripping the population growth rate also. It needs to be highlighted that India is a country where the extent of disparities is such that one state has achieved a literacy rate higher than 90 per cent, while on the other hand, there also exist states where the literacy rates are still dismal. Six Indian states account for about 70 per cent of all illiterates in India: Uttar Pradesh, Bihar, Madhya Pradesh, Rajasthan, Andhra Pradesh and West Bengal. Slightly less than half of all Indian illiterates (48.12%) are in the six Hindi-speaking states of Uttar Pradesh, Bihar, Rajasthan, Madhya Pradesh, Jharkhand, and Chhattisgarh. Large variations in literacy exist even between contiguous states. While there are few states at the top and bottom, most states are just above or below the national average.

Together with the quantitative expansion of education facilities, there is now a greater emphasis on the qualitative aspect as well. Before 1976, education was exclusively the responsibility of the states, the central government being concerned only with the coordination and determination of standards in technical and higher education. In 1976, through a constitutional amendment, education became the joint responsibility of both the centre and the states. Determined efforts were made to achieve the goal of universal elementary education and eradication of illiteracy in the age group 15–35. The government is also working towards achieving the goal of 'Education for All'. It is a commitment made in 2000 by the international community to provide quality education to all children, youth and adults. Non-formal education and open learning systems are being encouraged at all levels. However, in the field of removing illiteracy in the country, not much progress could be made on account of its huge population. This is evident from the vast magnitude of illiterate persons still found in the country.

Illiteracy in India

According to 2011 Census, 26 per cent people of India are illiterate. Whereas according to Census Report of SECC (Socio Economic Caste Census) 2011, more than a third of its 121.08 crore population are non-literate. This is higher than the 32 per cent recorded by the 2011 Census of India. About 6 per cent of 88.4 crore people in rural India are non-literate.

The attainment of goal of 'Education for All by 2015' appears to be difficult also because, as per the World Bank, our public spending on education is much lower than other countries. In 2010, for instance, India spent only 3.3 per cent of its GDP on education in comparison to 5.6 per cent by USA, 5 per cent by Russia and 5.9 per cent by France. Not only this, despite increase in the aggregate expenditure on education, the rate of increase is not necessarily keeping pace with budgetary expenditure, GDP growth or rate of inflation. The share of public expenditure on education, which was 4 per cent of country's GDP in 1990–91, declined since then. It, however, recovered to over 4 per cent only around the year 2000, but has been on a decline and nowhere near the oft quoted target of 6 per cent.

The problem of illiteracy among women in our country is worse though sex differentials have narrowed down significantly over the years. As mentioned earlier, though the absolute number of female illiterates has gone down by 1,71,22,197 during 2001–2011 but it is still high in comparison to other countries. In 2011 Census, the decadal difference in literacy rates for males and females stands at 6.88 and 11.79 percentage points respectively.

The position of children in terms of illiteracy is equally bad. Despite a major improvement in overall literacy rates, the number of children who are not in schools is still high. The literacy rate jumped from 52 per cent in 1991 to 65 per cent in 2001. The absolute number of non-literates dropped for the first time and gross enrolment in government-run primary schools increased from over 19 million in the 1950s to 114 million by 2001. In spite of all this, 20 per cent of children aged 6 to14 are still not in school.

Causes of Illiteracy

Illiteracy in India is more or less concerned with different forms of disparities that exist in the country. There are gender imbalances, income imbalances, state imbalances, caste imbalances, and technological barriers which shape the literacy rates that exist in the country. India possesses the largest illiterate population. Literacy rates stood at 82.14 per cent for men in 2011 and 65.46 per cent for women. It has been estimated that at the current rate of progress, India will attain universal literacy only until 2060. This low female literacy is also responsible for the dependency of women on men. Illiterate women keep on struggling hard and bear harshness of life and family. Thus, this all leads to the formation of a vicious circle.

Again, it is not a new concept that the rich households will have better access to educational facilities as compared to the poor households. Poor households due to the lack of skills and knowledge involve themselves with unskilled labour in order to save bread for the family. Thus, this reduces the focus from achieving education as the main focus deviates to earning income so as to be able to survive in the society. States that spend more on education seem to have a higher literacy rate as to the states which do not invest heavily in education.

Since many adults in India are illiterate, they do not understand the importance of getting education for their children. Other social evils like caste system, gender inequality also cause illiteracy. One of the primary reasons for dismal literacy rates is the ineffectiveness of primary schools in enrolling and retaining students. The teaching staff that is employed across the government-run schools is inefficient and unqualified. Unfortunately, there is a dearth of suitably trained, sincere and selfless teachers. Another reason which leads to the maximum dropouts among the children is the lack of proper sanitation. A study has stated that 59 per cent of the schools do not have drinking water facilities. There is a shortage of teachers as well. The funds earmarked for adult education are too inadequate, and whatever little has been set aside, it is not been utilized profitably. Lesser money than the actual budget allocation for education is utilized for the implementation of the schemes. Moreover, very little coordination exists among the different agencies engaged in adult literacy. Very often there is a duplication of work at most of the places.

The main causes of illiteracy are: (a) high rate of population growth in relation to low rate of adult population gaining literacy; (b) ineffectiveness of primary schools in enrolling and retaining students; (c) traditional outlook of low-class people in using the services of young children either for earning money or looking after infants in family instead of sending them to schools; (d) high level of poverty; (e) non-conducive educational policies of the colonial rulers to the spread of education; and (f) low allotment of funds for education.

In Indian context, the two major causes of illiteracy are paucity of schools as well as teachers. According to the report of the 8th All India Education Survey, released by NCERT, the ratio of student to teacher in the country is 1:32 across primary, upper primary and secondary levels. In addition, there is also poor sanitation in schools with no toilets and drinking water facilities. The survey revealed that one-fifth of total schools in rural areas do not have facility for drinking water and three out of ten schools do not have a usable toilet. Even half of them have no playground for children (*Indian Express*, 23 January 2013).

Disadvantages of Illiteracy

Illiteracy generates hundreds of problems. Because of illiteracy, people do not know how to earn well and how to spend well. As a result, they cannot come out of their poverty trap. Many do not have knowledge about food and nutrition, so they suffer from various kinds of diseases. In a word, illiteracy is the cause of the poor socio-economic condition, high mortality rate, low life expectancy, child labour and child marriage and high growth rate of population. Illiteracy frustrates all developmental programmes of the government. Again, in order to improve the poor condition of the illiterate people, the government has to spend a huge sum of money on different programmes. This affects other sectors and hinders the long-term development of the country. The population of a country is termed as its human resources. The educated and skilled manpower of a country is its great asset. But if the people are illiterate, they become a burden for the country. Illiterate people cannot contribute much to the social and economic development of the country.

1. Illiteracy is the main cause of poverty and vice versa.
2. One of the major cause of crimes is illiteracy: Due to illiteracy issue rates of crime are gradually increasing and health, productivity, and growth of the country are gradually decreasing.

3. Most illiterate people are unaware of the benefits of maintaining cleanliness and hygiene.
4. Illiteracy leads to overpopulation, which in turn leads to financial and resource constraints.
5. People's superstition and negative attitude about education.
6. Illiterate people find it very difficult to secure a good job and earn a livelihood.

How to Overcome Illiteracy

As illiteracy is the root cause of all evils, it should be the number one agenda of the government. Though government has taken various measures like making primary education free and compulsory, girl's education up to higher secondary level free and the highest allocation for education in our national budget, still the measures are inadequate. Government must ensure that the money is being utilized properly and effectively. Government need to set up more educational institutions, make reading materials cheap and available and guarantee employment after completing education. Private sectors, NGOs, academician and patrons of learning should come forward to spread the light of education in every house. We also have to make people aware of the importance of education. Media can play a great role in this regard. Reducing poverty is the most effective way of removing illiteracy from society. Hence, government must work in coordination with others to fight poverty and increase literacy rate.

There is no single way of solving the problem of illiteracy. It has to be carried out in multiple steps and at various levels. Illiteracy can be eradicated from society in the following ways: (a) To eradicate illiteracy, the government must take necessary steps to eradicate poverty. (b) Right to Education Act, ICDS (Anganwadi) Schemes, Sarva Siksha Abhiyan (SSA), Food Security to Children (Mid-Day Meal) Schemes, all need to be integrated. Such a measure would involve a definition of a child as we use different age groups every time for different laws and schemes. (c) The solution lies in political will and installation of proper monitoring mechanisms. (d) We should make people aware of the Right to Education Act and how it entitles free education in government schools to every child below 14 years of age. (e) Big industries and companies that employ manual contract labourers could definitely make arrangements for the education of their employees' children. (f) Promote education in all local languages. (g) Improve the content and delivery mechanism, when we have less time we cannot expect conventional primary school content will work.

Efforts to Improve Literacy Level

The Supreme Court in a ruling in 1993, said that children have a fundamental right to free education and thus, in the year 2003 the 'Right to Education' was incorporated in the Constitution under the 83rd Amendment, 2000. Despite this, India is not able to provide free and compulsory education for children up to fourteen years of age within ten years of the bill coming into effect under Article 45 of the Constitution.

Several other schemes too had been launched to ensure the right to education in the country. The National Policy on Education in the year 1986 declared that the whole nation must commit itself to drive away the menaces of illiteracy, especially among the young population. The National Literacy Mission in 1988 made literacy a community endeavour, which seems to bite the dust today as it has not been able to prevent dropouts among school children and illiteracy prevails. The Sarva Shiksha Abhiyan was launched in 2001 to ensure that all children in the 6–14 years of age-group attend school and complete eight years of schooling by 2010. An important component of the scheme is the Education Guarantee Scheme and alternative and innovative education, meant primarily for children in areas with no formal school within one-kilometre radius.

National Policy on Education

In India, the first resolution on National Policy on Education was adopted after independence in 1968. As stated at the outset, radical reconstruction of the education system in the country was proposed in it. Then, in 1986, the parliament approved the National Policy on Education (NPE). It sought a national system of education laying down: (a) a curricular framework to establish comparability of competence at the end of various stages of education all over the country, (b) reinforcing the integrative aspect of society and culture, and (c) establishing a value system necessary for an egalitarian, democratic and secular society. The new policy lists the specific steps in such detail that it has been described as nothing less than a charter not only for equality of access to education but also for equalization with regard to the status of the disadvantaged sections of society. It lays down that educational transformation, reduction of disparities, universalization of elementary education, adult education, and scientific and technological research would be accepted as national responsibilities for which adequate resources would be provided.

The concept of the national system of education implies that up to a given level, all students, irrespective of caste, sex or location, have access to education of a comparable quality. It envisages a common educational structure of 10+2+3 for all parts of the country. The break-up of the first 10 years comprises five years of primary education, three years of middle school, and two years of high school. Regarding elementary education, the NPE Policy proposed to ensure that all children who attained the age of 11 years will have had five years of schooling through the non-formal stream. Likewise, it proposed that all children will be provided free and compulsory education up to 14 years of age.

Regarding eradicating illiteracy, the NPE, 1986 proposed that in the 15–35 age group, a vast programme of adult and continuing education will be implemented through various channels like: (a) establishment of centres in rural areas for continuing education, (b) worker's education through the employers and concerned agencies of the government, (c) radio, television and films as mass and group learning media, (d) creation of learners' groups and organizations, (e) programmes of distance learning, and (f) organizing assistance in self-learning. In 1992, the NPE, 1986 was modified and a programme of action was formulated, which stipulated that about 100 million persons would be covered under the National Programme of Adult Education by 1995.

In the year 2003 the 'Right to Education' was incorporated in the Constitution under the Constitution (83rd Amendment), 2000. Then, in 2005, a new chapter was added to the educational reforms in the country when Right to Education (RTE) was passed by the Indian parliament.

Right to Education (RTE)

In 1950, India made a constitutional commitment to provide free and compulsory education to all children up to the age of 14, by adding this provision in Article 45 of the Directive Principles of State Policy. With the Constitution 86th Amendment Act on 12 December 2002, Article 21A was amended in order to introduce Right to Education as a fundamental right. The Right of Children to Free and Compulsory Education Act finally came into force on 1 April 2010. With the implementation of this Act, it is expected that issues of school drop out, out-of-school children, quality of education and availability of trained teachers will be addressed in the short to medium term plans.

The National Commission for Protection of Child Rights (NCPCR) has been designated as the agency to monitor provisions of the Act. The main provisions of the Act are:

1. Every child between the age of six to fourteen years shall have the right to free and compulsory education.
2. No child shall be liable to pay any kind of fee or charges or expenses which may prevent him or her from pursuing and completing elementary education.
3. Where a child above six years of age has not been admitted to any school or though admitted, could not complete his or her elementary education, then, he or she shall be admitted in a class appropriate to his or her age.
4. The appropriate government and local authority shall establish a school, if it is not established, within the given area in a period of three years from the commencement of this Act.
5. The Central and the State Governments shall have concurrent responsibility for providing funds for carrying out the provisions of this Act.

As per the provision of the Act, the Central Government has authorised the National Council of Educational Research & Training (NCERT) as the academic authority to lay down the curriculum and evaluation procedure for elementary education and develop a framework of national curriculum.

This Act is an essential step towards improving each child's accessibility to education. The Act also contains specific provisions for disadvantaged groups, such as child labourers, migrant children, children with special needs, or those who have a disadvantage owing to social, cultural, economical, geographical, linguistic, gender or any such factor.

Adult Education Programme

In the history of adult education, the concept of adult education has constantly changed and developed under various nomenclatures. The key concept used upto 1947 was 'basic education' which was based on traditional approach and focussed on the programme of night schools. Between 1949 and 1966, the concept used was 'civic literacy' which was based on life-oriented approach and focussed on social education. Between 1967 and 1977, 'functional literacy' concept based on work-oriented approach came to be emphasized in adult education which focussed on functional literacy programme, farmer's education and Shramik Vidyapeeths. From 1978 onwards, 'developmental literacy' concept based on social change approach came to be used more which focussed on total literacy campaigns.

The *basic literacy* concept evolved with the expansion of night schools which received grants-in-aid from 1929. The course in this scheme was spread over a period of two years and included simple lessons in ₹ 3, stories of historical importance, and elementary lessons in health, hygiene and first-aid. The instruction was imparted for 2–3 hours in the evening. During 1938–39, a series of Provincial Mass Literacy Campaigns were organized by different provincial governments. It was estimated that during 1938–42, about 1.38 crore persons became literate.

The concept of *civic literacy* was conceived in 1949 and modified in 1952 when it was integrated with Community Development Programme. It was implemented all over India during the first two five-year plans. It was estimated that nearly 35 lakh illiterates became literate during the First Five-Year Plan and about 40 lakh during the Second Plan.

The concept of *functional literacy* emerged during the 1960s. Defined as 'literacy integrated with the occupation of the learner and directly related to development', functional literacy was translated into action in 1968. Initially it was introduced in three districts but it expanded during next ten years and covered 144 districts out of 397 by 1977. During the Fourth Plan, nearly 30 lakh farmers joined the functional literacy classes.

By early 1970s, the concept of *development literacy* came to be evolved. Literacy was described not just the process of learning the skills of reading, writing and arithmetic but a contribution to the liberation of man and to his full development. In 1978, the government formulated the National Adult Education Programme (NAEP). The 1980s also witnessed the expansion of

University Adult Education in India when the University Grants Commission (UGC) provided grants to 93 universities.

National Adult Education Programme (NAEP)

The NAEP was launched on 2 October 1978 with the aim of providing education and promoting literacy among all illiterate persons, particularly in the age group of 15–35 years. The programme is a joint and collaborative effort of the central government, state governments, union territory administrations, voluntary agencies, universities, colleges and youth centres. The education under the NAEP is a package which envisages: (a) imparting literacy skills to the target illiterate population, (b) their functional development, and (c) creation of awareness among them regarding laws and policies of the government for the efficient implementation of the strategy of redistributive justice. Special emphasis is being placed on the education of women, SCs/STs and other weaker sections of society, who comprise the bulk of illiterate population in India.

Rural Functional Literacy Programme

The RFLP is a sub-programme of the NAEP which is fully funded by the central government and implemented by the states and union territories. The broad objectives of this programme are: (a) to develop abilities in the learners to read and write, and (b) to create awareness among the learners about their rights and duties and the benefits they can draw from various schemes of socio-economic development being implemented by the government.

The RFLP was launched in May 1986 by involving the NSS and other student volunteers in colleges and universities on the principle of 'Each One Teach One'. Starting on a modest scale of 2 lakh volunteers, it went up to 4.50 lakh in 1990 covering over 4.20 lakh learners. The programme has been designed keeping in view the needs and languages of the learners. The government has selected 40 districts to improve the quality of adult education. It is only after evaluation of the impact that the programme will be taken up in a big way to spread literacy in the minimum possible time.

The process of the Mass Programme of Functional Literacy involves a number of stages. These stages are:

(a) selecting master trainers who are to train the student volunteers;
(b) selecting, motivating and mobilizing the student volunteers who are genuinely and sincerely committed to literacy work;
(c) identifying illiterate persons in the age group of 15–35 who may be staying in the neighbourhood of an educational institution;
(d) forging a link between the student volunteers and the illiterate persons and assigning an area of operation for each volunteer;
(e) monitoring of the programme of the student volunteers by senior teachers/headmasters of schools;

(f) coordination with various development departments/agencies by way of visits of functionaries to the place where the volunteer is imparting literacy;
(g) telling the learners about the advantages of being literate;
(h) making available charts, posters and other materials to the learners;
(i) identifying genuine difficulties of the learners; and providing post-literacy activities for the neo-literates through libraries and reading rooms;
(j) coverage and support by the media and evaluation of the overall impact of the programme through University Departments of Adult and Continuing Education is of crucial importance.

Directorate of Adult Education

The Directorate of Adult Education, a subordinate office of the Department of Elementary Education and Literacy, Ministry of Human Resource Development, has been functioning as the National Resource Centre for Adult Education and Literacy Programmes in the country. It is the functional arm of the National Literacy Mission (NLM), which is responsible for monitoring, and evaluation of various schemes launched under the aegis of the Mission. The Directorate is also entrusted with the task of developing model teaching learning materials for the learners and neo-literates and harnessing all kinds of media facilities for furtherance of the objectives of the NLM. It provides professional, academic and technical guidance for the effective functioning of the Jan Shikshan Sansthans (previously known as Shramik Vidyapeeths).

The main activities of various units of the Directorate are:

1. Provision of academic and technical resource support for implementation of various programmes of the NLM.
2. Development of teaching material.
3. Organization of training and orientation programmes keeping in view the needs of ongoing programmes in the field.
4. Monitoring of the progress and status of literacy campaigns.
5. Production of media and harnessing of all kinds of electronic, print, traditional and folk media for furtherance of the objectives of the NLM.
6. Printing and publishing of different literacy campaigns success stories
7. Coordination, collaboration and networking with all the resource centres and other organizations and agencies.
8. Analysing the findings of the evaluation and research activities concerning the literacy campaigns.
9. Professional, academic and technical guidance concerning literacy activities and monitoring of Jan Shikshan Sansthans.

National Literacy Mission (NLM)

National Literacy Mission (NLM) was launched on 5 May 1988 as a Technology Mission to impart functional literacy to non-literates in the country in the age group of 15–35 years in a time bound manner. By 'literacy', the NLM means not only learning how to read, write and count but also helping people understand why they are deprived and helping them move towards change. This age group has been the focus of attention because they are in the productive and reproductive period of life. The National Education Policy, 1986, as modified in 1992, also has recognized National Literacy Mission (NLM) as one of the three instruments to eradicate illiteracy from the country, the other two being Universalization of Elementary Education (UEE) and Non-Formal Education.

The success of the Ernakulam literacy campaign in 1990 provided the much-needed clue to the manner in which the Mission can move to achieve its desired objectives. The campaign mode, which was adopted as the dominant strategy under the Mission, has proved to be the most appropriate in Indian conditions. Through these campaigns not only the ₹ 3 are imparted to the beneficiaries, they are also made aware of their rights and responsibilities towards their family, society and the country so that they can play appropriate roles in the development of the country as a whole. Thus, the campaigns have been launched not only for spreading literacy but also for family welfare, immunization, mother and child health care, conservation of environment, communal harmony, cohesion, national integration, etc.

The Mission's objective was to impart functional literacy to 80 million illiterate persons in 15–35 age group – 30 million by 1990 and additional 50 million by 1995. However, later on, the goal of the Mission became to attain a sustainable threshold literacy rate of 75 per cent by 2007.

The Mission also takes into its fold, children in the age group of 9–14, in areas not covered by Non-Formal Education programmes to reach the benefits of literacy to out-of-school children as well. The major thrust of these programmes is on the promotion of literacy among women, SCs/STs and other backward classes.

The NLM eventually aims at ensuring that the Total Literacy Campaign (TLC) and their sequel, the Post-Literacy Programme (PLP), successfully move on to Continuing Education (CE), which provides a life-long learning and is responsible for the creation of a learning society.

Total Literacy Campaign

As stated above, Total Literacy Campaign (TLC) has been the principal strategy of the National Literacy Mission (NLM) for eradication of illiteracy after the success of the campaign mode in Ernakulam district of Kerala.

The TLC has certain positive characteristics like being area-specific, time-bound, participative, delivery through voluntarism, cost effective and outcome oriented. Though the campaign emphasizes the achievement of predetermined levels of literacy and numeracy, there are other activities linked up with TLCs, such as campaigns for universal enrolment and retention in schools, immunization, conservation of environment, the small family norm, women's empowerment, etc.

The TLC has an assumed duration of 12 to 18 months of which half is devoted to preparation and half to actual teaching/learning activity. In exceptionally difficult areas, the duration is suitably extended. Two activities, namely, environment building as well as monitoring and internal evaluation are continued throughout the campaign.

The initial activity of environment building is closely followed by a door-to-door survey to identify potential learners and volunteer instructors. Suitable primers (in three parts) are developed through the State Resource Centres for adult education in accordance with the new pedagogic technique of 'Improved Pace and Content of Learning'.

The three-legged management structure of TLC consists of popular committees from district to village levels, the Zila Saksharata Samiti (ZSS) supported by the subject-specific sub-committees, and the officials of the district and block level administration.

Literacy campaigns are implemented by the Zila Saksharata Samitis, usually headed by district collectors. Both the central and state governments participate in funding in the ratio of 2:1 for normal districts while the ratio of central and state share for districts under tribal sub-plan areas is 4:1. Presently, per learner cost for a TLC is between ₹ 90 to 180.

Post-Literacy Programme

On the conclusion of Total Literacy Campaign (TLC), Post-Literacy Programme is implemented by the Zila Saksharata Samiti (ZSS) for the period of one year.

One of the major objectives of a Post-Literacy Programme is to enable the neo-literates to learn the application of literacy skills as a problem-solving tool, so that learning becomes relevant to living and working. In the limited time available during TLC, it is not possible to dwell adequately on the functionality and awareness components of the programme. Therefore, in post-literacy phase, these objectives take centre stage.

One of the first tasks in a Post-Literacy Programme is what is known as 'mopping up' operation. Those learners, who dropped out or could not achieve the NLM levels of literacy in the TLC phase, are enabled to achieve them through remediation or mopping up operation.

To ensure that there is no time lag between the conclusion of the basic literacy phase and the start of Post-Literacy Programme, which could result in a regression of neo-literates, NLM has laid a great deal of emphasis on the planning and launching of Post-Literacy Programme well in time.

Post-literacy specifically aims at remediation, retention and consolidation of literacy skills in the first phase through guided learning. In the second phase, learners are provided with a variety of supplementary reading material and library services to help them continue learning through self-directed processes.

The NLM has emphasized the integration of skill development programme with Post-Literacy Programme to enable the neo-literates acquire skills for their economic self-reliance.

The Post-Literacy Programme is to be regarded as the preparatory stage for Continuing Education Programme in the district. The duration of Post-Literacy Programme, which was initially for two years, has now been restricted to one year. The present per learner cost for Post-Literacy Programme has been enhanced to ₹ 90–130 per annum.

Continuing Education Programme

The Government of India had approved a new scheme of Continuing Education for Neo-Literates in December 1995. It provided a learning continuum to the efforts of the Total Literacy and Post-Literacy Programmes. The scheme was revised in November 1999, which retained the basic structure of CECs and further expanded its scope and content.

Under the scheme the main thrust is given to set up Continuing Education Centre (CEC) which will function as a focal point for providing learning opportunities such as library, reading room, learning centre, training centre, information centre, *charcha mandal,* development centre, cultural centre, sports centre and other individual interest promotion programme centre. One CEC is set up for a population of 2,000 to 2,500. For a group of about 10–15 CECs, there is a nodal CEC, which monitors and oversees the activities of those cluster of CECs. Besides the provisions of setting up of CECs, the scheme of continuing education also provides the opportunities to undertake diverse activities involving alternative and innovative approaches to cater to the needs of the learners. Taking into account local conditions and the resources available, various target specific activities such as Equivalency Programmes (EPs), Quality of Life Improvement Programmes (QLIPs), Income Generating Programmes (IGPs) and Individual Interest Promotion Programmes (IIPPs) could be organized for specific groups of beneficiaries.

The programmes of continuing education are being implemented under the aegis of ZSSs, which, along with district, block and gram panchayat level committees, are responsible to oversee the programme in the entire district.

Each CEC will be annually provided assistance of ₹ 25,000 as recurring and non-recurring grant, and nodal CEC ₹ 45,000 as recurring and non-recurring grant with an additional provision of house rent for few selected centres where no government or community building is available to run the centre. In the revised scheme a provision of *Sahayak Prerak* has been made who will be primarily responsible for conducting literacy classes during continuing education programme.

The scheme envisages 100 per cent assistance to the states for the first three years of the implementation. The state governments are required to share 50 per cent of the expenditure during the fourth and fifth year of the project, and thereafter take over the total responsibility for the programme.

The State Literacy Mission Authorities (SLMAs) have been authorized to sanction the projects for CE related to their states. Where SLMA has not been created the state government is required to examine and recommend their CE projects to the SLMA, which then discusses and sanctions the projects in its Project Approval Committee (PAC). Grants are placed at the disposal of SLMA/state governments on basis of the project for onward transmission to the respective ZSS or the implementing agency.

NLM's Contribution to Female Literacy

The provision of educational opportunities for women has been an important part of the national endeavour in the field of education since India's independence. Though these endeavours did yield significant results, gender disparity persists with uncompromising tenacity, more so in the rural areas and among the disadvantaged communities. It is with this concern that the Government of India launched the National Literacy Mission in 1988 for the eradication of adult illiteracy. Total literacy campaigns launched since 1988 under the aegis of the NLM have adopted a strategy that lays considerable emphasis on making efforts to:

1. Create an environment where women demand knowledge and information, empowering themselves to change their lives.
2. Inculcate in women the confidence that change is possible, if women work collectively.
3. Spread the message that education of women is a pre-condition for fighting against their oppression.
4. Highlight the plight of the girl child and stress the need for Universalization of Elementary Education (UEE) as a way of addressing the issue.

One of the most striking features of India's campaign against illiteracy has been its focus upon, and involvement of, women. From the information available, around 60 per cent of the learners are women and considerable numbers of the volunteers are also women and young girls. The gender gap is slowly but surely closing. Nonetheless, India's achievements today cannot mask the daunting obstacles still to be overcome.

Some of the significant ways in which the literacy campaigns have contributed to the promotion of female literacy and women's empowerment are as follows: (a) social awareness, (b) school enrolment, (c) self-confidence and personality development, (d) gender equity and women's empowerment, (e) status in the family, (f) educational equality, (g) women as entrepreneurs, (h) household savings and access to credit, and (i) health and hygiene.

Eradicating Illiteracy in India

Eradication of illiteracy has been one of major national concerns of the Government of India since independence. The Union Human Resources Minister explained the programme of major acceleration in education, while attending the Education For All (EFA) summit of nine highly populated countries held in Copenhagen in the second week of March 1995. The government's future plans were described as: (a) By the turn of the century, every child between the age of 6 and 14 years will have the opportunity to attend school and get educated. (b) There will be a sharp increase in the number of primary schools and teachers. (c) In rural areas, schools will be within the reach of every village. (d) Besides the universalization of primary education, there will be vocationalization of secondary education and rationalization of higher education. This will make education employment-oriented right from the secondary stage. (e) To deal with the dropouts, the government has a plan of expanding the open school system. Education for All emphasizes the need to provide access to education for traditionally marginalized groups, including girls and women, indigenous populations and remote rural groups, street children, migrants and nomadic populations, people with disabilities, and linguistic and cultural minorities. A comprehensive rights-based approach must be dynamic, accounting for different learning environments and different learners.

As stated earlier, eradication of illiteracy has been one of the major concerns of the governments both at central and state levels. In recent years, various initiatives have been taken by governments to eradicate illiteracy. Some of these are:

Elementary Education

Elementary education in India starts from the age of six. The government has made elementary education compulsory and free. The central and state governments have been expanding the provision of formal and non-formal primary education to realize the goal of Universalization of Elementary Education (UEE). The following schemes have been launched under this programme:

1. The Schemes for Providing Quality Education in Madrassas (SPQEM)
2. Education Guarantee Scheme (EGS) / Alternative and Innovative Education (AIE)
3. Education for Women's Equality
4. Kasturba Gandhi Balika Vidyalaya (KGBV)

Sarva Shiksha Abhiyan

Sarva Shiksha Abhiyan (SSA) is a Government of India flagship programme for achievement of Universalization of Elementary Education (UEE). The Sarva Siksha Abhiyan was launched to ensure that all children in the 6–14 years of age-group attend school and complete eight years of schooling by 2010. An important component of the scheme is the Education Guarantee Scheme and Alternative and Innovative Education, meant primarily for children in areas with no formal school within one kilometre radius. The programme seeks to open new schools in those habitations which do not have schooling facilities and strengthen existing school infrastructure through provision of additional class rooms, toilets, drinking water, maintenance grant and school improvement grants. SSA has a special focus on girl's education and children with special needs. SSA also seeks to provide computer education to bridge the digital divide.

Mid-Day Meal Scheme

Aiming at enhancing enrolment, retention and attendance and simultaneously improving nutritional levels among children, the Mid-Day Meal (MDM) is the world's largest school feeding programme, reaching out to about 12 crore children in over 9.50 lakh schools/EGS centres across the country. The meal is freshly cooked and wholesome. The Mid-day Meal Programme will also help to increase the literacy levels of the country and develop it.

Problems with Government Schemes

The Sarva Shiksha Abhiyan mainly incorporates decentralization for planning and management of elementary education because of which there is an absence of community participation and thus, most of the policies fail to generate a mass consensus. Also the mandates of institutions like Ministry of Human Resource Development (MHRD), National Council of Educational Research and Training (NCERT), National University of Educational Planning and Administration (NUEPA), National Institute of Open Schooling (NIOS) and National Council of Teacher Education (NCTE) clash with each other. Thus, there is no clarity on the objectives of all these bodies with respect to the spread of education. A major aspect that is slowly ruining the state of education is the commercialization of education both at the elementary and at the higher education levels. Private schools charge enormous fees which makes it difficult for the poor parents to send their children to the schools. The government should take steps to promote free education for the backward class of the society in government schools.

Adult Education

Literacy among adults has been recognized as a crucial input for nation building. The National Literacy Mission (NLM) was set up in May 1988 to impart a new sense of urgency and seriousness to adult education. Some of the other initiatives under adult education are:

1. Saakshar Bharat
2. Innovative Proposals in the Field of Adult Education
3. Scheme of Support to Voluntary Agencies for Adult Education and Skill Development
4. Creation of Directorate of Adult Education

Efforts by Voluntary Organizations

The government alone cannot solve the vast problem of illiteracy in the country. It is not possible to achieve the objective of total eradication of illiteracy entirely through governmental efforts. The government can undoubtedly take cognizance of the situation, identify the agencies, institutions and individuals, act as a catalytic agent to provide human material and financial resources, but it cannot promote literacy by itself. The efforts of the government – both central and state – will, therefore, have to be supplemented and strengthened by voluntary organizations and individuals who have a positive perception and commitment. The bulk of Indian illiterates live in the country's rural areas, where social and economic barriers play an important role in keeping the lowest strata of society illiterate. Government programmes alone, however well-intentioned, may not be able to dismantle barriers built over centuries. Major social reformation efforts are sometimes required to bring about a change in the rural scenario. In other words, we may also have to move from the concept of exclusive responsibility of the government for education to shared responsibility between the government and the community.

To conclude, Article 45 of our Constitution refers to 'endeavour to provide free and compulsory education for all children until they reach 14 years of age'. While many state governments claim to have enacted compulsory education laws but, in practice, no state has implemented such a law, that is, requiring local authorities to compel school attendance. In fact, instead of talking of 'compulsory' education, the decision-makers now talk of 'universal' education. Even, the New Education Policy of 1986 gave concrete expression to the shift away from the goal of compulsory schooling. Elementary education is now 'universalized' and not 'compelled'. The educational restructuring and the 'new' policy now focus on 'incentives' like free school meals, free uniforms, free books and skill-oriented teaching. Out of the estimated 105 crore population in the 7 and above age group, only about 77 crore is found to be literate as per the provisional totals of 2011 Census. Out of every 10 children who enter the first grade, only four complete four years of schooling. By shrugging off its duty to educate children, our society and our government are in effect denying the experience of childhood, that is, of play, experimentation, and self-discovery to millions of children. Retreat from the formal commitment to mandatory full-time schooling has unmistakably been a retrogressive step in economic development as well as in reducing the problem of child labour in the country.

It may therefore be inferred that the task of making some 30 crore people literate indeed needs perseverance and require ingenious efforts and a high degree of motivation on the part of both the learners and the instructors. Such a serious problem of illiteracy calls for drastic measures rather than the half-hearted approaches which we have so sedulously pursued all these years without any tangible results whatsoever. Mass illiteracy and child education have to be tackled on a war footing because of the sheer magnitude of the problem. After all, education is the backbone of a nation.

Conclusion

The present illiteracy rate is still high in our country, that is why we are lagging behind in all respects than many other nations. If we want to build a happy and prosperous nation, we must remove illiteracy from the country. Not only the government, but every literate person needs to accept the eradication of illiteracy as a personal goal. Every contribution by a literate person can contribute to eradicating the menace.

References

Census of India, 2011.

Education for All 2000–2015: Achievement and Challenges. EFA Global Monitoring Report, 2015.

McCullough, M.C., 'Illiteracy in India: Problems and Progress', *The Reading Teacher*, International Literacy Association and Wiley, Vol. 19, No. 2, November, 1965.

National Literacy Mission Programme, 1988.

National Policy of Education, 1986.

Right to Education Act, 2009.

Shah, S.V., *Indian Education: A Historical Perspective*, Directorate of Adult Education, New Delhi, 1993.

Sikligar, P.C., *Mid Day Meal Scheme and School Education*, LAP Lambert Academic Publishing, 2012.

12

Urbanization

Some Facts about Urbanization in India

- As per 2018 data, a large number of Indian cities have a population between 3,00,000 and 1 million inhabitants.
- There are 120 medium-sized cities of such population size and only five urban settlements with 20 million or more inhabitants.
- The seven largest cities in India will become even bigger by 2030.
- Prospects suggest that the population growth of India's capital New Delhi will increase about one third within the next decade up to 38.9 million people.
- Of the 121 crore Indians, 83.3 crore live in rural areas while 37.7 crore stay in urban areas, i.e. approx 32 per cent of the population.

Urbanization and urban growth are two different, yet interlinked concepts, but not necessarily complementary to each other. While urbanization refers to an increase in the percentage of urban population to total population, urban growth denotes an increase in the total urban population. Urbanization occurs because people move from rural areas to urban areas. This usually occurs when a country is still developing. Urbanization has become a common feature of Indian society. It denotes a diffusion of the influence of the urban centres in a rural hinterland. Urbanization can also be defined as a process of concentration of population in a particular territory. According to Mitchell, urbanization is a process of becoming urban, moving to cities, changing from agriculture to other pursuits common to cities. Population and economic growth have fostered urbanization in the country and the number of urban towns and cities have drastically increased. This growth is expected to continue in the years to come and India has to step up its game in order to catch up with this kind of change. Investments have to be made in order to better serve the country. There are several factors at play that have led to the urbanization in India – population growth and migration are the two major factors. Recently, a third factor has been seen as a huge contributor to the urbanization growth – the expansion of towns and cities. This factor is due to the high economic growth that the city has witnessed over the years.

The Census of India, 2011 defines *urban settlement* as – all the places which have municipality, corporation, cantonment board or notified town area committee. Urban areas have been recognized as 'engines of inclusive economic growth'.

After independence, urbanization in India is increasing at a very high pace, but at the same time, there are some problems, which are becoming barriers to balance equitable and inclusive development. Migration is the key process underlying growth of urbanization, and the process of urbanization is closely related with rural to urban migration of people. In most developing countries of the world where the rate of urban growth is relatively higher, the urban-ward migration is usually high. Rural to urban migration is by far the major component of urbanization and is the chief mechanism by which urbanization trends all the world-over have been accomplished.

Along with the growth of population in the last few decades, there has been a shift in the population from rural to urban areas. The increasing urbanization has led to problems like crime and juvenile delinquency, alcoholism and drug abuse, housing shortage, overcrowding and slums, unemployment and poverty, pollution and noise, and communication and traffic control among others. Even if cities are places of tensions and strain, they are also the centres of civilization and culture. They are active, innovative and alive. They provide opportunities to achieve one's aspirations. If the future of our country is linked with the development of rural areas, it is equally linked with the growth of cities and metropolitan areas. But before analysing these problems, let us understand the basic concepts.

Concepts of Urban, Urbanization and Urbanism

Urban

What is an 'urban area' or a city or a town? This term is used in two senses – demographically and sociologically. In the former sense, emphasis is given to the size of population, density of population and nature of work of the majority of the adult males; while in the latter sense, the focus is on heterogeneity, impersonality, interdependence, and the quality of life. The German sociologist, Tonnies (1957) differentiated between rural and urban communities in terms of social relationships and values. The rural *gemeinschaft* community is one in which social bonds are based on close personal ties of kinship and friendship, and the emphasis is on tradition, consensus and informality, while the urban *gesellschaft* society is one in which impersonal and secondary relationships predominate and the interaction of people is formal, contractual and dependent on the special function or service they perform. The emphasis on *gesellschaft* society is on utilitarian goals and competitive nature of social relationships. Other sociologists like Max Weber (1961: 381) and Georg Simmel (1950) have stressed on dense living conditions, rapidity of change and impersonal interaction in urban settings. Louis Wirth (1938: 8) has said that for sociological purposes a city may be defined as 'a relatively large, dense and permanent settlement of socially heterogeneous individuals'. Scholars like Ruth Glass have defined city in terms of factors like: size of population, density of population, main economic system, type of administration, and some social characteristics.

In India, the census definition of 'town' remained more or less the same for the period 1901–51, but in 1961, a new definition was adopted. Up to 1951, 'town' included: (1) collection of houses permanently inhabited by not less than 5,000 persons, (2) every municipality/corporation/notified area of whatever size, and (3) all civil lines not included within the municipal units. Thus, the primary focus in the definition of town was more on the administrative set-up rather than the size of the population. In 1961, certain tests were applied for defining a place as 'town'. These were: (a) a minimum population of 5,000, (b) a density of not less than 1,000 persons per square mile, (c) three-fourth of its working population should be engaged in non-agricultural activities, and (d) the place should have a few characteristics and civic amenities like transport and communication, banks, schools, markets, recreation centres, hospitals, electricity, and newspapers, etc. From 2001 Census, the towns and cities are classified as 'Tier I' with people 1,00,000 and above, 'Tier II' with 50,000 to 99,999, 'Tier III' with 20,000 to 49,999, 'Tier IV' with 10,000 to 19,999, 'Tier V' with 5,000 to 9,999 and 'Tier VI' with less than 5,000.

Sociologists do not attach much importance to the size of population in the definition of city because the minimum population standards vary greatly. The reason being every country has a criterion of minimum population for a place to be designated as 'urban'. As such, they give more importance to characteristics other than the population size. Theodorson and Theodorson (1969: 451) have defined 'urban community' as 'a community with a high population density, a predominance of non-agricultural occupations, a high degree of specialization resulting in a complex division of labour, and a formalized system of local government. It is also characterized by a prevalence of impersonal secondary relations and dependence on formal social controls'. According to Robert Redfield (*American Journal of Sociology*, January 1942), 'urban society' is characterized by a large heterogeneous population, close contact with other societies (through trade, communication, etc.), a complex division of labour, a prevalence of secular over sacred concerns, and the desire to organize behaviour rationally toward given goals, as opposed to following traditional standards and norms.

Urbanization

Urbanization is the movement of population from rural to urban areas and the resulting increasing proportion of a population that resides in urban rather than rural places. Thompson Warren in *Encyclopaedia of Social Sciences* has defined it as 'the movement of people from communities concerned chiefly or solely with agriculture to other communities, generally larger whose activities are primarily centred in government, trade, manufacture, or allied interests'. According to Anderson (1959: 11), urbanization is not a one-way process but it is a two-way process. It not only involves movement from villages to cities and change from agricultural occupation to business, trade, service and profession, but it also involves change in the migrants' attitudes, beliefs, values and behaviour patterns. He has given five characteristics of urbanization: money economy, civil administration, cultural changes, written records and innovations.

Urbanism

Urbanism is a way of life. It reflects an organization of society in terms of a complex division of labour, high levels of technology, high mobility, interdependence of its members in fulfilling economic functions and impersonality in social relations (Theodorson and Theodorson, 1969: 453).

Characteristics of Urbanism or Urban System

Louis Wirth (1938: 49) has given four characteristics of urbanism:

1. *Transiency*: An urban inhabitant's relations with others last only for a short time; he tends to forget his old acquaintances and develop relations with new people. Since he is not much attached to his neighbours, members of the social groups, he does not mind leaving their places.
2. *Superficiality*: An urban person has a limited number of persons with whom he interacts and his relations with them are impersonal and formal. People meet each other in highly segmental roles. They are dependent on more people for the satisfaction of their life needs.
3. *Anonymity*: Urbanites do not know each other intimately. Personal mutual acquaintanship between the inhabitants which ordinarily is found in a neighbourhood is lacking.
4. *Individualism*: People give more importance to their own vested interests.

Ruth Glass has given the following characteristics of urbanism: mobility, anonymity, individualism, impersonal relations, social differentiation, transience and organic type of solidarity. Anderson (1959: 2) has listed three characteristics of urbanism: adjustability, mobility and diffusion. Marshall Clinard (1957) has talked of rapid social change, conflict between norms and values, increasing mobility of population, emphasis on material things and decline in intimate interpersonal communication as important characteristics of urbanism. K. Davis (1949) has highlighted eight characteristics of the urban social system: social heterogeneity (people of different religions, languages, castes, and classes live in urban areas. There is also specialization in occupation), secondary association, social mobility, individualism, spatial segregation, social tolerance, secondary control and voluntary associations. Further, Louis Wirth (1938: 124) has given following characteristics of urbanism: heterogeneity of population, specialization of function, anonymity and impersonality and standardization of life and behaviour. Though these characteristics present an exaggerated picture of the urban man and his life, an analysis thereof is necessary.

(1) *Heterogeneity of population*: The growing population in cities can be largely attributed to migration from different areas which leads to people of different backgrounds and beliefs living together. This mixture of people affects the working of informal controls – mores and institutions – and reliance on formally designed mechanisms for regulating the behaviour of individuals and groups increases. People no longer share the common sentiments, and being exposed to new ideas imported from other cultures through contacts with migrants, they challenge the outmoded beliefs and practices and adopt such new attitudes and lifestyles which help them in improving their economic status and coping with problems of adjustment. The influence of family and neighbourhood decreases and people come into conflict on the question of rightness of behaviour.

(2) *Specialization of function and behaviour*: The heterogeneity and the large size of population of a city favour the development of specialization. Since the city has many facets of life and an individual can participate only in some of them, he becomes choosy and takes interest only in a few fields. Specialization in function encourages a diversity of life patterns. Doctors, engineers, businessmen, lawyers, bureaucrats, factory workers, teachers, clerks, policemen, for example, have different life patterns, different interests, and also different philosophy of life. Each specialist group makes its own contribution to the community and thus a division of labour is created. The cloth merchant say, sells only cloth, and depends on many other specialists to manufacture, process and distribute cloth so that it reaches his shop. Such a division of labour permits an individual to benefit from a broader range of services than his own knowledge and capabilities provide. Each inhabitant in the city becomes dependent on specialists such as physicians, masons, mechanics, shopkeepers, tailors, washermen, and so on. He need not learn the techniques of each profession.

Specialization provides an individual diverse opportunities to act, to express himself and to develop his potentialities. However, the contacts become secondary and formal and the sense of living a common life and having common concerns is destroyed. The relationship between two persons remains for a short duration till they gratify each other's purpose.

In a social order characterized by a heterogeneous population and diversity in behaviour patterns, there is a greater likelihood of confusion among several alternatives for proper behaviour in a given situation. For example, a student finds other student using unfair means and getting first division. He then thinks, should he do the same thing? One person finds another person giving ₹ 10,000 and getting a job of a police sub-inspector. He gets confused whether he should report the case and get the bribe-taker arrested, or should he develop an attitude of indifference? These moral, social, and legal dilemmas are overwhelming in the city life.

(3) *Anonymity and impersonality*: High population density in the city erodes a sense of personal identity leading to loneliness and a loss of a sense of belonging. Hundreds of people watch a movie in a picture-house, enjoy and laugh together but when the film ends, the common emotions disintegrate into anonymity and impersonality. On the other hand, this very anonymity is the crux of personal freedom. The lack of interest in others releases the individual from heavy pressures towards conformity. In many cases, his responsibility to others ends with payment. Even when he becomes a member of a voluntary group like a club for instance, his participation could be minimum. He does not have to win the acceptance of other members or to engage in the accommodative process of fitting himself into the frame of their expectations. He may observe others but he may not necessarily be carried away by their stimuli.

One advantage of anonymity is that individuals are not judged according to their parents' lower class status but are evaluated on the basis of their appearance and behaviour in casual contacts. The anonymity and impersonality of urban life gives an individual, who aspires for a higher status, a greater opportunity to take advantage of symbols of higher status, like wearing attractive clothing, improving his mode of speech and manner, so as to gain the acceptance and to impress persons of high positions, maintaining contacts with them and ultimately achieving the goals he seeks through these contacts.

(4) *Standardization of behaviour*: The urban life necessitates an individual to standardize his behaviour which ultimately helps him and others (with whom he interacts) to understand each other and make interaction simpler. For example, a shopkeeper finds the same questions being asked by a succession of customers. The customers are then seen as types – the person who haggles over price, the fellow who goes for quality, the man who is merely looking without any intention of buying, and so on. The experienced shopkeeper quickly judges the type of customer he is dealing with and uses the sales strategy he regards as most effective for a particular type of customer. This helps both the shopkeeper and the customer to handle the sales transaction in a simple and quick fashion. Such standardized expectations and behaviour are part of urban life. Markets, clubs, restaurants, buses, newspapers, TV, radio, and schools/colleges present a largely standardized picture. A person who is unable to fit into such a life finds himself out of step, and is faced with the problem of adjustment. The large size of the city population lends particular force to the standardization of behaviour. This does not mean that the divergence of individual orientations is not possible.

Sorokin and Zimmerman (1962: 56–57) have identified the following characteristics of the urban social system:

1. *Non-agricultural occupation*: While agriculture is the main basis of the rural economy, trade, industry and commerce are the chief supports of the urban economy. It is this difference in occupation that ensures that rural people work in natural environments. Urban people on the other hand work mostly in artificial and unnatural environment in which the heat, cold and humidity are controlled by innovative skills. According to James Williams, working in unnatural environment affects people's attitudes and behaviour patterns. It is, thus, because of the occupational differences that in urban areas we find liberals as well as conservatives, moderns as well as traditionalists, and unsociables as well as sociables.
2. *Size of population*: Urban communities are much bigger in size than rural communities. The availability of job opportunities on one hand, and the materialistic as well as educational, medical and recreational facilities on the other hand attract people to cities.
3. *Density of population*: In villages, people have to live near their fields to supervise the agricultural pursuits but in urban areas, people's residence depends on the location of their offices, market, children's school/college and so forth. This leads to a high density of population in areas which abound in these facilities. In India, the average density of population per square mile in metropolitan cities varies between 3,000 and 5,000 persons. This high density has its own benefits as well as disadvantages. The advantages are that social contacts multiply, all necessary facilities are easily approachable and selection of friends becomes easier. The disadvantages are that inhabitants have very formal and impersonal relations with each other and their mental stress increases.
4. *Environment*: Bernard has talked of following types of environment: material (climate), biological (animals and plants), social, physio-social (machines, gadgets, instruments) and psycho-social (customs, traditions, institutions, etc.) and composite (economic, political and educational systems). The urban environment is more polluted. Besides, because of being surrounded by educational institutions and hence being more educated, an urban dweller is more rational, secular, and competitive.
5. *Social differentiation*: In urban areas, people are differentiated on the basis of occupations, religion, class, living standards and social beliefs. Yet, they are dependent on each other and act as a functioning whole.
6. *Social mobility*: Urban areas provide opportunities for change in social status because of which, as compared to villages, there is more upward mobility in cities. The mobility may be horizontal or vertical. Besides social mobility, we also find geographical mobility in urban areas.
7. *Social interaction*: Relations among urban inhabitants are secondary and impersonal. People are more concerned with the status and skills of other persons than with their beliefs and ideologies. Control is also so formal that many a time it creates deviant behaviour.

8. *Social solidarity*: In comparison to mechanical solidarity in rural areas, there exists organic solidarity in urban areas. In such a solidarity, though each person has his own individuality and personality, he depends more on others for their specialized roles.

The above description of the characteristics of urbanism as a way of life gives a feeling as if personal relations, primary groups and social intimacy do not exist in the cities. If consciously developed organizations serve the interests of the individuals, the primary groups also admit members through birth. Primary group members are tied together by a fusion of concerns for one another. Their relations are more emotional and intensive. Within the group, a member performs variety of functions unlike specified functions in secondary groups. For example, in a family, a mother serves as a cook, a nurse, a moral instructor and a manager of tensions for the children and the family members. Although the social change has weakened the bonds of family, neighbourhood and peer groups yet the old kind of functioning of these groups has not completely stopped nor have the primary relations vanished. Performing obligatory roles in the family, maintaining social participation within the neighbourhood, sharing common interests of castes and, acting as a source of support to one's kin and friends continue to be important and significant features of urban life. A number of studies in India (like those by K.M. Kapadia, Sachchidanand, R.K. Mukerjee and M.S. Gore) have shown that rural people who migrate to cities continue to maintain links with their families and kin in the village. In cities too, they not only share their problems with persons belonging to the same and adjoining villages but also with members of their caste. This makes their adaptation to city life easier.

Growth of Urban Areas

While cities have existed since ancient times, until recently, they represented only a relatively small proportion of the population. The lives of the great majority of the people were predominantly shaped by the rural community or village. The massive growth of cities and metropolitan areas, and the shift of a significant proportion of the population to urban areas has been a characteristic feature of past six decades or so. Urbanization was an off-shoot of the industrial revolution which created a demand for a large number of workers at centralized locations.

The growth of cities depends not only on birth and death rates and migration but also on political, religious historical and economic factors.

As per the population totals of 2011 Census, of the total population of India (1,210.2 million), the urban population stands at 377.1 million and, in absolute numbers, has increased by 91 million in the last decade. Maharashtra has the highest urban population of 50.8 million (13.48% of the country's urban population) in the country. Thus, the growth rate of population in urban areas is 31.80 per cent.

Features of Urban Society

1. Urban society is known for its diversity and complexity.
2. It is dominated by secondary relations.
3. Formal means of social control such as law, legislation, police, and court are needed in addition to the informal means for regulating the behaviour of the people.
4. The urban society is mobile and open. It provides more chances for social mobility.
5. Joint families are comparatively less in number.
6. People are more class-conscious and progressive.
7. The status is achieved than ascribed.

Social Effects of Urbanization

The social effects of urbanization may be analysed in relationship to family, caste, social status of women and village life.

Urbanization and Family

Urbanization affects not only the family structure but also intra- and inter-family relations, as well as the functions the family performs. Several empirical studies of urban families conducted by scholars, like I.P. Desai, K.M. Kapadia and Aileen Ross, have pointed out that urban joint family is being gradually replaced by nuclear family, the size of the family is shrinking and kinship relationship is confined to two or three generations only. In his study of 423 families made in 1955–57 in Mahuva town in Gujarat, Desai (1964) found that 5 per cent families were nuclear (residentially as well as functionally), 74 per cent were residentially nuclear but functionally and/or substantially (in property) joint, and 21 per cent were joint in residence and functioning as well as in property. Of the 95 per cent joint families (joint in functioning and/or property, and/or residence), the degree of functionality was low in 27 per cent cases (that is, they were joint only in functioning), high in 17 per cent cases (that is, they were joint in functioning and property), higher in 30 per cent cases (that is, they were joint in functioning, property and residence but were two-generation families), and highest in 21 per cent cases (that is, they were joint in residence, functioning and property and were three-generation families). This shows that though the structure of urban family is changing, the spirit of individualism is not growing in the families.

Kapadia (1959) in his study of 1,162 families in rural and urban (Navsari) areas in Gujarat in 1955 found that while in rural areas, for every two nuclear families there were three joint families; in urban areas, nuclear families were 10 per cent more than joint families. Ross (1961) in her study of 157 Hindu families belonging to middle and upper classes in Bangalore in 1957 found that: (a) about three-fifth (or 60%) of the families are nuclear and two-fifth (or 40%) are joint; (b) of the joint families, 70 per cent are small joint (couple+unmarried children+married sons without children, or two or more married brothers with children) and 30 per cent are large joint families (parents of unmarried children+unmarried children+married sons with children); (c) the trend today is towards a break with the traditional joint family form into the nuclear family unit; (d) small joint family is now the most typical form of family life in urban India; (e) there is a cycle of family types; (f) a growing number of people now spend at least part of their lives in single units; and (g) relations with one's distant kin are breaking or weakening.

R.K. Mukherjee (1975) also, on the basis of his study of 4,120 families in West Bengal in 1960–61, has said that replacement of joint family by nuclear family units is a *fait accompli*.

Though intra-family and inter-family relations are changing, it does not mean that youngsters no longer respect their elders, or children completely ignore their obligations to their parents and siblings, or wives challenge the authority of their husbands. The important change is that the 'husband-dominant' family is being replaced by 'equalitarian' family where wife is given a share in decision-making processes. The parents also no longer impose their authority on the children nor do the children blindly obey the commands of their parents. The attitude of youngsters is motivated by respect rather than fear. I.P. Desai maintains that 'in spite of strains between the younger and older generations,, the attachment of the children to their families is seldom weakened'. M.S. Gore (1968) writes: 'even in joint family, the eldest male consults his children and this consultation is not formal'. Ross (1961), however, thinks that 'the feelings of family obligation and emotional attachment to family members will almost certainly weaken and the authority of the patriarch break down. When this happens, there will be little left for identity within the larger kinship group'. Our own feeling is that family in urban India (and for that matter in the whole country) will never disintegrate but it will remain a strong unit.

Urbanization and Caste

Caste identity tends to diminish with urbanization, education and the development of an orientation towards individual achievement and modern status symbols. Urbanites participate in networks which include persons of several castes. According to Rajni Kothari, the structure of particularistic loyalties has been overlaid by a more sophisticated system of social and political participation with crosscutting allegiances. Andre Beteille (1966: 209–10) has pointed out that among the westernized elite, class ties are much more important than caste ties.

The educated members of some castes with modern occupations sometimes organize as a pressure group. As such, a caste association competes as a corporate body with other pressure groups for political and economic resources. This type of organization represents a new kind of solidarity. These competing units function more as social classes than as caste structures.

Yet another change that we find today is the fusion of sub-castes and fusion of castes. Kolenda has identified three kinds of fusion: (a) on the job and in newer neighbourhoods in the city, persons of different sub-castes and castes meet. They are usually of approximately equal rank. Neighbourhood or office group solidarity develops. This has been found common in the government colonies in big cities; (b) inter-sub-caste marriages take place, promoting a fusion of sub-castes. This is because many a time it is difficult to find a sufficiently educated groom for an educated daughter within his own sub-caste, but one may find it in neighbouring sub-caste; and (c) democratic politics fosters the fusion of sub-castes and of adjacent castes.

Urban dwellers do not conform to caste norms strictly. There is a change in commensal relations, marital relations, social relations, as well as in occupational relations. Likewise, caste solidarity was not as strong in urban areas as in the rural areas. Caste panchayats were very weak in cities. G.S. Ghurye, K.M. Kapadia, A.P. Barnabas, Yogendra Singh, R.K. Mukerjee, M.N. Srinivas, Yogesh Atal and S.C. Dube have also referred to the impact of urbanization on caste.

Urbanization and Status of Women

The status of women in urban areas is higher than that of rural women. Urban women are comparatively educated and liberal. Some of them are working too. As such, they are not only aware of their economic, social and political rights but they even use these rights to save themselves from being humiliated and exploited. The average age of girls at marriage in cities is also higher than the corresponding age in villages.

However, in the labour market, women are still in a disadvantaged situation. The labour market discriminates against women and is opposed to equality of opportunity – understood in a comprehensive sense to include equality of employment, training and promotional opportunities. In this sense, change is not possible in the sex segregated labour market whose structures ensure that the career patterns of women will normally be marked by discontinuity, unlike the normal male career patterns which assume continuity. Because of the constraints of the sex segregated labour market, women tend to cluster in a limited range of occupations, which have low status and are poorly paid. Women normally prefer teaching, nursing, social work, secretarial and clerical jobs – all of which have low status and low remuneration. Even those women who have surmounted the hurdle to professional education are disadvantaged as they find it difficult to reconcile to the competing demands of a professional career and home.

It is difficult for women to remain single or to combine marriage with career. Apart from the general expectation that all wives must be housewives, it has been noted that women are called upon to sacrifice their career when the need arises, thereby subordinating their own career to that of their husbands. This often creates frustration among women, leading to psychotic illness in a few cases. Rural women, however, do not have to face such problems.

It has been further found that in the cities of India, the high level education among girls is significantly associated with the smaller family size. Though education of women has raised the age of marriage and lowered the birth rate, it has not brought about any radical change in the traditional pattern of arranged marriages with dowry. Margaret Cormack found in her study of 500 university students that girls were ready to go to college and mix with boys but they wanted their parents to arrange their marriage. Women want new opportunities but demand old securities as well. They enjoy their newly found freedom but at the same time wish to carry on with old values.

Divorce and remarriage are the new phenomena we find among urban women. Women today take more initiative to break their marriages legally if they find adjustment after marriage impossible. Surprisingly, a large number of divorces are sought by women on the grounds of incompatibility and mental torture.

Politically also, urban women are more active today. The number of women contesting elections has increased at every level. They hold important political positions and also possess independent political ideologies. It may, thus, be concluded that while rural women continue to be dependent on men both economically and socially. urban women are comparatively independent and enjoy greater freedom.

Urbanization and Village Life

During the past 70 years, urban development in our country has led to the centrifugal movement of village people to the urban areas that were located within fairly easy access of public utilities. Many migrated to cities because of the availability of jobs there. Those who continue to live in villages also enjoy many of the conveniences of city life, although they are miles removed from the urban centres. The excellent highways, automobiles, radio, television and newspapers keep the villagers in contact with the city culture and civilization. The combination of rural residence and urban employment, and urban residence and rural contact has resulted not only in certain modifications of social patterns but also in adjustments to a new way of life. They have become more liberal in their approach. Many cultivators have accepted the new farm practices. Not only have their values and aspirations changed but there is a change in their behaviour too. The *jajmani* system is weakening and inter-caste and inter-class relations are changing. There is a change even in institutions of marriage, family and caste panchayats. Instead of depending on traditional methods of treating the diseases, they now use modern allopathic medicine. Similarly, in elections, they give as much importance to the social status of the candidate as to his individual potentialities and his political background.

But this in no way means that traditions have ceased to be important in villages. Individualism has not been able to replace familism, nor has secularism been able to replace the bond with the sacred.

Causes of Urbanization in India

The main causes of urbanization are:

1. *Industrialization:* It is a major cause of urbanization. The growth of industries has contributed to the growth of cities. As a result of industrialization, people have started moving towards the industrial areas in search of employment. This has resulted in the growth of towns and cities. It has expanded the employment opportunities. Rural people have migrated to cities on account of better employment opportunities. Rural to urban migration is happening on a massive scale due to population pressure and lack of resources in rural areas.
2. *Social factors*: Many social factors such as the attraction of cities, a better standard of living, better educational facilities, the need for status also induce people to migrate to cities. Often they believe that the standard of living in urban areas will be much better in urban areas.
3. *Employment opportunities*: In the rural sector, people have to depend mainly on agriculture for their livelihood, but Indian agriculture greatly depends on monsoon too. In drought situations or natural calamities, rural people have to migrate to cities.
4. *Modernization*: Urban areas are characterized by sophisticated technology, better infrastructure, communication, medical facilities, etc. People feel that they can lead a comfortable life in cities and hence migrate to cities.
5. *Rural-urban transformation*: It is an interesting aspect that not only cities are growing in number but the rural community is adopting the urban culture. Rural communities are no longer retaining their unique rural culture. Rural people are following the material culture of urban people. Urban-rural transformation can be observed in the following areas:

   (a) Change in dressing habits.
   (b) Adoption of modern technology.
   (c) Enlightenment of women.
   (d) Modern transport and communication: cell phones have become common even among rural people.
   (e) Active involvement in politics.
   (f) The growth of infrastructure like banks, post offices, etc.
   (g) Awareness among rural consumers.
   (h) Increasing demand for sophisticated products like cosmetics, etc.

6. *Spread of education*: The literacy rate has increased among the rural people. They have become more modernized.

Thus, it can be noticed that there are significant changes in the lifestyle of the village people. Indian villages have adopted the urban culture and urban style of living. However, all villages in India are not transformed. Only certain villages situated close to the cities have been transformed.

Effects of Urbanization

A range of economic, political, social, cultural and environmental factors affect urbanization. Urbanization is encouraged socially and culturally through the media. With a high rate of urbanization, significant changes have taken place. The effects of urbanization can be summed up as follows:

Socio-cultural Impacts

1. Cities have a strong socio-cultural impact on their surrounding rural areas. The mass media depicts city life as superior to rural life, the 'standard' language is deemed that of the national capital, and better services are received in the city due to its wealth.
2. The fertility rate in cities is often lower than in rural areas due to the absence of agriculture, the cost of children, food and living space in cities, and family planning.

Socio-economic Impacts

1. As a city grows, the cost of housing and infrastructure also grows, since there is less water, land and building material available and greater congestion problems. As a city decays in this way, governments often do not meet the service needs of residents and urban development is dominated by private capital.
2. Unemployment grows, as do drug abuse, crime and homelessness.

Environmental Impacts

1. Waste is a major problem in large cities.
2. Air pollution results from overdependence on motorized transport and from burning of coal to supply energy.
3. Water pollution results from poor sewage facilities and disposal of industrial heavy metals into waterways.
4. Vast quantities of solid waste are produced in industries.
5. Traffic congestion and noise pollution are major environmental impacts of large cities.

Positive Effects of Urbanization

1. Improvement in economic conditions.
2. Growth of commercial activities and employment opportunities.
3. Social and cultural integration.
4. Efficient transport and communication facilities.
5. Better utilization of resources.
6. Better education facilities.

Adverse Effects of Urbanization

Urbanization can yield positive effects if it takes place up to a desirable limit. Extensive urbanization or indiscriminate growth of cities may result in adverse effects. They may be as follows:

1. *Problem of Overpopulation*: Concentration of population is a major problem of cities. It has resulted in the accommodation problem, growth of slums, etc.
2. *Disintegration of the Joint Family*: Joint family can not be maintained in cities on account of the high cost of living. People prefer to live in nuclear families.
3. *High Cost of Living*: High cost of living is a major problem in metro cities like Mumbai, Bangalore, etc. It is very difficult for lower income groups to maintain a decent standard of living.
4. *Increase in Crime Rates*: Urban centres are known for the high rate of crimes. Theft, dacoity, murder, cheating, pickpocketing, rape, etc. are common in urban centres.
5. *Impersonal Relations*: Urban centres are characterized by highly secondary relations. The concept of neighbourhood, community life are almost absent in cities. Urban life is highly monotonous. This may have an adverse psychological effect on individuals. People are often self-centred and they have no concern for the fellow human beings.
6. *Problem of Pollution*: In industrialized cities, pollution is a major problem. It may be caused by industries or by excessive movement of vehicles.
7. *Stress*: Urban life is characterized by stress which may even strain family relations. In cities, employment of women is almost inevitable to meet the increasing cost of living. Changing role of women in the family creates stress in the family which may result in divorce or strained relations.

Thus, urbanization has its own merits and demerits. Urbanization can not be avoided. But the negative effect of urbanization can be minimized. The challenge today is to minimize the negative effects and build the benefits. Infrastructure needs to be improved. Opportunities should be created within rural areas to prevent migration to cities.

Due to social and economic pressures, people from backward villages started to move towards urbanized centres in search of a job, where newly established industries and ancillary activities continuously offer job opportunities to those people migrating to cities. Infrastructure needs to be improved. Opportunities should be created within rural areas to prevent migration to cities.

The pace of urbanization is fast if the industrial growth is fast. The pace of urbanization gradually declines only when the proportion of urban population to total population of the country becomes too high.

Problems of Urbanization

Urban problems are endless. Drug addiction, pollution, crime, juvenile delinquency, begging, alcoholism, corruption and unemployment are a few of them. Let us analyse the incidence and prevalence of seven crucial problems that are not covered in other chapters of this book. These are: (a) housing and slums, (b) crowding and depersonalization, (c) water supply and drainage, (d) transportation and traffic, (e) power shortage, (f) sanitation, and (g) pollution.

Housing and Slums

Housing people in the city or abolishing 'houselessness' is a serious problem. Governments, industrialists, capitalists, entrepreneurs, developers, contractors, and landlords have been unable to keep pace with the housing needs of the poor and the middle class people.

Millions of people are required to pay excessive rent, that is, one which is beyond their means. In our profit-oriented economy, private developers and colonizers find little profit in building houses in cities for the poor and the lower middle class people, and they consider it gainful to concentrate instead in meeting the housing needs of the rich and the upper middle class. The result has been higher rents and a scramble for the few available houses. Almost half of the population are either ill-housed or pay more than 20 per cent of their income on rent. In some states, the Housing Boards and the City Development Authorities have tried to remedy the city housing problem with active financial support from the Life Insurance Corporation, HUDCO and such other agencies. They even charge the total housing cost in monthly instalments on an interest varying between 10 per cent and 12 per cent. But engineers and contractors profit a lot from these government efforts. They use poor quality material in construction and finish the houses contravening the laid down specifications. The buyer soon finds that the roof leaks, the plaster peels off, there are cracks in the walls, and the electric fittings break down. Such ventures bring bad name to housing boards and even to a few honest bureaucrats associated with such housing schemes. No wonder, housing in the cities continues to be a gigantic problem even today, after food and clothing.

The situation is more or less the same in all the metropolises in the country. The slum population, governmental efforts notwithstanding, is expected to show a sizeable increase in the future aggravating to the housing problem and the squalor conditions. The living conditions in slum areas are characterized by overcrowding, poor environmental conditions, scarcity of health and family welfare services and total absence of minimum level of residential accommodation. As a result, conditions of people living in slums is far more pathetic than in non-slum areas. Census provides a fair amount of information on India's slum – the number of Indian cities that have slums (2,600), the number of slums across the country (33,500), the population in these slums (6.6 crore), the infrastructure available (56% with access to water, 90% use electric power). The destiny of millions of slum dwellers depends upon our policymakers getting the right, and soon.

Rajiv Awas Yojana was launched in 2011 for creating 'slum-free India' as a pilot project for two years. But now it has been extended till 2022. It is applicable to all slums in the city whether notified or non-notified. It is also applicable to urban homeless and pavement dwellers.

Crowding and Depersonalization

Crowding (density of population) and people's apathy to other persons' problems (including their neighbours' problems) are some other problems growing out of city life. Some homes are so overcrowded that five to six persons live in one room. Some city neighbourhoods are extremely overcrowded. Overcrowding has very deleterious effects. It encourages deviant behaviour, spreads diseases, and creates conditions for mental illness, alcoholism and riots. One effect of dense urban living is people's apathy and indifference. City dwellers do not want to 'get involved' in other people's affairs. Some people do take interest in accidents and in cases of molestations, assaults and even murders but others choose to be mere onlookers.

Water Supply and Drainage

We have reached a stage where no city has round the clock water supply. Intermittent supply results in a vacuum being created in empty water lines which often suck in pollutants through leaking joints. Today, inhabitants of almost all metropolises in India get water supply for less than an hour a day. Many small towns have no main water supply at all and are dependent on tubewells. Even a relatively planned and serviced city like Jaipur, now has to reach as far as 150 km to the Bisalpur dam in Ajmer district for augmentation of water supply. Most towns and cities, which normally get good rain every year, have now been undergoing the agony of acute water shortage. What seems to be sadly lacking is a national water policy which would assess the total water resources and then allocate water.

When we look on the other side of the water supply, that is, drainage, we find the situation equally bad. One of the less known facts about India is that there is not a single city which is fully sewered. Not even Chandigarh can claim this distinction because the unauthorized constructions in and around it lie outside the purview of the main system. Because of the non-existence of a drainage system, large pools of stagnant water can be seen in every city even during summer months. Just as we need a national water policy, we also need a national and regional drainage policy.

Transportation and Traffic

The transportation and traffic scenario in all Indian cities is unhappy. A majority of people use buses and auto-rickshaws, while a few use rail/metro as transit system. The increasing number of scooters, motorcycles and cars makes the traffic problem worse. The number of buses plying in metropolitan cities like Delhi, Mumbai, Chennai and Kolkata is not adequate and commuters have to spend about one to two hours to get into a bus, which means leaving the house two hours in advance in the morning to reach their place of work and reaching home two hours late in the evening. The main reason for being in this mess is that the low income of the commuters forces them to live in areas with cheap accommodation which necessitates extensive travel. Further, since our citizens cannot afford to pay high fares for the use of a public transport system, the fares have to be kept very low which results in all city bus services sustaining such annual losses as hamper their expansion or maintenance a fleet adequate to meet city needs.

Power Shortage

Closely linked with transportation is the question of power shortage. On the one hand, the use of electrical gadgets has increased very much in cities, and on the other hand, the establishment of new industries and the expansion of the old industries has also increased dependence on electricity. Most states are not in a position to generate the power that they need with the result that they remain dependent on the neighbouring states.

Sanitation

Municipalities and municipal corporations in Indian cities are so riddled with corruption and inefficiency that they have time for all things, but the interest in sanitation of the city, particularly in removing garbage, cleaning drains and unclogging sewers. The sweepers rarely and reluntantly perform their assigned duties and every few months threaten to go on strike on the issue of wages, etc. The garbage disposal fleets operate to a third or half of their capacity. If removing garbage work is assigned to private contractors, they always complain of non-payment of money and stop working on slight pretexts. There is, thus, total lack of motivation to tackle the basic sanitation needs of the cities. The spread of unauthorized slums in congested urban areas and lack of civic sense among the settlers in these slums further adds to the growing mound of filth and diseases. Even the major cities of our country reflect the sanitation crisis.

Obviously, the basic problem is excessive urbanization and the resultant slumming of the cities. But, because our politicians use migrants as vote banks, they remain unconcerned with taking necessary civic action. Lack of understanding at the planning level, lack of coordination between the concerned agencies, mismanagement of municipalities and lack of necessary funds to be provided by the state governments will always remain as barriers in putting sanitation maintenance cycle in proper shape. If cities continue to treat sanitation and sewage as low-priority areas, overcoming health crisis in urban areas will be an insurmountable task in years to come. As a long-term remedy, what is needed is using new techniques of refuse collection, new technology for the disposal of garbage, a fundamental change in the municipal infrastructure and land use planning.

Pollution

Our cities and towns are major polluters of the environment. As stated above, most cities discharge 90 per cent of their entire sewage and industrial effluents untreated into the nearby rivers. Likewise, the small towns contribute their share of garbage and excreta to the nearest waterway through its open drains. Urban industry pollutes the atmosphere with smoke and toxic gases from its chimneys. Areas recording higher levels of air pollution abound with many ailments which particularly affect children below five years and people above fifty years of age. The high synergistic effect of sulphur dioxide, nitrogen dioxide, etc. causes these diseases.

The issue of environmental pollution in urban areas is considered so significant that even the Supreme Court, from time to time, ordered for the strict enforcement of environmental laws.

Suggestions for Urban Planning

There should be focussed attention to integrated development of infrastructure services in cities covered under the mission and there should be the establishment of linkages between asset-creation and asset-management. Through a slew of reforms for long-term project sustainability; green building concepts should be implemented.

Urban planning mechanisms need an overhaul to unify land record keeping, integrate land use with transport planning, and embed municipal plans into the district and regional plans.

1. Local bodies should fill vacancies.
2. Time-tested master plans should be strengthened instead of preparing quick fix city development plans.
3. Populist policies and reforms should have their logical conclusion and should be not done in great haste.
4. Land development should be the part of the planning of urban development.
5. Project management skills need to be enhanced and timely completion of projects.

Urban expansion in India will happen at a speed quite unlike anything the country or the world has seen before. It took nearly 40 years (from 1971 to 2008) for India's urban population to rise by nearly 230 million; it will take only half that time to add the next 250 million. This expansion will affect almost every state. For the first time in India's history, five of its largest states will have more of their population living in cities than in villages by 2039. Fifty per cent of India's population would begin to live in urban areas. The challenge over the next 30 years is to take advantage of the potential benefits of urbanization and agglomeration in an inclusive way.

Causes of Urban Problems

Following McVeigh and Schostak (1978: 198–205), who have linked urban problems in the United States to four factors, we can identify following five major causes of problems of urban life in India: (a) migration in and out of the city, (b) industrial growth, (c) apathy of the government, (d) defective town planning, and (e) vested interest forces.

Migration

People migrate to towns/cities because of the relatively better employment opportunities available there. In India, the migration has four patterns: rural to rural, rural to urban, urban to urban and urban to rural. Though rural to rural migration is by far the most prevalent form of movement but rural to urban and urban to urban migration is equally crucial.

The entrance of the rural poor into the city depletes sources of revenue. On the other hand, the rich people today prefer to live in sub-urban areas. This movement of the rich causes financial loss to the city. This migration to the city and away from the city aggravates problems.

Industrial Growth

While the annual urban population growth rate was 3.0 per cent (2011) in India, the industrial growth rate was 7.1 per cent per annum in February 2018. This growth was expected to take care of the additional job requirements in the cities. The tertiary sector also provides refuge to the migrants, though their earnings remain at low level.

Apathy of the Government

The administrative mismanagement of our cities is also responsible for the mess in which city dwellers find themselves. Municipal governments have not kept pace with city growth, either spatially or in terms of management infrastructure. There is neither the will nor the capacity to plan for the future. There is also no skill and capability to manage what exists. Until we improve the capacity of our cities to govern themselves, we cannot emerge from the urban mess. On the other hand, the state governments also put many restrictions on local governments in raising necessary funds for dealing with particular urban problems.

Defective Town Planning

A more alarming factor in the general deterioration in the standard of civic services is the growing sense of helplessness of our planners and administrators. From the Planning Commission downwards, there seems to be a fatalistic acceptance of the uncontrolled growth in our metropolitan cities. In fact, there is a feeling that very little is being done in our country to plan the growth of the cities in a proper way.

Vested Interests

The last cause of urban problems is the vested interests that work against people but enhance private commercial interests and profits. The city residents are usually powerless to affect decisions that the elite make to further their own interests, power and profit. When these powerful elite can make more money, they adopt plans and programmes no matter how many people are hurt in the process.

Solutions to Urban Problems

Some measures have to be adopted if we want to remedy urban problems. The measures suggested are as follows:

Systematic Development of Urban Centres and Creation of Job Opportunities

One important solution to our urban problems is the systematic development of the fast growing urban centres and planning an investment programme which, over the next 20 years or so, could give rise to a large number of well distributed, viable urban centres throughout the country. So far we have been focussing attention on programmes for providing wage employment in rural areas through schemes like MNREGS to hold people back in the villages. While there is ample justification for providing rural employment, this by itself is not enough. It is not possible to provide gainful employment in the agricultural sector beyond a certain point. For this purpose, we have to emphasize on programmes which can permit multifunctional activities to sustain people in cities.

Regional Planning along with City Planning

Urban planning is almost city-centred. We have always been talking of town and city planning but never of the planned development of the whole region so that population is logically dispersed and activities are properly distributed. City planning is an ad-hoc solution but regional planning could be a more lasting one. For example, instead of providing houses to slum dwellers in cities through city development authorities, if through regional planning migrants could be diverted to other areas which may provide attractive employment, the pace of growth of existing cities could be checked.

Encouraging Industries to Move to Backward Areas

Land pricing policy which gives land in large chunks at throwaway prices has to be replanned to encourage industries to move to backward areas/districts. This will also take care of linear development of metropolitan and big cities. A policy of the state taking over potential high value land in and around large cities with a view to exploit its full cost at a later date, also needs serious consideration.

Municipalities to Find Own Financial Resources

People do not mind paying taxes to the municipality if their money is properly utilized to maintain roads, provide sewage system, reduce water shortage and provide electricity. It is a well-known fact that cities suffer from crippling resource constraints. If deterrent punishment is given to the corrupt municipality officials, there is no reason why the municipal corporations should find it difficult in collecting money from the residents of the city. A city must bear the cost of its own development. High financial support from state government is becoming difficult. By revising property, water and electricity taxes, money can be collected and more money per head, per annum can be made available for providing necessary amenities. When any new industry or business is located in a city or on its periphery, it could be moderately taxed so that additional money becomes available to the local body.

Encouraging Private Transport

Why should city transport be a public monopoly? When the transport is handled by state employees, it has been noticed that they tend to have extremely rudely and callously. Backing of the trade union encourages them to go on strikes frequently. It is necessary that private transportation must be encouraged. Privately operated mini bus and tempo services will charge a little more fare but commuters would not mind paying this in view of the better services.

Amendment of Rent Control Acts

Laws which inhibit the construction of new houses or giving of houses on rent must be amended. Which landlord would like to spend lakhs of rupees on a two-three room tenement and give it on rent for ₹ 10,000–15,000 a month or so for the next 10 to 20 years without having the authority to increase the rent or get it vacated on appropriate grounds. A few states like Maharashtra has taken a lead in amending the Rent Control Act which has made thousands of houses available for rent. A similar step in other states would be welcome.

Adopting Pragmatic Housing Policy

In India, the policies of urban development and housing have come a long way since 1950. Actually, the pressure of increasing urban population and lack of housing and basic services were very much evident at the time of independence. Though, in almost every five-year plan, there has been an emphasis on solving urban problems, no concrete outcome has come out even after six decades of planning. Not only this, the government has also framed a number of policies, the recent one being the National Urban Housing and Habitat Policy, 2007, which intends to promote sustainable development of habitat in the country with a view to ensuring equitable supply of land, shelter and services at affordable prices to all sections of society. In fact, the government policy and planning has to be more down to earth. This is not to say that the concept of National Housing Policy (NHP) is irrational. The NHP strategy is broad-based. It seeks to provide easy access to finance as well as land and materials for building houses at reasonable rates. It also seeks to encourage manufacturers to use new type of building materials. Moreover, it seeks to review the entire gamut of laws relating to land tenure, land acquisition and ceiling to apartment ownership, municipal regulations and rental laws. But, these are all thorny issues. In recent years, we have seen that the NHP is oriented towards rich developers, landlords and contractors. The NHP has to discourage luxury housing and promote cooperative and group housing societies. It has to develop special schemes for the poor and low-income people. It has also to favour providing incentives to employers to build houses for the employees. Unless a more pragmatic NHP is adopted, it will be impossible to achieve the set goals.

Structural Decentralization

One proposal by innovative planners and some radicals envision a structural decentralization of local self-government itself. This could entail the creation of 'neighbourhood action groups', to be called 'community centres' consisting of representatives of residents and municipality officials. These centres will identify and act upon neighbourhood needs. For example, many new colonies have come to be established in many cities in which as many as 10,000 to 50,000 people reside. Thus, these colonies are small towns themselves. Some taxes like house tax, road tax, light tax, etc. could be passed on directly to these community centres instead of giving them to municipalities. The centres would direct the affairs of the neighbourhood without reference to the city municipal corporation and use the collected money in maintaining roads, lights and so forth. The argument for this kind of decentralized structure within the city is that the same system that allows lakhs of people a substantial control over their civic destiny denies them an effective role in shaping the institutions that shape their lives. Community centres will allow them to create their own exclusive environment.

The effects of urbanization and urbanism and the problems of cities can never be solved until urban planning is modified and radical measures are taken. These should not be based on the profit motive which would benefit a few vested interests. The use of land, technology, and taxes should be for the benefit of the people and not for the benefit of a few powerful interest groups. City dwellers have to become politically active and organize themselves and agitate to change the existing economic and social systems in the cities.

Urban Agglomeration

Urban agglomeration is a continuous urban spread constituting a town and its adjoining urban outgrowths or two or more physical contiguous towns together and any adjoining urban outgrowths of such towns. For the Census of India, 2001 it was decided that the core town or at least one of the constituent towns of an urban agglomeration should necessarily be a statutory town and the total population of all the constituents should not be less than 20,000 (as per 1991 Census). With these two basic criteria having been met, the following are the possible different situations in which urban agglomerations could be constituted: (a) a city or town with one or more contiguous outgrowths; (b) two or more adjoining towns with or without their outgrowths; (c) a city or one or more adjoining towns with their outgrowths all of which form a continuous spread.

India's Urban Challenges

Urbanization is an integral part of the process of economic growth. As in most countries, India's towns and cities make a major contribution to the country's economy. With less than one-third of India's people, its urban areas generate over two-third of the country's GDP and account for 90 per cent of government revenues. Urbanization in India has expanded rapidly as increasing numbers of people migrate to towns and cities in search of economic opportunity. Slums now account for one-fourth of all urban housing. Meeting the needs of India's soaring urban populations is and will, therefore, continue to be a strategic policy matter. Critical issues that need to be addressed include poor local governance, weak finances, inappropriate planning, critical infrastructure and a rapidly deteriorating environment.

The rapid rise in urban population, in India, is leading to many problems. India's urban growth rate is 2.07 per cent which seems to be significant. This has greatly caused slum problems, with so many people overcrowding cities and forcing people to live in unsafe conditions which also includes illegal buildings. Water lines, roads, and electricity are lacking which is causing a fall in living standards. It is also adding to the problem of all types of pollution.

Urbanization also results in a disparity in the market, owing to the large demands of the growing population and the primary sector struggling to cope with them.

Urbanization since independence has been focussed through respective five-year plans. The Eleventh Plan (2007–2012) introduced some innovative changes through capacity building, increasing the efficiency and productivity of the cities, dismantling the monopoly of the public sector over urban infrastructure, using technology as a tool for rapid urbanization.

The 2011 Census was the first one that collected data on people living in slums that have become commonplace in a rapidly urbanizing India. It found that around one out of every six households in urban India (17.4%) is in a slum and that well over one-third of all slum households in the country (38%) are in cities with a population in excess of a million.

Planning

1. Many urban governments lack a modern planning framework.
2. The multiplicity of local bodies obstructs efficient planning and land use.
3. Rigid master plans and restrictive zoning regulations limit the land available for building, constricting cities' abilities to grow in accordance with changing needs.

Housing

1. Building regulations that limit urban density – such as floor space indexes – reduce the number of houses available, thereby pushing up property prices.

2. Poor access to microfinance and mortgage finance, limit the ability of low-income groups to buy or improve their homes.
3. Policy, planning, and regulation deficiencies lead to a proliferation of slums.
4. Weak finances of urban local bodies and service providers leave them unable to expand the trunk infrastructure that housing developers need to develop new sites.

Service Delivery

1. Most services are delivered by city governments with unclear lines of accountability.
2. There is a strong bias towards adding physical infrastructure rather than providing financially and environmentally sustainable services.
3. Service providers are unable to recover operations and maintenance costs and depend on government for finance.
4. Independent regulatory authorities that set tariffs, decide on subsidies and enforce service quality are generally absent.

Infrastructure

1. Most urban bodies do not generate the revenues needed to renew infrastructure, nor do they have the credit-worthiness to access capital markets for funds.
2. Urban transport planning needs to be more holistic – there is a focus on moving vehicles rather than meeting the needs of the large numbers of people who walk or ride bicycles in India's towns and cities.

Environment

The deteriorating urban environment is taking a toll on people's health and productivity and diminishing their quality of life.

Steps Taken by the Government to Improve Urban Development

The Constitution (74th Amendment) Act came into effect in 1993, emphasizes to strengthen urban planning, regulation of land use, roads and bridges and providing urban amenities.

National Urban Transport Policy, 2006

Its main purpose is to provide affordable, comfortable, safe, rapid, reliable and sustainable urban transport system for the growing number of city residents commuting for jobs, education and recreation and other such needs within city limits.

Encouraging integrated land use and transport planning in all cities so that travel distances are minimized and access to livelihoods, education, and other social needs, especially for the marginal segments of the urban population is improved.

Continuous Improvements in Design and Management

1. Climate-oriented development,
2. Mass transit-oriented development,
3. People-centric technological applications,
4. Planning can be bottom up for future urbanization,
5. Smart PDS rationing, and
6. Social inclusive and economically diverse.

India's Seven Mission Programme

With the rapid rise of urbanization in India, the Seven Mission Programme was founded, which aims to fund cities to achieve intended milestones. The Seven Mission Programme includes the following plans:

1. 100 Smart Cities Mission
2. AMRUT (Atal Mission for Rejuvenation and Urban Transformation)
3. HRIDAY (National Heritage City Development and Augmentation Yojana)
4. Sardar Patel National Urban Housing Mission
5. National Mission on Sustainable Habitat
6. Clean India Mission
7. National Urban Information System.

Each of these intervention has its specific mandate, objectives and targets. Yet the outcomes of one are directly linked to the progress of other, ensuring comprehensive approach to development.

Swachh Bharat Mission

Swachh Bharat Mission was launched on 2 October 2014 with the objectives of eliminating open defecation, eradicating manual scavenging, promoting scientific processing of municipal solid waste, and bringing behavioural change about sanitation practices. The Swachh Bharat Mission aims to cover all rural and urban areas. The urban component of the mission is being implemented by the ministry of urban development and the rural component by the ministry of drinking water and sanitation. Clean urban areas will attract tourists and can increase the economic diversity of the urban dwellers and it will be also a source for revenue generation for Urban Local Bodies (ULB).

Smart Cities Mission

The Smart Cities Mission was launched on 25 June 2015. The government has planned to develop 100 smart cities in India in a phased manner. Union Budget 2018–19 allocated ₹ 2.04 lakh crores, covering 99 cities. The objective of Smart Cities Mission is to promote cities that provide core infrastructure and give a decent quality of life to its citizens, a clean and sustainable environment and application of 'smart' solutions. The focus is on sustainable and inclusive development. Area-based development will transform existing areas, including slums, into better planned ones, thereby improving livability of the whole city. The core infrastructure elements in a smart city would include:

1. adequate water supply,
2. assured electricity supply,
3. sanitation, including solid waste management,
4. efficient urban mobility and public transport,
5. affordable housing, especially for the poor,
6. robust IT connectivity and digitalization,
7. good governance, especially e-Governance and citizen participation,
8. sustainable environment,
9. safety and security of citizens, particularly women, children and the elderly, and
10. health and education.

Trends Supporting Urbanization in India

1. Private cities are now expanding due to the support of private companies. Private developers are building private housing projects that will exponentially grow in the years to come.
2. The Delhi–Mumbai Corridor is an infrastructure programme set to develop 'smart cities' and combine next-generation technology with infrastructural development.
3. The transport and logistics sector of India underlines the importance of interconnecting the different modes of transportation: road, rail, sea and air. An efficient multi-modal system is relevant in the development and successful growth of the infrastructural systems.
4. Special Economic Zones dot the landscape of India. Each of these zones is focussed on a particular sector such as IT, apparel and fashion, or petroleum and petrochemical industries.
5. Industrial townships are built to house employees close to the factories and manufacturing plants at which they work. After the success of the pioneering industrial township, Tata's steel town, the government is planning on developing more like it.
6. India's expected economic growth opens up expansion prospects for Indian airports. Domestic and international passengers are inevitably predicted to double in number in the years to come.

Spatial Planning in India

There are two types of planning systems laid out in the Indian urbanization and spatial development agenda to carefully combat the complications and explore the potential of urbanization.

1. A new institution named NITI Aayog (National Institution for Transforming India) is a new planning system which aims to target cooperation and active participation in the economic policy-making process led by the

state governments of India. This NITI Aayog was made to replace the Planning Commission of India.

2. The Ministry of Urban Development (MoUD), the Ministry of Housing and Urban Affairs (MoHUA), and the Town and Country Planning Organization (TCPO) will facilitate and support the nationwide urban and regional development planning. These organizations place their efforts on spatial planning for the improvement of the entire country.

Conclusion

Urbanization has undermined old forms of political mobilization based on caste and religious identities and favours local issues to be resolved on right based approach has its impact on all aspects of day-to-day life. Family structure has also been influenced by urbanization. In the rural society, the concept of family living is different from that in the urban society. In the urban society usually the families are nuclear, a very small percentage of households have joint families, whereas in rural society most of the households have joint families. This change in family structure is a direct result of urbanization. In urban areas, especially urbanization in the metropolitan cities, people of extremely divergent cultures live together. This has a positive impact. People come to know about each other's culture and they exchange their ideas, breaking the barriers which earlier used to exist between them. This results in cultural hybridization. There is no doubt that careful and strategic planning of urbanization can make the life of human beings more comfortable.

References

Anderson, Nels, *The Urban Community*, Holt, Rinehart and Winston, New York, 1959.

Anderson, N. and Iswaran, K., *Urban Sociology*, Asia Publishing House, Bombay, 1965.

Beteille, Andre, *Caste, Class and Power*, Oxford University Press, Bombay, 1966.

Clinard, Marshall, *Sociology of Deviant Behaviour*, Holt, Rinehart & Winston, New York, 1957.

Davis, K., *Human Society*, Macmillan, New York, 1949.

Desai, I.P., *Some Aspects of Family in Mahuva*, Asia Publishing House, Bombay, 1964.

Gore, M.S., *Urbanization and Family Change*, Popular Prakashan, Bombay, 1968.

Kapadia, K.M., 'The Family in Transition', *Sociological Bulletin*, 1959.

Kapur Mehta, A. and Shepherd, A. (eds.), *Chronic Poverty and Development Policy in India*, Sage Publications, New Delhi, 2006.

McVeigh, F.J. and Schostak, Arthur B., *Modern Social Problems*, Holt, Rinehart & Winston, New York, 1978.

Mukherjee, R.K., 'Family in India' in D. Narain (ed.), *Exploration in the Family and Other Essays*, Thacker & Co. Ltd., Bombay, 1975.

Premi, Mahendra K., *Population of India in the New Millennium: Census 2001*, NBT, New Delhi, 2011.

Ross, Aileen, *Hindu Family in its Urban Setting*, Oxford University Press, New Delhi, 1961.

Simmel, Georg, 'The Metropolis and Mental Life', in *The Sociology of Georg Simmel*, Kurt H. Wolf (ed.), Free Press, New York, 1950.

Sridhar, K.S. and Kashyap, Nevedita, 'Density Gradients and Their Determinants: Evidence from India'. *Regional Science and Urban Economics*, 37(3): 314–344. 30, 2007.

Sorokin, P. and Zimmerman, C.C., *Principles of Rural Urban Society*, Henry Holt, New York, 1962.

Theodorson, G.A. and Theodorson, A.G., *A Modern Dictionary of Sociology*, Thomas Coowell, New York, 1969.

Tonnies, F., 'Gemeinschaft and Gesellschaft', in Talcott Parsons et al. (eds), *Theories of Society*, Vol. 1, The Free Press of Glencoe, New York, 1887, 1957 and 1961.

Tripathi, S., 'Do Large Agglomerations Lead to Economic Growth? Evidence from Urban India'. MPRA Paper No. 38227, 2012.

Weber, Max, 'The Urban Community', in Talcott Parsons et al. (eds), *Theories of Society*, Vol. 1, The Free Press of Glencoe, New York, 1961.

Wirth, Louis, 'Urbanism as a Way of Life', *American Journal of Sociology*, Vol. 44, 1938.

13

Globalization and Consumerism

Two threads that weave our era, particularly the quandary of the contemporary times, are that of globalization and consumerism. Both have intervened social, cultural, economic and environment spheres and have even altered the sense of identity and generated new forms of subjectivity.

Consumerism has transformed citizens into global shoppers and globalization has transformed citizens of nation-states into global citizens. However, a simple definition of globalization would describe the term as the process by which businesses or other organizations develop international influence or start operating on an international scale. Meanwhile, consumerism is a social and economic order that encourages the purchase of goods and services in even greater amounts.

Consumerism is tied in with the concept of globalization – making the world one economy and marketplace – and popular culture plays an important role in connecting the two. According to one approach, consumerism is a virtue because popular culture makes people want material things, but another point of view looks at consumerism as a force breeding profit motive and hence exploitative.

GLOBALIZATION

Meaning

By the term globalization, we mean opening up of the economy for world market by attaining international competitiveness. Thus, globalization of the economy simply indicates interaction of the country relating to production, trading and financial transactions with the developed industrialized countries of the world. The term globalization has been used to describe different countries joining for economic, political and educational equality. The countries joining together think about themselves as a part of the world rather than as separate countries. Accordingly, the term globalization has four parameters:

1. Permitting free flow of goods by removing or reducing trade barriers between the countries.
2. Creating an environment for the flow of capital between the countries.
3. Allowing free flow of technology transfer.
4. Creating an environment for the free movement of labour between the countries of the world.

Thus, taking the entire world as a global village, all the four components are equally important for attaining a smooth path for globalization.

The term globalization also means international integration. An opening up of world trade, development of advanced means of communication, internationalization of financial markets, growing importance of MNCs, population migrations and increased mobility of persons, goods, and capital.

George Soros takes globalization to 'mean the development of global financial markets, the growth of transnational corporation, and their increasing domination over national economies' (2002: 1).

Tracing the History of Globalization

The industrial revolution in the 19th century was one of the major periods in the history of globalization, for there was a significant increase in the quantity and quality of products and it led to higher exports and better trade relations. Colonialism and imperialism further contributed to the trade and with the First World War, the period referred to as 'pre-globalization', came to an end.

Globalization, as it is understood in modern sense, came into existence after the Second World War. After the war, the leaders of the world decided to bring down the barriers and promote trade relations among countries across the globe. Moreover, with countries like India, Sri Lanka and Indonesia gaining independence, the need for economic cooperation among nations became essential.

The next step was establishment of United Nations Organization and, henceforth, the creation of World Trade Organization and International Monetary Fund. The International Monetary Fund (IMF, 2000) identifies four basic aspects of globalization:

1. *Trade and transactions:* With the beginning of the 20th century, international trade and business flourished, mainly because of improved transportation and communication, special economic zones and tax competition among governments and countries.
2. *Flow of capital:* It is through a rapid increase in cross-border movement of goods, service, technology and more importantly, capital, that national economies across the world become increasingly interdependent economically. This is also referred to as economic globalization, which

comprises the globalization of production, markets, competition, technology, corporations and industries (Joshi, 2009).

3. *Movement of people:* Cross-cultural contact across countries and nations has been possible as a result of globalization. International migration, for work or marriage, travel and transit, all have transformed people into global citizens.
4. *Distribution of knowledge, accessibility to information:* Internet can be looked at as both, a product and a catalyst of globalization.

However, for a better understanding, we could discuss globalization under the following broader categories:

1. *Economic:* According to Shangquan (2000), economic globalization refers to the increasing interdependence of world economies as a result of the growing scale of cross-border trade of commodities and services, flow of international capital and wide and rapid spread of technologies. It reflects the continuing expansion and mutual integration of market frontiers, and is an irreversible trend for the economic development in the whole world at the turn of the millennium. The rapid growing significance of information in all types of productive activities and marketization are the two major driving forces for economic globalization.
2. *Cultural:* Cultural globalization is the rapid movement of ideas, attitudes and values across national borders. As early as the 1960s, the Canadian literary critic Marshall McLuhan popularized the term 'global village' to describe the effect, that the ability to connect and exchange ideas instantaneously, would bring to the world. This sharing of ideas generally leads to greater interconnectedness and interaction between people of diverse cultures which can have both positive and negative results. Consequently, as technology has accelerated the process, it has sparked off considerable controversy.
3. *Political:* With global ecological changes, an ever more integrated global economy, and other global trends, political activity increasingly takes place at the global level. According to V.M. Moghadam, political globalization 'refers to an increasing trend toward multilateralism (in which the United Nations plays a key role), toward an emerging "transnational state apparatus", and toward the emergence of national and international non-governmental organizations that act as watchdogs over governments and have increased their activities and influence' (2005: 35).

In case of India, the economy was opened up in the early nineties, following a major crisis as a result of a foreign exchange crunch. The new economic reforms, thereafter, fell under the heads of liberalization, privatization and globalization (LPG). Thus, the LPG model aimed at making Indian economy the fastest growing and the most competitive in the world. The major measures initiated as part of the plan included devaluation, disinvestment, dismantling of the industrial licensing regime, allowing foreign direct investment and removal of quantitative restriction on imports, besides financial sector reforms.

Impact of Globalization

Globalization has, undoubtedly, led to growing competition across the globe. There are beneficial aspects that have increased production and efficiency. Competition for increasing market space has led to specialization and an improved division of labour. On the other hand, the 'costs' of globalization can lead to conflicts at various levels, especially since many of the beneficiaries of globalization have been the richer countries. The net result has not been convergence but rather divergence of incomes worldwide. There are also regional and global instabilities that are rooted in the interdependencies of economies.

The Positives

1. *Better organized markets:* For a growing economy, well-organized and effectual markets are essential. If there are willing buyers who are ready to pay for quality products and services that are on sale, a healthy balance can be maintained that facilitates an efficient market. With open economies and better trade, outsourcing of products/services is possible and, thereby, improvement in the quality, and that too at a reduced cost. A lower selling price could result in increased demand and affordability.
2. *Increased competition:* More the producers, better the quality of goods and services, as per the demand of the competition and consumers will only benefit from such a situation. As trade crossed international borders, there were more choices available and standards would be raised. Also, each producer will be in a constant process of improving the product and at times will bring down the prices.
3. *Promotion of free commerce and trade:* The abolition of various double taxes, tariffs and capital controls, reduction of transport cost and development of infrastructure have made free trade possible. Moreover, globalization has resulted in many businesses setting up or buying operations in other countries. When a foreign company invests in a country, perhaps by building a factory or a shopping mall, this is called 'inward investment' and the companies that operate in several countries are called multinational corporations (MNCs) or transnational corporations (TNCs). For example, the US fast-food chain McDonald's is an MNC, with nearly 30,000 restaurants in 119 countries. Global corporations provide impetus to development and growth of economy.
4. *New technologies*: Introduction of new technologies has resulted in increased productivity and efficiency. This has also facilitated better living standards.
5. *Cultural exchange:* Globalization leads to sharing of ideas, experiences and lifestyles of people and cultures. People can experience foods and other products, previously unavailable in their countries. Culturally speaking, globalization has brought in different ideologies and thought process amongst people.

6. *More tolerant:* Socially we have become more open and tolerant towards each other, and people who live in the other parts of the world are now not considered aliens. A condition is created where human rights could flourish.

The Negatives

1. *Interdependence:* Since all economies are connected together, when one market falls, the world's economy collapses. For instance, when the US market turns into a disaster, other countries are also affected because the US loses its buying power.
2. *Loss of economic sovereignty:* Often, it is the powerful countries, multinational firms and international financial institutions that end up controlling the economy of the weaker country and, as a result, national sovereignty has progressively and systematically undermined. Such cynicism has led to extreme forms of nationalism, populism, xenophobia and the emergence of fundamentalist and dissenting political movements.
3. *Exploitation:* An absence of strictly enforced international laws means that TNCs may operate in less economically developing countries (LEDCs) in a way that would not be allowed in a more economically developed country (MEDC). There is a risk that poor working conditions are imposed and local workers are given low wages. Globalization brings fear as well. Because of too much flow of capital amongst countries, it introduces unfair and immoral distribution of income.
4. *Outsourcing:* While it provides jobs to a population in one country, it takes away those jobs from another country, leaving many without opportunities.
5. *Environment effect:* Many believe that globalization is one of the most important factors that has aggravated environmental degradation. The amount of raw materials needed to run industries and factories is taking a toll on the natural reserves of planet earth, and pollution has severely impacted the quality of air.
6. *Loss of indigenous identity:* In the process of cross-interaction and sharing of ideas and innovations, the indigenous traditions and culture is lost.

Impact of Globalization on India

Positive Impacts

The following are some of the important advantages of globalization for a developing country like India:

1. Globalization helps to boost the long run average growth rate of the economy of the country through:
   (a) Improvement in the allocative efficiency of resources;
   (b) Increase in labour productivity; and
   (c) Reduction in capital-output ratio.

2. Globalization paves the way for removing inefficiency in the production system. The prolonged protective scenario in the absence of globalization makes the production system careless about cost effectiveness, which can be attained by following the policy of globalization.
3. Foreign direct investment (FDI) tends to increase at a much greater rate than the growth in world trade, helping boost technology transfer, industrial restructuring, and the growth of global companies.
4. Globalization usually restructures production and trade pattern favouring labour-intensive goods and labour-intensive techniques as well as the expansion of trade in services.
5. In a globalized scenario, domestic industries of a developing country become conscious about price reduction and quality improvement to their products so as to face foreign competition.
6. Globalization discourages uneconomic import substitution and favours cheaper imports of capital goods which reduces the capital-output ratio in manufacturing industries.
7. Globalization facilitates consumer goods industries to expand faster to meet the growing demand which would result in a faster expansion of employment opportunities.
8. Globalization enhances the efficiency of the banking insurance and financial sectors with the opening up to those areas to foreign capital, foreign banks, and insurance companies.
9. Globalization has resulted in dissemination of advanced management practices and newer forms of work organization, and sharing of internationally accepted labour standards.

Adverse Impacts

The following are some of the disadvantages for developing country like India:

1. Globalization paves the way for redistribution of economic power at the world level leading to domination by few economically powerful nations.
2. Globalization usually results in a greater increase in imports than the exports, leading to a growing trade deficit and balance of payments problem.
3. Although globalization promotes the idea that technological change and increase in productivity would lead to more jobs and higher wages but during the last few years, such technological changes have resulted in more loss of jobs than being created, leading to decline in employment growth rate.
4. Globalization has alerted the village and small-scale industries and sounded death-knell for them, as they cannot withstand the competition arising from well-organized MNCs.
5. Globalization is also posing a threat to agriculture. As with the two-way trading provisions, agricultural commodities market of poor and developing countries will be flooded with farm goods from other countries at a rate much lower than that of indigenous farm products, leading to a death-blow to many farmers.

6. A majority of multinational industries prefer cheap labour in the skilled and unskilled category and are willing to manufacture products in countries like India, which may harm the environment and may lead to commercial exploitation.
7. As a result of globalization, fast foods culture is growing in India. This has replaced home-cooked food. Traditional diets and recipes are yielding to highly processed and standardized items that have a lot of fat, sugar, and salt resulting in a global epidemic of diabetes, obesity, and other chronic diseases.

Economic Impact of Globalization

New multilateral agreements for services, intellectual properties and communications are more binding on national governments than any previous agreements. They also take on such new agendas as environmental and social conditions.

Globalization enables large companies to realize economies of scale that reduce costs and prices, which in turn supports further economic growth. Impact of globalization on industrial sector has resulted in extension of markets for the domestic companies. Highly advanced technologies are available at much cheaper prices. The contribution of export sector has increased in the overall GDP growth rate. With growing global markets for services, people can now execute trade services globally – from medical advice to software writing to data processing, that could never really be traded before.

Impact of Globalization on Education

There is immense shift observed in the educational sector due to globalization. With introduction of information technology, the Indian educational system is facing challenges of globalization and it offers opportunities to evolve new paradigm shifts in developmental education. Globalization promotes new tools and techniques such as e-learning, flexible learning, distance learning and overseas training.

Impact of Globalization on Agriculture

Agriculture occupied 43 per cent of India's geographical areas and 60 per cent of the population still depends on agriculture for their livelihood. Agriculture scientists are applying new technologies and instruments in growing crops. Special assistance and loans from world bank as well as other international financial institutions are provided which has resulted in large number of benefits for the agriculture sector.

Technological and Cultural Impact of Globalization

Telecommunication and software industries are booming in India. Entertainment sector in India has a worldwide market. Bollywood movies are distributed and accepted worldwide. Big international companies are investing in this sector. Famous international brands are investing in the Indian market resulting in changing of the fashion statement of Indians.

Conclusion

Globalization means a combination of economies and societies through cross country flow of ideas, goods, services, capital, finance and people. Globalization is described by theorists as the process through which societies and economies are integrated through cross border flows of communication, technology, capital, and information. There are few challenges due to globalization such as migration, competition, and changes in skills and technology. Globalization has proven advantageous to professional and skilled individuals, primarily from urban regions.

Flowing with globalization, India is shining in nearly every prospect. India is getting a global recognition and slowly moving towards becoming a major economic and political strength. Though the development is progressing rapidly, still many basic problems like rural poverty, corruption, and political instability remained unsolved. The process of globalization has changed the industrial pattern and social life of people. Today, in this age of information technology, new ways of communication have made the world a very small place. It is also true that globalization brings in its wake, great enquiry, mass impoverishment and misery. It almost irreversibly widens the gap between the developed and the developing nations. The process of globalization is that it is more harmful to the developing and the under developed countries. The choice for the developing countries like India lies not in total global integration, but less of global integration and more of self reliance and self sustenance with an emphasis on indigenous and traditional production and knowledge system.

CONSUMERISM

Consumerism is a social as well as an economic order which means the 'emphasis on or preoccupation with the acquisition of consumer goods'. Consumerism essentially means the growing wants and needs of an individual for goods and services. India is one of the largest and fastest growing economies in the world. The Indian consumer, due to his exposure of the global market, strives to get the best of the goods in their homeland. Consumer tastes and preferences are definitely changing the retail sector – both organized and unorganized strive hard to cater to the vast range of Indian consumers. The retail sector in India, with its present pace, is expected to grow at a rate of 25 to 30 per cent annually. Being the fifth largest retail industry in the world, the trends of the retail industry in India is quite remarkable. The consumer group can literally be divided into three clear groups:

1. The first group comprises of consumers who are extremely brand conscious and depend upon the high-end retail stores to satisfy their needs.
2. The second group is another extreme who satisfy their consumer needs from outlets that do not hold popular brands and are also much cheaper.

3. The third group, however, follows the middle path – they satisfy their consumer needs either from high-end retail outlets or the less popular retail outlets, as and when necessary.

Consumerism is a social and economic order that is based on the systematic creation and promoting a desire to purchase goods and services in greater amounts. As a social value, it encourages people to purchase as many things as they possibly can, without questioning the necessity. And, while buying is essential to the survival of businesses, individuals and society as a whole, consumerism encourages people to buy things, attempting to expand the 'want' of the people. Advocating that quality is more important than quantity, it tries to satisfy the consumers. Moreover, consumerism is largely a media-related idea with billions of dollars that are spent each year trying to convince people that if they do not have a particular company's products, then their lives will not be as good. Many would argue that consumerism has emerged through a historical process that has created a capitalist society. It is shaped by mass markets and cultural attitudes, which warrant an ever-growing consumption and is also, to an extent, driven by conspicuous consumption which is lavish spending on goods and services acquired mainly for the purpose of displaying income or wealth and maintaining social status.

Hindrances to the Growth of Consumerism

1. Lack of effective implementation of legislative measures.
2. Difficulty in disseminating consumer education.
3. Cumbersome legal process.

Impact of Consumerism

Consumerism has provided the required momentum for the growth of economies and has led to healthy competition in the trade markets. On the other hand, it is also the crux of problems like creation and maintenance of the false self, spiritual emptiness, detachment from nature, and sustainability. With the rise of consumerism, our global society has become increasingly focussed on consuming goods and services, as a means to feel good about ourselves and to drive the economies of the world (McKibben, 1989; Suzuki, 1997). Also, current levels of consumption are ecologically destructive and unsustainable, as is noted by Kanner and Gomes: 'The ecological impacts of manufacturing, transporting, marketing, packaging, and storing so many items is incredibly high' (1995: 84).

The Positives

1. *Consumerism stimulates the economy:* People regularly spend money in shops and online, and thereby, huge amounts are regularly pumped into local and global businesses. For an economy, stimulation is always a necessity.
2. *More awareness:* Consumers in the present times are more aware of their rights, the companies' rights and they are constantly being made aware

of exactly what they are buying. Be it nutritional information and health warnings or details about what a product is made up of, labels carry all information in a clear and concise manner.

3. *Higher growth:* More goods and services are available to choose from. Also, since companies begin to compete to improve sales, there is scope for innovation.
4. *More employment:* Increased production will increase employment opportunities.

The Negatives

1. *Left in debt:* A negative impact that consumerism has is that it makes anyone who cannot afford to buy the products bombarded with the feeling of being left out. This leads to a negative effect on people's attitudes and often leads to people getting the credit that they cannot afford to pay back. This means people are then dealing with debt, which makes them feel even worse than they did before. Hence, it is a vicious cycle.
2. *Decline in spiritual values:* Material wealth is the deciding factor about whether a society is highly developed or not. Spiritual values are undermined. This may not be suitable to a person, particularly who is appreciative of spiritual values.
3. *Ecological imbalance:* The natural habitat is being destroyed to create more goods and build more buildings affecting the climate. Global warming will eventually result in health problems. Industrial pollution is affecting people's health in many ways.
4. *Misuse of land and resources:* It is well documented that the depletion of resources and environmental degradation is directly related to consumption of goods and services (Brown, 2001; Brower and Leon, 1999; Gardner and Stern, 2002).
5. *Pollution:* Increased consumption leads to increased levels of pollution. For instance, take the case of automobiles: more consumption as a result of consumerism will add to pollution. Other examples include, industrial waste that is dumped into rivers and oceans, waste from the tourist industry, waste from agriculture, consumer waste such as household waste, excessive product packaging, the new 'throw-away' culture, and so on.
6. *Marginalization of poor:* Mass consumption increases in the wealthy nations that receive these exports at cheap prices and demands are further increased. Poor producers are further marginalized as the wealthy export producers use even more resources for the drive for further profits to meet this demand.

The main cause of the current environmental crisis is human nature. More specifically, all that we are doing is what all other creatures have ever done to survive, i.e. expanding into whatever territory is available and using up whatever resources are available and one day it may result into death in their own waste. The wants and desires of the people change according to time. The more their income, the better their purchasing power. But in case, they are not able to do so, then they feel dissatisfied. India is also progressing towards materialism, although this goes against its ancient philosophical approach towards materialism, which favours a simple, non-materialistic life. The eastern spiritualism and philosophy have always laid emphasis on simplicity. Gandhian principles and values favour a non-materialistic approach to life. Material wealth is the deciding factor about whether a society is highly developed or not. Spiritual values are underplayed. India is experiencing many societal changes, including the expanding role of women, increased individualism, shifting roles within families, and rising national pride. These shifts have the potential to fundamentally alter how Indian consumers spend. Personal relationships also get affected as people are busy trying to earn more to maintain their standard of living. Cheaper goods are imported from other countries, affecting the growth of locally based manufacturing industries. Consumerism has also resulted in ecological imbalances. The natural habitat is being destroyed to create more goods and build more buildings which is affecting the weather. Global warming will eventually result in health problems. Industrial pollution is affecting people in many ways. Crime rate also increases as wants to possess expensive gadgets increase. Thefts have become common and daylight robberies are taking place.

Rights and Responsibilities of Consumers

Consumer responsibilities refer to the responsibility of having awareness of the quality and safety of goods and services while purchasing. It also entails responsibility to speak out and to inform manufacturer and government about needs and wants. The consumer should also feel the responsibility to complain or inform business, along with other people, about discontentment with a product or service in an honest way. Under Section 6 of Consumer Protection Act, consumer has the following rights:

Right to choose: Consumers must be provided free choice and alternatives when it comes to choosing commodities and services offered by various companies. The government emboldens this right of fair commerce by ensuring limits on price gouging, underselling, patent ownership, monopolies, and anti-trust.

Right to be informed: This right ensures that proper informational programmes are in place that is easily accessible and helps consumers make purchasing decisions. Businesses must provide customers with complete and accurate information, permitting them to make informed decisions about products and services. This includes correct packaging, advertising, and full disclosure of past issues.

Right to safety: Consumers have the right to safeguard against injuries or physical harm (excluding automobiles). The main application of this right is in the healthcare, pharmaceuticals, food processing and Automobiles sector as these have a direct impact on health. It aims to protect consumers against immoral practices. This right needs each product, which can potentially be a danger to our lives, to be marketed after adequate and complete verification as well as validation.

Right to be heard: Consumers have the right to voice complaints, criticisms, grievances, and concerns regarding company practices and products in order to make sure that their interests are not harmed by such practices. It also includes the right to be represented in various forums formed to consider the consumer welfare.

Right to redress: The right to redress provides for consumers to receive a fair settlement of just claims, including compensation for misrepresentation, shoddy goods, or unsatisfactory services. It includes right to a settlement of the genuine grievances of the consumer.

Right to consumer education: It means the right to acquire the knowledge and skill to be informed throughout life.

Redressal Mechanism

The Act of 1986 prescribes for a quasi-judicial machinery for the purpose of redressal of consumer-related disputes. The fundamental principles upon which the working of these quasi-judicial body rests are the principles of natural justice. Further, the act empowers such bodies to give reliefs of specific nature and award appropriate compensation to the aggrieved party as they may find it fit in a particular case.

Conclusion

However, in order to understand the relation between globalization and consumerism, it is important to take note of the possible access to resources and markets on a global basis, production of consumers all over the world – which were not easily available before – and the essential understanding of globalization and the notion of consumerism. Through the working of the aforementioned factors, consumerism becomes a process that is triggered off by globalization and eventually the two make up an interrelated mechanism.

In the present world, some characteristics of consumption are: (a) choices of consumption are being influenced by certain actors, (b) what is to be produced and not is being decided by certain actors, (c) a uniformity of consumption patterns is being created throughout the world, and (d) material value influences relationships among people.

There is a structured system behind the present prevalent forms of consumption and consumerism that are operating by the actors of a global economy which have the power to control the global market forces of a globalized economy. Within this context, there are trends that have been identified around globalization and consumerism which have made consumerism an issue at present. Some of the trends of consumption in the present times are:

1. Inequality of consumption (not redistributing from high-income to low-income consumers).
2. Use of pollutant goods and production technologies instead of cleaner ones.
3. Promoting goods that discourage poor producers rather than promoting goods to empower poor producers.
4. Creating a priority among consumers for consumption to conspicuous display rather than to meeting basic needs.

Hence, globalization and consumerism today are accelerating the dynamics of the consumption-poverty-inequality-environment nexus. Moreover, two of the major criticisms of globalization and consumerism are unequal distribution of wealth and unsustainable consumption patterns. One major problem of consumerism is that consumption patterns today are not able to meet everyone's needs. The system that drives these consumption patterns contributes to inequality as well as unsustainability. Thus, globalization and consumerism create two important issues: (a) patterns and effects which exacerbate inequalities, and (b) unsustainable consumption and the depletion of the environmental resources.

The consumerism is critical to the contemporary forms of globalization and it is also essential to understand the relationship between globalization and consumerism: 'This connection could be grasped in the fact that globalization enables access to resources as well as markets globally. Furthermore, to this argument, it could be asserted that the emergence of consumerism parallels the emergence of free market. The globalization-led consumerism in its nature creates two important issues which could be taken into debate: the patterns and effects which exacerbate inequalities and the unsustainable consumption and depletion of the environmental resources'.

To conclude, the most recent obsession to have gripped the government of our country is to promote consumerism and globalization. Today, the focus is on raising the rate of economic growth calculated in aggregate terms, not on raising the living standards of those needing it most. It is assumed that some of the gains will eventually trickle down to the poor. There is no sign of that; instead, the gulf between the rich and the poor is widening. It is also argued that today India has maximum number of millionaires, but at the same time, the number of those living below the poverty line is also highest in the world. The basic problems of unemployment, illiteracy and economic disparity are not addressed. Agriculture, which sustains majority of our people, is neglected. Their fate is reflected in the rising number of suicides among farmers.

The victims of the cult of consumerism are not only the poor; all sections of our society are infected. The constant marketing campaign to buy more has led to spiralling indebtedness. Families have been disrupted, envy aroused and social tensions exacerbated. The root cause of the sickness is the view that sees progress and development purely in material terms. No other values are recognized, certainly not the ethical values of social justice and other non-material attributes of a healthy society.

References

Appudurai, Arjun, *Modernity at Large: Cultural Dimensions of Globalization*, University of Minnesota Press, Minneapolis, 2006.

Bentley, J.H., 'AHR Forum: Cross-cultural Interaction and Periodization in World History', *American Historical Review*, Vol. 101, 1996, pp. 749–70.

——, 'Asia in World History', *Education about Asia*, Vol. 4, 1999, pp. 5–9.

Brower, M. and Leon, W., *The Consumer's Guide to Effective Environmental Choices: Practical Advice from the Union of Concerned Scientists*, Three Rivers Press, New York, 1999.

Brown, L.R., *Eco-Economy: Building an Economy for the Earth*, W.W. Norton & Company, Inc., New York, 2001.

Frank, A.G., *Reorient: Global Economy in the Asian Age*, University of California Press, Berkeley, 1998.

Gardner, G. and Stern, P., *Environmental Problems and Human Behavior* (2nd edn), Pearson Custom Publishing, Boston, MA, 2002.

Joshi, Rakesh Mohan, *International Business*, Oxford University Press, New Delhi, 2009.

Kanner, A.D. and Gomes, M.E., 'The All-consuming Self', in T. Roszak, M.E. Gomes and A.D. Kanner (eds), *Ecopsychology: Restoring the Earth, Healing the Mind*, Sierra Club Books, San Francisco, CA, 1995.

McKibben, B., *The End of Nature*, Anchor Books, New York, 1989.

Moghadam, V.M., *Globalizing Women: Transnational Feminist Networks*, The Johns Hopkins University Press, Baltimore, MD, 2005.

Pramanick, S.K. and Ganguli, Ramanuj, *Globalization in India: New Frontiers and Emerging Challenges*, PHI Learning Pvt. Ltd., New Delhi, 2010.

Rajkobal, Praveena, 'Globalization, Consumerism and Unsustainable Consumption', Background Paper (Final), IGD Program, SPARC Colombo University.

Shah, A., Behind Consumption and Consumerism,<www.globalissues.org/Trade Related/ Consumption.asp> 2006.

Shangquan, Gao, 'Economic Globalization: Trends, Risks and Risk Prevention', *Economic and Social Affairs*, CDP/1, 2000.

Shiva, Vandana, *Stolen Harvest*, South End Press, London, 2000.

Soros, George, *On Globalization*, Public Affairs, New York, 2002.

Stearns, P.N., *Consumerism in World History: The Global Transformation of Desire*, Routledge, London, United Kingdom, 2001.

Suzuki, D., *The Sacred Balance: Rediscovering Our Role in Nature*, Greystone Books, Vancouver, British Columbia, 1997.

14

Crime and Criminals

Crime Report India (2016) – Highlights

1. Delhi records 40 per cent incidents of all the rape incidents in the country. A rape occurs in every five minutes in Delhi. There are 30 per cent of crimes against women uncured in Delhi alone.
2. *Crime against women:* There are 41,761 offences reported against women.
3. *Abduction of women:* A total of 9,256 abductions have taken place.
4. *Rape incidents:* There are 4,935 cases of rape.
5. *Sexual exploitation of children:* There are 4,473 children reported to have been sexually exploited in 19 metros (only those 19 cities are covered which have a population of more than 20 million).
6. *Domestic violence:* A total of 12,218 cases have been registered in 19 metros of the country.
7. Delhi experienced a 10 per cent hike in the criminal cases in 2016 as compared to 2015.
8. *Kidnapping:* In the year 2016, Delhi received 5,453 (48.3%) cases, Mumbai 1,876 (16.6%) and Bengaluru reported 879 (7.8%) cases of kidnapping in the country.
9. As per the definition of crime given by the Indian Penal Code, criminal cases were highest in Uttar Pradesh (9.5%) whereas with 8.9 per cent cases Madhya Pradesh was at the second spot and Maharashtra reported 8.8 per cent cases.
10. With 38.8 per cent share in the crimes committed in cities across the country, Delhi is at the top of the list. Following this, Bangalore is ranked second with 8.9 per cent crime and Mumbai is at the third spot, where 7.7 per cent of the country's criminal cases have been registered.
11. Criminal activities have increased across the country by 2.6 per cent in 2016 as compared to 2015.

The word 'crime' was originally taken from a Latin term *'crimen'* which means 'charge' or 'offence'. The Greek expression *'krimos'* is synonymous to a

Sanskrit word *'krama'* which means 'social order'. Therefore, in common parlance, the word crime is applied to those acts that go against social order and are worthy of serious condemnation. According to Adler, 'crime' is merely, 'an instance of behaviour prohibited by criminal law'. Crime in the Indian context is an activity that involves breaking the law and enforcement.

There are many types of different crimes. In some crimes, only one individual is involved and in some other crimes, there are many persons who are organized for the purpose of crime. There are such bands of criminals working at the national level and even there are bands of criminals whose field of crime is international. It is not only the males to be criminals but there are females and children also engaged in criminal acts. Sutherland, a criminologist, considers the seriousness of crimes and divides them broadly into two types of crimes: (a) Ordinary types of crime and (b) Serious types of crime. Bojore, another expert, classifies crimes into four main types depending upon their purpose or objective: (a) Monetary crimes: crimes are done to get money – theft, dacoity, fraud, forgery, contraband currency, etc. (b) Sexual crimes – rape, homosexuality, (c) Political crimes – espionage (international), treachery, treason etc. (d) Miscellaneous crimes – crimes other than the above types, e.g. quarrels, fights, kidnapping or addiction to narcotics, etc.

Sociologists and criminologists have been broadly concerned with locating the causes of crime and analysing the effectiveness of the criminal justice system. Recently, some scholars have moved beyond these narrow twin concerns and have raised questions about the enactment of laws, improving the police system, judicial activism, protecting the interests of victims, improving the condition in prisons and humanizing the deviant.

Concept of Crime

Let us first look at the concepts of crime and criminals and also identify various types of crimes and criminals. Since official statistics are based on the legal definition of crime, as the system of criminal justice is perceived from a legal approach, since all empirical studies on criminals focus on crime defined by law, and since legal definition of crime is considered to be precise, unambiguous and capable of measurement, let us examine this legal definition (of crime) first.

Tappan (1960: 10) has defined crime as 'an intentional act or omission in violation of criminal law committed without defence or justification'. Five elements are important in this definition: (a) It should be an act or omission of an act, that is, a person cannot be punished for his/her thoughts. (b) The act must be voluntary and committed when the actor has control over his actions. (c) The act should be intentional, whether the intent be general or specific. A person may not have a specific intent to shoot another person and kill him, but he is expected to know that his action might result in injury or death of others. (d) It should be a violation of a criminal law (as distinct from a non-criminal law or civil and administrative law). This is necessary so that the state can take action against the accused. (e) It (the act) should be committed without defence or justification. Thus, if the act is proved to be in self-defence, or committed in insanity, it will not be considered a crime even if it causes harm or injury to others. Ignorance of law is usually not a defence.

Hall Jerome (1947: 8–18) has defined crime as 'legally forbidden and intentional action, which has a harmful impact on social interests, which has a criminal intent, and which has legally prescribed punishment for it'. Thus, according to him, no action is to be viewed as crime unless it has five characteristics: (a) it is legally forbidden, (b) it is intentional, (c) it is harmful (to society), (d) it has criminal intent, and (e) some penalty is prescribed for it.

Crime has also been defined in non-legal or social terms. Mowrer has defined it as 'an anti-social act'. Caldwell (1956: 114) has explained it as 'those acts or failures to act that are considered to be so detrimental to the well-being of a society, as judged by its prevailing standards, that action regarding them cannot be entrusted to private initiative or to haphazard methods but must be taken by an organized society in accordance with tested procedures'. Thorsten Sellin (1938) has described it as 'violation of conduct norms of the normative groups'. Clinard (1957: 22) has, however, maintained that all deviations from norms are not crimes. He talks of three types of deviations: (a) tolerated deviation, (b) deviation which is mildly disapproved, and (c) deviation which is strongly disapproved. He perceives the third type of deviation as crime. Let us take one example in order to understand it. Gandhiji not only himself deviated from caste norms but also prompted others not to follow them. Yet, Gandhiji was not considered a deviant because his deviation was for the good of the society. The deviation that harms the society is strongly disapproved.

Criminologists with a sociological perspective have not claimed that there is no place for the legal definition of crime in criminology. They have only drawn attention to situations in which people who engage in 'criminal' behaviour are either not caught or are acquitted by courts because of inadequate evidence or legal loopholes or pressures. Taking the reconciliatory position between legal and social definitions of crime, Reid (1976: 5) has said that the legal definition may be used for compiling statistics on crime and for assigning the label 'criminal', but the studies undertaken for studying causation of crime should include such persons also in their sample of 'criminals' who admit their crime but are not convicted by court.

Crime, Criminal and Criminology

Six questions are important in criminology today (Young, 1975: 249–52). These are:

1. How is an individual's criminal behaviour explained? At the point of committing crime, is the offender perceived as acting out of free-will or is he seen as compelled by some forces beyond his control?
2. How is the functioning of social order perceived? Is order in society understood as based on the consent of the vast majority or is it largely based on the coercion?

3. How is crime defined? Is crime seen as the violation of the legal code or as a behaviour that offends the social code of a particular community?
4. How is extent and distribution of crime viewed? Is crime viewed as a limited phenomenon committed by a small number of people, or as the extensive phenomenon engaged in by a large proportion of the population?
5. How are the causes of crime explained? Are the causes of crime located primarily within the individual (that is, his personality) or is crime seen as the product of the wider society within which the individual lives?
6. What is the policy regarding criminals? Is the policy of punishing the offender appropriate or is the policy of treatment of the criminal accepted?

These questions can be framed on the basis of dichotomies as follows:
(i) Individual's behaviour: free-will versus determinism
(ii) Functioning of social order: consensus versus coercion
(iii) Definition of crime: legal versus social
(iv) Extent and distribution of crime: limited versus extensive
(v) Causes of crime: individual versus social
(vi) Policy towards criminals: punishment versus treatment

Following Fitzgerald (1975: 248–307) and Young et al. (1975), a chart (Table 1) can be presented to point out dichotomous reactions of seven different paradigms on these six questions.

Characteristics of Crime

1. Harm should have been caused, mere intention is not enough.
2. Anti-social behaviour is not crime unless prohibited by law.
3. It is an act which is both forbidden by law and inciting the moral sentiments of the society.
4. The act must be conducted which brings harmful results.
5. The harm caused must be natural consequences of the voluntary act.
6. There must be legally prescribed punishment.
7. Crime calls for punishment and if it is not punished, the society would take the law in its own hands.
8. State interference is very effective in preventing crime since it cannot be controlled in any other way.

Theoretical Explanations of Criminal Behaviour

In presenting these facts and features, the idea is to point out the weakening of motives for conformity to social norms and the disruption of social relationships and social bonds. The unrest is increasing almost in all sections of our society. There is unrest among youth, peasants, industrial workers, students, government employees and the minorities. This unrest increases frustrations and strains which lead to the violation of legal and social norms. It is, thus, the organization and the functioning of the existing sub-systems and structures in our society that are more responsible for the increase in crime. Various sets of ideas about crime causation have been developed by a

Table 1

Reactions of Different Paradigms on Important Questions of Crime and Criminals

Questions and Dichotomous Reactions	*Classicism*	*Positivism (Bio, Psy, Social Theories)*	*Conservatism*	*Strain Theory*	*New Deviancy Theory*	*Liberalism Reformism Theory*	*Marxism*
1. How is individual behaviour determined ? (free will vs determinism)	Free will	Determinism	Freewill	Determinism	Determinism	Determinism	Determinism
2. How is functioning of social order perceived ? (consensus vs coercion)	Consensus	Consensus	Coercion	Consensus	Coercion	Coercion	Coercion
3. Definition of crime (legal vs social)	Legal	Social	Social	Social	Legal	Legal	Legal
4. Extent of crime (limited vs extensive)	Limited	Limited	Extensive	Limited	Limited	Limited	Limited
5. Causes of crime (individual vs social)	Individual	Social	Individual	Social	Social	Social	Social
6. Policy towards criminal (punishment vs treatment)	Punishment	Treatment	Punishment	*	*	Treatment	*

* They emphasize changing the functioning of social structures and social systems.

number of scholars, stemming primarily from Durkheim, moving to scholars like Merton, Cohen, Miller, Cloward and Ohlin. We shall attempt to analyse some of these viewpoints.

Table 2

Theoretical Explanations of Causes of Crime

Theoretical Explanation	*Propounder*	*Year*	*Main Thesis that Crime is Result of*
1. *Classicist*	Beccaria	1764	(i) Man's rational motivation (ii) Hedonism or pain/pleasure principle
2. *Biogenic*			Inherited traits
(i) Evolutionary Atavism Theory	Lombroso	1876	Physical stigmata or defective organisms
(ii) Goring's Theory	Charles Goring	1919	Defective anatomical factors
(iii) Hooton's Theory	Hooton	1939	Biological inferiority
(iv) Physiological Make-up Theory	Sheldon	1940	Mesomorphic physique
3. *Psychogenic*			Defective personality
(i) Psychiatric Theory	William Healy	1915	Mental disorders or emotional disturbances
(ii) Psycho-analytical Theory	Adler, Abrahamsen, etc.	1952	Instincts
4. *Sociogenic*			Learnt and conditioned by social environment
(A) Processual Explanation			
(i) Differential Association Theory	Sutherland	1939	Associations with and social influences of criminalistic norms
(ii) Labelling Theory	Howard Becker	1963	Consequences of the application by others of rules and sanctions to an 'offender'
(B) Structural Explanation			
(i) Economic Theory	Fornasari & Bonger	1894, 1916	Economic conditions
(ii) Geographical Theory	Dexter, Quetlet, etc.	1904	Geographical factors like climate
(iii) Sociological Theory			
(a) Anomie Theory	Merton	1938	Strains caused by disjunction between goals and means
(b) Differential Opportunity Theory	Cloward & Ohlin	1960	Differentials in legitimate and illegitimate means to success-goals
(c) Delinquent subculture Theory	Cohen	1955	Rejection of dominant values and development of delinquent values
(d) Containment Theory	Walter Reckless	1967	Unfavourable self-concept

The theoretical explanations of criminal behaviour have been classified into six groups: (a) biological or constitutional explanations, (b) mental subnormality, illness and psycho-pathological explanations, (c) economic explanation, (d) topographical explanation, (e) (human) environmental explanation, and (f) 'new' and 'radical' explanation.

Reid (1976: 103–251) has classified the theoretical explanations as: (a) classical and positive theories, (b) physiological, psychiatric and psychological theories, and (c) sociological theories. He has further sub-classified the sociological theories in two groups: (i) social structural theories (including Merton's, Cohen's, Cloward and Ohlin's, Matza's, Miller's, and Quinney's theories), and (ii) social process theories (including Sutherland's and Howard Becker's theories).

We will discuss these theories by dividing them in four groups: (a) classicist, (b) biogenic, (c) psychogenic, and (d) sociogenic.

Classicist Explanation

Classicist explanations of crime and punishment were developed in the second half of the eighteenth century. In fact, these theoretical explanations developed as reaction to the enlightened thinkers and political reformers against the arbitrary systems of justice and the barbarous codes of punishment which prevailed up to the eighteenth century. They demanded a legal system that would defend the interests of criminals and protect their rights and liberties. They believed in the 'contract theory' of the origin of state (propounded by Rousseau), that is, regulating the conduct of free individuals who were bound to one another within the society by a free and 'legal' contract between free and equal individuals. Thus, individuals were conceived as free, rational and sovereign individuals, capable of defining their self-interests and rationally thinking of the consequences of their actions. They, therefore, thought of state/society not as something sovereign but as something which individuals had contracted to establish for their individual and mutual benefit. Thus, they sought to limit the power of the state to defence of the rights and liberties, as well as safety and security of the individual.

The propounder of the classicist explanation was an Italian thinker Beccaria who was influenced by the writings of scholars like Bentham and John Howard. Beccaria and his classical school maintained that (a) human nature is rational, free, and governed by self-interest, (b) social order is based on consensus and social contract, (c) crime is the infringement of the legal code and not of social norm, (d) distribution of crime is limited and is to be ascertained through a 'due process', (e) crime is caused by an individual's rational motivation, and (f) in punishing the offender, the principle of 'restraint' should be observed.

The main postulates of Beccaria's classical explanation (Schafer, 1969: 106) developed in 1764 were:

1. Man's behaviour is purposive and rational and is based on hedonism or pleasure-pain principle, that is, he consciously chooses pleasure and avoids pain.
2. Punishment should be assigned to each crime so that the pain would outweigh any pleasure from the commission of crime.
3. Punishment should not be severe and deterrent but it should be proportionate to crime and also be predetermined, prompt, and public.
4. The law must apply equally to all citizens.
5. The legislatures should clearly enact the law and prescribe specific punishment for its violation. The judges should not interpret the law but should only decide whether a person committed the crime (violated the law) or not. In other words, courts should only determine innocence or guilt and thereafter prescribe the set punishment.

The major weaknesses in the classical explanation were: (a) all criminals were to be treated alike without differentiating them on the basis of age, sex or intelligence; (b) no importance was given to the nature of crime (that is, whether the crime was a felony or misdemeanour) or the type of the criminal (that is, whether he was a first offender, a casual offender, a habitual offender, or a professional offender); (c) explaining an individual's behaviour merely on the doctrine of 'free-will' and suggesting punishment on the principle of 'utilitarianism' is only an armchair philosophy which considers crime in the abstract and lacks a scientific approach in the objective and empirical measurement; (d) there was no provision for justifiable criminal acts; and (e) Beccaria and Bentham were more concerned with reform in the criminal law like mitigation of severity of punishment, removal of defects in the Jury system, abolition of transportation and capital punishment and adoption of a prison philosophy and regulating morality, than in controlling crime or development of criminological theories.

The British neo-classicist criminologists revised the classical theory in 1810 and 1819 and provided for judicial discretion and introduced the idea of minimum and maximum sentences (Vold, 1958: 25–26). Describing the concept of equal justice as unreal, they suggested giving importance to age, mental condition and extenuating circumstances in fixing punishment to criminals. Children under seven years of age and mentally diseased persons were to be exempted from the law. However, in spite of these changes, the neo-classicists accepted the principles of free-will and hedonism. As such, this school also has not been considered as a scientific school of criminology.

Biogenic Explanation

The positivists rejected the concept of 'free-will' advocated by the classicists and the neo-classicists and emphasized the doctrine of 'determinism'. Lombroso, Ferri and Garofalo were the major positivists who emphasized the biogenic or hereditary aspects of criminal behaviour. (Heredity is the parental contribution made through 46 chromosomes. Of these, two determine the sex of the infant and 44 affect other qualities of the body. The combinations and permutations among the genes determine the infant's particular genotype, that is, genetic contribution of an organism).

Lombroso, an Italian physician and professor of Clinical Psychiatry and Criminal Anthropology and described as the 'Father of Criminology', propounded the Theory of Evolutionary Atavism (also called Theory of Physical Criminal Type or Theory of Born Criminals) in 1876. He claimed that the criminal is of a different physical type than the non-criminal (1911: 365). A criminal suffers from many physical abnormalities. As such, he can be identified by a number of characteristics or stigmata, like asymmetrical face, large ears, excessively long arms, flattened nose, retreating forehead, tufted and crispy hair, insensibility to pain, eye defects and other physical peculiarities. Lombroso not only pointed out differences in physical characteristics between criminals and non-criminals but he also gave characteristics that distinguished criminals according to the type of crime they committed.

Charles Goring, an English psychiatrist and philosopher, criticized Lombroso's theory on the basis of his own study in which he measured the characteristics of 3,000 English convicts and a large number of non-criminals in 1913. He maintained that there was no such thing as a physical criminal type. However, he himself explained crime on the basis of hereditary factors (1919: 11) using the statistical treatment of facts, or what is called the statistico-mathematical method. But Goring's work was also criticized because (a) he committed the same errors in statistical analysis for which he had criticized Lombroso. He measured intelligence not by the available Simon-Binet tests but by his own impression of the mental ability of the criminals, (b) he completely ignored the impact of environment on crime, (c) the sample of non-criminals which included undergraduate university students, inmates of a hospital, mental patients and soldiers was defective, and (d) he was violently prejudiced against Lombroso (Reid, 1976: 120–21).

Though, Ferri and Garofalo too had supported Lombroso but he (Lombroso) modified his theory at the end of his life and said that all criminals are not 'born criminals'. There are 'criminaloids' (who are individuals of normal physical and psychological make-up), occasional criminals, and criminals by passion. The main criticisms against Lombroso's theoretical explanations are: (a) his collection of facts was confined to organic factors and he neglected the psychic and social factors; (b) his method was mainly descriptive and not experimental; (c) his generalizations about atavism and degeneracy left a gap between theory and fact. He adjusted facts to fit into his theory; (d) his generalization (about atavism) was drawn from a single case and is, therefore unscientific; and (e) his use of statistics was actually not tested by the data. In spite of these criticisms, Lombroso's contribution to the development of criminological thought has been recognized on the basis that he redirected emphasis from the crime to the criminal.

Interest on biogenic variables was revised by a Harvard physical anthropologist Hooton in 1939. On the basis of his 12 year study of 13,873 male prisoners compared to a small number of 3,203 male non-offenders, he concluded that the primary cause of crime is 'biological inferiority'. The four conclusions he drew from his study (1939) were: (a) criminal behaviour is the direct result of inherited biological inferiority as shown by characteristics like sloping foreheads, thin lips, straight hair, body hair, small ears, long thin necks and sloping shoulders, (b) particular types of crime are caused by particular types of biological inferiority. Tall and thin men tend to be murderers and robbers, tall and heavy men tend to be cheats, short statured and thin men tend to be thieves and burglars, and short heavy men are prone to commit sexual crimes, (c) criminals are organically inferior, and (d) elimination of crime can be effected only by the sterilization of the physically and mentally unfit persons.

He further held that in every society, there are a few geniuses, hordes of mediocres, masses of morons, and regiments of criminals. He gave three types of biologically inferior people: (a) who are organically unadaptable, (b) mentally stunted, and (c) sociologically warped.

His theory was, however, criticized by Albert Cohen, Alfred Lindesmith and Karl Schuessler (see Sutherland and Cressay, 1965: 118–19; Vold, 1958: 59–64; Gibbons, 1977: 139–40) on the arguments that: (a) his control groups of non-offenders were small in size and represented types that could be expected to be superior intellectually (university students) and physically stronger (firemen); (b) the sample of criminals was unrepresented as it was drawn only from an imprisoned population; (c) his research methodology was defective; (d) he had no explicit criterion of 'biological inferiority'; and (e) he offered no evidence that physical inferiority is hereditary.

Sheldon related crime with physiological make-up or body constitution in 1940. He classified individuals on the basis of their physique (or body types) into three groups: endomorphic, ectomorphic and mesomorphic. Individuals with the first type of physique (with small bones, short limbs, and soft, smooth and velvety skin) love comfort and luxury and are essentially extroverts; those with the second type of physique (with lean, fragile, delicate body, small delicate bones) are introverts, full of functional complaints, sensitive to noise, who complain of chronic fatigue, and shrink from crowds and individuals; and those with the third type of physique (with strong muscles and bones, heavy chest and large wrists and hands) are active, dynamic, assertive and aggressive. Sheldon developed scales for measuring the body-type dimensions in which individuals were scored on each component between 1 to 7 scores. However, Sheldon's hypothesis that there is a relationship between delinquent behaviour and body-types and that the delinquents are somewhat more mesomorphic in body structure than are the non-delinquents has not been convincingly proved. Crime is a social process and not a biologically determined pattern of behaviour.

If we were to compare the main points of the classical school with the positivist school, we could say that (a) the former emphasized the legal definition of crime, the latter rejected the legal definition; (b) the former believed in the doctrine of free-will, the latter believed in determinism; (c) the former did not use empirical research, while the latter did; (d) the former concentrated on crime (in suggesting punishment), the latter on the criminal, (e) the former suggested death penalty for some offences, the latter recommended abolition of death penalty; and (f) the former was in favour of a definite sentence, the latter was in favour of an indeterminate sentence.

Besides the above theories, some studies on identical twins have also laid emphasis on heredity as an important factor in crime. For example, Lange (1931) compared the behaviour of male twins in several prisons with the non-institutionalized twins. He found that in the case of identical twins (born of a single fertilized ovum), 10 of the 15 pairs were concordant (both members of a twin pair having the same characteristics) while in the case of fraternal twins (born of separate ova), 15 of the 17 pairs were discordant (both twin members having different characteristics).

Kranz (Cf. Rosenthal, *Genetic Theory and Abnormal Behaviour,* 1970) in his 1936 study of twins and criminality found 66 per cent twins concordant among identical twins and 54 per cent among fraternal twins. Christiansen (Cf. Reuck and Porter, *The Mentally Abnormal,* 1968) in his study of 6,000 pairs born between 1880 and 1890 in Denmark found that with respect to criminal behaviour, identical twins were concordant in 66.7 per cent cases as compared to 30.4 per cent of the fraternal twins.

The criticism against explaining criminal behaviour in terms of inherited factors is that the similarities of the behaviour of identical twins could be the result of living in the same environment and be totally unrelated to heredity. Second, if heredity is the cause of crime, there should be no cases of identical twins where one is a criminal and the other is not. On similar lines, the studies of family lines (Jukes by Dugdale in 1877; Kallikaks by Goddard in 1911, etc.) as evidence of inherited criminality have also been rejected.

Psychogenic Explanation

The psychogenic theories trace crime in some defect in the personality of the offender or 'in the inside of the person'. The psychological theory emphasizes feeblemindedness (low Intelligence Quotient or IQ), the psychiatric theory on the mental disorders, and the psychoanalytical theory on the undeveloped ego, or drives and instincts, or guilt-feelings or inferiority complex.

Henry Goddard (1920) reported results on intelligence tests in 1919 and maintained that the greatest single cause of delinquency and crime is feeble-mindedness (very low IQ). He said that feeblemindedness is inherited and is rarely affected by life events. He emphasized that a criminal is not born but made. But Goddard did not believe that every feeble-minded person was a criminal. He may be a potential criminal but whether he becomes one would be determined by two factors: his temperament and his environment. Thus, though feeblemindedness may be hereditary, criminality is not hereditary.

In 1928–29, Sutherland and Cressay (1965: 357–75) analysed 350 reports on studies on intelligence tests covering little less than two lakh criminals and delinquents to examine the relationship between crime and mental deficiencies. They discovered that: (a) 50 per cent criminals were diagnosed as feeble-minded in the studies conducted between 1910–14, but only about 20 per cent were found criminals in studies in the period 1925–28; (b) there was a negligible difference in the mental age of criminals and non-criminals; (c) the discipline among low-mentality prisoners was the same as among high-mentality prisoners; and (d) conformity to parole conditions of the feeble-minded and the ordinary parolees was almost equal. They, thus, concluded that low mentality of the feeble-minded is not a significant cause of criminality.

Psychiatric Explanation

William Healy, a psychiatrist in Chicago, disagreeing with his physician colleagues that juvenile delinquency was caused by defective organisms or anatomical factors emphasized on personality defects and disorders, or 'psychogenic traits' as the cause of crime. In broader terms, psychogenic traits cause those ways of behaviour which are established in the infant or the young child through emotional interaction within the family. These traits refer to extroversion or introversion, dominance or submission, optimism or pessimism, emotional independence or dependence, self-confidence or its absence, egocentrism or sociocentrism, and so on (Johnson, 1978: 155). In narrower terms, however, the term 'psychogenic' is referred to 'mental disorder' or 'emotional disturbances'. Analysing psychological factors Healy found a greater frequency of personality disorders among delinquents than among non-delinquents.

Psychiatrists have given three types of mental disorders or psychoses (that is, individuals manifesting severe decompression, distortion of reality and loss of contact with reality): (a) schizophrenia (exhibiting tendency to retreat from reality through delusions and hallucinations), (b) maniac-depressive disorder (exhibiting fluctuations in mood), and (c) paranoia. The estimate is that only 1.5 per cent to 2 per cent criminals are psychotic, of whom the schizophrenic is the most common among such offenders.

A study of 10,000 felons in New York between 1932 and 1935 also pointed out that only 1.5 per cent were psychotic, 6.9 per cent were psycho-neurotic, 6.9 per cent were psychopathic and 2.4 per cent were feeble-minded. Thus, 82.3 per cent of offenders were diagnosed as 'normal'. Another study of Paul Schilder (*Journal of Criminal Psychopathology*, October 1940: 152) in 1937 in New York pointed out that 83.8 per cent offenders were 'normal'. Faris and Dunham's (1939) study of 500 males in Illinois hospital showed that schizophrenia was a negligible factor in the causation of crime. Thus, all these investigations show that the psychiatric theory has proved untenable.

Serious methodological errors have been pointed out in Healy's researches too: (a) his samples are small and unrepresentative; (b) his terms are either not defined or vaguely defined, for example, 'normal emotional control' and 'good living conditions'. How are these factors to be measured; and (c) research fails to explain why some children who have the traits believed to be characteristic of delinquents do not become delinquents and why some children who do not have those traits do become delinquents. By now, we might conclude that psychiatric theory stands rejected.

Psycho-analytical Explanation

Sigmund Freud, who developed the psycho-analytical theory at the end of the nineteenth and the beginning of the twentieth century, did not advance a theory of criminality. But his approach and the three elements of Id, ego, and superego have been used by others like Adler, Abrahamsen, Aichhorn and Friedlander to explain criminal behaviour. Id is an individual's raw instinct or desire or drive or urge; ego is the reality; and super-ego is an individual's conscience or moral pressure. Super-ego constantly tries to suppress the Id while the ego is the acceptable balance between the Id and the super-ego. The Id and superego are basically unconscious while the ego is the conscious part of the personality.

The three propositions of psychoanalytic thoughts are: (a) behaviour is largely the product of unconscious psychological-biological forces (drives or instincts); (b) criminality arises out of conflicts related to these basic drives; and (c) to modify undesirable (criminal) behaviour, the person must be guided towards insight into the unconscious roots of his responses so that he can develop control over such impulses. In a well-balanced personality, Id, ego and super-ego work in relative harmony. But in abnormal cases (neurotic individuals), imbalance and disharmony occurs. When the super-ego is not sufficiently developed, the released repressed instincts may lead to anti-social behaviour. Conflict in the unconscious mind gives rise to feelings of guilt with a consequent desire for punishment to remove the guilt feelings and restore a balance of good against evil. The individual then commits the criminal act, leaves clues for apprehension in order to be caught and punished (Vold, 1958: 93).

August Aichhorn (1955) was the first scholar to use Freud's psychoanalytical approach in studying delinquents. He found several kinds of delinquents: some neurotic, some aggressive and lacking in super-ego development, some with little capacity for repressing their instinctual drives, and some having distorted cravings for affection.

Alfred Adler explains crime in terms of 'inferiority complex'. An individual commits crime to 'get attention' which helps him to compensate for his sense of inferiority. But Adler's theory is criticized for placing greater emphasis on the 'rational' side of an individual's behaviour and for oversimplification.

David Abrahamsen has explained crime in terms of an individual's resistance to tendencies and situations. He developed a formula:

$$C = T + \frac{S}{R}$$

where 'C' stands for crime, 'T' for tendencies, 'S' for situation, and 'R' for resistance. Criminal behaviour will result if the individual has strong criminalistic tendencies and low resistance.

Sociologists have not favourably reacted either to Abrahamsen's explanation or to psychoanalytic explanation that causes of crimes are unconscious. They say, it is an oversimplification to reduce causative factors to three factors in mathematical terms. Likewise, the explanation that the criminal commits crime because he subconsciously desires to be punished as a result of his guilt feelings cannot be accepted for all crimes because in some cases, the individual commits crime, feels guilty, and is then punished. Mannheim has also said that punishment is no deterrent for the criminal. Thus, arguments against the psychiatric theory are: (a) there is methodological and logic-of-science error in psychiatric theory; (b) the terms are vague as no operational definitions of Id, ego, super-ego or unconscious are given; (c) protective techniques are open to subjective interpretation of the analyst; (d) the researches are based on small samples and inadequate control groups; (e) so long as an individual is the focus of the approach, generalizations cannot be made regarding patterns of behaviour; and (f) this theory in fact does not explain anything in terms of the causation of criminal behaviour.

Sociogenic Explanation

While the physiological, psychiatric and psychological theoretical explanations emphasize that crime is either inherited and results from a physical or a mental factor, or is the consequence of suppressed childhood experiences, sociologists argue that criminal behaviour is learned and it is conditioned by the social environment. Sociologists have used two approaches in studying the causation of crime: the first approach studies the relationship between crime and the social structure of society; and the second approach studies the process by which an individual becomes a criminal. Thus, sociological explanations may be classified in two categories: (a) structural explanations which include economic explanation, geographical explanation and sociological explanations of Merton and Clifford Shaw and sub-culture explanations of Cohen and Cloward and Ohlin, and (b) processual explanations which include explanations of Sutherland, Howard Becker and Walter Reckless.

Economic Explanation

This explanation analyses criminal behaviour in terms of the economic conditions in society. It holds that the criminal is a product of the economic environment which provides him his ideals and his goals. It was the Italian scholar Fornasari who talked of the relationship between crime and poverty in 1884. He maintained that 60 per cent of the population of Italy is poor, and of the total crimes in Italy, 85 per cent to 90 per cent criminals belong to this section of the poor. In 1916, a Dutch scholar Bonger also emphasized the relationship between crime and the capitalistic economic structure. In a capitalistic system, man concentrates only on himself and this leads to selfishness. Man is interested only in producing for himself, specially in producing a surplus which he can exchange for profit. He is not interested in the needs of others. Capitalism, thus, breeds social irresponsibility and leads to crime.

In 1938, a British criminologist Cyril Burt (1944: 147) analysing juvenile delinquency found that 19 per cent juvenile delinquents belonged to extremely poor families and 37 per cent to poor families. He concluded that though poverty is an important factor in crime, it is not the only factor. In 1915, William Healy studied 675 juvenile delinquents and found that 5 per cent belonged to the destitute class, 22 per cent to the poor class, 35 per cent to the normal class, 34 per cent to the comfort class, and 4 per cent to the luxury class. Thus, since 73 per cent delinquents belonged to classes which were economically normal or well-off, poverty cannot be considered to be a very important factor in delinquency.

Karl Marx's view of economic determinism advocated that private ownership of property results in poverty which distinguishes those who own the means of production from those whom they exploit for economic benefit. The latter turn to crime as a result of this poverty. Thus, though Marx did not specifically develop a theory of criminal causation but he believed that the economic system was the sole determinant of crime.

Sutherland and Cressay (1965) have also said that: (a) we find more criminals in poor families because it is easy to locate them, (b) criminals belonging to upper classes use their influence and pressures in escaping arrests and convictions, and (c) reactions of administrators are biased in favour of the upper class people. Thus, today, most behavioural scientists reject the theory of economic determinism in criminal behaviour.

Geographical Explanation

This explanation evaluates crime on the basis of geographical factors like climate, temperature and humidity. It is supported by scholars like Quetlet, Dexter, Montesquiu, Kropotokin, Champneuf and many others. According to Quetlet, crimes against persons predominate in south and increase in summers, while crimes against property predominate in north and increase in winters. Champneuf supported this hypothesis of relationship between the nature of crime and the climate on the basis of his study conducted in France between 1825 and 1830. He found 181.5 property crimes against every 100 crimes against persons in north France, and 98.8 property crimes against every 100 crimes against persons in south France. On the basis of his study of property crimes conducted between 1825 and 1880, the French scholar Laccasagne also found the highest number of property crimes in December, followed by January, November and February. In the study on the effect of weather on an individual's behaviour made in 1904, the American scholar Dexter found that crime and geographical environment are highly related with each other. In 1911, a Russian scholar Kropotkin established that the rate of murder in any month/year can be predicted by calculating the average temperature and humidity of the preceding month/year. For this, he gave a mathematical formula $2(7x+y)$, where 'x' is temperature and 'y' is humidity. Multiplying the average temperature 'x' of last month with 7 and adding the average humidity of the last month 'y' to it, if we multiply the total figure with 2, we will get the number of murders to be committed in the given month.

The geographical explanation has been criticized on the ground that geographical factors may affect individual behaviour but the direct relationship between crime and geographical factors cannot be accepted as given by the scholars. Had such relationship existed, the number and nature of crime in a given geographical environment would have been the same at all times, which is not so. Hence, this theory is invalid.

Sociological Explanations

Sutherland's Theory of Differential Association

E.H. Sutherland propounded the Differential Association Theory in 1939. He says, two explanations have mainly been forwarded for criminal behaviour: situational and genetic or historical. The former explains crime on the basis of situation that persists at the time of crime, and the latter explains crime on the basis of a criminal's life experiences. He himself used the second approach in developing the theory of criminal behaviour. Suppose, a hungry boy comes across a shop and finds the shopkeeper absent and steals a loaf of bread. In this case, it is not because the shopkeeper was absent and he was hungry that the boy committed the theft, but it is because he had learnt earlier that one can satisfy his hunger by stealing things. Thus, it is not the situation which motivates a person to commit theft, it is his learnt attitudes and beliefs.

Sutherland's main thesis is that individuals encounter many inharmonious and inconsistent social influences in their life-time and many individuals become involved in contacts with carriers of criminalistic norms, and as a consequence become criminals. He called this process 'differential association' (Sutherland and Cressay, 1965: 77–79).

The theory states that criminal behaviour is learnt in a process of communication with other persons, principally in small, intimate groups. This learning includes the techniques of committing the crime. The specific direction of motives, drives, rationalizations and attitudes is learned from definitions of the legal codes as favourable or unfavourable. A person becomes criminal or delinquent because of an excess of definitions favourable to violation of law over definitions unfavourable to violation of law. This is the principle of differential association. Differential associations may vary in frequency, duration, priority and intensity. The process of learning criminal behaviour by associations with criminal and anti-criminal patterns involves all of the mechanisms that are involved in any other learning. While criminal behaviour is an expression of general needs and values, it is not explained by those needs and values since non-criminal behaviour is an expression of the same needs and values.

Sutherland's theory was supported by James Short Junior on the basis of his study of 176 school children (126 boys and 50 girls) in 1955 (Giallombardo, 1966: 85–91). Short measured the degree of. presumed exposure to crime and delinquency in the community, the frequency, duration, priority and intensity of interaction with delinquent peers and knowledge of and association with adult criminals.

But Sutherland's theory has been attacked by many scholars like Sheldon Glueck, Mabel Elliott, Caldwell, Donald Cressey, Tappan, George Vold, Herbert Bloch, Jeffery Clarence, Daniel Glaser and others. The major criticism is that it is difficult to empirically test the principles and measure 'associations' and the priority, intensity, duration, and frequency of relationships. According to Tappan, Sutherland has ignored the role of personality or role of biological and psychological factors in crime. Vold (1958: 194) has maintained that he has ignored the role of secondary contact and formal groups in criminality. Clarence Ray Jeffery holds that Sutherland's theory fails to explain the origin of criminality, since criminality has to exist before it can be learnt from someone else. Elliot (1952: 402) says, Sutherland's theory explains the systematic crimes but not the situational ones. According to Cressey, Sutherland does not fully explore the implications of the learning process itself as it affects different individuals. Bloch (1956: 158) is of the opinion that it is virtually impossible to measure associations in comparative quantitative terms. Glueck (1951) maintains that an individual does not learn every behaviour from others; many acts are learnt naturally. Caldwell (1956) says that individuals become what they are largely because of the contacts they have but both the constitutional or inborn hereditary structure and the intensity of the environmental stimuli must be appraised as well. Daniel Glaser (1956) modified Sutherland's theory a little to explain from whom an individual learns crime. He called this new theory as 'Differential Identification Theory' and said that a person pursues criminal behaviour to the extent that he identifies himself with real or imaginary persons from whose perspective, his criminal behaviour seems acceptable. He further says that one of the persistent problems in the Theory of Differential Association is the obvious fact that not everyone in contact with criminality adopts or follows the criminal pattern. What, therefore, is the difference in the nature or quality of the association that in one case it leads to acceptance of the attitudes and behaviour of a group of one individual but in the case of another individual it leads only to acquaintance with but not an acceptance of the behaviour characteristics of the group.

Merton's Theory of Anomie

R.K. Merton (1968), reacting against the biological and psychiatric theories (that crime is the result of inherited traits) first attempted to explain deviant behaviour in 1938 in a paper published in the *American Sociological Review*. He elaborated his thesis further in 1949 and 1957 and distinguished between social and cultural structures. Cultural structure, according to him, refers to goals and interests men pursue, while social structure refers to means or approved methods which regulate and control the pursuit of goals and interests. The cultural system of society enjoins all men to strive for goals by means of normatively regulated or approved forms of behaviour. However, opportunities to reach these goals through socially approved means are unequally distributed. Deviant behaviour ensues when social structure restricts or completely closes a person's access to the approved modes of reaching these goals. In other words, the disjunction between goals and means causes strains which in turn leads to a weakening of men's commitment to the culturally prescribed goals or institutionalized means, that is, to a state of anomie. Thus, Merton's thesis is that some social structures exert a definite pressure on some persons to engage in non-conformist rather than conformist conduct.

Merton (1968: 192–93) has identified five modes of adaptation available to those who react to goals and means of society: conformity, innovation, ritualism, retreatism and rebellion. Conformity describes the acceptance of goals and also of the means of the society. Innovation represents the acceptance of the goals but the rejection of the means. For example, a student accepts the goal of passing the examination and obtaining a degree but uses unfair means to pass. Thus, Merton points out that poverty does not cause crime but when poverty is linked with a cultural emphasis on monetary success as a dominant goal and a poor individual cannot compete, because of his poverty, for the cultural values, then criminal behaviour is the normal outcome. Ritualism is the rejection of the goals but acceptance of the means. For example, a student goes to college but does not attend his classes and instead spends time in the college canteen. Retreatism involves the rejection of both goals and means. For example, when an individual fails to achieve his goals by legitimate means and at the same time cannot adopt illegitimate means because of his prior socialization, he rejects both goals and means and becomes a drunkard, drug addict or a vagrant rebellion is characterized by the rejection of the goals and the means and an attempt to adopt new goals and means.

Merton's theory has been criticized by Cohen, Clinard and Lemert. Their main arguments are: (a) Merton's theory is incomplete because he has not explained who will reject the goals and who will reject the means; (b) only structure has been given importance; an individual's personality has been ignored; (c) strains do not necessarily lead to deviant behaviour; (d) the theory neglects the important role of social control; (e) Merton's assumption that deviant behaviour is disproportionately more common in lower classes is not correct; (f) anomie may be the cause rather than the effect of circumscribed life chances; (g) Cohen has argued that Merton has not explained the determinants of the mode of adaptation of an individual; (h) Cohen has also said that Merton has failed to account for the 'non-utilitarian' crime and juvenile delinquency in which people engage only for fun and not to meet specific goals of the society; for example, vandalism or a car-theft for joy-rides; and (i) finally, the theory does not take into account the social-psychological variables or the social structural elements which might explain the priority of one adaptation over the other by the individuals.

Cloward and Ohlin's Theory of Differential Opportunity

Cloward and Ohlin (1960) integrated Sutherland's and Merton's theories and developed a new theory of criminal behaviour in 1960. Whereas Sutherland talks of illegitimate means and Merton talks of differentials in legitimate means, Cloward and Ohlin talk of differentials in both legitimate and illegitimate means to success-goals. The important elements of this theory are: (a) an individual occupies a position in both the legitimate and illegitimate opportunity structures, (b) relative availability of illegitimate opportunities affects the resolution of an individual's adjustment problems, and (c) faced with limitations on legitimate avenues of accessibility to goals and unable to revise his aspirations downward, he experiences intense frustration, resulting in exploration of non-conformist alternatives.

Schrag (1972: 167) systematically organized Cloward's theory and gave its four postulates: (a) middle-class goals, specially economic goals, are widespread, (b) every organized community provides legitimate opportunities for attaining these goals, (c) access to legitimate means varies from class to class, and (d) within given community, illegitimate opportunities may or may not be available. But Schrag himself has criticized the theory of Cloward and Ohlin based on the above postulates on two counts: (a) the theory fails to explain why a young person who belongs to a lower class does not become involved in the activities of delinquent gangs, and (b) who will use illegitimate means to achieve the goals? Schrag has answered the second question himself. He says that three types of persons are susceptible to indulging in deviant behaviour or join delinquent gangs: (a) those who blame the system for their failures and/or adjustment problems, (b) those who think, they possess the official criteria but not the pragmatic criteria, and (c) those who are alienated from conventional norms or a legitimate system.

Cloward and Ohlin have identified three types of delinquent sub-cultures: the criminal, the conflictory, and the retreatist. The first emphasizes orderly activity oriented to economic gain; the second emphasizes violence and gun-fighting; and the third emphasizes drug use and other 'kicks'. The first tends to arise in areas where successful and big-time criminals reside and they have a high status in the conventional community and mutually acceptable relations with political machines and law enforcement officials. This sub-culture does not manifest violence. The second is found in areas where there is no alliance between the criminal and the conventional elements. This subculture features violence and/or threat of violence as a method of getting status. In such neighbourhoods, young people tend to organize themselves in a community of gangs contending with one another for 'rep' through the show of violence and toughness. The third is found in areas where either repressive police measures make street-fighting too dangerous or where moral and other inhibitions against the use of violence exist. Individuals denied access to criminal and conflictive opportunities tend to withdraw into a world of narcotic drugs.

Short, Tennyson and Rivers have supported Cloward and Ohlin's theory on the basis of their study on the perception of legitimate and illegitimate opportunities pertaining to education and occupation among 500 Negro and white lower-class gang boys and middle-class non-gang boys from the same neighbourhood. Walter Reckless also undertook a project to examine Cloward's theory. Some of the questions pertaining to the perception of opportunities were: (a) 1 probably won't be able to do the kind of work that I want to do because I don't have enough education, (b) if a kid like me works hard, he can get a lead, (c) my family can't give me the opportunity that most kids have, (d) most people are better off than I am, (e) I am as well off as most people are, and (f) a guy like me has a pretty chance of going to a college.

On the basis of the responses received, Reckless found that Cloward's theory is partly correct, that is, it explains some crimes but not all crimes.

The important criticisms against Cloward and Ohlin's theory are: (a) the main contention in the theory that there are two kinds of opportunities – legitimate and illegitimate – is not so simple as it seems. The distinction, although real, is 'analytical' rather than 'concrete', that is, there are some things that are legitimate opportunities and other things that are illegitimate opportunities, but the same things are always both; for example, notes prepared by students on small pieces of paper can be used as unfair means in examinations as well as legitimate simple means for remembering points a day or two before the examinations. Similarly, a gun can be used for killing as well as defending oneself; (b) Cloward and Ohlin maintain that the lower-class youths have two orientations: (i) orientation toward membership in middle-class, called 'lifestyle' orientation, and (ii) orientation toward economic improvement, called 'economic' orientation. Cloward's thesis is that candidates for delinquent subculture are those who wish to retain lower-class membership but aspire to improve their economic status (Johnson, 1978: 179). But Gordon says, these two orientations do not exist separately; (c) Cloward has not specified the initial conditions for the emergence of various types of sub-culture; (d) there is class-bias in this theory; (e) some concepts cannot be operationalized; for example, opportunity structure, perception of opportunity, denial of legitimacy or double failure; and (f) the personality factor has been completely ignored.

Cohen's Theory of Value Orientation or Delinquent Sub-culture

Albert Cohen's (1955: 65–66) theory mainly deals with the problems of status adjustment of working-class boys. Cohen holds that the young people's feelings of themselves depend largely upon how they are judged by others. The situations in which they are judged, most notably the school situation, are largely dominated by middle class values and standards, which in fact is the dominant value system. These standards include such criteria as neatness, polished manners, academic intelligence, verbal fluency, high level of aspirations, and a drive for achievement. Young people of different origins and backgrounds tend to be judged by the same standards in the society, so that young people of lower classes find themselves competing for status and approval under the same set of rules. However, they are not equally well equipped for success in this status game. For this and other reasons, the lower-class children are more likely to experience failure and humiliation. One way they can deal with this problem is to repudiate and withdraw from the game and refuse to recognize that these rules have any application to them. But, this is not quite that simple because the dominant value system is also, to a degree, their value system. They have three alternatives before them: (a) to adopt the 'college-boy response' of upward mobility (thrifty, hardwork, cuts himself from the activities of peers), (b) to adopt the 'stable corner-boy response' (does not surrender the upward mobility idea but is neither thrifty nor cuts himself from peers nor incurs hostility of either middle-class persons or delinquent boys), and (c) to adopt 'delinquent response' (completely repudiates middle-class standards). Of these alternatives, most of the children adopt the third response. They resort to reaction formation. They reject the dominant value system and develop new values which are non-utilitarian (because they do not benefit economically), malicious (because they enjoy at others' cost and suffering), and negativistic (because they are opposed to the accepted values of the larger society).

The propositions in Cohen's theory may be stated briefly as follows: The working-class boy faces a characteristic problem of adjustment which is qualitatively different from that of the middle-class boy. His problem is one of 'status frustration'. His socialization handicaps him for achievement in the middle-class status system. Nevertheless, he is thrust into this competitive system where achievement is judged by middle-class standards of behaviour and performance. Ill-prepared and poorly motivated, he is frustrated in his status aspirations by the agents of middle-class society. The delinquent sub-culture represents a 'solution' to the working-class boy's problem, for it enables him to 'break clean' with the middle-class morality and legitimizes hostility and aggression without moral inhibitions. Thus, the delinquent sub-culture is characterized by non-utilitarian, malicious and negativistic values as an attack on the middle-class where their egos are most vulnerable. It expresses contempt for a way of life by making its opposite a criterion of status.

Cohen's above theory has been critically examined both as a theory of the delinquent sub-culture and as a theory of delinquency. Sykes and Matza, Merton, Reiss and Rhodes, Kobrin and Finestone, Kitsuse and Dietrick and Wilensky and Labeaux have questioned various propositions and implications of his thesis. The main criticisms are: (a) a gang member does not reject middle-class values and standards but adopts techniques of neutralization to rationalize his delinquent behaviour; (b) if Cohen's theory is accepted, the delinquency rate of lower-class boys should be higher in areas where they are in direct competition with middle-class boys and their rate should be lowest in areas where lower-class is universal. But Reiss and Rhodes (1961) found that the more the lower-class boy was in minority in school and in his residential areas, the less likely was he to become a delinquent; (c) Kitsues and Dietrick have challenged Cohen's statement that the working-class boy measures himself by middle-class norms; (d) his description of delinquent sub-culture as non-utilitarian, malicious and negativistic is inaccurate; (e) Cohen's description of the working-class boy's ambivalence toward the middle-class system does not warrant the use of the 'reaction formation' concept; (f) the methodological basis of the theory renders it inherently untestable; and (g) the theory is ambiguous concerning the relation between the emergence of the sub-culture and its maintenance.

Becker's Labelling Theory

Howard Becker (1966) propounded his theory in 1963. Before him, Frank Tennenbaum (1938), Edwin Lemert (1951), John Kitsuse (1962) and K. Erikson (1962) had also used an approach called the 'Social Reaction Approach' or the 'Social Interaction Approach' as different from the 'Structural Approach' used by Merton, or the 'Cultural Approach' used by Cohen and Cloward and Ohlin. This theory does not deal with the question as to why a person becomes a criminal but tells why the society labels some people as criminals or deviants. Some men who drink heavily are called alcoholics while others are not; some men who behave oddly are committed to hospitals while others are not. Thus, according to this theory, what is important in the study of deviance is the social audience, not the individual person. Becker also maintained that what is important in crime is not the act of an individual but the reaction of the society in terms of rules and sanctions. Erikson has also said that what distinguishes a delinquent from a non-delinquent is not the characteristic found in him but the characteristic assigned to him by others. According to Becker (1966: 9), deviance is not a quality of the act a person commits but rather a consequence of the application by others of rules and sanctions to an 'offender'. The deviant is one to whom that label has successfully been applied; deviant behaviour is behaviour that people so label.

According to Becker, whether or not labelling occurs depends upon (a) the time when the act is committed, (b) who commits the act and who is the victim, and (c) the consequences of the act. Thus, whether a given act is deviant or not depends in part on the nature of the act and in part on what other people do about it. Becker suggests that a distinction be made between rule-breaking behaviour and deviance. Deviance is not a quality that lies in the behaviour itself, but in the interaction between the person who commits an act and those who respond to it. Becker has also suggested that certain types of groups are more likely to be labelled deviant than others; for example, groups that do not have political power and, therefore, cannot put pressure on the officials for not enforcing the law, groups which are seen to threaten the persons in power, and groups which have low social status.

What are the effects on the individual who is labelled. The official response to the behaviour in question may initiate processes that push the 'delinquent' individuals towards further delinquent conduct, and at least, make it more difficult for them to re-enter the conventional world. If on the other hand, an individual does not receive official response to his delinquent acts, he may continue committing them while receiving no help in changing his behaviour (Wheeler and Cottrell, 1966: 22–27).

Criticism against the labelling theory is that it gives a good logic but does not explain the cause of crime. It entirely avoids the question of causation. Jack Gibbs (1982: 219) has posed four questions: What elements in the scheme are intended to be definitions rather than substantive theory? Is the ultimate goal to explain deviant behaviour or to explain reactions to deviation? Is deviant behaviour to be identified exclusively in terms of the reaction to it? Exactly, what kind of reaction identifies behaviour as deviant?

Reckless' Theory of Self-Concept and Containment

Walter Reckless (1967: 522) has said that the important question that must be answered in explaining criminal behaviour is why, given the alternatives of law-abiding and law-violating behaviour, do some people turn to one or the other behaviour. He advocates that self concept is the key factor in explaining the choice among alternatives of behaviour. A favourable self-concept directs an individual toward law-abiding behaviour, and an unfavourable self-concept directs him towards delinquent behaviour. Reckless has further said that there are two important aspects of control: inner control and outer control, and that depending upon the balance of these control systems, the individual can take either a deviant or a conformist route. His assumption is that strong inner and reinforcing outer containment, constitutes an isolation against normative deviancy, that is, violation of the socio-legal conduct norms.

Confinement and Correction of Criminals

Two methods are mainly used in our society in punishing/treating the criminals: imprisonment and release on probation, though some serious offenders are given capital punishment, and fines are imposed on some minor offenders.

Prisons

The management of prisons falls exclusively under the domain of the state government, as per the Seventh Schedule of the Constitution. In every state, the prison administrative machinery works under the chief of prisons who is a senior ranking IPS officer. Indian prisons face three long-standing structural constraints: overcrowding, due to a high percentage of undertrials in the prison population, understaffing and underfunding. The inevitable outcome is sub-human living conditions, poor hygiene, and violent clashes between the inmates and jail authorities. Indian prisons are overcrowded and understaffed. Unless these issues are dealt with, prisons will remain hellish for the socio-economically disadvantaged.

The conditions in Indian jails were horrible up to 1919–20. It was after the recommendations of 1919–20 Indian Jails Reform Committee that changes like classification, segregation of prisoners, education, recreation, assigning productive work and opportunities for maintaining contacts with family and society were introduced in maximum security prisons (that is, central jails, district jails and sub-jails). Later on, three medium security jails or model jails were also established in three states with an emphasis on *Panchayati Raj*, self-managed canteens and the wage system, but these jails were ultimately converted into central jails. Minimum security prisons or open jails were started in Uttar Pradesh in 1952. At present, the open jail system has been working successfully in India. Around 28 prisons in the country follow the system, and most states have at least one of them. Prisoners have to fulfil certain conditions before being admitted to an open jail, like spending one-third term of imprisonment in an ordinary jail, having a record of good behaviour, possessing physical and mental fitness, and being in the age group of 20 to 50 years. The capacity of open jails varies from 100 to 3,000; the highest capacity (3,000) being allocated in Sitarganj Camp in Nainital district in Uttar Pradesh. Some open jails provide training only in agriculture, some only in industries and some both in agriculture and industries. The average stay of a prisoner in an open jail varies from two to three years.

A prison is a unisex world where every inmate is stigmatized and has to carry on tightly scheduled activities in the company of strangers. The inmates are deprived of liberty, privileges, emotional security, and hetero-sexual relations. To face these psychological and social problems, inmates follow the 'inmate code' of the 'inmate system' which is just contrary to the formal code of the prison system. Some examples of the inmate code/norms are: do not work hard, do not cooperate with the officials, do not quarrel/argue with other inmates, do not reveal secrets to officials, always keep on expressing dissatisfaction with food, clothes, work, and so forth. Donald Clemmer has described the internalization of these values and norms as the process of 'prisonization'. His contention is that every prisoner is prisonized; prisonization takes place in stages; the degree of prisonization could be low, medium or high; prisonization depends upon factors like age, term of imprisonment, nature of crime, relations with outside world, cell inmates and work colleagues; and the length of time served in jail. The prisonized inmate could be deprisonized as well as reprisonized. Studying the effects and the effectiveness of the prison system on the basis of an empirical study of 252 prisoners in three central jails in Rajasthan in 1977–78 (Ahuja, 1981), it was found that though the process of prisonization was found in Indian jails too, but every prisoner was not prisonized as claimed by Clemmer. Studying conformity to prison/inmate norms on the basis of three factors, namely, contact with inmates/officials, identification with staff/inmates norms, and loyalty to inmates/officials, it was found that 24 per cent inmates were conformists (who identified with prison norms, were bound by loyalty to staff and had great contacts with prison officials), 42 per cent were non-conformists, 27 per cent were partial conformists and 7 per cent were isolationists. Further, analysing the absorption of inmate/prison norms by assigning scores to answers of 15 questions, it was found that 48 per cent inmates conformed to inmate norms, 45 per cent to prison norms and 7 per cent were neutral. This shows that the rate of absorbing inmate norms is about the same as that of absorbing prison norms and most of the inmates remained in an ambiguous position in accepting or rejecting prison/inmate norms. It was also found that prisonization was not related to age, nature of offence, term of imprisonment, and the phase of imprisonment as claimed by Clemmer. However, it was related with the type of inmates with whom a prisoner lives/works. Thus, rejecting Clemmer's model, a new model was developed, called 'Self Image Model', for explaining the process of adjustment of inmates in a jail. This model is based on four elements: self-image, value conformity, actual conformity and prisoners' prestige.

On the basis of this study of three prisons, it is maintained that a balanced policy of liberalization and strictness regarding the inmates in the prison should be adopted for punishing/treating the offenders through imprisonment. Other measures needed to make the prison system more effective and in correcting the deviants are: undertrials should not be kept with convicts in the same prison; inmates should be provided access to their files; there should be proper diagnosis before assigning barrack/work to the prisoners; inmates should be given freedom of choosing the work of their choice; release on parole should be made easier and more effective; private industries should be encouraged to come to prisons; effective channels should be provided to the inmates for expressing their grievances; a system of indeterminate sentence should be introduced; sending offenders to prison for a short term (less than six months) should be discouraged (at present 85 per cent of our prisoners are short-termers); a Bureau of Prison Industries should be established at the state level, and the prisoners should be associated with the management of prisons through the Advisory

Committees (this system will be different from the *Panchayati Raj* system in prisons). Knowing that there is no connection between the severity of prison conditions and incidence of crime, why should we not try to devise programmes which may induce prisoners to turn over a new leaf? What we need today is an alternative to a prison.

According to the Prison Statistics India 2015 report by the National Crime Records Bureau (NCRB), India's prisons are overcrowded with an occupancy ratio of 14 per cent more than the capacity. New Delhi's Tihar Jail is the country's largest and most crowded prison with over 15,000 prisoners are lodged in a space meant for not more than 6,200 across the 400-acre prison complex. Sixty-seven per cent of the people in Indian jails are undertrials – those detained in prisons during trial, investigation or inquiry but not convicted of any crime in a court of law. More than 25 per cent of under-trial prisoners in 16 out of 36 states and union territories have been detained for more than one year. With over a staggering 3.1 crore cases pending in various courts of the country as on 31 March 2016, jails across the country will remain overcrowded in the absence of any effective systemic intervention.

As a matter of fundamental rights guaranteed by the Indian Constitution, undertrials are presumed innocent till proven guilty. But they are often subjected to psychological and physical torture during detention and exposed to sub-human living conditions and prison violence. Many lose their family neighbourhood and community ties and, more often than not, their livelihoods. Moreover, prison time attaches a social stigma to them as individuals and as community members. Even their families, relatives and communities are not immune to disgrace and humiliation. Even after their acquittal, undertrials find their employability severely jeopardized for none of their faults.

Undertrials tend to have restricted access to legal representatives. Many undertrials are poor people accused of minor offences, locked away for long periods because they are not aware of their rights and cannot access legal aid. Lack of financial resources and a robust support system, and the limited ability to communicate with lawyers from within the jail premises hamper their ability to defend themselves in the court of law. This happens despite a landmark Supreme Court ruling, that Article 21 of the Constitution entitles prisoners to a fair and speedy trial as part of their fundamental right to life and liberty.

Undertrials often remain behind bars for years despite the provisions of Section 436A of the Code of Criminal Procedure, which came into effect in 2005. This section mandates the release, on a personal bond with or without surety, of under trial detainees who have been imprisoned for half the maximum sentence they would have received if convicted for the offence they are charged with. This section does not apply to those who could be sentenced to death or life term. According to Prison Statistics 2014, 39 per cent of those charged for crimes under the Indian Penal Code could not be punished with life term or death penalty.

Severe Staff Crunch

While 33 per cent of the total requirement of prison officials still lies vacant, almost 36 per cent of vacancies for supervising officers is still unfulfilled. Delhi's Tihar jail ranks third in terms of a severe staff crunch. The manpower recruited inside this prison is almost 50 per cent short of its actual requirement. As the nation's capital, Delhi has the most over-crowded jails and suffers from an acute shortage of prison guards and senior supervisory staff. States like Uttar Pradesh, Bihar and Jharkhand have the most scantily guarded jails, seeing over 65 per cent staff vacancies among jailers, prison guards and supervisory levels.

In the absence of adequate prison staff, overcrowding of prisons leads to rampant violence and other criminal activities inside the jails. In separate incidents, 32 prisoners escaped in Punjab in 2015, while in Rajasthan, the number of such cases has risen to 18. Maharashtra witnessed the escape of 18 prisoners. In 2015, on an average, four prisoners died every day. A total of 1,584 prisoners died in jails, 1,469 of which were natural deaths and the remaining 115 were attributed to unnatural causes. Two-thirds of all unnatural deaths (77) were reported to be suicides, while fellow inmates murdered 11, nine of which were in jails in Delhi. About 12,727 people are reported to have died in prisons between 2001 and 2010.

In the absence of a robust Whistleblower Protection Act and structural changes to address the issues of overcrowding and understaffing, India's prisons will continue to be heaven for politically connected criminals and hell for socio-economically disadvantaged undertrials, some regular media uproars notwithstanding.

Open Prisons

Open prisons refer to the prisons that involve minimum security and is mainly dependent on the self-discipline of the inmates. The rules of these prisons are less stringent as compared to the rules of the other prisons. For this reason, they are also known as open-air camps, prisons without bars or minimum security prison. Open jail means 'prisons without walls, bars and locks'. The jail does not confine them completely but requires them to earn their living to support their families, living with them inside the jail.

Prisons in India are governed by the Prisons Act, 1900 and each state follows their prison rules and manuals. India has a maximum number of central jails, sub-jails, which are controlled jails, and 63 open jails.

Open prisons have relatively less stringent rules as compared to the controlled jails. They go by many names like a minimum-security prison, open-air camps or prison without bars. The fundamental rule of an open prison is that the jail has minimum security and functions on the self-discipline of the inmates.

Inmates in open prisons are free to go out of the prison after a first roll call and have to return before the allotted second roll call. The jail does not confine them completely but requires them to earn their living to support their families, living with them inside the jail.

Every state law defines the eligibility criteria of inmates who can be in an open prison. The principal rule is that an inmate eligible for open-prison has to be a convict. The All-India Committee on Jail Reforms recommended that life convicts, who offer good prognosis should be transferred to semi-open and open prisons.

Probation

Probation is defined as the postponement of final judgment or sentence in a criminal case, giving the offender an opportunity to improve his conduct and to readjust himself to the community, often on certain condition imposed by the court and under the guidance or supervision of an officer of the court. It aims at rehabilitation of offenders by returning them to society during the period of supervision rather than sending them into an unnatural and socially unhealthy atmosphere of prisons.

Advantages of Probation

1. It is most useful in the case of juvenile delinquents.
2. It gives hope for the rehabilitation of the offender who has not committed the offence.
3. Probation is a way of sending a good idea into the mind of offenders.
4. It is helpful for both hardcore and youthful offenders.
5. It helps in reducing the crowding in the jails.

Disadvantages of Probation

1. The warning of further punishment should also be incurred in the mind of prisoners. Here, there is no threat in the mind of the prisoner.
2. It decreases the average penalty.

Parole

According to J.L. Gillin, 'Parole is the release from a penal or reformative institution, of an offender who remains under the control of correctional authorities, in an attempt to find out whether he is fit to live in the free society without supervision'.

Objectives of Parole

1. To enable the inmate to maintain continuity with his family life and deal with family matters;
2. To save the inmate from the evil effects of continuous prison life; and
3. To enable the inmate to retain self-confidence and active interest in life.

Merits of Parole

1. It creates hopes among other prisoners.

2. Once a prisoner is released on parole, the opinion of the society is liberal.
3. Securing family life of the parolee.
4. It eradicates overburden of the jails.
5. It is also economical to the state. The cost of expenditure of parolee also decreases.
6. It creates threats on the mind of the parolee to maintain good conduct in the society.

Demerits of Parole

1. If there is any negligence in the selection of the parolee, it results in serious consequences.
2. The parole board is bound to act on the aid and advice of the jail authority.
3. It is not necessary that the prisoners who are maintaining their good conduct in the prisons will maintain their good conduct in the society.
4. Political interference.
5. Ill-treatment and doubtful behaviour by the society makes them impediment in their character development.

The Distinction between Probation and Parole

1. *Nature*: Probation is judicial in nature whereas parole is quasi-judicial in nature.
2. *Sentence*: In probation, no such formal penalty is imposed, if imposed it is not executed. But parole is granted after serving a part of the sentence in prison.
3. *Substitute for punishment*: Probation is granted as a substitute for the punishment, but parole is granted after completing a part of the sentence.
4. *Punishment and treatment*: Probation is only a treatment in which the sentence is suspended. But parole implies both punishment and treatment.
5. *Stage*: Probation is probably the first stage of correctional scheme whereas parole is the last stage of the correctional scheme.

Probation and Parole: A Comparative Study

Probation is a way of sending a good idea in the mind of offenders. The object of probation is to keep delinquent away from evil consequences and offer him an opportunity to lead a socially useful life without violating the law. On the other hand, parole has emerged as one of the most acceptable forms of the correctional device in modern penology. Parole is the most appropriate methods of treatment of offenders for their reformation and rehabilitation in the normal society after the final release.

Probation is an alternative to a prison. It is suspension of sentence of an offender by the court and releasing him on certain conditions to live in the community with or without the supervision of a probation officer. The system was introduced in India in 1958 by passing the Probation of Offenders Act. Though Section 562 in 1898 The Code of Criminal Procedure (CrPC) permitted release of an offender on probation but it applied only to juvenile delinquents and first offenders. There was no provision for supervision and only first class magistrates were empowered to grant probation.

The probation system has certain advantages over the prison system. These are: no stigma is attached to the offender released on probation; there is no break in the probationer's economic life; his family does not suffer; the offender does not feel frustrated; and economically it is less expensive. The disadvantages are that the offender is put in the same environment in which he committed the crime; there is no fear of punishment; and no individual attention is paid to probationers. However, these criticisms are not logical. Further, probation can be made more effective through new measures. These could be: changing the concept of probation and treating it not as a suspension of sentence but as an alternative to imprisonment (with this, the probationer will not be imprisoned for the original offence for which his sentence was suspended but will only be penalized for violating the conditions); making social investigation compulsory in all those cases where the offender is released on probation; not making supervision compulsory for all probationers; making conditions for release flexible; introducing indeterminate sentence system and, not linking probation services with any other department but establishing a separate directorate for it at the state level.

Summarizing the problem of correction, it may be concluded that criminologists have always been tied to two explicit interests: first, the managerial interest in making the correctional system more efficient and second, the humanitarian interest in reforming the system. These two interests are often considered incompatible but they might not be so when perceived in terms of 'rehabilitative ethics'. Treatment can be seen both as more efficient and more humanitarian.

New Age Crimes in India

India is facing a threat of new crimes and enormous increase in the number and technological sophistication of old crimes, to which it must respond. In recent decades, new technologies have led to new types of crimes, such as identity theft and credit card fraud. The Indian system of policing and the criminal investigation is still stuck in the old ways of information gathering and beating out a confession from the suspects. The police force is completely untrained on modern methods of criminal investigation and is not primed to gather scientific evidence to present a watertight case in the court. This is why the gap continues between reporting of crime, arresting a criminal and finally ensuring successful prosecution of the accused. All developed nations now follow basic human rights principles and have done away with physical means to elicit a confession from a potential suspect. Modern techniques are applied to confirm innocence or psychologically breakdown a suspect into confessing a crime. There is no choice but to learn and implement strategies to seriously attempt crime prevention and crime control.

Cyber Crimes

Cyber crimes can be defined as the unlawful acts where the computer is used either as a tool or a target or both. Cyber crimes include illegal access, illegal interception, system interference, data interference, misuse of devices and fraud. In today's digital world, the amount of personal data being generated, transmitted and stored on to various digital devices is growing. The critical nature of this data and the complexity of the systems that support its transmission have created a gamut of cyber risks and crimes. To encourage the use of digital payment methods by a larger proportion of population, redressal of such cyber-crimes should be given utmost priority by mobile service providers and concerned authorities. A 77 per cent rise in number of cyber crime cases was observed in 2017, compared to 2016 (NCRB).

Types of Cyber Crimes

Cyber crimes can be categorized in two ways:

1. The crimes in which computers are the target. Examples of such crimes are hacking, virus attacks, DOS attack, etc.
2. The crimes in which the computer is used as a weapon. These types of crimes include cyberterrorism, IPR violations, credit card frauds, EFT frauds, pornography, etc.

E-crimes such as money frauds, hacking of bank accounts, online scams and social media threats like stalking, pornography, bullying, defamation and online harassment are tremendously increasing. The internet has been misused for terrorism, copyright infringement, fraud, software piracy, illegal trafficking, and web defacement. According to the National Investigation Agency, every sixth cybercrime in India is committed through social media. Different kinds of cyber crimes are:

1. *Theft*: This crime occurs when a person violates copyrights and downloads music, movies, games, and software.
2. *Unauthorized access*: It means any kind of access without the permission of either of the rightful or person in charge of the computer, computer system or computer network. This is a type of crime wherein a person's sensitive information can be accessed. Some hackers hack for personal monetary gains, such as to stealing the credit card information, transferring money from various bank accounts to their own account followed by withdrawal of money. Government websites are the most targeted sites for the hackers.
3. *Malicious software*: These are internet-based software or programmes that are used to disrupt a network. The software is used to gain access to

a system to steal sensitive information or data or causing damage to software present in the system. Malware or malicious software can be used for stealing, encrypting or deleting sensitive data as well as for hijacking computing functions.

4. *Web hijacking*: Web hijacking means taking forceful control of another person's website. In this case, the owner of the website loses control over his website and its content.
5. *Child pornography*: The internet is being highly used as a medium to sexually abuse children. The children are viable victims to the cybercrime. Computers and internet have become a necessity for every household, the children have got an easy access to the internet. There is an easy access to the pornographic contents on the internet. Paedophiles lure the children and start actual exploitation of the children by offering them some money or falsely promising them good opportunities in life. Under the Protection of Children from Sexual Offence (POCSO) Act, 2013, whoever uses a child or children for pornographic purposes shall be punished with imprisonment upto five years and liable to fine.
6. *Identity theft*: This has become a major problem for people using the internet for cash transactions and banking services. In this cybercrime, a criminal accesses data about a person's bank account, credit cards, social security, debit card and other sensitive information to syphon money or to buy things online in the victim's name. It can result in major financial losses for the victim and even spoil the victim's credit history.
7. *Cyber stalking*: This is a kind of online harassment wherein the victim is subjected to a barrage of online messages and emails. Typically, these stalkers know their victims and instead of resorting to offline stalking, they use the internet to stalk. However, if they notice that cyberstalking is not having the desired effect, they begin offline stalking along with cyberstalking to make the victims' lives more miserable.

Cyber Laws

The Internet has now become part and parcel of human life. Internet access is a fundamental right under Article 19 of the Constitution. It is the most important source of information and communication and is used for multifarious purposes such as entertainment, online shopping, job hunt, banking, commerce, online study and networking, etc. However, it poses challenges to our existing legal system as it deals with jurisdiction issues, difficulty in tracing the culprit, public unawareness and underreporting of cases. Our law needs to be stricter and enforcement mechanisms more effective to tackle the problem. To combat the crimes related to internet the Information Technology Act, 2000 was enacted with the prime objective to create an enabling environment for commercial use of IT. The IT Act, 2000, is primarily meant to be legislation to promote e-commerce. It is not very effective in dealing with several emerging cyber crimes like cyber harassment, defamation and stalking. Although, the Information Technology Act, 2000 modishly deals with cyber-crimes but it does not specifically cover all internet-based crimes. Online infringement of intellectual property rights, cyber-squatting, tax evasion, online sale of illegal articles and money laundering cases occur very frequently but these crimes are not explicitly covered under IT Act. There is a need to amend the IT Act so as to cover other internet-based crimes. New threats relating to bitcoins and cryptocurrency are required to be defined clearly. The IT Act specifies the acts which have been made punishable. The Indian Penal Code, 1860 has also been amended to take into its purview cyber crimes.

A Cyber Security Policy adopted in 2013 was aimed at creating safe and secure cyber space. The policy had several action points. Important ones relate to setting up a National Cyber Security Centre, Malware Monitoring and Cleaning Centre, National Critical Information Infrastructure Centre, etc. We, however, need to review the 2013 policy and take corrective steps to strengthen the system to enhance resiliency of cyber infrastructure in the country, particularly critical infrastructure.

Since users of computer system and internet are increasing worldwide, where it is easy to access any information easily within a few seconds by using internet which is the medium for huge information and a large base of communications around the world. Certain precautionary measures should be taken by netizens while using the internet which will assist in challenging this major threat. With the increase in the number of netizens, the internet has been misused by some criminal elements against persons, property, government and society. Indeed, the use of internet has made our modern lifestyles easier, but when we see the other side of the coin, there are many limitations attached to it. The lure of the virtual word has also given rise to many new types of crimes. The widespread use of social media has also provided a clear platform to cyber criminals to take an undue advantage of those vulnerable.

Mob Lynching

The Webster's dictionary describe 'lynching' as – putting to death by mob action without legal approval. Lynching is an act of violence by a mob. There has been a number of incidences of mob violence in the country in the last three years. The governing sentiments of mob sometimes pertain to child lifting, witchcraft, cow protection, cattle or any other theft and caste-related violence. Lynching and vigilant attacks are usually targeted on Muslims and Dalits.

The crowd is of general perception that judiciary and police administration cannot provide justice and there is a chance that accused will go scot free. This shows that people in the country have lost their trust in judiciary on law and order. In fact, people have to understand that their act of providing 'instant justice' is itself a crime. Mob lynching is the result of a particular set of social or psychological factors and circumstances.

The Protection from Lynching Act, 2017 provide effective protection of the constitutional right of persons and to prevent the lynching of innocents. The Supreme Court in its judgment on 17 July 2018 laid down a string of preventive, punitive and remedial measures to curb incidences of mob vigilintism. Supreme Court guidelines for a tough anti-lynching law sees tardy progress. A separate law is needed as lynching is not defined in the IPC or CrPC. In order to combat a crime, we need to define it first. The object of the anti-lynching law will also ensure accountability in the police force.

References

Ahuja, Ram, *Sociological Criminology*, New Age International Publishers, New Delhi, 1996.

——, *The Prison System*, Sahitya Bhawan, Agra, 1981.

——, 'A Prisoner is a Human-being', *Times Weekly, Times of India*, Bombay, 27 May, 1973.

Aichhorn, August, *Wayward Youth*. Meridian Books, New York, 1955.

Becker, Howard (ed.), *Social Problems: A Modern Approach*, John Wiley and Sons Inc., New York, 1966.

Bloch, Herbert A., *Man, Crime and Society*, Random House, New York, 1956.

Bonger, William A., *Criminality and Economic Conditions*, translated by Henry P. Horton, Little Brown and Co., Boston, 1916.

Burt, Cyril, *Young Delinquent*, University of London Press, London, 1944.

Caldwell, Robert G., *Criminology*, University of Pennsylvania Press, Philadelphia, 1956.

Clemmer, Donald, *The Prison Community*, Christopher Publishing House, Boston, 1940.

Clinard, Marshall B., *Sociology of Deviant Behaviour*, Holt, Rinehart & Winston Inc., New York, 1957.

Cloward, Richard and Ohlin, Lloyd, *Delinquency and Opportunity: A Theory of Delinquent Gangs*, The Free Press, Glencoe, Illinois, 1960.

Cohen, Albert K., *Delinquent Boys: The Culture of the Gang*, The Free Press, New York, 1955.

——, *Deviance and Control*, Prentice Hall Inc., Englewood Cliffs, New Jersey, 1966.

Crime in India, National Crime Records Bureau, New Delhi, 2012.

Elliot, Mabel, *Crime in Modern Society*, Harper & Bros., New York, 1952.

Faris, R.E.L. and Dunham, H.W. *Mental Disorders in Urban Areas: An Ecological Study of Schizophrenia and Other Psychoses*. University of Chicago Press, Chicago, 1939.

Fitzgerald, Mike, *Crime and Society*, Routledge, London, 1981.

Gibbons, Don, *Society, Crime and Criminal Careers* (3rd edn), Prentice Hall, New Jersey, 1977.

Giallombardo, Rose, *Juvenile Delinquency*, John Wiley & Sons, New York, 1966.

Gibbs, Jack (ed.), *Social Control: Views from the Social Sciences*, Sage, Beverly Hills, CA, 1982.

Glaser, Daniel, 'Criminality Theories and Behavior Images', *American Journal of Sociology*, 61, March 1956.

Glueck, Sheldon, *Delinquents in the Making*, Harper, New York, 1951.

Goddard, Henry Herbert, *Human Efficiency and Levels of Intelligence*, Princeton University Press, Princeton, NJ, 1920.

Hall, Jerome, *General Principles of Criminal Law*, Bobbs-Merrill, Indianapolis, 1947.

Johnson, Elmer H., *Crime, Correction and Society* (4th edn), The Dorsey Press, Homewood, Illinois, 1978.

Merton, R.K., *Social Theory and Social Structure*, The Free Press, New York, 1968.

Reckless, Walter, *The Crime Problem*, Meridith, New York, 1967.

Reid, Sue Titus, *Crime and Criminology*, The Drydon Press, Hinsdale, Illinois, 1976.

Reiss, A.J. and Rhodes, L.E., 'The Distribution of Juvenile Delinquency in the Social Class Structure', *American Sociological Review*, 26, 1961.

Ruttonshaw, G.N., *Juvenile Delinquency and Destitution in Poona*, Deccan College, Poona, 1947.

Schafer, Stephen, *Theories in Criminology*, Random House, New York, 1969.

Schrag, Clarence, 'Delinquency and Opportunity: Analysis of a Theory', *Sociology and Social Research*, Vol. 46, 1972.

Sellin, Thorsten, *Culture, Conflict and Crime*, Social Science Research Council, New York. 1938.

Sutherland, E.H. and Cressay, D.R., *Principles of Criminology* (6th edn), The Times of India Press, Bombay, 1965.

Tappan, Paul, *Crime, Justice and Correction*, McGraw Hill, New York, 1960.

Vold, George B., *Theoretical Criminology*, Oxford University Press, New York, 1958.

Voss, H.L. (ed.), *Society, Delinquency and Delinquent Behaviour*, Little Brown, 1972.

Wheeler, Stanton and Cottrell, Leonard S. Jr., *Juvenile Delinquency: Its Prevention and Control*, Russell Sage Foundation, New York, 1966.

Young, Jock et al., *Critical Criminology*, Routledge & Kegan Paul, London, 1975.

15

Juvenile Delinquency

Juvenile delinquency statistics include:

1. The peak age for offending falls between 15 and 19 years of age.
2. 52 to 57 per cent of juvenile offenders continue offending into their mid-20s.
3. By the age of 30, only 16 per cent to 19 per cent of juvenile delinquents continue to offend.
4. If a juvenile starts offending before the age of 12, he is more likely to continue offending into adulthood.
5. The average onset of gang involvement is 16 years of age.
6. The average onset of drug use is 16 to 17 years of age.
7. According to National Crime Records Bureau data, 2018, over the past three years, on an average one juvenile is dying due to drug overdose every 10 days in India.

According to the National Crime Records Bureau (NCRB) statistics of 2011, juvenile crimes comprise 1.1 per cent of IPC offences, of which nearly 2 per cent of their offences were brutal of the total violent crimes were registered. Further, NCRB statistics state that among the IPC offences by juveniles, 64 per cent of juveniles were between the age of 16–18. There was a minimum of 32.5 per cent of offences by the age cluster of 12–16 yrs. And 3.6 per cent by the age cluster of 7–12 years. With regard to sexual offences, data has revealed that there has been a sharp rise in rapes committed by juveniles. While in 2010, the figure was at 858, it became 1,149 in 2011 and 2,054 in 2016.

At least one juvenile is arrested on charges of rape every four hours on an average in India, since the last three years. Similarly, one juvenile is apprehended every two hours for assault on women with intent to outrage their modesty. Five such juveniles are charged with one cognizable crime or the other.

Owing to the rise and brutality of sexual assaults particularly by juveniles on young girls and women, there has been an increasing sense of urgency to create legal avenues for some deterrence to warn of the under-age perpetrators.

In recent years, India has seen manifold increase in crimes committed by minors. While analysing the factors responsible for the spurt in crime rate, the experts believe that the rural-urban conflict is at the core of these crimes in cities, especially underage crimes. An increase in a number of rural people migrating to cities in search of better life opportunities, however, do not prepare them for the urban value system. The children are often neglected, as both parents are working and unable to spend time with them. The children do not get the attention and right values essential for upbringing. They feel neglected, frustrated and distressed which leads to crimes.

Who is a Juvenile?

Juvenile means anyone who has not yet reached the age of adults in terms of childishness or immaturity.

Difference between a Juvenile and a Minor

A minor refers to a person who is not yet an adult in the eyes of the law. Juvenile, on the other hand, indicates legality. In technical terms, it does mean young but has a negative connotation to it. It tends to imply immaturity and childishness and in legal terms, it refers to a young person who has been accused of a crime. In this context, a juvenile is sort of the opposite of a minor, as minor indicates an innocent child whereas juvenile tends to imply a young criminal.

William Caxton in the year 1484, used the word delinquent to refer to a person who was found guilty. Juvenile delinquency means the involvement by the teenagers in an unlawful behaviour who is basically under the age of 18 and commits an act which is considered as a crime. In India, the first legislation dealing with children in conflict with law or children committing a crime was the Apprentices Act, 1850. It provided that children under the age of 15 years found to have committed petty offences will be bounded as apprentices.

Juvenile delinquency is also termed as Teenage Crime. Basically, juvenile delinquency refers to the crimes committed by minors. Juvenile delinquency occurs when a minor violates a criminal statute. When a juvenile commits a crime, the procedures that take place differ from those of an adult offender. In all states, juvenile court systems, and juvenile detention facilities deal specifically with underage offenders. While it is common for state statutes to consider people under the age of 17 as minors, the justice system can charge minors as adults, if the crime committed is very serious. Juvenile delinquency is the participation by a minor child, usually between the ages of 10 to 17, in illegal behaviour or activities. Juvenile delinquency is also used to refer to children who exhibit a persistent behaviour of mischievousness or disobedience, so as to be considered out of parental control, becoming subject to legal action by the court system. Juvenile delinquency is also known as 'juvenile offending', and each state has a separate legal system in place to deal with juveniles who break the law. To explore this concept, consider the following juvenile delinquency definition.

Definition of Juvenile Delinquency

Juvenile Justice Act, 2000 has defined juvenile in conflict with the law as a juvenile who is alleged to have committed an offence and has not completed the eighteenth year of age as on the date of commission of such offence.

The crimes by teenage boys or girls are generally done without having proper knowledge of it as they know very little about the world. Basically, juvenile delinquency refers to the involvement by the teenagers in unlawful behaviour who is usually under the age of 18 and commits an act which would be considered a crime. A child is known as a delinquent when he/she commits a mistake which is against the law and which is not accepted by the society. Thus, a 'juvenile' or 'child' means a person who has not completed eighteen years of age and violates the law and commits an offence under the legal age of maturity. The difference between a delinquent child and an adult criminal is important from the case-work approach. The difference between the two is made by the conduct involved, the methods employed by the court, the philosophy and methods applied in treatment, and the individuals' status, reputation and civil rights in the community after adjudication.

Classification of Juvenile Delinquents

Juvenile delinquents have been classified by different scholars on different basis. For example, Hirsh (1937) has classified them in six groups on the basis of the kinds of offences committed: (a) *incorrigibility* (for example, keeping late hours, disobedience, etc.), (b) *truancy* (staying away from school), (c) *larceny* (ranging from petty theft to armed robbery), (d) *destruction of property* (including both public and private property), (e) *violence* (against individual or community by using weapons), and (f) *sex offences* (ranging from homosexuality to rape).

Eaton and Polk (1969) have classified delinquents into five groups according to the type of offence. The offences are: (a) minor violations (including disorderly conduct and minor traffic violations), (b) major violations (including automobile thefts), (c) property violations (d) addiction (including alcoholism and drug addiction), and (e) bodily harm (including homicide and rape).

Trojanowicz (1973: 59) has classified them as accidental, unsocialized, aggressive, occasional, professional and gang-organized.

Psychologists have classified juvenile delinquents on the basis of their individual traits or the psychological dynamics of their personality into five groups: mentally defective, psychotic, neurotic, situational and cultural.

Nature and Incidence

There are two main types of offenders:

1. *Repeat Offenders*: These juvenile delinquents begin offending or showing other signs of anti-social behaviour during adolescence. Repeat offenders continue to engage in criminal activities or aggressive behaviours even after they enter adulthood.
2. *Age-specific Offenders*: This type of juvenile delinquent behaviour begins during adolescence. The behaviours of the age-specific offender end before the minor becomes an adult. Age-specific offenders leave their delinquent behaviour behind when they enter adulthood. They often engage in substance abuse and have greater financial problems than adults who were never delinquent as juveniles.

Of the total delinquencies committed by the juveniles, hardly 2 per cent come to the notice of the police and the courts. The statistics complied by the National Crime Records Bureau (NCRB), and published in *Crimes in India,* 2011, gives some indication of the incidence of juvenile delinquency in India.

According to the report 'Why Children Commit Offences' published by Delhi Commission for Protection of Child Rights (DCPCR) in June 2015 focussed on children in conflict with the law in Delhi. The report looks at multiple issues like the socio-economic profile of children with a criminal record, the nature of the offence that these children were accused of and analysed the factors that push children towards deviant behaviour. The report highlighted the role of the family, the community, the school and education as well the peer influence. The report after studying 182 children in observation homes, special homes found that poverty is one of the biggest contributing factors in children taken to crimes. Most of the children had undergone multiple deprivations with low economic households, uneducated parents; disrupted families. The children were dropouts and working independently to support their families.

A study of B.R. Sharma, Sangeet Dhillon noted that childhood incidents and experiences are significant in the development of criminality; on the other hand, it does not mean criminals expose their criminality early in life. Sociological theories of juvenile delinquency, put prominence on the environment, social structures and the learning process. The study also mentioned individual factors for Juvenile delinquency. Individual factors are personality traits like submissiveness, defiance, hostility, impulsiveness, feeling of insecurity, fear, lack of self-control and emotional conflicts whereas situational factors are family, companions, movies, school environment, work environment, etc.

The study of Haveripeth P.D. describes that causes of juvenile delinquency are negative influence of movie and media, urbanization, lack of recreation, negative environment, availability of weapons, association with deviant peers, parental substance use.

Some of the most common causes which are associated with juvenile crimes are Poverty; Drug Abuse; Anti-social Peer Group; Easy availability of firearms; Abusive parents; Nuclear Family; Family Violence; Child sexual abuse and Role of Media. However, as far as India is concerned, it is Poverty and the effect of media, especially the social-media which make juveniles more inclined towards criminal activities.

Characteristics

Following are some of the important characteristics of juvenile delinquency in India:

1. Juvenile delinquency is more an urban than a rural phenomenon. The metropolitan cities (with a population of more than 10 lakh) produce more juvenile delinquents than small cities and towns.
2. Children living with parents and guardians are found to be more involved in the juvenile crimes.
3. Poor economic background is another important characteristic of juvenile delinquency in India.
4. Juvenile delinquency is more a lower class phenomenon. Almost all studies conducted in our country on juvenile delinquency and its relation to the socio-economic order show that those at the bottom strata have been found to have the highest rates. The extent to which this is true varies under different conditions, but one general point that has been made in almost all studies is that the impact of socio-economic status shows its effect most strongly the further one goes into the delinquency adjudication process.
5. More juvenile delinquents are first offenders and only a little more than one-tenth are recidivists or past offenders.
6. Though some delinquencies are committed in groups, having adult members also, the number of juvenile gangs having support of organized adult criminals is not much in our country.

Causes of Juvenile Delinquency

No one is a born criminal. Circumstances make them so. Sociocultural environment, both inside and outside of the home, plays a significant role in shaping one's life and overall personality. There are many factors contributing towards the criminal nature of the youth. Most of these youths come from families of discord or abuse. Peer pressure and the neighbourhood also influence the development of a child. Poverty is also one of the main causes for a delinquent youth. Although education plays an important role in making the future citizens, the system somewhere lacks in the ability to hold the attention of non-bookish and non-academic individuals and thus, contributes towards many cases of juvenile delinquency. Delinquents are typically those who take studies like a burden and on being rebuked, turn towards crime. There are numerous reasons behind juvenile delinquency, such as:

1. *Lack of knowledge*: They know very little about the outside world. They sometimes commit a crime unknowingly.
2. *Poverty*: One of the main causes for a delinquent to commit a crime.
3. *Trauma*: Trauma of any childhood or teenage incident may have a negative effect on mind. It can also be a physical injury or wound to the body.
4. *Vicious films and movies*: Watching any stuff like murder, violence, etc. may again negatively affect the mind of the teenager.
5. Family disturbance, discord or abuse.
6. Peer pressure and neighbourhood.

Some of the most common causes of juvenile delinquency are as follows:

Family

The family is the basic socialization agency for the children. Children learn basic concepts about good and bad from their family, they make their values and set the norms of society. Family can make or break the personality of the children. In the family, the most important role is played by the parents and siblings. Most of the adolescents who show delinquent behaviour in any form related to families that could not give a firm foundation to the children. Broken families, single-parent families, separated families, frequent parents' fight, lack of trust and confidence among the parents, criminal parents or psychological problems in parents can be the most important reason behind juvenile delinquency. The other reason can be sibling rivalry or unequal treatment between children. Parents and elder siblings have the responsibility to mould the personality of the children. When parents or siblings do not show moral behaviour or they commit crime, children or younger siblings also get the motivation to do something bad resulting in delinquent behaviour.

Economic Problems in the Family

Often the cause of juvenile delinquency is economic problems in the family. Youth belonging from poor economical status easily get involved in criminal activities. They want to improve their status and for this purpose, they use the negative path. In this regard often people do not support teenagers which belong from poor status and they turn towards criminal activities.

Psychological Problems in the Family

Psychological problems in parents or siblings can also be a risk factor for juvenile delinquency. Mental illnesses or other psychological problems like depression, frustration, aggression or hyper behaviour showed by the parents can make the child feel deprived and inferior among friends. Sometimes children adopt depression and anger from parents or elder siblings.

Social Problems in the Family

In many families, parents or elder siblings are involved in various social problems. There can be various problems like gender discrimination, age discrimination, racial discrimination, child labour or violation of animal rights. Children and youth learn what they see in their family. In many rich families parents do not feel shame in child labour and children can not understand that child labour is against society and against morality. Social problems cause stress and due to stress teens get involved in violence.

Moral Problems in the Family

Morality is the most important concern among teens today. Teens should know how to respect family and other people. They should give due respect to everyone they know and meet. Some parents do not take care of their elders, and it is a known fact that such children who see their parents disrespecting their elders, never respect their parents and elder siblings.

Parenting Style

Parenting style also matters and many researchers say that it is one of the biggest reason why teens commit a crime. Parents are sometimes very harsh and they punish their children for small issues. Children start disrespecting their parents and they become violent.

Peer Group Influence

Peer group is a very strong force that can cause delinquent behaviour in the adolescent. Sometimes youth do not get acceptance in any group as they do not have a strong personality and due to peer group rejection, they commit crimes. When friends commit crime, adolescents often learn to do it and they cannot understand the consequences of the crime. Adolescents can also show delinquent behaviour when they cannot get similar resources as their friends have. Parents should ensure that their children are hanging out with friends who belong to their class as this will prevent adolescent jealousy which can cause several crimes in adolescents. Parents should also see that their children are going out with good friends that belong to respectable families. They should not become part of any gang.

Gangs and Cliques

Youth can easily become part of a gang or clique during their age. They think it appropriate to be powerful and to be part of a large group. Often strong groups and gangs are ones that are indulged in negative actions. Peer group influence can be positive and it can be negative.

Abusive Behaviour

Abusive behaviour is the first step towards committing crimes. When teens become part of a clique that is abusive and that does not know how to behave, the teen also get involved in negative means.

Lowering the Age of Juvenile Delinquent in India

The Government of India, in view of the public outrage, constituted a committee to look into rape laws under the chairmanship of Justice J.S. Verma but unfortunately it made no such recommendation. Almost everybody will agree that there is something wrong with a system that allows someone who has raped and brutalized a girl, resulting in her death, to walk free after just three years because he was a 'juvenile'. All over the world, laws distinguish between adults and juveniles but many countries do not make this distinction absolute and rigid. They strike a balance by calibrating the age below which a person is considered juvenile to the nature of the crime. For those charged with heinous crimes like murder or rape, the age limits are lower. So, in our country too, an individual must be tried for the severity of the crime he is accused for and his age must not be kept in view.

Against the backdrop of all this, many sensible persons have raised their voice in this regard because sentencing a person to such a mild punishment of just three years in a children's home will encourage other criminally-minded youth also and this trend has already been set if we see the Mumbai's gang-rape incident.

Types of Delinquency

Delinquency exhibits a variety of styles of conduct or forms of behaviour. Each of the patterns has its own social context, the causes that are alleged to bring it about, and the forms of prevention or treatment most often suggested as appropriate for the pattern in question. Howard Becker (1966: 226–38) has referred to four types of delinquencies: (a) individual delinquency, (b) group-supported delinquency, (c) organized delinquency, and (d) situational delinquency.

Individual Delinquency

This refers to delinquency in which only one individual is involved in committing a delinquent act and its cause is located within the individual delinquent. Most of the explanations of this delinquent behaviour come from psychiatrists. Their argument is that delinquency is caused by the psychological problems stemming primarily from defective/faulty/pathological family interaction patterns. Researches of Healy and Bronner, Albert Bandura and Richard Walters, Edwin Powers and Helen Witmer, and Henry Mcyer, Edgar Borgatta are based on this approach. Healy and Bronner (1936) compared delinquent youths with their non-delinquent siblings and analysed the differences between them. Their most important finding was that over 90 per cent of the delinquents compared to 13 per cent of their non-delinquent siblings had unhappy home lives and felt discontented with their life circumstances. The nature of unhappiness differed: some felt rejected by parents and others felt either inferior to or jealous of siblings or suffered from mental conflict. They indulged in delinquency as a solution to these problems, as it (delinquency) either brought attention from parents or provided support from peers or reduced their guilt feelings. Later studies also identified important aspects of family relations leading to delinquencies. Bandura and Walters compared the aggressive actions of white delinquents with those of non-delinquent boys with no clear sign of economic hardship. They found that delinquents differed from non-delinquents a little in their relationship with their mothers but more in their relationship with their fathers. Thus, father-son rather than mother-son relations seemed more crucial in delinquency, as delinquent boys could not internalize moral values because of the absence of good role models in their fathers. In addition, their discipline was also more harsh and stern.

Group-supported Delinquency

In this type, the delinquencies are committed in companionship with others and the cause is located not in the personality of the individual or in the delinquent's family but in the culture of the individual's home and neighbourhood. The studies of Thrasher (1936) and Shaw and McKay (1931) talk of this type of delinquency. The main finding in understanding why the young became delinquent was their association and companionship with others already delinquent. This was later put very clearly by Sutherland, who developed the theory of differential association. Unlike the psychogenic explanations, this set of ideas focusses on what is learnt and who it is learnt from rather than on the problems that might produce a motivation to commit delinquencies.

Organized Delinquency

This type refers to delinquencies that are committed by developing formally organized groups. These delinquencies were analysed in the United States in the 1950s and the concept of 'delinquent sub-culture' was developed. This concept refers to the set of values and norms that guide the behaviour of group members, encourage the commission of delinquencies, award status on the basis of such acts and specify typical relationships to persons who fall outside the groupings governed by group norms. Cohen (1955) was the first person to refer to this type of delinquency. He was followed by Cloward and Ohlin (1960) and a few others.

Situational Delinquency

The above mentioned three types of delinquencies have one thing in common. In all of them, delinquency is viewed as having deep roots. In individual delinquency (according to the psychogenic explanation), the roots of delinquency lie primarily within the individual; in group-supported and organized delinquencies (the sociogenic explanation) the roots (of delinquency) lie in the structure of the society with emphasis either on the ecological areas where delinquency prevails or on the systematic way in which social structure places some individuals in a poor position to compete for success. The situational delinquency provides a different perspective. Here the assumption is that delinquency is not deeply rooted, and motives for delinquency and means for controlling it are often relatively simple. A young man indulges in a delinquent act without having a deep commitment to delinquency because of less developed impulse control and/or because of lesser reinforcement of family restraints and because he has relatively little to lose even if caught. Matza (1964) is one scholar who refers to this type of delinquency. However, the concept of situational delinquency is undeveloped and is not given much relevance in the problem of delinquency causation. It is a supplement to rather than a replacement of other types.

Factors Involved in Juvenile Delinquency

Researchers generally agree that a number of factors play an important part in a youngster's delinquencies. We can divide these factors into two groups: individual factors and situational factors. The former include personality traits like submissiveness, defiance, hostility, impulsiveness, feeling of insecurity, fear, lack of self-control and emotional conflict while the latter may be sub-divided into five groups: family, companions, school environment, movies and work environment. We will mainly discuss here the family's contribution to delinquency.

Family

Many theorists consider family as the most significant factor in the development of juvenile delinquency. Class status, power group relations and class mobility, are also directly or indirectly related to the family environment. Psychological theorists like Irving Kaufman, Sidney Berman and August Aichhorn are primarily concerned with the causation of delinquency in early childhood experiences, emotional deprivations and child-rearing processes, which influence the formation of the personality and the development of attitudes, values, and a lifestyle. The abnormal expression of behaviour expressed in an anti-social form is the result of these factors according to the psychologists. Whereas, the psychologist is concerned with the identification of individual variables, such as motivation, drives, values, and needs, the sociologist is concerned more with the social environment, the factors in the social system, and the functioning of the institutions that promote delinquency. Thus, the psychologists focus on internal control while the sociologists focus on external control.

Family environment producing delinquent behaviour may be analysed with reference to a broken home, family tension, parental rejection, parental control, and family economics. A normal family is described as one which is structurally complete (with both parents alive), functionally adequate (each member performing his/her expected roles which reduces conflicts), economically secure (gratifying important needs of the members) and morally strong (each member conforming to the moral values of the culture). The family is abnormal if it lacks any of these characteristics.

Factors in Juvenile Delinquency

Individual factors

1. Submissiveness
2. Defiance
3. Hostility
4. Impulsiveness
5. Feeling of insecurity
6. Fear
7. Emotional Conflicts
8. Lack of Self-control

Situational factors

- Family
  1. Parents' discipline
  2. Parents' affection
  3. Cohesiveness of family
  4. Conduct-standards of home
  5. Substitute parents
  6. Father's work habits
  7. Economic condition of family
  8. Conjugal relations of parents
  9. Broken Homes
  10. Affection of siblings
  11. Household duties
  12. Culture refinement of home.
- Peer Group Relations
- School Environment
  1. Adjustment to school mates
  2. Attitudes toward school
  3. Failure in classes or academic interests
- Movies
- Working Environment

The broken family (where one parent is absent because of parental separation, divorce or death) fails to provide affection and control to the child. Glueck and Glueck (1968: 12) found in their study of delinquents and non-delinquents that more than half of the delinquents studied were reared by one parent, whereas only 10 per cent of the non-delinquents were reared by one parent. Monahan (1957: 250–58), Browning (1960: 3744), Gold Martin, Slocum and Stone (1965), and Peterson and Becker (1965) also found that a significantly greater number of delinquents than non-delinquents were from broken homes.

Family tension is also a major contributing factor to delinquent behaviour. Abrahamsen (1960: 43) found that family tension results from hostility and hatred. The youngster does not feel secure and content in the tension-filled family environment. Long-term tension reduces family cohesiveness and affects parents' ability to provide a conducive atmosphere to satisfactory child-rearing and family problem-solving. McCord, McCord and Zola (1959) also found that cohesive homes produced fewer delinquents whereas homes where tension and hostility existed were good breeding grounds for future delinquents.

Parental rejection or emotional deprivation has much to do with juvenile delinquency. If a rejected or a neglected child does not find love and affection as well as support and supervision at home, he will often resort to groups of a deviant nature outside the family. Studies have found that mutual rejection of parent and child markedly affects positive relationship and can ultimately result in delinquent behaviour. Jenkins (1957: 528–37) found that parental rejection had a direct effect on the child's development and growth of a conscience. He stated that lack of adequate conscience, combined with feelings of hostility for being rejected, led to aggression. Andry (1960: 64) also has maintained that delinquents were the recipients of less parental love both in quantity and in quality than were the non-delinquents.

Just as a broken home, family tension and parental rejection can affect the capability of the family structure, methods of parental control or forms of discipline also can play a part in the development of delinquent behaviour. The type of discipline used by parents in rearing children varies from situation to situation and from child to child. An authoritarian approach to discipline, affects the child in his peer group relationships as the child will not be able to interact freely with his peers. Conversely, a too lenient attitude will not provide the child with the necessary controls to guide his behaviour. Unfair or partial discipline fails to form an adequate conscience in the child, prevents the adults from serving as a model to be imitated by the child, and reduces the adolescent's wish to avoid hurting the parent and the delinquent behaviour. Glueck and Glueck (1968: 15–16) found that the parents of delinquents used physical punishment more than verbal discussion. Both the parents were less consistent in their disciplinary measures than were the parents of non-delinquents. If the methods of disciplining are classified as love-oriented discipline, punitive discipline, lax discipline and erratic discipline (punitive and lax), the last three types can be related to delinquency.

Emotional instability and behavioural disturbances in one or both of the parents also lead to a child's delinquent behaviour. The child of the parents who are constantly in conflict often exploits the situation and gets away with a great deal of misbehaviour.

Lastly, family economics is also an important contributing variable in delinquency. A family's inability to provide for the material needs of the child can create insecurity and affect the amount of control that the family exerts over the child, because he often seeks material support and security outside the home. Peterson and Becker (1965) have pointed out that the homes of delinquents are often physically deteriorated which can affect the boy's perception of himself and can act as a repellent, driving him away from the home. It should, however, be pointed out that economic status and material possessions do not explain middle and upper class delinquency. The economic condition of the family can be one of many contributing factors in a multiproblem family.

Dealing with Family Issues

The family should have a positive attitude towards life and towards society. Parents and elder siblings should show the children positive values, norms and standards of society. In this way, the children will be able to show the right behaviour to the society. The family is the role model of every child and a model behaviour by the parents and siblings can give motivation to the child to behave positively. The government should support families that have poor economic status so that they can improve their financial condition. Parents should also teach children the importance of respecting the laws of society. Parents should tell their children the consequences of breaking laws that the government has made for public safety and betterment. Parents should make sure that they observe equality of rights, justice and condemn discrimination.

There are many organizations who deal with the problem of juvenile delinquency. They are established to help those children who are involved in it. They increase their thinking ability, decision-making skills, instil in them a sense of security and give them the love and affection that they may have been deprived of. Parents are also counselled to detect early signs of maladjustments, so that any tendency towards delinquency may be destroyed at the roots. There are rehabilitation centres and consultancies also run by the government who treat such children and make them a good person.

Neighbourhood

The impact of the neighbourhood on the child is more in the urban areas than in the rural areas. After the family, the child spends a good part of the day in company of children in his neighbourhood. The neighbourhood can contribute to delinquency by blocking basic personality needs engendering culture conflicts, and fostering anti-social values. On the other hand, it can supplement the influence of the home in the maintenance of social values. Congested neighbourhoods with inadequate recreation facilities deny the natural play impulses of children and encourage the formation of delinquent gangs. Picture houses, cheap hotels and video-halls in the neighbourhoods become breeding places of vice and delinquency.

Cinema and Pornographic Literature

Movies and comic books featuring immorality, smoking, drinking and brutality leave a strong impression on the young minds of the children and the adolescents. Many a time, they teach the techniques of crime and delinquency. Several children are arrested in different parts of our country for emulating these techniques to commit thefts, burglaries and kidnapping. They claimed to have seen such techniques succeed in the movies. These movies also develop attitudes conducive to delinquent behaviour by arousing desires for easy money, suggesting questionable methods for their achievement, inducing a spirit of toughness and adventurousness, arousing sexual desires, and by invoking daydreaming.

Sociology of Juvenile Delinquency

The major sociological theorists who have contributed to the criminological knowledge of delinquency are Merton, Frederick Thrasher, Clifford Shaw and Henry McKay, George Herbert Mead, Albert Cohen, Cloward and Ohlin, Walter Miller and David Matza. These are briefly summarize here :

Merton's *Anomie Theory* is that when there is a discrepancy between the institutionalized means that are available within the environment and the goals that individuals have learnt to aspire for in their environment, strain or frustration is produced and norms break down and deviant behaviour may result (1938: 672–82). Merton, thus, does not discuss individual motivational factors in deviance (that is, in selecting one of the five alternative modes of behaviour suggested by him) or he fails in explaining why all persons in similar situations do not choose deviance.

Fredrick Thrasher's *Gang Theory* concentrates on group delinquency and explains positive peer influence as Cohen's, Cloward's and Miller's theories did later on (1936: 381). Thrasher does not say that the gang is a cause of delinquency but he says that gang facilitates delinquency. Explaining the process whereby a group takes on certain behavioural characteristics and then transmits them to its members, he says that a gang originates during the adolescent years from spontaneous play groups and conflict with other groups, transforms it into a gang for protecting its members' rights and satisfying the needs which their environment and their family could not provide. Gradually, the gang develops distinct characteristics such as a mode of operation and disseminates criminal techniques, excites mutual interests and attitudes and provides protection to its members. Thrasher emphasized that not all gang activities were necessarily devious and that much of the gang members' time was spent in normal athletic activities as well as in other teenage endeavours. His thesis, thus, mainly describes how environmental pressure is conducive to delinquent behaviour.

Shaw and McKay's *Cultural Transmission Theory* holds that delinquency is transmitted through personal and group contacts and that lack of effective social control agencies contributes to the high incidence of delinquency in some parts of the large cities (1931: 386). These 'delinquency areas' are the low-income and physically deteriorated areas whose members suffer from economic deprivations. Furthermore, the boys in these areas are not necessarily disorganized, maladjusted or anti-social. It is the exposure to delinquency traditions present in these areas which makes them delinquents. But for this exposure, they would have found their satisfaction in activities other than delinquency. Shaw and McKay acknowledge that other factors may cause certain youngsters to become involved in delinquent activities, but they feel that these factors are secondary to the economic and social factors that exist in the community. It is this learned phenomenon of delinquency which is developed in Sutherland's theory also.

George Herbert Mead's *Role Theory and Theory of the Self* explain why only a limited number of persons assume criminal identities while the majority of people remain law-abiding (1934: 577–602). He says, becoming a delinquent and assuming a criminal identity involves more than merely associating with law violators. The associations have to be meaningful to the individual and supportive of a role and self-concept that he wants to become committed to.

Albert Cohen's *Working-Class Boy and Middle-Class Measuring Rod Theory* (1955: 119) maintains that delinquency is mainly a working class phenomenon. He states that the working-class boy finds himself at the bottom of status hierarchy whenever he moves into the middle-class world. To the degree to which he values middle class status either because he values the good opinion of the middle class persons or because he has, to some degree, internalized middle class standards himself, he faces the problem of adjustment. A delinquent sub-culture deals with the problems of adjustment (that is, status problems) by providing a criteria of status which these children can meet. Not having learnt the behaviour that will equip them to deal with the competitive struggle for their success, the working class boys feel frustrated, react against middle class values and standards, and adopt their very antithesis, that is, non-utilitarian, malicious and negativistic values. Group or gang delinquent activity legitimizes and supports aggression against middle class institutions.

Cloward and Ohlin's *Success and Opportunity Structures Theory* copes with the discrepancies of Sutherland's, Merton's and Mead's theories and explains the types of alternatives available as a result of strain and lack of legitimate alternatives to satisfy the needs (1960: 86). Faced with limitations on legitimate avenues of access to their goals and unable to revise their aspirations downward, the lower-class youths experience intense frustrations which results in their exploring nonconformist and illegitimate alternatives. Cloward and Ohlin's theory is difficult to test and evaluate empirically.

Walter Miller's *Lower-Class Boy and Lower-Class Structure Theory* rejects 'delinquent sub-culture' and talks of 'lower-class culture' itself which comes about as a result of the process of immigration, migration and mobility (1958: 6). Those persons who are left behind as a result of these processes comprise the lower class. They develop a distinct pattern of behaviour (which is not necessarily reactive against any other class) based on distinctive (lower-class) traits like toughness, smartness, excitement, fate and autonomy. The street group provides the lower-class adolescent boy an opportunity to act tough and become involved in masculine activities. Many of his activities, thus, revolve round his desire to become a 'real man'. The major criticism of Miller's theory is that today with mass communication, it is difficult to believe that the distinct lower-class culture, which Miller describes, can exist in such a pure form. Lower class is bound to be influenced by the other classes.

David Matza's *Delinquency and Drift Theory* rejects the deterministic orientation of the Positive School that delinquent behaviour is caused almost entirely by emotional and environmental factors (1964: 11). Matza feels that man is neither totally free (as the Classical School assumes) nor is he totally constrained (as the Positivist School assumes), but he is somewhere between being controlled and being free. Drift stands midway between freedom and control. The youngster, therefore, drifts between criminal and conventional action. Even though most of the youngster's activities are law-abiding, he can periodically drift into delinquency because the normal conventional controls that usually inhibit delinquent behaviour become neutralized as a result of the drifting process. Once he indulges in delinquency, he drifts back to conventionality. Matza, thus, emphasizes on the 'will to crime'. It is this 'will' which explains why some youngsters choose delinquent behaviour while most of their peers within the same environment choose socially acceptable modes of adaptation. He also explains why delinquency is not an 'either-or' proposition. Most youngsters exist somewhere along the continuum between convention and crime. Total commitment to delinquency is uncommon.

Two major types of theories include *psychodynamic theory* and *social learning theory*. The *psychodynamic theory* places its emphasis on the notion that one of the main causes of juvenile delinquency is children's abnormal personalities that were created and developed in earlier life. Since then these 'unconscious mental processes' (Siegel and Welsh, 2012) have been controlling the adolescents' criminal behaviour. The Id is the drive for immediate gratification and can explain delinquency acts such as shoplifting or burglary. The ego is the realization of real life and helps control the Id. Superego develops through interactions with parents and other responsible adults and develops the conscience of moral rules. This psychodynamic approach states that traumatic experiences during early childhood can prevent the ego and superego from developing properly.

Social learning theory is also a major theory that implies that criminal behaviour is learned through close relations with others, it asserts that children are born good but learned to be bad. This theory states that all people have the potential to become criminals because modern society presents many opportunities for illegal activity but one has the choice to not engage. If a child is raised in a clean community that has strong morals and if that child has positive role models at home and in the community, he or she is more likely to grow up achieving their goals. Opposing that scenario, when a child is growing up in a poor neighbourhood where he or she is surrounded by gangs, drugs, and violence every day, it is very likely that this child will grow up committing crimes (McDavid and McCandles, 1962).

Social learning theory posits that humans learn social behaviour by observing others' behaviour and the consequences of that behaviour, forming ideas about what behaviours are appropriate, trying those behaviours, and continuing them if the results are positive. This theory does not view aggression as inevitable but rather sees it as a social behaviour that is learned and shaped by its consequences, continuing if it is reinforced (Lore and Schultz, 1993). From this perspective, male violence against women endures in human societies because it is modelled both in individual families and in the society more generally and has positive results: it releases tension, leaves the perpetrator feeling better, often achieves its ends by cutting off arguments, and is rarely associated with serious punishment for the perpetrator.

One of the mechanisms through which social learning occurs is social information processing – the decoding or interpreting of social interactions, making decisions about appropriate responses on the basis of the decoding, and carrying out a response to see if it has the intended effect. It has been hypothesized that violent men may be deficient in the skills necessary to accurately decode communications from women.

Psychological theories explain juvenile delinquency with individual-level constructs that exist inside of all people and interact with the social world.

According to Sigmund Freud (1925), who theorized that the personality consists of three parts: the Id, ego, and superego. The Id, which is present at birth, consists of blind, unreasoning, instinctual desires and motives. The Id represents basic biological and psychological drives and does not differentiate between fantasy and reality. The Id is antisocial and knows no rules, boundaries, or limitations. If the Id is left unchecked, it will obliterate the person. The ego grows from the Id. It deals with reality and teaches children to delay gratification because acting on impulse will get them into trouble. The superego develops from the ego and is the norms, and values the child has acquired. The superego is responsible for feelings of guilt and shame. In mentally healthy children, the three parts of the personality work together. When the parts are in conflict, children may become maladjusted and ready for delinquency.

B.F. Skinner (1953), who theorized that children learn conformity and deviance from the punishments and reinforcements that they receive in response to their behaviour. He believed that their behaviour is the result of the consequences. He concluded that children and adolescents repeat rewarded behaviour and terminate punished behaviour.

In his social learning theory, Albert Bandura (1977) suggests that children learn by modelling and imitating others. For example, children learn to be aggressive from their life experiences and learn aggression in different ways. For example, by seeing parents argue, watching their friends fight, viewing violence on television and listening to violent music. What children learn is that aggression is sometimes acceptable and can produce the desired outcome. The ideas of Skinner and Bandura would later be adopted by sociologists.

If we now take all the sociological theories of juvenile delinquency together, it may be said that all sociologists have put emphasis on the environment, social structures and learning process unlike the psychologists who consider the individual and his motivational patterns important in delinquency.

There is not one set answer on why our youth is turning to criminal behaviour, but there are plenty of biological, sociological and psychological theories that can help acquire reasonings and knowledge to better understand juveniles. Once these theories have been carefully analysed, applying them to juveniles in a case by case scenario can help deter and keep children from choosing a life of criminal behaviour.

Methods of Treating Delinquents

Many approaches and methods can be used in treating the delinquent. Some important methods are: (a) psychotherapy, (b) reality therapy, (c) behaviour therapy, (d) activity therapy, and (e) milieu therapy. Punishment is not discussed as a treatment method because it is no longer viewed as a viable technique of treatment, though some do feel that pain serves as a deterrent to further criminal action. Restrictions and reprimands can be effective supplements to the major treatment approach utilized but punishment cannot become an end in itself.

The two basic approaches in dealing with youngsters are the individual and the group method of treatment. Of these, it is generally the individual method which is used by psychologists, psychiatrists sociologists and social workers, though psychologists sometimes do use the group method as well. Sociologists usually take a 'social engineering' approach to delinquency, that is, they deal with the conditions of the social structure that breed delinquency, while psychologists treat the individual and emphasize his interpersonal dynamics. Sociology is regarded as a theoretical discipline researching the causes and effects of crime and delinquency. The profession of social work is the 'practical arm' of the sociologists (Trojanowicz, 1973: 229). As such, the above-mentioned six therapeutic methods are generally utilized by psychologists, psychiatrists and social workers. We will briefly discuss each method separately.

Psychotherapy treats emotional and personality problems by psychological means, that is, by changing the attitudes and feelings about significant persons (say, parents) in the client's (delinquent's) past. When the early relationship of the youngster with his parents was not satisfactory, his emotional development was often retarded, with the result that he was often impulsive in his attempt to satisfy his infantile urges, not satisfied in the normal manner within his family. Satisfying these urges and impulses can take the form of anti-social behaviour. Through psychotherapy, the delinquent is allowed by the therapist to operate in an atmosphere of love and acceptance, where the person does not have to fear severe rejection or physical punishment. This is due to the transference established in which the client and the therapist feel comfortable in exchanging communication. Thus, this therapy involves facilitating the solving of conflicts and providing positive alternatives to behaviour adaptation by the client.

Reality therapy is based on the view that people who are unable to fulfil their basic needs, act in an irresponsible manner. The object of the reality therapy is to help the delinquent person act in a responsible manner, that is, refrain from anti-social activity. This therapy can be given by any one (police officer, counsellor, teacher, social worker, family member or a friend) because it does not emphasize nebulous psychiatric terms, extensive testing or time-consuming case conferences. This method differs from the psychotherapeutic method in the sense that the latter is concerned with the past behaviour while this is concerned with the present behaviour. Whereas the basis of psychotherapy is that a person cannot change his present behaviour unless he can clearly tie it to the events in the past, the basis of the Reality therapy is that the past is insignificant. In this therapy, since a child is treated as a responsible person and not as an unfortunate youngster, it transmits strength to the youngster. The child is expected to obey rules but he is not rejected when he breaks one.

Behaviour therapy is modifying the learnt behaviour of the delinquent through the development of new learning processes. Behaviour can be changed through positive or negative reinforcements, that is, rewards or punishments. Negative or unpleasant reinforcements (like restrictions) will reduce/eliminate negative behaviour (that is, delinquent activity), while positive or pleasant reinforcements (like rewards) will maintain/increase positive behaviour (like success on the job and in school). This requires determining each individual's 'reinforcers,' that is, those aspects which the individual (delinquent) will strive to achieve to gain personal satisfaction. Money, praise, attention, food, privileges, admission in school, freedom to play with children, and good clothes can be considered as positive reinforcers, while threats, confinements, ridicule, physical punishment and depriving of money are negative reinforcers. For modifying behaviour, both the reinforcers can be employed.

Activity therapy: Many children do not have the verbal ability to communicate effectively in a conventional individual or group situation. In activity therapy method, a group of 6–8 children are gathered/invited to meet at a specific time/place to engage in play or some artistic endeavour. The atmosphere is permissive and the youngsters can use their time as they wish. Thus, a moderately neurotic child finds great release in a permissive environment where he can express his hostility and aggression in creative work, play, or mischief. As his behaviour does not call for retaliation, punishment, or disapproval; pent-up emotions find appropriate release.

Milieu or environment therapy attempts to produce an environment that will facilitate meaningful change and satisfactory adjustment. This is used for persons whose deviant behaviour is a reaction to unfavourable life conditions.

Apart from the above methods, three more methods are also used in the treatment of juvenile delinquents. These are: (a) Social case work, that is, assisting the maladjusted youngster in coping with his problems. Although similar in many respects, technically social case work, is different from psychotherapy. Whereas a social case-worker could be a probation officer, prison counsellor, mental health worker, or hospital social worker, a psychotherapist is essentially a doctor by profession. The case worker prepares the case history of the client to explore his background, environment and relationships with his family, friends and school fellows and evaluates his personal strengths and weaknesses so that a treatment plan can be devised and carried out. This method however, is often unsuccessful with the delinquents because on the one hand, it is difficult to obtain the delinquent's co-operation as he has no trust in the case worker and on the other hand, the delinquent's family also resists and feels threatened by the case worker's 'probing'. (b) Individual counselling, that is, re-educating a delinquent to enable him to understand his immediate situation and solve his problem. In this method, no attempt is made to affect a fundamental change of the client's personality. (c) Vocational counselling, its main purpose is to increase the delinquent's knowledge of his career choices, job specifications and qualifications and training needed for successful employment. The positive attitudes, skills and habits that the youngster develops and refines in the work situation can be carried over to the community and can positively affect his relationships with others.

Custody in Juvenile Institutions

Remand Homes, Certified Schools, Reformatory Schools, Borstal Schools and Probation Hostels are the important institutions used for the custody and correction of the juvenile delinquents in India. Children Acts were enacted long back in different states for the treatment and protection of young offenders, and the custody, trial and punishment of the juvenile delinquents. Both the 1986 Act and Children Acts suffered from many deficiencies in the absence of a uniform law for the country as a whole. Some of these deficiencies were: (a) the upper age limit in defining a 'child' varied from state to state; (b) all states had not provided for juvenile courts; (c) the institutional facilities were devoid of any well-defined criteria and norms to regulate capacity, staff, and programmes; (d) no minimum standards for basic needs, living conditions or therapeutic services existed; and (e) in most states, neglected children were huddled together with juvenile delinquents.

The Juvenile Justice (Care and Protection of Children) Act of 2000 is the primary legal framework for juvenile justice in India. It provides a differential approach towards prevention and treatment of juvenile delinquency in the country. This law, brought in compliance of Child Rights Convention, and repealing the earlier Juvenile Justice Act of 1986, has been further amended from time to time.

The 2000 Act contains statutory provisions to handle cases relating to minor offenders, called as 'delinquents', 'juveniles in conflict with law' or as 'children in need of care and protection'. Its Section 2(k) defines a 'juvenile' or a 'child' as a person who has not completed 18 year of age while 2(l) says a 'juvenile in conflict with law' means a juvenile who is alleged to have committed an offence. Regarding determination of the age of a juvenile, the Act calls for a 'due inquiry' by competent authority – usually the Juvenile Justice Board. Rules under the Act lay down that medical opinion on the age of an accused be sought only if he fails to produce matriculation or an equivalent educational certificate, or a birth certificate in absence of the former.

Besides, like previous laws, this Act also has many serious flaws. For example, whenever a juvenile is arrested for an alleged offence, he requires to be immediately produced before the Juvenile Justice Board (JJB). The law says that the Board, irrespective of the offence, should release him on bail, with or without any surety. Even, there are no provisions for rarest of rare cases in this Act. However, certain provisions leave some discretion with the Board's magistrate to pass orders in exceptional cases. Section 15(g), which was brought after an amendment, states that the Board can order putting a juvenile, between the ages of 17 and 18, in a special home for a period of not less than two years.

Section 16 talks about penalizing orders that cannot be passed against juveniles and imposes an absolute prohibition on a life term or death sentence or even any duration of jail term. At the same time, the proviso to this section says that if the 'Board is satisfied that the offence committed is so serious in nature or that his conduct and behaviour have been such that it would not be in his interest or in the interest of other juvenile in a special home to send him to such special home and that none of the other measures provided under this Act is suitable or sufficient,' it may seek the assistance of the state government for placing him in an appropriate institution. On receiving a report from the Board, the government may arrange for keeping a juvenile under protective custody at a place, but not for more than three years or till he turns 18.

Even if a juvenile turns 18 during the course of sentence, he will continue to stay in the children's or observation home. Not only this, Section 44 of the Act provides for establishment or recognition of after-care institutions by the state government for lodging juveniles after their release from observation homes. However, the period of such stay for a juvenile over 17 but less than 18 has been limited to three years or till he attains the age of 20 years.

In India, juveniles accused of a crime or detained for a crime are brought before the Juvenile Justice Board (JJB), established in all states as per the requirement of the Juvenile Justice (Care and Protection of Children) Act, 2000 (amended in 2006). Under this Act and provisions of the Criminal Code Procedure children are not to be taken to a regular criminal court. The purpose of a separate court is socio-legal rehabilitation and reformation and not punishment.

The JJB consists of a metropolitan magistrate or a judicial magistrate of the first class and two social workers, at least one of whom should be a woman. All three people form a bench to function as a unit. Though they have different roles they are required to coordinate for the best interest of the child. When a child has been found guilty of a crime, the social workers are vital to deciding the best course of action for the rehabilitation of that child. JJBs are meant to resolve cases within a four-month period. Backlog of cases can be addressed with an increased number of sittings.

A child is usually brought before the JJB by a police officer or person from the Special Juvenile Police Unit (SJPU). Any organization or person who brings a child before the court should inform their local police units first. The police has 24 hours to produce a child before the court once he/she is arrested. The person or police officer who brings the child before the JJB is required to complete a report of the arrest/detainment. Once the child has been brought before the JJB he/she is registered into the closest Observation Home. In most circumstances the juvenile can be released on bail by the JJB. If the police wish to interrogate the child or conduct a test identification parade, the JJB has to give an order allowing so and it can only be conducted in the presence of the superintendent of the home. The home probation officer (PO) in charge will also submit a report on the child.

With the police report and PO report the JJB calls for the child's plea. If the child pleas guilty the JJB will pass appropriate orders for the child. To prevent coercion, the JJB can dismiss the child's guilty plea if it feels it was forced. If the juvenile pleads not guilty the JJB must further investigate by calling witnessing and accusers to testify before the court. The juvenile is given then opportunity to address the evidence brought before the court and also bring witnesses to the court. According to the evidence the JJB will then pass an order disposing of the case as it sees fit. The JJB is a child-friendly space that should not be intimidating or overwhelming for the child.

Remand Homes or Observation Homes

These homes are meant for children during the pendency of their trial in the JJBs, but they are also used for keeping the homeless, destitute and neglected children. The stay here is used for evaluating their personality traits and behaviour. As such, these homes are viewed more as observation homes than as places of detention.

The important characteristics of a good Remand Home are: segregation, education, training, recreation facilities, health care, controlled discipline and effective supervision. Since the child in the Remand Home comes into contact with the law for the first time, if the environment is not kept conducive, the child might become suspicious and defiant towards the courts.

In India, Remand/Observation Homes do not exist in all states. According to 1993 figures, Remand Homes are found only in 14 out of 25 states and in one union territory. The highest number of Remand Homes are found in Maharashtra, followed by Gujarat, Karnataka, Tamil Nadu, Kerala, Uttar Pradesh, Bihar, Andhra Pradesh and West Bengal. Of about 154 Remand/Observation Homes, a little more than half are run by the government and a little less than half by voluntary agencies. There are separate homes for boys and girls. Of the total inmates in the Remand Homes, 15 to 20 per cent are juvenile delinquents and the rest are homeless, destitute and neglected children. Of the total inmates, two-thirds belong to the 7–14 years age group while the remaining one-third are either below seven years or between 14 and 18 years of age.

Certified or Reformatory Schools

Juveniles given detention order by the JJBs are kept in Reformatory Schools for a minimum period of three years and a maximum period of seven years. Inmates of about 18 years age are transferred to Borstal Schools. These schools, meant only for boys, remain under the supervision of prison department. Each school having a capacity of 80–100 inmates is divided into 4–5 dormitories and each dormitory has 4–5 cells. Each school has a superintendent, deputy superintendent, deputy jailer, assistant jailer, doctor, 3–4 instructors, 2–3 teachers and some wardens. Training is given in tailoring, toy-making, manufacturing leather goods, and agriculture. Each training programme is of two years. The inmate gets the raw material from the school and the things manufactured by him are sold in the market and the profit deposited in his account. After the deposits have reached a fixed amount, the inmate has to produce things only for state use. The inmate even gets basic education up to the fifth standard and he has to appear in the examinations (at the end of the year) conducted by the Inspector of Schools. If the inmate wants to study beyond the fifth standard, he is admitted in the outside school. Since no work is forced upon the inmates here, they live like family members. However, no follow-up records are maintained by the schools after the release of the inmates. Second, the training programmes are too old and traditional.

Borstal Schools

Provision was made in the 1920s for the segregation of adolescent offenders from the adults so that correction services, free from the authoritarian atmosphere, be made possible for the young offenders. Borstal Schools were thus established for youthful offenders in the age group of 16–21 years. Up to 1993, there were Borstal Schools only in nine states in the country: Tamil Nadu (1926), Andhra Pradesh (1926), Bihar (1926), Punjab (1926), Madhya Pradesh (1928), Maharashtra (1929), Uttar Pradesh (1938) and Kerala and Karnataka (1943). As of 31 December 2016, there are 21 functioning Borstal Schools in India, with a combined total capacity for 2,218 inmates. The capacity of each school varies from 100 to 350 inmates. Though these schools function under the general supervision of the Inspector General of Prisons, each school however, has its own Visiting Committee consisting of one sessions judge, one district magistrate, district level school officer and four non-government members. No inmate is kept here for less than two years or more than five years. Thus, only those delinquents are sent to these schools who are awarded more than three years term. Each school is divided into houses and each house has a House Master. Each house is further divided into groups and each group has a monitor. These monitors are selected from amongst the inmates themselves. There is a grading system too in the school: ordinary, star and special star grades. Those inmates who violate the norms are demoted to penal grade, but in ordinary cases, they are promoted from one grade to the other. No inmate is eligible to be released from the school unless he has reached the special star grade. On admission in the school, he is first observed for three months and given some ordinary work like, say, gardening. On being kept in the ordinary grade, he is assigned some training programme, depending on his education and potential. Each promotion entails more freedom and more privileges. The daily routine includes two hours' basic education and 5–6 hours' vocational training. Every inmate gets 15 days' leave in one year to visit his home. Normally, the inmate remains in continuous contact with his family members through correspondence and their visits. Some schools have created a *panchayat* system too and have thus associated the inmates with the management of the schools. In many cases, inmates are released from the schools before the expiry of the term also. Before the release from the Borstal School, the Discharged Prisoners Aid Society is informed so that it can chalk out the after-care programme for the released inmate.

Probation Hostels/Homes

These institutions, established under the Probation of Offenders Act, are meant to provide residential care and treatment to the offenders released under probation under the supervision of a probation officer. The inmates are given complete freedom to go to the market and also to take up jobs of their choice.

An evaluation of all types of juvenile institutions shows that though inmates' lifestyle is satisfactory and they enjoy better freedom but the institutions suffer from being overcrowded, the management is centralized, the training programmes are too traditional and inmates are not given individual attention. The budget allocation for them is also too low. One study made long ago (1968) to evaluate the juvenile correctional institutions was by the Indian Council of Social Welfare under the directorship of S.D. Gokhale. In this study, 229 inmates released during the period of five years were interviewed. It was found that the (a) training given in these institutions does not help the inmates to get jobs, (b) institutions do not provide facilities for formal school/college education, (c) counselling and case work facilities are inadequate, (d) individual attention is not paid to the inmates, and (e) institutions have limited budgets which prevents them from making adequate planning.

A study of 27 institutions for the socially handicapped children in Rajasthan (including Juvenile Reformatory, Observation Homes, Probation Home and Children Home) pointed out that: (a) institutional facilities are underutilized and occupancy rate of institutions is much below their capacity; (b) the quality and the content of vocational training is poor. It does not equip the inmate with skills essential for him to rehabilitate himself economically after being discharged from the institution; (c) space and physical amenities for inmates fall short of the minimum standards laid down by the Central Social Welfare Board; (d) protection services during institutionalization (against tough and aggressive inmates, homosexual assaults, snatching of eatables and other things by fellow inmates) and after discharge (against old accomplices, police harassment, immoral traffickers, etc.), are not provided; and (e) facilities to inmates for communicating with family members, kin and friends are inadequate. Even if it is assumed that some changes must have been introduced in these homes, it can be safely surmised that there is a great need of restructuring these homes.

After the independence, with an aim to provide care, protection, development and rehabilitation of neglected or delinquent juveniles, our parliament enacted the Juvenile Justice Act, 1986. It was an act which brought uniform system throughout the country. Section 2(a) of the Act defined the term 'juvenile' as a 'boy who has not attained the age of 16 years and a girl who has not attained the age of 18 years'.

Later on, the parliament enacted the Juvenile Justice (Care and Protection) Act, 2000 which raised the age bar to 18 years for both girl and boy. The Juvenile Justice (Care and Protection) Act, 2000 lays down that juvenile in conflict with the law or juvenile offenders may be kept in an 'observation home', while children in need of care and protection need to be kept in a 'Children Home' during the pendency of proceedings before the competent authority. As per the Juvenile Justice (Care and Protection) Act, 2000, a juvenile shall not be treated as an adult even if he/she is involved in any criminal acts for the purpose of trial and punishment in the court of law. For the betterment of the children, the Juvenile Justice Act, 2000 has introduced Special Trial Process.

Juvenile Justice (Care and Protection of Children) Act, 2015

The Juvenile Justice Act, 2015 was enacted to replace the existing Indian juvenile delinquency law, Juvenile Justice (Care and Protection of Children) Act, 2000, so that juveniles in conflict with the law in the age group of 16–18 years, involved in heinous offences can be tried as adults. It is an Act to consolidate and amend the law relating to children alleged and found to be in conflict with law and children in need of care and protection by catering to their basic needs through proper care, protection, development, treatment, social re-integration, by adopting a child-friendly approach in the adjudication and disposal of matters in the best interest of children and for their rehabilitation through processes provided, and institutions and bodies established for matters connected therewith.

Key Provisions

Change in nomenclature from 'juvenile' to 'child' or 'child in conflict with law', across the act to remove the negative connotation associated with the word 'juvenile'.

1. The inclusion of several new definitions such as orphaned, abandoned and surrendered children; and petty, serious and heinous offences committed by children.
2. Clarity in powers, function and responsibilities of Juvenile Justice Board (JJB) and Child Welfare Committee (CWC).
3. Special provisions for heinous offences committed by children above the age of sixteen years.
4. Adoption provides for detailed provisions relating to adoption and punishments for not complying with the laid down procedure.
5. The inclusion of new offences committed against minors.
6. Penalties for cruelty against a child, offering a narcotic substance to a child, and abduction or selling a child have been prescribed.
7. Mandatory registration of Child Care Institutions.

Protective Factors

Protective factors are traits or experiences that help counteract risk factors. These protective factors may reduce the likelihood of delinquent behaviour:

1. *Youth resilience:* Include hopefulness, spirituality, positive view of self, overall positive attitude, trust in others, sense of empowerment, realistic belief in one's ability to succeed, motivation, sense of purpose, positive future orientation, and taking responsibility for oneself.
2. *Social connectedness:* Signs of social connectedness include warm, supportive relationships with parents and other adults, friends who disapprove of anti-social behaviour, and positive school climate.

3. *Cognitive and social-emotional competence:* Signs include realistic belief in one's ability to succeed, personal goals, self-esteem, thinking about the consequences of one's behaviour, personal failings, and personal strengths.

There are some measures which may help in reforming these children:

1. Instil in them a sense of security and give them the love and affection that they may have been deprived of.
2. Parents should be counselled to detect early signs of maladjustments, so that any tendency towards delinquency may be destroyed at the roots.
3. A sense of moral and social values should be instilled in them from the very beginning.
4. Bring about a change in the community that encourages such behaviour.
5. Schools should adopt the option of skill management and vocational training so that children who are not academic by nature have the option of developing a skill which will give them the opportunity to earn a livelihood even without formal education.
6. Once the delinquent behaviour has been detected, one must remember to reject the behaviour and not the individual.

Preventive Programmes for Juvenile Delinquency

There may be two kinds of preventing programmes for the juvenile delinquency:

1. *Individual programme*: The individual programme involves the prevention of delinquency through counselling, psychotherapy, and proper education. Such programmes include – Parent Education, Recreational Programme, Educational Curriculum and Activities and Removal of Inferiority Complex.
2. *Environmental programme*: Environmental programme aims at changing the socio-economic conditions which are likely responsible for promoting delinquency. These programmes include – community activities for kids, parental care, family atmosphere and enforcement of the law.

Juvenile delinquency being mainly an urban phenomenon, both private and public agencies have to be involved in delinquency prevention, particularly because of the complexities of the urban society.

The three approaches to delinquency prevention are: (a) organizing activities that contribute to healthy personality development and adjustments of children, (b) controlling environment of children contributing to delinquency, and (c) organizing specific preventive services for children. The first approach links the delinquency prevention with: (i) general improvements in the institutional structure of the society, for example, family, neighbourhood, school, (ii) raising the income levels of poverty-stricken families, (iii) providing job opportunities to children, (iv) establishing schools, (v) improving job conditions, (vi) providing recreational facilities in neighbourhoods (vii) improving marital relations through family counselling services and family social work, and (viii) imparting moral and social education. Preventive activities of the second type include community organization and the efforts of welfare and child care agencies. Preventive activities of the third type include probation and parole services, Certified and Borstal Schools, Children Homes, Probation Hostels, and so forth.

The preventive programmes have also been classified (Trojanowicz, 1973: 188) as: (a) pure prevention or primary prevention, which attempts to inhibit delinquency before it takes place, and (b) rehabilitative prevention or secondary prevention, which deals with youngsters who have been adjudicated delinquents by the court.

Lejins (1967: 3) has classified the prevention programmes as: (a) punitive prevention, (b) corrective prevention, and (c) mechanical prevention. The first is the threat of punishment based on the idea that punishment will forestall criminal acts; the second refers to an attempt to eliminate potential causes before the criminal behaviour actually takes place; and the third emphasizes placing obstacles (like increased security measures or increased police protection) in the way of the potential criminal so that he will find it difficult to commit an offence.

The agencies concerned with the prevention of delinquency between the 1950 and the 1990s in India were voluntary children's organizations administering child welfare, schools, social welfare departments, rescue homes, orphanages and psychiatric centres. The efforts of voluntary organizations were less coordinated, while those of government departments more planned and systematically organized.

An overview of the functioning of the government institutions (Children Homes, Certified Schools, etc.) for 'rehabilitative prevention' is given in the earlier pages (with a discussion on 'Custody in Institutions'). We will briefly discuss here the 'pure prevention programmes'. The most important areas where the government needs to take up some measures like providing educational, recreational, and vocational training facilities for preventing delinquencies are the slum areas in cities. A big chunk of population lives in slums in big cities. If theories propounded by Thrasher, Shaw and McKay, Cohen, and Cloward and Ohlin, regarding learning of delinquencies from environment and lack of neighbourhood cohesiveness have some justification, it is necessary that the government takes up some measures for the welfare of the children in these areas and for their better integration into community life.

Family is another institution which needs greater attention. The role of functionally inadequate families, structurally incomplete or broken families, poor families, immoral families and undisciplined families in juvenile delinquency has already been elaborated. Unless these disorganized families are reorganized, and environment or milieu therapy is provided, frustrated and emotionally disturbed children cannot be prevented from developing a relationship with delinquents.

Police running recreation units for children is a new concept. Juvenile units in police department in cities like Mumbai and Delhi have undertaken these tasks. The police-school liaison programme on similar lines will go a long way in removing hostility and mutual suspicion between the police and youngsters; in the police helping teachers in handling problem youth; and, in improving the police image in general.

Initiating community programmes for educating the youngsters regarding the detrimental effects of using drugs and becoming involved in devious social behaviour is yet another measure in the prevention of juvenile delinquency. Drug abuse in recent years has increased among school children and slum-dwellers. Providing counselling services to these children experimenting with drugs will be an effective means of combatting illicit drug use in particular and juvenile delinquency in general.

Programmes for run-away children also need attention. Homes for these children, to give them a chance to reflect on their own situations with the assistance and guidance of staff members need to be established in big cities and towns. These homes can help in promoting a positive communication between run-away children and their parents and guardians so that serious problems can be resolved.

Suggestions

In order to make full use of the legal provisions available for juvenile, the state may initiate the following steps:

1. Through a programme of education, promotion and organization, form groups of local citizens and assist these groups in conducting activities aimed at the prevention and control of juvenile delinquency, making use of local people and resources for the following purposes:
   (a) Combatting local conditions known to contribute to juvenile delinquency.
   (b) Advise local and state officials, public and private agencies and lay groups on the needs and possible methods of the reduction and prevention of juvenile delinquency and the treatment of delinquent children.
   (c) Consultation with the schools and courts of this state on the development of programmes for the reducing and preventing delinquency and the treatment of delinquents.
   (d) Assisting any community within the state by conducting a comprehensive survey of the community's available public and private resources, and recommend methods of establishing a community programme for combatting juvenile delinquency and crime, but no survey of that type shall be conducted unless local individuals and groups request it through their local authorities, and no request of that type shall be interpreted as binding the community to follow the recommendations made as a result of the request.

2. Evaluating the rehabilitation of children committed to the department and prepare and submit periodic reports to the committing court for the following purposes:
   (a) Administering within the state any Juvenile Justice Acts and programmes that the governor requires the department to administer.
   (b) Visiting and inspecting jails, detention facilities, correctional facilities, facilities that may hold juveniles involuntarily, or any other facility that may temporarily house juveniles on a voluntary or involuntary basis.
   (c) Applying for allocating, disbursing and accounting grants that are made available pursuant to Juvenile Justice Acts, or made available from other states or private sources, to improve the criminal and juvenile justice systems in the state. All money from Juvenile Justice Act grants shall, if the terms under which the money is received require that the money is deposited into an interest-bearing fund or account, be deposited in the state treasury to the credit of the juvenile justice programme purposes fund, which is hereby created. All investment earnings shall be credited to the fund.
   (d) Assisting, advising and making any reports that are required by the governor, attorney general or general assembly.

Conclusion

India is perhaps the only country in the world which has the dubious distinction of having a maximum number of laws to regulate the conduct of society. It is the only country where almost all aspects of human behaviour are sought to be governed by laws rather than through education or innate enlightenment which is the preserve of every egalitarian society. In this fast-changing world where the development of science and technology keeps us on the run with rapidly occurring incredible changes that affect our lifestyles, we can not remain contented or being confined in a strait jacketed idealist frame of laws which have no bearing on the present day situation. We have to be pragmatic and realistic rather than narrow-minded with a kind of idealism that hardly works now. The state, as well as the society, have a responsibility towards our children in the sense that they would not become wayward and remain in the social mainstream; hence, 'care and protection' must be the main motto and not punishment.

The development of a sound public policy regarding all aspects of delinquency prevention and control requires both planning and evaluation by rigorous research methods. This requires coordination between the government agencies, universities, police, judiciary and social workers.

Juvenile crimes cannot be stopped only through the proper implementation and amendments of the Juvenile Justice Act. The problem of child crime like many other social problems is linked up with the imperfections and maladjustment of our society.

References

Abrahamsen, David, *The Psychology of Crime*, Columbia Press, New York, 1960.

Ahuja, Ram, *Sociological Criminology*, New Age International Publishers Ltd., 1996

Andry, R.G., *Delinquency and Parental Pathology*, Methuen and Co. Ltd., London, 1960.

Bandura, A., *Social Learning Theory*, Prentice Hall, Englewood Cliffs, NJ, 1977.

Becker, Howard S., *Social Problems: A Modern Approach*, John Wiley & Sons Inc., New York, 1966.

Berman, Sidney, 'Anti-social Character Disorder', in Ruth S. Cavan (ed.), *Readings in Juvenile Delinquency*, J.B. Lippincott and Co., Philadelphia, 1964.

Cloward, Richard and Ohlin, Llyod E., *Delinquency and Opportunity: A Theory of Delinquent Gangs*, The Free Press, Glencoe, Illinois, 1960.

Cohen, Albert, *Delinquent Boys: The Culture of the Gang*, The Free Press, Glencoe, Illinois, 1955.

Crime in India, National Crime Records Bureau, New Delhi, 2011.

Freud, Sigmund, *Collected Papers*, Hogarth Press, London, 1925.

Giallombardo, Rose, *Juvenile Delinquency*, John Wiley & Sons Inc., New York, 1960.

Gibbons, Don C., *Deviant Behaviour* (2nd edn), Prentice Hall Inc., Englewood Cliffs, New Jersey, 1976.

Glueck, Sheldon and Glueck, E., *Delinquents and Non-Delinquents in Perspective*, Harvard University Press, Cambridge, 1968.

Gokhale, S.D., *Impact of Institutions on Juvenile Delinquents*, United Asia Publications Ltd., Bombay, 1969.

Haveripeth, P.D., 'Contributing Factors of Juvenile Delinquency', *International Journal of Innovative Research and Development*, 2(1): 8–16, 2013.

Healy, W. and Bronner, A.F., *New Light on Delinquency and Its Treatment*. Yale University Press, New Haven, 1936.

Jenkins, R.L., 'Motivation and Frustration in Delinquency', *American Journal of Orthopsychiatry*, 27, 1957.

Juvenile Justice (Care and Protection of Children) Act, 2000 and 2015.

Knadten, Richard D. and Schaper, Stephen, *Juvenile Delinquency: A Reader*, Random House, New York, 1970.

Lejins, Peter, 'The Field of Prevention', in William Amos and Charles Welfond (eds), *Delinquency Prevention Theory and Practice*, Prentice Hall, New Jersey, 1967.

Lore, R.K. and Schultz, L.A., 'Control of Human Aggression: A Comparative Perspective', *American Psychologist*, 48(1), 1993.

Matza, David, *Delinquency and Drift*, John Wiley & Sons Inc., New York, 1964.

McCord, W., McCord, J. and Zola, I.K., *Origins of Crime*, Columbia University Press, New York.

McDavid, John W. and McCandless, Boyd R., 'Psychological Theory, Research, and Juvenile Delinquency', *The Journal Criminal Law and Criminology*, 53(1), 1962.

Mead, George Herbert, *Mind Self and Society: From the Standpoint of a Social Behaviorist*, University of Chicago, Chicago, 1934.

Merton, Robert K., *Social Theory and Social Structure*, The Free Press, Glencoe Illinois, 1957.

Merton, Robert K., 'Social Structure and Anomie', *American Sociological Review*, 3(5): 672–682, 1938.

Miller, Walter, 'Lower Class Culture as a Generating Milieu of Gang Delinquency', *Journal of Social Issues*, No. 3, 1958.

Monahan, Thomas P., 'Family Status and the Delinquent Child', *Social Forces*, Vol. 35, No. 3, 1957.

Neumayer, Martin H., *Juvenile Delinquency in Modern Society*, D. Van Nostrand co., Inc., 1977.

Peterson, D.R. and Becker, W.C., 'Family Interaction and Delinquency', in Herbert C. Quay (ed.), *Juvenile Delinquency*, Van Nostrand, Princeton, 1965.

Rao, Venugopal, *Juvenile Delinquency: Role of the Police*, working paper in a seminar organized by CBI, Ministry of Home Affairs, Delhi, 25–27 November, 1965.

Reckless, Walter G., *Handbook of Practical Suggestions for the Treatment of Adult and Juvenile Offenders*, Government of India, New Delhi, 1956.

Siegel, Larry J. and Welsh, Brandon C., *Juvenile Delinquency: Theory, Practice, and Law*, Cengage Learning, Belmont, CA, 2012.

Sharma, B.S. Dhillon. 'Juvenile Delinquency in India: A Cause for Concern'. *J Indian Acad Forensic Med.*, 31(1): 68–70, 2009.

Shaw, Clifford and McKay, Henry D., *Social Factors in Juvenile Delinquency*, U.S. Government Printing Office, Washington, 1931.

——, *Juvenile Delinquency and Urban Areas*, The University of Chicago Press, Chicago, 1942.

Skinner, B.F., *Science and Human Behavior*, Macmillan, New York. 1953.

Tappan, Paul W., *Crime, Justice and Correction*, McGraw Hill, New York, 1960.

Thrasher, Frederick, *The Gang*, The University of Chicago Press, Chicago, 1936.

Trojanowicz, Robert C., *Juvenile Delinquency: Concepts and Control*, Prentice Hall Inc., Englewood Cliffs, New Jersey, 1973.

16

Domestic Violence and Abuse

The word 'domestic' in this context means within the family or house. Use of violence by any member of the family against another person or the entire family to fulfill ones wishes is termed domestic violence. The home which should be the safest place for a woman has become a place where she faces a regime of terror and violence at the hands of somebody close to her or should be able to trust. These women suffer both physically and psychologically. They are unable to take their own decisions, voice their opinions or protect themselves and their children for fear of further repercussions. Sometimes, even their basic human rights are also denied.

Definitions

The definition of domestic violence varies depending on the context in which the term is used. In common parlance, it is violence or physical abuse directed towards spouse or domestic partner – usually by a man against a woman. According to *Innocenti Digest* (June 2000), the term includes violence by an intimate partner and other family members, wherever this takes place and in whatever form.

According to Ganley and Schechter (1996), domestic violence is a pattern of coercive and assaultive behaviours that include physical, sexual, verbal and psychological attacks and economic coercion that adults or adolescents use against their intimate partner.

According to another source (www.domesticviolence.org), domestic violence and emotional abuse have been described as behaviours used by one person in a relationship to control the other. Partners may be married or unmarried, heterosexual, gay or lesbian, living together, separated or dating. Examples of abuse are: (a) name-calling or putdowns, (b) keeping a spouse from contacting one's family or friends, (c) withholding money, (d) stopping a spouse from getting or keeping a job, (e) actual or threatened physical harm, (f) sexual assault, and (g) stalking intimidation.

Anyone can be a victim of such violence irrespective of age, sex, race, culture, religion, education, employment or marital status. Although both men and women can be victims, but mostly these are women. Besides women, children in homes where there is domestic violence are also likely to be abused and/or neglected. Even if a child is not physically harmed, he/she may suffer emotional and behavioural problems.

Domestic Violence and Civil Harassment

A common misconception about domestic violence is that it is a sub-category of civil harassment. However, civil harassment references its own particular type of 'violence' or 'harassment'. Domestic violence concerns the sphere of violent or abusive actions that are perpetrated by and on family members or couples. The relationships between victims and perpetrators are important part of this definition. Civil harassment also refers to many different types and varieties of violence and abuse, but only those acts that are non-domestic in nature can form the basis for civil harassment. Civil harassment occurs when one person annoys, harasses, injures, or threatens another person.

Domestic Violence Facts

1. Domestic violence (also called intimate partner violence, domestic abuse, dating violence, spousal abuse, and intimate partner abuse) is any form of maltreatment that takes place in a heterosexual or homosexual romantic relationship between adults or adolescents.
2. Intimate partner abuse is a major public health problem. It is affecting more than 2 million women and 8,00,000 men and resulting in homelessness, injury, or death of victims, billions of dollars in health-care costs, and lost work productivity. Intimate partner abuse, in some ways, continue to be endorsed in all societies.
3. While domestic abuse strikes couples of all races, religions, social economic status and sexual orientations, risk factors for men or women becoming victims or abusers include poverty, lack of a high school education, witnessing family violence as a child and attitudes of male domination and substance abuse, especially alcohol abuse.
4. Women with disabilities are more likely to experience domestic violence, emotional abuse and sexual assault than women without disabilities. Women with disabilities may also feel more isolated and feel they are unable to report the abuse or they may be dependent on the abuser for their care. Like many women who are abused, women with disabilities are usually abused by someone they know, such as their partner or family member.
5. The warning signs for individuals to consider if they suspect they are the victim of intimate partner violence includes feeling demeaned, assaulted, or excessively controlled by their partner.

6. Warning signs friends, family members, and coworkers can look for if they wonder whether the person they care about is the victim of domestic abuse include frequent absence from school or work, numerous injuries the victim tries to explain, low self-esteem, a change in their personality, fear of conflicts, passive-aggressive behaviour, blaming him or herself for the problems in their relationship, isolation from others or stress-related physical symptoms.
7. Health professionals unfortunately only screen for intimate partner abuse in about 20 per cent of the patients seen. Domestic violence is most effectively assessed when the professional asks questions that call for more than a 'yes' or 'no' answer and do not directly inquire about domestic abuse, at least earlier during an assessment interview.
8. Domestic abuse is treated by establishing and maintaining the safety of the victim, providing appropriate legal consequences to the batterer, addressing the emotional impact on the victim and the problems of the abuser, particularly if one of the problems includes alcohol or other substance abuse.
9. The prognosis of domestic violence can be quite negative if it goes on untreated, in that the emotional and physical consequences of continued abuse can be severe and even end in homicide. Treatment and enhancing social supports to the victim can improve prognosis.
10. Prevention of domestic violence involves providing economic opportunity, mentors, role models, organized community programmes for youth and families, a school environment that promotes prevention of abusiveness in any relationship and adult family members who are nurturing and who provide consistent and structured support.

Forms of Domestic Violence

Domestic violence is abuse by one partner against another in an intimate relationship such as dating, marriage, cohabitation or a familial relationship. Domestic violence is also known as domestic abuse, spousal abuse, battering, family violence, dating abuse and intimate partner violence (IPV). Domestic violence can be physical, emotional, verbal, economic and sexual abuse. Domestic violence can be subtle, coercive or violent. It is the inflicting of physical injury by one family or household member on another; and a repeated or habitual pattern of such behaviour. Violence can be criminal and includes physical assault (hitting, pushing, shoving, etc.), sexual abuse (unwanted or forced sexual activity), and stalking. Although emotional, psychological and financial abuse are not criminal behaviours, they are forms of abuse and can lead to criminal violence.

There are different types of domestic abuse, including emotional, psychological, physical, sexual, and financial abuse. Many abusers behave in ways that include more than one type of domestic violence and the boundaries between some of these behaviours are often quite blurred.

Physical

Physical violence is most likely what comes to most people's minds when we talk about domestic violence. Violence Prevention Alliance (VPA) – a network of WHO member-states, international organizations and civil society organizations working to prevent violence – defines physical violence as 'the intentional use of physical force or power, threatened or actual, against oneself, another person, or against a group or community, that either results in or has a high likelihood of resulting in injury, death, psychological harm, maldevelopment, or deprivation'. It involves behaviour intended to cause feelings of intimidation, pain, injury, or other physical suffering or bodily harm. It may also include acts of hitting, slapping, punching, choking, pushing, burning, etc. which may result in physical injury. Physical abuse can also include behaviours such as denying the victim of medical care when needed, depriving him/her of sleep or other functions necessary to live, or forcing him/her to engage in drug/alcohol use against his/her will.

Sexual

When someone forces another person to have sexual intercourse by way of physical force, the threat of force, intimidation, or by use of a weapon, it is considered rape, which is one form of sexual violence. In other words, sexual violence is any situation in which force or threat is used to obtain participation in unwanted sexual activity. Coercing a person to engage in sexual activity against his/her will, even if that person is a spouse or intimate partner with whom consensual sex has occurred, is an act of violence. WHO has defined sexual violence as any sexual act, attempt to obtain a sexual act, unwanted sexual comments or advances, or acts to traffic, or otherwise directed, against a person's sexuality using coercion, by any person regardless of their relationship to the victim, in any setting, including but not limited to home and work.

Sexual violence is not something that happens only between strangers. In fact, a good number of rapes occur between individuals who know each other. In many countries, it is now against the law for a man to force even his wife to have sex with him. It is called *spousal or marital rape.*

Other forms include forced sexual activity (oral sex, sodomy, etc.), forced sex with animals, forcing a person to have sexual intercourse or sexual activity with another person, or forced sexual activity with objects.

Emotional/Psychological

Emotional or psychological abuse can be verbal or non-verbal. Its aim is to chip away at the confidence and independence of victims with the intention of making him/her compliant and limiting their ability to leave. Emotional abuse includes verbal abuse such as yelling, name-calling, blaming and shaming, intimidation, threats of violence and controlling behaviour. Emotional and verbal abuse can have short-term and long-lasting effects that are just as serious as the effects of physical abuse. Emotional and verbal abuse also includes insults and attempts to scare, isolate or control.

Emotional abuse (also called psychological abuse or mental abuse) includes humiliating the victim privately or publicly, controlling what he/she can and cannot do, withholding information from him/her, deliberately doing something to make him/her feel diminished or embarrassed, isolating him/her from friends and family, implicitly blackmailing him/her by harming others when he/she expresses independence or happiness or denying him/her access to money or other basic resources and necessities. Degradation in any form can also be considered as psychological abuse.

Emotional abuse also includes verbal abuse and is defined as any behaviour that threatens, intimidates and undermines the victim's self-worth or self-esteem or controls his/her freedom. This may include threatening the victim with injury or harm, telling him/her that they will be killed if they ever leave the relationship and public humiliation. Constant criticism, name-calling, and making statements that damage the victim's self-esteem are also common verbal forms of emotional abuse.

People who are being emotionally abused often feel as if they do not own themselves; rather, they may feel that their significant other has nearly total control over them. Women or men undergoing emotional violence often suffer from depression, which puts them at increased risk for suicide, eating disorders and drug and alcohol abuse.

Honour Based Violence

'Honour' based violence (HBV) is a form of domestic abuse which is perpetrated in the name of so-called 'honour'. The honour code which it refers to is set at the discretion of male relatives and women who do not abide by the 'rules' are then punished for bringing shame to the family. Infringements may include, a woman having a boyfriend, rejecting a forced marriage, pregnancy outside of marriage, interfaith relationships, seeking a divorce, inappropriate dress or make-up and even kissing in a public place.

Forced Marriage

A forced marriage is a marriage that is performed under duress and without the full and informed consent or free will of both parties. Forced marriages are associated with a high rate of domestic violence. This violence perpetrates inside marriage and is related to the customs and traditions of such marriage.

Economic or Financial Abuse

Economic or financial abuse aims to limit a victim's ability to access help. Tactics may include controlling the finances, withholding money or credit cards, making someone unreasonably account for money spent/petrol used, exploiting assets, withholding basic necessities, preventing someone from working, deliberately running up debts, forcing someone to work against their will and sabotaging someone's job.

Economic or financial violence is a form of abuse when one intimate partner has control over the other partner's access to economic resources. It may involve preventing a spouse from resource acquisition, limiting the amount of resources to use by him/her, or by exploiting his/her economic resources. The motive behind this may be to diminish victim's capacity to support himself/herself, thus, forcing him/her to depend on the perpetrator financially, which includes preventing him/her from obtaining education, finding employment, maintaining or advancing careers and acquiring assets.

In addition, the abuser may also put the victim on an allowance, closely monitor how he/she spends money, spend his/her money without his/her consent and creating debt, or completely spend his/her savings to limit available resources.

Apart from the above, there are also country-specific forms of domestic violence, such as acid throwing or attack, honour killings, bride burning or dowry violence, etc. These are discussed in details in chapter on crimes against women.

Reasons Behind Domestic Violence

Incompetency of understanding each other, never letting go even minor things, lack of tolerance, an unnecessary composition in own family, undue shows, improper liberty, TV serial, kitty parties, social instigation, etc. are the reasons which work behind domestic violence. Local customs and traditions are often responsible for maintaining certain forms of domestic violence. Such customs and traditions include male-child preference, child and forced marriages, dowry, the hierarchic caste system and the importance given to 'family honour'.

Causative Factors

There are many causative factors in domestic violence. It mainly occurs within the framework of patriarchy. There are several theories linked to the causes – from psychological (personality traits and mental behaviour) to social (family structure, learned behaviour, etc.) The reasons could be:

1. childhood socialization, growing up seeing abuse in parents,
2. previous experiences of abuse in relationships,
3. psychological disorder of anger or sadism,
4. sense of insecurity in marital bond, and
5. frustration at work.

Some other reasons for domestic violence pointed out by sociologists and feminist scholars like Buzawa and Buzawa (cited in Shirwadkar, 2009: 145) are unequal distribution of power in society leading to women occupying positions inferior or subordinate to men. According to them, historical and social acceptance of gender stereotyped roles, which legitimize and justify aggression against women, contribute to family violence against women.

Within the broader context of violence against women, exploring the issue of domestic violence or violence within the family, the United Nations

Commission on the State of Women, in its Vienna Declaration, noted that from the existing empirical evidence regarding causation of violence, four generalizations could be drawn as under:

1. Violence in the family occurs primarily by men against women.
2. Most victims of violence within the family and society are the weakest owing to their sex (women are considered to be the weaker sex), age (children, elderly) and physical fitness (disabled). It can also be in terms of dependency relationships of various natures (e.g., economic or employment status in an organizational setting, and so on).
3. Violence occurs when the imbalance of power is challenged and the perpetrator fails to recognize and respect the victim's basic human rights, fundamental freedom, dignity and right to peace and security, and acts accordingly.
4. Violence has always existed in various forms but it is only during the last decade that violence against women has been increasingly acknowledged to be a serious issue in terms of both magnitude and effect (Bokil in Shirwadkar, 2009: 237–38).

Discourse on domestic violence is not as loud and widespread as it should be. This is mainly because this subject is so easily hushed away as a matter of personal nature to be resolved within the family itself. Very recently concluded popular reality show on television 'Satyamev Jayate' aired an episode on this issue titled as 'Danger at Home'. This sensitized both media and society as many alarming facts were exposed. There was a mention of two separate studies, one organized by the Ministry of Health and Family Welfare, Government of India and the other by the Planning Commission, which showed that somewhere between 40 and 80 per cent of women in India are victims of domestic violence (www.satyamevjayate.in/issue 07/learnmore, accessed on 22 August 2013).

Consequences of Domestic Violence

There are varied consequences of domestic violence depending on the victim, the age group, the intensity of the violence and frequency of the torture they are subjected to. Living under a constant fear, threat and humiliation are some of the feelings developed in the minds of the victims as a consequence of an horrible violence.

One of the severe effects of domestic violence against women is its effect on her children. It is nature's phenomenon that a child generally has a greater attachment towards the mother for she is the one who gives birth. As long as the violence subjected to the mother is hidden from the child, he/she may behave normally at home. The day when a mother's grief and suffering is revealed, a child may become upset about the happening deeply. Children may not even comprehend the severity of the problem. They may turn silent, reserved and express solace to the mother. When the violence against women is openly done in front of them since their childhood, it may have a deeper and gruesome impact on their mindset. They get used to such happenings at home and have a tendency to reciprocate the same in their lives. It's common especially in rural homes in India which are victimized by the evil of domestic violence.

Researchers have found that some people are more likely to become the victims of domestic violence. A likely victim:

1. has a poor self-image,
2. puts up with abusive behaviour,
3. is economically and emotionally dependent on the abuser,
4. is unsure of his or her own need,
5. has the belief that he or she can change the abuser,
6. feels helpless to stop the violence,
7. believes that jealousy is proof of love, and
8. has low confidence.

One well-known approach to treating domestic abuse in families is the Duluth model. It is also called the Domestic Abuse Intervention Project (DAIP) and focuses on women as the victims and men as the perpetrators of intimate partner violence. This treatment model takes the approach of empowering women by providing them information, resources and support, which has been found to significantly decrease the violence in victims' lives over time. It also uses legal resources as a means of keeping women safe and holding males who engage in battering accountable for their actions.

Coping Mechanism

The subtle and complex phenomenon of domestic violence has not only called for various analytical perspectives but also various practical approaches for its resolution. The analytically perspectives have dealt with the sociological factors affecting domestic violence, the economic dependence of women and their consequent vulnerability and the issues of sexuality. The practical approaches, on the other hand, have dealt with the role of law, judiciary, state and social policy. But the broad conclusion is that the coping with this menace becomes difficult because marriage and family are considered as institutions in the private domain where state and judiciary cannot intervene.

This situation has prompted for search of alternate sociological approaches. At present, most of the assistance is provided to the victim through counselling and legal services by the feminist groups or welfare-oriented NGOs. But, the scope and outreach of such services is limited in view of the gigantic nature of the problem. Moreover, these are not pro-active services. Unless a woman approaches them, they do not provide assistance. In this regard, the area that is not sufficiently researched into is, how domestic violence can be addressed through women's collectivities like self-help groups (SHGs) (Bokil in Shirwadkar, 2009: 238–40).

According to Ranjana Kumari (also in Shirwadkar, 2009: 220–21), we should democratize our institutions for combatting domestic violence. The three steps in this regard could be: (a) democratization of family to allow women to be equal partner in decision-making; (b) no discrimination between sexes in society; and (c) equal representation of women in state.

Poonacha, in her paper, in Shirwadkar (2009: 25–26), writes: 'Strategies to cope with domestic violence may broadly be classified as those that seek to prevent/eradicate violence and those that react/respond to such instances. The preventive measures can further be classified as three-fold, namely, research and documentation, social action and awareness generation. The first step requires research and documentation on the nature and extent of violence. It is from a clear social analysis of violence and an understanding of the use and limitations of the legal system that it would be possible to devise preventive strategies that are communicated to the field staff and social workers of the organizations. Second, social action to prevent violence requires neighbourhood vigilance and the creation of new socio-economic options (through employment opportunities and skill training) for women who are likely to face violence. It also requires the empowerment of women with the knowledge of their rights and enabling them to access information about the various government welfare schemes. Last, the awareness generation programme exposes the extent to which women's rights are violated through media campaigns and publicity programmes that seek to create gender-just laws and reform of the prevailing criminal justice system'.

Poonacha further writes: 'Reactive measures can also be categorized as three-fold: (a) research and documentation of cases and experiences to understand the lapses in investigation and the legal system; (b) emotional, material and legal support to the survivor to enable her to rebuild her life as well as that of her children; and (c) efforts to raise community/neighbourhood opinion against domestic violence and the mobilization of the entire community to oppose violence and support the woman. Additionally, there is need for shelter homes, short stay homes, legal aid, counselling and child care facilities'.

The Indian Scenario

It is really surprising that despite spread of education and awareness, domestic violence is on the rise all over the world. A study by WHO shows that domestic violence cuts across all the countries of the world. In India too, all forms of abuse covered under the term 'domestic violence', such as physical, sexual, verbal, emotional and economic, are common. It was for the first time when the Indian National Family and Health Survey-3 (NHFS-3) in 2005–06 addressed these concerns and officially recorded the data pertaining to the domestic violence in the country. Accordingly,

1. One in three out of every married woman report of having been slapped by their husband.

2. Between 12 and 15 per cent report having their arms twisted, being pushed, shaken, kicked, dragged, or beaten up, or having something thrown at them.
3. Ten per cent report that their husbands have physically forced them to have sex.
4. One in seven every married woman has suffered physical injuries as a result of spousal violence.
5. For most women who have ever experienced spousal violence, the violence first occurred within the first two years of their marriage.

Every third woman in India suffers sexual and/or physical violence at home. According to the National Family Health Survey (NHFS-4), 27 per cent of women have experienced physical violence since the age of 15 in India. Domestic violence cases, where women reported physical abuse in rural and urban areas, were at 29 per cent and 23 per cent, respectively. The most common type of spousal violence is physical violence (27%) followed by emotional violence (13%).

The experience of physical violence stems from the most common perpetrators, which includes mothers or step-mothers (56%), fathers or step-fathers (33%), sisters or brothers (27%), and teachers (15%). The percentage justifying abuse is marginally lesser among younger women. About 47.7 per cent of girls between the age of 15 and 19 agreed with violence by husbands. The most common perpetrators of sexual violence on unmarried women were other relatives (27%), followed by a current or former boyfriend (18%), their own friend or acquaintance (17%) and a family friend (11%).

The following three studies together provide an understanding of the degree of domestic violence being experienced by Indian women in a rural setting, the possible protective factors and the existing options available to women outside of family and friends. They also point to new directions for strategies to reduce, and hopefully eliminate, domestic violence in India.

Leela Visaria's study on five villages in Kheda district is a preliminary exploration of the prevalence of domestic violence against women. An Analysis of Primary Survey Data study presents a picture of domestic violence as reported by 346 married women. The findings of the study point to several interesting dimensions such as the lower incidence of violence among joint families, the difference in the impact of the higher educational status of men compared to that of women on levels of violence, and the complex linkages between correlates of violence, forms of abuse, and reasons given for abuse. Her study also indicates some of the possible links between the gender division of labour within the household and incidents of violence. The study highlights the lack of options for women in rural communities to address domestic violence.

The second study, by Nishi Mitra of the Tata Institute of Social Sciences (TISS), focuses specifically on the governmental and non-governmental interventions and responses being implemented in the states of Maharashtra and Madhya Pradesh. This study undertakes a non-random, cross-sectional survey of various actors involved in interventions. A qualitative analysis of purposively selected samples of state and NGO responses were also undertaken. Counselling oriented towards preserving family inviolability is found to be a predominant response in the state sector. The non-governmental sector does attempt to extend the range of services provided by offering an array of rehabilitative programmes.

The focus of the SNDT University study by Veena Poonacha and Divya Pandey is on the interventions and responses being implemented in the states of Gujarat and Karnataka. The study provides a comprehensive examination of the range of responses through in-depth case studies of organizations. A finding of the study is that the prevailing types of response or intervention strategies, among both state and non-governmental sectors are in essence reactive to individual complaints and are, therefore, short-term in their impact. The study, however, also points to the emergence of a variety of innovative, grassroots efforts to address domestic violence more proactively.

But, it is also pertinent to mention that the reported cases of domestic violence in the country represent only the tip of the iceberg, whereas the majority of cases are invisible both socially and institutionally. The worst problem in India is that the victims do not feel victimized. The way women are brought up in India explains why only one-fourth of them seek help to end violence meted out by their husbands.

In India, domestic violence was recognized as a criminal offence in 1983. The offence chargeable under Section 498-A of the Indian Penal Code (IPC) that relates to domestic violence is any act of cruelty by a husband (or his family) towards his wife. However, till 2006, there was no separate civil law addressing the specific complexities associated with domestic violence, including the embedded nature of violence within familial networks, the need for protection and maintenance of abused women, and the fact that punishment and imprisonment for the husband may not be the best resolution in every case. Accordingly, after a decade-long process of consultations and revisions, a comprehensive domestic violence law, known as the Protection of Women from Domestic Violence Act 2005, took effect in 2006.

Protection of Women from Domestic Violence Act, 2005

The Protection of Women from Domestic Violence Act, 2005 was brought into force by the Government of India from 26 October 2006. For the purposes of this Act, any conduct of the respondent shall constitute domestic violence if he, (a) habitually assaults or makes the life of the aggrieved person miserable by cruelty of conduct even if such conduct does not amount to physical ill-treatment; or (b) forces the aggrieved person to lead an immoral life; or (c) otherwise injures or harms the aggrieved person. However, nothing contained in clause (c) above shall amount to domestic violence if the pursuit of course of conduct by the respondent was reasonable for his own protection or for the protection of his or another's property.

Scope

The law is primarily meant to provide protection to the wife or female live-in partner from domestic violence at the hands of the husband or male live-in partner or his relatives, it also extends its protection to women living in a household with sisters, widows or mothers. Domestic violence under the act includes actual abuse or the threat of abuse whether physical, sexual, verbal, emotional or economic. Harassment by way of unlawful dowry demands from the woman or her relatives would also be covered under this definition.

The key elements of the law include the prohibition of marital rape and the provision of protection and maintenance orders against husbands and partners who are emotionally, physically, or economically abusive. In a nutshell, the salient features of the Act are as follows:

1. It seeks to cover those women who are or have been in a relationship with the abuser where both parties have lived together in a shared household and are related by consanguinity, marriage or a relationship in the nature of marriage, or adoption; in addition relationship with family members living together as a joint family are also included. Even those women who are sisters, widows, mothers, single women, or living with the abuser are entitled to get legal protection under the proposed Act.
2. The term 'domestic violence' includes actual abuse or the threat of abuse that is physical, sexual, verbal, emotional and economic. Harassment by way of unlawful dowry demands to the woman or her relatives would also be covered under this definition.
3. One of the most important features of the Act is the woman's right to secure housing. The Act provides for the woman's right to reside in the matrimonial or shared household, whether or not she has any title or rights in the household. This right is secured by a residence order, which is passed by a court. These residence orders cannot be passed against anyone who is a woman.
4. The other relief envisaged under the Act is that of the power of the court to pass protection orders that prevent the abuser from aiding or committing an act of domestic violence or any other specified act, entering a workplace or any other place frequented by the abused, attempting to communicate with the abused, isolating any assets used by both the parties and causing violence to the abused, her relatives and others who provide her assistance from the domestic violence.
5. The Act provides for appointment of Protection Officers and NGOs to provide assistance to the woman with regard to medical examination, legal aid, safe shelter, etc.
6. The Act provides for breach of protection order or interim protection order by the respondent as a cognizable and non-bailable offence punishable with imprisonment for a term which may extend to one year

or with fine which may extend to twenty thousand rupees or with both. Similarly, non-compliance or discharge of duties by the Protection Officer is also sought to be made an offence under the Act with similar punishment.

The Protection of Women from Domestic Violence Act 2005 (PWDVA) provides for more effective protection to the rights of women guaranteed under the Constitution who are victims of violence of any kind occurring within the family and for matters connected therewith or incidental thereto. Domestic violence includes all forms of physical, emotional, verbal, sexual, and economic violence, and covers both actual acts of such violence and threats of violence. In addition, the PWDVA recognizes marital rape and covers harassment in the form of unlawful dowry demands as a form of abuse, and including not only physical violence, but also other forms of violence such as emotional, verbal, sexual, and economic abuse. It is a civil law meant primarily for protection orders and not meant to penalize criminally. The protection of women from Domestic Violence Act 2005 differs from the provision of the Penal Code – Section 498A of the Indian Penal Code – which provides a broader definition of domestic violence.

Actually, in all societies, family matters are seen as personal and not to be intervened by any outsider. In India, societal attitudes that convey acceptance or justification of domestic violence have made the situation more worse. In a shocking revelation by UNICEF's 'Global Report Card on Adolescents 2012', not just Indian men, but even adolescents – in the 15–19 age group – feel that wife beating is justified. Not only this, over half of the Indian adolescent girls, or around 53 per cent, think that a husband is justified in beating his wife.

Remedies for Combatting Domestic Violence

In the present scenario, strict and stringent steps need to be taken out against the growing evil of domestic violence. Some of the steps which can be taken to mitigate the rising crime of domestic violence can be:

1. The basic support system needs to be established which may include immediate medical assistance to the victim, shelter and emotional support and counselling.
2. The Indian Parliament must come out with a more stringent law to protect the rights of women who are victims of violence of any kind occurring within the family so that it would work as a preventive measure to eradicate the crime.
3. New legislation is needed to provide for granting 'Interim Relief' (A big sum of money that is paid by the perpetrator) to a victim of a severe sexual assault. The money may be utilized for rehabilitation of the victim. Rehabilitation of the victims of brutal sexual assaults should be the State's responsibility. The legislation should provide for enhanced punishment for violence perpetrated against women with mental illness.

4. The role of non-governmental organizations in controlling the domestic violence and curbing its worse consequences is crucial. They must encourage more and more people to report any case of domestic violence so that proper action may be taken against the culprits.
5. Police plays a major role in tackling the domestic violence cases. They need to be sensitized to treat domestic violence cases as seriously as any other crime.
6. Studies on prevalence, risk and protection factors as well as consequences need to be carried out.
7. An awareness programme for protection of women should be launched by the government because domestic violence in one or another way, affects the national productivity and lesson to protect and respect the women.
8. Prosecution shortcoming in the handling of domestic violence case must be addressed and conviction rate should be increased in cases like domestic violence to create fear in the mind of violator or abuser.
9. There is a need to inform, educate and communicate to the society about domestic violence and the existing laws to protect women against domestic violence. Efforts in this respect through community participation along with social welfare will be a better sustainable solution to the problem. As long as we as a culture accept and tolerate violence against women, men will continue to be abusive.

Violence against women in the country is getting more frequent and alarmingly huge. It is creating pressure and heavy responsibility on the shoulders of social workers. However, there is an urgent need for women to be empowered and responsible for themselves in order to understand all the rights and take benefits. Emphasis should be given on female education so as to make them self-reliant through capacity building and skill development.

Much is said about safety of women in public places but statistics show that women are equally vulnerable in their own homes. It can be stated that the domestic violence or violence within family is a big social problem today and unless and until serious efforts for its solution are not made, women will continue to be denied justice. The violence can be stopped both by the victim as well as the perpetrator. The women have to gather courage to say 'No' to it and walk out if necessary, but the onus of stopping the violence is on source – the man who carries it out.

Conclusion

Domestic violence is a multifaceted problem and characterized by repetitive and patterned acts of dominance and coercion. The abuser often uses different tactics to make their weaker partner submit to them as well as exercise power and control over them. These include intimidation, economic deprivation, isolation and all forms of abuse – physical, verbal, sexual, and psychological. Although, there is no specific cause for domestic violence, women at the highest risk of being the victim of domestic violence include those with male partners who abuse drugs (especially alcohol), are unemployed or underemployed, afflicted by poverty and have been in a romantic relationship with the victim. Unmarried individuals in heterosexual relationships tend to be more at risk for becoming victims of intimate partner abuse. A mindset that gives men power over women puts individuals at risk of becoming involved in an abusive relationship, either as a perpetrator or as a victim. Modern laws protect the rights of women and individuals from domestic violence, still, the number continues to rise. The future of finding solutions to domestic violence includes continuing to improve the effectiveness of treatment and to strengthen legal protection for victims, as well as accountability and treatment for abusers.

References

Bokil, Milind, 'Ending Domestic Violence: Self-Help Groups Can Help', in Swati Shirwadkar (ed.), *Family Violence in India: Human Rights, Issues, Actions and International Comparisons*, Rawat Publications, Jaipur, 2009.

Buzawa, Eve S. and Buzawa, Carl G., *Domestic Violence: The Criminal Justice Response, (Studies in Crime, Law and Justice)*, Vol. 6, Sage, New Delhi, 1990, pp. 15–19.

Daga, A.S., Jejeebhoy, S.J. and Rajgopal, S., *Domestic Violence Against Women: An Investigation of Hospital Casualty Records*, Mumbai, 1999.

Domestic Violence Act, 2005.

Ganley, A.L. and Schechter, S., *Domestic Violence: A National Curriculum for Children's Protective Services*, Family Violence Prevention Fund, San Francisco, CA, 1996.

Jawarkar, A.K., Shemar, H., Wasnik, V.R., Chavan, M.S., 'Domestic Violence against Women: A Crossectional Study in Rural Area of Amravati District of Maharashtra, India'. *Int J Res Med Sci*, 2016, 4: 2713–8.

Kumari, Ranjana, 'Globalizing India and Domestic Violence against Women', in Swati Shirwadkar (ed.), *Family Violence in India: Human Rights, Issues, Actions and International Comparisons*, Rawat Publications, Jaipur, 2009.

Mitra, Nishi, *Domestic Violence in the States of Maharashtra and Madhya Pradesh*, Tata Institute of Social Sciences (TISS), Mumbai, 1999.

Poonacha, Veena, 'On the Fringes of Human Rights Discourse: Violence against Women in Intimate Relationships', in Swati Shirwadkar (ed.), *Family Violence in India: Human Rights, Issues, Actions and International Comparisons*, Rawat Publications, Jaipur, 2009.

Poonacha, Veena and Divya Pandey, Domestic Violence in Karnataka and Gujarat, Research Centre for Women's Studies (RCWS), SNDT Women's University, Mumbai, 1999.

Shirwadkar, Swati (ed.), *Family Violence in India: Human Rights, Issues, Actions and International Comparisons*, Rawat Publications, Jaipur, 2009.

Sood, Sooshma, *Violence against Women: Instigators of Wife Battering*, Arihant Publishers, Jaipur.

Visaria, Leela, *Violence against Women in India: Evidence from Rural Gujarat*, Gujarat Institute of Development Studies, Ahmedabad, 1999.

17

Alcoholism

Alcoholism is also known as alcohol-use disorder. It is a general term for the problems of uncontrollable consumption of alcohol. It deteriorates the health of the drinker and in medical term, it is considered a disease. Alcoholism is a chronic, often progressive disease in which a person craves alcohol and drinks despite repeated alcohol-related problems (like losing a job or a relationship). Alcoholism involves a physical dependence on alcohol, but other factors include genetic, psychological and cultural influences. By pharmacological definition 'alcohol is a drug and may be classified as a sedative, tranquillizer, hypnotic or anaesthetic, depending upon the quantity consumed'.

Alcoholism has many negative connotations in India. Not only is it considered an unfavourable practice but also banned on 'dry days'. Republic Day (26 January), Independence Day (15 August), and Gandhi Jayanti (2 October) are commonly observed 'dry days' across the country. They are considered as the national holidays, so every state is bound to celebrate this day as a dry day. There are also other celebrations and festivals in India which are considered as dry days. The days preceding or following the state/national election are also usually dry days.

The problem of alcoholism, until a few decades ago, was considered a moral problem and a sign of social irresponsibility. After the introduction of the prohibition policy in some states, it was viewed as an illegal act. Now, it is considered by some scholars more of a complicated, chronic and immensely costly disease than a type of a deviant behaviour. The victim does not need the punitive treatment but treatment by specialists – psychiatrists, doctors, social workers and others – who will help him in his personality reconstruction.

Alcoholism has much in common with the problem of drug abuse. Both consist essentially of the habitual use of chemical agents to produce a temporarily pleasant mental state. In either case, the results can be extremely dangerous. Addicts in both require therapy rather than penal action. However, in spite of these similarities, the two problems are considerably different and require separate discussion. Most drinkers in India are rare, infrequent and moderate drinkers and the compulsive drinkers or alcoholics are only a minority. Drinking is not as dangerous as drug addiction.

Alcohol is not a stimulant; it is a depressant or inhibitor on the central nervous system. Alcohol relaxes the customary controls on behaviour and the drinker becomes less restrained and feels more free. But taking alcohol even once in a while leaves the possibility of a habit-forming phenomenon open and the drinker may start taking it frequently and in large quantity which could have tragic and disastrous effects. It may affect him physically, destroy his ability to work and earn, ruin his family life, and demoralize him utterly. An innocent recreation, thus, may spoil the whole life of the drinker. But before analysing the causes and effects of alcoholism, let us understand some basic concepts.

The Concept

Alcoholism is a condition in which an individual loses control over his alcohol intake in that he is constantly unable to refrain from drinking once he begins (Johnson, 1973: 519). According to Keller and Vera (1955: 619–644), alcoholism is characterized by the repeated drinking of alcoholic beverages to an extent that exceeds customary use or compliance with the social customs of the community and that adversely affects the drinker's health or interferes with his social or economic functioning.

An alcoholic is different from an 'occasional drinker'. Any person who takes alcohol is a 'drinker', while a 'compulsive drinker' who cannot live without taking alcohol is called an 'alcoholic'. According to Waskin (1964: 362), an alcoholic is an excessive drinker whose dependence upon alcohol has reached such a degree that it results in a noticeable mental disturbance or an interference with his bodily and mental health, his interpersonal relations, and his smooth social and economic functioning; or one who shows the early signs of such developments. Clinebell (1956: 17) has defined an 'alcoholic' as one whose drinking interferes frequently or continuously with any of his important life adjustments and interpersonal relationships.

Broadly speaking, alcoholism has been characterized by four factors: (a) excessive intake of alcoholic beverages, (b) individual's increasing worry over his drinking, (c) loss of the drinker's control over his drinking, and (d) the disturbance in functioning in his social world.

Richard Blum (1973: 508) has referred to drinking in two contexts: (a) in the context of prescribed social pattern where drinking is integrated in the culture of the society and it is perceived as part of everyday life, (for example, in Italy, the United States) and people do not find any psychological potential in it; and (b) in the context of perceiving alcohol use as disruptive to culture and society and people find addictive potential in it (as in India) and view drinking as a means of seeking pleasure and escape. Drinkers have been classified as 'non-addicts', 'addicts' and 'chronic alcoholics'. Non-addicts are categorized as 'experimenters' and 'regulars'. Don Cahalan has given a five-fold classification of alcohol drinkers on the basis of the frequency of drinking (and not the quantity of alcohol taken):

1. *Rare users,* who drink once or twice a year.
2. *Infrequent users,* who drink once or twice in two-three months, that is, less than once a month.
3. *Light drinkers,* who drink once or twice a month.
4. *Moderate drinkers,* who drink three or four times in a month.
5. *Heavy drinkers,* who drink every day or several drinks during the day.

The last category of drinkers is also described as 'hard core' drinkers.

Extent of Alcoholism

India is showing a phenomenal increase in alcohol consumption in recent years, though the consumption levels are still very low vis-à-vis the global standard. India's per capita alcohol consumption has more than doubled between 2005 (2.4 litres) and 2016 (5.7 litres), revealed the Global Status Report, 2018. Of the total consumption, 4.2 litres are consumed by men and 1.5 litres by women. The rise in alcoholic liver diseases is fast growing in India and it is a result of excessive alcohol consumption.

Fewer studies have assessed the prevalence among middle-aged and elderly populations. Sethi and Trivedi (1979) found alcohol misuse to be 11.3 per cent among the 55–64 year age group and 16.8 per cent among the 65–74 year age group in a rural population in north India. Varma et al. (1980) found 18.3 per cent of the 50+ age group to be current users of alcohol and 23.3 per cent to be 'ever' users of alcohol. Mohan et al. (2001) found that the current use of alcohol to be varying between 19.6 and 27.8 per cent amongst the 50+ age group in the three sites. Current heavy users, i.e. those consuming 75 ml or more of absolute alcohol in a day, accounted for between 79.9 and 84.1 per cent of this 50+ age group of users.

Research in the past few years has conclusively demonstrated that nearly one in three male adults consume alcohol. It has been estimated that India has nearly 70 million alcohol users which include 12 million users who are dependent on alcohol, but does not include millions of social drinkers. A recent National Household Survey of Drug Use recorded alcohol use in only 21 per cent of adult males. In the total spectrum of alcohol consumption in the country, only about 50 per cent is documented and the rest is undocumented.

Despite the overall low consumption, patterns of alcohol consumption vary throughout the country. For example, alcohol use is relatively high in north-eastern and southern states of India and Goa as compared to other parts of country. The prevalence of current use of alcohol ranged from a low of 7 per cent in the western state of Gujarat (officially under prohibition) to 75 per cent in the north-eastern state of Arunachal Pradesh.

Indian made foreign liquor (IMFL) and beer are the preferred drinks in younger age groups, while country made liquor and rum are common in rural India. Home-made or local brews continue to be popular in select communities, especially in north-eastern parts, Goa, etc. Significantly, higher use has been recorded in peri-urban/transitional areas. Interestingly, these are the areas with growing income levels and are, thus, entering the spiralling loop of alcohol use and its harm.

Alcohol use is also directly associated with education, social class and occupation. Alcohol use among the poor communities contributes to increasing expenditure on alcohol on one hand and increasing resources spent for managing alcohol related problems on the other.

The average age of starting alcohol use has reduced from 28 years during the 1980s to 17 years in 2007. Once begun, the average duration generally lasts for more than 10 years. What starts as experimentation and pleasure-seeking, often becomes an addictive process. The amount of drinking also increases with age and duration. Social drinkers generally graduate to become hazardous and pathological drinkers over time. More than 50 per cent of regular alcohol users also fall into the category of hazardous drinking.

India is generally regarded as a traditional 'dry' or 'abstaining' culture. Yet, it has one of the largest alcohol beverage industries in the world. Even in the South-East Asia region it is the dominant producer of alcohol (65%) and contributes to about 7 per cent of the total alcohol beverage imports into the region.

The National Institute of Mental Health and Neurosciences (NIMHANS) report (2011) further indicates that the bulk of alcohol produced in India is mainly from sugarcane molasses. Roughly 52 per cent of alcohol produced in India is for potable purposes. Among the potable forms of alcohol, IMFL and country liquor account for nearly 60 to 70 per cent of the total alcohol consumed. Alcohol is also one of the important sources of revenue for the governments.

Process of Becoming an Alcoholic

A 'drinker' has to pass through various stages to become an 'alcoholic'. According to an American psychiatrist Jellinek (1946: 368), an alcoholic has to pass through the sequence of seven phases: (a) blackouts, in which the individual is not able to find a solution to his individual problems, (b) sneaking drinks, in which he takes alcohol without being observed, (c) increased tolerance, in which he tolerates the increased effects of drinking. (d) loss of control, in which he fails to control the desire of not taking alcohol, (e) development of an alibi system, in which he gradually starts neglecting his social roles, (f) going on periodic benders, in which he keeps on drinking regularly, and (g) regular matutinal drinking, in which he regularly starts taking alcohol in the morning.

Jellinek (1946) has also explained the process of becoming an 'alcoholic' in the following four stages:

1. *Pre-alcoholic symptomatic phase*: In this phase, taking advantage of social sanction, an individual starts drinking to reduce tensions and solve his personal problems. Linking drinking with relief, he keeps on searching for those opportunities in which he may drink. The frequency of drinking increases as he starts losing his capacity to overcome conflicts in life.
2. *Prodigal phase*: In this phase, along with the increase in the frequency of drinking, there is increase in the quantity of the drink too. However, he develops a guilt feeling and knows that gradually he is becoming an abnormal person.
3. *Crucial phase*: In this phase, his drinking becomes conspicuous. He develops rationalizations to stand social pressures and to assure himself that he has not lost control over himself. However, he does not lose his self-respect. Gradually, he starts alienating himself from others as his physical and social deterioration becomes obvious to them.
4. *Chronic phase*: In this phase, he starts drinking even in the morning. He faces prolonged intoxication, impaired thinking, indefinable fears, tremors, and loss of certain skills. He is all the time obsessed with drinking and feels restless without alcohol.

Though every alcoholic does not necessarily pass through all these four stages and in the same sequence, most of the alcoholics have to go through this process.

Alcoholics may be classified in three groups: steady (balanced and supported), periodic, and plateau (expanse of high level). The *steady* alcoholic is one who is not constantly saturated with alcohol. The *periodic* alcoholic abstains from drinking for considerable periods of time and then goes on binging. The *plateau* alcoholic is one who drinks more deliberately than either of the above two types and tends to seek the maximum effects from alcohol. He seems to need to maintain a certain level of saturation at all times but does have the capacity to spread the effect of his alcohol over a long period of time (Landis, 1959: 21–22).

In terms of social status, the alcoholics are classified as the low bottom and the high bottom types. The former refers to the person who has hit the bottom of social status, while the latter is one who still maintains a fairly respectable status in spite of his drinking.

What is sociologically important in alcoholism is the socialization to accept alcohol. Indian culture does not view alcohol drinkers as normal. As such, people are not mentally prepared to accept alcohol as an important part of social life. While in the western society, phrases like 'Have a drink' or 'Would you care for a drink' are common in evening gathering, in India, on the other hand, we usually talk of 'Have a cup of tea'. Thus, alcoholism is a serious social issue in our culture. Though in comparison to drugs, drinking is considered less harmful and even trivial by many parents who themselves drink, still, liquor is not perceived as respectable. Occasional drinking may be tolerated but regular drinking is condemned. We must, therefore, clearly distinguish between a person who uses alcohol in moderation and one who is a 'problem drinker', or between a person who drinks responsibly and one who drinks in a manner that causes problems to himself, to his family, and to society.

One of the big problems of alcoholism is that the individuals do not recognize themselves as an alcoholic. An American psychiatrist Robert V. Seliger has developed a check-list of some twenty questions. If the answer to even a few of these questions is 'Yes,' the individual may well take it as a warning of serious trouble ahead. Here are some of the questions from the check-list: (a) Do you lose time from work due to drinking? (b) Is drinking making your home-life unhappy? (c) Is drinking affecting your reputation? (d) Have you ever felt remorse after drinking? (e) Have you got into financial difficulties as a result of drinking? (f) Do you turn to lower companions as a result of drinking? (g) Does your drinking make you careless of your family's welfare? (h) Has your ambition decreased since drinking? (i) Do you crave for a drink at a particular time daily? (j) Does drinking cause you to have difficulty in sleeping? (k) Has your efficiency decreased since drinking? (l) Is drinking jeopardizing your job or business? (m) Do you drink to build up your self-confidence?

The Legal Age for Alcohol Consumption

The permitted age for drinking alcohol varies from state to state – ranging between 18–25 years. And even the consumption and purchasing age of alcohol are different in the states. This difference, in purchasing and consumption of alcohol, creates confusion and results in difficulty in implementation of the law of consumption age of alcohol.

Liquor Laws in India

1. Alcohol is something whose demand and the sale does not fall but can rise only with time. There are various laws regarding liquor in India and there is no uniformity in these at all.
2. The subject of alcohol is included in the state list under the seventh Schedule of the Constitution of India. Thus, the law which governs the sale and consumption of alcohol varies from state to state. In most of the states of India, a ban on alcohol did exist during pre-independence days but was lifted after India became independent, except in the state of Gujarat. Till now alcohol is banned in Nagaland, Mizoram, Gujarat, Bihar and Kerala. Moreover, Andhra Pradesh, Tamil Nadu, Haryana and Manipur experimented with a partial or complete ban on liquor.
3. The license is needed to sell the alcohol and in some particular states, so are the consumers. Usually, liquor stores, pubs, clubs, discos, bars, hotels and restaurants are licensed to sell alcohol.
4. In addition to this, beaches and houseboats may hold the license to sell alcohol to tourists. The sellers are required to hold a license to sell alcohol, otherwise, the selling of alcohol is illegal and prohibited.

Implementation of the Alcohol Laws in India

Drunkenness is defined as the condition produced by a person who has taken alcohol in a quantity sufficient to cause him to lose control of his faculties to such an extent that he is unable to execute the occupation on which he is engaged. Not only alcohol is injurious to health, but the crime rate gets raised too. Drink and drive cases are very common in most of the states of India. The state government has made liquor laws to govern the sale and consumption of the alcohol and makes amendment time to time to do alternation when new laws are needed. And as a result of this attempt, the permitted age for consuming alcohol differs in the various states. Through these laws, states make efforts to save the future of youth and next generation of the country. The laws made with a motive to lower the rate of consumption of alcohol are violated rigorously. People who are habitual drinkers tend to avoid the state liquor laws to drink liquor. It is very essential for the nation to ensure that legal drinking age should be strictly followed and there should be the diligent participation of the law enforcement agencies towards this. There is a need for laws with strict punishments to make sure the implementation of those laws as well.

Causes of Alcohol Abuse

There are numerous causes or reasons for alcohol dependence or addiction to alcohol or alcoholism, such as:

1. *Depression*: Depression is a mental illness that is caused by various factors such as the loss of a loved one, the lack of self-esteem, unhappiness, despair, and dejection. A person who is depressed finds life an unbearable burden and to overcome all the unpleasant thoughts, finds comfort in alcohol. Unfortunately, alcohol is a depressant and as much as the person taking it may achieve that temporary high, once the effect wears off, the depression sets in and this time much worse than before. It, therefore, becomes a habit as the affected person continuously drinks to stay high and keep away the bad memories and thoughts.
2. *Hopelessness*: Even when tough times set in, people look forward to a better future knowing that what is happening is only temporary. Hopelessness, on the other hand, is the inability to foresee brighter days. A person can be hopeless of ever finding love because of too many failed relationships. Job failure and career stagnation can also lead to a state of hopelessness in an individual's professional life. To numb the unpleasant feeling, such people look to alcohol as a remedy. Since drinking does not offer any solution but a temporary high, alcoholism sets in.
3. *Mental Stress*: This can be caused by anxiety, tension, worry, excessive workload, or trauma. When your desk is full of pending work, coupled with the need to balance family and work life, mental stress may set in. Anxiety, worry or tension caused by unsolved issues may also lead to mental stress. To cope with the pressure, one might find alcohol as an

attractive solution. People who find it difficult to strike a balance between their professional and personal lives may become alcoholics as the pressure becomes too much. The same may happen in a situation of marital strife that leads to mental stress. The affected spouse or spouses may turn to alcoholism to cope with the ensuing stress.

4. *Pleasure*: Some people start off as social drinkers then eventually become alcoholics. The habit of taking a few drinks after work or during the weekend may turn into an alcohol addiction especially for a person who does not have the ability to regulate his or her drinking. Taking alcohol for pleasure can create a social life pattern that results in alcoholism.
5. *Compulsive habit*: There are people who work as wine-tasters. They taste wine and write reviews based on texture, smell and the actual taste of the product. It is a job that may turn into an alcohol addiction if left unchecked. Individuals in such areas of work may develop compulsive habits and end up as alcoholics.
6. *Peer influence*: Young people are the most affected by influence. The need to fit in can often lead to the development of bad social habits such as alcoholism. The constant parties and weekend rendezvous are basically characterized with a lot of boozing and other illicit substances. Bad peer influence is one of the leading causes of alcohol and substance abuse among young people. The group mentality is an ideal foundation for social vices and bad habits that may affect an individual for much of his or her adult life.
7. *Accepted cultural norm*: In some cultures, taking alcohol is a habit that is not frowned upon. In fact, it is the way of life. In such cultures, it is not uncommon to find people indulging in alcohol as early as the wee hours of the morning. Alcoholism may thus, set in due to such cultural norms.
8. *Other causes*:
   (a) childhood incident which affects badly (trauma),
   (b) difficult upbringing and childhood,
   (c) easy availability of alcohol, and
   (d) showing off in front of friends.

Spending most of the times with different types of people who are already addicted to alcohol.

In interpreting the causes of alcoholism, the important thing to bear in mind is that, of those who consume alcohol, about 90 per cent do not become alcoholics. The key to alcoholism is in the *motive* for repeating the drinking. Therefore, explaining alcoholism only in terms of factors like personality structure will be inadequate. No wonder, a psychogenic view is described as an oversimplified explanation of alcoholism. One psychological view is that practically all alcoholics show the mark of deprivation of emotional needs during childhood. Clinebell (1956: 45) reports four main types of parental attitudes which happen to be associated with alcoholism in adulthood and all of which tend to produce trauma and emotional deprivation in the child: (a) authoritarianism, (b) overt rejection, (c) moralism, and (d) success worship. These factors are the key ones in the formation of an insecure personality resulting in falling prey to alcohol is indicated by the fact that psychological studies of alcoholics repeatedly mention the following personality traits: a high level of anxiety in interpersonal relationships, emotional immaturity, ambivalence towards authority, low frustration tolerance, low self-esteem, feelings of isolation and guilt (1956: 49). These psychological traits are not the result of alcoholism but are the causes of alcoholism. They are often present in many alcoholics before they take to excessive drinking.

According to some scholars, there seems to be a definite connection between alcoholism and personality maladjustment. Initially, a person drinks to seek refuge for his problems of life or to find a temporary respite from his troubles. Gradually, he starts drinking more and more frequently until he becomes utterly dependent on it. However, psychologists maintain that only those people take to frequent drinking who are emotionally immature and lack self-confidence.

Around what personal problems of adjustment do anxiety, tension, guilt and frustration arises. According to Bacon (1959: 208), the main problems are: an individual's opinion of himself; gaining and holding respect and affection of others; conflict with others through self-assertion, criticism, out-and-out aggressions; overall security as to ownership, prestige, personal safety as they are tied up with money; responsibilities accepted in the achievement of specific goals; and sexual matters.

The sociological reasons for taking alcohol are essentially the same as for taking drugs. However, a distinction can be made in the causes of drinking alcohol and taking illicit drugs. Since alcohol is socially more acceptable than drugs, drinking reduces a person's fears, worries and anxieties. Besides, alcohol is more easily available than drugs. It is also cheaper than many drugs like heroin, cocaine and LSD. The main sociological causes of taking alcohol are: (a) environmental pressures, (b) peer pressure, and (c) a dominant sub-culture.

The question is: Why do certain persons choose drinking as an answer to environmental pressure while others do not? Here, certainly personality and cultural factors are the major conditioning elements in the individual's experience. Cultural taboos and lack of availability of liquor due to the prohibition policy keeps many people away from being exposed to its use. One may conclude from this that alcoholism can be explained only on the basis of a holistic approach rather than a single-factor approach.

A question is raised whether pressures can be located in the culture itself both to cause and to contain alcoholism. It is said that some cultures are able to develop effective controls over the individual than others. A research in the United States shows that there are very few teetotallers among the Jews (13%), compared to Catholics (21%) and Protestants (41%).

In France, Germany and the United States, the use of wine has been very common. It is only recently that alcoholism has become a major crisis in the life of the people of these countries. Once people start using alcohol because of the cultural sanctions, they use it frequently, especially in situations of insecurity and anxiety.

The current approach is that alcoholism is to be understood in terms of character and motivation. An alcoholic is a sick man. He is not to be looked upon with ridicule, condemnation and blame. He has fallen a victim to a set of complexes, attitudes and habits which bind him until the process of self-destruction is inevitable.

Major Concerns Relating to Alcoholism

Alcoholism is one of the leading causes of liver cirrhosis and failure. About 10 per cent of strokes, tuberculosis, hypertension, and epilepsy are caused by excess alcohol consumption. Alcohol-related deaths and deaths caused by diseases due to alcoholism are a major cause for concern in the country. In 2012 alone about 3.3 million deaths in India were attributed to alcohol consumption. This amounts to some 5.9 per cent of the global deaths that year.

On the 'years of life lost' scale, which is based on alcohol-attributable years of life lost, India has been rated 4 on a scale of 1 to 5. This implies that the alcohol consuming population of our country loses most years of their life because of drinking and its consequences.

Apart from the health concerns, chronic alcoholism is one of the greatest causes of poverty in the country. According to various studies, primary bread earners are ten times more likely to report alcohol abuse in the country. The regular consumption of alcohol is also inversely proportional to the family income. This means that consumption increases significantly with diminishing income.

Consumption of alcohol is a social taboo in most parts of India. While Islam as a religion does prohibit the consumption of alcohol but Hinduism mentions it as one of the moral evils, alcoholism in India is linked more with the economic and family circumstances than with religious dictates.

Alcoholism is also often blamed for domestic violence and poverty. Sometimes women, mostly wives of alcoholics, have formed groups that have forced alcohol shops to close. Efforts by women activists, women's organizations, and even ordinary housewives in rural areas have started struggling hard over the past several years to convince men against liquor consumption and force government to introduce prohibition.

In the flux of values and economic relations of our multilayered society, four denominators can still describe the major pillars of alcohol-related problems in India: (a) lack of information (c) adulteration of alcohol (d) inefficient alcohol regulation policies and (e) the paucity of appropriate medical intervention.

Consequences of Alcoholism

Alcohol has now become a common word in Indian society. With the impact of globalization, urbanization, industrialization, media influence and changing lifestyles, alcohol has entered the lives of Indians in a big and unrestricted manner. The consequences of alcoholism – in terms of personal misery, family budget, family discord, loss of wages, failure of health, accidents and cost in damage claims, cost of hospital treatment, cost in custodial treatment in jail, monetary damage in courts, and inducement to crime – are almost disastrous. Social deviance and social problems emerge from the use and abuse of alcohol. Though the number of annual arrests for public drunkenness is not much in our country, it is a known fact that a large number of alcoholics are not arrested because of the fact that arrest is not considered a good solution to the problem. A good number of persons arrested for crimes like rape, burglary, murder and theft are those who committed them while under the influence of alcohol. Alcohol is a major factor in highway accidents. Besides, it contributes to thousands of deaths every year. The National Crime Records Bureau (NCRB) suggested that in 2015 about 1.5 per cent of the total 4.67 lakh road accidents were caused by drunken driving or 'drug driving', resulting in injuries to 6,295 people. The offence, the report said, resulting in 2,988 deaths, at more than 8 deaths a day.

A high percentage of admissions to hospitals, particularly mental hospitals, is related to persons with 'alcoholic disorders' or a 'drinking problem'. Other socially deviant acts related to alcohol/drugs are thefts, bribes, wife battering, and suicides. Studies on suicide point out that the suicide rate is 50 times higher among alcoholics/drug users than non-alcoholics and non-drug users.

Since alcoholics/drug users directly affect four or five other persons (wife, parents, children, siblings, close friends, co-workers), the problem affects millions of people in the country. Families of alcoholics and drug users suffer the most. Even family violence, family unrest and divorce is caused by alcoholism. Drinking affects the business, the office efficiency and factory production also. Absenteeism, low output and poor judgement leading to work-related accidents, costs the government billions of rupees. Most factory-owners indicate a lack of interest and deny the existence of these problems among their employees in the factories/offices to save themselves the botheration of adopting effective measures for prevention.

Alcoholism poses a threat to every aspect of the addict's life. Besides physical effects, most also suffer from psychological effects. This could include unexplained mood swings, anxiety, severe depression, suicidal thoughts and tendencies, angry outbursts and acts or violence. All of these things are caused by dependency on alcohol. The drinker thinks that alcohol will reduce his tension, guilt, anxiety and frustration. But, the fact is that it reduces his operational efficiency to below the minimum level necessary for social existence or even for a bare existence. A drinker harbours the mistaken notion that alcohol can make association and interpersonal activity easier in society. But, in reality, alcohol breaks down an individual's participation in associations and thus socially weakens the individual. It impairs socially valuable ideas. Disadvantages of alcoholism can be summed up as below:

1. It hampers the drinker in both ways, physically and mentally.
2. Alcoholism can cause cancer in many parts of the body mainly in kidney, liver, stomach, etc.
3. It also hampers the digestive system of the body.
4. Alcoholism can also create depression and behavioural changes. This can affect personal life and relationships of a person with friends and families.
5. Alcohol consumption can have adverse social and economic effects on the individual drinker, the drinker's immediate environment and society as a whole. Indeed, individuals other than the drinker can be affected, for example, by traffic accidents or violence. It has an impact on society as a whole in terms of the resources required for criminal justice, health care and other social institution. Alcohol consumption can affect work performance in several ways:
   (i) *Work accidents:* In Great Britain, up to 25 per cent of workplace accidents and around 60 per cent of fatal accidents at work may be linked to alcohol. In India about 40 per cent of work accidents have been attributed to alcohol use.
   (ii) *Productivity:* Heavy drinking at work may reduce productivity. Performance at work may be affected both by the volume and pattern of drinking. Co-workers perceive that heavy drinkers have lower performance, problems in personal relationships and lack of self-direction, though drinkers themselves do not necessarily perceive effects on their work performance.
   (iii) *Unemployment:* Heavy drinking or alcohol abuse may lead to unemployment and unemployment may lead to increased drinking.

Societal Costs of Alcoholism

The societal costs linked to alcohol use can be broadly categorized as direct and indirect, tangible and intangible. Direct costs are the medical costs linked to treatment , transport costs, rehabilitation costs and in the event of death, funeral costs. Indirect costs include property damage, litigation costs, loss of insurance, and others. Intangible costs are those due to absence from work, decreased productivity, absenteeism, sickness leave, loss of school for children and many others. Besides, governments also incur huge expenditure for managing harmful effects of alcohol use. The collective costs of all these are also difficult to estimate.

Treatment of Alcoholics

Alcoholism is more treatable than drug addiction. There have been many successful treatment programmes. Since there is a continuum between use and abuse, there are various kinds of programmes for different degrees of drinking. Psychotherapy, environment therapy, behaviour therapy, and medical therapy are suggested and used for different types of drinkers. In medical therapy, hospitals and clinics give alcoholic patients the drug 'Antabuse' (technically called Tetra Ethylthiu Ramdisul Fide) (Walsh and Furfey, 1958: 151). This drug is inexpensive and is taken orally. It produces no effect whatever unless the patient drinks alcohol; in that case, it quickly produces extremely violent and unpleasant but not dangerous symptoms. Thus, it can guard the drinker against relapse.

In psychotherapy, resocialization is reinforced through counselling and through group therapy. In environment therapy, the drinker is made to change the environment where his behaviour may be easily controlled. In behaviour therapy, his fears and inhibitions are removed to enable him to develop self-confidence and self-reliance. Thus, the following treatment measures are mainly used to treat drinkers and alcoholics:

1. *Detoxification in Hospitals*: For alcohol addicts, the first step is 'detoxification'. Alcoholics need medical care and medical supervision. Tranquilizers are used for treating their withdrawal symptoms like convulsions and hallucinations. High potency vitamins and fluid electrolyte balance are also used in their physical rehabilitation.
2. *Role of Family:* Involving an alcoholic's family in his treatment and rehabilitation enhances the chances of success by 75 to 80 per cent. The family members do not preach; nor do they blame or condemn the alcoholic. They minimize his problems, offer him sincere and unselfish help and guidance, and never abandon him.
3. *Alcoholics Anonymous*: One of the most effective social therapies which uses group interaction is Alcoholics Anonymous. It is an organization of ex-alcoholics which started in the United States in the early 1940s and today has lakhs of persons as its members. In India, the branches exist in all the metropolitan cities, while in some cities, the branches have been recently established. Alcoholics Anonymous (AA) is an organization, a group of people, fellowships of men and women, who share their experience, strength and hope with each other that they may solve their common problem (i.e. alcoholism) and help others recover from alcoholism. In AA, even such alcoholics are found who were dismissed by medical fraternity as 'hopeless cases', who had been admitted in the psychiatric units for the proverbial nth times, who had no desire to be treated but were dragged to the hospitals by relatives and friends to 'reform' them. Having failed to reform in these units, they are brought to AA. There are cases in AA who had been in and out of AA at least eight to ten times, who after 'leaving' AA hit the bottle again, yet they are brought back to AA and again learn to stay off the bottle, seeking the help of the group of fellow alcoholics. These are the people who believe that medicine can treat the physical complications of alcoholism but it cannot cure the disease. The cure has to come from within and that is what AA offers.

At one time, generally 30 to 40 members are found in an AA who are from all walks of life, cutting through religion and financial status (*Family*, July 1995: 104–5). Most members are sober, some inebriated, but all very seriously involved in what is going on. The AA meetings mostly comprise of three parts: (a) a talk by the chairperson that is open, frank and hard-hitting, (b) autobiographical stories, and (c) open session.

What really drives people to quit alcohol after joining AA? In the outside world, an alcoholic is considered a social outcaste and feels forever chastened, which adds to his problems. In AA, all members share his situation and suddenly the alcoholic realizes that there is a hope for reform. The organization helps the 'patient' in healing by humanely reaching out to him as he has a real desire to stop drinking. The fellowship offers strength and hope.

4 *Treatment Centres*: These centres have been developed in some cities as alternatives to hospital treatment. Each centre has about 10–20 residents. Here, not only counselling takes place in a supportive environment but residents are made to follow certain anti-drinking rules too.

5. *Changing Values through Education*: Some voluntary organizations undertake educational and information programmes to alert the alcoholics to the dangers of excessive drinking. Social workers help the drinkers in coping with life and changing the social values and attitudes about drinking.

Risk Factors/Effects of Alcoholism

Alcoholism has many negative impacts that can affect the health of an individual, social life, professional life and financial life. Some of the effects of alcohol abuse are:

1. *Mental disorder*: Alcoholism affects the functioning of the brain and can lead to memory loss and psychological problems. Since alcohol is categorized as a depressant, it may amplify mental disorders such as depression and stress. A depressed alcoholic can develop suicidal tendencies more so when the effects of alcohol wears off.
2. *Health impact*: Alcohol abuse has several negative impacts. People addicted to alcohol may become frail and of poor health as a result of poor eating habits. This opens the door for diseases and a host of infections. Excessive drinking can also cause liver cirrhosis which is a common killer health condition among alcoholics. Since judgment is usually impaired when one is drunk, poor decision-making can lead to risky sexual behaviour and infections.
3. *Addiction*: Alcohol addiction is also termed as alcohol dependence. An alcoholic cannot function before indulging in alcohol or getting some liquor in the body system. Alcoholics do not know how to operate in a

sober state. It is a negative impact of addiction that affects alcoholics as well as those addicted to drugs and other substances.

4. *Abuse*: Alcoholism leads to alcohol abuse. A person with a compulsive drinking habit will keep on drinking even when he or she is inebriated. To such people, there is never a point when alcohol becomes too much. Alcohol abuse can lead to alcohol poisoning when there is too much liquor in the body system.
5. *Wastage of money*: Alcoholics will prioritize drinking over other important life decisions. An alcoholic can spend a lot of money on liquor at the expense of feeding the family or making serious investment decisions. Poor judgment when an individual is drunk can also lead to bad financial decisions. A person can buy an item that is not needed and thereby cause wastage of money.
6. *Relationship problems at home and issues at work*: Alcoholism can lead to relationship problems at home and result in issues in the workplace. An alcoholic spouse may become abusive towards his or her partner it leads to unhappiness in the relationship and may cause marital strife. An alcohol addict may also have problems interacting with friends and other family members due to the bad habits. Alcoholism also affects the professional life of a person. Alcohol addiction can lead to disorganization in the office, poor quality of work output, and bad decision-making skills.
7. *Low self-esteem*: Alcohol addiction can lead to low self-esteem. It can lead to the inability to take advantage of existing opportunities due to the low self-esteem.
8. *Unfulfilled career*: A person addicted to alcohol may never truly realize his or her potential career-wise. Alcoholism kills motivation and affects job performance leading to career stagnation. An alcoholic cannot be trusted with the management of an organization and may often be overlooked when promotion opportunities arise.

Prohibition

Gandhiji regarded the consumption of liquor as a major social evil and favoured complete prohibition in India. With this in view, the Constitution of India included Article 47 in the Directive Principles of State Policy, which states, 'The State shall endeavour to bring about prohibition of use, except for medicinal purposes, of intoxicating drinks and drugs which are injurious to health'. After independence, some states took up the programme of prohibition earnestly and some half-heartedly. In the last five decades or so, most of them have given up prohibition even though most leaders pay lip-service to the programme. Things have gone so far that in some states even chief ministers, ministers and their close relatives are running distilleries for manufacturing liquor, and their supporters and relatives are blessed with liquor licences. Individual politicians have thus developed vested interests in the manufacture and sale of liquor. The excuse they offer in justification against not introducing prohibition is that their governments will lose huge revenue without which they cannot launch their development projects.

After independence, Madras Province and Bombay State implemented prohibition between 1948 and 1950, and total prohibition was in operation in Madras State, Maharashtra, Gujarat and 11 districts of Andhra Pradesh from 1958 to 1969, and other sizeable areas in Assam, Madhya Pradesh, Orissa (now Odisha), Karnataka and Kerala. One-fourth of India's population was under prohibition by 1954, and in the same year, the Prohibition Enquiry Committee set April 1958 as the target to achieve national prohibition.

A renewed push for prohibition occurred under the Morarji Desai government in 1977, but it failed to achieve nationwide prohibition. The negative effects of prohibition including wide-scale sale of spurious and cheap liquor, the rise of organized crime and bootlegging due to the growth of a black market for alcohol, a large police force required to implement prohibition and loss of employment connected to the alcohol industry reduced demands for prohibition and led to calls for regulation of alcohol.

Role of Women

Women activists, women's organizations and even ordinary housewives in both urban and rural areas can spearhead the struggle to convince men against liquor consumption and force governments to introduce prohibition. They can demand the political parties to include prohibition in their poll manifestoes. It was in 1993 when a small group of neo-literate women in Dabbagunta village in Nellore district in Andhra Pradesh, fed up with the drunkenness of their men, attacked a liquor shop, drove away its owners and destroyed the stocks of indigenous wine. The spark provided by the unorganized women of a small dusty village caught the imagination of the womenfolk all over Andhra Pradesh, from where the agitation spread to other states in the country.

Control on Alcoholism

With the failure of the prohibition model, state governmental control has come to be focussed on the regulation of the liquor trade. The state governments, under the open licence system, leave the alcoholic beverage trade to private enterprise under licensing and regulation, the nominal public objectives being to eliminate people with criminal or questionable financial histories and to control the physical location of licensed liquor shops. Every state government earns crores of rupees every year when it auctions the contracts.

Radicals argue that as long as our social structure and economic system continues to produce inequality, unemployment, poverty, injustice, and role-strains and tensions, alcoholism will persist. Since the present social systems operating in our society produce more frustrations and deprivations, the rate of drinking would only accelerate in future. What is, therefore, needed is a policy and programme to produce more jobs, permit fair competition and reduce corruption and nepotism in appointments and promotions. If the lives of people are made meaningful, rewarding and satisfying, the need for alcohol would not exist or it will be minimized. Second, educating about the harm and hurt that alcohol can bring to a person's life and to society will help control the use of alcohol. Parents can impart education on the dangers of becoming an alcoholic as well as punish the deviants and create the necessary fear. Parents' education should be concerned with shaping the attitudes and behaviour conducive to non-drinking. Lastly, schools and colleges can also educate young students about the psychological and sociological effects of alcohol and alcoholism.

It is indeed a tragedy that our governments and political parties have not been able to follow the ideals we cherished during our struggle for independence. Gandhiji could not think of an independent India without prohibition. For him, prohibition was an integral part of the freedom movement. He categorically declared that if he were to be appointed dictator of the country for one hour, his first action would be to close all liquor shops without paying compensation. According to him, the evil of drinking was worse than theft and even prostitution, as it was the mother of both these evils.

Alcohol prohibition in India is in force in the states of Gujarat, Kerala, Bihar, Nagaland and Manipur; as well as in the Union Territory of Lakshadweep. All other Indian states and union territories permit the sale of alcohol. The present state of affairs can be summed up as: 'everybody wants prohibition but nobody wants it to be implemented'. No wonder, some committees/commissions appointed by some state governments recommend implementation of total prohibition 'in stages'. The problem of alcoholism calls for a concerted attack which may embrace treatment, social measures, education and research.

Alcohol Ban in India: Pros and Cons

In favour:

1. With the alcohol ban, problems of domestic violence will be reduced.
2. When alcohol is available abundantly, chances of drinking is higher.
3. A total ban on alcohol in 'Lakshadweep' is a big success.
4. Alcohol consumption is highly prevalent in the poorer sections of society. A ban on alcohol will save them from the financial drain.
5. Prohibition of alcohol limits, prevents alcohol addiction. The addiction can ruin people's lives, jobs, families, and obviously themselves too.
6. There is a direct correlation between alcohol consumption and an increase in crime.
7. Drunk Driving Prohibition reduces accidents and damages through drunk driving.

Against:

1. Prohibiting alcohol leads to loss of taxes and jobs.
2. In most cultures and religions, social drinking is an acceptable practice.
3. People who want alcohol will still be able to purchase it or make it even though at a higher cost and from sordid locations.
4. Smuggling and liquor mafias will be increased.
5. Use of alternative additives such as drugs will be increased.
6. If the alcohol ban is implemented, people will be arrested and prosecuted for just taking alcohol. That may not be a serious crime to get punished.

Solutions

Alcoholism is a disease that has a solution. These are the ways in which alcohol addiction can be treated or prevented:

1. *Discourage drinking*: Alcoholism can be prevented by discouraging drinking. The government and relevant stakeholders can carry out awareness campaigns to educate the society on the dangers of alcohol addiction. The campaign can be done on social media, print media, and television so that it can reach the target audience. Drinking while driving should also be prohibited.
2. *Depression treatment centres*: Psychiatrist treatment and not alcohol is the solution to depression. Depression treatment centres would, therefore, serve as a good treatment mechanism for those suffering from depression. Many people in the society do not really understand that depression is a mental disorder. Having treatment centres and creating awareness would destigmatize it and get help to those in need.
3. *Detoxification*: People addicted to alcohol can get professional help and kick the bad habit. Rehabilitation centres are ideal places for detoxification. An addict will be accorded treatment and given the necessary support to overcome alcoholism. Rehab is usually a good treatment option for those who, even, after the intervention of friends and family members cannot overcome the habit. An individual may be directed to attend a rehabilitation centre by a court of law, employer or in other cases forcibly taken to the centres by concerned friends and relatives.
4. *Ban alcohol*: An alcohol ban can also play an important role in combatting alcoholism. Limiting drinking hours in bars and other social places may discourage public drinking. The government can enact legislations to ensure that this is legally enforceable and to act as a deterrent to those that might want to flout the directive.
5. *Peer counselling*: Peer guidance and counselling can help the youth avoid the negative influence of peer influence and place them on the right paths to academic excellence and career progression. It can be used to guide youth properly and help them overcome issues such as low self-esteem that may lead to depression and hence, alcohol abuse. Peer

counselling centres can be set up in schools, campuses, places of worship, and places of work so that the young people can get help and keep away from negative behaviour. Community peer counselling centres are also ideal places to seek guidance and find help.

Other suggestions for implementing the prohibition: (a) Refusing permission to open new liquor shops, (b) Punishing government servants who drink, (c) Strict restrictions on drivers and pilots, (d) No liquor shops on the wayside, (e) No licence for distillation or brewing liquor (f) Discontinuing advertisements on drinks, and (g) Stoppage of drinking in public places.

It is very important that the patient is willing to quit the habit of alcohol. Otherwise any detoxification or rehabilitation will not able to solve the problem of alcohol addiction. What is needed of people is to be informed of the beneficial and harmful effects of alcohol, shed away taboos that do not serve any good and understand that addiction is a disease that can be cured in most instances and the sooner one intervenes the better one can expect the outcomes to be. What is needed of the government is to have a smart regulation of alcohol that will add to revenue, ensure the quality of alcohol and spread information on the ills of alcoholism without making it the forbidden fruit.

Conclusion

Alcoholism is a disease (chronic illness) with many negative impacts. People who are addicted to alcohol abuse take it without any moderation. The health implications of alcohol abuse are numerous and may prove fatal if left untreated. A variety of factors such as mental stress, issues at work, marital strife, hopelessness and depression may push one toward alcoholism. Alcohol does not solve any of the problems. It is thus, better to find a solution to the existing problems instead of turning to alcohol to find solace. Addicts should be given the necessary support and help to overcome their addiction problems.

References

Blum, Richard, *Drug Dealers: Taking Action*. London, Jossey Bass, 1973.

Clinebell, Howard J., *Understanding and Counselling the Alcoholic*, Abingdon Press, New York, 1956.

Gold, Herry and Scarpiti, Frank (eds), *Combating Social Problems*, Holt, Reinhart & Winston, New York, 1967.

Jellinek, E.M., 'Phases in Drinking History of Alcoholics', *Quarterly Journal of Studies on Alcohol*, Vol. 7, June, 1946.

Johnson, Elmer H., *Social Problems of Urban Man*, The Dorsey Press, Homewood, Illinois, 1973.

Keller, Mark and Vera, Efron, 'The Prevalence of Alcoholism', *Quarterly Journal of Studies on Alcohol*, Vol. 16, December, 1955.

Landis, Paul H., *Social Problems*, J.B. Lippincott Co., Chicago, 1959.

McVeigh, Frank and Shostak, Arthur, *Modern Social Problems*, Holt, Rinehart & Winston, New York, 1978.

Mohan, D., Chopra, A., Ray, R. and Sethi, H., 'Alcohol Consumption in India: A Cross Sectional Study', in Room, R., Demers, A., Bourgault, (eds) *Surveys of Drinking Patterns and Problems in Seven Developing Countries*, World Health Organization, Geneva, 103–114. 2001.

NIMHANS, 'Alcoholism-related Harm: Implications for Public Health and Policy in India', Bangalore, 2011.

Sethi, B.B., Trivedi, J.K., 'Drug Abuse in a Rural Population'. *Indian Journal of Psychiatry*. 1979; 21: 211–6.

Shepard, J.M. and Voss, H.L., *Social Problems*, Macmillan Publishing Co. Inc., New York, 1978.

Varma, V.K., Singh, A., Singh, S. and Malhotra, A., 'Extent and Pattern of Alcohol Use and Alcohol-related Problems in North India'. *Indian Journal of Psychiatry*, 22: 331–337, 1980.

Walsh, Maty E. and Furfey, Paul H., *Social Problems and Social Action*, Prentice Hall Inc., Englewood Cliffs, New Jersey, 1958.

Waskin, Richard (ed.), *Social Problems*, McGraw Hill & Co., New York, 1964.

18

Drug Abuse and Drug Addiction

'Say "no" to drugs and "yes" to life'; 'drug abuse is life abuse'; 'born free, live free'. These are the messages which are delivered by the Ministry of Welfare, Narcotics Control Bureau, and every man of importance to the deluded youth of India. Has drug abuse really become such a social problem in our country?

Drug abuse and addiction, now both grouped as 'drug use disorder', is a condition that is characterized by a self-destructive pattern of using a substance that leads to significant problems and distress, which may include tolerance to or withdrawal from the substance. Drug abuse or addiction is caused by the habitual taking of addictive substances. It focuses on the pattern of drug use and the effects drugs are having on a user's life.

1. Drug use has negatively impacted performance in work or school.
2. Risky acts endangering the drug user or others, are committed as a result of drug use, for example, drinking and driving.
3. Continuation of drug use in spite of the negative consequences it is having on relationships.
4. Legal or financial problems as a result of drug use.

Drug addiction contains that the user is experiencing negative consequences from drug use and refuses to quit using the drug. However, with drug addiction, the addict has developed a tolerance to the drug, increasing the used amount, and experiences withdrawal symptoms when abstinent. Drug abuse and addiction takes place over time. Drug abuse frequently, but not always, leads to drug addiction. Although drug abuse and drug addiction are different terms, but they are related.

Addiction is a chronic disease characterized by drug seeking and use that is compulsive, or difficult to control, despite harmful consequences. Addiction does not start overnight. The initial decision to take drugs is voluntary for most people, but repeated drug use can lead to brain changes that challenge an addicted person's self-control and interfere with their ability to resist intense urges to take drugs. Some people become addicted to drugs while others do not. No one factor can predict if a person will become addicted to drugs. A combination of factors influences risk for addiction. The more risk factors a person has, the greater the chance that taking drugs can lead to addiction. It takes time to build up a tolerance to the drug of choice, to develop cravings for the drug and to experience problems due to use of illicit substances. Drug abuse often starts first. Though at its worst it can look like an addiction. Specific symptoms that are used to diagnose drug use disorders include the following:

1. Difficulty with concentration and minor memory problems.
2. Irritable depression like anger.
3. Repeated arguments with loved ones.
4. Repeatedly using drugs to cope with problems.
5. Physical symptoms when abstaining from drug use.
6. Physical problems as a result of using drugs.
7. Repeatedly using more drugs or using drugs for longer than intended.
8. Spending less time on life obligations due to drug use.
9. Needing more and more of the drug than one used to.

In addition to drug tolerance, drug addiction symptoms include:

1. Experiencing withdrawal symptoms when not using the drug.
2. Unable to stop using the drug even after repeated attempts to do so.
3. Consumes large and even dangerous amounts of the drug.

Aberrant Behaviour

Drug abuse may be perceived both as an aberrant behaviour as well as a social problem. In the former sense, it is regarded as an evidence of individual's social maladjustment; in the latter sense, it is viewed as a widespread condition that has harmful consequences for society. In several western countries, drug abuse was regarded as an important social problem since long but in India, it is only since last three decades that it has come to be considered a crucial social problem. It is said that India has become not only an important transit centre for drugs (from where drugs are smuggled from some countries and sent to other countries), but the prevalence of drug use is also alarmingly increasing. According to one estimate, India has about one million heroin addicts alone. The illegal drug trade in India is estimated to generate between ₹ 10 to 20 thousand crores annually. Likewise, the quantity of illicit drugs seized over the years has increased manifold. The use of illicit drugs today is not confined to the street urchins and the lower classes; more and more middle and upper class youth are succumbing to drugs.

In spite of this, drug abuse in India is still considered more as an aberrant behaviour than an anti-social or a non-conforming behaviour. By this, one means that the aberrant person conceals his transgression from social norms of the society, violates norms without questioning their legitimacy, and attempts to escape the penalties for violating norms without proposing changes in them. The aberrant person is believed to be out to satisfy his private interests.

Merton (1979: 829–32) has distinguished between 'aberrant' and 'non-conforming' behaviour to show the significance of various kinds of norm violations. The 'non-conformist' challenges the legitimacy of the norms (goals and/or means) and he publicly rejects and advocates the substitution of new norms, but the 'aberrant person' neither questions the legitimacy of norms nor seeks replacement of old norms with new norms. No wonder, sociologists perceive drug abuse in India as aberrant behaviour, and drug users and addicts as aberrant persons, who unlike non-conformists, are not interested in improving social conditions or benefiting mankind.

Several researches have been conducted on drug abuse in India in the last three decades by medical scientists, psychiatrists and sociologists. This author conducted two studies on drug abuse among college/university students in 1976 and 1986 in Rajasthan not only to analyse the problem of extent of drug abuse but also to study its causes and suggest measures for controlling it. Before examining the findings of these researches, let us first try to understand the basic concepts in drug abuse terminology.

Basic Concepts

The concepts of drug, drug abuse, drug dependence, drug addiction and abstinence syndrome need some clarity. *Drug* is a chemical substance associated with distinct physical and/or psychological effects. It alters a person's normal bodily processes or functions. But, this definition is too broad. In medical parlance, a drug is a substance prescribed by a physician or manufactured expressly for the purpose of treating and preventing disease and ailment by its chemical nature and its effect on the structure and functions of a living organism. In the psychological and sociological contexts, drug is a term for habit forming substance which directly affects the brain or nervous system. More precisely, it refers to 'any chemical substance which affects bodily function, mood, perception, or consciousness which has potential for misuse, and which may be harmful to the individual or the society' (Jullian, 1977). In this sense, the frequent use of drug is considered so dangerous and sometimes even immoral and anti-social that it arouses a variety of indignant and hostile sentiments on the part of general public. Some drugs are, however, relatively innocuous and are not addictive or accompanied by harmful physiological effects. The use of such drugs stands in marked contrast to the use of illegal drugs like heroin, cocaine and LSD or the consumption of legal drugs like alcohol, tobacco, barbiturates and amphetamines, all of which are associated with distinctly harmful physical effects on the person habituated to them.

Drug abuse is the use of illicit drug or misuse of legitimate drug resulting into physical or psychological harm. It includes smoking *ganja* or hashish, taking heroin or cocaine or LSD, injecting morphine, drinking alcohol and so forth. These are sometimes referred to as being 'high on speed' or 'trip' or 'getting kicks'.

Drug dependence denotes habitual or frequent use of a drug. The 'dependence' can either be physical or psychological. Physical dependence occurs with the repeated use of the drug when the body has adjusted to the presence of a drug and will suffer pain, discomfort or illness if the use of the drug is discontinued.

Addiction is generally referred to describe physical dependence. Thus, 'addiction' or 'physical dependence' is 'a state whereby the body requires continued administration of the drug in order to function'. Body functioning is interfered with, if the drug is withdrawn, and withdrawal symptoms appear in a pattern specific for the drug. The total reaction to deprivation is known as *abstinence syndrome*.

The chronic drug user develops a feeling that he must constantly increase the dose in order to produce the same effect as that from the initial dose. This phenomenon is called 'tolerance'. It represents the body's ability to adapt itself to the presence of a foreign substance. However, tolerance does not develop for all drugs or in all individuals; though with certain drugs (for example morphine), addicts have been known to build up great tolerance very quickly. 'Cross tolerance' refers to the fact that tolerance development for one drug may also result in tolerance for similar drugs.

Psychological dependence occurs when an individual comes to rely on a drug for the feeling of well-being it produces. The word 'habituation' is sometimes used to refer to psychic or psychological dependence. The difference between 'habituation' and 'addiction' is that habit is not compulsive as addiction is. Addiction to a drug means that the body becomes so dependent to the toxic effects of the drug that one just cannot do without it. The characteristics of drug addiction are: (a) an overpowering desire or need (compulsion) to continue taking the drug and to obtain it by any means; (b) a tendency to increase the dose; (c) a psychological and generally a physical dependence on the effects of the drugs; and (d) an effect detrimental to the individual and to the society.

The criteria for diagnosis of addiction are as follows:

1. Using larger and larger amounts of the drug of choice in order to achieve the same results experienced initially.
2. Less interest in old hobbies and interests or career/school pursuits.
3. Withdrawing from friends and family.
4. Patterns of behaviour that revolve solely around getting or staying high.
5. Multiple attempts to cut down or stop drug use without success.
6. Continued use of drugs and alcohol despite continued and growing problems related to their use.

Nature and Impact of Abusable Drugs

The abusable drugs may be divided into eight categories: stimulants, inhalants, cannabinoids, depressants, opioids and morphine derivatives, anabolic steroids, hallucinogens and prescription drugs.

Stimulants speed up the body's nervous system and create a feeling of energy. They are also called 'uppers' because of their ability to make you feel very awake. Stimulants have the opposite effect of depressants. When the effects of a stimulant wear off, the user is typically left with feelings of sickness and a loss of energy. Constant use of such drugs can have many negative effects on the user. In order to prevent extreme negative side effects of these drugs and the impact they have on life, drug treatment centres are often recommended. Cocaine, methamphetamines, amphetamines, ritalin and cylert are main stimulants.

Inhalants are sniffed or huffed and give the user immediate results. Unfortunately, these immediate results can also result in sudden mental damage. When inhalants are taken, the body becomes deprived of oxygen, causing a rapid heartbeat. Other effects include liver, lung and kidney problems, affected sense of smell, difficulty walking and confusion. Types of inhalants include glues, paint thinner, gasoline, laughing gas and aerosol sprays.

Cannabinoids result in feelings of euphoria, cause confusion and memory problems, anxiety, a higher heart rate, as well as staggering and poor reaction time. These drugs include hashish and marijuana.

Depressants slow down activity in the central nervous system of your body. These drugs are also called 'downers' because they slow the body down and seem to give feelings of relaxation. Depressants are available as prescription drugs to relieve stress and anger, although drowsiness is often a side effect. The 'relaxation' felt from these drugs is not a healthy feeling for the body to experience, to stop abuse of this drug, drug treatment is suggested. The major depressants are barbiturates, benzodiazepines, flunitrazepam, gamma-hydroxybutyrate, methaqualone, alcohol and tranquillisers.

Opioids and morphine derivatives can cause drowsiness, confusion, nausea, feelings of euphoria, respiratory complications and relieve pain. These include codeine, fentanyl and fentanyl analogs, heroin, morphine, opium, oxycodone HCL, hydrocodone bitartrate and acetaminophen.

Anabolic steroids are taken to improve physical performance as well as to enlarge muscles and increase strength. Negative effects of steroids include baldness, cysts, oily hair and skin, acne, heart attack, stroke and change in voice. Hostility is also a frequent side effect of anabolic steroids. Types of drugs include anadrol, oxandrin, durabolin, stanozol and dianabol.

Hallucinogens change the mind and cause the appearance of things that are not really there. Hallucinogens affect the body's self-control, such as speech and movement, and often bring about hostility. Other negative effects of these drugs include heart failure, increased heart rate, higher blood pressure and changes in the body's hormones. These drugs include LSD (lysergic acid diethylamide), mescaline, psilocybin, cannabis and magic mushrooms.

Prescription drugs can be very helpful drugs when used properly and under the guidance of a qualified physician. These drugs can be used as aids in surgery, to treat medical conditions and while controlling various symptoms. Misuse and abuse of prescription drugs however can be very dangerous. Types of drugs include opiods (codeine, oxycodone, morphine), central nervous system depressants (barbiturates, benzodiazepines) and stimulants (dextroamphetamine, methylphenidate).

Extent and Nature of Drug Abuse

Any substance (usually chemical) which influences our bodies or emotions when consumed may be called a drug. Drug affects bodily function, mood, perception or consciousness which has the potential for misuse and which may be harmful to the individual or the society. These substances may be medicinal. The use of such drugs is usually legal. Some drugs may be non-medicinal in nature. Their use is illegal. Using drugs to cure or prevent an illness or improve one's health may be called drug 'use'. Using drugs (medicinal/non-medicinal) in quantity, strength, frequency or manner that damages the physical or mental functioning of an individual, is termed as drug abuse.

How widespread is the use of illegal drugs and the misuse of legal drugs in our country? According to recent surveys, India has at least 7.5 crore drug addicts. The number has been increasing at an alarming rate. A study, conducted by the Postgraduate Institute of Medical Education and Research (PGIMER), has claimed that drug abuse has increased among youngsters in the 16–25 age group.

Mostly it is the younger generation that fall an easy prey to it. What started off as casual use among a minuscule population of high-income group youth in the metros, has now permeated to all sections of society. Indian produced pharmaceuticals, heroin and alcohol are amongst the most abused drugs. It is said that with a turnover of around $ 500 billion, it is the third largest business in the world, next to petroleum and arms trade. Actually, in India, the cultural values are changing, the poorer class is suffering with economic hardship while at the same time there is a massive rise in the upper class. All this, combined with the dwindling support of family (due to increase work and western life), is leading to drug abuse and addiction.

Besides, over the past few decades, India has seen a rise in industrialization and urbanization, which has caused large migrations to its cities. This is causing their traditional culture and way of life to slowly loosen. The individual Indians and their new way of life is causing them to be very vulnerable to the stresses and strains of the modern way of life. These stresses and strains may cause the person to turn to drugs to calm their thoughts and deal with everyday life.

India's approach towards narcotic drugs and psychotropic substances is enshrined in Article 47 of its Constitution which mandates that the 'state shall endeavour to bring about prohibition of the consumption except for medicinal purposes of intoxicating drinks and of drugs which are injurious to health'. The Narcotic Drugs and Psychotropic Substances Act, 1985 was enacted with stringent provisions to curb this menace. The Act prohibits, except for medical or scientific purposes, the manufacture, production, trade, use, etc. of narcotic drugs and psychotropic substances. It also envisages a minimum term of 10 years imprisonment extendable to 20 years and fine of ₹ 1 lakh extendable up to ₹ 2 lakh for the offenders. It has been further amended by making provisions for the forfeiture of properties derived from illicit drugs trafficking.

Besides, several measures involving innovative changes in enforcement, legal and judicial systems have been brought into effect. The introduction of death penalty for drug-related offences has been a major deterrent. Comprehensive strategy involving specific programmes to bring about an overall reduction in use of drugs has been evolved by the various governmental agencies and NGOs and is further supplemented by measures like education, counselling, treatment and rehabilitation programmes. At international level, India has also bilateral agreements on drug trafficking with 13 countries, including Pakistan and Burma.

Effects of Drug Abuse and Addiction

Drug use can hurt the people who take drugs and the people around them, including families, kids and babies who are not yet born. Drug use can also lead to addiction, a long-lasting brain disease in which people can not stop taking drugs on their own, even when they know that bad thing could happen if they keep using them. Drug abuse is the increasing desire to obtain and use increasing amounts of one or more substances to the exclusion of everything else. Drug abuse affects the body and mind of the user. One specific effect of drug abuse is the creation of physical drug dependence, a person who abuses drugs may not realize that they have a problem until pronounced effects of drug abuse are seen, often physically. While drug abuse effects on the body vary depending on the drug used, all drug abuse negatively impact one's health. Common effects of drug abuse on the body include sleep changes and decreased memory and cognitive abilities. Other common physical problems include abnormal vital signs like respiration, heart rate and blood pressure, chest or lung pain, nausea, vomiting, diarrhoea, stomach pain, skin can be cool and sweating or hot and dry

One of the primary effects of drug abuse can be found within the definition of drug abuse itself: an increasing, intense desire to use the drug above all else. Drug craving can shift a person's entire mental focus on obtaining the drug. Side effects of drug abuse then include preoccupation with where to get the drug, how to get money for the drug, and where and when the drug can be used. Psychological drug abuse effects commonly include changes in mood. A person may be anxious, thinking about when they can next use the drug, or depressed due to drug side effects. Other psychological side effects include aggressiveness or irritability, selfishness and moreover, one of the side effects of drug use may be bizarre, out of character, behaviour that further separates the drug abuser from their loved ones. The effects of drug abuse can also include decreasing performance at work or school. This decreased performance may lead to disciplinary action, expulsion or dismissal, creating money problems and possibly even legal troubles. Discontinuing participation in sports and giving up hobbies are other effects of drug abuse.

Drugs are chemicals that affect the body and brain. Different drugs can have different effects. Some effects of drugs include health consequences that are long-lasting and even permanent. They can continue even after the person has stopped taking the substance. People suffering from drug and alcohol addiction also have a higher risk of unintentional injuries, accidents and domestic violence incidents. The impact of drug abuse and dependence can be far-reaching, affecting almost every organ in the human body.

Health Problems

1. Weaken the immune system, increasing susceptibility to infections.
2. Substance abuse can lead to abnormal heart rates and heart attacks.
3. Stop bones from growing properly.
4. Cause cardiovascular conditions ranging from abnormal heart rate to heart attacks. Injected drugs can also lead to collapsed veins and infections of the blood vessels and heart valves.
5. Cause nausea, vomiting and abdominal pain.
6. Cause the liver to have to work harder, possibly causing significant damage or liver failure.
7. Severe muscle cramping and general weakness.
8. Cause seizures, stroke and widespread brain damage that can impact all aspects of daily life by causing problems with memory, attention and decision-making, including sustained mental confusion and permanent brain damage.
9. Injecting drugs can result in collapsed veins and infections in heart valves.
10. Sharing the needles used to inject certain drugs can give diseases like Hepatitis C, Hepatitis B and HIV.
11. Produce global body changes such as breast development in men, dramatic fluctuations in appetite and increases in body temperature, which may impact a variety of health conditions.

Injuries and Death

Use of drugs and alcohol also have an increased risk of death through both suicide and homicide. Alcohol specifically results in accidental injuries and deaths. People who live with substance dependence have a higher risk of all bad outcomes including unintentional injuries, accidents, the risk of domestic violence and death.

Effects on the Brain

Drug use can hurt the body and the brain, sometimes forever. Although initial drug use may be voluntary, Long-term use also causes changes in other brain chemical systems and circuits as well, affecting functions that include learning, judgment, decision-making, stress, memory and behaviour.

Birth Defects

Illicit drugs such as marijuana, cocaine, ecstasy and other amphetamines, and heroin may pose various risks for pregnant women and their babies. Some of these drugs can cause a baby to be born too small or too soon, or birth defects or learning and behavioural problems.

Legal Consequences

Drug and alcohol abuse not only has negative effects on health but can also have legal consequences. Driving under the influence of drugs or alcohol can lead to a suspended driver's license, usually for 6 months to 2 years and also heavy fines.

Financial Problems

Drugs and alcohol are expensive. Substance abuse also impacts productivity and success at work. The legal issues tied to drug use will have to find a way to pay for legal counsel.

Other Problems

1. Fighting and violence inside and outside the home.
2. Trouble at school.
3. Trouble at work or losing a job.
4. Trouble in relationships.
5. Child abuse or neglect.
6. Rash driving and accidents.
7. Arrests and jail.

Motivations in Drug Usage

What are the causes of drug abuse? These may be classified under four heads: (a) psychological causes, like relieving tension, easing depression, removing inhibitions, satisfying curiosity, removing boredom, getting kicks, feeling high and confident, and intensifying perception; (b) social causes, like facilitating social experiences, being accepted by friends, and challenging social values; (c) physiological causes, like staying awake, heightening sexual experiences, removing pain, and getting sleep; and (d) miscellaneous causes, like improving study, sharpening religious insight, deepening self-understanding, and solving personal problems, etc.

My study (of 4,081 college/university students) revealed that of the 1,469 students who consumed drugs, 85.5 per cent took drugs because of psychological reasons, 15.2 per cent because of physiological reasons, 10.9 per cent because of social reasons, and 28.4 per cent because of miscellaneous reasons (the total is more than 100 per cent because each category was taken separately). The detailed analysis pointed out that (a) the largest number of drug-using students comprised individuals who were devoted to pleasure, seeking new excitement and thrill, (b) a small number took drugs as an escape mechanism or to alleviate distress, and (c) a very small number of students receiving drugs in the course of medical treatment for the relief of pain continued to take them long after the treatment was over.

My view is that drug abuse is a learnt behaviour, acquired by individuals in interaction with peers, acquaintances, family members and others in three ways: through persuasion, through unconscious imitation and through reflective thinking. In the analysis of the sources of getting drugs, it was found that (a) drugs were generally obtained from the non-medical sources (friends, acquaintances, family members, home cupboard), (b) medical sources were used more by girls than by boys, and (c) the non-medical source mentioned most often was 'friend'.

Like analysing causes of drug abuse, it is equally essential to analyse the causes of abstinence, that is, why the non-users abstained from taking drugs or the 'past users' discontinued them. My study of students showed that the important causes of abstinence and discontinuation were: personal (49.3%), physiological (23.8%), social (22.4%), religious (22.3%), and economic (4.1%). The personal causes were: lack of interest/curiosity, personal dislike or hatred for the use of drugs, and non-availability of or non-accessibility to drugs; the physiological causes were: risk of physical/mental dangers or deteriorating health, risk of dependence on the drug, and having had a bad experience of 'being on a trip'; the social causes were: pressure of friends, influence of parents, risk of social disapproval; the religious cause was the moral principles; and the economic cause was that individual had either no money to purchase drugs or found drugs too expensive.

Role of Family and Peer Group in Drug Abuse

Family and peer group associations are the primary potent influences upon the direction which individual takes and maintains in his life. A hypothesis in my own study of drug abuse among college/university students was that drug usage was influenced by the quality of affectionate family relationships. This term (affectionate family relationship) was operationalized on the following bases: (a) parents take an interest in the career of their children and are conscious of their parental obligations, (b) relations between parents of drug users, between drug users and their parents and between users and their siblings are based on harmony and solidarity, (c) parental control is neither very harsh nor very lenient so as to give an opportunity to the child for self-expression, (d) the size of family is so manageable in terms of family income that no child in the family suffers from unfulfilment of the necessities of life, (e) parents broadly conform to social and moral norms setting examples for their children to follow, and (f) the child exhibits a feeling of trust and security in the parents by taking them into confidence and by seeking their advice and help in facing perplexing problems.

The study revealed that in a good number of cases, the families of drug users were not 'normal' and family relationships were not 'affectionate'. In testing the relationship between drug usage and 'staying away from parents', it was found that residence with parents was as important in the incidence of drug usage as residence in hostel. In other words, family background is significant in drug usage. The nature of family control, the discipline imposed by the parents over the children, the parents' interest in their friends, leisure activities and their future career prospects and parents remaining conscious of their obligations towards their children were found to be important factors which determine the children's inclination to step into the world of drugs. The drinking/smoking and drug taking behaviour of family members also had a bearing on the use of drugs. It may therefore, be maintained that family environment is an important factor in drug usage.

Like the family, peer group pressure was also found influential in drug usage. About 81 per cent drug users had friends who were drug users. Another 44 per cent drug users were initiated into drug use by their friends. Approximately 31 per cent drug users always took drugs in the company of their friends. As many as 63 per cent drug users got first knowledge of drugs from their friends, and 17 per cent users had first taken drugs in their friends' house. All this shows that peer group culture has a significant effect on the drug use behaviour.

On the basis of the above analysis, it may be pointed out that the main causes of drug abuse are: family environment, mental condition, social factors like oppressive social system and power structure, subcultures (slum areas, college/hostel sub-cultures, etc.), peer pressures, personality factors (dependent personality) and pursuit of pleasure and fun.

Theories of Causation

The theoretical explanations of drug usage may be grouped broadly under four heads: physiological, psychological, socio-psychological and sociological.

According to the *Physiological Theory,* people take drugs because of physiological aberrations and deficiencies or owing to bodily adaptation to chemical properties of the drug. Mordones, Silkworth, Randolph and Nimwich, are the scholars who have explained drug usage in terms of chemical reactions. But this theory, though widely accepted in the first two decades of this century has been found inadequate ever since the psychological and sociological attributes of people who use drugs have been pointed out by the empirical studies.

The psychologists have explained drug use and drug dependence mainly in terms of Reinforcement Theory, Personality Theory, Power Theory, and the Weakened-Self Theory. In the Reinforcement Theory, Abraham Wilker (Stark, 1975: 102) has maintained that the pleasurable sensations produced by drugs reinforce their use. The Personality Theory has explained drug usage in terms of satisfying certain psychological needs or compensating for certain psychological shortcomings. It refers to distinctive personality traits associated with drug dependence and emphasizes on 'dependent personality' as the cause of drug dependence. Chein (1969: 13–30), Knight (1937: 538), and Robert Freed Bales (1962: 157), the main supporters of this theory, hold that people with dependent personalities require emotional support and attention from others and failure to get it is substituted by drug usage. Chein in his study of narcotics in New York city found that persons with personality traits like passivity, low self-esteem, little ability for self-direction, distrust of other people, difficulty in handling frustrations and anxieties, inadequate masculine identification and failure to resolve childhood conflicts, take to drugs. McClelland (1977) challenging the Personality Theory has propounded Power Theory and has explained drug usage (alcohol) as an expression of a person's need for power. The light and occasional alcohol user gets a feeling of enhanced social power while the heavy alcoholic gets a feeling of enhanced personal power. In the Weakened Self Theory or Fear Theory, Peele and Brodsky (1975) have maintained that drug addiction is a response to fear and insecurity to the conditions of modem life.

All these psychological theories are incomplete in three ways: (a) they fail to explain how the personality traits, exclusive to drug users, are developed by the users, (b) they fail to explain why this syndrome leads to drugs or alcohol rather than to some other behaviour like suicide, and (c) they fail to identify personality traits exclusive to drug addicts or alcoholics and why people with similar personality profiles do not take to drugs.

In the *Socio-Psychological Labelling Theory*, Becker (1963) and Erickson (1964: 21) have maintained that a person becomes a drug dependent or an alcoholic under the pressure of being labelled as an addict or an alcoholic. But it fails to explain why people first engage in drug behaviour that gets them socially labelled as deviant addicts.

The *Sociological Theory* holds that it is the circumstances or social environment which make people drug addicts. Sutherland's *Differential Association Theory*, when applied to drug usage, explains drug taking as behaviour learnt from other persons, principally in small intimate groups. The *Social Learning Theory*, which is the expansion of Differential Association Theory and the Reinforcement Theory, has been propounded by Akers and Burgess. When the Reinforcement Theory merely assumes that drug dependence is conditioned learning, the Social Learning Theory examines the social sources of reinforcers that operate in the learning process. The reinforcement comes from association with persons favourably defining the drug use. The *Strain Theory* focusses on the intense pressures put on individuals that cause them to deviate from the internalized norms. According to Merton, the source of this pressure is the discrepancy between goals and means. Those who fail to achieve their goals through legitimate means become so frustrated that they turn to the use of drugs and alcohol. Merton calls them 'retreatists'. The *Sub-cultural Theory* holds that different groups within the society are socialized into different sets of norms and deviance is a judgement imposed by an outside group. Thus, what may appear to be deviant behaviour is really conformity to a set of norms espoused by one group but rejected by another. When young people claim that adults are hypocritical to ban cannabis in a society where alcohol drinking is socially permissible, and when adults denounce cannabis as more dangerous substance than alcohol, two sub-cultures are fighting over whose norms shall prevail. Thus, drug use is the result of clash in sub-cultural values of the young and the adults.

All the above sociological theories have their own perspectives, but each theory leaves a number of questions unanswered. In my own Social Bond Approach (1982: 120), I have explained drug abuse in terms of weakening of social bond between individual and society due to maladjustment (in status), unattachment (to social groups), and non-commitment (to social roles). It is individual's attachment to others, commitment to his social roles, and adjustment to various situations that determine his values about what is good or desirable, his behaviour patterns and his motives in deviating from the dominant values of the culture. It is only by recognizing the role and analysing the nature of these three factors in particular or social bond in general that we will be able to point out the structural or the institutional measures to control drug abuse.

Measures to Combat Drug Trafficking, Treating Addicts and Preventing Drug Abuse

Over the last three-four decades, India has been facing the problem of increasing trafficking in drugs, particularly transit traffic in respect of heroin and hashish from the Middle East region destined to western countries. As a result of this transit traffic, metropolitan cities like Mumbai, Delhi, Kolkata, and Chennai have become vulnerable to drug trafficking. Almost daily, we read news about drug trafficking. The narcotic authorities seize drugs worth crores of rupees in almost every corner of the country. However, in recent times, Punjab has emerged as a major transit and destination point for drugs coming from Pakistan. Drug trafficking has reached a new high in the state. The latest report of the Narcotic Control Bureau reveals that the seizure of high-priced heroin from Punjab was more than the total seizures in the country. Most of the heroin seized in Punjab enters through Pakistan as the state shares a 550 km long international border with it. The smugglers have not even spared the country's capital and have made it the hub of drug trafficking in the country.

The 'profits' generated by drug trafficking are used in many ways: (a) for financing politicians and developing lobbies in bureaucracy, judiciary, police, prisons and media; (b) for investment in shell corporations that take over legitimate business organizations; (c) in purchasing arms for terrorism (it has been found that militants in Kashmir and Punjab and LTTE and ISI organizations use drug trafficking as the main source of obtaining money for purchasing weapons); and (d) intelligence agencies also take help of drug traffickers to assist terrorist activity. But, the fact is that all these 'profits' are nothing but subversion of democratic processes.

In order to combat trafficking in drugs, among the various measures adopted by the government, one was the enactment of an Act in 1985, called Narcotic Drugs and Psychotropic Substances Act.

Narcotic Drugs and Psychotropic Substances Act

The Act relates to drug addicts, too. It lays down imprisonment of one year or fine or both for illegal possession in small quantity for personal consumption of any narcotic drug or psychotropic substance. It also empowers the court to release an addict for undergoing medical treatment for detoxification or de-addiction from a hospital or an institution maintained or recognized by the government. In keeping with this, the Act requires the government to establish as many centres as it thinks fit for identification, treatment, education, after-care, rehabilitation and social reintegration of addicts.

Electronic Cigarettes Act

E-cigarettes are battery-operated device that heat a substance, which may or may not contain nicotine, to create vapour for inhalation. E-cigarettes do not contain tobacco and therefore are not regulated under the cigarettes and other Tobacco Products Act, 2003. In August 2018, the Ministry of Health and Family Welfare had released an advisory to all states requiring them to not approve any new e-cigarettes and restrict the sale and advertisement of e-cigarettes. The legislation was notified on 5 December 2019, making the production, import, export, transport, sale or advertisement of such 'alternative' smoking devices a cognizable offence attracting jail term and fine. Fifteen states including Delhi, Maharashtra and UP have since banned e-cigarettes in the interest of public health.

Action Plan for Drug Abuse

The Ministry of Welfare, Government of India has also evolved a four-point action plan on drug abuse: (a) community-based action for identification, motivation, counselling, treatment and after-care, (b) generation of awareness about the consequences of drug abuse, (c) training for service providers, and (d) association of non-governmental organizations in the implementation of the programme and providing funds to them for the establishment of counselling and de-addiction facilities. The National Institute of Social Defence at one time was engaged in training functionaries of governmental and non-governmental agencies engaged in drug abuse prevention. In the last one decade, hundreds of de-addiction centres have come up all over the country. Private nursing homes and government hospitals have opened new wings to treat addicts.

Some state governments have also undertaken programmes to impress upon the university authorities to mount a special vigil against drinking and drug abuse in hostels and campuses. In the voluntary sector too, a number of counselling and guidance centres have been established in different cities. These centres are engaged in supplying information regarding the sources of treatment, coordinating with rehabilitation agencies, data collection, dissemination of knowledge, liaison with enforcement agencies and psychological aid by way of individual and group therapy.

However, the drug de-addiction programme in our country has not made any significant headway. However, for the purpose of reduction in drug demands, the Ministry of Social Justice and Empowerment, Government of India has been implementing a scheme for prevention of alcoholism and substance (drugs) abuse since 1985–86 under which 41 counselling centres and 401 drug de-addiction centres are functioning in the country for counselling, treatment and rehabilitation of drug addicts. The Ministry has also set up a National Centre for Drug Abuse Prevention (NCDAP) in the National Institute of Social Defence for capacity building and training of NGOs working in the field. Besides, the Government of India has also constituted a National Consultative Committee on De-addiction and Rehabilitation (NCCDR) to advise government both at the centre and in the states on the entire gamut of issues related to prevention, de-addiction and rehabilitation of drug abusers.

Ways to Prevent Substance Abuse

While it's practically impossible to prevent anyone and everyone from using drugs, there are things we can all do to avoid drug and/or alcohol abuse. By sharing this knowledge with those closest to you, you yourself may be able to prevent them from doing drugs, too. Here are the top five ways to help prevent drug abuse:

1. *Effectively deal with peer pressure*: The biggest reason teens start using drugs is because their friends utilize peer pressure. No one likes to be left out, and teens (and yes, some adults too) find themselves doing things they normally would not do, just to fit in. In these cases, you need to either find a better group of friends who will not pressure you into doing harmful things, or you need to find a good way to say no. Teens should prepare a good excuse or plan ahead of time, to keep from giving into tempting situations.
2. *Deal with life pressure:* People today are overworked and overwhelmed, and often feel like a good break or a reward is deserved. But in the end, drugs only make life more stressful – and many of us too, often fail to recognize this at the moment. To prevent using drugs as a reward, find other ways to handle stress and unwind. Take up exercising, read a good book, volunteer with the needy or create something. Anything positive and relaxing helps take the mind off using drugs to relieve stress.
3. *Seek help for mental illness:* Mental illness and substance abuse often go hand-in-hand. Those with a mental illness may turn to drugs as a way to ease the pain. Those suffering from some form of mental illness, such as anxiety, depression or post-traumatic stress disorder should seek the help of a trained professional for treatment before it leads to substance abuse.
4. *Examine the risk factors*: A history of substance abuse in the family, living in a social setting that glorifies drug abuse and/or family life that models drug abuse can be risk factors.

5. *Keep a well-balanced life*: People take up drugs when something in their life is not working, or when they're unhappy about their lives or where their lives are going. Look at life's big picture, and have priorities in order.

   Other prevention strategies include:

1. Increasing taxes on tobacco and alcohol products to reduce use, particularly among young people.
2. Reducing the availability of excess prescription medications.
3. Restricting advertising of addictive substances, particularly to young people.
4. Restricting the marketing of addictive substances in ways that appeal to youth.
5. Resist social pressures to engage in substance use.
6. Strengthen self-esteem.
7. Improve decision-making and communication skills.
8. Manage stress and anxiety.

Drug prevention programmes are designed to provide the education and support necessary to diminish drug dependency in communities, schools and the workplace. Drug abuse prevention has become an important first step in informing specific individuals about the dangers of addiction, prevention techniques and where to find recovery help if necessary.

Control Over Drug Abuse

The control over drug abuse can be made possible by adopting the following measures:

1. *Imparting education about drugs*: The target population for educational measures for prevention should be young college/university students particularly those living in hostels and away from the control of their parents, people living in slums, industrial workers, truck drivers and rickshaw pullers. The method of imparting education should be such that people involve themselves actively and there is a free exchange of valuable information. The type of education which would be more effective would be one whereby they are able to discard a good deal of inaccurate and misleading knowledge about artificial euphoria and acquire information which is more authoritative pertaining to physical and psychological effects of the so-called mood modifying drugs, their pharmacological properties and their medical uses. Parents have to play an important role in imparting education.
2. *Changing physicians' attitudes*: A change in the attitude of doctors in prescribing too many drugs can go a long way in controlling the abuse of drugs. The doctors have to show a greater care in not ignoring the side effects of the drugs. Though drugs help many, yet there are dangers of

over-dependency. Once a patient gets a prescription from a doctor that cures his ailment, he ceases to consult the doctor and continues to use the drugs indiscriminately or excessively whenever he suffers from the same ailment. Thus, people come to depend more on medication than on physician which is a dangerous practice.

3. *Undertaking follow-up study of addicts* treated under detoxification programmes.
4. *Giving deterrent punishment to policemen* and other law enforcers found working in collusion with drug peddlers.
5. *Parents need to play a crucial role in controlling drug usage among their children:* Since parental neglect, over-hostility, rejection and marital disharmony play an important role in perpetuating drug addiction, parents have to take more care in keeping the family environment congenial and harmonious. Since addiction does not develop overnight and it involves a process of evolution of losing interest in studies, activities and hobbies, indulging in irresponsible behaviour, irritability, impulsive conduct, and having a dazed expression, parents can locate the early signs by being alert and can make sure that the child withdraws from the habit. In preventing drug abuse, the role of parents could be: (a) communicate openly with the children, listen to their problems patiently, and teach them how to handle the problems, (b) take interest in children's activities and their circle of friends, (c) set an example for children by not taking drugs or alcohol, (d) keep track of prescribed drugs in home, and (e) learn as much as possible about drugs.
6. *The teachers too can help a lot in the prevention of drug abuse in the following manner*: (a) they can discuss dangers of drug abuse with the students by talking informally and openly; (b) they can keep themselves interested in their students' interests and activities; (c) they can encourage them to volunteer information of any incident of drug abuse; (d) they can talk about the problems of adolescence and guide students how to solve them; (e) they can help them in selecting career options and setting goals; and (f) they can encourage them to discuss their (students') crises (of family, peer group, money, etc.) with them and help them to the best of their abilities in facing these crises.

Prevention of Drug Abuse and Addiction

As with most other chronic diseases, such as diabetes, asthma, or heart disease, treatment for drug addiction generally is not a cure. However, addiction is treatable and can be successfully managed. People who are recovering from an addiction will be at risk for relapse for years and possibly for their whole lives. Research shows that combining addiction treatment medicines with behavioural therapy ensures the best chance of success for most patients. Treatment approaches tailored to each patient's drug use patterns and any co-occurring medical, mental and social problems can lead to continued recovery. India has over 500 deaddiction centres nursing addicts back to health, but stakeholders say that efforts to cut supply of drugs have been insufficient.

To conclude, it may be said that drug abuse has become a growing threat to humanity. Drugs pose complex problems for law enforcement agencies, while drug traffickers and mafias play havoc with the social structure of our country by wielding enormous power with ill-gotten wealth and influence. Drug users who take drugs to seek instant remedies to their depression, frustration and anger suffer physically, economically, emotionally as well as socially. Since 1991, 26 June is observed every year as an International Day against Drug Abuse and Illicit Trafficking to create awareness among drug abusers as well as those who are engaged in waging war against drugs. Our main task in policy and action is not only to control supplies of drugs but also to reduce demand for drugs. Prevention, treatment and rehabilitation all require a positive and life-affirming campaign. Persuasion, motivation, coercion, compulsion and punishment are the measures all of which have to be used so that drug abusers can be made to resist the temptation for drugs and live a wholesome drug-free life. Families and voluntary organizations also can play an important role in bringing back the recovered addicts into the mainstream of social life.

The United Nations adopted a Global Programme of Action to be implemented at the national, regional and global levels. Besides focussing on enhanced communication, more effective exchange of information and renewed commitment on the part of governments, it has suggested four specific measures to be adopted: First, prevention should become an integral element of drug control efforts worldwide. Second, multidimensional drug control programme involving all sections of government and society should be formed. Third, the international drug control treaties should be ratified and implemented as the basis of a global framework for co-operation. These treaties can provide a legal foundation for effective drug control co-operation. Lastly, regional partnerships involving neighbouring governments should be used as effective mechanisms for containing the illicit drug problem. Drug abuse, thus, can be contained only through cooperative and dedicated efforts.

References

Ahuja, Ram, *Sociology of Youth Subculture*, Rawat Publications, Jaipur, 1982.

Akers, Ronald L., *Deviant Behaviour: A Social Learning Approach*, Wadsworth, Belmont, CA, 1973.

Becker, Howard S., *The Outsiders*, Free Press, New York, 1963.

Blachly, Paul H., *Drug Abuse*, Charles C. Thomas, Illinois, 1970.

Carey, Jarnes L., *The College Drug Scene*, Prentice Hall, Englewood Cliffs, New Jersey, 1968.

Chein, Isodore, 'Psychological Functions of Drug Use', in H. Steinberg (ed.), *Scientific Basis of Drug Dependence: A Symposium*, Churchill Livingstone, London, 1969.

Hirschi, Travis, *Causes of Delinquency*, University of California Press, Berkeley, 1969.

Jullian, Joseph, *Social Problems*, Prentice Hall, Englewood Cliffs, New Jersey, 1977.

Lindesmith, Alfred, 'The Drug Addict as a Psychopath', *American Sociological Review*, Vol. 5, December, 1940.

McClelland, David, *The Drinking Man*, Free Press, New York, 1977.

Merton, Robert K. and Nisbet, Robert A., *Contemporary Social Problems* (3rd edn), Harcourt Brace Jovanovich, New York, 1979.

Nowlis, Helen H., *Drugs on the College Campus*, Anchor Books, New York, 1969.

Peele, Stanton and Brodsky, Archie, *Love and Addiction*, Taplinger, New York, 1975.

Stark, Rodney, 'Alcoholism and Drug Addiction', in Rodney Stark (ed.), *Social Problems*, Random House, Toronto, 1975.

Young, Lock, *The Drugtakers: The Social Meaning of Drug Use*, MacGibbon & Kee, London, 1971.

19

AIDS

AIDS (Acquired Immuno-Deficiency Syndrome) is a disease which is caused by a virus called Human Immunodeficiency Virus or HIV. This virus is fatal and dangerous because it destroys the immune system (the capacity of the body to fight diseases) in the human body and remains in the body for years together without any visible symptoms. This virus is even smaller than bacteria and is not observable even with the microscope. It can be transmitted to other persons in a number of ways. AIDS is the last stage of infection due to the virus. It takes about eight to ten years between getting infected with HIV and developing AIDS. No vaccine has been invented till today as a cure for AIDS or for protecting people from the HIV, though some scientists claimed in October 1995 that it was likely to be invented in the foreseeable future. And, three decades into the quest to develop a vaccine against the HIV, the success is yet to be achieved.

In the United States and some other countries like France, Belgium, Uganda, Zambia, Tanzania, Zimbabwe, etc. the AIDS emerged in the 1980s, though the first case was detected in America in 1959. In India, the first case of HIV infection was reported in May 1986 in Madras (now Chennai). The National Institute of Virology, Pune, and the Christian Medical College, Vellore, started 'screening operations' in 1987 on the recommendations of AIDS Task Force of Indian Council of Medical Research, New Delhi. It screened 3,027 persons of high risk groups and detected a good number of cases as being seropositive (Thomas, 1994: 12).

HIV Facts and Figures

India has about 21.40 lakh people who are living with HIV/AIDS as compared to 21.17 in 2015. Children (less than 15 years) account for 6.54 per cent, while two fifths (40.5%) of total HIV infections are among females. Over 87,000 get new HIV infections in India annually, according to the National AIDS Control Organization's latest estimates released in 2018. Due to its large population size, India has the third largest HIV epidemic in the world. India has witnessed a major reduction in its AIDS burden with new HIV cases dropping by 26.6 per cent and AIDS-related deaths declining 56.8 per cent between 2010 and 2017 backed by a sustained effort.

As per the released, India HIV estimation 2015 report, national adult (15–49 years) HIV prevalence in India is estimated at 0.26 per cent (0.22%–0.32%) in 2015. In 2015, adult HIV prevalence is estimated at 0.30 per cent among males and at 0.22 per cent among females.

Just eight states accounted for two-thirds of the 87,500 annual new HIV infections in India, Telangana led with 11 per cent of the new infections, Bihar and West Bengal accounted for 10 per cent each, followed by Uttar Pradesh (8%), Andhra Pradesh and Maharashtra (7% each), Karnataka (6%) and Gujarat (5%). On account of the heterogeneity of infection between states, different prevention methods and care services have to be adopted.

HIV/AIDS in India

HIV is an infectious disease but is not easily transmitted through the environment such as air, water, food, etc. Therefore, it is a non-communicable disease. If untreated, AIDS is a progressive life-threatening disease. Treatment significantly prolongs life expectancy. There is no cure for HIV/AIDS, but there are medications that can dramatically slow the progression of the disease. The main causes or the modes through which the virus enters the body are:

1. The virus transmission is facilitated when either partner has another sexually transmitted disease (STDs).
2. Through the transfusion of HIV infected blood or the blood products or by sharing contaminated needles, syringes and other such instruments. These include needles and syringes shared by intravenous drug users and those that are induced for injections without proper cleaning and sterilization.
3. HIV is a sexually transmitted infection (STI). It can also be spread by contact with infected blood or from mother to child during pregnancy, childbirth or breastfeeding.

The enormity of the problem and the concern generated by it globally was, for the first time, realized in the last week of January 1988 when a historic and unprecedented meeting took place in London. It was the World Summit of Ministers of Health from 148 countries along with health experts when a single disease syndrome was discussed at that level. The historic London Declaration, emerging from the meeting stated: 'In the absence at present of a vaccine or cure for AIDS, the single most important component of National AIDS Programme is *information* and *education*' (Parvi, 1992: 89).

The government established the National Aids Control Organization (NACO) and the National Aids Control Programme (NACP) to oversee policies related to HIV and AIDS prevention in 1992. In addition, State Aids Control Societies (SACS) were set up to support blood safety.

NACP's second phase emerged in 1999. This second phase promoted behaviour change to hinder the spread of HIV such as a programme for preventing transmission from mothers to children and providing antiretroviral treatment generally Phase-III (2007–2010).

In 2007, NACP (the third phase) delegated local levels and NGOs (non-governmental organization) more responsibilities and jurisdiction over welfare services for those affected. There was also an increased focus on high-risk groups and control outreach programmes. This phase has, therefore, placed the highest priority on preventive efforts by integrating prevention with care, support and treatment through a four-pronged strategy.

In India, as elsewhere, AIDS is often seen as 'someone else's problem' – as something that affects people living on the margins of society, whose lifestyles are considered immoral. People living with HIV have faced violent attacks; been rejected by families, spouses, and communities; been refused medical treatment; and even, in some reported cases, denied the last rites before they die. The challenges India faces to overcome this epidemic are enormous. Yet India possesses all the resources needed to achieve universal access to HIV prevention and treatment.

In 2009, an estimated 2.4 million people (aged 15–49) were living with HIV, slightly lower than the 2.5 million reported in 2001. However, India remains just behind South Africa and Nigeria in number of persons living with HIV (UNAIDS, 2010). According to National Aids Control Organization (NACO) report for 2009–10, women accounted for 38 per cent of people living with HIV while children accounted for 4.4 per cent.

With a concentrated HIV epidemic, India's HIV prevalence continues to be high among key affected populations (6–8 times that of the general population). High HIV prevalence among female sex workers is observed in the south and rising trend is evident in the north-east. Higher HIV prevalence among injecting drug users (IDUs) is also found in north-eastern states. However, it is localized in nature, and both rising and declining trends are observed in different north-eastern states, thus, indicating the dual nature of the epidemic. In 2006, new sites of high HIV prevalence among IDUs were identified in the states of Punjab, Tamil Nadu, West Bengal, Kerala and Maharashtra. HIV prevalence among MSM is highest in the states of Karnataka, Andhra Pradesh, Manipur, Maharashtra, Delhi, Gujarat, Goa, Odisha, Tamil Nadu and West Bengal. Nationally, HIV prevalence is notably higher among IDUs and men who have sex with men than among female sex workers and other population groups. Still, sex work continues to act as the most important source of HIV infections due to the large number of clients becoming infected by sex workers.

Vulnerability and risk factors that could contribute to spread of the epidemic in India include gender discrimination, stigma and discrimination, and inadequate human resource and technical support that lead to slow progress in the scale-up of prevention, care and support programmes. Furthermore, there is a need to strengthen capacity and systems to effectively implement certain HIV programmes such as a strategic information management system, cohort tracking of anti-retroviral treatment (ART), and ensuring quality data on children affected or infected by HIV as well as operational and functional governance structures.

In 2017, 79 per cent of people living with HIV were aware of their status, of whom 56 per cent were on anti-retroviral treatment (ART). HIV can be suppressed by combination ART consisting of three or more anti-retro (ARV) drugs. ART does not cure HIV infection but suppresses viral replication within a person's body and allows an individual's immune system to strengthen and regain the capacity to fight off infections. India's 'test and treatment' policy provides free anti-retroviral treatment (ART) used to treat HIV and AIDS, free to everyone who test positive. The scale-up of the ART programme has led to a 71 per cent decline in AIDS-related deaths in India. India's 'test and treatment' policy provides free anti-retroviral treatment (ART) used to treat HIV and AIDS free to everyone who test positive. The scale-up of the ART programme has led to a 71 per cent decline in AIDS-related deaths in India.

Risk Factors in Spread of HIV

Several factors put India in danger of experiencing the rapid spread of HIV if effective prevention and control measures are not scaled up throughout the country. These risk factors include:

1. *Migration and mobility*: Migration for work takes people away from the social environment of their families and community. This can lead to an increased likelihood to engage in risky behaviour. Concerted efforts are needed to address the vulnerabilities of the large migrant population.
2. *Low Status of Women*: Infection rates have been on the increase among women. Power relations and the low status of women, as expressed by limited access to human, financially unequal, and economic assets, weakens the ability of women to protect themselves and negotiate safer sex both within and outside of marriage, thereby increasing their vulnerability.
3. *Widespread stigma*: HIV/AIDS comes with huge stigma and discrimination. Stigma towards people living with HIV is recognized as a major barrier to HIV prevention. The most affected groups, often marginalized, have little or no access to the legal protection of their basic human rights. Addressing the issue of human rights violations and creating an enabling environment that increases knowledge and encourages behaviour change is thus, extremely important in the fight against AIDS.
4. *The development of 'opportunistic' infections:* AIDS can also contribute to the development of some forms of cancer. The presence of the virus can also lead to other problems such as lesions to the nervous or digestive systems, or to the muscles or kidneys.

5. *Targeted interventions for most at-risk populations:* Although, India is increasing the coverage of targeted interventions for the most at-risk populations, it will be critical to sustain these efforts and expand more rapidly in those areas and among those population groups, which are lagging behind and hard to reach.

High Risk Groups and Means of Transmitting the Virus

HIV infection is not contagious in the same sense as measles, chickenpox, tuberculosis, cholera, plague or small-pox. It mainly spreads through a sexual route and blood to blood contact. It may be said that HIV spreads mainly through four sources: (a) sex with an infected partner – heterosexual as well as homosexual, (b) transfusion of blood and blood products infected with HIV, (c) injecting drugs with infected syringes or needles, and (d) infected mother to her unborn child, there being 30–50 per cent chance of transmission with each delivery. As stated previously in India, HIV had been transmitted mainly via sexual intercourse (87%), followed by unsafe blood transfusion, infected needles/syringes, etc. It is thus a myth to believe that HIV infection spreads through mosquitoes, holding/embracing/kissing each other, shaking hands, coughing, sneezing or spitting, sharing of public toilets, swimming pools, sharing meals or eating from the same plates and cutlery, through clothes and bed sheets, by attending the same school or workplace, etc. There are no reports of doctors, nurses and other health care workers becoming infected with HIV or developing AIDS from direct contact with a patient.

According to UNICEF, India has a low HIV prevalence of only 0.34 per cent. Yet, in terms of individuals infected, it is home to the third largest number of people living in the world. The vast majority (85.6%) of HIV infections in India occur through sexual transmission, whereas nearly 5 per cent is attributable to parent-to-child transmission. The epidemic disproportionately affects women, accounting for 40 per cent of the total infections in the country. And, the epidemic is more pronounced in urban areas than rural ones and decreases with education levels.

We will now analyse the main sources of transmission of virus, i.e. prostitutes, homosexuals, intravenous drug addicts, blood donors, pathological laboratories, and mothers with HIV infection giving birth to children.

Prostitutes (female sex workers) sell sex. There are believed to be about 20 lakh prostitutes distributed over 817 red-light areas in different parts in India. This does not include the number of call girls (*Social Welfare*, Delhi, June 1990). A large number of these prostitutes and call girls are infected with HIV who pass on the infection to their customers. There is also a view that prostitutes are at a lower risk of infecting their clients and at a higher risk of getting infected by them. Therefore, along with targeting the preventive programmes to prostitutes they should also cover their clients.

Drug addicts, who take drugs by injection, carry the possibility of spreading the HIV infection through infected needles. The use of drugs is spreading rapidly among students, industrial workers, truck and auto-rickshaw drivers, and cycle-rickshaw pullers and people living in slum areas. A good number of drug users gradually become so addicted to drugs that they start taking them by self-injection. Sometimes the same syringes are used by many drug-addicts increasing the possibility of spreading the HIV infection. In Manipur, where 40 to 50 per cent of intravenous drug users are HIV positive, many have been sent to jail, in some cases even by their own parents. Among them are children of senior government officials as well as of those in business, politics and academics (*Seminar*, August, 1992: 13).

Blood donors too transmit the HIV infection. According to Central Drugs Standard Control Organization, in November 2012, there were 2,545 licensed blood banks in our country, of which 981 were government banks and the remaining 1,564 were private banks. There are some professional blood donors, whose blood sometimes contains the HIV. When their blood is transfused to patients without proper testing, the HIV is transmitted. The pathological laboratories too similarly transmit the HIV when they supply blood without scientific testing.

HIV positive pregnant women transmit the virus to the new-born children. On one hand, about 65 per cent of the pregnant women remain anaemic and require blood transfusion and, on the other hand, the prostitutes give birth to about 50 lakh children every year. They are thus doubly vulnerable to transmitting the HIV.

Use of *blade* for shaving, particularly the one used by the barbers, is also a risk factor in spreading the HIV.

Origin of the Pandemic

Renee Sabatier (1988: 34–35) has pointed out three explanations of the origin of HIV virus: One, it originated from an old human disease unknown to science for a long time. Two, it has originated from species other than human-beings, like apes, monkeys who suffered from natural virus. Three, it accidentally originated in laboratories while conducting experiments. Of these three explanations, the first one is more acceptable to the scholars. It was a young American physician who specialized in clinical immunology who noticed way back in 1981 some extremely unusual features in a group of otherwise healthy young homosexual men. This syndrome, therefore, was initially called guy-related immunodeficiency or GRID (Parvi, 1992: 3). He noticed that their bodies were being invaded by germs which are always present in our environment but hardly ever attack normal human-beings. Ordinarily, these germs are seen in persons whose immune system is damaged due to the intake of some drugs or who have received radiation treatment for cancer. His search alerted the entire scientific community and a French virologist reported in 1983 the isolation of a new virus from patients who suffered from this newly described disease. The isolation of this virus causing the disease was further researched in the USA and other countries by virologists and biologists and the virus was given a new name of Human Immunodeficiency Virus (HIV). These virus particles have a tendency of moving from one to another human body. After invading the body, they enter their target cells and remain there completely disguised and safe for years together until they convert the infection into an active *disease*. The irony is that it is very difficult to detect asymptomatic HIV infected persons because they feel and look normal and rarely visit doctors. Without blood test, there is no way to detect such an infection.

Stages in the Development of the Disease

AIDS is a disease which is caused in a slow and gradual process. Theoretically, four stages have been identified in the development of HIV infection (Malaviya, 1992: 16–20):

1. *Initial HIV infection*: In this stage, with the entering of HIV virus in the body, some people come to experience temporary serocon version disease within few weeks which resembles influenza or flu with symptoms like fever, bodyache and headache. The immune system in the body produces antibodies (one kind of substance) which does not destroy the HIV virus. After this, no characteristic develops for months and years together; but during this period a person can spread the HIV infection to others through sex, shared needles, blood transfusion, etc.
2. *Persistently enlarged glands*: In the next stage of HIV infection, a person develops enlarged but painless glands in the neck and armpits which are free of any symptoms. They continue to persist for months and years without producing any apparent ill-health. The early symptoms of AIDS are fatigue, weight-loss, chronic diarrhoea, prolonged fever, cough, night sweats and lymph gland enlargement. These characteristics are considered as first symptoms of AIDS in the developed countries but in the developing countries, since these symptoms cannot be differentiated from the ordinary infections, people do not think of going for early treatment.
3. *AIDS-related complex*: In this stage, the virus damages the immune system which produces symptoms like attacks of diarrhoea, sweating, loss of weight and extreme weakness.
4. *Full-blown AIDS*: This stage is reached after an average of nine to ten years from the time of containing the HIV infection. The immune system is totally destroyed and many infections and cancers are produced. The patient becomes very weak and always feels tired. This stage is easily recognized by doctors. A man does not survive for more than three to four years after this stage.

Malaviya (1992: 18) is of the opinion that the progress of HIV infection towards clinical illness varies from case to case. On an average, about 20 per cent of infected persons become symptomatic at the end of five years, 50 per cent at the end of ten years, and about 80 per cent will be sick at the end of twenty years.

How does one know whether one has contracted HIV infection? There are certain tests for detecting the presence of this infection. When a person comes to suffer from some disease, he develops what is called 'pathogens'. These pathogens are identified so that the immune system in human body can destroy them through the internal defences. The HIV virus affects the immune system and produces 'anti-bodies'. The presence of these anti-bodies in the body (called HIV anti-bodies) suggests infection, which can be identified through blood samples.

Two most common tests are: one called 'ELISA' and other called 'Western Blot' test. First test is simple and gives result within a few hours. Second test is extremely difficult, expensive and time-consuming. It is done to confirm the first test and is 50 times more expensive than the first one. These days, by carrying out the ELISA test by certain kits, the results obtained are taken as a definite affirmation of HIV infection.

Implications

It is difficult to visualize the devastating effects of the pandemic in our lifetime and beyond. What initially appeared to be an illness confined to few homosexuals has in one decade affected millions of men, women and children worldwide. AIDS is not just a health problem; rather, it is a societal problem with important social, cultural and economic dimensions. It threatens the basic social institutions at the individual, family and community levels. Its economic consequences are equally serious as it could claim up to half of national expenditure for health if the needs of AIDS patients were to be fully met. AIDS selectively, yet definitively, attacks people in their economic and socially most productive years and those responsible for the support and care of others. Consequently, when the earners are dead, they leave behind families without any source of livelihood. Thus, not only the HIV infected people initially face emotional trauma and later on social isolation and in the last one or two years suffer from serious body problems, but economically too they are shattered. The victims are sacked from their jobs, disowned by their families and communities, rejected by their friends, refused treatment by doctors, turned down by schools, colleges and universities, and even imprisoned and humiliated. Their families too suffer economically, psychologically and socially. After the bereavement of the young and married victims, their wives suffer from the problems of widowhood and their children from the problems of orphanhood.

It is also argued that the rapid spread of HIV/AIDS is linked with globalization, which makes it easier for people to travel and may promote some risk behaviours. It also creates much higher costs of health care for governments.

Caring for the Infected

The facilities presently available for the care of AIDS patients are woefully inadequate. Soon after reporting of the first HIV/AIDS case in the country, the government recognized the seriousness of the problem and took a series of important measures to tackle the epidemic. A high-powered National AIDS Committee was constituted in 1986 and a National AIDS Control Programme was launched a year later. In the initial years the programme focussed on generation of public awareness through mass communication programmes, introduction of blood screening for transfusion purposes and conducting surveillance activities in the epicentres of the epidemic. In 1992 the government formulated a multi-sectoral strategy for the prevention and control of AIDS in India. It is implemented through the National AIDS Control Organization (NACO) at the national level and State AIDS Cells at the state/UT levels.

As a result of these measures, awareness levels which were almost insignificant at the beginning of the epidemic have substantially increased in urban areas even though the level of awareness in rural areas continues to remain low. Some very successful intervention programmes among the high-risk groups, like commercial sex workers, men having sex with men and injecting drug users, were carried out through the dedicated involvement of NGOs. Emphasis has also been laid on control of STDs by strengthening STDs clinics at the district level by early diagnosis and proper management of STDs.

Several important actions have also been taken to ensure blood safety by modernization and strengthening of blood banks, introduction of licensing system for blood banks and gradual phasing out of professional blood donors. Introduction of component separation facilities has also helped in proper clinical use of blood for transfusion. This has resulted in reduction of the percentage of infections occurring through blood transfusion.

There is a lack of trained HIV physicians in India. Few hospitals and physicians provide health care for people living with HIV/AIDS, partly because of reluctance among healthcare personnel to deliver treatment to this population. Reasons for this reluctance include personal values and prejudices, an inaccurate perception of occupational risks entailed in health care, and the belief that HIV negative patients will refuse to share health care facilities with people living with HIV.

Counselling centres also need to be established where the therapist counsellors may interact with the patients (HIV carriers as well as AIDS patients), provide them psycho-social support and give them knowledge about dosage of medicines, special diets, etc. and about the prevention of transmission. Jacob John (*Seminar*, August 1992: 43) is of the opinion that counselling needs can be grouped into four broad areas: (a) pre-test counselling for assessing the need for an HIV test and suggesting preventive strategies against HIV infection to the individual; (b) post-test counselling to those whose results have been negative, reemphasizing change in behaviour; (c) counselling to those who are known to be HIV positive to help them to encounter emotional shock and depression and suggest strategies for care and treatment and prevention of infecting others; and (d) counselling the full-blown patients who are in the last stage of the disease. Caring of these patients with compassion could help them to die with dignity. Supporting the family of the patient would be equally essential as the members would be under considerable stress with their resources having already stretched to the limit.

In performing his roles in various stages, the counsellor has to remain in close contact with medical, social and other agencies. This calls for effective training and skill. Naturally, a large number of counsellors cannot be recruited and trained within the available resources. Therefore, persons fit to be trained for these roles could be amongst doctors, nurses, psychologists, social workers and para-medical staff. It should also be remembered that training in counselling requires an ongoing practical, supervised input with a high trainer-trainee ratio.

Link Between Sexually Transmitted Diseases and AIDS

Sexually transmitted diseases (STDs) make it easier for HIV to pass from one person to another. Chancroid, chlamydia, gonorrhea, syphilis and trichomoniasis increase the risk of HIV transmission by two to nine times. Nine out of eleven studies of syphilis and HIV infection found an association between the two. Syphilis increased with the risk of HIV infection three-fold to eight-fold for heterosexual men. Herpes doubled the risk of HIV infection for women and heterosexual men. Six studies found that chlamydia, gonorrhea and trichomoniasis increase the risk of HIV transmission to women by three to five times (*Population Reports*, Series L, No. 9, June 1993: 6).

STDs are more often treated and cured. It is, therefore, essential that cases with STD symptoms are diagnosed in their early stages and controlled with better drug supply through primary care clinics. Thus, following measures in this connection can improve care for patients with STDs: (a) conduct surveys to identify the level of untreated infection, (b) make clinics hospitable, (c) diagnose and treat patients in one visit, (d) offer sympathetic and helpful counselling, (v) conduct educational campaigns about STDs, and (e) provide services for high-risk population. Measures like these will prevent the spread of HIV infection and AIDS in large number of cases.

Role of Voluntary Organizations

The task being gigantic and the work that needs to be done for the patients infected with HIV or suffering from AIDS for many years being unprecedented in terms of scale and efforts, government alone cannot be expected to take up the total control programme. Voluntary organizations too, have to be involved in 'behaviour change' programme. The World Health Organization (WHO) has also emphasized its need. But, it appears that, at present the voluntary organizations are unwilling and consider themselves unable to respond to this need of associating themselves with efforts to contain AIDS. Knowing that the origin of HIV infection is related to inadequate health care, subordination of women, illiteracy, poverty and such other traditional problems, the voluntary organizations can surely address themselves to these social realities. Focussing on the social factors influencing the vulnerability of people to HIV infection, the voluntary organizations can provide information, services and other social support systems to people in danger of catching the disease. Before catching the infection, knowledge about the spread of HIV infection can be imparted by community-based social workers. It is well recognized that women are much more vulnerable to HIV infection than men. The reasons for this are not medical but are rooted in a social environment that actually promotes this vulnerability. The capacity to motivate and sustain the involvement of the vulnerable people will determine the success of the voluntary organizations. After being infected with virus, the need for psychological and social support is as crucial as medical support and non-government organizations can easily provide these services. When lakhs of people suffer from a certain disease, total dependence on the medical system will be unwise and will surely result in a failure. There is a simultaneous need to prepare communities to be able to cope with caring for the diseased people and to find resources for this within the community itself. The voluntary organizations can surely make genuine effort towards this support system. Besides helping the patients, the voluntary organizations can also help the children, families and other dependents of the sufferers who become victims of isolation and discrimination.

Issues for Prevention and Control of HIV/AIDS

Institutional capacity: The national response still faces institutional constraints, both structural and managerial, to continue to scale up at the national and state levels. It is critical that these factors be addressed as the programme expands its response to the epidemic. State level performance varies significantly. There is a need for tailored capacity – building activities and increased attention to performance-based financing approaches.

Use of Data to Tailor the Response: There is a need for greater use of data for decision making, including the use of programme data and epidemiological data at district and state levels to tailor the response. India has successfully arrested the HIV epidemics and can end it by 2030.

There are several myths surrounding HIV and AIDS, so it can be sometimes difficult to differentiate between fact and fiction. It is important to look at this issue because of the magnitude of its implications when such an infection strikes. Fortunately, preventive measures and the development of medication have contributed to limiting its consequences, there is still a lot to be done to raise public awareness on the issues surrounding the disease, at a national level.

According to the National Strategic Plan (NSP), by 2020, the focus of the national programme will be on achieving the following fast-track targets:

1. 75 per cent reduction in new HIV infections.
2. 90-90-90: 90 per cent of those who are HIV positive in the country know their status, 90 per cent of those who know their status are on treatment and 90 per cent of those who are on treatment experience effective viral load suppression.
3. Elimination of mother-to-child transmission of HIV and Syphilis.
4. Elimination of stigma and discrimination.

By 2024, it hopes to achieve:

1. 80 per cent reduction in new HIV infections.
2. Ensuring that 95 per cent of those who are HIV positive in the country know their status, 95 per cent of those who know their status are on treatment and 95 per cent of those who are on treatment experience effective viral load suppression.

Protective Programmes

Initially when the first case of AIDS was detected in the United States, it was said that this pandemic is 'western' and it cannot appear in India. Few years later, when the first AIDS case appeared in Madras (now Chennai) in 1986, many states believed that it would not reach them. In 1996, when officially it was stated that there are more than 1,000 AIDS cases and about 22,000 HIV carriers, and unofficially it was estimated that there were lakhs of HIV carriers in the country and when there is a projection that by the end of this century, the largest population of HIV carriers in the world (about one-fourth of the world HIV population) will be in India, our governments – central and state – are yet to enunciate clear-cut strategies to combat the spread of the virus. It is not likely that we will have a vaccine or a cure for AIDS in the near future, though serious efforts are constantly being made in this direction, its spread, therefore, can only be controlled through preventive education for behavioural change.

Some measures have been suggested for protecting and preventing the AIDS and HIV infection. These are: *One*, since sex with infected person is the highest risk factor in AIDS, the greatest need is to educate people TV, radio, newspapers and other mass media. The required awareness can be produced through course content in the educational institutions too. AIDS Advisory Centres may also be established for imparting the required knowledge to the people. Seminars, symposia, and workshops too can be organized from time to time for imparting the required knowledge. *Two*, some training is necessary for doctors and nurses so that they can impart some knowledge to the patients regarding the symptoms of HIV infection and AIDS. *Three*, persons suffering from STDs are also a significant risk factor in HIV transmission. Though data are limited, there appears to be a high incidence of

STDs among tribal poor, rural poor and urban slum-dwellers in India, and these conditions do provide a fertile ground for the spread of the virus. Unlike AIDS, STDs can be treated. Hence, programmes for the prevention and control of STDs should be given high priority. *Four,* blood or blood products must be tested for HIV before transfusion. *Five,* the HIV tests should be made free and confidential for persons who indulge in the high-risk activities and who may themselves want to know whether they are HIV infected or not and for persons who receive a transfusion of blood not properly screened for HIV infection. However, testing for diagnosis raises several ethical problems. Should individuals at risk for HIV be encouraged to take the test? How forceful should such encouragement be? How should those who are tested be counselled? Can and should the test results be kept confidential? Suppose a pregnant woman comes for a test and is found infected with HIV. Should she be compelled to go for abortion or can she be permitted to continue her pregnancy because the studies have demonstrated that there is the risk of only 25 to 50 per cent of transmission of HIV from mother to the child. These issues raise nagging dilemmas that cannot be easily resolved. There is an urgent need for framing of policies on all these issues after careful thinking. *Six,* doctors should ensure that injecting equipment is sterilized. As far as possible, the use of disposable syringes should be encouraged. *Seven,* condoms should be freely distributed or supplied at cheap rates in red-light areas to prostitutes. *Eight,* drug users should be persuaded to stay away from intravenous drug use. *Lastly,* voluntary organizations should help spread knowledge on AIDS to different vulnerable groups through innovative and community-based approaches.

Doctors and health care centres in our country are prejudiced about HIV/AIDS with the result that patients are denied admission in hospitals and neglected in treatment by not regularly visiting them in the isolated wards. This has resulted in panic reactions. Such reactions are counter-productive. Such effective strategies have to be designed and developed which can help the HIV/AIDS victims to overcome fear and hysteria. Counselling families, individuals in neighbourhood, and members of social-support networks is also an important need because eventually they have to bear a major responsibility for the sick and the survivors.

HIV infection are transmitted mainly through behaviour which is private, secret and often hidden. As such, the infection or even the suspicion of infection leads to stigma and discrimination. Discriminatory practices have targeted persons that are subsumed under 'high risk' groups, like prostitutes, drug users and homosexuals. These persons are categorized according to the presumed risk that they are identified with. Such categorization not only challenges the rights of the individuals but the categorized persons are also victimized under the guise of preventing AIDS. This undermines efforts to reach these persons and seek their active cooperation in the fight against AIDS.

Finding funds to fight AIDS is a serious problem in our country because the potential costs are staggering. On one hand, diverting funds from other problems to AIDS control may distort health priorities, while on the other hand, if proper funds are not made available, the economic consequences may be more devastating. In 1990, India had received a loan of 85 million dollars from the World Bank for AIDS control but will these funds suffice? Along with finding more sources of funds, the political will has to be generated, joint action has to be mobilized and the sustainable strategies have to be located for creating necessary awareness. The efforts made so far in dealing with the HIV infection/AIDS pandemic cannot be described as totally inadequate. A beginning has been made, today is better than yesterday and tomorrow is what we look forward to. Certain issues can be dealt with legally by enacting laws (say, by making blood screening mandatory, keeping HIV patients' status confidential, prescribing anti-discriminatory provisions, making it obligatory for doctors not to deny services to HIV/AIDS patients, and so on) and certain issues can be faced socially by creating the required social environment and providing certain social services.

HIV Prevention Programmes in India

NACO is the body responsible for formulating policy and implementing programmes for the prevention and control of the HIV epidemic in India. NACP-IV (2012–2017, extended to 2020), aims to reduce annual new HIV infections by 50 per cent through the provision of comprehensive HIV treatment, education, care and support for the general population and build on targeted interventions for key affected groups and those at high risk of HIV transmission.

Future Challenges

It is noteworthy that newer pockets of high HIV prevalence among different risk groups in low-prevalence states have emerged over the past decade. The Indian HIV programme has evolved, expanded and implemented various new initiatives over the years. The national HIV programme has, so far, been a success story, however, challenges and gaps remain, including stigma and discrimination and access to testing services for people from certain sections of society. The other major challenge that the programme faces is funding. With declining funding from external donors, access to the domestic budget has progressively increased but has been slow. As a result, newer policies and strategies such as 'test and treat' might be difficult to implement. The Indian government needs to align its policies and strategies with the global target of ending AIDS by 2030. It will require acceleration of current efforts and scale-up of innovations in order to change the trajectory of the response.

Despite all the challenges inherent in HIV-vaccine development and delivery, a preventive vaccine for AIDS remains the best hope to end the global epidemic. Researchers, public health leaders, governments, private organizations and companies, and affected communities must work together closely to accelerate research and delivery of HIV vaccines.

Some measures have been suggested by protecting and preventing the aids and HIV infection. The greatest need is to educate people through TV, radio, newspaper and other mass media. It is also required to introduce awareness through course content in the educational institutions. The medical fraternity in our country is prejudiced about HIV/AIDS with the result that patients are denied admission in hospitals and neglected in treatment by not regularly visiting them in the isolation wards. This has resulted in panic reactions. Such rejections are counter-productive. Effective strategies have to be designed and developed which can help the patients in overcoming fear and hysteria. Counselling families, neighbourhoods and members of social-support networks is also an important need because eventually, they have to bear a major responsibility for the sick and the survivors. The trained medical staff can impart information about AIDS to the patients and to their relatives. Since persons suffering from STDs are also a significant risk factor it is important to give high priority to the programmes for the prevention. The HIV tests should be made free and confidential for persons who indulge in high-risk activities. The medical staff should ensure the use of disposable syringes and other operating equipment. The drug-users should be persuaded away from using intravenous drug abuse. The voluntary organizations should help spread knowledge on AIDS to different vulnerable groups through innovative and community-based approaches. Non-governmental organizations working through peer educators with women in prostitution in India have had remarkable success in raising awareness of the basic facts of HIV transmission and AIDS care. Thousands of cases of AIDS have been prevented by this work, some of which has been supported financially or in kind by the government.

By focussing on the overarching goal of controlling and ultimately ending the HIV and AIDS pandemic, a scientifically challenging research agenda is essential to develop the necessary interventions, together with a full-scale implementation of effective approaches. Despite all the challenges inherent in HIV-vaccine development and delivery, a preventive vaccine for AIDS remains the best hope to end the global epidemic. Researchers, public health leaders, governments, private organizations and companies, and affected communities must work together closely to accelerate research and delivery of HIV vaccines.

Conclusion

As per Claeson and Alexander, given the complexity and heterogeneity of HIV, India will need to be flexible to address the changing environment, including the growing economy and income inequities that influence rural-to-urban migration, knowledge, attitudes, and risk-taking practices and the interrelated changes in sexual mores. To conclude, the achievements of

India in the prevention and control of HIV/AIDS are truly noteworthy. India's local manufacture of generic antiretroviral drugs has significantly contributed to its success. According to the UNAIDS report, India purchased 80 per cent of the generic drugs and saved billion dollars in the past five years. It also provides generous support to other Asian countries. To continue such achievements, India needs to strategically focus on current and future challenges with an eye to sustainability.

In summary, a multifaceted approach incorporating biomedical, behavioural, and structural interventions is crucial if we are to have universal access to HIV prevention. Although some countries, including India, have made substantial progress on this front, it will be important not only to provide services but also to measure the effect of each of these services in reducing HIV among high-risk groups and in the general population. HIV prevention must remain a top priority if we hope to finally reduce the HIV pandemic. Expanding access to treatment is at the heart of a set of targets for 2020 which aim to bring the world on track to end the AIDS epidemic by 2030.

References

Annual Report 2015–16, National AIDS Control Organization (NACO), 2016.

Cantwell, Alan, *AIDS: The Mystery and the Solution*, Aries Rising Press, Los Angeles, 1991.

Cahill, Kevin M. (ed.), *The AIDS Epidemic*, St. Martin Press, New York, 1983.

Feldman, D.A. and Johnson, T.M. (eds), *The Social Dimensions of AIDS: Methods and Theory*, Praeger Publishers, New York, 1986.

Gong, Victor (ed.), *Understanding AIDS: A Comprehensive Guide*, Rutgers University Press, New Brunswick, 1985.

Gupta, Sudhir (ed.), *AIDS: Associated Syndromes*, Plenum Press, New York, 1986.

Malaviya, A.N., *Seminar*, Special Issue on AIDS, August, 1992, pp. 16–20.

Nag, Moni, *Sexual Behaviour and AIDS in India*, Vikas, Delhi, 1996.

Panos, Dossiers, *AIDS and the Third World*, Panos Institute, London, 1988.

Parvi, Khorshed M., *Challenge of AIDS*, National Book Trust, New Delhi, 1992.

Renee, Sabatier (ed.), *Blaming Others: Prejudice, Race and Worldwide AIDS*, Panos Institute, London, 1988.

Thomas, Gracious, *AIDS in India*, Rawat Publications, Jaipur, 1994.

UNAIDS, *Report on the Global AIDS Epidemic*, 2010.

Vita, D., Vincent, T., Hellman, S. and Rosenberg, S. (eds), *AIDS: Etiology, Diagnosis, Treatment and Prevention*, J.B. Lippincott, New York, 1985.

World Health Organization, *Guidelines for Counselling about HIV Infection and Disease*, WHO AIDS Series 8, WHO, Geneva, 1990.

20

Terrorism

Terrorism has pushed the world into a perilous new age of insecurity. In India, we have been facing this for more than four decades. Earlier, we have faced the problem of insurgency in North-East India while dealing with the Naga and the Mizo rebels and the terrorism of the Naxalites in Bengal. Today, terrorism is perceived as a problem capable of destabilizing not only national but international politics also. Terrorism in recent times has affected both the developed and the developing countries. What has made terrorism a significant instrument for achieving desired goals and ends by persons using the terrorist techniques are factors like conviction in the purity of the 'cause', fanatical loyalty, desire for self-sacrifice, a sense of absolutism, and financial and material support from abroad.

For the purpose of this chapter, insurgency has been taken to mean an armed violent movement, directed mainly against security forces and other government targets, to seek territorial control. Terrorism has been taken to mean an armed violent movement directed against government as well as non-government targets. It involves pre-meditated attacks with arms, ammunition and explosives against civilians, and resorting to intimidation tactics such as hostage-taking and hijacking, but not seeking territorial control.

The Concept

The words terrorism, insurgency, civil war, revolution, guerrilla war, intimidation and extremism are most often interchanged and used very loosely. What is common in all is 'violence'. Terrorism is an organized system of intimidation. It is broadly defined as 'violent behaviour designed to generate fear in the community, or a substantial segment of it, for political purposes'. Walter Laqueur uses a simple and broad definition, 'terrorism is the illegitimate use of force to achieve a political objective by targeting innocent people'. The common definition of terrorism is the systematic use or threatened use of violence to intimidate a population or government and thereby, affect political, religious, or ideological change. It is also defined as 'a method whereby an organized group or party seeks to achieve its avowed aims chiefly through the systematic use of violence' (*Encyclopaedia of Social Sciences*). All those activities which kill the humanity are called terrorism. Terrorism is the unlawful act done by a group of people. A group of people who take the support of terrorism is known as terrorists. They only use violent acts intending to create and enhance the level of terror in the society and country.

The UN General Assembly Resolution 49/60, adopted on 9 December 1994, contains a provision describing terrorism: 'Criminal acts intended or calculated to provoke a state of terror in the general public, a group of persons or particular persons for political purposes are in any circumstance unjustifiable, whatever the considerations of a political, philosophical, ideological, racial, ethnic, religious or any other nature that may be invoked to justify them'.

According to the UN Security Council Resolution 1566 (2004), the term 'terrorism' includes criminal acts, including against civilians, committed with the intent to cause death or serious bodily injury, or taking of hostages, with the purpose to provoke a state of terror in the general public or in a group of persons or particular persons, intimidate a population or compel a government or an international organization to do or to abstain from doing any act.

The United States has defined terrorism under the Federal Criminal Code. Title 18 of the United States Code defines terrorism and lists the crimes associated with terrorism. The Section 2331 of Chapter 113(B), defines terrorism as: '... activities that involve violent ... or life-threatening acts ... that are a violation of the criminal laws of the United States or of any state and ... appear to be intended (i) to intimidate or coerce a civilian population; (ii) to influence the policy of a government by intimidation or coercion; or (iii) to affect the conduct of a government by mass destruction, assassination, or kidnapping; and ... (C) occur primarily within the territorial jurisdiction of the United States ...'. According to the US Patriot Act of 2001 terrorist activities include:

1. threatening, conspiring or attempting to hijack airplanes, boats, buses or other vehicles;
2. threatening, conspiring or attempting to commit acts of violence on any 'protected' persons, such as government officials; and
3. any crime committed with 'the use of any weapon or dangerous device,' when the intent of the crime is determined to be the endangerment of public safety or substantial property damage rather than for 'mere personal monetary gain'.

The European Union defines terrorism for legal/official purposes in Article 1 of the Framework Decision on Combating Terrorism (2002). This provides that terrorist offences are certain criminal offences set out in a list comprised largely of serious offences against persons and property which given their nature or context, may seriously damage a country or an international organization where committed with the aim of: seriously intimidating a population; or unduly compelling a government or international organization to perform or abstain from performing any act; or seriously destabilizing or destroying the fundamental political, constitutional, economic or social structures of a country or an international organization.

Terrorist acts are directed against persons who, as individual agents or representatives of authority, interfere with the consummation of the objectives of such a group. A 'terrorist' is one who imposes the punishment meted out by his/her organization upon those who are held to interfere with the revolutionary programme. The terrorist does not merely threaten; death or destruction is part of his/her programme of action. If he/she is arrested, he/she does not try to prove his/her innocence but he/she spreads his doctrines.

Though the long-term objectives of terrorism, insurgency and revolution are similar, that is, overthrow of the existing regime or order, but the short-term objectives and strategies or methodology may be quite different.

One view is that the above definitions refer only to that terrorism which is practised by the 'opponents of the state'. There is another terrorism which is practised by the 'state apparatus'. The above definitions do not include the latter type of terrorism. The greatest practitioners of the art of terrorism, like Hitler, Stalin, Mao, Yahya Khan, Mussolini and Franco, cannot be termed as 'terrorists' with these definitions in mind. Terrorism practised by the state refers to violence based on extra-legal methods. It may, however, be clarified that all violence practised by the state is not terrorism. In fact, an organized state sometimes has to use violence for certain objectives. The democratic states generally use legal apparatus to achieve their objectives; it is only the totalitarian states which employ terror. But then all totalitarian states are not terrorists. Similarly, at times, the democratic states can also resort to using terror.

The common definition of terrorism does not include all types of violence used by the organized groups. That violence which is motivated by consideration of pure personal aggrandizement is excluded from terrorism. This excludes common organized crimes like dacoity and robbery. However, all murders and dacoities organized by ideological groups like the Naxalites fall within the purview of terrorism.

Terrorism has also been differentiated from intimidation and insurgency. In 'intimidation', the intimidator merely threatens injury to collect a ransom but in 'terrorism' and 'insurgency', the terrorists and the insurgents actually use violence. Terrorism is not a fight between individuals but a struggle between social groups and political forces. It has little to do with intimidating individuals as individuals. The terrorists punish those individuals whom their organization considers guilty of interfering with their programme aimed at the removal of the undesired social or governmental system. According to Wilkinson (1974), terrorism in politics is a weapon of blackmail, coercion, and imposition of minority will against and upon a majority decision.

Terrorism is different from 'mob violence' also. The latter is unplanned and uncontrolled, guided by some immediate motivation which may not even be rational and is not based on any precise programme. The former has a definite goal and is planned. It aims at demoralizing a governmental authority and undermining its power. However, at times, terrorism may also use mob violence as its method.

The difference between terrorism and insurgency is that an insurgent has the support of a large section of the local population while a terrorist need not have such support. Again, an insurgent is a national of a country which is in revolt against the constitutional government of his country and fights to overthrow the government by guerrilla warfare. The terrorist may or may not be a national of the country in which he operates (Saxena, 1985: 14–35).

The above definitions enable us to put forth six basic definitional components of terrorism. These are: (a) terror purpose (that is, creating fear in the minds of the primary target), (b) instrumental or immediate victims, (c) primary targets (population or broad groups and others), (d) an outcome of death to instrumental targets and damage to or destruction of property, (e) violence, and (f) political purpose.

Terrorism appears in many forms – from planting a crude, home-made bomb, hand-grenade or other explosive in a shopping centre, a railway station, a bus-stand or a bus, a train or an aeroplane to kidnapping and assassination of important personalities. The main aim of terrorists is to wreak havoc upon those whom they regard as obstacles or enemies or oppressors.

Characteristics

Terrorism is characterized by a technique of perpetrating random and brutal intimidation, coercion, or destruction of human lives and property, and used intentionally by subnational groups operating under varying degrees of stress, to obtain realistic or illusory goals. The main characteristics of terrorism are:

1. it is against the state or community,
2. it has a political purpose,
3. it is illegal and unlawful,
4. it aims at intimidating and creating impact of fear and panic not only for the victim but also for the people at large, caused for the purpose of coercing or subduing,
5. it is accompanied by a feeling of impotence and helplessness on the part of the masses,
6. it stops rational thinking,
7. it leads to reaction of fight or flight, and

8. it contains arbitrariness in violence as victims' selection is random or indiscriminate.

Objectives

The goals of terrorists may vary from movement to movement but the main objectives of terrorism are the same in all terrorist movements. These are: (a) cause the regime to react and also to overreact. Reaction is required to compel the government/community to concede the demand of the terrorists. Overreaction or indiscriminate reaction is required to demonstrate the repression by the regime so that the people are alienated and their sympathy is achieved. The security forces used by the government (because of overreaction) to protect the VIPs and the public installations will reduce the amount of security forces available to protect the general public, which will enhance their feeling of insecurity and helplessness and also increase the sense of terror amongst them; (b) mobilize mass support and urge potential sympathizers to greater militancy, or increase the involvement of more people. In a foreign territory, the objective of terrorist activity is to influence people rather than win friends. The chief objective in these places is a show of strength and to demonstrate the incapacity of the regime to protect people and maintain order; (c) eliminate opponents and informers and remove threat to the movement and also ensure obedience of the followers; and (d) give publicity or magnify their cause and strength.

According to Baljit Singh (cited in Alexander and Finger, 1977: 8), the overall objectives of terrorism are: (a) to gain popular support, (b) to disrupt and destroy the military and psychological strength of the regime, and (c) to break internal stability and check growth. If the premise is accepted that political terror primarily aims at the psyche rather than at military hardware, then the killing of selected important but unpopular public officials and politicians may boost the terrorists' morale, create sympathy among the people and provoke the regime to adopt repressive measures that further alienate the people.

Jay Mallin (1971: 9) has suggested five basic short-term objectives of political terrorism: (a) morale building within the ranks, (b) advertising the movement, (c) disorientation and psychological isolation of the people, (d) elimination of opposing forces, and (e) provocation of the government.

Origin and Development

Political terrorism as an instrument of power came of age during the French Revolution of 1793. Terror incorporated two facets in this Revolution: a state of anxiety within a group, and the tool that induced fear and violent acts aimed at influencing political behaviour of the state. After the French Revolution, political terrorism did not score any significant success until 1921, when the IRA in Ireland used it against the British. Following the World War II (i.e. after 1939), political terrorism re-emerged on the international scene. Besides India, it was used in Algeria, Cyprus and Kenya for political independence through activities including intimidation, sabotage, abduction and killing.

During the 1960s, political terrorism entered another phase. According to Baljit Singh (cited in Alexander and Finger, 1977: 7), the two most significant quantitative changes in terrorism during 1960s were: its trans-national character and its emergence as a self-sufficient strategy, that is, terrorists attempted to operate independently of the larger political arena. This was made possible through a revolution in communication and modern urban civilization. Between 1969 and 1975, more than forty countries were involved in terrorist activities.

Alexander and Finger (1977: xi) are of the opinion that the major reasons for terrorism lie in the very nature of modern civilization itself and are inherent in the modern industrial system. They have given following causes for the origin and development of terrorism:

1. The present complex technological society is extremely vulnerable to unsuspected and ruthless attacks of terrorism because transportation centres, communication facilities, factories and agricultural fields cannot always be protected against the random acts of dedicated and determined terrorists.
2. Highly sophisticated weapons like missiles, and remote controls are now relatively easy to obtain for various terror movements. In future, the terrorist groups will probably have access even to chemical and nuclear weapons and instruments of death and destruction.
3. With modern warfare capabilities, the 'powerless' terrorist groups have been transformed into subnational groups with formidable strengths, capable of creating states within states, thereby undermining the ability of legitimate governments to rule or to survive (the LTTE in Sri Lanka, the Khalistan Commandos and Kashmir militants in India and the PLO in Israel are some examples of such strong sub-national groups).
4. Communication and transportation opportunities have enabled an international network of terrorism to develop with a certain degree of centralized organizational structure. Collaboration among ideologically linked groups and among those with common political interest has developed relationships involving financing, training, supply of combat materials, organizational assistance and joint attacks. This pattern of 'comradeship' is inevitably expanding the areas of international violence.
5. Through revolution in communications, terrorists are able to target their violence not only against immediate victims but also direct it at a wide audience as well for psychological intimidation and blackmail. The media coverage also exports the terroristic techniques and inspiration to other terrorist groups.

In addition to above factors, the other factors which have substantially contributed to terrorism are: the weak nations' will to weaken the strong nations, which motivates them to support the subnational groups of strong nations in their terroristic activities; financial support of rich non-residents to terrorist groups on religious and cultural basis; feasibility of using smuggling and drug trafficking methods by the terrorists and, thus, getting money for purchasing modem weapons; confrontations between the East and the West as well as between the ideologies of the Leftists and the Rightists; the rise in religious, linguistic, ethnic and national consciousness of groups throughout the world; the feelings of deprivation and frustration among the minorities struggling for their liberation and a legitimate right to self-determination and, the growth of opposition by citizens to repressive regimes and dictators ruling their countries. The strategies and tactics employed by political terrorists are generally directed at three groups: the people, the regime in power and the terrorist organization itself.

Types of Terrorism

Different types of terrorism have been defined, according to the kind of 'attack agents' an attacker uses or by what they are trying to defend. The types of terrorism are as follows:

State terrorism: State terrorists can use force or the threat of force, without declaring war, to terrorize citizens and achieve a political goal. It has also been argued that states participate in international terrorism, often by proxy war.

Bioterrorism: Bioterrorism refers to the intentional release of toxic biological agents to harm and terrorize civilians, in the name of a political or other cause.

Cyberterrorism: Cyber terrorists use information technology to attack civilians and draw attention to their cause. Cyber terrorism refers to an attack on information technology itself in a way that would radically disrupt networked services.

Eco-terrorism: Environmental extremists sabotage property to inflict economic damage on industries or the natural environment.

Nuclear terrorism: This includes attacking nuclear facilities, purchasing nuclear weapons, or building nuclear weapons or otherwise finding ways to disperse radioactive materials.

Narco-terrorism: Narco-terrorism has been used to indicate situations in which terrorist groups use drug trafficking to fund their other operations.

Perspectives on Terrorism

Terrorism has been perceived by different scholars with different perspectives. We may identify four such perspectives: historical, political, sociological and legal (Figure 1).

The *historical* perspective focusses on the origin, development and qualitative changes in different phases in terrorism.

The *political* perspective perceives political terrorism as a political violence movement managed by an organized political group(s) either at national or at international level.

Figure 1
Perspectives on Terrorism

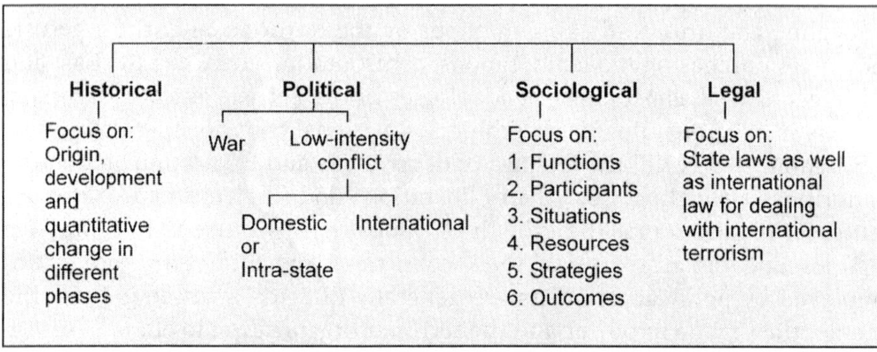

The *legal* perspective concentrates on state laws as well as international laws for cooperation among various states in dealing with international terrorism.

In the *sociological* perspective, Jordan Paust (Alexander and Finger, 1977: 19) focusses on: (a) the types of participants engaged in terrorism as terrorists, targets, victims, and so forth, (b) the objectives of the participants, (c) the situations of actual interaction, (d) the type of resources at the disposal of each type of participant, (e) the strategies of terror utilized (killing, kidnapping, bombing, looting and hijacking) and, (f) the outcome of the terroristic process (deaths, injuries, destruction of property, etc.).

Mass Support

What is the nature and extent of mass support to the ideology, goal and methodology of the terrorists? Many a time it happens that the masses accept a particular ideology but not the goal, or they accept the goal but not the strategies of the proponents of terrorism. Even when one agrees with the goal, he may not support the movement or may not go beyond a certain point. Thus, the quantity and quality of mass support varies from one terrorist movement to other terrorist movement. Verma (Tiwari, 1930: 233) has given some indicators of the characteristics of mass support. These are: supporting the ideology or cause, agreeing with methodology, providing money and material, nonviolent participation in rallies, supplying arms and ammunition, providing shelter or harbouring, vocal or written (in media, etc.) support, and active participation in movement (violent support). Verma has also arranged these indicators in ascending order and has given three types of civil strife: terrorism, insurgency and revolution. According to him, terrorism is characterized by very little mass support but the participants go all the way from ideology to extreme violence. Insurgency or guerrilla warfare is characterized by the small number of insurgents or guerrillas supported by a very large segment of population. This happens when the cause is removal of colonial rule or resisting a foreign ruler. Revolution is characterized by much larger number of participants and mass uprising.

Terrorism in India has attracted more youngsters, particularly the unemployed, the misguided and the idealistic youth. As long as there are causes which arouse intense emotions, the idealistic youth will be led to have romantic visions of terrorism for a cause. When a nation loses its purpose owing to a corrupt leadership with vested interests, frustrations and deprivations, this will lead the aggressive youth to extremist tendencies like Naxalism, or parochial issues in Punjab, or religious issues in Kashmir. Some examples of terrorist groups which have attracted the youth outside India are: the IRA in Ireland, Black Septemberists in Jordan, Baader Meinhof in Germany, LTTE in Sri Lanka and the Red Army in Japan.

Support Base

The success of terrorism depends to a large extent upon its support base which includes not only the political and social support but also support in terms of money, weapons and training. Terrorists obtain money from different sources like donations and taxes from people, through bank robberies, by smuggling and selling drugs, and collecting ransom for hostages and hijacked planes. Weapons are often looted from people or snatched from police stations or purchased from abroad.

Terrorism in India

India is among the 25 least peaceful nations to live in, according to the Global Peace Index, 2013. The country was placed 141 among 162 nations having lost more than two lives a day or a staggering 799 persons to internal conflicts in 2012 (*Times of India,* 12 June 2013).

Terrorism in India is essentially the creation of politics. The four types of terrorism India had/has to face are: Khalistan-oriented terrorism in Punjab, militants' terrorism in Kashmir, Naxalite terrorism in Bengal, Bihar/Jharkhand, Chhattisgarh and Andhra Pradesh, and the ULFA terrorism in Assam. Earlier we had faced this problem in Nagaland (1951), Mizoland (1966), Manipur (1976), Tripura (1980) and (of Gorkhaland) in Bengal (1986). The Sikh terrorism in Punjab was based on a dream of a 'theocratic state through secession'; the Nagaland and the Mizo terrorism was based on the 'identity crisis'; the Manipur and Tripura terrorism was based on 'the grievance situation', and the Naxalite terrorism in Bengal, Bihar/Jharkhand and Andhra Pradesh is based on 'class enemity'.

The regions with long term terrorist activities today are Jammu & Kashmir, Central India (Naxalism) and Seven Sister States (independence and autonomy movements). In the past, the Punjab insurgency led to militant activities in the Indian state of Punjab as well as the national capital Delhi (Delhi serial blasts, anti-Sikh riots). As of 2006, at least 232 of the country's 608 districts were afflicted, at differing intensities, by various insurgent and terrorist movements. Terrorism existing in India includes religious terrorism, narco-terrorism, ethno-nationalist and left-wing terrorism.

Ethno-nationalist Terrorism

This form of terror focusses either (a) on creating a separate state within India or independent of India or in a neighbouring country, or (b) on emphasizing the views/response of one ethnic group against another. Violent Tamil nationalist groups from India to address the condition of Tamils in Sri Lanka, as well as insurgent tribal groups in North-East India are examples of ethnic-nationalist terrorist activities.

Religious Terrorism

This form of terror focusses on religious imperatives, a presumed duty or in solidarity with a specific religious group, against one or more religious groups. Mumbai 26/11 terror attack in 2008 organized by an Islamic group in Pakistan is an example of religious terrorism in India. The maximum number of terrorist incidents and deaths of innocent civilians have occurred due to religious terrorism. While the intensity of the violence caused by terrorism of a non-religious nature can be rated as low or medium, that of religious terrorism has been high or very high. It has involved the indiscriminate use of sophisticated improvised explosive devices, suicide bombers, the killing of civilians belonging to the majority community with hand-held weapons and resorting to methods such as hijacking, hostage-taking, blowing up of aircraft through IEDs, etc.

Kailash Kumar Chatry (2012) studied four (Sikh, Kashmiri Muslim, Hindu and Naga Christian) religious communities to explain the religious nature of terrorism in India. The thesis argues that, in contrast to the existing explanations, religion (religious ideologies) and historical and socio-political factors are intensely interconnected for the rise of the terrorism in India. It is proposed that rebuilding of the communal harmony, by utilizing the interconnecting social threads of the coexisting sections of the Indian society, is essential for the deconstruction of the religious terror in India.

Left-wing Terrorism

This form of terror focusses on economic ideology, where all the existing socio-political structures are seen to be economically exploitative in character and a revolutionary change through violent means is essential. The ideology of Marx, Engel, Mao, Lenin, and others are considered as the only valid economic path. Maoist violence in Jharkhand and Chhattisgarh are examples of left-wing terrorism in India.

Narco-terrorism

This form of terror focusses on creating illegal narcotics traffic. Drug violence in northwest India is an example of narco-terrorism in India.

The Terrorists

All this discussion brings us to the basic question of the terrorist personality. What are the conditions and factors which create such a personality?

How does such a personality evolve and reach a point of no return? How does it emerge as a pure machine of destruction, insensitive to the objective reality around, and unresponsive to pity and compassion? How may such a personality be recovered and restored to moral health? Some scholars may argue that these are the questions of technology which fall within the scope of the science of psychology and not sociology. But others may view them as problems of social psychology. The truth is that no one is born as a terrorist. We have, to totally reject the role of heredity, genes, blood, etc. in terrorist's personality. Equally, no theory of a 'bruised childhood' or of an 'evil neighbourhood' and environment is going to explain a terrorist's behaviour. For each abused youth who turns into a terrorist, there are scores of youths who nurse no such injuries and traumas and in fact become a part of the social order. Recent studies have shown that over 80 per cent of the terrorists in advanced countries come from reasonably affluent families (D.S. Maini, *Hindustan Times*, 9 April 1995). Each terrorist personality is thus an individual case, though it may end up as having almost all the marks of its tribe.

Psychologists have advanced theories to explain the working of the terrorist mind and the making of the terrorist personality. For example, Lawrence Zelic Freedman writing on 'Perspectives on Terrorism' has offered four hypotheses in this regard (see D.S. Maini): (a) *the affirmation of self-esteem,* where an ego has been deeply hurt and denied identity; (b) *depersonalization,* i.e. the surrender of one's personality in the service of a group; (c) *a method of establishing intimacy,* i.e. becoming a terrorist as a means to enforce recognition and thus establish a subjective relationship with one's victim; and (d) *a belief in 'the magic of violence',* wherein the elements of secrecy, mystery and wonder fuse to propel the terrorist towards an unknown territory. To this list, Maini adds other factors like: (a) a big business linking-up with the underworld and the local magic, (b) a form of revenge to redress insult, (c) as an aspect of messianic (confusing) politics, (d) as an intolerable urge for action, (e) as a surrogate sexual activity, and (f) as a group narcissim (mental state in which there is self-worship). All this indicates that the phenomenon of terrorism is a complex issue of inflamed sentiment, thought and passion, and of action and abstraction.

There is thus bound to be a certain arbitrariness in classifying the types of terrorists. For instance, while the American Professor of Psychiatry Frederick J. Hacker has given three types of terrorists: the crazy, the criminal, and the crusading, the Russian scholar Viktor Vitiuk (1985) has classified them as the 'idealists', the 'filibusters', and the 'lost souls'. While the chances are that a person may become a terrorist in a slow process, there is a possibility of suddenly becoming a terrorist due to an impulsive and a passionate response to a given situation-a personal injury, a communal trauma, a political tragedy, etc. For terrorists of Punjab, for instance, all these factors in varying degrees had their validity. What ultimately sustains a terrorist in the face of various contradictions and compulsions is a cause, an idea, or a dream. Ultimately, it is a leader, a charismatic figure, who will bind him to the group to keep him going, since his own authority is illusory and deceptive and his power of manipulating reality is a receding vista. His dreams require a feedback and he gets this nourishment from his image. He then continues to be a terrorist even when the leader is gone from the scene, killed or executed.

Then what are the chances of a terrorist's return to the path of sanity and normalcy? While developing a terrorist's philosophy, since he remained willing even to give his life for the cause he was fighting, he remains a terrorist throughout his life. Yet, the rigours of life and the corrective processes may contribute to his recovery. A mother's love, a secular politician's appeal, a woman's attraction may hasten the process. But then there always remains the possibility of his bouncing back into the life of terrorism.

Chief Terrorist Groups Operating in India

There are, at present, as many as 66 terrorist/separatist groups active across the country. Indian terrorist groups have external links with like-minded terrorist groups in other countries. The link between the Marxist groups of Indian with Maoist groups of Nepal, Sri Lanka and Bangladesh; the link between the indigenous Kashmir organizations with the religious, fundamentalist and jihadi organizations of Pakistan; the link between organizations such as the Students Islamic Movement of India with *jihadi* elements in Pakistan and Saudi Arabia; and the link between the Pakistani pen Islamic jihadi organizations operating in India with al-Qaeda and the Taliban are well known. Countries host groups that play a major role in terrorism in India are:

Pakistan: Pakistan-based extremists have long played a part in the conflict over Indian-controlled Kashmir. Experts say that Pakistan's Inter-Services Intelligence(ISI) agency supported Kashmiri militants.

Bangladesh: The rise of Islamist extremism in Bangladesh, near the Indian border, has caused fears of a spillover into India's Northeast by growing illegal immigration from Bangladesh and cooperating with Pakistan's ISI in 'nefarious designs against India'. Bangladesh has long served as a sanctuary and training ground for Northeast separatist militants such as the United Liberation Front of Assam.

Nepal: There are indications that the success of Maoist rebels in neighbouring Nepal has bolstered left-wing extremist groups in India. Nepalese and Indian Maoists offer each other ideological and possibly military support. The Terrorism Knowledge Base reports that the two groups launched their first joint attack in 2005.

Here are some of the chief terrorist groups operating in India:

Jaish-e-Mohammed: Jaish-e-Mohammed, meaning 'Army of Mohammed,' is another Pakistan-based terrorist group operating in Jammu & Kashmir. Founded in 2000 by the former leader of the now-defunct group

Harkat-ul-Ansar, Jaish-e-Mohammed seeks to drive India out of Jammu & Kashmir and transfer control of the region to Pakistan and has instigated several terrorist attacks in the valley to further their aim.

Lashkar-e-Taiba (LeT): This is an Islamist militant group which is operating in Pakistan and even in India's Jammu & Kashmir region. It is said to be funded by Pakistan and is responsible for carrying out many massive terrorist attacks in India. LeT, which has ideological, but unconfirmed operational ties to al-Qaeda aims to win sovereignty for Jammu & Kashmir and spread Islamic rule across India. LeT is suspected of involvement in the December 2001 attack of New Delhi's Parliament, the 2006 Mumbai train bombings, and the February 2007 blast of a train running between India and Pakistan.

Harkat-ul-Jihad-i-Islami (HUJI) was founded in 1980, is based in Pakistan and Kashmir, primarily attacks Indian military targets. But it is believed to be linked to the abduction and slaying of five Western tourists in Jammu & Kashmir in 1995.

Jamaat-ul-Mujahideen is a small pro-Pakistan militant group formed in India-controlled Kashmir in 1990. Followers are mostly Kashmiri but include some Pakistanis. It is thought to be responsible for 2004 grenade attacks against political targets in India.

Maoist: This terrorist group was created by the merger of Naxalite groups, after talks between leftist militants and Indian government broke in the year 2004.

United Liberation Front of Assam (ULFA): ULFA has sought to establish an independent socialist state in Assam since its founding in 1979. In the 1990s, ULFA's attacks on political leaders, security forces, and infrastructure provoked a harsh response from the Indian government, causing it to lose some support among the residents of Assam.

The irony is that even though these terrorist groups take the onus of the bomb blasts and other terrorist activities carried out by them, most of the times the government is not able to reach out to them and take the required action against them.

India has to fight on its own with the terrorism being funded and encouraged by the neighbouring countries. We have to empower ourselves, tackle our problems in our own ways. Terrorism has to be dealt firmly with determined efforts and indomitable political will with the full and all-out support of all political parties and every citizen.

Naxalism signifies a particular kind of militant and violent armed struggle by the peasants and tribals who accept Marxist-Leninist ideology. In spite of Naxalism being termed as the biggest problem in *adivasi* areas, the social problems are actually much wider in the form of unemployment, poverty and an untold number of socio-economic injustices.

Naxalites are powerful and effective in some areas in India because of the unresolved contradictions and issues in our society. They have proved effective because they have an ideology that inspires youth apart from having an organizational structure and armed groups. Proper enforcement of land ceiling laws, utilization of the funds provided to the government to the maximum could be the solution to this problem. The central reason for the advancement of Naxalism is the vast exploitation of the poor and the scheduled castes. People, who have been displaced, should be given proper rehabilitation along with police protection. Security, as well as development, has to run hand in hand.

Deadliest Terrorist Attacks in India in the Last 25 Years

Mumbai–Maharashtra (1993)

The city of Mumbai was rocked by a series of bomb explosions within a span of two and half hours (1.30 pm to 4 pm) on 12 March 1993. The explosions were caused at commercial centres and other landmarks of Mumbai. The incidents were an outcome of a criminal conspiracy, in which 257 persons lost their lives and 713 others sustained injuries. The conspiracy was hatched by Dawood Ibrahim in conjunction with Pak establishment.

Indian Parliament Attack (2001)

Five terrorists belonging to Jaish-e-Mohammed (JeM) and Lashkar-e-Taiba (LeT) targeted the nation's safest building – Parliament – on 13 December 2001. The attack led to the death of five terrorists, six Delhi Police personnel, two Parliament Security Service personnel and a gardener. All five terrorists were also killed by the security forces and were identified as Pakistani nationals. The terrorists set off massive blasts and used AK-47 rifles, explosives, and grenades for the attack. Senior Ministers and over 200 members of parliament were inside the Central Hall of Parliament when the attack took place. Security personnel sealed the entire premises, which saved many lives.

Akshardham–Gujarat (2002)

The Akshardham Attack was a terror attack at the Akshardham Temple in Gandhinagar, in 2002. Two terrorists attacked the temple complex killing 31 people. The National Security Guards ended the siege by killing both the attackers. Over seventy others were injured in these attacks.

Mumbai–Maharashtra (2006)

A series of seven bombs exploded in local trains of Mumbai in a short span of 11 minutes. The bombs were set off in pressure cookers. A total of 187 people were killed and 817 others sustained injuries. In 2015, 12 people were convicted in this case.

Samjhauta Blasts (2007)

An explosion occurred in two unreserved coaches of Samjhauta/Attari Express at Diwana near Panipat. The Samjhauta Express, a twice-weekly train service connecting Delhi and Lahore. Bombs were set off in two carriages, both filled with passengers, just after the train passed Diwana station. 68 people were killed and 15 others sustained injuries. Among those killed were Indian and Pakistani citizens, including a few policemen.

Mumbai–Maharashtra (2008)

In November 2008, 10 Pakistani members of Lashkar-e-Taiba, an Islamic militant organization, carried out a series of 12 coordinated shooting and bombing attacks lasting four days across Mumbai. The attacks, which drew widespread global condemnation, began on Wednesday, 26 November and lasted until Saturday, 29 November 2008, killing 175 (including 9 terrorists) people and 291 others sustained injuries. The only terrorist who was caught alive.

Pulwama–Kashmir (2019)

Militants from Pakistan based Jaish-e-Mohammed (JeM) terrorist organization targeted a CRPF convoy in Jammu & Kashmir's Pulwama district on 14 February 2019, with a car-borne IED, destroying vehicles and killing 40 jawans. The 78-vehicle convoy was on its way from one transit camp in Jammu to another in Srinagar. JeM was also behind the recent terror strikes in the Uri headquarters and Pathankot air base. The Pulwama terror attack is the biggest in the last twenty years. The government data shows that there has been a 176 per cent rise in the number of terrorist incidents in Jammu & Kashmir between 2014 and 2018.

Terrorism in Punjab

Sikh terrorism in Punjab was based not on 'grievance situation', but on 'identity crisis of Sikhs', or on the idea of a 'theocratic state' through secession and partition of the country. It (terrorism) entered a dangerous phase in 1984–85. Earlier, during 1982–83, scores of innocent people, mostly Hindus were killed in a reckless spree. In the later phase, along with Hindus, Sikhs were also killed.

The imperialist forces interested in balkanizing India and in weakening, destabilizing and even disintegrating our country, had been supporting, encouraging and abetting the demand of Khalistan. The internal factor which helped the terrorists in Punjab was the spread of Hindu communalism. The Hindu communalists held the entire Sikh community responsible for the crimes of terrorists. They kept on harping on the slogan of revenge and retaliation. Their (communalists') assertion that 'Sikhs are Hindus' provided the argument to the separatists that unless there is Khalistan, Sikhism will be absorbed in the Hindu religion. The anti-Sikh riots in Delhi at the time of the assassination of Mrs Indira Gandhi had resulted in killing of more than 300 Sikhs. The fact that no action was taken against those who were involved in these riots was exploited by the extremists in Punjab to spread terrorism and gather mass support for their action.

The strategies and tactics adopted by the Khalistan-oriented terrorists were: (a) undermining the authority of the administration by issuing their own orders and demonstrating their strength by killing the deviants, (b) projecting themselves as the defender of Sikhs and Sikh religion, (c) killing innocent people, looting banks and shops and creating terror, (d) forcing the Hindus of Punjab to migrate to other states and providing opportunities to Sikhs from other states to migrate to Punjab, and (e) developing a nexus with smugglers for raising funds in Punjab.

Naxalism

The Ministry of Home Affairs, Government of India describes the objectives of Naxalites (also called Maoists) as destroying 'state legitimacy ... with the ultimate object of attaining political power by violent means'. They are also considered a terrorist organization under the Unlawful Activities (Prevention) Act 1967 of India.

The Naxalite movement first came to the forefront in the late 1960s. The name originates from Naxalbari, a village in West Bengal, where the uprising began in 1967. Naxalbari became famous for the left-wing revolt that took place in West Bengal. Naxalism signifies a particular kind of militant and violent armed struggle by the peasants and tribals who accept Marxist-Leninist ideology. Maoists engage in guerrilla-style warfare to fight for the rights of landless workers and tribals. These Maoists are known in India as Naxalites. 'The Maoists', whose numbers are estimated at more than 50,000, believe that the country is ruled by a servile bourgeois elite and that the whole system needs to be overthrown by an armed force. Today, the Naxalites operate mainly in mineral-rich, isolated regions and their control area stretches from the south to the northeast of the country, including the states of Andhra Pradesh, Jharkhand, Chhattisgarh and Bihar among others. The rebels have engaged in guerrilla-style warfare against Indian security forces, claiming to fight for the rights of what they consider to be exploited people, such as landless workers who lack access to minimum wages and basic amenities, such as health care and education. The movement has managed to survive for more than four decades because of the brutal nature of economic and social relations prevailing in the Indian countryside. Naxalite movement attempted to achieve equity in the society by means of a mass movement and struggle, and they did achieve it to some extent but at the cost of the economic development of the state. The movement has now advanced to the hilly and forest regions of around eight different states, with more than 150 districts believed to be under its direct influence. Naxal violence has resulted in the death of over 10,000 civilians and displaced 12 million people since 1980s with a significant rise in the number of killings in Naxalism-hit states. In spite of Naxalism being termed as the biggest problem in *adivasi* areas, the social problems are actually much wider in the form of unemployment, poverty and an untold number of socio-economic injustices.

The Naxals have lost track of their ideology and have become a menace as they not only control parts of India's so-called tribal belt but also resort to extortion from rich landowners and businessmen. Naxalism is the single biggest internal security challenge ever faced by our country. India's current development model, which gives priority to industry, resulting in the displacement of millions of people, needs to be re-examined if a solution to this decades-long unrest is ever to be found. A vibrant and active civil society needs to apply moral pressure on the Maoists, thus, making them adhere to constitutional norms and the rule of law.

In spite of the government laying down a clear plan to tackle the left-wing extremism like launching a Police Modernization Scheme in areas affected by Naxal movements, the bill for safeguarding land rights and the police and paramilitary organizations' approach to the 'Naxalite' problem exposed weakness within state governments. Various state governments, from time to time, banned Maoist outfits, without developing any consistent policy to deal with such elements. Without understanding their needs and issues, such bans, along with preventive detention or anti-terror laws that allowed the police to come down heavily on such groups, created a feeling of unrest amongst the Naxals. Development is, without a doubt, very necessary in today's age but the Central and State governments should make sure that it is not done at the cost of citizens. There has been a range of violence which has had no direct consequence on the rights of people but invariably ended up harming masses by way of disruption in the elections, destruction of schools, trains and rail lines, etc. Naxalites are powerful and effective in some areas in India because of the unresolved contradictions and issues in our society. They have proved effective because they have an ideology that inspires youth apart from having an organizational structure and armed groups. Proper enforcement of land ceiling laws, utilization of the funds provided to the government to the maximum could be the solution to this problem. The central reason for the advancement of Naxalism is the vast exploitation of the poor and the scheduled tribes. People, who have been displaced, should be given proper rehabilitation along with police protection. Security, as well as development, has to run hand in hand. A mutual under standing, therefore, should prevail which can end Naxalism. Naxalites have been attacking police establishments and public infrastructures causing insecurity and instability to the area.

Terrorism in Kashmir

India has been facing this problem from the early 1990s and has also fought two wars with Pakistan on this issue, but the governments have not been able to take hard decisions and evolve a definite coherent policy. Our policy makers have been chasing the mirage of soft options and have been following a weak-kneed approach in dealing with the terrorists. Terrorism in Kashmir assumed a new shape 1988 onwards. The militants launched a bloody battle to underline their separate identity. The neighbouring countries, particularly Pakistan, determined to see turmoil continuing in the valley, are providing training and weapons to the militants even today. The people have also been so brain-washed that they talk of the excesses of the police and the para-military forces. For the militants, the criticism of the government by the people means that people are more than willing to support them. On the other hand, the Hindus have been forced by the militants to leave Kashmir. It is claimed in one report that nearly two lakh Hindus fled Kashmir valley between 1988 and 1991. The Hindus claimed that the fundamentalists and militants had infiltrated every sphere of the government in the valley till the middle of 1996 and that 'what ruled the roost' was not the writ of the government but that of the militants. They maintained that the pro-Pakistan forces had overtaken the valley and in a way, there was a collapse of the administration and the terrorists wanted them to quit the valley. The civilian Muslims now claim that they are innocent and are being unnecessarily harassed. There is no dearth of weapons in the valley, nor is there any dearth of frustrated youths to operate them. Hizb-ul-Mujahideen was claimed to have a cadre strength of 20,000 with at least 10,000 persons being trained in camps across the border and in the valley. The Jammu & Kashmir Liberation Front (JKLF) still clings on to the concept of an independent state (Azad Kashmir) as opposed to a merger with Pakistan, whereas other militant groups like Lashkar-e-Taiba and Jaish-e-Mohammad favour a Pakistani Kashmir. All militants at one time had developed a feeling that they had to unite against a common enemy – the Indian Armed Forces.

The rise in violence indices in Jammu & Kashmir may warrant a rethink in strategy. Besides the military strategy, political, economic, and cultural strategies too have to be used in combatting Kashmir uprisings. The bridges of trust have to be built by far-sighted political initiatives.

ULFA Terrorism

Terrorism in Assam emerged from 1980 onwards. Assamese already had raised the issue of removing 'foreigners' and deleting their names from the electoral rolls. When the government failed to take action, there were agitations in February 1983 elections in which 5,000 persons lost their lives. After the AASU movement when the Assam Gana Parishad (AGP) came to power in 1986, it was felt that the State would develop. But the factions soon led to the split of the AGP. The United Minorities Front (UMF) and the United Liberation Front of Assam (ULFA) emerged as two militant organizations. The All Bodo Students' Union (ABSU) also demanded a separate state resulting in considerable violence. The ULFA stepped up its campaign of murder, loot and kidnapping. The terrorist activities spread panic not only among the non-Assamese but also amongst the Assamese people. The army action – named Operation Bajrang – against the secessionist militant organization subdued it to the extent that the militant activities did not interfere even with the elections in June 1991. It was hoped that the formation of the new Congress government in June 1991 would rout or weaken organizations like the ULFA Bodo Security Force, and the ASDC and that the new government would be able to contain the terrorist activities of the militant organizations in the state. But the abduction of persons from different parts of the state and the killing and the looting of the people belied these expectations. The eight-year Bodoland movement was formally ended in 1994 when the Bodo Peoples' Action Committee (BPAC) and the All Bodo Students Union (ABSU) agreed to accept a Bodoland Autonomous Council within the state of Assam. This Council (of 40 members) was to have full autonomy to make the development plans relating to 38 specified subjects and jurisdiction over roughly 15,000 sq km spread over seven districts of Assam. However, the agreement between the government and the Bodos has not borne the expected fruit. Even the AGP government and successive governments have failed to contain the ethnic violence and almost daily we read about the acts of violence in the state in newspapers.

Besides the above-mentioned political aspect of terrorism (in Punjab, Kashmir, Assam, etc.) in India, it has one more aspect too, what may be called the 'Islamic aspect'. India is the only major power that is the odd-man-out amidst the 'Islamic Crescent' that stretches from Saudi Arabia to Indonesia. A product of the 1970 and the Pakistan's talk of 'Islami Bomb', this phenomenon resurged with the Iranian Revolution. The emergence of fundamentalist forces in the Arab world posed the principal threat to governments in many countries.

Causes of Terrorism: Theoretical Explanations

Following Gurr (1970: 47), the causes of terrorism may be explained on the basis of the Theory of Relative Deprivation. According to this theory, political collective violence may be described as a consequence of gap developing between the value expectations of a given group of people and the value capabilities of the group. Gurr has talked of three types of deprivations:

1. *Declivity deprivation* occurs when the value capabilities of a given population decline drastically but the value expectations remain the same. Bolsheviks' collective political violence in Russia in 1917 was due to this type of deprivation. The Russian people, after World War I, were a discontented lot, and the failure of the government to terminate the Russian involvement in the war led to a swing in popular sentiment in one group (Lenin and his party) that promised immediate peace.
2. *Aspirational deprivation* occurs when the value capabilities of the given population remain the same but value expectations increase. Terrorism in the Kashmir valley is due to this type of deprivation. Similarly, the ULFA terrorism in Assam is the result of the demands for immediate equality as opposed to the continuing discrimination and prejudice against them.
3. *Progressive deprivation* occurs when value expectations increase and the value capabilities decline. The Khalistan-oriented terrorism is the best example of this.

The process of modernization and the 'ethnicity explosion' leads to widespread feelings of relative deprivation.

Causes of Terrorism in India

There are several causes of terrorism. Some may be genuine and some less-genuine. Some genuine causes include socio-economic, political motivation and frustration, regional disparities, intervention into religious, social and personal freedom of the people, communalism and secessionism, etc. And other less-genuine reasons for the growth of terrorism are illiteracy, increase of population, the soft attitude of government towards criminals and economic offences, etc. But, it does not mean that these less-genuine reasons are not responsible for the emergence of terrorism. The responsible factors of the emergence of terrorism may briefly be classified as under: (a) socio-economic factors, (b) political factors, and (c) regional disparities.

Socio-economic factors: Socio-economic causes refer to gross economic inequalities in which there is exploitation of man by man. Economic inequality and widening gap between rich and poor is undoubtedly a very important cause leading to terrorism in human society. There are a number of examples of terrorism, particularly, the revolutionary terrorism, occurring, in the different states, due to the real conditions of discrimination, deprivation, frustration, injustice, misery, poverty and unemployment among a large section of people in a society. Economic causes contribute to intense terrorism in India. Andhra Pradesh, Madhya Pradesh, Odisha, and Bihar are prime examples. The economic factors include rural unemployment, exploitation of landless labourers by those who own land and lack of land reforms. These economic perceptions and grievances of gross social injustice have led to the rise of ideological groups of terrorists existing under different names. Socio-economic factors of terrorism result into various problems in the society. These are: (a) unemployment, (b) poverty, (c) illiteracy, (d) homelessness, desperation and lack of opportunity, (e) wrong policies of government, (f) accumulation of wealth in few hands, (g) deprivation of basic rights, and (h) violation of fundamental freedoms.

Political factors: Economic dissatisfaction may cause political violence. The political cause is also a source of terrorism in India. This is seen essentially in Assam and Tripura. The political factors that led to insurgency-cum-terrorism included the failure of the government to control large-scale illegal immigration of Muslims from Bangladesh, to fulfil the demand of economic benefits for the sons and daughters of the soil, etc.

Regional factors: religious causes are also a source of terrorism. In Punjab, before 1995 some elements of Sikh belonging to different organizations shifted to terrorism to the development of an independent state known as Khalistan for the Sikhs. In J&K since 1989, Muslims associated with various organizations shifted to terrorism for conflicting objectives.

Ethnic causes, mainly seen in Nagaland, Mizoram, and Manipur due to feelings of ethnic separateness also contribute to terrorism.

Combatting Terrorism: Models

Terrorism is too serious a problem to be left to politicians alone. General awareness among the masses and pressures on people are the only way out. The one thing we have to understand is that terrorism is like a common cold. It runs its own course and there is need for patience. Basically, there are three models of combatting terrorism: the Indian, the American and the Israeli. A comparison of these three models is necessary for furthering our understanding.

The Israeli Model

Terrorism in Israel has been prevailing for the last four decades. Initially, for about one and a half decades (1953 to 1967), the Palestinians living in the west of Jordan and in the Gaza strip carried out their resistance through cross border raids by sneaking into Israel. The Israelis responded by carrying out airborne raids and by intruding into Jordan and destroying Palestinian camps with tanks. Since these attacks caused extensive damage to Jordanian army and property, the public opinion in Jordan turned against supporting the PLO. Along with Jordan, other Arab countries also prevented the PLO from carrying out its activities from their soil. Jordan launched a purge in September 1970 against the Palestinians and killed about 15,000 of them. The PLO base in Lebanon also was eliminated when Israel invaded Lebanon in 1982. Israel, thus, dealt with the PLO terrorists by eliminating their bases. The Palestinians then adopted the tactics of hijacking Israeli civilian aircrafts and also kidnapping the Israeli civilians and demanding the release of their jailed colleagues in Israel. The Israeli government never yielded to such terrorist threats and in retaliation attacked the Palestinian camps. Though the Israeli policy of non-negotiation with the terrorists was often criticized but Israel never budged from its position, maintaining that once they gave into hijackings and kidnappings, they would multiply manifold. Thus, the four primary components of the Israeli strategy in dealing with terrorist violence are: (a) refusal to negotiate with terrorists, (b) retaliatory raids on the bases of terrorists, (c) strict security measures, and (d) covert violence against Palestinians (even innocent) connected with terrorists and sympathizers of Palestinians. Thus, the Israeli model of combatting terrorism is based on 'counter-terror' and 'anti-terror' rather than passive defensive measures.

The American Model

The United States has global economic interests and is vulnerable to terrorism. The most potent weapon of America to fight terrorism has been its economic clout like cutting off trade and technology export. When this fails, the US bombs the enemy country supporting terrorists. This method was adopted for Cuba in 1962 and for Libya in 1986 when its leader Colonel Gaddafi supported terrorist movements like those of the PLO or of the IRA of Northern Ireland or of the HUK rebels of Philippines, or of the terrorist gangs in Latin America. The same method was adopted by America when it invaded Cambodia for giving shelter to Vietcong during the Vietnam war. In Afghanistan too, the same strategy was adopted by America when it supported Talibani rivals against the pro-Soviet government. Thus, the American model of combatting terrorism was 'counter-terror campaign' and invasion.

The Indian Model

India has been facing severe problems of violence and terrorism since the 1960s. The insurgency in the north-east in the 1960s and the 1970s was tackled by the government more through political methods. The violence in Jammu & Kashmir also falls more into the category of insurgency rather than pure terrorism. 'Operation Blue Star' of the military on 6 June 1984 in Punjab and 'Operation Black Thunder' in Assam designed to counter terrorism totally failed. They were anti-terrorist measures (implemented mainly through the police forces and partially through the military forces) rather than counter-terrorist measures. The hallmark of the policies in the former measures are: frequent road checks, sentries at vulnerable points and elaborate security for the VIPs. The countries which supply the bulk of arms, or give shelter to terrorists or finance terrorism have not been called to account. Even there, the emphasis is on passive measures like border fencing or lodging mild protests. No wonder, even after 50 years, India has not been able to control terrorism. The government in most cases succumbs to the demands of the terrorists as happened in Kashmir, Andhra Pradesh and Bihar.

Thus, the three models (Israeli, American and Indian) of combatting terrorism are different in content as well as in temperament. In a way, they reflect the power of the states. The American model is 'counter-terror' model which is based on hitting at the very roots of terrorist support. The Indian model is anti-terrorist model. The Israeli model is 'blend of counter-terror and anti-terrorist measures'. The terrorist menace cannot be eliminated either through anti-terror or counter-terror approaches. Besides the police and the military measures, the socio-political issues have also to be tackled. The militant bases in the countries, at least the neighbouring countries, supporting the terrorists, needs to be attacked and destroyed. The policy in dealing with such countries has to be deterrent.

The Government of India cannot face the problem of terrorism merely by enlisting public sympathy or by blaming countries of giving support to terrorists. Helping terrorists in a hostile country is a fact of life which no organized government in modern times can ignore. India has to evolve its own system of dealing with terrorists.

TADA and POTA

The Terrorist and Disruptive Activities (Prevention) Act, 1987, was at one time the main law to deal with cases of terrorism and organised crime, but due to rampant misuse, it was allowed to lapse on 23 May 1995. The Act defined a 'terrorist act' and 'disruptive activities', put restrictions on the grant of bail, and gave enhanced power to detain suspects and attach properties. The law made a confession before a police officer admissible as evidence. Separate courts were set up to hear cases filed under TADA.

In wake of the 1999 IC-814 hijack and 2001 Parliament attack, a more stringent anti-terrorism legislation was enacted which came in the form of The Prevention of Terrorism Act (POTA), 2002. A suspect could be detained for up to 180 days by a special court. A separate chapter to deal with terrorist organisations was included. The Union government could add or remove any organisation from the schedule. However, reports of gross misuse of the Act by some state governments led to its repeal in 2004.

Agencies Responsible for Fighting Terrorism in India

A number of intelligence, military, and police organizations within the Indian government contribute to counterterrorism efforts. These include state-run police forces, special security forces to guard airports and other high-profile targets, and paramilitary forces that patrol the borders and assist the police when necessary. Besides these, India has several intelligence agencies that monitor terrorist activities. The Research and Analysis Wing (RAW) is the external intelligence agency and the Intelligence Bureau (IB), a division of the Home Affairs Ministry, collects intelligence inside India. A Joint Intelligence Committee analyses intelligence data from RAW and IB as well as from a handful of military intelligence agencies, which usually provide tactical information gathered while carrying out counter-terrorist operations.

Some methods which may prove to be helpful to our government in this regard are (Saxena, 1985: 33–34):

1. seeking cooperation of the citizens by the police to get information about the terrorists;
2. reducing the finance at the disposal of the terrorists to contain their operations;
3. refusing to accept any demands of any group of terrorists;
4. giving swift and judicial punishments to arrested terrorists. The greater the delay in prosecution and greater the detention in the jail as undertrials, the greater the possibility of their escape;
5. adopting more effective intelligence methods in retrieving information about the terrorists, their associates, their modus operandi, and their sources of finance and weapons, etc.;
6. improving security measures continuously at important places; and
7. giving more scientific training to forces dealing with terrorists.

Sociology of Terrorism

How does terrorism disrupt the political system or social organizations? How does terrorism act as a method for hastening social change? How does terrorism explain the social relationship between a frustrated minority and the ruling political elite, or between a group which feels deprived and a group which has the monopoly on the use of force? A holistic sociological perspective of terrorism will be possible only when we discuss large-scale political events not only in aggregate numerical terms but also in impact terms, that is, we focus not only on quantitative macropolitics but also on qualitative micropolitics.

Terrorism demoralizes and demobilizes populations and disintegrates societies, though it is also true that terrorism in some instances serves as an integrative mechanism binding people together in a common cause. Terrorism may involve the problem of law and order, that is, of killing or kidnapping of one group by other group because of its religious affiliations or sub-cultural differences, but it does not disrupt the social systems. Nor is terrorism a special method for hastening historical change. No terrorist movement has ever succeeded in achieving its goals. Terrorists, therefore, do not shape the course of historical events.

For understanding terrorism, it is necessary to measure the amount of violence engaged in by the terrorists to effect their desired ends, the quantum of force utilized by the police and the armed forces to prevent social change, and also to measure the types of violence. Using this perspective to terrorism in India, the number of people killed and kidnapped in Bihar in one year is much more than the killings and kidnappings in Punjab or Kashmir. When a terrorist takes a life in the name of social justice, he faces a problem of social accounting at one level and moral constraint at another. One might also speak of the results of the use of terror to overthrow state authority. Suppose we accept the temporary disruption of the normal administrative activities of politico-social systems, do we not face the same results whenever we are faced with any social or natural calamity? Does the killing of one or two, or even a few important political leaders by the terrorists change the structure of politics? By and large, the nature of political process in the society is not interfered with, nor it is interrupted by these killings. Quantitatively, thus, the killings by terrorists may not be significant but they do involve the qualitative traumas. This is the problem we faced in the assassinations of Indira Gandhi and Rajiv Gandhi by the terrorists. As a result, we may not label terrorist activities 'unsuccessful', but at the same time, we cannot view them as 'successful' too in terms of the limited numbers involved. Sociologically, therefore, terrorists may not be able to topple the social order but they do loosen that order symbolically by weakening the legitimating capacities of administrative officials and the power elite. To board an aeroplane, one might agree to get his luggage checked or go through the security measures for approaching an important person; nevertheless, one has a perfect right to raise questions about these new social costs. These symbolic changes as the result of consequences of terrorism may be irritable but their transitory nature is invariably important for social evaluation. The social impact of terrorism which may totally affect the society on a long-term basis, thus, should be the central focus in any system of analytic measurement. It may, therefore, be concluded that the claims that terrorism disintegrates society or affects the survival of the system will not be very correct.

Nevertheless, mechanisms have to be created to prevent acts of terror. Terrorism and political violence have become the bane of Indian society today. Both are leading the country towards anarchy and chaos. Terrorists kill in the name of religion and region, in the name of language and culture. It is time that the prevalent frustration and a sense of deprivation amongst people, particularly the youth, be checked. On one hand, the government has to deal with the terrorists with a very firm hand, and on the other the minorities have to be protected and right atmosphere has to be created for the functioning of a genuine democracy. The terrorism of the terrorists of terrorizing the terrorized has to be contained. For decades, the country and numerous families have suffered pain owing to terrorism.

The Global Terrorism Index measures the direct and indirect impact of terrorism, including its effects on lives lost, injuries, property damage and the psychological after effects. It is a composite score that ranks countries according to the impact of terrorism from 0 (no impact) to 10 (highest impact). India Terrorism Index – actual data, historical chart and calendar of releases – was last updated in April 2018. India's score was 7.53. According to a report issued by Global Terrorism Index 2014, India was ranked among the top ten countries to be significantly affected by terrorist activities in 2013.

The Economic Impact of Terrorism

According to economists, the already damaged economy of India, as a result of the global financial crisis, will further be affected by recent terrorist activities in the country. The immediate impact of terrorism is loss of lives, loss of money and destruction of property, but the worst loss of them all is fear and anxiety that negatively affects economic activities. Transportation, tourism, and hospitality sectors are amongst the first areas to feel the pain. Now, the new band of terrorists has spread hatred wings in other parts of the world. It appears the entire world has to work with the constant vigil, tooth, and nail, against the menace, before the orgy of destruction spree through the length and breadth of the world. Terrorism could be wiped off the scene, provided the think-tank of the developed and developing world unite for the cause.

Action Required to Check Terrorism

1. All the parties should take the hardest possible actions against terrorists. Instead of politicizing, all the parties should work towards eliminating terrorism. There should be no blame game.
2. As an independent country, we have to exercise our rights. India's law is too soft to handle terrorism. Drastic steps should be taken against extremists.
3. Prevention is better than cure. The very first thing is to strengthen our intelligence services. There should be a proper security plan in place and there should be routine checkups.
4. All the state governments should act equally on terror. They should not ignore security alerts and make sure that it is happening at all levels.

5. Our police force needs to be improved to a large extent, because they are not equipped with modern amenities to confront terrorists. Now only the Army and NSG can confront them. First of all, they have to develop a good attitude to fight against terrorism as well. Police force need to be trained properly to deal with terrorism.
6. There should be a proper coordination among foreign, home and defence ministry.

Fundamentalism

Some people use 'fundamentalism' synonymous with terrorism because it is an ideology of extremists, a feeling of self-righteousness, and moral correctness of one's cause and one's objective. It convinces the believer that others and their causes are wrong, and they should be corrected, even by resorting to coercion, and they should be defeated or converted, and if need be, even eradicated. One definition of fundamentalism goes as 'a usually religious movement or point of view characterized by a return to fundamental principles, by rigid adherence to those principles, and often by intolerance of other views and opposition to secularism'.

Although, all the religions, more or less, have patches of fundamentalist upsurge, but no religion is so closely knit with politics as is Islam. That is why the most talked about example of fundamentalism cited these days is of Islamic fundamentalism though there are also Christian fundamentalism, Hindu fundamentalism, etc.

Fundamentalism usually has a religious connotation that indicates unwavering attachment to a set of irreducible beliefs. In the broadest sense, fundamentalism is an extreme adherence to the core rules of any set of beliefs. Its adherents are often told that their religious views must be obeyed to the absolute letter of the law, and any violation of the law is unforgivable. It makes people of other religious beliefs inferior in the eyes of fundamentalists, and the results tend to be very violent. Religious fundamentalism is a form of extremism. Communalism also inspires fundamentalism and strict dogmatic observation of one religion's doctrines as superior to other religions or non-fundamentalists. The issues of communalism and fundamentalism have actually the same ideologies that most Indian politicians officially support today: secular democracy and religious pluralism.

Religious fundamentalism has risen to worldwide prominence since the 1970s. It has taken place from a large variety and interaction of factors and forces such as political, social, economic, etc.

References

Alexander, Y. and Finger, S.M., *Terrorism: Interdisciplinary Perspectives*, John Jay Press, New York, 1977.

Athal, Anil A., 'Terror Tactics', *Gentleman*, April, 1991, pp. 56–60.

Chatry, Kailash Kumar, 'Understanding the Religious Nature of Terrorism in India: Four Case Studies with an Analysis for Proposal and Resolution', Ph.D. Thesis, University of Birmingham, Birmingham, UK, 2012.

Crenshaw, Martha (ed.), *Terrorism, Legitimacy and Power: The Consequences of Political Violence*, Wesleyen University Press, Moddletown, 1983.

Gurr, Ted Robert, *Why Men Rebel*, Princeton University Press, Princeton, 1970.

Laqueur, W., *Terrorism*, Weidenfeld and Nicholson, London, 1977.

Mallin, Jay, *Terror and Urban Guerrillas*, University of Miami Press, Coral Gables, 1971.

Marwah, Ved, *Uncivil Wars: Pathology of Terrorism in India*, HarperCollins India, Delhi, 1996.

Naunihal, Singh, *The World of Terrorism*, South Asian Publishers, New Delhi, 1989.

Rapoport, D.C. and Alexander, Y. (eds), *The Morality of Terrorism: Religious and Secular Justification*, Pergamon Press, Elmsford, 1982.

Saxena, N.S., *Terrorism: History and Facets in the World and in India*, Abhinav Publications, New Delhi, 1985.

Sheth, Pravin N., *Global Terrorism: Meeting Borders, Hardened Walls*, Rawat Publications, Jaipur, 2005.

Sterling, Clarie, *The Terror Network*, Holt, Rinehart & Winston, New York, 1981.

Terrorism: International Journal, Vols. 1–6, 1977–1983.

Verma, Smita (ed.), *Underdevelopment and Naxalism in India: Reflexive Discourse and Debates*, Rawat Publications, Jaipur, 2018.

Vitiuk, Viktor, *Leftist Terrorism*, Progress Publishers, Moscow, 1985.

Wardlaw, Grant, *Political Terrorism: Theory, Tactics and Countermeasure*, Cambridge University Press, London, 1984.

Wilkinson, Paul, *Political Terrorism*, Macmillan & Co., London, 1974.

21

Corruption

Facts about Corruption in India

1. The biggest drawback of the country which has the largest democracy in the world is not population but corruption.
2. Corruption is often strong in countries with the lowest per capita incomes. Sadly India is one of them having low per capita income.
3. There is currently no exclusive legislation to check corruption in the private sector in India.
4. Corruption is primarily seen in instances like jobs, businesses, promotions, election campaigns, sports, etc.
5. Most corrupt sectors are Infrastructure, Real estate, Metal, Mining, Power and utilities and Aerospace.
6. Pharmacy, retail, consumer products and education sector are found to be less corrupt sectors.
7. Excessive regulations, complicated taxes and licensing systems, opaque bureaucracy, monopoly, and the lack of transparent laws and processes are some of the causes of corruption in India.
8. Because corruption is willfully hidden, it is impossible to measure it directly; instead, proxies for corruption are used.
9. In the private sector, corruption increases the cost of business through the price of illicit payments themselves.
10. Giving gifts, meals, refreshments or travel, funds spent on liaising and bonus payments are some of the hot tactics used in documentation by which the bribe is being hidden.
11. The Government of India's RTI site, the Right to Information Act (2005) and equivalent acts in the states, have reduced corruption to some level and opened platform for grievances.
12. Transparency International's most recent Global Index ranked India 81st, down a few places from the year before.

Corruption is a complex social problem that affects all societies. India is no exception. It is no longer considered a *soft* state as political scientists once used to call it. It has now become a kleptocracy, a *consideration* state, where everything to be had for a consideration. Here, it is said, obvious does not happen. For example, if a person wants a government job, he/she has to pay lakhs of rupees to the higher officials irrespective of satisfying the eligibility criteria. In every government office, one either has to give money to the employee concerned or arrange for some sources to get the work done. There is adulteration, duplication and underweighing of products in food and civil supplies department by unscrupulous workers. They not only cheat the consumers but also play with the health and lives of innocent people. In the assessment of property tax one has to pay bribes even if the house is built as per rules and regulations.

Political corruption is also worst in India. Today, corruption has taken the shape of such a common menace that people do not mind giving bribe even for getting a lawful work done.

Concept

Corruption is broadly defined by the World Bank to mean the use of public office for private gain. In simple terms, it may be described as 'an act of bribery'. It has also been described as 'the use of public power for private profits in a way that constitutes a breach of law or a deviation from the norms of society'. D.H. Bailey has explained it as 'misuse of authority as a result of consideration of personal gain which need not be monetary' (cited in Douglas and Johnson, 1971). Andriski considers it as 'the use of public power for private advantage in ways which transgress some formal rule or law' (cited in Clarke, 1983). Szeftel has observed that 'corruption is behaviour which is deviance from norms and duties governing the exercise of public role or office for private gains' (cited in Clarke, 1983). This private gain is achieved by ignoring prohibitions against certain acts, by exercising legitimate discretion to act, or by fulfilling obligations to act. J. Nye (1967: 410) states that 'corruption denotes the abuse or misuse of public offices for personal gains'. Corruption is also described as 'deviation from formal duties of public role for pecuniary or status gains'.

Thus, in its broadest sense, corruption is the lack of integrity – whether intellectual, moral or financial. And, when integrity fails, the entire society collapses.

A corruption equation has been given as follows (Klitgaard 1988):

$$C = M + D - A$$

In the equation, C stands for corruption, M for monopoly, D for discretionary powers, and A for accountability. The equation states more the monopolies over particular decision (M) exist in a country, the larger will be the corruption. Similarly, the greater the discretionary powers (D) granted to administrators, the greater will be the corruption. However, the more administrators are held accountable (A) for their actions, lesser will be the corruption, and hence a minus sign in front. All the above three causal claims may be true under certain circumstances, but the Klitgaard Formula implies that they are generally true.

Corruption is spread in the society in several forms. Of these, the major ones are: bribe (money offered in cash or kind or gift as inducement to procure illegal or dishonest action in favour of the giver), nepotism (undue favour from holder of patronage to relatives), misappropriation (using other's money for one's own use), patronage (wrong support/encouragement given by patron and thus misusing the position), and favouritism (unduly preferring one to other).

Types of Corruption

1. *Nepotism*: Favouritism shown by public officials to relatives or close friends.
2. *Fraud*: Cheating the government through dishonesty.
3. *Embezzlement*: Stealing money or other government property.
4. *Administrative corruption:* Corruption that alters the implementation of policies.
5. *Political corruption*: Corruption that influences the formulation of laws, regulations, and policies.
6. *Grand corruption* consists of acts committed at a high level of government that distort policies or the central functioning of the state, enabling leaders to benefit at the expense of the public good. With grand corruption, highly placed individuals exploit their positions to extract large bribes from national and transnational corporations, who appropriate significant payoffs from contract scams, or who embezzle large sums of money from the public treasury into private bank accounts. It is also when politicians design legislation to work in their favour. Grand corruption mostly occurs in large procurement projects such as the building of roads, dams, hospitals, airports, mining, oil/gas concessions, construction projects and in arms and defence contracts, in new weapons technology, aircraft purchase, warships, and artillery pieces. Grand corruption involving public officials is referred to as kleptocracy.
7. *Petty corruption:* Petty corruption involves smaller sums and typically more junior officials. It is the low-level corruption that citizens face every day in their encounters with corrupt public officials, in the struggle to obtain public services such as healthcare, education, paying taxes, and obtaining licenses. This type of corruption is referred to as petty because the amount of money required for petty corruption is lower. However, even though the sums are low in stand-alone cases, petty corruption often add up to quite a large sum of money. So even in the case where there is very little grand corruption with the elite, a large amount of petty corruption

in the lower offices of government or outside of government can do just as much harm, if not more.

8. *Corruption for good causes:* It may sound absurd but sometimes intention of doing good work leads to the road of corruption. The NGOs and the social service foundations sometimes get involved in corruption by giving a false certificate to the donor for tax saving and fame, in return for money.

Factors that Stimulate the Growth of Corruption

Globalization: Globalization of Indian market flooded the market with luxury goods. To increase the purchasing power, people involve in corruption. *Bureaucracy:* The absolute power and authority given to the public servants involved with administrative job give them enough opportunity to engage in corruption.

Democratic Pluralism: The multiparty democracy or the democratic pluralism leads to corruption. Every political party needs a huge amount of money to buy the vote or the media. So they involve in corruption to make money for the party. They know after the stipulated period they may not return to the power. So, they try their best to earn as much as possible during the governance of their party.

Capitalism: The free and open trade and privatization of public property leads to capitalism and corruption. The businessman demands as much as he wants and the poor have to pay to buy the basic needs of life. To do all these things, the industrialist needs political support and they pay money to purchase the contract at a low cost and encourage corruption.

Corruption: A Historical Perspective

Corruption is a global phenomenon. It is found almost in every society in one or the other form since time immemorial. In ancient times, the judges received bribes in Egyptian, Babylonian and Hebrew societies. In Rome, bribe was a common feature in elections to public offices. In France, judicial offices were sold during the fifteenth century. England was described a 'sink-hole' of corruption in the seventeenth and the eighteenth centuries. In the nineteenth century also, corruption was so rampant in Britain that Gibbon described it as the most infallible symptom of constitutional liberty (*Seminar*, No. 421, September 1994).

In India too, corruption has prevailed from time immemorial in one form or the other. Kautilya has referred in his *Arthasastra* (Samasastry, 1967: 15–17) embezzlement by government servants out of the state revenue. He has mentioned about forty types of embezzlement and corrupt practices adopted by government servants. During Ashoka's regime, corruption prevailed on a lower scale (Majumdar, 1960: 113). In medieval society, scope for corruption was minimum because only few authorities existed for the collection of taxes. So long they amassed wealth, they were praised rather than censured. During the British rule, bribes were accepted not only by the Indian officials but by the highly-placed British officials too. Clive and Warran Hastings were found corrupt to an extent that they were tried by the parliamentary committee after their return to England. The expansion of the economic activities during the first and second world wars opened new vistas of corruption in the country (Hallaya, 1948: 13–51). War-time controls, restrictions and scarcities provided ample opportunities for bribery, corruption and favouritism. After independence, though top political elite at the national level remained very honest for sometime but after the third and the fourth general elections, the new political elite lost people's confidence of being honest. The government employees in all public concerns at all levels started accepting huge bribes even for small considerations. Today, both at the central and the state levels, the number of politicians and bureaucrats with an honest image can be counted on fingers.

India was ranked at 94th position, out of 176 nations in 2012, according to Transparency International's Corruption Perception Index. Today, corruption in India has reached an all-time high with rates being exactly double the global prevalence. Globally, while 27 per cent people paid bribes when accessing public services and institutions in 2012, in India, the percentage of persons who did the same was 54. Political parties have been found to be the most corrupt institution in India with a corruption rate as high as 4.4 on a scale of 5 (1 being the least corrupt and 5 highest).

The highest amount of bribe was collected by police (62%), followed by those involved in registry and permit (61%), educational institutions (48%) and land services (38%). India's judiciary has also been found guilty of involving in taking bribes. These findings are based on a survey of 1.14 lakh people in 107 countries conducted by the Transparency International's Global Corruption Barometer, 2013.

Corruption Among Public Servants

Corruption among public servants has always existed in one form or the other although its shape, dimensions, textures and shades have been changing from time to time and place to place. At one time, bribe was paid for getting wrong things done, but now the bribe is paid for getting right things done at the right time.

Which acts have been called 'corrupt' in public service? Though the term 'corruption' has wide connotations, the following patterns of behaviour among public servants can be described as 'corrupt' within the provisions of law (Malhotra, 1992: 254–256): (a) acceptance of gratification as reward for work done in an official capacity, (b) obtaining any object or pecuniary advantage illegally, (c) fraudulent misappropriation of public property, (d) being in possession of financial resources or property disproportionate to one's known sources of income, (e) misuse or abuse of official position, (f) 'borrowing' money for purchasing a costly article from a person with whom one has official dealings with a 'known' understanding that the 'borrowed money' will not be returned, (g) accepting gifts by 'persons of position' from persons with whom they have 'positional' relations, (h) disregard of neglect of rules purposely to help the citizen in avoiding dues/tax/duty due to be paid to government, (i) refusal to do a duty on some plea which may benefit the other party (e.g. police officer not registering a case to protect a criminal).

Extensive corruption in government departments/ministries has almost become a tradition. There are at least five ministries in the union government which are regarded as gold mines for making money. These are: Defence, Railways, Petroleum, Power, and Communication. The annual budget of these ministries runs in billions. While commissions between 15 and 40 per cent are not uncommon in defence purchases, the import of oil and natural gas also yields a big kickback. We have also seen the examples of communication (2G Spectrum) and railways ministries where scandals involving lakhs of crores of rupees were surfaced. In both the cases, the concerned ministers were found to be involved. While the 2G scam amounts to about ₹ 1,76,000 crore (according to CAG), in the railway scam the minister's nephew was alleged of accepting ₹ 90 lakh from a Railway Board member for promoting him as Member (Electricals). It is pertinent to mention that the Member (Electricals) has huge financial powers being responsible for around 35 per cent of total spending, amounting to about ₹ 2,500 crore, of total railway budget.

Four other departments where corruption is rampant are Public Works, Police, Excise, and Revenue. The Public Works Department gets a huge portion of budget and plan provision for civil engineering works like construction of buildings, maintenance of roads, digging drains, construction of dams, and so on. Corruption in this department prevails from top to bottom at all stages, like selection, purchase of materials, execution of work, payment of bills, and settlement of disputes. It is said that out of the total cost sanctioned for the project, about 70 per cent is invested in the work, 20 per cent on contractor's profit, and 10 per cent goes into various officers' pockets.

The Police Department is said to be the most corrupt department where bribes are taken by constables upwards to high status officers. What is surprising is that the police takes money both from the accused and the complainants. The powers enjoyed by the police are so wide that they can accuse, arrest, and harass even an honest person. Cases of beating the poor people (e.g. rickshaw-pullers, labourers, shopkeepers, vendors, etc.) on small pretexts and taking away all the money in their pockets, accepting money from truck drivers, taking *hafta* (weekly fixed amount) from shopkeepers and the like are very common cases of corruption.

The scope of corruption is greater where substantial decisions are taken, e.g. assessment and collections of taxes, sanctioning contracts, passing bills, issuing cheques, approving supplies, and so forth. A predetermined percentage is paid to the officials and this money is shared by all in the establishment. In railways, for example, money is paid for the allotment of wagons, booking parcels of perishables goods, passing damage claims, and so on. In many establishments, while awarding contracts, a fixed percentage is taken as a rule. Similarly, failure to pay commission results in delay in getting the bills passed and receiving the cheques. Often, dishonest contractors and suppliers wanting to deliver inferior goods or getting approval of substantial work, spend a portion of their ill-earned profits for getting their work done. Tax evasion, sub-standard construction, supplying goods in small quantities, and charging heavily for the repair of government vehicles, are other examples of corruption.

Corruption is noticeable not only at the top but it also extends all the way down. Assistant and junior engineers, middle and low rank officials in government departments like telephones, state electricity boards and water-works, cops in police, inspectors in revenue and excise departments, clerks in secretariats, and junior staff in railways accept bribes in return for big and small favours. In many establishments, junior officials have a fixed rate of kickbacks as an unwritten rule. The amount may, however, vary from department to department or as per nature of the contract/transaction. The corruption is so pervasive in the government departments that even a former Prime Minister Rajiv Gandhi had to state in a public meeting that out of every ₹ 100 sanctioned by the government for any public programme, the people actually get the benefits worth only ₹ 20. No wonder that the corruption has emerged as the most pernicious threat to governance in India. There is perception of its encompassing all spheres of public life. The presence of administration in the form of a public official – either police or civil – is today considered as synonymous to corruption, exploitation and repression in India.

Share of kickbacks in India keeps on shooting up every year that some people started calling it humorously a 'kickback nation'. In an article published in *Business Standard* (13 July 2013), unravelling the sordid nexus among businessmen, politicians and bureaucrats, Veena Sandhu and T.E. Narasimhan write: 'The world of kickback is murky and difficult to unravel .... In such a scenario, the magnitude of the country's kickback can only be speculated, at best estimated, but is impossible to accurately calculate'.

Political Corruption and Scams

It is a well-known fact that a large number of politicians not only in India but almost in all countries are corrupt. People never feel shocked when politicians' corruption is divulged. Honest politicians are a rare breed today. Corrupt politicians not only go scot-free, unharmed and unpunished but they manage to strut on the political stage as honourable leaders. Examples of politicians like Lal Bahadur Shastri and Sardar Vallabh Bhai Patel are rare who had very little bank balance at the time of death. In this land of ours, while a thief who commits theft for feeding his hungry children after remaining unemployed for a long time is promptly put behind the bars, those who plunder the country masquerade as honourable citizens with all the paraphernalia merely because they happen to be big-wigs in politics or are close to centres of power.

Recently, in its landmark judgement, the Supreme Court of India had attempted to correct an anomaly in the Representation of People Act when it held that there was no reason why elected representatives should be specially protected from disqualification pending appeal when they are convicted for offences specified in the Act.

In the last four decades or so, several scandals and financial irregularities, including paying of massive commissions, pay-offs and kickbacks, have been reported in our country. Mostly, it is the chief ministers, ministers, leaders holding important political positions, bureaucrats and big businessmen who are reported to be involved in these scams. But nothing tangible has been done in uncovering, tracing, apprehending, prosecuting and punishing the culprits on the plea of 'inadequate evidence'. We will point out here the most notorious scandals/scams that broke in India after independence (also see Table 1).

Table 1

Major Corruption Scams in India after Independence (1981–2018)

Year Scam	*Nature*	*Amount involved (in crores)*	*Persons involved*
1981 Pay-off	Garnering crores of rupees illegally	30	CM of Maharashtra
1987 HDW	A big commission was paid by the German submarine company	20	
1987 Bofors	Purchase of guns from a Swedish firm for the military	64	High-ranking politicians
1991 Telgi	Printing of fake stamp papers	43,000	Abdu Karim Telgi
1992 Securities	Manipulating banks and stock market	10,000	Harshad Mehta, stock market player
1994 Sugar import	Importing sugar on high prices	650	Union Food Minister
1995 JMM	Taking/giving money to exercise vote in parliament	2.8	PM, ministers, MPs and industrialists
1996 Hawala	Bribing for gaining favours	810	Top politicians of different parties and bureaucrats
1996 Fodder (Bihar)	Large-scale misappropriation and fraudulent transactions in dealing with public fund	950	CM, ministers, politicians, bureaucrats and mafia groups
1996 Urea	Paying crores of rupees in advance for urea to a Turkish company that was not supplied even in two years. A part of it was however supplied in September 1996 but was returned being sub-quality.	233	Sons and kins of former PM/central ministers and Directors of NFL

Cont'd...

...Cont'd

Year	*Scam*	*Nature*	*Amount involved (in crores)*	*Persons involved*
1996	Bank	Financial irregularities by banks between 1991 and 1995	2,358	Politicians, bureaucrats and bank officials
2001	Stock market	Swindling investors	1,50,000	Ketan Parekh, stock market player
2002	Taj heritage corridor	Construction of Taj corridor near Taj Mahal in Agra		CM/ministers of Uttar Pradesh
2002	Foodgrain (Uttar Pradesh)	Grain worth crores of rupees meant for poor was sold in open market	35,000	Politicians/bureaucrats of state
2005	Oil for food	Taking illegal payments from an international programme		Former Union Foreign Minister and his son
2006	IPO	Use of faked and benami demat accounts by financiers and stock market players to illegally reserve IPO shares	61	Rupalben Bansal of Indiabulls
2008	Cash for vote	Bribing MPs for winning confidence in Lok Sabha		UPA politicians
2009	Madhu Koda	Money laundering	4,000	CM of Jharkhand
2009	Satyam	Manipulation and falsification of company accounts	24,000	Chairman of company
2010	CWG	Overpriced deals were made		Chairman of organizing committee
2010	2G spectrum	Issuance of illegal licences for spectrum	1,76,000	Union Communication Minister and top bureaucrats of the ministry
2012	NRHM (Uttar Pradesh)	Siphoning off and massive booty from NRHM	10,000	Politicians and senior bureaucrats of the state
2012	Coalgate	Giving undue benefits to companies in allotting coal blocks	1,85,591	PMO, ministers and bureaucrats
2013	Railgate	Accepting bribe for promotion	10	Union Railway Minister and his kin and a Member, Railway Board
2013	Saradha Group chit fund	Running of fake schemes	20,000	T. Sudipta Sen and Associates
2013	Augusta Westland chopper deal	Purchase of helicopters for military	36,000	Christian Michel Rajiv Saxena
2016	Kingfisher Airlines	Loan from 17 PSB Banks	9,000	Vijay Mallya
2018	PNB Fraud	Fake LOU Issued	11,600	Nirav Modi and Mehul Choksi

Antulay Trust Pay-off Scam (1981): A.R Antulay, the then Chief Minister of Maharashtra, allegedly garnered ₹ 30 crore from businesses dependent on state resources.

HDW Submarine Scam (1987): The German submarine maker was black-listed after allegations that commissions worth ₹ 420 crore had been paid in the 1987 deal in India.

Bofors Scam (1987): It was a major corruption scam involving the then Prime Minister, Rajiv Gandhi and several others who were accused of receiving kickbacks from Bofors of Sweden for winning a bid to supply 155 mm field howitzer. The scale of the corruption was far worse than any that India had seen before and directly led to the defeat of Gandhi's ruling Indian National Congress party in the November 1989 general elections. The Swedish company paid ₹ 64 crore (US$12 million) in kickbacks to top politicians.

Telgi Scam (1991): One of the largest scams which was estimated at ₹ 43,000 crore in which fraudster Abdul Karim Telgi printed fake stamp papers and appointed 300 agents to sell them in bulk to banks and foreign investors, insurance companies, stock market players and other, earning about ₹ 200 crore.

Securities Scam (1992): Harshad Mehta manipulated banks and the stock market, pushing shares like ACC from ₹ 500 to ₹ 10,000. The stacked-up claims of the brokers were a staggering ₹ 10,000 crore.

Sugar Import Scam (1994): In this scam, the then Union Food Minister, was accused of importing sugar at high prices that resulted in a loss of ₹ 750 crore to the state exchequer.

JMM Scam (1995): It was a bribery scam that involved four MPs for JMM and three MPs for receiving ₹ 40 lakh each in July 1993 for exercising their vote to defeat the no-confidence motion in the Parliament against Narasimha Rao's government. A former PM, four union ministers, two CMs and two industrialists have also been charged with corruption and criminal conspiracy.

Hawala Scam (1996): This scam, estimated to be of the order of ₹ 810 crore, involved politicians, who allegedly received kickbacks totalling 18 million dollars from *hawala* brokers.

Fodder Scam (1996): This scam broke out in 1996 in the town of Chaibasa in Bihar when the animal husbandry department embezzled funds of around ₹ 950 crore meant to purchase cattle fodder, medicines and animal husbandry equipment in Bihar.

Urea Scam (1996): The scam came into light after a shortage of fertilizer in 1996 was reported, a clutch of businessmen in connivance with top officials of the National Fertilizer Limited, fleeced the government of ₹ 233 crore for the import of urea, which was never delivered.

Bank Scam (1996): The scam involved financial irregularities by public sector banks between 1991 and 1995 resulting in a loss of ₹ 2,358 crore. Loans were arbitrarily sanctioned to several parties owning *benami* companies in India and Singapore. Besides bank officials, several politicians and bureaucrats were also involved.

Stock Market Scam (2001): Stock market king, Ketan Parekh used UTI, Calcutta Stock Exchange and his own index K-10 to swindle investors. When the scam was unearthed, it was reported that he had wiped off ₹ 1.5 lakh crore of market capital.

Taj Heritage Corridor Scam (2002): It is an alleged scam wherein the then Chief Minister of Uttar Pradesh and a minister in her cabinet, were charged with corruption. The Taj Corridor Project was intended to upgrade tourist facilities near the Taj Mahal.

UP Foodgrain Scam (2002–10): Uttar Pradesh foodgrain scam, also dubbed as mother of all scams, took place between years 2002 and 2010. The grain worth ₹ 35,000 crore, meant to be distributed via PDS to the poor under several schemes, like Antyodaya Anna Yojana, Jawahar Rozgar Yojana and Midday Meal Scheme, was diverted to the open market. Some of it was traced at the Nepal and Bangladesh borders, as in 2010 security forces seized ₹ 1.17 crore worth of foodgrains like paddy and pulses being smuggled to Nepal, another ₹ 60.62 lakh worth of grains were confiscated on the Indo-Bangladesh border. The scam first was exposed in 2003, in Gonda district during the distribution of foodgrain meant for the Sampoorna Grameen Rozgar Yojana. After initially ordering an inquiry into the scam, the Chief Minister withdrew it. The Special Investigation Team (SIT), set up by the Mulayam Singh government in 2006, lodged over 5,000 FIRs. The latest of the scam series in India, initially referred as the 'UP rice scam' could be the biggest of them all, even outdistancing the 2G spectrum scam. The scam involves goofing up of rice worth ₹ 2,00,000 crore. It was a scam that stretched to almost seven years and 300 FIRs.

Oil for Food Scam (2005): In this scam some politicians were found to be involved in the international Oil-for-Food Programme. The Volcker Report, commissioned by the United Nations, named then Union Foreign Minister Natwar Singh and his son Jagat Singh as beneficiaries of illegal payments.

IPO Scam (2006): This was the first post-liberalization market-related scam estimated to be of the quantum of ₹ 61 crore. Benami and fake demat accounts were used by financiers and stock market players led by Rupalben Bansal of Indiabulls to illegally reserved IPO shares. Small investors became victims when those shares were sold on the first day itself making huge profits on the difference in the issue price and the listing price.

Cash for Vote Scam (2008): In this scandal, the governing coalition at the Centre, was alleged for bribing MPs in order to survive a confidence vote on 22 July 2008. The vote in the Lok Sabha arose after the Communist Party of India (Marxist)-led Left Front withdrew support from the government on the issue of Indo-US nuclear deal.

Madhu Koda Scam (2009): In this scam, the Enforcement Directorate charged Madhu Koda, Chief Minister of Jharkhand with money laundering estimated at ₹ 4,000 crore. The ED raided his hotels and companies in Mumbai and Kolkata and also discovered that he owned assets in Thailand, Indonesia, Singapore and Dubai. He allegedly also had coal mines worth ₹ 8.5 crore in Liberia. A one-time labourer, Koda had 1,800 bank accounts across the world.

Satyam Scam (2009): It was a corporate scandal where Chairman Ramalinga Raju of Satyam Computers confessed that the company's accounts had been falsified. The global corporate community was shocked and felt cheated itself when Raju resigned on 7 January 2009 and confessed that he had manipulated the accounts worth $1.47 billion.

CWG Scam (2010): Suresh Kalmadi, who was the chairman of the Organizing Committee of the Commonwealth Games, was the main accused. It consisted of a number of corrupt deals involving overstated contracts. For example, Kalmadi handed out a ₹ 141 crore contract to Swiss Timing for its timing equipment; the deal was inflated by ₹ 95 crore.

2G Spectrum Scam (2010): The illegal undercharging by government officials to various telecom companies during the allocation of 2G licences for cellphone subscriptions gave rise to the 2G spectrum scam. According to the CAG, the scam amounts to about ₹ 1,76,000 crore, whereas the CBI estimates it at ₹ 30,984 crore only. Politicians named as accused in the chargesheet filed by the CBI include A. Raja, then Union Communication Minister and M.K. Kanimozhi, Rajya Sabha member and daughter of former Chief Minister of Tamil Nadu Karunanidhi.

Uttar Pradesh NRHM Scam (2012): Under Mayawati's regime, this scam caused a loss of ₹ 10,000 crore to the state exchequer. Politicians and senior bureaucrats are alleged to have siphoned off a massive booty from the National Rural Health Mission (NHRM), a Central Government programme meant to improve health care services in rural areas. Several former ministers of Mayawati's Bahujan Samaj Party are being investigated by the CBI. The scam came into the light after two Chief Medical Officers (CMOs) were murdered in a broad daylight in Lucknow.

Coalgate (2012): It is one of the scams in which Prime Minister's office has been alleged to be involved. The CAG has accused the Centre of giving undue benefits to companies by distributing 155 coal blocks in an arbitrary manner instead of auctioning to the highest bidder during 2004–2009, causing a loss of ₹ 1,85,591 crore to the state exchequer.

Railgate (2013): Infamously known as Railgate, it involves then Railway Minister and his nephew for allegedly accepting a bribe of ₹ 90 lakh from a Railway Board member for promoting him as Member (Electricals).

Saradha Group Chit Fund Scam (2013): The Saradha Group Chit Fund scam caused a loss of ₹ 20,000 crore to the common people. The scam that involves running fake schemes has also led to many suicides across the state of West Bengal.

Augusta Westland Chopper Deal Scam (2013): Money laundering aspect of irregularities allegedly linked to the purchase of helicopters from Agusta Westland.

Vijay Mallya's Fraud, Criminal Conspiracy Regarding Unpaid Loans (2016): Loans amounting to ₹ 9,000 crore were given to erstwhile Kingfisher Airlines (which was grounded on 20 October 2012). A group of 17 Indian banks are trying to collect approximately ₹ 9,000 crore (US$1.3 billion) in loans which Mallya has allegedly routed to gain 100 per cent or a partial stake in about 40 companies across the world. Several agencies are investigating Mallya for charges including financial fraud and money laundering. Mallya owes an estimated ₹ 13,000 crore to different banks, if one takes into account the accrued interest on the principal loan amount. Assets worth ₹13,000 crore belonging to him had been seized.

PNB Fraud Scam (2018): Nirav Modi a diamantaire and others had allegedly fraudulently obtained Letters of Undertaking (LoUs) from the connivance with some bank officials of Punjab National Bank. The fraud is pegged at over $2 billion. An LoU is a guarantee given by an issuing bank to Indian banks that have branches abroad for granting a short-term credit to the applicant. Modi and others are being probed under various criminal laws after the fraud came to light in January 2018.

Since independence, there has been no dearth of political corruption in India. In every decade till today, scams and scandals have dolled the Indian political scenario.

Judicial Corruption

The judiciary is the most important institution visualized by the makers of our Constitution to guarantee clean and good governance. One of the three pillars of governance – executive, legislature and judiciary – it performs the crucial role of interpreting the law. This empowers it to interpret the spirit of the Constitution and articulate the basic framework of legislation. It is therefore obvious that if the judiciary has to retain its credibility and efficacy by preserving its own institutional integrity, it must ensure that only persons with impeccable integrity and competence are elevated to the bench right from the level of lower judiciary.

The issue of judicial corruption in India has become a live issue, especially after 2005, when the RTI Act was passed. The scams of 2010 which inter alia included the allegations of corruption against the former Chief Justice K.G. Balakrishnan have also added a sense of urgency and wide publicity to the issue. Even the judges themselves have been criticizing the prevalence of corruption in the judiciary recently. Apparently, there seems to be much soul-searching going on in the higher judiciary. All this may reflect the growing concern amongst citizens across the country about the lack of ethics at all levels of our public life today.

A striking aspect of our judicial system is the enormous delay in arriving at decisions, often leading to denial of justice. The number of pending cases is about 30 million and at the present rate of disposal, even if courts were not to take on any new cases, it would take 300 years to wrap up the existing ones (Vittal, 2012:148).

For the judiciary to check corruption effectively, as mentioned above, the people managing it must be honest and independent-minded and also render justice without fear or fervour. Besides, the disposal of cases within a specified time would help enhance their productivity. Lastly, the infrastructure of the judiciary should be strengthened.

Corruption in Corporate Sector

The corporate sector is an important link in the vicious cycle of corruption comprising *neta-babu-lala-jhola-dada* (Vittal, 2012: 190). India has a long tradition of entrepreneurship. The link between government and business also has a long history everywhere in the world. In any system of governance, business enterprises and their owners play a vital role. The post-liberalization period, due to market-based competition, was visualized as an era of reduced corruption. But, unfortunately, this did not happen in India; instead corruption has mutated into more vicious forms, leading to crony capitalism.

The scams of recent years again brought into sharp focus the corporate sector's role in governance. If the corporate sector is corrupt, it can corrupt other sectors easily because of its financial clout. Good corporate governance has, therefore, become a necessity. And that depends on the corporate leadership's ability. Not only there should be transparency in every decision-making operation but also accountability on the decision taken, that in turn means protection of the interests of both the stakeholders and shareholders.

To realize the goal of maintaining a clean corporate sector, regulators are extremely important. They must be fair and independent. According to Vittal (2012: 195), corporate cleanliness can be maintained by following:

1. legal requirements that make it mandatory to observe certain norms, procedures, systems;
2. alert shareholders and media which can highlight malpractices; and
3. an independent judiciary that can intervene when things go beyond control.

Let us hope that with our experience of three decades of liberalization and over four decades of permit-licence raj, the corporate sector and the government will be able to work out pragmatic and clean models for the future.

Causes of Corruption

Several factors have been pointed out as causes of corruption or public dishonesty. *First* is the emergence of political elite who believe in interest-oriented rather than nation-oriented programmes and policies. In fact, the post-British *Raj* (rule) has been described as the '*raj* of ministers and bureaucrats'. The political elite in the first two decades after independence were honest, dedicated and nation-oriented to the extent that they always worked for the country's progress. Later on, particularly after the fourth general elections in 1967, such persons came to hold political power both at the Centre and in the states who worked only on the basis of some vested interest, say, interest of self, family, caste, region, party, and so forth. Their policies and programmes incidentally might have been nation-oriented, but essentially they were 'interest-based'. They encouraged the bureaucrats too to follow suit. A majority of bureaucrats in our country are 'ritualists' and remain concerned more with perks and privileges than with 'development-oriented' policies for the society. The politicians and bureaucrats thus started using their power and position for illegal benefits. The emergence of the new business leaders who wanted profits even by sharing them with the people in power became equally responsible for the mushroom growth of corrupt practices among the public servants. Corruption also emerges from the power of the government officials of taking decisions, say, issuing licences, assessing income tax, giving extensions and so on. It is not the rules but the interpretation of the rules which enables officers to receive kickbacks and pocket the bribe. Many officers pay thousands and lakhs of rupees to get themselves posted in particular places only because those places enable them to earn thousands and lakhs of rupees every month as illegal gratification. The *second* cause is the economic policy of the government. Most of the recent scandals have been in areas where either purchase policies or prices are controlled by the government. Sugar, fertilizers, oil, military weapons, electronic equipment, spectrum, etc. are some examples. One NRI businessman some years ago claimed in the court that he had to pay Chandraswami, with verbal assurance from a former Prime Minister, to get a contract for selling pulp to India. Similar kickbacks were paid in Bofors, telecom and many other scams. The real issue is freeing the economy from the clutches of misguided government regulations. But a slap-dash approach to privatization will also not do. Clear and transparent rules are needed. Arbitrary decision-making by certain individuals (like minister, or director-general or secretary) is an invitation to corruption. The Enron project in Maharashtra ran into trouble because the negotiations and the terms of the deal were shrouded in secrecy. *Third*, corruption is caused by scarcity. When things required are in short supply, people in power demand 'consideration' to ensure their regular supply or increase their cost. This happens whenever there is high demand but low supply of commodity of daily use like cement, sugar, oil, etc. *Fourth*, corruption is caused as well as increased because of the change in the value system and ethical qualities of men who administer. The old ideals of morality, service, honesty and sacrifice are regarded as an achronistic, and accepting 'favours' as a 'need' than a folly or an aberrant behaviour. *Fifth*, corruption can be traced to ineffective administrative organization. Lack of vigilance, enormous powers to the ministerial staff, unaccountability, defective information system, etc. give scope to officials not only to be corrupt but remain unaffected even after following corrupt practices.

Causes of corruption can also be categorized as economic, social, political, legislative and judicial. The *economic* causes include: craze for higher living standards, inflation, licence system, profiteering tendencies, and lack of morality in business community. The *social* causes include: materialistic outlook of life, erosion in social values, illiteracy, acquisitive cultural traits, feudalistic hangover, peoples' toleration, public indifference, and exploitative social structure. The *political* causes include: political patronage, ineffective political leadership, political apathy, political immorality, election funding, nexus with politicians, and political sub-culture. The *legislative* factors are: inadequate legislation, loopholes in law, and callousness in implementation of laws. The *judicial* causes include: expensive judicial system, judicial indifference, lack of commitment among judges, and frequent acquittals of the accused on technical grounds.

Thus, the most important factor responsible for corruption is the nature of human being. People in general have a great thirst for luxuries and comforts and as a result of which they get themselves involved in all unscrupulous activities that result in monetary or material benefit. Besides moral and spiritual values are not given utmost importance in educational system, which is highly responsible for the deterioration of society. At the same time, the punishments imposed on the criminals are inadequate.

Factors Responsible for Corruption

1. The most important factor is the nature of the human being. People in general, have a great thirst for luxuries and comforts, as a result of which they get themselves involved in all unscrupulous activities that result in monetary or material benefits.
2. Moral and spiritual values are not given utmost importance in the educational system, which is highly responsible for the deterioration of the society.
3. The salary paid to employees is very less and as a result of which they are forced to earn money by illegal ways.
4. The punishments imposed on the criminals are inadequate.
5. Political leaders have spoiled the society completely. They lead a luxurious life and do not even care about the society.
6. People of India are not awakened and enlightened. They fear to raise their voice against anti-social elements prevailing in the society.
7. Corruption starts at the higher levels and it carries its way to the lowest levels. The common man finds it difficult to bypass and get things done.

Level/Spread of Corruption in India

The most corrupted fields in India are:

Government officials: Government officials are the most corrupted in India. Without giving bribe, it is very difficult to get the work done in a government office. Hence, the work efficiency also gets corrupted and altered as per the interests of the people in power.

Police: The police system is also corrupted in India. Even to file an FIR and to get a copy of it, people need some source or to give bribe to the police.

Politicians: The politicians and their relatives are mostly involved in corruption by using the influence of party source. Corruption remains the central issue of Indian politics.

Judiciary: The judiciary system of India is badly involved in corruption to give favoured judgment and delaying the delivery of judgment.

Media: Today, media is also engaged in corruption. Influencing the voters and arising false sentiment in return for money is the main business of the media.

NGOs: The last but not the least, the NGOs are involved in corruption. In the back of tax relief rule, they encourage the fostering of corruption.

Impact of Corruption

Corruption affects society in various ways. It hinders economic development of the country, creates violence and lawlessness in the society making the life of common man miserable. It also perpetuates inequalities, deepens poverty, causes human suffering, dilutes the fight against terrorism and organized crime, and tarnishes India's image globally. The impact of corruption is multifold, encompassing political, economic, social, environmental and issues of national security.

Political: The political corruption is manifested in weakened public trust in political institutions, reduced political participation, perversion of the electoral process, and loss of legitimacy of the democratic institution and democracy itself.

Economic: Corruption reduces economic efficiency by increasing the cost of public transactions, acting as an additional tax on business thereby reducing foreign direct investment, reducing genuine business competition. There is a debate about the relationship between corruption and growth. One the one hand, there is the orthodox 'sand in the wheels' view, which says bribes misallocate resources, lowering investment and growth. The other is the 'greasing the wheels' school, which suggests graft can help growth.

Social: The effect of corruption on the social fabric of society is perhaps the most alarming damage of all. It undermines people's trust in the political system, its institutions and leadership. Corruption distorts the value systems. This results in a disillusioned public, a weak civil society, which attracts unscrupulous leaders to political life. Eventually, there is a risk that demanding and paying bribes could become the norm.

Environmental: Environmental degradation is an indirect but serious consequence of corrupt systems. Environmentally devastating projects are given preference in funding because they are easy targets for syphoning off public money into private pockets.

Issues of national security: Corruption within security agencies can lead to a threat to national security, through the distortion of procurement, recruitment of incompetent persons, providing an easy route for smuggling of weapons and terrorist elements into the country and money laundering.

Globally, there is a general consensus amongst most academics and policymakers that the debilitating effects of corruption permeate through all aspects of public life. Several studies have shown that corruption not only stifles growth, it also perpetuates inequalities, deepens poverty, causes human sufferings, dilutes the fight against terrorism and organized crime, and tarnishes India's image globally.

While talking of corruption, should we be concerned only with big financial deals and scams, or types of corruption called political, bureaucratic, industrial, institutional, etc. or we should also be concerned with those corruption cases which remain invisible but pervade our daily life and corrode the very fibre of our moral fabric. Some people feel that we should filter corruption into various grades. While according to one view, 'amount' should be the criterion of corrupt act, according to other, 'need' should be the focus. A few rupees spent to gain a major benefit is not worth bothering about. Yet another view is that 'price' paid for the required 'service' is in order. Corruption comes in only when the price is paid but for which no service has been done. But what about adulteration in food or spurious drugs sold to us and things like that? Generally, such cases in our daily life are not regarded as 'corruption'. Is cheating in an examination a type of corruption? Is increasing marks in an answer-book by an examiner on getting 'recommendation' from a colleague or a friend or a kin (but not by accepting money) corruption? In their defence, examiners say that they only 'oblige' and how can 'obligation' be corruption? Many clerks go to the offices and sign the attendance registers but are never found on their seats. They become 'available' only when they are offered money for the file they move. This is corruption.

Some people say that while corruption is found even in most developed countries like the United States, Japan, England, France, Canada and Germany, why should we unnecessarily get perturbed about it in India? These people forget that nature of corruption in the developed countries is different from the one we find in our own country. Corruption in these countries exists only among the highest echelons of business giants, while in India we have to pay for the railway reservation, for getting admission not only in a professional institution but even for a child in a good primary school, for driving the two-wheeler without a helmet, for getting the arrear bill passed, for getting the tax refund, and so on. Thus, while in other countries, money is paid for getting illegal things, in India it is paid for getting legal and authorized things. And, this is really disturbing that the corruption is now accepted as a normal course of interaction between the citizen and the public official. All these affect the day-to-day living of the common man. As such, we have to be concerned with such corrupt acts too.

We should not forget that corruption has affected our society in several ways: (a) It has retarded economic development of the country. (b) It has created violence and lawlessness in the society since the corrupt man has the money power to influence the executors of law to serve him. (c) It has given rise to casteism, linguism and communalism. (d) It has diminished morality and destroyed the individual character. (e) It has heightened inefficiency, nepotism, and lethargy and has created indiscipline in all fields of administration, making the life of a common man miserable. (f) It has reduced the credibility of the officials in the eyes of the masses. (g) It has increased black money in the country. (h) It has led to adulteration of eatables, spurious drugs and shortage of many consumer items. (i) It has destabilized the governments both at the centre and in the states. (j) Corruption distorts markets and the allocation of resources because it reduces the ability of the government to impose necessary regulatory controls and inspection to correct for market failures. We have, therefore, to focus on both types of visible and hidden corruption cases which stir up our conscience.

Measures Taken to Contain Corruption

The framework for fighting corruption in India has largely been based on two approaches. These are the promulgation if anti-corruption laws and vesting police and other similar law-enforcement institutions with the powers to investigate crimes relating to corruption more efficiently and effectively.

There are some specific measures to control increasing corruption. These are as follows:

1. The Right to Information (RTI) Act gives one all the required information about the government, such as what the government is doing with our tax payments. Under this act, one has the right to ask the government about any problem which one faces. There is a public information officer (PIO) appointed in every government department, who is responsible for collecting information wanted by the citizens and providing them with the relevant information on payment of a nominal fee to the PIO. If the PIO refuses to accept the application or if the applicant does not receive the required information on time then the applicant can make a complaint to the respective information commission, which has the power to impose a penalty up to ₹ 25,000 on the errant PIO. A study of CMS-ICS 2018 found that less than 2 per cent of the respondents had used RTI to seek information. Those used RTI, i.e. sought information, asked from public services namely, Education, Land Registration, Municipal Corporation or Block office and Revenue Office. Among states, most of the RTI applicants came from Delhi, Rajasthan and Telangana states. Motivating citizens to use RTI to bring transparency and accountability in public services should be taken up more vigorously.
2. Another potent check on corruption is the Central Vigilance Commission (CVC). It was set up by the government to advise and guide central government agencies in the areas of vigilance. If there are any cases of corruption or any complaints thereof, then that can be reported to the CVC. CVC also shoulders the responsibility of creating more awareness among people regarding the consequences of giving and taking of bribes and corruption.
3. Establishment of special courts for speedy justice can be a huge positive aspect. Much time should not elapse between the registration of a case and the delivery of judgment.

4. Strong and stringent laws need to be enacted, which gives no room for the guilty to escape. To the extent possible, there is a need to cut back on the multiplicity of unnecessary and complex laws to ensure a fair, equitable and just system. These should then be administered without fear or favour.
5. In many cases, the employees opt for corrupt means out of compulsion and not by choice. Some people are of the opinion that the wages paid are insufficient to feed their families. If they are paid better, they would not be forced to accept a bribe.

Prevention of Corruption Act, 1988

Among the anti-corruption laws in India, the Prevention of Corruption Act, 1988 is the most important. It consolidated the provisions of the Prevention of Corruption Act, 1947, some sections of the Indian Penal Code, the Criminal Procedure Code, and the Criminal Law Act, 1952. The sole idea was to bring all relevant provisions in single Act. Finding that bribery and corruption among public servants had considerably increased during and after the Second World War and many unscrupulous officers had amassed huge wealth, and the existing provisions of the IPC and the CrPC were inadequate to tackle this problem, the Prevention of Corruption Act, 1947 was passed. In the Criminal Procedure Code, offences relating to public servants are not cognizable, but the 1947 Act made it obligatory for the court to make certain presumptions of guilt against the accused. The 1947 Act shifted the burden of proof from the prosecution to the accused. The investigation against the accused was to be made by an officer not below the rank of Deputy Superintendent of Police. The 1947 Act declared such corrupt acts as offences as taking bribe, misappropriation, obtaining a pecuniary advantage, possessing assets disproportionate to income, and abusing official position. However, the authority for prosecution was vested only in the departmental authorities and not in the Central Bureau of Investigation.

The 1988 Act enlarged the scope of the term 'public servant' and included a large number of employees within its ambit. Besides the employees of the central government and the union territories, the employees of public undertakings, nationalized banks, office bearers of cooperative societies of the central and the state governments receiving financial aid, employees of the University Grants Commission (UGC), vice-chancellors, professors and scientists in institutions receiving financial aid from the central or state governments or even from the local authorities have all been declared as public servants. However, the MPs and MLAs, even though performing 'public duties', have been kept out of the ambit of the Act. The Act covers all the 'corrupt' acts as covered by the 1947 Act (bribe, misappropriation, obtaining pecuniary advantage, possessing assets disproportionate to income, etc.). The Act extends to whole of India except Jammu & Kashmir and applies to all Indian citizens, whether living in the country or outside it.

If the offence against the public servant is proved in the court, it is punishable with imprisonment of not less than six months but extending to a maximum period of five years. Six months imprisonment is thus mandatory and the courts have no discretion in this regard. If public servant is found committing offence habitually, he is to be punished with imprisonment of not less than two years but not more than seven years, and along with a fine.

Prevention of Money Laundering Act, 2002

The Prevention of Money Laundering Act, 2002 was enacted in January 2003. The Act along with the rules framed thereunder have come into force with effect from 1 July 2005. The Act defines offence of money laundering as whosoever directly or indirectly attempts to indulge or knowingly assists or knowingly is a party or is actually involved in any process or activity connected with the proceeds of crime and projecting it as untainted property, shall be guilty of offence of money laundering. It prescribes obligation on banking companies, financial institutions and intermediaries for verification and maintenance of records of the identity of all its clients and also of all transactions and for furnishing information of such transactions in prescribed form to the Financial Intelligence Unit-India (FIU-IND). It also empowers the Director of FIU-IND to impose fine on banking company, financial institution or intermediary if they or any of its officers fails to comply with the provisions of the Act as indicated above.

The Act empowers certain officers of the Directorate of Enforcement to carry out investigations in cases involving offence of money laundering and also to attach the property involved in money laundering. The Act envisages setting up of an adjudicating authority to exercise jurisdiction, power and authority conferred by it essentially to confirm attachment or order confiscation of attached properties. It also envisages setting up of an appellate tribunal to hear appeals against the order of the adjudicating authority and the authorities like Director, FIU-IND.

The Act envisages designation of one or more courts of sessions as special court(s) to try the offences punishable under the Act and offences with which the accused may, under the Code of Criminal Procedure, 1973, be charged at the same trial. The Act also allows Central Government to enter into an agreement with government of any country outside India for enforcing the provisions of the Act, exchange of information for the prevention of any offence under the Act or under the corresponding law in force in that country or investigation of cases relating to any offence under the Act.

Besides, the Right to Information Act, 2005 also contains some provisions which can be used for containing corruption. Among its major objectives are containing corruption, making public servants accountable by empowering citizens to get information and improving transparency.

The Lokpal and Lokayuktas Act, 2013

The Lokpal and Lokayuktas Act, 2013, commonly known as the Lokpal Act, is an anti-corruption act, which 'seeks to provide for the establishment of the institution of Lokpal to inquire into allegations of corruption against certain public functionaries and for matters connecting them'. The Lokpal will have the power of superintendence and direction over any investigation agency including CBI for cases referred to them by the ombudsman.

Salient Features

The Act allows setting up of anti-corruption ombudsman called Lokpal at the centre and Lokayukta at the state level. The Lokpal will consist of a chairperson and a maximum of eight members. The chairperson can be current or former judges of the Supreme Court or Chief Justices of High Courts. Members should have at least 25 years of experience in matters related to anti-corruption policy, vigilance, public administration. finance, law and management. The Lokpal will cover all categories of public servants, including the Prime Minister. But the armed forces do not come under the ambit of Lokpal. The Act also incorporates provisions for attachment and confiscation of property acquired by corrupt means, even while the prosecution is pending. The states will have to institute Lokayukta within one year of the commencement of the Act.

A five-member selection panel comprising the Prime Minister, the Lok Sabha Speaker, the Leader of the Opposition, the Chief Justice of India and an eminent jurist nominated by the President, select the Lokpal.

Role of Lokpal and Lokayukta

1. Lokpal is a multi-member body and an active politician. A person convicted of any offence involving moral turpitude cannot become a member of Lokpal.
2. Similarly, every state shall establish a Lokayukta by a State Act, if it is not established before passing this Act.
3. Lokpal will constitute an inquiry wing to conduct the preliminary inquiry into any offence alleged to have been committed by a public servant punishable under the Prevention of Corruption Act, 1988. If the complaint is found to be true, the Lokpal can ask the government to take disciplinary action against the public servant and also file a case in a special court to be set up by the centre.
4. Jurisdiction of Lokpal includes Prime Minister, all union ministers, MPs, all officers, etc.
5. Powers of Lokpal includes superintendence over CBI, confiscation of assets or other benefits which have arisen by means of corruption, its inquiry wing has powers of a civil court, etc.
6. Independence of Lokpal ensures that the institution is not prone to misuse of powers.

Some of the provisions of this Act also defeat its purpose. These provisions are:

1. This Act does not provide protection to whistleblowers who complaints to Lokpal or Lokayukta.
2. Although this Act covers all ministers including PM, some crucial institutions of democracy like the judiciary, media and NGOs are left out of this Act.
3. Since states have been given complete freedom to decide on appointment, composition and powers of Lokayukta, there are chances that Lokayukta may remain weak institution in some states.
4. Lokpal will supervise CBI only on cases referred to it by Lokpal. However, CBI will continue to face the issue of independence on other cases/issues.

The Lokpal and Lokayukta Act, 2013 Amended to Include NGOs

The Lokpal and Lokayukta Act 2013 (LLA, 2013) has been amended to include senior management personnel working with NGOs to disclose their assets and liabilities if their NGO receive foreign donations and funds from the Union Government. Any NGO receiving more than ₹ 10 lakh annually from foreign sources under FCRA 2010 will now be covered under the amended law. The law will apply to the functionaries and officers of the NGOs. The officers and functionaries of NGOs shall have to file annual returns declaring their assets and other prescribed particulars every year under LLA. Some of the main provisions of the amended Lokpal and Lokayukta Bill are:

Lokayukta: Each state should set up Lokayukta by law within 365 days. But the states will have the freedom to determine the nature and type of Lokayukta.

Penalty: Public servants can face imprisonment up to 7 years. While criminal misconduct and habitually abetting corruption can attract jail term up to 10 years.

Jurisdiction: The prime minister, ministers, current and former legislators, government employees, employees of firms funded or controlled by Centre, societies, and trusts that collect public money, receive funds from foreign sources come under the purview of the anti-corruption law. However, bodies creating endowments for or performing religious or charitable functions have been excluded.

Central Vigilance Commission

A Committee on Prevention of Corruption was appointed by the Government of India in 1960 under the chairmanship of K. Santhanam. This committee gave its report in 1962. The recommendations pertained to various aspects of corruption. It was on the basis of the recommendations of this committee that the Central Vigilance Commission (CVC) was set up in

1964 by the government to advise and guide Central Government agencies in the areas of vigilance. If there are any cases of corruption or any complaints thereof, then that can be reported to the CVC. CVC also shoulders the responsibility of creating more awareness among people regarding the consequences of giving and taking of bribes and corruption. The CVC is a non-statutory body whose jurisdiction and functions can be amended not by the parliament but by a government order. It deals with cases of corruption against the gazetted officers of central government, union territories, officers of PSUs, and nationalized banks. It is independent of government and works as an autonomous body like the Union Public Service Commission. Its role is merely advisory. It is a one-man commission headed by the Central Vigilance Commissioner, assisted by a Secretary, five Branch Officers and eleven Commissioners for Departmental Inquiries (CDIs).

The main functions of the CVC are: (a) to undertake an inquiry into any complaint of corruption against a public servant; (b) to advise the disciplinary authority about the type of proceedings to be initiated against accused person involved in corruption; (c) to direct the CBI to register a regular case; and (d) to exercise general check and supervision over the vigilance and anti-corruption work in ministries/departments/banks/public undertakings. The CVC has also taken certain proactive actions recently, such as advising all central government departments on quicker disposal of pending corruption cases. The CVC has an online complaint management system where individuals can register complaints in this regard and has an online whistleblower complaint mechanism available on its website.

Combatting Corruption

There are many myths about corruption which have to be exploded if we really want to combat it. Some of these are: corruption has become a way of life and nothing can be done about it; or that corruption is a post-independence phenomenon and it is the result of giving too much freedom and licence to the people in democracy; or that the poor people of underdeveloped countries are generally dishonest and untrustworthy by nature and easily tempted, while people of the developed countries are less prone to corruption; or that corruption exists only at the lower and the subordinate levels; or that corruption is found more among the illiterate than the educated people; or that corruption spreads mainly because of politicians. All these fallacies are too crude and we have to guard against them while planning measures to contain corruption.

Some methods have been suggested for reducing corruption. These are: *First*, we have to focus on law, procedure and administration. Laws and rules pertaining to the organization and behaviour of persons in specific situations with specific status are essential. 'Bad' laws/rules have to be changed or repealed. If the law/rule is too harsh, complicated, and ambiguous, it leads to corruption. The multiplicity and complexity of laws make compliance, deterrence, and effective enforcement difficult and, in many cases, impossible. Laws should not be such that they leave too much scope for discretion.

Discretion will have to be commensurate with the status of the officer and the type of the role assigned to him. 'Administrative' factors include both structural and functional aspects. How is an organization structured will determine the lacunae for corruption. 'Functioning' refers to the 'ongoing' process of working which refers both to the quantity and the quality of work, supervision, magnitude of lapses permitted, and so on. *Second,* artificial shortages and scarcities which facilitate illegal gratification have to be controlled. *Third,* vigilance should be increased. It is a myth that vigilance hampers efficiency; on the contrary, it improves it. Suspect officials of doubtful integrity should be kept away from sensitive posts. Surprise checks should be carried out at vulnerable points of corruption. *Fourth,* liberalization policy should be introduced very cautiously. Eventually, liberalization and free market may reduce corruption but at present 'liberal sanctions' are granted in return for a 'consideration'. *Fifth,* expenses in elections have to be strictly controlled. *Sixth,* cooperation of people has to be obtained for successfully containing corruption. We will elaborate the last two measures.

Why are cases of corruption not reported by the people to the police? It is because they are afraid (that the corrupt will harm them), indifferent (that it is not their duty to reform the society) and pessimists (that the corrupt are influential and powerful people and no action will be taken against them). Yet, there are people who do try to bring corrupt cases to the notice of the concerned authorities. These are the people who have a feeling of uneasiness, who have a sense of guilt and who get comfort of mind for doing something good for the community. Corruption is a monster which can be vanquished only by the collective efforts of the people. If they make sure that the dishonest politicians do not get elected to legislatures, half the battle is won. But the big question is: will it ever happen?

In a democratic country like India, will people ever realize that they have to play a crucial role in combatting evils like corruption? In fact, much of the corruption exists because of people's tolerance or complete lack of public outcry against it, as well as the absence of a strong public forum to oppose it. While many intellectual, educated, well-informed and articulate citizens remain worried about this monstrous problem in the country, they fail to channelize their resentment into strong public opinion against it. A concerted effort by the responsible and enlightened citizens can surely make a serious dent in the corruption level. Even our university youths can take up such society-oriented goals and organize movements for curbing the evil.

Yet other effective method of containing corruption could be to introduce method which will enable political parties to secure electoral funds in a bonafide manner, or the central government may finance elections through an election fund. This system is being followed in Germany, Norway and Sweden and some advanced countries of Europe. The political parties may be funded by the state in accordance with the votes polled by them in the previous general elections. The money may be fixed per vote, say two rupees per vote or so on. The idea of state funding of elections has also been discussed in our parliament more than once in recent years. In view of our huge annual budget, it would hardly be 1–2 per cent of the total budget outlay. If the government thinks that even this paltry sum cannot be set aside, an election cess, like education cess, on the voters may be imposed. This state funding of elections will no doubt reduce corruption to a large extent. State funding of elections will not only eliminate contributions from corrupt businessmen and interest groups but will also contribute to free and fair elections, drawing men of integrity in assemblies, equalizing the amount spent by various political parties, and so forth.

Besides the above measures, appointing Lokpal to look into the charges of corruption at the highest echelons of power, could prove to be an effective measure in containing corruption. At present, Lokayuktas in most states have been rendered impotent because of the numerous disabilities. Learning from their experiences, the powers of the Lokpal should be widened. His recommendations should have a statutory force.

The one thing that needs to be ensured is proper, impartial, and unbiased use of various anti-social regulations to take strong, deterrent, and timely legal action against the offenders, irrespective of their political influences or money power. Firm and strong steps are needed to curb the menace and an atmosphere has to created where the good, patriotic, intellectuals come forward to serve the country with pride, virtue, and honesty for the welfare of the people of India. So long corruption fails to attract legal, moral and social censures, there is no hope of eliminating or even reducing it. It may not be possible to root out corruption completely at all levels but it is certainly possible to roll it down or to contain it within the tolerable limits. Corruption is a cancer which every Indian must strive to obliterate. Honest and dedicated persons in public life known for their honesty and integrity, reduced government control in the economy, popularly called liberalization policy, and control over electoral expenses could be three most important prescriptions for corruption. People have tolerated the corrupt persons for long. It is now time that containing corruption is taken seriously by the dedicated political rulers.

The finding of the survey, CMS-India Corruption Study 2017, conducted by New Delhi based think tank Centre for Media Studies (CMS), which compares corruption in public services between 2005 and 2016, reinforces that it has made a dent in graft with its various anti-corruption initiatives. According to the report, around one-third of the households surveyed experienced corruption in public services at least once in 2016 compared to 53 per cent of households in 2005. While 73 per cent of households perceived an increase in corruption level in public services in 2005, only 43 per cent reported an increase in 2016. The report also says that the estimated total amount paid as bribes went down from ₹ 20,500 crore in 2005 to ₹ 6,350 crore in 2016. The report covers over 3,000 households in rural and urban areas across 20 states including Andhra Pradesh, Assam, Bihar, Chhattisgarh, Delhi, Gujarat, UP and Rajasthan.

12th Report of the CMS (Centre for Media Studies) for the year 2018 mentions that – [General Perception about Corruption in Public Service] – while 38 per cent of the households across India feel that the level of corruption has increased, while another 37 per cent of households feel that the level of corruption in public services has remained the same as before.

Suggestions to Deal with Corruption

To fight corruption, the following steps can be taken:

1. *Strict law/anti-corruption court*: Though there is anti-corruption bureau functioning in India, the absence of a stricter anti-corruption law made it ineffective. A strict law and enforced implementation of it by the special anti-corruption court can keep a check on it.
2. *Appointment process*: The appointment process of bureaucrats and ministers should include checking all the past records and efficiency basis and not by lobbying or by influence. The appointment of a corrupt official on the post of anti-corruption bureau head cannot solve the problem. So the appointment process should be very clean and impartial.
3. *Control on capitalist*: The government should keep control of the capitalists and industrialist. A close watch should be kept on them to control the undue advantage taken by them in the name of free marketing.
4. *Controlled democracy*: There should be controlled democracy with a limited number of the political party. Limitation on wealth accumulation and limitation on high income should be there. It will bring down the gap of inequality and corruption.
5. *Adoption of a code of conduct and ethics:* Not only for civil servants but also for all public functionaries, media, political parties, professionals, and the corporate sector based on constitutional principles and moral values.
6. *Setting up of strict laws* and along with them, strict enforcement of these laws will help in fighting corruption. Exposing corruption can be difficult. Appointing internal agencies to keep an eye on corruption may simply lead to more opportunities for graft. Often, citizen-led groups are formed to keep an eye on specific industries or government processes. These are called watchdog groups, and they rely on independent, generally non-profit charters to preserve a reputation of integrity.
7. *Investigating agencies:* There are bodies like CBI (Central Bureau of Investigation) and CVC (Central Vigilance Commission) to look into cases of high officials getting involved in corruption. There should be no control of the government on these bodies and they should act independently to bring in effective results.
8. *Encouraging professional skills:* Research indicates that India can control corruption by training its civil servants to a more professional level with skills in auditing, accountancy, and legal matters. If this step would have been taken at the time of liberalization, the scenario could have been much different from oversight and scrutiny from within the administration would have increased. Moreover, there would have been

a greater understanding and respect for administrative procedures, thereby reducing corruption and increasing development in India.

9. *Anti-social regulations:* The one thing that needs to be ensured is proper, impartial, and unbiased use of various anti-social regulations to take strong, deterrent, and timely legal action against the offenders, irrespective of their political influences or money power. Firm and strong steps are needed to curb the menace and an atmosphere has to be created where the good, patriotic, intellectuals come forward to serve the country with pride, virtue, and honesty for the welfare of the people of India.
10. *Bureaucracy:* Bureaucracy, which is the backbone of good governance, should be made more citizen-friendly, accountable, ethical and transparent.
11. *Citizen activism and empowering:* Apart from the government action to eliminate corruption from public services, citizens too have a major role to play individually or in group. Citizen activism expects that on coming across any incidence of corrupt practices in public services, the citizen should inform the concerned public complaint officer or grievance redressal officer about the unfair practices in the public service. Also, as a citizen of the country, from time to time, citizens may raise their voice against corrupt practices in public services and the desired changes at policy level to plug source(s) of corruption in public services; bring more transparency and accountability in public services.

A few more measures can be suggested to eradicate corruption from the society. These are: (a) political commitment; (b) administrative accountability; (c) procedural simplification; and (d) civil society activism.

Conclusion

The biggest hurdle in the prevention of corruption is the lack of public awareness. Corruption is a heinous crime as compared to that of traditional crimes. Corruption directly attacks the national economy, affecting the development of the country. It is necessary to be curbed and removed by adopting the proper legal system. At present, there is no law to deal with corruption in the private and corporate sector. To prevent corruption in the Indian society to a remarkable extent, a strong political will, effective anti-corruption laws with effective anticorruption agencies, effective adjudication, effective administration, good governance and strong public support are essentially and immediately required to be implemented and followed. Awareness among people will bring out the change in the society.

Corruption is an intractable problem; it is like diabetes, which can only be controlled but not totally eliminated. It may not be possible to root out corruption completely at all levels but it is possible to contain it within tolerable limits.

References

Abbulraheem, 'Corruption in India: An Overview – Causes, Consequences and Remedial Measures', *Social Action*, Vol. 59, October–December 2009.

Choudhry, P.C., 'Corruption', *Seminar*, No. 421, September, 1994.

Clarke, Machael (ed.), *Corruption: Causes and Consequences*, Pinter, London, 1983.

Douglas, Jack and Johnson, J., *Official Deviance*, Lippincott Co., Philadelphia, 1971.

Gupta, K.N., *Corruption in India*, Anmol Publications Pvt. Ltd., New Delhi, 2001.

Hallaya, M., *Corruption in India*, 1948 (quoted by P.C. Choudhry in *Seminar*, No. 421, September, 1994).

Klitgaard, R. *Controlling Corruption*, University of California Press, Berkeley, 1988.

Kohli, Suresh, *Corruption in India*, 1975 (quoted by P.C. Choudhry in *Seminar*, No. 421 September, 1994).

Kumar, C. Raj, *Corruption and Human Rights in India*, Oxford University Press, New Delhi, 2011.

Levine, Victor T. et al., *Political Corruption: The Ghana Case*, Transaction Publishers, New Brunswick, New Jersey, 1957.

Majumdar, K.C., *Ancient India*, Motilal Banarasidass, New Delhi, 1960.

Malhotra, K.L., *Facets of Vigilance*, Malhotra Publications, Delhi, 1988 and 1992.

Mathur, K.M., 'Corruption in Administration', Working Paper for DIG Police Seminar held at Internal Security Academy, Mount Abu, from 12–17 October 1992.

Monteiro, J.B., *Corruption*, Manaktalas, Bombay, 1966.

Myint, U., 'Corruption: Causes, Consequences and Cures', *Asia-Pacific Development Journal*, Vol. 7, No. 2, December 2000.

Nye, J., 'Corruption and Political Development: A Cost-Benefit Analysis', *American Political Review*, Vol. 61, No. 2, 1967.

Samasastry, R., *Arthasastra* (translated), Mysore Printing House, Mysore, 1967.

Sandhu, Veena and Narasimhan, T.E., 'Kickback Nation', *Business Standard*, 13 July 2013.

Santhanam Committee Report on 'Prevention of Corruption', Government of India, 1964.

Sunday Times of India, Calcutta, 27 November–3 December, 1994.

Szeftel, Morris, 'Corruption and the Spoil System in Zambia', in Machael Clarke (ed.), *Corruption: Causes and Consequences*, Pinter, London, 1983.

Vittal, N., *Corruption in India: The Roadblock to National Prosperity*, Academic Foundation, 2003.

Vittal, N., *Ending Corruption: How to Clean up India*, Penguin/Viking, New Delhi, 2012.

Writh, Ronald and Simpkins, Edgar, *Corruption in Developing Countries*, Allen & Unwin, London, 1963.

22

Tribal Unrest

India is a plural society and the central thread that seems to weave it together is 'co-existence' of groups that vary in economic, sociocultural and intellectual development. However, the balance keeps oscillating between confrontation and harmonization among different peoples. The co-existence of established states and independent tribal communities living according to their own rules and customs dates back to the earliest times of recorded Indian history. Tribals are generally called *adivasis* implying 'original inhabitants' of the land. The scheduled tribes are notified in 30 States/UTs and the number of individual ethnic groups, etc. notified as scheduled tribes are 705. The tribal population of the country, as per 2011 Census, is 10.43 crore, constituting 8.6 per cent of the total population. 89.97 per cent of them live in rural areas and 10.03 per cent in urban areas. The decadal population growth of the tribals from Census 2001 to 2011 has been 23.66 per cent against the 17.69 per cent of the entire population. As per the 2011 Census, about 80 per cent live in the Central Indian belt of Andhra Pradesh, Odisha, Jharkhand, Chhattisgarh, Madhya Pradesh and northern Maharashtra. There are also 'denotified and nomadic tribes' who have never been counted by India's census.

History of Tribals in India

Even at the times when the subcontinent was thinly populated and beyond the limits of centres of higher civilization, there were vast tracts covered in forests and inaccessible areas, where populations on very different levels of material and cultural development lived side by side without encroaching upon each others' territories. Even at times of the greatest efflorescence of Hindu culture, there were no organized attempts to draw aboriginal tribes into the orbit of caste society.

In fact, a social philosophy based on the idea of the permanence and inevitability of caste distinctions saw nothing strange or incompatible in the persistence of primitive lifestyles on the periphery of sophisticated civilizations. No doubt, there were areas where the infiltration of advanced populations into tribal territory resulted in a closer interaction between aboriginals and Hindus. In such regions, cultural distinctions were blurred, and tribal communities became gradually absorbed into the caste system, though usually into its lowest strata. For example, the untouchable castes of Cheruman and Panyer of Kerala were probably at one time independent tribes, and in their physical characteristics, they still resemble the neighbouring tribal groups that have remained outside the caste system.

Aboriginals who retained their tribal identity and resisted inclusion within the Hindu fold fared better than the assimilated groups and were not treated as untouchables, even if they indulged in practices, such as the eating of beef, which Hindus considered polluting. For instance, the Raj Gonds, some of whose rulers vied in power with Rajput princes, used to sacrifice and eat cows without debasing their status in the eyes of their Hindu neighbours. The Hindus recognized the tribes' social and cultural separateness and did not insist on conformity to Hindu patterns of behaviour, and this respect for the tribal way of life prevailed as long as contacts between the two communities were of a casual nature. The tribal people, though considered strange and dangerous, were taken for granted as part of the world of hills and forests, and a more or less frictionless co-existence was possible because there was no pressure and demand of the population, and hence no need or reason to deprive the aboriginals of their land.

This position persisted during the entire Mughal period. Now and then, the campaign of a Mughal army extending for a short spell into the wilds of tribal country would bring the inhabitants briefly to the notice of princes and chroniclers, but for long periods the hillmen and forest dwellers were left undisturbed.

The Impact of Colonialism

Under British rule, however, a new situation arose. The extension of a centralized administration over areas which had previously lain outside the effective control of princely rulers deprived many of the aboriginal tribes of their autonomy. Though most British administrators had no intention of interfering with the tribesmen's rights and traditional manner of living, the establishment of law and order in outlying areas exposed the aboriginals to the pressure of more advanced populations. In areas which had previously been virtually unadministered, and hence unsafe for outsiders who did not enjoy the confidence and goodwill of the aboriginal inhabitants, traders and moneylenders could now establish themselves under the protection of the British administration. Often they were followed by settlers, who succeeded in acquiring large tracts of the aboriginals' land.

The process of land alienation took place by imposing on tribal populations, systems of land tenure and revenue collection developed in advanced areas. The government unintentionally facilitated the transfer of tribal land to members of other ethnic groups. The deterioration of the aboriginals' position, which in many parts of Peninsular India began as early as the middle of the 19th century and continued into the 20th century, occurred despite the fact that many British officials sympathized with the tribesmen and some of the most fervent advocates of tribal rights were found among the officers of the Indian Civil Service. Yet, the recommendations for reforms contained in numerous reports were seldom implemented in full, and even where they were incorporated in legislation, they did not always prove effective.

Unable to resist the gradual alienation of their ancestral land, the aboriginals of many regions either gave way by withdrawing further into hills and tracts of marginal land or, if no such refuge areas were left, had no other choice than to accept the economic status of tenants, sharecroppers, or agricultural labourers on the very land their forefathers had owned.

There was only one part of British India where a policy of non-interference and protection enabled the tribal populations to retain their land as well as traditional lifestyle. In the hill regions of Northeast India which enclose the Brahmaputra valley in the shape of an enormous horseshoe, tribes, such as Nagas, Mishmis, Adis, Miris, Apa Tanis and Nishis, were the sole inhabitants of a vast region of rugged mountains and narrow valleys into which the peoples settled in the plains of Assam had never penetrated. A small volume of barter trade between hills and plains was carried on by tribesmen from the foothills, but most of the hill people never set foot in the Brahmaputra valley. When in the second half of the 19th century and during the first decades of the 20th century the British extended their administrative control over part of the hill regions, they did not encourage the entry of plainsmen but devised a system of administration which allowed the hillmen to run their affairs along traditional lines.

As late as the 1930s, the entire administration of the Naga Hills district, for instance, was in the hands of one deputy commissioner stationed at Kohima and one sub-divisional officer, whose headquarters was Mokokchung. With the help of a few clerks and a small force of Assam Rifles, these two officers maintained peace and order in a vast hill region where bridle paths were the only means of communications. No plainsman was allowed to acquire land in the hills, and the indigenous system of land tenure was retained virtually unchanged. This policy protected the hill people from exploitation and land alienation.

Post-Independence Scenario

It is not surprising that the introduction of a much more elaborate and less flexible system of administration in the years following 1947 sparked off a great deal of unrest, for tribesmen used to running their own affairs reacted violently to interference from a host of officials lacking in understanding of local customs. However, no analysis of the relations between aboriginal tribes and the governments in power can be complete without consideration of at least some of the rebellions by which tribal populations tried to shake off the yoke of those who had invaded their habitat, usurped their ancestral land, and mercilessly robbed them of the fruits of their labours. Soon after Independence, the basic principles for the development of the scheduled tribes were clearly enunciated by Pandit Jawaharlal Nehru, the first Prime Minister of Independent India, in the form of five principles known as 'Tribal Panchasheel'.

India is home to about 700 tribal groups with a population of 104 million, as per 2011 Census. These people constitute the second largest tribal population in the world after Africa. As industries encroached upon their lands, many communities were displaced and some even continued to wage a struggle to either protect their homes or demand a fair compensation. Recognizing their rights to forest areas and forest management practices is critical to understand their struggle for survival. Loss of forest cover, mining and the expansion of hybrid crops remain direct threats to the food security of these people who count on forest resources and wild food. There is a need for scientific discourse on the impact of climate change on species that grow in the wild and are used by tribals living close to forests. As legal loopholes, poor enforcement of existing safeguards, bureaucratic apathy and corporate neglect of human rights try to further isolate these people and muffle their voices. It is time we had a look at the encouraging and disturbing developments that took place over the last few years.

These tribal communities have traditionally controlled vast tracts of land and its resources, such as forests and coal, through well-established community institutions. Twenty-seven per cent of India's population depends on non-timber forest produce for subsistence and income. 'This dependence is particularly intense for half of India's 104 million tribal people, the most disadvantaged section of society, who live in forest fringe areas,' says a 2014 report by the Food and Agriculture Organization. These tribal and rural households, which are dependent on wild foods, risk losing nutrition, health, medicine and economic stability. The centre has for long protected their autonomy through various constitutional provisions. The state governments have acknowledged this. But as the value of natural resources touches an all-time high, the governments turn their eyes to the largely untapped region, perhaps the most resource-rich landscape in the country.

Degradation of forest resources due to industrialization have forced the tribals to look for an alternative source of livelihoods. The gold symbiotic relationship between nature and human being got disturbed. Forest has become a dream for them. The tribals who used to sell the forest product in the market earlier have become the buyers of the same. Introduction of various development programmes by the government and the emergence of new industries in the locality have given an alternative source of livelihood for the tribals. The rural non-farm sector has become a major source of livelihood for the poor tribals. Some tradition patterns are still flowing at present time but lots of changes come in livelihood the pattern of tribal people.

The Struggle of Tribal People

The struggle is not new, in fact, it began even before independence when Britisher's forced these tribal people into agriculture and they were forced to choose between their traditional form of living and survival. It stayed a problem even after independence as the Indian government became custodian of all the forest and the tribal lands through 5th and 6th Schedule and these areas came under the tribal ministry. It made the tribals to think that their remaining autonomy is also taken over from them, their forests and their lands have been taken away from them and agriculture is forced over them. After independence, the tribal struggle may be classified into three groups:

1. Struggles due to the exploitation of the outsiders.
2. Struggles due to economic deprivations.
3. Struggle due to separatist tendencies.

Classification of Tribal Movements

According to Ghanshyam Shah, different scholars have evolved different typologies of tribal movements. Mahapatra (1972) applies the typologies widely used for social movements to tribal movements.

1. *Reactionary*: The reactionary movement tries to launch a movement to bring back 'the good old days'.
2. *Conservative*: The conservative movement tries to maintain the status quo.
3. *Revisionary or revolutionary*: The revisionary or revolutionary movements are those which are organized for 'improvement' or 'purification' of the cultural or social order by eliminating 'evil' or 'low' customs, beliefs, or institutions.

Surajit Sinha (1968) classified the movements into: ethnic rebellion, reform movements, political autonomy movements within the Indian union, secessionist movements, and agrarian unrest.

K.S. Singh (1983) makes more or less the same classification except that he uses the terms 'Sanskritization' instead of reform movement and 'cultural movements' instead of ethnic movements.

The tribal movements may also be classified on the basis of their orientation into four types:

1. Movements seeking political autonomy and formation of a separate state,
2. Agrarian movement,
3. Forest-based movements,
4. Socio-religious movements.

S.M. Dubey (1982) divides the tribal movements in Northeast India into four categories:

1. Religious and social reform movements

2. Movements for separate statehood
3. Insurgent movements
4. Cultural rights movements

In fact, there is a very thin line dividing the second, third, and fourth types. However, these typologies do not include the recent movements around the issues of forest rights and environment and displacement of the tribals due to the 'development' programmes of the state and the market.

Briefly, we might reformulate the typologies as follows:

1. Ethnic movements, which include culture/religion identity.
2. Agrarian and forest rights movements.
3. Environmental movements.
4. Involuntary displacement and rehabilitation movements.
5. Political movements around the nationality question for a separate state.

Most of the tribal movements were the result of oppression and discrimination, neglect and backwardness and apathy of government towards the tribal problems.

Tribals adopted two paths to achieving goals:

1. *Non-violent path* of bargaining and negotiating with the government and using a variety of pressure tactics without resorting to violence/revolts.
2. *Militant path* of revolts or mass struggles based on developing the fighting power of the exploited/oppressed tribal strata.

The consequences of both these paths are different. One indicates struggle oriented to reforms, while the other indicates the structural transformation of the community. The fact that tribals continue to face problems and also continue to feel discontented and deprived, brings to the fore the conclusion that both paths have not helped them to achieve their goals.

Anyone familiar with the oppression and exploitation that aboriginals of regions such as the Telengana of Andhra Pradesh have suffered at the hands of landgrabbers, landlords, unscrupulous traders and moneylenders, and, regrettably, many minor officials must be surprised not by the fact that now and then tribal groups rose against their oppressors in violent outbursts, but that organized rebellions were so few and so short-lived. If any of the tribes of Arunachal Pradesh or even of such settled hill regions as the Garo or Mikir hills had been exposed to injustices as severe as those suffered by Gonds, Kolams, Koyas and Reddis, murder and violence would have been the order of the day, but most of the tribes of the Deccan are on the whole so gentle and inoffensive that extreme provocation is necessary before they take the law into their own hands.

Rebellions of aboriginal tribesmen against the authority of the government are among the most tragic conflicts between ruler and ruled. Whatever course the clash may take, it is always a hopeless struggle of the weak against the strong, the illiterate and uninformed against the organized power of a sophisticated system. There may be loss of life on both sides, but it is always the aboriginals who court ruin and suffer economic distress. We do not refer here to the past risings of martial frontier tribes whose aims were basically political, but to the rebellions of primitive aboriginal tribes of Peninsular India, such as the Santal rebellion in Bihar, the Bhil rebellion in Khandesh, and the Rampa rebellion in the East Godavari district. All these uprisings were defensive movements; they were the last resort of tribesmen driven to despair by the encroachment of outsiders on their land and economic resources. As such they could all have been avoided had the authorities taken cognizance of the aboriginals' grievances and set about to remedy them, not as it happened in most cases *after* the rising, but *before* the pressure on the tribesmen made an outbreak of violence unavoidable.

The Legislations

The various orders passed from time to time with the purpose of ameliorating the conditions of the tribal population of the East Godavari Agency Tract were ultimately consolidated in legislation known as the Agency Tracts Interest and Land Transfer Act, 1917. The regulation of this Act formed a model for similar legislations in other tribal areas, and we shall therefore quote some of its main sections. In order to save the tribals from the exploitation of moneylenders, the Act laid down that (a) interest on any debt or liability shall not as against a member of a hill tribe be allowed or decreed at a higher rate than 24 per cent per annum nor shall any compound interest or any collateral advantage be allowed against him; and (b) the total interest allowed or decreed on any debt or liability as against a member of a hill tribe shall not exceed the principal amount.

Even more important were the sections restricting the transfer of land from tribals to outsiders. The relevant Section (4) contained the following provisions:

1. Notwithstanding any rule of law or enactment to the contrary, any transfer of immovable property situated within the Agency tract by a member of a hill tribe shall be absolutely null and void unless made in favour of another member of a hill tribe or with the previous consent in writing of the Agent or of any other prescribed officer. [Agent was the revenue officer comparable to the collector of a normal district.]
2. Where a transfer of property is made in contravention of Subsection (1), the Agent ... may on application by anyone interested decree ejectment against any person in possession of the property claiming under the transfer and may restore it to the transferor or his heirs.

It is only fair to admit, however, that in the period 1917–47 the condition of the tribal populations in the East Godavari Agency Tract was relatively favourable, and that the massive invasion of tribal land by outsiders occurred only after 1947.

The need for special protection of aboriginal tribes was not confined to the areas notified as Agencies, and in 1919 an Act known as the Government of India Act, 1919, provided that 'the Governor-General in Council may declare any territory in British India to be a 'Backward Tract' and that any act of the Indian Legislature should apply to such Backward Tracts only if the Governor-General so directed'.

The legislation of 1919 was a forerunner of the Government of India Act, 1935, and the Government of India (Excluded and Partially Excluded Areas) Order, 1936. 'Excluded areas' were backward regions inhabited by tribal populations to which Acts of the Dominion Legislature or of the provincial legislatures were to apply only with the consent of the governor of the province. The intention of this provision was to prevent the extension of legislation designed for advanced areas to backward areas where primitive tribes may be adversely affected by laws unsuitable to their special conditions. Though at the time Indian nationalists saw in it a device to retain British control over selected areas, after the attainment of independence the Government of India adopted a somewhat similar policy in regard to several territories on the Northeast Frontier.

The Indian Constitution of 1950 also provided for the notification of scheduled tribes (STs) and their protection by a special legislation. Regarding the administration of the Scheduled Areas, the governor of each state which includes a Scheduled Area is bound to submit a report to the President of India annually or whenever required. The states periodically prepare lists of STs, and these have to be confirmed by parliament. As STs in receipt of various benefits, there has been considerable pressure from backward classes for inclusion in this list.

The National Tribal Policy (NTP), first proposed in 2004, met with much opposition from civil society for adopting an assimilationist approach. It was criticized for trying to include tribal people with mainstream population, thus violating their rights and diluting their distinctiveness. It was also frowned upon for being a stand-alone document, not factoring in other applicable laws like the Panchayat Extension to Scheduled Areas Act or the Land Acquisition Act and instead loosely speaking about measures like land rights, without any actual commitment.

In 2006, the Ministry of Tribal Affairs drafted a fresh policy. The draft handled the 'assimilation' issues that were diluting their unique identity and, instead, used an approach of 'integration'. For example, in Northeast India, over a 100 tribal ethnic minorities are dependent on shifting cultivation. Half of Meghalaya's population, the Khasi tribes in particular, practise this method of farming for survival. While the 2004 draft coerced them to give up this 'primitive' method, pointing out that the tribes 'do not seem to have any emotional attachment to land as an asset', the current draft approaches this issue realistically by acknowledging that it is the only possible farming practice in interior areas that, in fact, promotes collective ownership of natural resources. While the 2004 draft makes vague suggestions like 'encouraging qualified tribal doctors to serve tribal areas,' the new draft proposes integrating indigenous and modern medicine for the tribal population. Such changes make the 2006 draft realistically address contemporary tribal issues such as evictions from forests, indebtedness and conflict and unrest, which were earlier never addressed. Yet, the drawback it suffers from the most is the lack of any action points or a timebound strategy to act upon.

What then is the significance of NTP in the Indian context? Since independence, the major policy initiatives with regard to tribes have been Nehru's outlined 'Panchsheel' (a five-pointer guideline to develop a tribal policy) and constitutional provisions protecting STs. Various laws and schemes regarding different aspects of STs were formulated, each ambiguous and contradicting the other. This has deepened the sense of exclusion and alienation of *adivasis* in India, which has been manifesting itself in the form of tribal unrest. The emergence of Naxalism in Chhattisgarh has been capitalizing on this very same tribal discontent. 'It is a paradox that the poor tribals are living in areas which are rich in minerals, forest resources and other natural bounties. The solution lies in giving rights to the ST communities over natural and financial resources, addressing economic deprivation.

In the wide range of current political debates in India lies a core question: Who is a 'Scheduled Tribe'? With the many ambiguities regarding the nature of the term, any comprehensive policy on the STs should have had an authoritative clarification on this term. However, the NTP merely points out the outdated and derogatory nature of criteria used for scheduling tribes so far – 'primitive traits, distinctive culture, geographical isolation, shyness of contact and backwardness'. The policy needs to outline new criteria from the perspective of deprivation and exclusion.

In the transient state of globalization, the *adivasis* in the country are faced with new aspirations and problems, and so the choice to retain or rebuild their cultural and political identities should be left to them. A National Tribal Policy should be based on the principle of freedom for every tribal society to opt either the old lifestyle or to go for the modern life, or choose access to both lifestyles. India, along with 143 member-state nations of the UN, adopted the Declaration on the Rights of the Indigenous Peoples in September 2007. Article 3 of the Declaration states: 'Indigenous peoples have the right to self-determination. By virtue of that right, they freely determine their political status and freely pursue their economic, social and cultural development'. And yet, the NTP is far from proposing the right to self-determination to help tribal communities choose their path of development as their fundamental right.

While the policy is a remarkable attempt to capture a holistic view of the contemporary tribal situation in the country, the extreme delay in approving the policy, its inability to fix concrete goals, and the lack of a participatory approach render it inadequate.

The strategy for implementing the policy includes reorienting institutional arrangements in the tribal areas, strengthening and revamping of the administrative machinery, linking devolution of funds to improvements in Tribal Development Index so as to bring the STs and tribal areas at par with the national level by 2020 and preparation of a separate tribal-centric strategy for each sector besides devising an appropriate personnel policy to ensure the presence of government functionaries in far-flung tribal areas.

The policy seeks to address the issue of tenurial insecurity among tribals by amending state anti-alienation land laws, amending the Indian Registration Act and establishing fast-track courts to deal with tribal alienation. Efforts will be made to strengthen the regulatory and protective regime through enforcement of relevant Acts or their amendment.

Exploitation and Unrest of the Tribes

For ages, tribals are considered the primitive segment of Indian society. They lived in forests and hills without any contact with civilizations. During British rule, they consolidated their position and their political aspirations and administrative needs necessitated to open up the entire country. The British introduced the system of land ownership and revenue. The annual tax was trebled, which was beyond the paying capacity of tribal cultivators. The tribal population faced all types of exploitation such as unfriendly forest laws and regulations, lack of legislation to prevent the passing of tribal land into the hands of non-tribals, lack of credit facilities, ineffective government measures to rehabilitate tribal population, delay in implementation of recommendations of different committee, and discrimination in implementation of reform measures.

Many non-tribal began to settle in the tribal areas offering credit facilities. Initially, it provided relief to tribals, but gradually the system became exploitative. Over the years, the tribal population faced all types of exploitation. This aroused the tribal leaders to mobilize the tribals and start agitations.

Some Major Causes of Tribal Unrest

Majority of the tribal are engaged in agriculture and non-formal economic activities such as food gathering and hunting; rarely they are engaged in the formal occupation. Exploitation and marginalization of tribals have been intensified due to India's rapid economic growth demanding mineral resources be extracted from tribal habitats. Sustainable and subsistence tribal livelihood is under threat from the flow of global and local capital in the exploitation of their physical environment. Growth-oriented economic development model demands rapid industrialization and promotes mega development projects, and mineral resource extraction to accelerate national production. Tribal response to the exploitation and marginalization has ignited severe social unrest and protest. Tribal unrest and discontentment are a cumulative effect of a number of factors. Some of the vital factors are as follows:

Government Failures

The failure of the government to take appropriate measures to rehabilitate the tribal population, both before and after independence, has disappointed the tribals. Independent India's Constitution envisages a comprehensive and well-designed scheme of action for the tribal protection and development. The state governments are vested with the responsibility of implementing the constitutional provisions. Unfortunately, these constitutional provisions have remained non-operational. Land continues to pass out of the tribal's to non-tribal's hands. Moneylenders continue to exploit them. There has been a heavy influx of outsiders into the tribal areas and they have grabbed most of the opportunities.

Inadequate Laws for Tribals

The provisions laid down by the Constitution have rarely provided justice to the tribals. This holds good with almost all laws – forest, revenue, excise, criminal or civil laws – which have basically two major lacunae: they have snatched away the tribal rights over land, forest and resources, and second, they have failed to recognize the traditional legal system and management practices of the tribals with regard to either resources or to the social systems. Even laws which are protective of tribal interests have not been implemented with earnestness as a result of which land alienation prevails as the most serious problem until today. The ignorance and docility of tribal people in confronting the exploitation of non-tribals has shifted to a gradual awareness of laws and assertion of their rights.

Unjust Development Policies of the Government

If one traces the historical process of development intervention by the government in the tribal areas, he can perceive a very illogical, insincere and shortsighted attempt at defining 'development' in the hill regions. Government policies have always been in contravention of the laws of the Scheduled Areas and there was little respect paid to the implementation of these laws. Moreover, the abundant resources of land, water or forests have been utilized for the benefit of external societies and people but never for the development of the local communities. Further, they have only been displaced, at times more than once and never or meagrely compensated for their loss of resources or livelihoods. This is true of irrigation, drinking water, electricity or any other development projects.

The present policies of the government are to violate, circumvent or amend the laws which protect the interests of the poor tribals, falling over backwards to help private companies or industries commercially prosper, like mining industries, tourism, paper mills, film or wood-based industries. The experience with such unscrupulous development policies of the government is spurning the tribals, especially the youth, into the tantalizing calls of extremist exhortations.

Non-Tribal Nature of All Development Activities

The underlying non-tribal nature of any development approach is a serious factor to reckon with. Non-tribals dominating the government machinery in the tribal areas not only feel bitter about the various welfare programmes designed for tribals, but also get into an exploitative relationship with the local traders, contractors and police. This results in very few benefits actually reaching the tribals. While tribals revere the natural resources as life sustaining forces, the non-tribals outlook is one of utilitarian and short-term commercial exploitation. This disregard for tribal-nature symbiosis is causing not only a threat to tribal survival but is also leading to depletion of resources in the tribal regions.

The ignorance of tribals has given advantage in flourishing of trade and business by non-tribals who hold the reins of the economic and political powers in the tribal region and the functioning of the government machinery. Whether directly or indirectly they have total control over the lands and resources of the tribals. This suppression of rights through the nexus with the politicians and police has emboldened the tribals to strike back with the aid of extremist forces.

Attitudes and Prejudices

The officials and employees of the government posted in tribal areas approach the tribals with all the prejudices of non-tribal society. The tribals are considered uncouth savages, steeped in crude superstitions and rituals due to their ignorance of external mechanisms of life. Their culture and social systems are looked down upon and it is with condescension that they relate to tribals when they visit the tribal villages. There is anger among the tribals at this ill-treatment which is now showing itself in various forms of protest.

Ineffective Development Programmes

There is a discernible lack of concentration on addressing the basic issues of the tribals on the part of the government administration. Many programmes implemented for the tribals look into the peripheral needs of the people and display apathy towards the primary causes of unrest, mainly land alienation and land-related problems. Tribals being inseparably bonded to land and forest face serious problems with non-tribals and the in regaining their control over their lands. The present administration chooses to ignore this aspect.

Absence of Efficient Tribal Leadership

Tribals should be able to develop their own leadership to fight against exploitation and to secure justice. But unfortunately, various vested interests have prevented the emergence of powerful tribal leaders. There is virtually a vacuum of tribal leadership. This has very badly affected their development.

It is clear from the above that various social, political, economic and legal factors have contributed to the problem of tribal unrest. Thus, it is the cumulative result of a number of factors:

1. Indifference from administrators and bureaucracy in dealing with tribal grievances.
2. Harsh and unfriendly forest laws and regulations.
3. Lack of legislation to prevent the passing of tribal land into the hands of non-tribals.
4. Lack of credit facilities.
5. Ineffective government measures to rehabilitate the tribal population.
6. Delay in the implementation of recommendations of the different committee.
7. Discrimination in the implementation of reform measures.
8. Lethargy, indifference, and lack of sympathy from administrators and bureaucrats in dealing with tribal grievances.
9. Lack of interest and dynamism among the political elite to solve tribal problems.

Possible Remedies

Depressing as it is, there is scope for setting straight the disturbing situation of the tribal region. What is necessary is the genuine interest of the government in making a serious effort at remedying the causes of unrest. Some factors which could be looked into are:

1. *A sensitive administration:* The government has to recognize that the tribal people have a distinct sociocultural structure and the administration has to understand and respect these systems while designing and implementing development programmes. Programmes should be sympathetic to tribal needs addressing the real issues and conflicts. It should be emphasized that the machinery should work without social and political biases towards tribal communities. For instance, any conflicts or disturbances that arise between tribals and non-tribals should be dealt by the police, revenue and other officials with anti-tribal and pro-non-tribal stand.
2. *More powers to the people:* Governance of tribal areas cannot be undertaken with the same method adopted in the plans. Conflicts of customary laws versus universal laws, conflicts over control over resources and tribal – non-tribal disputes in the tribal areas all over the country have led to the formulation of the New Panchayati Raj Act which lays emphasis on the local self-governance and empowering the Gram Sabha in Scheduled Areas. The state governments should, in all sincerity, implement this Act without any dilutions.
3. *Balanced development policies:* The state governments should follow a people-friendly development policy with regard to any programmes or projects planned in the tribal areas. It should first consider the social and economic progress of the local communities in the overall development

planning in the region instead of displacing people, destroying their livelihoods and taking up only an apparent development.

4. *Inconsistencies in laws and policies:* The existing inconsistencies in the constitutional laws and the changing trends in the policies of the state governments, which are in violation of the protective laws, are causing unequal and discriminative programmes with regard to tribal communities. If clarity in laws and implementing policies are followed, there would not be any necessity for people and organizations to question the projects of the government.
5. *Education:* Ignorance and illiteracy of tribals are the basic problems of any development. Government should also take it up as a thrust activity to bring literacy and education to the tribals. Government institutions like ITDA have a responsibility to make the tribals aware of their laws and programmes so that education in all aspects is achieved.

Measures Taken for the Development of Tribal Areas

The government has laid greater emphasis on the development of tribal area since independence. Some of the measures for the development of tribal areas are as follows:

An important landmark was opening of 43 Special Multi-purpose Tribal Block during the Second Five-Year Plan (1956–61), later called Tribal Development Blocks (TDBs) and of a Tribal Sub-Plan (TSP) within the State plan in the Fifth Five-Year Plan (1974–79), marked a shift in the approach when the Tribal Sub Plan (TSP) based on the integrated area development approach for the direct benefit of the STs was launched. During the sixth plan, Modified Area Development Approach was adopted to cover smaller areas of tribal concentration aims at development for tribals staying outside the integrated tribal development areas and formation of the Large-scale Multipurpose Cooperative Societies (LAMPS), Tribal Development Agencies, Integrated Tribal Development Area Projects (ITDA), Modified Area Development Approach (MADA), Micro Projects for Primitive Tribal Groups (PTGs) reflected the course of tribal development administration in the country.

Government provides grants under Article 275(1) of the Constitution for raising the level of infrastructure in the Scheduled Areas and economic development of the scheduled tribes. It is also implementing various centrally-sponsored schemes under which financial assistance is given to the states and UTs for construction of hostels and coaching facility for ST students for competitive examinations, research and training, setting up of ashram schools, vocational training centres, educational complexes for ST girls in low literacy pockets and development of primitive tribal groups.

The government has enacted the Scheduled Tribes and Other Traditional Forest Dwellers (Recognition of Forest Rights) Act, 2006 which recognizes and vests the forest rights and occupation in forest land in forest dwelling scheduled tribes and other traditional forest dwellers who have been residing in such forests, for generations, but whose rights could not be recorded.

Impact of Extremism on Development Activities

Tribal areas were totally closed and neglected by the government till the insurgence of extremist forces who have the credit of making the government focus its attention on the development of tribal areas and in improving the conditions of the tribals. A variety of approaches and strategies like top-down approach, regional planning, target group approach, integrated development, participatory development, joint forest management, watershed management, and poverty alleviation programmes have formed part of the development approach.

Interestingly, the latest developments in the strategies of the extremists seem to have a populist and welfarist approach while so far it has been a political and social movement. Today, the extremists are declaring that they would assist the tribals in activities like providing credit and banking facilities, medical aid, irrigation and agricultural programmes, etc. They are also encouraging the people to regenerate forests but with species specified by them. It has to be observed what impacts this parallel development approach from the underground would have on the tribals and the government. However, it is seen that some of the divisions of the Naxalite groups are dealing with the tribal situation arbitrarily the repercussions of which have to be taken note of by the larger society.

Current Scenario

The basic problem of the tribal people, as of the vast majority of the non-tribal population, is that of poverty. The problem of the low standard of living, starvation, malnutrition, illiteracy, disease, poor sanitary and housing facilities, etc. all are common to the tribal and a vast majority of the non-tribal population. They have been subjected to exploitation for centuries together by the non-tribals such as moneylenders, forest contractors, traders, landlords, officials and politicians. Compared with the exploitation of the non-tribal rural poor, the exploitation of the tribals is more monopolistic in nature. They continue to be subjected to this exploitation because they do not generally move out of their immediate environment in search of employment opportunities. This is due to lack of awareness of such opportunities on the part of the tribals.

The tribal populace constitutes a dominant part in the north-eastern states of Mizoram, Meghalaya Nagaland, and Lakshadweep. The states with no scheduled tribe gatherings are Punjab, Chandigarh, Haryana, Delhi, and Pondicherry. The majority of the occupation falls into the essential occupations, for example, farming and chasing.

In numerous parts of India, tribal population experience endless diseases and infections, out of which water-borne sicknesses are life debilitating. They likewise experience the ill effects of insufficiency maladies. The Himalayan tribes experience the ill effects of goitre because of the absence of iodine. Infection and tuberculosis are additionally basic among them.

Efforts made from the beginning of the planned era (1951) through various developmental plans, policies, special strategies and programmes, have registered a definite quantifiable improvement in the socio-economic status of the tribals. However, the progress made by them could not bring them anywhere nearer to the mainstream society as the gap in their socio-economic status continued to prevail, not only as a matter of prime concern but also as a task to accomplish during the tenth plan. Achievements and the persisting gaps remain under the three core sectors of education, health and economic development.

Tribal communities continue to be vulnerable even today, not because they are poor, assetless and illiterate compared to the general population; but often their distinct vulnerability arises from their inability to negotiate and cope with the consequences of their integration with the mainstream economy, society, cultural and political systems, from all of which they were historically protected by their relative isolation. The requirements of planned development brought with them the dams, mines, industries and roads, all located on tribal lands. With these came the concomitant processes of displacement followed by ineffective implementation of PESA, 1996.

The 73rd and 74th Constitutional Amendments of 1993 followed by their extension to Scheduled Areas through the Panchayats (Extension to the Scheduled Areas) PESA Act, 1996, are landmark achievements in conferring powers and authority to the Panchayats and Gram Sabhas. But, unfortunately, the same is not being enforced in the right spirit, as the PRIs are yet to stabilize on a firm footing. The state governments should, therefore, take appropriate measures immediately to translate the legislation into reality so that tribals will have full say in their own affairs. There is no doubt that there has been a significant change in the lives of the tribals especially in the past 70 years of independence. Tribals continue to occupy the lowest economic strata, their areas of habitation are least developed in infrastructure and other aspects of development.

References

Dubey, S.M., 'Inter-Ethnic Alliancc, Tribal Movements and Integration in North-East India', *Tribal Movements in India*. Vol. I. Edited by K.S. Singh, Manohar, Delhi, 1982.

Mahapatra, L.K., 'Social Movements among Tribes in India' in K.S. Singh (ed.), *Tribal Situation in India*, Indian Institute of Advanced Study, Simla, 1972.

Mishra, Lakshmidhar, Annotated bibliography on forced/Bonded Labour in India (Part II, Articles/monographs/reports), International Labour Office, Bangkok 2002.

Oraon, Vijay, 'Changing Patterns of Tribal Livelihoods', Department of Humanities and Social Sciences, National Institute of Technology Rourkela, 2012.

Prasad, Kiran Kamal, *Understanding and Eradicating Bonded Labour in India*. Jana Jagrati Prakashana, Bangalore, 2008.

Press Information Bureau, Government of India, Ministry of Labour & Employment, 23 July 2018.

Report of the expert group on Bonded Labour, National Human Rights Commission, New Delhi, 2006.

Satyarthi, Kailash, 'We Shall Fight; We Shall Win', Bonded Liberation Front, New Delhi.

Sengupta, Nirmal, 'Reappearing Tribal Movements', *Economic and Political Weekly*, Vol. 23, Issue No. 23, 4 June, 1988.

Shah, Ghanshyam, *Social Movement in India*, Sage Publications, New Delhi, 1990, pp. 95–96.

Singh, K.S., *Birsa Munda and His Movement 1874–1901*, Oxford University Press, Delhi, 1983.

Sinha, Surajit, 'Tribal Solidarity and Messianic Movement', Review Article, *Contributions to Indian Sociology* (New Series 2), 1968.

Vyas, N.N., *Bondage an Exploitation in Tribal India*, Rawat Publications, Jaipur, 1980.

23

Bonded Labour

Bonded labour is the existing form of slavery. A man keeping another man in perpetual bondage for his selfish and personal objectives is the type of man's cruelty to man which is not confined to a particular country or a particular region but is found as a global phenomenon for hundreds of years, right from the Biblical days to the present era. The first Global Slavery Index, published by the Australia-based Walk Free Foundation, ranked India on the top with 13.9 million modern slaves out of a total of 26 million in the world. Modern slavery includes traditional slaves, those in debt bondage, forced labour or forced marriage, kids sold and victims of trafficking. According to International Labour Organization (ILO) estimates of 2013, over 21 million people across the world are trapped as forced labour. Today, the ILO estimates a minimum 11.7 million in forced labour in the Asia-Pacific region, the majority of whom are in debt bondage. However, the nomenclature changed from period to period and place to place: slave, serf, villein, and bonded labour. In India, this type of exploitation of man by man has remained prevalent in the name of *begar* and *ryot* for years. The term 'bonded labour' or *bandhua mazdoor* is of recent origin. Lakhs of bonded labourers continue to be exploited and carry the yoke of neglect, suffering and frustration in abject silence. In fact, the system of bonded labour, as prevalent in Indian society, is a relic of feudal hierarchical society. A considerable interest has come to be shown in the bonded labour during the past three decades by the social workers, social scientists, NGOs and the government because it is considered incompatible with our social ideal of egalitarianism and human rights. Not only adult males and females but children as well are condemned to be suffering under this bondage.

In India, the bonded labour system finds its genesis in the country's peculiar socio-economic culture. Like various other social evils prevailing in India, bonded labour is also an off-shoot of our caste-system. Mainly, it is a person belonging to the so-called higher castes who are the exploiters and person belonging to the so-called lower castes are the exploited.

Due to the weak economic and social conditions within the society, the SC/STs and Dalits are forced to sell their labours for nominal or no remuneration to the village landlord or moneylender. It is a practice continuing from ancient times and in some parts of the country is still prevalent. Bonded labour is one of the specific forms of forced labour (*begar*) in which a person is forced to sell labour to pay his/her debt. However, not all bonded labour is forced, but most forced labour practices are of bonded nature either by coercion or by compulsion.

Bonded labour is a hidden phenomenon as a majority of them are found in the informal sector. Bonded labour means the employment of a person against a loan or debt or social obligation by the family of the child or the family as a whole. It is a form of slavery. Children who are bonded with their family or inherit a debt from their parents are often found in the agricultural sector or assisting their families in brick kilns and stone quarries. Individual pledging of children is a growing occurrence that usually leads to trafficking of children to urban areas for employment and has children working in small production houses versus factories. Bonded labourers in India are mostly migrant workers, which opens them up to more exploitation. Also, they mostly come from low caste groups such as Dalits or marginalized tribal groups. Bonded child labourers are at very high risk for physical and sexual abuse and neglect, sometimes leading to death. They often become psychologically and mentally disturbed and do not get the opportunity to learn many social skills or survival skills.

The Concept

For developing a conceptual framework, we have to understand two terms: 'bonded labour system' and 'bonded labour'. The 'bonded labour system' refers to the relationship between a creditor and a debtor who obtains loan owing to economic compulsions confronting his day-to-day life and agrees to abide by the terms dictated by the creditor. The important term of the agreement is that the debtor agrees to mortgage his services or the services of any or all the members of his family for a specified or unspecified period. The relationship built on the agreement is on such unequal terms that while for every labour or service, there must be some fair remuneration equivalent to the price of labour in the market, under the bonded labour system, the service is rendered for the debt or in lieu of the interest accruing to the debt. The debtor either works without receiving any remuneration or if at all there is any remuneration, it is much less than the minimum wage (notified under the Minimum Wages Act) or the prevailing rate of market wage.

The Bonded Labour (Abolition) Act, 1976 defines 'bonded labour system' as the system of forced labour under which a debtor enters into an agreement with the creditor that he would render service to him either by himself or through any member of his family or any person dependent on him, for a specified or unspecified period, either without wages or for nominal wages, in consideration of loan or any other economic consideration obtained by him or any of his ascendants, or in pursuance of any social obligation, or in pursuance of any obligation devolving on him by succession. The agreement has other consequences too, such as, forfeiting the debtor the freedom of employment, denial of freedom of movement in any part of the country, and denial of the right to sell any of his property or product of his labour at market value.

The term 'bonded labour' has been defined by the National Commission on Labour as 'labour which remains in bondage for a specific period for the debt incurred'. The Commissioner for Scheduled Castes and Scheduled Tribes explained the term 'bonded labour' in its 24th report as 'persons who are forced to work for the creditors for the loan incurred either without wage or on nominal wage' (Sharma, 1990: 52).

The 'bonded labour' is different from 'contract labour' employed in industries, mines, plantations, docks, etc. The contract labour includes workers who are not directly recruited by the establishment, whose names do not appear on the pay roll, and who are not paid wages directly by the employer. In theory, the contract labourers in India are covered by the Factory Act, 1948, the Mines Act, 1952, the Plantations Labour Act, 1951 and the Dock Workers Act, 1948 so as to give them benefits as are admissible to labour directly employed. However, the advantages of employing both bonded labour and contract labour are the same: (a) the labour is engaged at the lower cost, (b) the employers have not to extend the fringe benefits to the workers, and (c) the employers are not under any obligation of providing welfare and security measures to the workers as stipulated in various Acts. The system of contract labour in our country was, however, abolished in September 1970 by an Act called Contract Labour (Regulation and Abolition) Act.

Debt bondage, as per the Bonded Labour System (Abolition) Act (BLSAA) occurs when a loan/advance from an employer results in the worker being in the following situation:

1. fully or partly forced to work for the employer until he/she repays the debt incurred;
2. has not paid the minimum wage;
3. has to forfeit the freedom to change the employment/means of livelihood;
4. forfeit the right to move freely throughout the territory of India; and
5. forfeits the right to sell the product of his/her labour at a market value.

The two basic features of bonded labour are: indebtedness and forced labour. The forced labour can hereditarily descend from father to son or be passed on for generations together. During the period of bondage, the debtor cannot seek employment from any other person. In economic terms, this means that he cannot 'sell his labour in the market at market value'. The bonded labour system is mostly found among agricultural labourers in villages, though today it has extended to workers working in stone quarries, brick kilns, *bidi* factories, glass factories, fireworks factories, textile and carpet factories, gemstones factories, etc. Large number of women and children are employed as bonded labour in these non-farming sectors. In cities, children are employed as bonded labour in restaurants or often end up being employed as bonded beggars or fall prey to sex trade.

The bonded labourers are known by different names in different parts of India. For example, in Andhra Pradesh and Karnataka, they are known as *Jeethams*, in Gujarat and Madhya Pradesh as *Halis*, in Bastar district in Madhya Pradesh as *Kabadis*, in Hyderabad as *Bhagela*, in Rajasthan as *Sagris*, in Bihar as *Kamias* or *Kamiantis*, in Odisha as *Gothees*, in Tamil Nadu as *Pandiyals*, in Kerala as *Adiyas*, *Paniyas* and *Kattunaikens* and in Uttar Pradesh as *Koltas*. According to a few recent systematic surveys, non-agricultural sector now has a very significant number of bonded labourers. Following types of bonded labour continue to be significant: (a) bonded labour that is a vestige of traditional social relations; (b) bonded labour in agriculture; (c) bonded labour in the rural and urban unorganized and informal sector; and (d) child bonded labour.

It would be wrong to think that bonded labour is a thing of past as it can be found even today in not only agriculture but also in other sectors of employment including brick kilns, stone quarries, salt fields, leather manufacturing units, etc.

Causes

Though the main causes of origin, growth and perpetuation of bonded labour system are economic but the social and religious factors too support the custom. The *economic* causes include: extreme poverty of the people, inability to find work for livelihood, inadequate size of the landholdings to support family, lack of alternative small-scale loans for the rural and urban poor, natural calamities like drought, floods, etc. destruction of the standing crops, plague and other diseases leading to death of men and animals, absence of rains, drying away of wells, meagre income from forest produce, and inflation and constant rising prices. The *social* factors include: high expenses on occasions like marriage, death, feast, birth of a child, etc. leading to heavy debts, caste-based discrimination, lack of concrete social welfare scheme to safeguard against hunger and illness, non-compulsory and unequal educational system, and indifference and corruption among government officials. Sometimes, the exploitation by some persons in the village also compels people to migrate to some other place and seek not only employment on the employer's conditions but also get protection from the influential persons. The *religious* arguments are used to convince the people of low castes that religion enjoins them to serve people of high castes. Illiteracy, ignorance, immaturity and lack of skill and professional training sustain such beliefs. Broadly speaking, it may be maintained that bondage originates mainly from economic and social pressures.

Under the bonded labour system, a person is given no or nominal numeration in return for his labour. It is also known as debt-bondage because bonded labour is generally demanded as a means of repayment for a loan. The system was designed to enable a few socially and economically powerful sections of society to exploit the weaker sections of the society.

The Legislation

The pernicious and fastidious practice of bonded labour existed in many states in India. After independence, it could not be allowed to continue to blight the national life any longer. There are a few constitutional provisions that safeguard the system of bonded labour from being practiced:

1. *Article 21*: This is the most important and foremost safeguard against any exploitation of human lives and their liberty. It is part of the Basic Structure of the Constitution and cannot be amended. It secures the right to life and right to live with human dignity to every person in India. So, any practice of bonded labour would be in contravention of this Constitutional provision since bonded labour deprives a person of numerous liberties.
2. *Article 23*: Expressly provides for the abolition of forced labour. This not only prohibits bonded labour but also covers the practice of *begar* and other similar forms of human trafficking are prohibited and any contravention of this provision shall be an offence punishable in accordance with law. Parliament has enacted the Bonded Labour System (Abolition) Act, 1976. The Act makes the system of bonded labour a punishable offence.
3. *Article 39*: This directs the state to secure the right to an adequate livelihood. It also directs the state to formulate its policies with an object that no citizen is forced out of economic necessity to enter into avocations which are not suited to them.
4. *Article 42*: This is also a directive principle of state policy which states, 'the state shall make provision for securing just and humane conditions of work...'. This means that the state must ensure that every person has a working condition which is just and humane for them.
5. *Article 43*: This is the directive which directs the state to secure conditions for work ensuring a decent standard of life.

However, no serious effort was made to give effect to constitutional provision and stamp out the shocking practice of bonded labour. The Forced Labour (Abolition) Convention adopted by the International Labour Organization (ILO) in 1919 was ratified by India only in November 1954. Some states in India had also enacted laws for abolishing the bonded labour. For example, the Bihar Kamianti Act was passed in 1920, the Madras Agency Debt Bondage Regulation in 1940, Kabadi System Regulation in Bastar in Madhya Pradesh in 1943, Hyderabad Bhagela Agreement Regulation in 1943, Odisha Debt Bonded Abolition Regulation in 1948, Rajasthan Sagri System

Abolition Act in 1961 (which was amended in 1975), and Kerala Bonded Labour System (Abolition) Act in 1975. But it was only after the announcement of the 20-point programme on 1 July 1975 that the legislative exercise at the national level began with some amount of seriousness and urgency. An ordinance was enacted in October 1975 which was later replaced by the Act passed in February 1976, called the Bonded Labour System (Abolition) Act. With this all the state laws became inoperative after the enactment of the Act by the union government in 1976.

Based on the Constitution, Parliament has enacted the Bonded Labour System (Abolition) Act, 1976. The Act makes the system of bonded labour a punishable offence. This not only prohibits bonded labour but also covers the practice of *begar* and other forms of human trafficking in India. All the state laws became inoperative after the enactment of the Bonded Labour System (Abolition) Act (BLSAA).

Salient features of the Act are:

1. The bonded labour system shall stand abolished and every bonded labourer shall stand free and discharged from any obligation to render bonded.
2. Liability to repay bonded debt shall be deemed to have extinguished.
3. Property of the bonded labourer to be freed from the mortgage, etc.
4. District magistrates entrusted with the responsibility of implementing the provisions of the Act.
5. Vigilance committees mandated to be constituted at district and sub-divisional levels.

The Act implies: (a) identification of bonded labourers; (b) release of bonded labourers; (c) action against offenders, i.e. creditors who had forced agreement upon the debtor; (d) holding of regular meetings of the vigilance committees at the district and *tehsil* level; (e) maintenance of the prescribed registers; and, (f) conferring of judicial powers to executive magistrates. The Act also provides for the rehabilitation of the bonded labourers who are freed from their creditors. The 1976 Act was amended in 1985 in which it was clarified that the contract workers and interstate migrant workers, if they fulfil the conditions laid down in the Bonded Labour System (Abolition) Act, 1976, will be considered as bonded labour.

The main problem that is faced in the implementation of the 1976 Act is the identification of the bonded labourers. Neither the administrators at the district and *tehsil* levels admit the existence of the bonded labourers in their areas nor the creditors accept that any bonded workers are serving them, nor the workers themselves are willing to give statements that they are being forced to work as bonded labourers since long. It is the social workers attached to non-political social action groups and voluntary organizations who identify the bonded labourers. The other handicap which aggravates the problem is the economic rehabilitation of the released labourers. The economic rehabilitation includes: finding jobs for them, getting them minimum wages, giving them training in skills, horticulture, animal husbandry, etc. promoting their traditional arts and crafts, allotment of agricultural land, helping them in developing the allotted land, helping them in getting the raw material, providing them either land for constructing houses or low-cost dwelling units, arranging bank loans or credit for them, helping them in the processing of forest produce, educating them and their children, arranging for their medical care, etc. All these are herculean tasks. Besides ensuring the economic rehabilitation, the state governments are also expected to arrange for their psychological rehabilitation and integration of various schemes of central and state governments. In chalking out plans and strategies of rehabilitation, the freed labourers are to be given the choice between various alternatives (Sharma, 1990: 54).

Based on the recommendations of Gurupadaswamy Committee, The Child Labour (Prohibition and Regulation) Act, 1986 was passed. This Act prohibits the employment of children below the age of 14 in factories, mines and in other forms of hazardous employment, and regulates the working conditions of children in other employment. The Act imposes a prohibition on employment of children in dhabas, restaurants, hotels, motels, tea shops, resorts, spas or other recreational centres, etc.

The central legislature has made substantial changes in the provisions of the CL Act, 1986 in the year 2016. The name of the CL Act has been changed to 'Child and Adolescent Labour (Prohibition and Regulation) Act, 1986'. The main features are:

1. A complete prohibition has been imposed on employment of child labour (i.e. a person below the age of 14 years) in any establishment whether hazardous or not.
2. A child is permitted to work only to help the family, in a family enterprise or as child artist after school hours or during vacations.
3. The amendment has introduced the concept of adolescent labour between the age of 14–18 years and permits employment of adolescent labour except in hazardous processes or occupation.
4. The number of hazardous occupations and processes has been reduced from 83 to only 3. The offences under the Act have been made compoundable and cognizable notwithstanding the provisions of the Criminal Procedure Code.
5. It provides for setting up of the Child and Adolescent Labour Rehabilitation Fund, in which all the amounts of penalty have to be realized. The Act provides for increased penalty and imprisonment which shall not be less than six months and may extend up to two years and fine which may vary between ₹ 20,000 to ₹ 50,000.

Apart from the above mentioned constitutional provisions and safeguards, there are a few more legislations in consonance with this major law in India such as Contract Labour (Regulation and Abolition) Act 1970, Minimum Wages Act, 1948, and the Inter-State Migrant Workmen

(Regulation of Employment and Conditions of Service) Act, 1979 and even the Indian Penal Code 1860.

1. The Indian Penal Code recognizes the offence of unlawful compulsory labour and imposes a punishment of imprisonment for a term extendable to one year or with a fine or both.
2. The Minimum Wages Act, 1948 sets the minimum wage for certain enumerated occupations and requires that overtime is paid to whoever working beyond the 'normal working day'.

Misery and Suffering in Bondage

The former Chief Justice of India Justice P.N. Bhagwati described the bonded labourers as 'non-beings, exiles of civilization living a life worse than that of animals, for the animals are at least free to roam about as they like and they can plunder or grab food whenever they are hungry, but these outcasts of society are held in bondage and robbed of their freedom even. They are confined to an existence where they have to live either in hovels or under the open sky and be satisfied with whatever unwholesome food they can manage to get, inadequate though it may be to fill their hungry stomachs. Not having any choice, they are driven by poverty and hunger into a life of bondage, a dark bottomless pit from which, in a cruel exploitative society, they cannot hope to be rescued' (*Yojana*, 1–15 May 1987: 32–33).

The 32nd Round of National Sample Survey Office (NSSO) gave an estimate of 3,43,000 bonded labourers in 16 major states. Of these, 98 per cent are said to be bonded due to indebtedness and 2 per cent due to customary social obligations. The highest number is believed to exist in three states of Andhra Pradesh, Karnataka and Tamil Nadu, followed by Odisha, Uttar Pradesh, Bihar and Madhya Pradesh. A Human Rights Watch report from 2003 estimates that 3,50,000 children work as bonded labour in silk thread and weaving industry in the Karnataka and Varanasi districts alone. In Tamil Nadu, no meaningful effort has been taken to wipe out bonded labour in the state due to the misconception that only stray case of it exists. But, the truth is that it is prevalent very much and in many forms like *Sumangali Thittam*. The Tamil Nadu State Legal Services Authority (TNSLSA) has launched a special programme to weed out bonded labour in the state (*The Times of India*, Madurai, 7 August 2013). The secretaries of the District Legal Services Authorities (DLSAs) have been directed to form a core group called District Taskforce for Bonded Labourer (DTBL) to achieve the purpose. The DTBL, first of its kind in the country, it will consist of a judicial officer of the rank of junior division civil judge, two-panel lawyers, an NGO member who works on the abolition and rehabilitation of bonded labour, an official nominated by the district collector (not below the rank of tahsildar), one or two para-legal volunteers and local panchayat chairman/member. The DTBL team will collect information about the prevalence of bonded labour system in their respective districts, and thereafter prepare a plan for the rescue, release and rehabilitation of the bonded workers.

In states like Kerala, where land reforms have been implemented by statute, bonded labour has been virtually eliminated. It has been pointed out that the majority of the bonded labourers work as agricultural labourers in villages and belong to the outcaste or tribal communities. Of the total labour force in the rural areas, about 33 per cent are engaged in non-agricultural activities, 42 per cent work as cultivators and 25 per cent as agricultural labourers. Of those who work as agricultural labourers, 48 per cent belong to scheduled castes (SCs) and 33 per cent to scheduled tribes (STs). Being unskilled and unorganized, the agricultural labourers have little for their livelihood other than personal labour. The bonded agricultural labourers occupy the lowest rung of the rural ladder. Social and economic stratification in a village is linked with land and caste which in turn govern the economic and social status of the people. The bonded labourers thus live in pitiable and miserable conditions. They are socially exploited because though in theory they are assured food, clothes, free tobacco, etc. but in practice they get the food that is leftover, and clothes that are discarded by family members. They are made to work for 12 to 14 hours a day and are forced to live with cows and buffaloes in shed. And, if they fall ill, they are hardly provided health care.

The International Justice Mission (IJM), in partnership with the Rural Development and Panchayat Raj Department, has launched a research study on the prevalence of bonded labour in Karnataka. The research study covered three districts – Bengaluru Rural, Bengaluru Urban and Ramanagara – in Karnataka. As part of the research, 4,306 labourers in the three districts were surveyed between April and June 2015. The study captured data on 15 distinct industries across 3,765 work-sites. This also included interviews with 39 labourers who had migrated to Karnataka in the last three years in search of job opportunities. Findings extrapolated that of the estimated total number of 16 lakh labourers across the three districts, about 33 per cent (approximately 5.5 lakh) could be bonded labourers. About 92 per cent of these labourers belonged to the SC/ST communities. The industries where this is most prevalent include brick klins, plantations, rock quarries, rice mills, tobacco and fish farms. There was evidence of trafficking in 59 per cent of bonded labour cases. The study, which was peer-reviewed and published in the *International Journal of Human Trafficking* in 2018, found that 50.5 per cent bonded labourers in the three districts were paid below-minimum wages and 37 per cent of them worked all seven days of the week. Given that about 64 per cent of these people were illiterate, it is unclear whether they understood the terms of their employment.

Rehabilitation

Under the Bonded Labour System (Abolition) Act, 1976, bonded labourers have a right to immediate rehabilitation. It is the state's duty to suitably rehabilitate its bonded labourers.

Getting the bonded labourers identified and freed was the statutory obligation of the state governments only but from November 1987 onwards, the voluntary organizations also came to be authorized both for identification and rehabilitation. The Indian government does not collect nationwide data on the age, gender and occupation of the bonded labourers who are released or rehabilitated. However, as per information collected from various states, over 3,13,000 bonded labourers have been identified and released since the Act was passed. The lack of implementation in identifying bonded labour gives impunity to the creditors, jeopardizes all measures, and has resulted in a wide gap between policy and reality. But this uncertainty only underlines the fact that accurate estimates of bonded labour are hard to establish, so the current government's claims to having abolished it are decidedly weak on this score. The Government of India's unique scheme of MGNREGA which guarantees 100 days of paid labour in a year has played an important role in securing the stability of rural workers. But to say bonded labour has been eradicated through a government scheme is to misunderstand the basic concept. By definition, bonded labourers are denied the freedom to leave their place of work and are not allowed to work elsewhere by employers for a variety of reasons – past debts being a key one. As a result, they are cut off from access to state or central government benefits and schemes, such as the MGNREGA, to which they are entitled. They simply do not have the freedom to engage in such schemes. The first step in any plan to effectively address the issue of bonded labour must be a concerted effort to ensure their freedom through a robust identification system and official release. It is only once bonded labourers are free that schemes such as the MGNREGA and other government welfare programmes can be converged and made easily accessible to promote the intended benefits to the vulnerable community.

Rehabilitation is both physical and psychological. Physical rehabilitation is essentially economic whereas psychological rehabilitation has to be built up through a process of assurance and reassurance. The two must go side by side. The first prerequisite of psychological rehabilitation is that the freed bonded labourers must be wrenched away from the old habitat and be rehabilitated at a place where they will no longer be subject to the ruinous influence of the erstwhile bonded labour-keepers. Unless they are psychologically assured that after release from bondage, debt will not regulate their destiny any longer, there is every possibility that they may slide back to debt bondage.

Basically, there are three phases of rehabilitation:

(a) Immediate physical subsistence after release.
(b) Short-term measures to help the freed workers to start a new life (for example, allotment of a house site, assistance for construction of a house, allotment of a plot of agricultural land, supplying a pair of bullocks and agricultural implements, or provision of avenues of gainful employment, etc.).

(c) Long-term measures (such as, arranging credit, training in new skills, developing existing skills, providing a remunerative price support, ensuring non-formal literacy of adult members and formal literacy for children, securing medical care, protection of civil rights, etc.).

It is thus, the rehabilitation which will give the freed bonded labourers the status of beings so that they may be able to identify themselves with the mainstream of a civilized human society and realize the dignity worthy of human existence.

In order to assist the state governments in the task of rehabilitation of freed bonded labourers, the government has revamped the Centrally Sponsored Plan Scheme into 'Central Sector Scheme for Rehabilitation of Bonded Labourers, 2016', with effect from 17 May 2016. Under the revamped Scheme, financial assistance is provided for rehabilitation of a rescued bonded labourer at the rate of ₹ 1 lakh for an adult male beneficiary, ₹ 2 lakh for special category beneficiaries such as children including orphans or those rescued from organized and forced begging rings or other forms of forced child labour, and women and ₹ 3 lakh in cases of bonded or forced labour involving extreme cases of deprivation or marginalization where the District Magistrate deems fit, ₹ 20,000 is provided as immediate assistance. The Scheme also provides for financial assistance of ₹ 4.50 lakh per district to the states for conducting the survey of bonded labourers, ₹ 1 lakh per district for evaluatory studies and ₹ 10 lakhs per state per annum for awareness generation.

Lacunae in Effective Rehabilitation

Qualitatively reviewing the implementation of the rehabilitative programmes for the bonded labourers in different states, we find that some states, like Odisha, Uttar Pradesh, Kerala and Andhra Pradesh, point out the welcome features of identification and rehabilitation but some need to introduce many innovative changes. The following visible lacunae in the implementation of the programme need to be dealt with immediately:

First, instead of treating the programme in isolation as the programme of a particular ministry/department, there has to be coordination among various concerned ministries/departments like those of agriculture, animal husbandry, irrigation, forest, fisheries, etc. so that the programme is dealt with as an integrated national programme. *Second*, since the social milieu and the social structures which promoted the bonded labour system in the past continue to dominate the village life and the economy even today, they need to be probed into and changed with commitment. *Third*, the development departments are so much burdened with schemes like MNREGS, etc. that their programmes mostly remain time-bound and target-oriented without taking into account the needs, aptitudes and preferences of the beneficiaries. The need is, therefore, to design programmes in such a manner that they serve as target group-oriented rather than target-oriented. *Fourth*, with poor infrastructure and lack of qualified and committed staff and resources, the beneficiaries are not provided protective covers on a long-term basis with the result that very often productive assets turn into liabilities. *Fifth,* middlemen operate like parasites and take away the limited fruits and benefits of rehabilitation to their advantage. What is required, therefore, is carefully and rationally formulated scheme with varied linkages, keeping an eye on the type of infrastructure already available. *Sixth,* the freed bonded labourers, who come from the lowest strata of the society and represent the extremes of poverty and destitution, are unable to exercise the choice of a particular scheme which may be most profitable to them. Their dependence on the concerned officials in selecting a particular scheme for them deprives them of the real benefits of rehabilitation. This dependence needs to be reduced. *Lastly,* the attitude of the erstwhile bonded labour keepers, people at large and officials in various departments, has not changed at all. Even when the erstwhile masters and landlords assault their labourers, their land is forcibly taken away, their children are not permitted to pass through the paddy fields of the landlords to reach schools, their animals are whisked away by their exploiters, and they complain to police, approach doctors for help, lodge complaints with the officers of the concerned departments, they (officers, police, doctors, etc.) are not at all moved by their pathetic stories and remain callous, unresponsive, insensitive and ineffective to help them. Without a change in the attitude of the people and the officials, the freed labourers cannot withstand the organized onslaughts against them by the more influential sections of the society. Their ignorance, illiteracy and lack of capacity to fight for their rights will always hamper them to enjoy the gains of freedom and development.

Changing social systems and social structures to benefit the poor who become the bonded labourers is not easy. Let us take two illustrations. A tribal needs money to pay bride-price for his own or his son's marriage. He obtains loan by mortgaging his services and thus becomes a bonded labourer. Similarly, suppose an individual is convicted by the court for illicit distillation and is heavily fined. Since he has no money to pay fine, he takes a loan from an influential person by pledging his labour and becomes a bonded labourer. Now, is abolishing the custom of bride-price possible? Is imposition of the fine by the court for an illegal action wrong? Many economic needs cannot be gratified by the poor individuals without seeking loans. In such cases, what is needed is careful scrutiny of the agreements for obtaining loans so that pledging the labour as security may be prevented and the system of bonded labour may be controlled.

The 'group approach' to development will bring the freed bonded labourers together, enable them to pool their resources, get help from various agencies, departments and banks, and integrate themselves for a common purpose for a qualitative and permanent rehabilitation. Such a group effort can be land-based, craft-based or asset-based for success. This requires proper selection of beneficiaries, the place where they are to be rehabilitated, selection of skills to be taught to them, and building awareness among the beneficiaries themselves by converting them into willing partners in a joint venture for their rehabilitation, progress and advancement.

The crucial problem is that if the freed bonded labourers are not rehabilitated, they will suffer more. The question before them would be: should they choose hunger or slavery, freedom or security, hard work in serfdom or crime to support family and the resultant fear of imprisonment? A Planning Commission report says that the progress of rehabilitation work is very slow. The state government officials lack initiative or remain indifferent to identification and rehabilitation programmes. The social workers too face many handicaps in their work. It is hoped that the central aid and the involvement of voluntary organizations will make the identification and rehabilitation programmes of the bonded labourers more effective.

Initiatives of the National Human Rights Commission (NHRC)

The Supreme Court in a writ petition – Public Union for Civil Liberties vs State of Tamil Nadu & Others – directed the National Human Rights Commission (NHRC) in 1997 to get involved in the monitoring of the implementation of the Bonded Labour System (Abolition) Act, 1976. Since then, the NHRC has been focussing on states where bonded labour is prevalent. During 2011, it took stock of the situation and the following charter of activities has been taken up on the issue of bonded labour:

1. Constitution of core group on bonded labour.
2. Organizing national level seminars on elimination of bonded labour system. One such seminar was organized in 2011 in New Delhi.
3. Workshops to be conducted in bonded labour-prone states to sensitize District Magistrates, Sub-Divisional Magistrates, SSPs and officers from the Labour Department. The Commission has altogether organized five such workshops.
4. Carry out surprise visits to bonded labour-prone areas.
5. Development of an instructional manual on bonded labour.
6. Revised format for monitoring of bonded labour in states.
7. Review existing schemes of the central and state governments on bonded labour.
8. Recommending state governments for organizing orientation training programmes in each bonded labour-prone district.
9. Recommending states to constitute a state-level monitoring and coordination committee under the chairmanship of Chief Secretary with secretaries to government of various departments as members.

In 2000, the NHRC also constituted an expert group chaired by S.R. Sankaran, for identification of bonded labour-prone districts, industries and occupations and for various aspects relating to legislation and implementation. The expert group, in its report submitted to the NHRC in 2001, concluded that although the Ministry of Labour had identified 13 states and

172 districts as being bonded labour-prone; the system is prevalent in almost all states (NHRC, 2001).

From its inception till January 2017, 14,614 cases were received by the National Human Right Commission, out of which 13,266 have been disposed of. There have been several initiatives by the National Human Rights Commission to curb this practice. Apart from that, even the Supreme Court has condemned this practice.

Bonded labour is a multidimensional problem. Therefore, for its eradication, a multidimensional approach is needed. It is desirable that every concerted effort must be made to wipe out this evil social practice from Indian soil. Mere passing of laws is not sufficient to eradicate this social evil. Preventive efforts must recognize the social dimensions of bondage, and thereby address it through public sensitization and rights awareness, adult literacy, organizing workers, income generation and vocational skills development. The strategies to eliminate bonded labour need to go beyond the symptoms to address the root causes (labour market segmentation, entrenched social discrimination, lack of financial services, lack of outreach of social partners in the informal economy). The multifaceted and deeply rooted nature of those causes requires an integrated and long-term strategy.

In 1978, the Central Government established a scheme to provide assistance in rehabilitating bonded labourers. This scheme has been revised in 1986, 1995, 1999, and 2000. The latest revision is the 2016 scheme. The 2016 scheme is noteworthy as it recognizes the differential needs of marginalized groups trapped in bonded labour. It provides cash assistance of ₹ 1 lakh for male bonded labourers, ₹ 2 lakh for female and child bonded labourers and children rescued from forced labour or organized or forced begging, and ₹ 3 lakh for differently-abled, physically challenged, trafficked, commercially sexually exploited, transgender, and other severely vulnerable bonded labourers.

Effective Concern

The plight of the bonded labourers continues to be a serious social problem and a matter of concern for public, government, judiciary, social scientists and social workers. For this purpose, it is necessary that researches be sponsored by different funding agencies to ascertain the extent and the nature of the problem, examine handicaps in identification, utility of various rehabilitation schemes, coordination of activities between central government, state governments and voluntary organizations, necessity of amending the 1976 Act, determining responsibilities and accountability of the concerned officers, and introducing after-care programmes for the freed bonded labourers. Unless serious efforts are taken to save the bonded labourers from ruthless exploitation for vested interests, the problem will continue to be a social menace. The total abolition of the system of bonded labour through legislation may not be feasible in the foreseeing future, yet doing away with the legislation may cause further distress to the victims.

Removing poverty, unemployment and illiteracy, which are believed to be the three basic causes of the bonded labour system, is also not easy. The formulation of future plans, programmes and projects for the bonded labourers would require a broad approach and action at various levels.

The problem of bonded labour has, thus, to be fought at various fronts – social, psychological and legal. We have to educate the exploited not to succumb to pressure tactics. We have to tell the exploiters that law cannot be circumvented and has to take its course in democratic India. We have to create committed opinion among the masses. We have to involve not only intellectuals but also the enlightened citizens to carry the message to those who matter. We have to enforce laws rigidly. We have also to impress upon the politicians to tackle the issue with concerted interest and missionary zeal. The system based on exploitation by a few socially and economically powerful persons, trading on the misery and suffering of large numbers of men, and holding them in a bondage constitutes a shameful feature of our national life. The bondage of the economically impoverished segments of society for a small debt is totally incompatible with the egalitarian socio-economic order promised to Indians. Wiping out this system is basic and crucial to human dignity and conformity to constitutional values. As long as there is poverty, unemployment, underemployment, landlessness, migration, indebtedness, the pernicious bonded labour system will continue to prevail.

Suggestions to Curb Bonded Labour

1. An effective and quicker criticism redressed machinery need to be set up for proper disposal of cases relating to bonded labour.
2. There should be a strict enforcement of the welfare and labour law.
3. A statewide public awareness campaign should be released regarding the legal prohibition of bonded labour.
4. Efforts must be made to create a database of bonded labourers. It is not an easy task but would be the first step towards their liberation and rehabilitation.
5. Amend the Child Labour (Prohibition and Regulation) Act, 1986, so that household enterprises and government schools and training centres are no longer exempted for prohibitions on employing children.
6. The bonded labourers ought to be rehabilitated as soon as viable after their release. Productive and profits generating schemes should be formulated in advance, otherwise they will once more fall back upon the machine of bonded labour after their release.

Conclusion

Bonded labour is one of the worst violations of human rights and also the dignity of life. It is a crime against humanity, anathema of civilised humanity, denial of inalienable human rights, the antithesis of decent work and a blot on civilised society that jolts the conscience of the entire nation.

There are several factors which are causing the continuance of this system of forced labour. Often, the usurious rate of interest is one of the leading factors which contribute to its continuance. Apart from that, the faulty system of adjustment of wages with the amount lent, prevalent ignorance, illiteracy, etc. are all factors contributing to the continuance of bonded labour.

References

Indian Labour Journal, August, 1989.

Indian School of Social Sciences, *Bonded Labour in India*, India Book Exchange, Calcutta, 1976.

Report of the National Commission on Labour, Government of India, 1969.

Sharma, A.N., 'Bonded Labour', *Welfare of Special Categories of Labour*, Tata Institute of Social Sciences, Bombay, 1990, pp. 51–56.

Srivastava, Ravi S., 'Bonded Labour in India: Its Incidence and Pattern', ILO Working Paper, June, 2005.

Yojana, Special Issue on 'Could We Break Their Shackles?', Vol. 31, No. 8, 1–15 May, 1987.

24

Agrarian Crisis, Distress and Farmers' Suicides

India is an agrarian country with around 70 per cent of its people depending directly or indirectly upon agriculture. The agrarian crisis in India is like a ticking time-bomb and it is crucial to rectify the mistakes which are contributing to it. Decisions on agriculture need to be taken on Indian agriculture and thus the economy as a whole. If the policies continue to put industrial growth before the farmers' needs, matters are going to worsen a lot. Business interests are important but not at the expense of farmers. Farmers are the real providers of food security for everyone. Steps should be taken to remove the middlemen between the farmers and consumers. This would ensure price stability of the essential commodities and the burden of increasing price would be based on both the farmers and consumers.

Nevertheless, there are two reasons to be concerned that Indian agriculture may indeed be facing a wider and deeper crisis: (a) the long-term growth trend in production and productivity of agriculture, considerably less than required to sustain the projected high overall growth rates in the coming decade, may actually be slowing down; and (b) the growing economic and social disparities between agriculture and the rest of the economy and between rural and urban sectors.

The slowing down of agricultural growth is widely attributed to the slowing down of investment, especially public investment. The Planning Commission seems to share this perception and sees increased investments in irrigation and watershed development as the means to achieve the projected growth. But what is relevant is not the magnitude of investment but its contribution to increasing production capacity. For a variety of reasons peculiar to agriculture, production capacity has not increased in proportion to the quantum of investment. Earlier, problems have worsened as farm incomes have been squeezed by slower output growth, higher costs and increased vulnerability to a changing climate. And there is a slew of new problems resulting directly from government policies, the outlay on surface irrigation, which accounts for the bulk of public investment in agriculture, is concentrated on projects that have taken an unconscionably long time to complete. Costs have risen and outlays have not resulted in any significant additions to the irrigated area. The efficacy of public investments in soil and water conservation is in serious doubt. They are marked by huge waste and corruption, and there are hardly any mechanisms at the local level to manage the works and ensure the potential for expansion is properly exploited. They have had hardly any impact on raising product potential or productivity of rain-fed lands.

Overcoming this barrier calls for a major reorientation on the following lines:

1. Shifting public investment towards modernization of surface irrigation works (to facilitate higher yield per unit of water used) and for watershed development.
2. Prioritizing incomplete irrigation projects after strict cost-benefit analysis and monitor implementation.
3. Limiting the government's role in laying down the broad principles and institutional framework. Entrust direct management of land, water, and common service facilities to autonomous organizations functioning within well-specified rules.
4. Enforcing better preventive and punitive measures to contain gross violations of rules governing access to, and use of resources.
5. Conducting a critical review of the research system in public institutions to make it more effective.
6. Changing policies relating to pricing of yield and input to avoid waste.

India's Urban Consumer-Driven Economic Policies

The political economy of India is driven more by the urban consumers than the rural producers. This is reflected in the urgency to impose price controls in case of price rise (imposing minimum export prices, bringing items under essential commodities, etc.) and a lacklustre withdrawal once the price is under control. Contrast this with how we have been imposing minimum import price to secure our steel sector. This differential treatment to the primary sector also limits profit margin and thereby hinders farmers' chances of breaking free from the cycle of indebtedness.

There is a widespread perception that the 'agrarian crisis' is more or less an outcome of natural calamities like drought which no one can fight. Governments over the years have used this misperception in their favour to hide their inefficiencies in problem-solving. This was also a period marked by imprudence in the use of land, water, fertilizers, and other key inputs due to failures of governance, poor management of public systems catering to agriculture and pricing, and subsidy policies inimical to the prudent use of resources and effective exploitation of the potential of available technology. With the scope for expanding area being exhausted and the scope for further expansion of irrigation getting diminished, the institutional barrier comprising governance, the quality of public systems, and economic policies have become the most serious impediment to agricultural growth.

According to Chandrasekhar (2017), the policy shifts of the reform era have not been in favour of agriculture. Though, an early argument was that agriculture would gain from liberalization and deregulation. Moreover, the market has worked against farmers in unusual ways:

1. Over the years, subsidies have been reduced in the case of important inputs raising their costs.
2. The government's reform programme has deregulated and, therefore, increased prices of inputs.
3. Fiscal conservatism has adversely affected public investment in irrigation and flood control.
4. The system of technical extension services for farmers has been allowed to decay.
5. Imports of agricultural commodities have dampened domestic prices. The dilution of government intervention in the form of minimum support prices, procurement and public distribution is undermining the medium-term viability of agricultural production in India.

According to National Institution for Transforming India (NITI Aayog) the average income growth of a farming family, in 2011–2016, was only 0.44 per cent, which basically means that income for farmers was stagnant, while their income mirrors inflation month-on-month in the same period, food inflation is at 2.8 per cent. All of these have adversely affected productivity, raised costs and squeezed margins. As a result, the viability of crop production has been eroded.

The Centre for Study of Developing Societies (CSDS), based in Delhi, found that given an option, majority of farmers in the country would prefer to take up some other work. Poor income, bleak future and stress are the main reasons why they want to give up farming. Around 18 per cent of respondents surveyed said it was because of family pressure that they are continuing with farming. The CSDS study report, 'State of Indian Farmers', says that benefits of government schemes and policies are being mostly given to big farmers having landholding of 10 acres (4.05 hectare) and above. Only 10 per cent of poor and small farmers with average land holding of 1–4 acres (0.4 to 1.6 ha) have benefited from government schemes and subsidies. The farmers blamed the state and central governments for their present condition as 74 per cent of those interviewed alleged they do not get any farming-related information from officials of the agriculture department.

Agriculture in India is undergoing a structural change, leading to a crisis situation. The relative contribution of agriculture to the GDP has been declining over steadily. In developing countries like India, agriculture occupies a dominant position in GDP since the secondary and tertiary sectors are not fully developed. As the economy gets diversified with considerable contributions from the secondary and tertiary sectors, particularly IT and service sectors, the share of agriculture goes down. This does not mean the importance of agriculture has gone down. It only means that the other sectors have grown. The trends in the area, input use, capital stock and technology also reflect the agricultural downfall. All these trends indicate that the agricultural sector in India is facing a crisis today. It is argued that the root cause of the crisis was that agriculture is no more a profitable economic activity when compared to the other enterprises. It means that the income derived from these activities is not sufficient enough to meet the expenditure of the cultivators. And therefore, unless agriculture is made a profitable enterprise, the present crisis cannot be solved. The related factors responsible for the crisis include dependence on rainfall and climate, liberal import of agricultural products, reduction in agricultural subsidies, lack of easy credit to agriculture and dependence on moneylenders, the decline in government investment in the agricultural sector and conversion of agricultural land for alternative uses. It is argued that the consequence of the agricultural crisis in India is very vast and likely to hit all the other sectors and the national economy in several ways. India's last national census, 2011, recorded nearly 15 million fewer farmers than there were in 1991. Many of those fell from being farmers to being landless agricultural labourers, into the ranks of the agrarian underclass. In specific, it has adverse effects on food supply, prices of food grains, cost of living, health and nutrition, poverty, employment, labour market, land loss from agriculture and foreign exchange earnings. The factors contributing to the crisis include environmental degradation, decrease in landholding size, plateauing of crop yields from the present farm technology, and withdrawal of state support. Moreover, the rapid growth of India's gross domestic product has not created enough opportunities for rural calamities. This leads to distress due to following reasons:

1. *Lack of Direct Integration with the Market*: Although initiatives like the national agricultural market and contract farming are helping integrate the farmers' produce directly with the market, cutting the role of intermediaries, but the reality is still lagging behind.
2. *Lack of Awareness*: The digital divide, as well as the literacy gap, has made the marginal and small farmers particularly vulnerable due to their inability to utilise the positives of government policies. This is reflected in the continued unsustainable cropping practices – like cultivating sugarcane in water-deficit regions.
3. *Water Crisis*: The concentration of these suicides in the water-deficit regions of states like Maharashtra, Karnataka, is a manifestation of how the water crisis and thereby failure to meet production demands have intensified the menace. This is particularly true in the backdrop of continued failed monsoons.

4. *Interstate Water Disputes*: What has added to the already prevalent crisis is the unwillingness to cater to each other's water needs amongst the states. A case in point is the recently resurfaced Kaveri dispute that saw Karnataka and Tamil Nadu battle out water shortage both in and outside the tribunal even to the extent of non-compliance with the tribunal award.
5. *Climate Change:* Climate change has acted as the last nail in the coffin by resulting in furthering of the uncertainties associated with the already uncertain monsoon system and hence agricultural production. While incidents like flash floods have led to crop losses, deferred monsoons have seen production shortfall year-in and year-out.
6. *Changes in the Global Market*: Such changes seriously threaten the security of farmers operating in this sector. Especially small-scale farmers from the low-caste and indigenous sector – who often lack market knowledge, land tenure, and resources to afford advanced agricultural technology – are increasingly left behind.

India is an agrarian economy with around two-third of its working population depending directly or indirectly upon agriculture. Agriculture contributes 23 per cent to India's Gross National Product. Though the share of agriculture and allied sector in the country's GDP has declined steadily over the years, it is still the largest sector and plays an important role in the overall socio-economic development of the country. India has achieved the self-sufficiency in the production of food grains in a few decades of its political emancipation.

The recent crisis in agriculture sector in India is mainly the result of the marginalization of agrarian economy in national policy since the initiation of economic reforms in the 1990s. Besides, farmers' indebtedness is also the main cause of distress in the agriculture sector. According to a survey conducted by National Sample Survey Office (NSSO), nearly half of India's farmers are in debt. Of the 89.35 million rural households engaged in farming in India, nearly 43.42 million or 48.6 per cent run into debt. Similarly, poor returns to cultivation and absence of non-farm opportunities are also indicative of the larger socio-economic malaise in rural India. The features of the current agrarian crisis are briefly elaborated as follows:

1. There is an excessive dependence of a large section of the population on agriculture. This also indicates that rural non-farm employment opportunities are limited.
2. The much talked about green revolution had a greater focus on rice and wheat under irrigated condition bypassing crops and regions under rainfed or dry land conditions. There has been a failure to capitalize on the vast network of institutions to provide and regulate new technology (including the usage of biotechnology), and a virtual absence of extension service.
3. Supply of credit from formal sources to the agricultural sector is inadequate leading to greater reliance on informal sources at higher interest burden.

4. With changing technology and market conditions, the farmer is increasingly being exposed to the uncertainties of the product as well as markets.
5. Cultivation costs have risen manifolds, but the farmers' incomes have stagnated or declined. Seed, fertilizer and pesticides are firmly in the hands of corporations. Agricultural credit from public-sector banks increased significantly in the past two decades benefiting agribusiness, not farmers.

Addressing the Farm Crisis

The policymakers need to recognize four key factors about Indian agriculture. First, productivity per worker is abysmally low. Reasons include very small plot sizes, inadequate investments in irrigation, limited mechanization and technology adoption. Second, value addition in Indian is low, especially for small farmers. Third, the status quo is ecologically unsuitable in many parts as there is a decline in groundwater level in India. Finally, the status quo is fiscally unsustainable, the fiscal pressure of subsidies, price supports, and loan waivers are so severe that it would be cheaper and better for the country to just pay (economically unviable) farmers to not grow anything rather than subsidising economically and ecologically unsustainable cultivation. Thus, it is essential to design policy options that alleviate farmer suffering in a visible manner, and facilitate the structural transformation. Policy schemes imposed by India's government, including land leasing reforms, loan waivers, increases in Minimum Support Price (MSP) for agricultural products and compensation to farmers for crop loss have so far failed to reverse this trend.

Sustainable Solutions

1. The more inclusive alternative approach is to identify the vulnerable farmers based on certain criteria and give an equal amount as a financial relief to the vulnerable and distressed families.
2. Raise income from agricultural activities to make agriculture a profitable enterprise and attract the farmers to continue the crop production activities.
3. Strengthen the repayment capacity of the farmers by improving and stabilizing their income.
4. Improved technology, expansion of irrigation coverage, and crop diversification towards high-value crops are appropriate measures for raising productivity and farmers' income.
5. Another major source of the increase in farmers' income is remunerative prices for farm produce. The minimum support prices (MSP) are benchmark prices at which the government procures agricultural produce from farmers. Prices below MSP are considered unprofitable.
6. Removal of old regulations and restrictions on agriculture to enable the creation of a liberalized environment for investment, trading and marketing.

7. States must undertake and sincerely implement long-pending reforms in the agriculture sector with urgency.
8. The drastic changes in the present economic policies related to agriculture are made. The government should augment its investment and expenditure in the farm sector. Investment in agriculture and its allied sectors including irrigation, transport, communication, rural market, rural infrastructure and farm research, should be drastically increased and the government should aim at the integrated development of the rural areas. Rural prosperity also generates industrial demand.
9. Government can adapt the important ways to alleviate the farmers' crisis:
   (a) *Reduce Post-harvest Loss*: The challenge ahead of the government is to reduce the loss that farmers suffer after the harvest. Most medium-scale and lower-scale farmers lack local processing and preservation technologies, resulting in massive wastage.
   (b) *Reducing Middleman Costs*: A limit on the prices that intermediaries can charge, reducing the huge gap between farm prices and consumer prices is a must. Small farms also suffer from their reliance on middlemen to sell their product. As a result, they are sometimes compelled to sell it at less than the cost of producing it.
   (c) *Interest-free Loans*: Providing interest-free loans to farmers can help to revive the agriculture sector. The interest can be charged only farmers get to sell their crop and still do not repay the loan.
   (d) *Crop Insurance*: To compensate for the uncertainty caused by climate change, an effective crop insurance programme is required to protect farmers from bad yields. The existing insurance provides little protection.
   (e) *Structural transformation*: That improves agricultural productivity per worker and frees up farmers to shift to higher earning occupations. This will require shifting public funds away from subsidies, MSP increases, and loan waivers, and using these funds for productivity-enhancing investments, increased research in productivity-enhancing technologies and accelerating their adoption and risk for farmers through ex-ante crop insurance based on rainfall rather than ex-post loan waivers.
   (f) The combination of low productivity, economic unavailability, and fiscal, and ecological burden of subsidies is taking Indian agriculture close to a breakpoint. Sustainably improving farmer welfare requires a clear understanding of the issues and a focus on improving productivity per worker, and economically sound policies that farmer can see as being beneficial to them.

It is time that the government deals with the agrarian crisis with all seriousness. Otherwise, farmers will have no choice but to take it to the streets. The agrarian crisis needs to be handled with a human touch. Lakhs of farmers have committed suicide and those who failed in these attempts have been imprisoned under the law. This shows the collective failure of both society and the state.

Broadly the problems in Indian agriculture are the following:

1. Excessive dependence of a large section of the population on agriculture i.e. nearly two-third of the population.
2. The consistent decline in the size-class of holding along with poor returns from cultivation indicates that income for farm households is very low.
3. There has been a failure to take advantage of the new technology and market conditions are exposing the farmer to the uncertainties of the product as well as the markets.
4. The neglect of agriculture in plan resource allocation has led to a decline of public investments in irrigation and other related infrastructure.
5. Supply of credit from proper sources to the agricultural sector is inadequately leading to greater dependence on familiar sources at higher interest burden.
6. The two classes of farmers, namely tenant farmers and sharecroppers are still largely excluded from institutional credit because they do not own land titles.

These factors push the farmers into various economic, social, political, individual and environmental crises which are forcing the farmers to commit suicides.

Farmers' Suicides

Farmers' suicides in India became the centre of considerable concern in the 1990s when a journalist first highlighted the large number of suicides among them. The first state where suicides were reported was Maharashtra. Official reports initially denied it but as more and more cases came to light, the government began to accept that farmers in India were under considerable stress.

In the beginning it was believed that most of the suicides were happening among the cotton growers, especially those from Vidarbha. A look at the figures given by the State Crime Records Bureau, however, was sufficient to indicate that it was not only the cotton farmers but farmers as a professional category were suffering, irrespective of their holding size. Moreover, it was not only the farmers from Vidarbha but all over Maharashtra which showed a significantly high suicide rate.

The crucial question is, who is a farmer? Because in the eyes of the government only those in whose name the land is registered are seen as farmers. The rest escape consideration. This is problematic because most people toiling in the fields are landless labourers who work for a pittance. The landed farmers are generally big farmers with large land holdings. Mostly marginal farmers and small farmers are committing suicide. The small and marginal land holdings (less than 2 hectares) account for 72 per cent of land holdings, and this predominance of small operational holdings is a major limitation to reaping the benefits of economies of scale. Since small and marginal farmers have a little marketable surplus, they are left with low bargaining power and no say over prices.

Marginal farmer households account for well over 80 per cent of rural households. Their tiny plots of land can no longer sustain whole families, especially in rain-fed agriculture, which accounts for two-third of India's total cultivable area. Landless or marginal farmers lack the resources to either buy or lease more land or invest in farm infrastructure-irrigation, power, farm machinery, etc.

The large majority of small farmers are dependent on the rains. A weak monsoon or even a delayed monsoon – timing matters – means a significant loss of output. The next risk is weak soil fertility, pests and plant diseases. The third risk is the price. Even a good harvest can be bad news for the small farmer, placing him at the mercy of the trader. The better the crop, the lower would be the price. Their crop is usually sold to traders at rock bottom post-harvest prices in the village itself or the nearest *mandi*. Despite subsidies on power, fertilizers, etc. input costs have been rising faster than sale prices, about 52 per cent of agricultural households are estimated to be in debt, and the average size of the household debt is ₹ 47,000. There is a strong correlation between crop failure and the incidence of farmer suicides.

The highest number of farmer suicides were recorded in 2004 when 18,241 farmers committed suicide. The farmer's suicide rate in India has ranged between 1.4 and 1.8 per 1,00,000 total population, over a 10-year period through 2005. India is an agrarian country with around 70 per cent of its people depending directly or indirectly upon agriculture. Farmer suicides account for 11.2 per cent of all suicides in India. Activists and scholars have offered a number of conflicting reasons for farmer suicides, such as monsoon failure, high debt burdens, government policies, personal issues and family problems. There are also accusation of states manipulating the data on farmer suicides. Various reasons have been offered to explain why farmers commit suicide in India, including floods, drought, debt, use of genetically modified seed, public health, use of lower quantity pesticides due to fewer investments producing a decreased yield. There is no consensus on what the main causes might be but studies show suicide victims are motivated by more than one cause, on average three or more causes for committing suicide.

Since 2014, for a better analysis, NCRB has divided suicides in the agriculture sector in two categories – farmers and agricultural labourers. Data from 2015 showed that bankruptcy, indebtedness and farming-related issues were the leading causes of suicide by farmers, accounting for over 58 per cent of deaths. Going by landholding status, the data showed that nearly 73 per cent of farmers who committed suicide were small and marginal cultivators owning less than two hectares of land.

As per NCRB's 2015 report, 12,602 farmers and agricultural labourers committed suicide, marking a 1.1 per cent fall in 2016. The farm sector witnessed 11,458 suicides in 2016, a normal monsoon year. According to a report by NDTV published in July 2018, around 639 farmers ended their lives between March and May 2018 due to crop failure, indebtedness and failure to repay bank loans. The latest numbers come in the backdrop of widespread farmer protests across several states, calling for loan waivers and remunerative crop prices.

A study conducted in 2014, found that there are three specific characteristics associated with high-risk farmers: 'those that grow cash crops such as coffee and cotton; those with "marginal" farms of less than one hectare; and those with debts'. The study also found that the Indian states in which these three characteristics are most common had the highest suicide rates and also accounted for 'almost 75 per cent of the variability in state-level suicides'. Available research suggests that farmer suicides have arisen to a greater extent recently, due to an agrarian crisis affecting the most vulnerable farmers. This has multiple manifestations, including a lack of agricultural investment and irrigation improvement, use of cash crops, the increased use of no institutional credit sources, and the reduction of trade barriers. Maharashtra is the worst affected state. In the last 20 years, nearly 3,00,000 farmers have ended their lives by ingesting pesticides or by hanging themselves. Farmers usually take out bank loans against land to buy seeds and fertiliser and acquire irrigation equipment. Long droughts, poor yields, and unseasonal rains and indebtedness contribute to the struggles that lead to suicides.

Agriculture is a state subject and so the state governments take appropriate measures for development of agriculture, while the central government supplements the efforts of the states. Taking cognisance of the problem of agrarian distress and consequent farmers suicide in the country, the central government has undertaken a study 'Farmers suicide in India: causes and policy prescription'. It is an-all India coordinated study conducted in work plan 2016–17 period by Bengaluru-based Institute of Social and Economic Change (ISEC). Another study was undertaken by Indian Council of Agricultural Research (ICAR) and National Institute of Agricultural Economics and Policy Research (NIAP) under *Mera Gaon Mera Gaurav* initiative in few villages around Delhi could not establish, any significant adverse effect of demonetization on input availability, market arrivals of produce and area sown in rabi season.

Most studies identified indebtedness as the predominant single factor associated with farmers' suicides. Dongre and Deshmukh (2012) found that Vidarbha region of Maharashtra ranked debt as the most important reason for farmer suicides, followed by addictions, environmental problems, and price issues, amongst others Kale found that in a small sample from Vidarbha, 95 per cent of farmer suicide victims were indebted. An investigation of the socioeconomic causes of farmer suicide in Karnataka also found that agricultural debt was given as the primary factor, leading to farmer suicides. Chhikara and Kodan estimated that for marginal and small farmers in Haryana respectively, 23.7 per cent and 20.7 per cent of loans were taken out to fulfil social obligations such as ceremonies and marriages. Another factor that could be altering farmer suicide rates is the substantial grants given to the families of farmers who die by suicide in various states. It has been suggested that this may provide an incentive for suicides.

Reasons for Farmers' Suicides

1. *Cost of chemicals and seeds*: Be it the fertilisers, crop protection chemicals or even the seeds for cultivation, farming has become expensive for the already indebted farmers.
2. *Costs of agricultural equipment*: The input costs, moreover, are not limited to the basic raw materials. Using agricultural equipment and machinery like tractors, submersible pumps, etc. add to the already surging costs. Besides, these secondary inputs have themselves become less affordable for the small and marginal farmers.
3. *Labour costs*: Likewise, hiring labourers and animals is getting costlier too. While this may reflect an improvement in the socio-economic status of the labourers, driven primarily by MGNERGA and hike in minimum basic income, this has not gone too well with boosting the agriculture sector.
4. *The surge in input costs*: A major cause of the farmers' suicides in India has been the increasing burden on the farmers due to inflated prices of agricultural inputs. The culmination of these factors is seen in the overall increase in the cost of cultivation.
5. The main reason behind farmer suicide is bankruptcy/indebtedness and family problems which claimed 1,163 and 1,135 farmer's lives respectively. For over a decade, farmer suicides in India have been a serious public policy concern. More recently, this has led to a shrill media outcry and much politicking. The government response to the crisis of farmer suicide has mostly been simplistic and sometimes aggravating. The main issue with the offering special packages, to deal with such a problem is that it is reactionary rather than preemptive long-term policy. Suicides are characterized by a prior history of difficulties and, in most cases, a mental illness that renders the person vulnerable to suicidal behaviour, for which there is a need to have a deeper understanding of factors that trigger and contribute to suicides among different demographic categories.
6. *Distressed due to loans*: NCRB data points out that in 2,474 suicides out of the studied 3,000 farmer suicides in 2015 the victims had unpaid loans from local banks. This is clear enough an indication for drawing correlations between the two. Moreover, a shift away from the usual trend also revealed that of the loans taken by these farmers, only 9.8 per cent were loans from moneylenders. Another source of strong linkages between

farmer suicides and indebtedness is indicated from the fact that Maharashtra had 1,293 suicides for indebtedness, Karnataka had 946. Both these states witnessed one of the highest incidences of farmer suicides as well as indebtedness.

Farmers indebtedness, bankruptcy and farm related issues, i.e. fragmentation and subdivision of land holdings, are the root causes of farmers suicides. Farming is the only occupation which can be started without any pre-training or coursework. One learns this from experience, from generation to generation. A person who is not fully prepared for farming, starts this work and suffers a huge loss owing to ill effects of nature, i.e. bad monsoon, crop failure, etc. His pessimism and indebtedness makes the condition even worse. All these adverse conditions push the farmer in the vicious circle of poverty, drug addiction and suicidal tendencies. In essence, the factors responsible for framers' suicides can be summed up as follows: monsoon failure, climate change, government policies, unsustainable production, subsequent farmer indebtedness leading to failure of strengthening the economic state of the farmer, mental health, personal issues and family problems.

There is a widespread perception that the unbearable burden of debt and increased competition from imports are symptomatic of a crisis in Indian agriculture. Both these phenomena are real – the inability to bear debt has led to farmers' suicides on an unprecedented scale. However, suicides are concentrated mostly in low rainfall, poorly irrigated regions and among a rather small fraction of the population. Southern Indian states have higher rates of suicides than some northern states. The most common cause of suicide in South India is a combination of social issues, such as interpersonal and family problems, financial difficulties, and pre-existing mental illness. The high suicide rates in southern states of India may be because of social acceptance of suicide as a method to deal with difficulties.

Loan waivers, though temporarily necessary for the revival of farming, do not provide conditions for a secure credit system in the long term. The waiver of loans implies that banks will have to be compensated by the government for the amount involved. This means that large sums of money, which could have otherwise gone to strengthen agricultural infrastructure and research – such as seed production, soil health enhancement, and plant protection, will not be available. Farmer suicides have been studied by a number of institutions and the underlying causes are many. But the generic cause is the economic condition of the family, aggravated by the drought-induced failure of crops. While past experience shows that there is no problem with the implementation of the loan waiver, it does not provide a long-term solution and comes in the way of adequate allocation for agricultural development.

Loan waivers do not alleviate agrarian crises that have deep structural roots in India's economy, including uneven access to subsidies, skewed land ownership patterns, and degeneration of government-supported agricultural extension programmes. Farm loan waivers can be avoided if the government uses its Electronic National Agricultural Market (e-NAM) effectively. The e-NAM can play a vital role in strengthening the farm value chain and enhance the incomes of Indian farmers significantly.

The government subsidies are being availed by big and medium farmers. The smaller farmers for whom subsidies are actually meant are sidelined. The 'land to the tiller' policy needs to be implemented in India so that those who are actually doing farming get the benefits due to them. What happens under the current system is that whenever crop failure happens due to natural calamities such as drought, floods, etc. it is the landowners who get the compensation and not the land tiller. This is sheer injustice due to the lacunae in the system. The other major issue which needs to be solved is the issue of ensuring water for the crops. It needs to be implemented on the ground before it can be properly lauded. Finally, this shows the collective failure of both the society and the state; the time has come to ensure that no farmer is pushed to the brink because human lives matter above all.

Research by various scholars identified a variety of reasons for farmers' suicide in the country. The agricultural indebtedness has been cited as the most important reason for this. The drying up of institutional credit and exploitative informal credit trap in the face of rising costs and declining profitability have led to pervasive indebtedness among farmers.

According to activist and physicist Vandana Shiva, rapid increase in indebtedness is at the root of farmers taking their lives. Debt is a reflection of a negative economy. Two factors have transformed agriculture from a positive economy into a negative economy for peasants: the rising of costs of production and the prices of farm commodities. Both these factors are rooted in the policies of trade liberalization and corporate globalization. Shiva further writes that the factors that have caused 2,00,000 suicides in India are rooted in the policies of trade liberalization and corporate globalization which ensnare farmers in a spiral of indebtedness, generating despair.

Contrarily, according to Madhya Pradesh Human Rights Commission, indebtedness is not the only cause of suicides among farmers, but at least 20–25 compelling reasons too have been driving hundreds of farmers in Madhya Pradesh to kill themselves. In another study of Punjab by Satyanarayana and Sanjay (2014), it was revealed that debt is not a sufficient condition for the suicides, but the processes of recovery of debt and the normative support and egoistic tendencies are found as some of the sufficient conditions. Actually, the phenomenon of suicides among cultivators is such a complex one that it is very difficult to point out one particular reason for this.

Aruna Burte, Sangeeta Rege and Padma Deosthali opine that the farmers are unable to cope up with the sudden changes in cropping patterns, market fluctuations and use of pesticides to increase the yield. These are direct results of agricultural policy driven by market forces. When the crops fail, they are in debt, which they have no means to repay. They are not able to perform the role of provider for the family. All these factors are to be taken into consideration while understanding an individual farmer committing suicide.

In joint family system, each member was secure. The joint families in olden days extended moral support to their members at the time of crisis. The majority of victims who committed suicides were surprisingly from nuclear families. Even Durkheim in his monumental contribution 'La Suicide' speaks of the co-relationship that exists between family size and incidence of suicides. According to him, there exists an 'inverse relationship between family size and tendency towards suicides'. Durkheim (1952: 355) writes: 'A person is almost certainly well insured morally when isolated and left to himself than when constantly under beneficent discipline of family surroundings'. Deshpande also feels that failure of social institutions to instil and establish confidence among those who are on the verge of breakdown is one of the main factors responsible for the suicides among farmers.

Sangalad and Hudder (2011), have also pointed out the failure of crops, increasing prices, financial stress, unwillingness to adopt scientific farming practices, mental illness and depression, scarcity of water and electricity, etc. as the contributory factors for suicides by farmers.

A.R. Vasavi (2005), in his paper, drawing upon a socio-anthropological approach, reviews data from five states of India where suicides by agriculturalists have taken place since 1998. Linking macro and micro economic factors to social structural and symbolic meanings, the article highlights the ways in which a range of new risks and contradictory social trends render the lives of agriculturists into distress conditions. Such conditions of distress are compounded by the social structuring of commercial agriculture that has led to the 'individualization of agriculturists'. These trends combine with the larger context of neo-liberal India, where agricultural issues and agriculturists are in a state of 'advanced marginalization', and account for the making of distress in which large numbers of agriculturists have taken their lives.

According to Srijit Mishra (2007), the increasing incidence of farmers' suicides in the country is symptomatic of a larger crisis, which is more widespread. A few scholars have also cited drought as the major cause for farmers' suicides. Agriculture in India is almost dependent on monsoon as 80 per cent of country's farmland relies on flooding during monsoon season, so inadequate rainfall can cause droughts, making crop failure more common. In regions that have experienced droughts, crop yields have declined, and food for cattle has become scarcer. Agricultural regions that have been affected by droughts have subsequently seen their suicide rates increase. In the specific context of Andhra Pradesh, campaign groups claim that suicides have been caused by food speculators manipulating cereal prices, and GM companies which are selling expensive cotton seeds and fertilizers. According to them, in order to buy GM seeds, some farmers got into unmanageable debt whereas others were crippled by fluctuations in food prices. And, when it became too tough, some of them decided to take their own lives.

In brief, India is transforming rapidly into a primarily urban, industrial society with industry as its main source of income and the government and society both have become unconcerned about the condition of the countryside, particularly farmers. Thus, in the absence of any responsible counselling, either from the government or civil society, there were many farmers who did not know how to survive in the changing economy.

Government Responses to Farmers' Suicides

Some of the major relief packages, debt waiver and other schemes announced by the government are summarized below:

1. *2006 Relief Package:* Primarily aimed at 31 districts in the four states of Andhra Pradesh, Maharashtra, Karnataka, and Kerala with a high relative incidence of farmers' suicides, the package provided debt relief to farmers, improved supply of institutional credit, improved irrigation facilities, employed experts and social service personnel to provide farming support services, and introduced subsidiary income opportunities through horticulture, livestock, dairy and fisheries.
2. *Agricultural Debt Waiver and Debt Relief Scheme, 2008:* Agricultural debt waiver and debt relief scheme in 2008 benefited over 36 million farmers at a cost of 65,000 crore rupees. This spending was aimed at writing off part of the loan principal as well as the interest owed by the farmers.
3. *2013 Diversify Income Sources Package:* In 2013, the Government of India launched a special livestock sector and fisheries package for farmers suicide-prone regions of Andhra Pradesh, Maharashtra, Karnataka and Kerala. The package was aimed to diversify income sources of farmers.
4. The ₹ 75,000 crore *Pradhan Mantri Kissan Samman Nidhi (PM-KISAN) cash transfer scheme* has been launched on 24 February 2019 for small and marginal cultivators, ₹ 6,000 would annually be transferred in three installments under the scheme into the bank accounts of farmers with less than two hectare land holding. The PM-Kisan Scheme covers farmers with clear land titles. It does not cover sharecroppers who are more than 50 per cent of farmer's population. It is difficult to transfer money to them. There are no middlemen in this scheme and it is being implemented with complete transparency. Payments are made through a centralised financial software. The software validates a payment only when there is an accurate match of three data points – Aadhar, land record and bank account.

Apart from these Central Government initiatives, there are many efforts from the state government's side like Maharashtra Bill to regulate farmer loan terms, 2008 and Kerala Farmers' Debt Relief Commission (Amendment) Bill, 2012.

Prevention Strategies

After the suicides by farmers in various parts of the country, both the central government and respective state governments have announced measures to deal with distress. But unfortunately, these measures have not completely stopped farmers from committing suicide. The reports of suicides by farmers are continuously coming from different states. Actually, the systematic risks in agriculture are qualitatively and quantitatively different today than a few decades ago. Increasing commercialization and heavy investments in inputs added technology and credit risks to the traditional weather risk to this liberalization added market risks. All these have been accentuated by receding state support since the nineties. Public investment in agriculture, institutional credit, research and extension services, a rationalized marketing structure and healthy rural development expenditure, which are all essential to overcome these risks, have declined since the nineties. The Planning Commission itself acknowledged a perceptible stagnation in the fortunes of the agricultural sector during the post-liberalization period, and much of the distress that the farmer faces today is demonstrably due to deliberate policy changes that the economic reforms entailed (Posani, 2009).

Some scholars and experts have also suggested measures to effectively bring down the suicides among farming community. According to Vandana Shiva, for instance, the strategies to prevent farmers to suicide may include a shift from GMO and non-renewable seeds to organic, open pollinated seed varieties which farmers can save and share, from chemical farming to organic farming, and from unfair trade based on false prices to fair trade based on real and just prices. And, the farmers who have made this shift are earning more than the farmers growing Monsanto's Bt-cotton. Similarly, others are of the view that risk mitigation strategies should go beyond credit. Long-term strategies require more stable income from agriculture, and more importantly, from non-farm sources. Private credit and input markets need to be regulated. A challenge for the technological and financial sector is to provide innovative products that reduce costs while increasing returns. The institutional vacuum of organizing farmers needs to be addressed through a federation of self-help groups (SHGs) or alternative structures.

Sangalad and Hudder (2011) have suggested the following measures:

1. Farmers Counselling Centres should be established at the *Mandal Panchayat* level with the appointment of trained staff comprising a social worker, psychologist, agricultural scientist, doctor and elected representative of Mandal Panchayat.
2. Proper training should be imparted to the farmers by agricultural experts regarding use of pesticides and fertilizers.
3. Awareness should be created among farmers regarding scientific farming of different crops to get better yield and good price for their products.
4. An Advisory Council should be formed for the prevention of farmers' suicides both at the district and state levels to advise and supervise the members of the Counselling Centres.
5. It should be made mandatory to the college level NSS units to organize camps in the villages and create awareness in the farming community about the effect of suicide and its impact on other members of the family.
6. Encourage the farmers to adopt the allied activities like dairy, poultry, etc. along with farming activities.

7. Encouragement of networks of relatives, friends, neighbours and members of the faith community to decrease isolation, which is one of the strongest risk factors for suicides.

The policy implication from the above discussion calls for an emphasis on the larger crisis. However, the trend can be reversed through active participation of the governmental institutions in addressing the real issues of the farmers that are driving them to suicides. Social responsibility or the involvement of civil society can also go a long way to help the farmers.

Suggestion to Prevent Farmers' Suicides in India

1. Farmers should be educated and training and farming awareness programmes should be started for them.
2. Eligibility criteria of the farmer should be determined.
3. Farmers should be compensated for the bad monsoon period.
4. The government should adopt an appropriate price policy for the farmers so that they get an optimum reward for their hard work.
5. To check the fragmentation and division of holdings, self-employment programmes should be started in rural areas.
6. Farmers should avoid the unproductive expenditure like expenditure on marriages, false rituals, etc.
7. Develop the banking habits among the small and marginal farmers so that they save enough to meet their emergency needs for natural calamities like earthquake, floods, famines, etc.
8. Farmers should be given credit facilities to start agriculture subsidiary activities.
9. Policies of integrated pest management to prevent pest damage – an all-inclusive approach that integrates biological, chemical, mechanical and physical methodology should be used to prevent crop damage.
10. Helping fertilizer industries to cut down on fertilizer costs, through internal funding rather than external borrowing should lower the input costs.
11. Leveraging advancements in science and technology by ensuring that state seed policies focus on new genotypes, contract farming and sensitization to adverse weather conditions.
12. Farm equipment policy must focus on imported equipments to provide for cheaper local manufacture, some incentives like grant of duty credit scrips may be tried.
13. Subsidies must be rerouted towards capital generation and the implementation must be ensured in a timely fashion.
14. Corporate Social Responsibility (CSR) must be encouraged in the agricultural sector, particularly towards capacity-building and the skill development.
15. Institutional financing must also be ensured to be adequate and inclusive rather than catering to the elites within the farming community.

16. Cooperative farming must be promoted amongst small and marginal farmers to ensure that they are not left lurking while the big farmers reap the benefit at their cost.
17. Doubling the farmer income by 2022 is a healthy aim, but loan waivers can not be the answer. Instead, sustainable agriculture that thrives on re-investment and restructuring is the way ahead.
18. Small and marginal farmers can be provided one-time state assistance to rid their personal debts taken from local moneylenders at exorbitant rates. The money so given as assistance must be recorded as interest-free loan from the government payable only in case the land is sold by these farmers. This will ensure that while the economic status of farmers will improve, the money will not be misused. The land shall not be allowed to be mortgaged to anyone except banks for crop loan only.

Direct Interventions

1. Options for restructuring loans must be used wherever possible.
2. Insurance claim settlements must be speedy and just.
3. NABARD and local administration must take control of the situation and play a greater role in curbing farmers' suicides.
4. Efforts like Agro-Climatic zoning, education through DD Kisan, Soil Health Card Scheme, various crop insurance and facilitative schemes like PM Krishi Sinchayi Yojana will go a long way in helping out.
5. Community-led awareness must be taken employing a role model approach highlighting the progress of farmers who have benefited from sustainable and climate-tailored agricultural practices.

Conclusion

Determining a single defining cause for farmer suicides in India is impossible. What can be inferred is that an amalgamation of factors has led to a picture of large-scale farmer indebtedness that combined with a volatile ecological climate and socio-economic landscape has left hundreds of thousands, if not millions of farmers vulnerable to a situation of such crushing debt and desperation that many have come to take their own lives.

References

Chandrasekhar, C.P. and Ghosh, Jayati, 'The Crisis in Agriculture', *Business Line*, 23 October 2017.

Chhikara, Kuldip S. and Kodan, Anand, *International Journal of Advance Research in Management and Social Sciences*, Vol. 1, No. 1, July 2012.

Dongre, A.R. and Deshmukh, P.R., 'Farmers' Suicides in the Vidarbha Region of Maharashtra, India: A Qualitative Exploration of Their Causes', *Journal of Injury and Violence Research*, January 2012; 4(1): 2–6.

Durkheim, Emile, *Suicide: A Study in Sociology*, tr. John A. Spoulding and George Simpsons, London: Routledge and Kegan Paul.

Mishra, Srijit, 'Risks, Farmers' Suicides and Agrarian Crisis in India: Is There a Way Out?' Mumbai: Indira Gandhi Institute of Development Research, Working Paper 2007, 14 September 2007.

Muralidharan, Karrthik, 'The Policy Options to Address Farm Crisis', *Hindustan Times*, 24 March 2019.

Posani, Balamuralidhar, 'Crisis in the Countryside: Farmer Suicides and the Political Economy of Agrarian Distress in India', Working Paper 09–95, Development Studies Institute, London School of Economics and Political Science, 2009.

Ramakumar, R., 'Large Scale Investments in Agriculture in India', *IDS Bulletin*, Volume 43 Number, July 2012.

Sangalad, Purnanand Nagappa and Hudder, Malakajappa Gynappa, 'Agrarian Distress and Farmers' Suicides in Karnataka: Strategy for Prevention', *International Multidisciplinary Research Journal*, 1/3:01–05, 2011 (available online: http//irjs.info).

Sainath, P., In India, Farmers Face a Terrifying Crisis, *The New York Times*, 13 April 2018.

Satyanarayana, A. and Sanjay, 'Does Indebtedness Lead to Suicides among Cultivators?', in Ishwar Modi, *Polity, Civil Society and Development*, Jaipur: Rawat, 2014.

Shiva, V., The Future of Food: Countering Globalisation and Recolonisation of Indian Agriculture. *Futures*, 36(6–7): 715–32, 2004.

The Kerala Farmers' Debt Relief Commission (Amendment) Bill, 2012, Government of Kerala.

Vasavi, A.R., 'Suicides and the Making of India's Agrarian Distress', paper presented at the seminar on 'Agrarian Distress and Farmers' Suicides in India' organized by the Governance and Policy Space Project of the Centre for Economic and Social Studies, Hyderabad from 24 to 26 February, 2005 at Acharya Nagarjuna University, Guntur (Andhra Pradesh).

25

Black Money

Some Facts About the Black Money in India

1. India's black economy is estimated to be 60 per cent of GDP. It is larger than the income generated by agriculture and industry put together. It is almost impossible to estimate the actual amount of black money in any economy. For this reason, it is not included in the GDP of a country.
2. Ninety per cent of the black money is in India. Around 10 per cent of the black money generated in the country goes abroad. This 10 per cent is invested in foreign and part of it comes back to India via round-tripping. India ranks third in a line-up of countries with money hidden abroad.

The black money is referred to by more than thirty different names all over the world – parallel economy, informal economy and so on, but none of these are appropriate terms to describe the black money in India. Black money is an elusive term. It is, as its name suggests, 'tainted' money – money which is not clean or which has a stigma attached to it. Different persons have understood this expression differently and the term has not yet acquired a precise connotation. However, black is a colour which is generally associated with evil. Black money consists of all the activities in which black incomes are generated and not reported to direct tax authorities. The money generated through any or all unrecognized and illegal sources, be it from land, corruption, fraud or any other unfair mean is collectively trashed under the label of black money by the law of any country. Black money is largely attributed to tax evasion. Black money proceeds are usually received in cash from underground economic activity and, as such, are not taxed. Recipients of black money must hide it, spend it only in the underground economy, or attempt to give it the appearance of legitimacy through money laundering. Black money is linked to corruption, crime, and black economy.

Black money is generated in many ways, such as tax-evasion, under-invoicing and over-invoicing, in all cases by a violation of laws, rules, licensing procedures, excise, income tax and foreign exchange regulations, capital gains and wealth tax. There are other sectors as well, but these are some of the largest segments where unaccounted money circulates. These sectors then feed the political parties and individual politicians with large sums of cash on an 'as and when' needed basis. In return, they get favours from the politicians and government largesse for substantial profit gains, and the cycle of black money continues.

In the past few years the public discourse on the issue of black money has come in the forefront. Black money is both an economic and a social problem. While in the latter context, it is perceived as a problem with adverse sociological effects on society, like social inequalities, social deprivations, etc. in the former context, it is perceived as a parallel economy, an underground economy or an unofficial economy that is the consequence of the economic policies of the government and has damaging effects on country's economy and nation's socialist planning development. While problem like poverty affects those people who are poor, unemployment affects those who are unemployed, alcoholism and drug abuse affect those who consume them, black money is a problem which does not affect those who possess it but the common man in society. No wonder, it has been described as a problem with a difference.

The Concept

Black money is tax-evaded income. It can be earned both through legal and illegal means. Its legitimate source is that the income-earners do not reveal their whole income for tax purposes. For example: government doctors earning money by private practice even when they get non-practising allowance, teachers earning money through tuitions, examinations and book royalty and not including it in income tax returns, advocates charging much higher fee than shown in their account books, and so forth. Its illegitimate source is bribe, smuggling, black marketing, selling commodities at prices higher than the controlled prices, taking *pugree* for house, shop, etc. selling house at a high premium price but showing it at a much lower price in the account books, and so forth.

Calculating the Magnitude of Black Money

It is not easy to calculate the magnitude of black money in any society. The economists across the world adopted different measures but could not estimate the amount involved in black money. Norway and Sweden used questionnaire method for eliciting answers from persons whether they had participated in illegal activities as buyers or sellers. Italy attempted to estimate the underground economy by finding out the difference between the size of the labour force officially reported and actually employed. This enabled to determine the productivity in the underground sector. The United Kingdom tried to assess parallel economy by comparing the official estimates of the Gross National Product (GNP) made from the consumption side with those made from the income side. In the United States, Guttman assumed that only cash is used in illegal transactions. He tried to find out the difference between currency required for economic transactions in a fixed period and actual currency held outside banks in the same period.

In India, the estimates of black money made so far have followed two distinct approaches, viz., (a) N. Kaldor's approach of quantifying non-salary incomes above the exemption limit of income tax; and (b) the Edgar Feige's method of working out the transaction income on the basis of currency-deposit ratio and deriving from it the 'black' income of the economy. Kaldor in his report (1956) estimated non-salary income on the basis of the break-up of national income into: (a) wages and salaries, (b) income of the self-employed, and (c) profit, interest, rent, etc. Excluding wages and salaries from the contribution to net domestic product, he derived total non-salary income. An estimate of the actual non-salary income assessed to tax was made for each sector in order to arrive at the total non-salary income assessed to tax. The difference between the estimated non-salary income above the exemption limit and the actual non-salary income assessed to tax measures the size of 'black' income.

Channelization of Black Money

Money generated illegally has to be parked somewhere and a large part of the money is invested in sectors that include:

1. *Building and construction industry*: Most of the black money is held not in the form of cash, but in the form of real sector assets. The real estate sector is one of the largest holders of illicit income and unaccounted funds. A large number of transactions are not reported and a vast number are under-reported. As the realty sector contributes 11 per cent to GDP, this huge amount of under-reporting is a huge dent in the treasury. Due to rising prices of real estate, the tax incidence applicable on real estate transactions in the form of stamp duty and capital gains tax can create incentives for tax evasion through under-reporting of the transaction price.
2. *Bullion and jewellery market*: The purchase allows the buyer the option of converting black money into gold and bullion, while it gives the trader the option of keeping his unaccounted wealth in the form of stock, not disclosed in the books or valued at less than the market price. One reason for people to invest in gold is that people may buy gold bars, coins, etc. easily and can be converted back into money anytime.
3. *Financial markets transactions*: IPO manipulations, rigging of the market such as the use of shell companies.
4. *Non-profit organizations*: Taxation laws allow certain privileges and incentives for promoting charitable activities which are misused and manipulated.
5. *Informal sector and cash economy*: Cash transactions, large unbanked and under-banked areas contribute to the large cash economy in India.

6. *Trade-based money laundering (TBML)*: Disguising the proceeds of crime and moving value through the use of trade transactions in an attempt at legitimizing their illicit origins.
7. *Tax havens*: Tax havens are typically small countries/jurisdictions, with low or nil taxation for foreigners who decide to come and settle there. Strong confidentiality or secrecy regarding wealth and accounts, very liberal regulatory environment and allow the opaque existence, where an entity can easily be set up without indulging in any meaningful commercial activity and yet claim to be a genuine business unit, merely by getting itself incorporated or registered in that jurisdiction. This makes them highly desirable locations for multinational entities wishing to reduce their global tax liabilities. Multinational entities consisting of a network of several corporate and non-corporate bodies set up medium companies in tax havens and artificially transfer their income to such companies in view of the low tax regime there.
8. *Investment through innovative derivative instruments*: Investments in instruments like Participatory Notes (P-notes) is one such example.

Magnitude of the Black Economy

There is at present no official assessment on the quantum of black money in India and abroad. A recent study by US-based think tank Global Financial Integrity (GFI) said an estimated USD 770 billion in black money entered India during 2005–2014. Nearly USD 165 billion in illicit money exited the country during the same period, the latest report by the global financial watchdog said. The issue of black money has attracted a lot of public and media attention in the recent past. So far, there are no reliable estimates of black money generated and held within and outside the country. These estimates are based on various unverifiable assumptions and approximations. A number of studies have been made to estimate the quantitative dimensions of the problem in the economy. The studies identify the different sources of black income as follows:

1. Income-tax evasion
2. Corporation tax evasion
3. Excise duty evasion
4. Customs duty evasion
5. Black income from exports
6. Evasion of state taxes
7. Bribes and illegal commissions
8. Goods supply to the black market
9. Unaccounted stock-market profit
10. Interest earned from unorganized credit markets

The Government of India had asked three think tanks – National Institute of Public Finance and Policy (NIPFP), National Institute of Financial Management (NIFM) and National Council of Applied Economic

Research (NCAER) – to arrive at an estimate of black money in the country. The three used various methodologies and gave an estimate of nearly ₹ 28 lakh crores to this parallel economy (*Business Standard*, 13 January 2013). With the three reporting wide variations, the government concluded that 'the unaccounted income and wealth inside and outside the country do not appear amenable to credible estimation in the context of India' or put simply: there is a lot of black money, but it is not possible to measure it precisely.

Arun Kumar, the eminent economist and India's leading expert on the subject, holds that black economy is estimated to be 62 per cent of the GDP. which is larger than the income generated by agriculture and industry put together, which is about 39 per cent of GDP. Because of its existence, the country's economy has been losing on an average 5 per cent growth. If we add 5 per cent to the rate of growth over the past four decades or so, the size of our economy would be ₹ 1,050 lakh crore instead of ₹ 150 lakh crore as it is now. We would have become the world's second largest, behind the US. The per capita income of the country would have been ₹ 7.4 lakh instead of about ₹ 1 lakh as it is at present. In other words, every one of us would have been seven times richer on average.

Estimates of Black Money Stashed Abroad

It may be useful to see how India compares with other countries in the world on estimates of black money or black or shadow economy. The World Bank Development Research Group on Poverty and Inequality and Europe and Central Asia Region Human Development Economics Unit in July 2010 estimated 'shadow economies' of 162 countries from 1999 to 2007. It reported that the weighted average size of the shadow economy (as a percentage of 'official' GDP) of these 162 countries in 2007 was 31 per cent as compared to 34 per cent in 1999. For India, these figures were 20.7 per cent and 23.2 per cent respectively, comparing favourably with the world average. Shadow economy, for the purpose of study, was defined to include all market-based legal production of goods and services that are deliberately concealed from public authorities for any of the following reasons:

1. to avoid payment of income, value added or other taxes,
2. to avoid payment of social security contributions,
3. to avoid having to meet certain legal labour market standards, such as minimum wages, a maximum working hours and safety standards; and
4. to avoid complying with certain administrative procedures, such as completing statistical questionnaires or other administrative forms.

As in the case of total size of black money, there are many scholars/ studies which have estimated the extent of black money of Indians stashed away in Swiss banks using different methods and have also arrived at different figures of black money even for the same year. There have also been media reports in recent years that have extended several estimates of black money, especially the unaccounted money held by Indians abroad. So, it is not possible to estimate the magnitude of black money either within the country or abroad. Studies conducted by National Institute of Public Finance and Policy (NIPFP), National Institute of Financial Management (NIFM) and National Council of Applied Economic Research (NCAER) have concluded that unaccounted wealth held by Indians outside the country till 2010 could be as high as $490 billion, besides black money parked within the country.

Causes of Generating Black Money

Unrealistic Taxation Policy

Complex tax laws which are not easily comprehendable by common people will lead to short cuts and tax evasion. High personal income tax rates also cause people to try and evade taxes. Moreover, various types of lacunae in the tax system also encourages generation of black income. Ineffective enforcement of tax laws is also a cause for black money.

Growth in Public Expenditure

Rapid growth of government spendings has been a major contributory factor in generating black money. Due to this rise of public spending for multiple governmental programmes and activities, the unscrupulous elements in public service and public life could find ample opportunities for generating black income and wealth by dubious methods.

Scarcity

Black money is also caused by scarcity and defective public distribution system. When essential goods become scarce, people have to pay higher than the controlled prices, which generates black money. The scarcity of cooking gas, cement, kerosene, sugar, refined oil, etc. for example, in the part, have always resulted in illegitimate transactions and black money.

Inflation

The increase in prices of commodities like petrol, etc. in international market, due to high increase in duties and taxes imposed by the government, the conspicuous consumption created by people with unaccountable money, diverting resources from production to speculation – all these cause inflation which in turn creates black money. As the matter of fact, inflation is both the cause as well as consequence of the growth of black money in the Indian economy.

Elections and Political Funding

Each election in the country involves lakhs of crores of rupees. In the present times, for contesting Lok Sabha election, a candidate normally spends more than five crore rupees and for Vidhan Sabha election, more than one crore. It is estimated that a single Lok Sabha election alone could see political parties spend around ₹ 10,000 crore to pay for poll expenses. Politicians also need to draw on business resources to nurse their constituencies. Given the mind-boggling numbers, black money naturally is built into the system. For funding politicians, even honest corporate houses have no option but to find ways to generate unaccounted money. Since the expenditure allowed by law for a candidate is limited and the companies are allowed to give up to 5 per cent of their profit in a year as donations to political parties for elections (as per Section 293A of the Companies Act, 1956), the elections are generally financed by the black money holders. These people expect political patronage and economic concessions which are obtained with the consent and the connivance of political elite in power in the form of artificial controls on commodities, laxity in the means of distribution, etc. All these methods generate black money.

Real Estate Transactions

Real estate transactions are always seen as a big generator of black money as transaction values are depressed to evade stamp duty and also absorb cash. In these days, due to rising prices, purchasing a house and/or land is considered to be very profitable. Establishing unapproved colonies on agricultural land is illegal. The transaction value shown by the colonizers in registration deeds is much less than the actual amount or the market value. This enables the seller of the land to evade capital gain tax. The high rates of stamp duty is a major cause for under-valuation of property and unreported deals, or both. Another hurdle is the Urban Land Ceiling Act, which reduces the supply of land and creates a black market.

Prohibition of Certain Activities

Gambling, betting, smuggling, illicit sale of liquor, match fixing, trafficking, etc. have become a source of easy money where people get more return than the amount invested. All such activities go undereported and such incomes are totally black. A large amount of black money is generated from this addictive play of gambling all in the name of luck while everything is pre-decided and the common man just falls prey ending up wasting his hard-earned income.

Agricultural Income

The unwillingness of the government to bring agricultural income in the ambit of income tax has also contributed to generation of black money. Big industrial houses, over the past few decades, have entered the agriculture sector in a big way by acquiring large farms, growing and producing nothing. The black money accrued from other sources is sought to be converted into white by showing it on the agricultural income account.

Social Effects of Black Money

Besides the economic effects, there are many social consequences of black money also. In economic terms, black money robs the exchequer of its due share, increases economic inequality and hampers programmes of economic development. Socially, it increases social inequality, creates frustrations among honest people, increases crimes like smuggling, bribery, etc. and adversely affects social service programmes for the uplift of the poor and the weaker sections of society. It also distorts the measurement of true rates like growth rate, inflationary rate, unemployment rate, poverty, etc. which in turn affects the government's policies for containing these problems.

Impact of Black Money on Indian Economy

Black money is a socio-economic evil. The major impacts of black money are discussed below:

1. *Less tax for the government*: Black money is largely attributed to tax evasion. Its direct impact is the loss of the government revenue.
2. *Uncontrollable inflation*: Black money generated through corruption leads to inflation in prices as the bribes burden in various goods and services is passed onto consumers. This causes the prices of commodities to increase to a level beyond normal.
3. *Dual economy*: The increase in the amount of black money over a period of time leads to the parallel economy. Such a parallel economy will ruin the entire economic development of the country.
4. *Lavish consumption spending*: Black money is disposed of by lavish spending and on extravagant elections, etc. This has also led to many social evils and deteriorated the values of life of the common people.
5. *Deteriorate the general moral standards of the society*: Black money is largely responsible for the deterioration of general moral standards of the society. Social values of honesty, hard work, thrift and simplicity get eroded. Even the political institutions and organizations lose their credibility as they also gradually become a part of the entire system of black income generation.
6. *Widening the gap between the rich and the poor*: When the black money grows faster, the rich becomes richer and the poor becomes poorer. The money generated through any or all unrecognized and illegal sources, be it from land, corruption, fraud or any other unfair mean is collectively trashed under the label of black money by the law of any country.
7. *Parallel economy*: India is facing the problem of shortage of capital. The major reason is the parallel economy.

There are two major issues – first, without an adequate factual basis, a large magnitude/amount of black money and unaccounted wealth stashed abroad every year. Second, government response to address this issue has been inadequate. While it symbolises something which violates moral, social or legal norms, it also suggests a veil of secrecy shrouding it. The term black money consequently has both these implications. It not only stands for money earned by violating legal provisions-even social conscience-but also suggests that such money is kept often secret and not accounted for. There is a perception that people do not pay taxes because the taxation levels are high.

The Income Tax Act forces an income tax payer to disclose not only his income but also his 'source' of income. For the last two categories above, the declaration of the source of income is the primary reason for not paying income tax. It is not the tax rate that holds them back but declaring the source of income. The loser is the government. The portion of a country's income that is tied to its black economy affects the economic growth of the country. Its direct impact is the loss of government revenue. Since these funds hardly enter the banking system, money that could be used by banks to fund small business owners and entrepreneurs. It also deprives the government to spend on infrastructure and public services like healthcare, and education. In addition, black money underestimates the financial health of a nation.

Black money is generated in many ways, such as tax-evasion, under-invoicing and over-invoicing, in all cases by a violation of laws, rules, licensing procedures, excise, income tax and foreign exchange regulations, capital gains and wealth tax. But the most important and socially dangerous form of black money generation is related to the production, distribution and hoarding of commodities.

The most common source of black money is illegal means through black market or underground economy. Through these portals, drug trafficking, weapons trading, terrorism, prostitution, selling counterfeit or stolen goods such as credit cards, and selling pirated versions of copyrighted items such as software and musical recordings are traded. Most black money holders attempt to convert the money into legal money, also known as white money. This is typically done through money laundering. Money laundering can be attempted in a number of ways. One way is the use of shell companies. Money laundering is a way to conceal illegally obtained funds. Money laundering can also be perpetrated using the hawala system of transactions. The hawala system is an informal and cheap method of transferring money from one region to another without any actual money movement and without the use of banks. It operates on codes and contacts and no paperwork and disclosure is required. Another way of money laundering is by fraudulent record keeping.

Black money can be classified into two types:

1. *Productive black money:* This black money is converted into white money at the cost and ploughed back into consumption or productive investment. The effect here is to increase the cost of money but not too bad for the economy as a whole.
2. *Non-productive black money:* This is the most distortive effect. Most black money cannot be used for productive purposes and must be invested either in gold or in real estate, where it leads to artificial demand and raising of prices. Gold artificial demand means more import of gold and weakening of currency. Real estate artificial demand distorts the supply of land resource which has a major impact on the overall economy.

Measures of Control

Over the past 70 years, the government has at various times announced several schemes offering opportunities to bring black money overboard. Some of these schemes are – introducing the scheme of special bearer bonds, demonetizing high denomination currency notes, stringent raids, and scheme of voluntary disclosures. Various attempts have been made to stop tax evasion but results have been futile in a large number of cases.

Demonetization

In India, demonetization was done for the first time in 1946 and the value of demonetized notes was about ₹144 crore. Demonetization of high denomination currency worth ₹ 1,000 and ₹ 5,000 and ₹ 10,000 was again attempted in 1978. Till August 1981, notes worth ₹ 125 crore were demonetized. Again on 8 November 2016, the Government of India announced the biggest-ever demonetization exercise. India has ever seen by abruptly withdrawing ₹ 500 and ₹ 1,000 notes from public use in a bid to clamp down on black money, fake currency menace, terror funding and corruption. The government claimed that the action would curtail the shadow economy and crack down on the use of illicit and counterfeit cash to fund illegal activity and terrorism. According to the Reserve Bank of India report for 2017–18, about 99.3 per cent of the demonetized currency has come back to the banking system. The demonetization has also not led to any drastic increase in cashless payments, this factor deserves greater attention. Demonetization as a measure of checking black money is not at all successful and it is also very much unpopular.

Tax Deducted at Source (TDS)

TDS is a type of tax that is deducted from an individual's income on a periodic or occasional basis. Since TDS is collected at the source of one's income, it effectively reduces evasion of tax by getting the income taxed, whether completely or moderately at that point of time. Payments such as salaries, interest payment, commission, fees to lawyers and freelancers, etc. are subject to TDS.

For salaries, the percentage of TDS will be based on income slabs rates. Similarly, each type of income has its own percentage of tax that is calculated when the amount meets a certain limit. Since TDS is collected at source without the calculation of investment that is eligible for tax deductions, hence, an individual can declare and submit his investment proof in order to file a return and claim for the TDS refund. TDS is based on the principle of 'pay as and when you earn'. TDS is a win-win scenario for both the taxpayers and the government. Tax is deducted when making payments through cash, credit or cheque, which is then deposited with the central agencies.

Encouraging Cashless Transaction

The term cashless transaction indicates reducing the use of physical cash for payments. Instead of cash, digital payments are made to settle the payments. Besides convenience, digital transaction gives more scope for the recording of transactions and in this way it is a first step against the spread of unaccounted money or black money. Second, the problem of counterfeit notes can also be avoided when payment is settled digitally.

1. *Mobile wallet*: This is basically a virtual wallet available on mobile phone various service providers offer these wallets via mobile apps, which may be downloaded on the phone. One can transfer the money into these wallets online using credit/debit card or net banking.
2. *Plastic money*: This includes credit, debit and prepaid cards. The latter can be issued by banks or non-banks and can be physical or virtual. These can be bought and recharged online via net banking and can be used to make online or point-of-sale purchases, even given as gift cards.
3. *Net banking*: This does not involve any wallet and is simply a method of online transfer of funds from the bank.

Voluntary Disclosure Schemes

Voluntary disclosure scheme was attempted at various times such as in 1951, 1976, 1997 and 2016. The direct taxes enquiry committee mentioned rightly – 'they were more or fewer schemes of converting black money into white on payment of what turned out to be, in most cases, a small amount of conscience money'.

Special Bearer Bond Scheme

The special bearer bond scheme 1981 also failed to analyse the black money to a large extent. A total amount of ₹ 964 crores was subscribed to the special bearer bond.

Tax Raids and Seizures

Raids are conducted from time to time by the tax enforcement machinery on the premises of the people who are suspected of possessing black money.

An information technology-based 'Project Insight', introduced by the Income Tax Department to strengthen the non-intrusive information-driven approach for improving tax compliance effective utilization of available information.

Some scholars have maintained that all these measures have touched only the tip of the iceberg. The main drawback in these schemes is that they touch the problem of black money already created but they do not go into the root cause of generation of black money and that is why a person is prepared to take the risk of keeping black money despite so many problems. Unless this problem is tackled, the menace of black money will continue to increase.

It has been suggested that the problem of black money and parallel economy can be contained by reducing taxes in some areas, giving incentives for voluntary disclosure of income, overhauling the economic intelligence unit, curbing administrative corruption at various levels, exempting tax on money spent on house construction, doing away with control policies, and so forth. Isolated attempts may not yield much but a package of mutually reinforcing measures along with a strong political will and the commitment of political elite may prove to be successful to a large extent.

Recent Initiatives by the Government

The following recent initiatives were taken by the government to curb black money:

1. The Black Money (Undisclosed Foreign Income and Assets) and Imposition of Tax Act, 2015 came into force on 1 July 2015. It seeks to check the black money menace with stringent provisions for those stashing illegal wealth abroad. The Bill provides for separate taxation of any undisclosed income in relation to foreign income and assets. Such income will henceforth not be taxed under the Income-tax Act but under the stringent provisions of the new legislation.
2. The government is also trying to automate information exchange with several countries, including Switzerland, to clamp down on black money.
3. *Benami Transaction Bill 2015:* Predominately an anti-black money measure with the purpose to seize unknown property and prosecute those indulging in such activities. The amendment fast-tracks procedure in dealing with Benami properties and ensures stringent punishment for offenders. The Bill increases penalty to rigorous imprisonment from 1 to 7 years and a fine which may extend to 25 per cent of the fair market value of the *Benami* property. The Bill will go a long way in improving the image of the Indian real estate sector.
4. *The Income Declaration Scheme, 2016:* The Scheme was a one-time opportunity to all people, who have not declared correct income in the past to come forward and declare such undisclosed income. The scheme was effective from 1 June 2016 to 30 September 2016. Total tax on undisclosed income was 30 per cent and a surcharge 25 per cent. So, surcharge and penalty amounting to 45 per cent of the total undisclosed income.
5. *The Prevention of Corruption (Amendment) Act, 2018*: Introducing changes to the existing anti-corruption law. Among other changes, the Amendment Act has made bribe giving a specific offence and has introduced the concept of corporate criminal liability for acts of bribery. Significant changes include: (a) the inclusion of bribe-giving as a specific offence, (b) that commercial organization can be liable for bribe-giving, (c) the introduction of a fixed timeline of two years for the conclusion of a trial-extendable up to four years, (d) the removal of the protection given to bribe givers who appear as witnesses, and (e) the introduction of stricter punishments for perpetrators of bribery.

The problem of 'black money' has to be tackled in a realistic and in an intelligent manner at the same time. Since it is not a problem with the poor but with the well-off people, it should be handled carefully. The following measures will be of some help in controlling, if not eliminating this problem:

1. The standards of public morality must be raised. In this regard, politicians, ministers, senior civil servants, intellectuals and the media people must play an important role.
2. Public expenditure must come down and there must be stringent monitoring of expenditure, especially of public sector projects.
3. There must be much more effective supervision of private sector investment expenditures, particularly where there is greater reliance on development finance institutions and banks.
4. The tax system must be realistic. Unduly high rates of tax are counter-productive. It would lead to tax evasion, whether it is income tax, wealth tax, capital gains tax or transfer tax on real estate and at a later stage creating black money.
5. Exchange rates should be realistic reflecting our comparative prices and competitive position in the world economy.
6. Tax collection machinery must be made more efficient than what it is now. Honest officials in this department must be profusely rewarded.
7. Attractive incentives must be given for voluntary disclosures of income.
8. Administrative corruption at different levels must be stopped.

Suggestions

The black money menace is still untamed and a lot more needs to be done to tackle it. Some of the strengthening steps that can be taken are:

1. *Appropriate legislative framework:* Related to Public Procurement, Prevention of Bribery of Foreign Officials, Citizens Grievance Redressal, Whistleblower Protection, UID Aadhar.
2. *Setting up and strengthening institutions dealing with illicit money:* Directorate of criminal investigation cell for the exchange of information, income tax overseas units – ITOUs at Mauritius and Singapore have been very useful, strengthening the foreign tax, tax research and investigation division of the CBDT.
3. *Developing systems for implementation:* Integrated Taxpayer Data Management System (ITDMS) and 360-degree profiling, setting up of cyber forensic labs and work stations, implementation of Goods and Services Tax and Direct Tax Code.
4. *Imparting skills to personnel for effective action:* Both domestic and international training pertaining to the concerned area. For instance, the Financial Intelligence Unit-India makes proactive efforts to regularly upgrade the skills of its employees by providing them opportunities for

training on anti-money laundering, terrorist financing, and related economic issues.
5. *Electoral reforms:* Elections are one of the biggest channels to utilize the black money. Appropriate reforms to reduce money power in elections.
6. Establishment of special courts for speedy justice can be a huge positive aspect. Much time should not elapse between the registration of a case and the delivery of judgment.
7. Strong and stringent laws need to be enacted which gives no room for the guilty to escape.

Conclusion

Black money is a term used in common parlance to refer to money that is not fully legitimate in the hands of the owner. This could be for two possible reasons – first is that the money may have been generated through illegitimate activities not permissible under the law, like crime, trafficking (human, drugs, arms), terrorism, and corruption, all of which are punishable under the legal framework of the state. Second and perhaps more likely reason is that the wealth may have been generated and accumulated by failing to comply with the tax requirements. Black money in India is decades old problem, it has become real threat post liberalization. Illegal activities such as crime and corruption, non-compliance with taxation requirements, complex procedural regulations, cultural and social practices, globalization along with weak institutional, policy, legal and implementation structures have further augmented the black money economy. Black money in India is a serious issue hampering the country's growth. The best way is to have strict checks in place, better laws, better processes, more digitalization, more power to the income tax department, etc. Strict punishment should be given to those avoiding taxes. Black money has a major impact on social, economic and political levels of our lives which has a significant effect on the institutions of governance and conduct of public policy in the country.

References

Agarwal, Lalit Mohan (ed.), 'White Paper on Black Money', *Journal of Securities Academy & Faculty for E-education*, Vol. 72, 2012.

Business Standard, 13 January, 2013.

Chopra, O.P., 'Unaccounted Income: Some Estimates', *Economic and Political Weekly*, Vol. XVII, Nos. 17 and 18, 24 April and 1 May, 1982.

Gupta, P. and Gupta, S., 'Estimates of the Unreported Economy in India', *Economic and Political Weekly*, Bombay, Vol. XVII, No. 13, 16 January, 1982.

Hindustan Times, New Delhi, 23 February 2019.

Kaldor Report, *The Economic Weekly*, 15 December 1956.

Kumar, Arun, *Understanding the Black Economy and Black Money in India*, Aleph, New Delhi, 2017.

Mahajan, V.S., *Recent Developments in Indian Economy*, Deep and Deep Publications, New Delhi, 1984, pp. 56–60.

Myint, U., 'Corruption: Causes, Consequences and Cures', *Asia-Pacific Development Journal*, Vol. 7, No. 2, December 2000.

Pendse, D.R., 'Black Money: Its Nature and Causes', *The Economic Times*, 19 March, 1982.

Rani, Kavita and Kumar, Sanjiv, 'Black Money in India: A Conceptual Analysis', *Indian Journal of Research*, Volume 3, Issue 1, January 2014.

Sarkar, Sukanta, 'The Parallel Economy in India: Causes, Impacts and Government Initiatives'. *Economic Journal of Development Issues*, Volume 11–12, No. 1–2, pp. 124–134, 2010.

Singh, Vijay Kumar, 'Controlling Money Laundering in India: Problems and Perspectives', presented at the 11th Annual Conference at the Indira Gandhi Institute of Development Research, January 2009.

Varghese, K.V., *Economic Problems of Modern India*, Ashish Publishing House, New Delhi, 1985, pp. 242–254.

Index